Sustainable Digital Marketing for Fashion and Luxury Brands

The book is an excellent resource for students, academics and practitioners. It covers comprehensively the conceptual foundations of sustainable digital marketing in the context of fashion and luxury brands, and then elucidates the scope and of the practice with relevant applications before outlining key strategies and techniques that can employed to win in this space. The book is quite accessible and is excellently edited – benefiting from a diverse range of expert contributors from around the world.

—Professor Sam Kamuriwo, *Professor of Strategy and Innovation at Bayes Business School, City University of London, UK*

Sustainable Digital Marketing Strategies for Fashion and Luxury Brands: Theory and Practice captures a compelling list of practices and avenues that support a sustainable marketing strategy approach. This book provides a seamless transition of discussion from theoretical to the practical recommendations for successful sustainable marketing; therefore, the book is an excellent source for marketing students, researchers and marketers that plan to develop sustainable marketing strategies for fashion and luxury industry.

—Yllka Azemi, *Associate Professor of Marketing, Indiana University Northwest, USA*

Sustainable Digital Marketing Strategies for Fashion and Luxury Brands is an invaluable resource for students and professionals. The book offers a comprehensive exploration of how to integrate sustainability practices with marketing strategies tailored specifically for the fashion and luxury sectors. Skillfully blending theory with practical application, the authors highlight key concepts like online communities and social media influences that support brand sustainability, illustrated through engaging case studies. The book further explores the critical role of technological innovations in moving the industry forward in the post-digital era. Offering practical strategies and insights, it helps professionals make informed decisions in a complex market environment.

—Professor Zhenqiang Li, *Dean of the School of Economics and Management, Hunan Institute of Science and Technology, China*

A seminal contribution to the field of digital marketing in fashion and luxury! Sustainable Digital Marketing Strategies for Fashion and Luxury Brands: Theory and Practice brings together an oustanding collection of experts to provide a comprehensive and authoritative overview of the latest research and practices on the subject. The editors have done an exceptional job in curating a collection of chapters that are both theoretically rigorous and practically relevant. This book is an essential resource for scholars, researchers, and practitioners seeking to understand the complexities of digital marketing in the fashion and luxury industries. A truly outstanding achievement!

—Professor Daniel K. Maduku, *College of Business, University of Doha for Science and Technology, Qatar*

This book is a fascinating journey into the metamorphosis of luxury, shaped by the emerging trends of sustainability and digitisation. Its main contribution is to analyse how these forces are reshaping the luxury industry, influencing its marketing strategies and practices and redefine new alternatives in terms of customer orientation

—Professor Michela Matarazzo, *University of Sannio, Italy*

Sustainable Digital Marketing Strategies for Fashion and Luxury Brands offer's a critical and timely examination of how digital marketing can drive sustainability in an ever-innovating marketing industry. The book narrows the gap between academic theory and practical application, not only provides new ideas for fashion and luxury brand marketing, but also meets the needs of consumers who are increasingly pursuing environmental protection. For marketing professionals, industry leaders and scholars advancing sustainability in the digital era, this book enhances the role that digital marketing strategies play in fostering sustainability.

—Professor Zheng Zhuqun, *Dean of Foreign Languages School of Fujian Jiangxia University, PRC*

Wilson Ozuem · Silvia Ranfagni ·
Cindy Millman
Editors

Sustainable Digital Marketing for Fashion and Luxury Brands

Theory and Practice

palgrave
macmillan

Editors
Wilson Ozuem
Business School
University for the Creative Arts
Epsom, Surrey, UK

Silvia Ranfagni
Economics and Business
University of Florence
Florence, Italy

Cindy Millman
Business School
University for the Creative Arts
Epsom, UK

ISBN 978-3-031-82466-1 ISBN 978-3-031-82467-8 (eBook)
https://doi.org/10.1007/978-3-031-82467-8

This Palgrave Macmillan imprint is published by the registered company Springer Nature Switzerland AG
The registered company address is: Gewerbestrasse 11, 6330 Cham, Switzerland

Foreword

Sustainability is increasing impacting on the fashion and luxury brands driven by growing consumer and retailer's concerns as well impending policy and legislative change particularly from Europe. COVID-19 created huge disruption to supply chains in the sectors leading to increase concerns over human health and worker vulnerabilities. This coupled with growing concerns over climate change has led to a 5th green consumer wave that impacting on global economies. This handbook brings together to a series of academics and practitioners from around the world to highlight theory and practice on how growing sustainability awareness and action is starting to impact on digital marketing from the needs for improved understanding of changing customer needs, to promotion and messaging. The volume is divided into 3 sections with 28 chapters: Foundations of Sustainable Digital Marketing; Scope and Applications; and Strategies and Techniques. Access better data on environmental and social impacts of fashion and luxury brands through their lifecycles from material sourcing to post-purchase use will be a growing imperative into the future and information-backed claims will be increasing importance, with greenwashing increasing regulated.

Digital and non-digital marketeers working for brands, suppliers and agencies will all need to respond and adapt to the changing paradigm to survive and prosper into the future. Raised awareness, understanding and action in relation to sustainability in education, research and practice in the fashion and luxury sector will be essential if trends are to be understood, opportunities are to be seized and challenges minimised. This volume should be essential reading for those working in digital marketing or contemplating future careers in the area.

Professor Martin Charter
Director
The Centre for Sustainable Design
University for the Creative Arts
UCA
Farnham, Surrey, UK

Sustainable Digital Marketing Strategies for Fashion and Luxury Brands: Theory and Practice

The volatile and dynamic global business environment requires that companies exhibit greater flexibility in their ability to swiftly adapt and respond to market fluctuations. Among the driving forces behind these transformations, corporate social responsibility and sustainability mandates are becoming increasingly urgent. Sustainability has emerged as a pivotal concern for both marketing academics and practitioners. This recent surge in attention is driven by the stark contrast between the economic prosperity of the past decades and the growing concerns over wealth inequality and environmental degradation (Dao et al., 2011; Ranfagni & Ozuem, 2022). The disruption caused by the COVID-19 pandemic has recently accentuated the need for sustainable digital marketing strategies and innovation in the fashion and luxury brand sector. These substantial disruptions have the potential to significantly alter the positioning strategies of fashion and luxury brands, especially considering the substantial influence of digital technologies on sustainable practices. More importantly, there has been an increasing appreciation for sustainable luxury, especially within the fashion industry. Consumers are now assigning more value to this concept, and it is increasingly acknowledged as a pivotal factor contributing to the enduring success of brands. Digital marketing is dynamic and remains a broad emerging field. The digital marketing environment is increasingly shifting to sustainable consumption; this had led to market competition and other organisational challenges. Given the participation of fashion and luxury brands in the omnipresent computer-mediated marketing environments (CMMEs), it can be argued that a robust digital ecosystem is pivotal in empowering companies to formulate strategies that effectively address sustainability challenges, deliver sustainability value to stakeholders and achieve a sustained competitive advantage.

This edited volume aims to broaden the contribution of digital marketing strategies to sustainability. Our goal in this handbook is to provide an authoritative, comprehensive and accessible resource on how the current state of digital marketing strategies impacts sustainable practices and consumption. This volume is thematic with a clear emphasis on the variety of emerging digital marketing strategies that influence sustainable practices across fashion and luxury brands. Each chapter sets the scene, as it were, before it delves into the main debates and controversies as they play out in contemporary CMMEs and sustainability. The book is divided into three main parts: Part I, titled 'Foundations of Sustainable Digital Marketing'; Part II, 'Scope and Application'; and Part III, 'Strategies and Techniques'.

Part I: Foundations of Sustainable Digital Marketing

In Chapter 1, 'Postdigital iconicity of runways: redefining sustainability in high-end fashion marketing', Annette Kallevig and Vésma Kontere McQuillan set the scene of the book. The chapter discusses the postdigital era. The merging of digital and physical marketing channels has birthed postdigital runway shows in high-end fashion that blur traditional lines. This exploratory conceptual work delves into the extended marketing opportunities associated with the postdigital runway show and its potential as a vehicle for sustainable marketing within the high-end fashion industry through influencer mediation. By examining an iconic fashion event, the influencers attending it and the content they produce through the lens of Erving Goffman's theory of identity construction, this chapter critically examines how a postdigital runway show can genuinely facilitate sustainable practices while maintaining its iconic status.

In Chapter 2, 'Online brand communities: digitally sustaining fashion brands' sustainability', Michelle Willis explores how online brand communities were developed as a digital initiative to increase communication and closeness between followers, loyal customers and brands, and to establish customers' long-term and sustainable trust in brands. As digital media increase their reporting of sustainability movements and initiatives, online communities are attracting members who extend the responsibility of sustainable practices to fashion and luxury brands.

In Chapter 3, 'Brand building using digital marketing tools: insight into an innovative hybrid model', Silvia Ranfagni, Massimo Rosati and Silvia Frescucci begin with a theoretical exploration of the contemporary role of branding; they look into its historical origins and trace its evolution, which ultimately culminates in its adaptation to the digital landscape. The chapter then discusses modern online analytics tools, such as Google Trends, Pinterest Trends, SEMrush, Not Just Analytics, Keywords Everywhere and Google Forms, highlighting their crucial role in market analysis, identifying emerging trends and comprehending competition. The chapter focuses on the cosmetics sector in Italy and describes the process of building a new brand.

In Chapter 4, 'Fostering meaningful interactions through user-generated content: reshaping how fashion brands interact with consumers', Samar Ghurab and Raye Ng offer a deep understanding of how user-generated content (UGC) has emerged as a transformative force within the fashion industry; it provides a dynamic conduit through which fashion brands interact with their audience, foster brand loyalty and drive sales. This is particularly evident in the democratisation of the fashion landscape. Historically, the fashion industry was characterised by exclusivity in which a limited number of high-end brands dictated trends and consumers passively received them. However, the rise of UGC has shifted this power dynamic and empowered individuals to become active participants in shaping fashion narratives.

In Chapter 5, 'Chinese online literature: sustainability and customers' value co-creation on an online brand platform', Liya An, Ling Lin and Caroline Jawad examine how Chinese online literature, which has been thriving for over two decades, demonstrates remarkable vitality and economic potential. Conversely, Western discussions often overlook internet literature and focus instead on experimental forms of electronic literature. Yet, Chinese internet literature transcends mere literary expression, it has evolved into a lucrative industry. While Western scholarship prioritises cutting-edge forms, Chinese internet literature encompasses a vast array of works produced by passionate netizens, which form the foundation of its commercialisation.

In Chapter 6, 'Social media and discursive practices in the global fashion industry', Samuel Osei-Nimo and Cindy Millman discuss the complex relationship between social media, discursive practices and sustainability in luxury fashion firms. This chapter discusses the importance of sustainability for post-pandemic recovery and explores how social media serves as a power and knowledge mechanism in shaping sustainable fashion discourses. Through a Foucauldian lens, they analyse how technologies influence the construction, dissemination and regulation of sustainable practices, and shed light on the power dynamics at play.

In Chapter 7, 'Luxury hotels' corporate social responsibility communications and online brand communities', Mei Kun (Vicky) Loi addresses luxury hotels' corporate social responsibility (CSR) communications on online brand communities (OBCs) in social media and the level of consumer engagement with CSR communications. The study follows a CSR framework proposed by Cherapanukorn and Focken (2014) to evaluate the CSR communications of five luxury hotel brands in Scotland. The four dimensions of the CSR framework are environment, community, employees and supply chain. The results show that luxury hotel CSR communications were evident on OBCs in social media albeit minimal.

In Chapter 8, 'Persuasive communication and emotional appeals: the contribution of psychology', Sara Bocci Benucci and Cristian Di Gesto examine how persuasive communication serves as a foundational element that underpins the success of campaigns targeting potential consumers.

This chapter delves into the significance of persuasive communication within the luxury brand landscape, with a particular focus on leveraging emotional appeals in crafting advertising campaigns within the realm of social media. Emotional branding and the strategic deployment of emotional appeals play a critical role in luxury brand marketing; companies need to adjust their strategies to effectively engage consumers and sustain their competitive advantage in the ever-evolving luxury market.

Part II: Scope and Application

In Chapter 9, 'Digital fashion in the metaverse and innovation for sustainability in fashion', Marta Giovannetti and Elena Cedrola focus on the research and practice in the fashion industry in the metaverse by concentrating on the sustainability challenges found within this sector. The metaverse can emphasise the search for sustainability, particularly in research and development, innovation and communication. This allows companies to think about sustainable transition, circular business models, minimising environmental damage and satisfying the needs of selected target customers. For the users active in the metaverse, interaction with the brand through digital experiences or objects can in fact constitute a form of experimental and immersive market research.

In Chapter 10, 'Social media influencers: transition from fast fashion to slow sustainable causes', Wilson Ozuem and Michelle Willis review a wide range of influential actors who display various types of fashion styles and consumption experiences through digital technologies. Beyond the aesthetics, the fashion and luxury industry attracts a wide range of social media influencers (SMIs) seeking to channel their values and aspirations into content and digital initiatives that have implications for their long-term sustainability. Fashion SMIs can also engage with social movements that are separate from, but relevant to, the fashion industry. Some of these social movements stand against the fast fashion industry and advocate for the slow sustainability of fashion, whereas others address the misrepresentation of cultural and society groups through fashion.

In Chapter 11, 'Repositioning of Chinese luxury spirit: Kweichow Moutai', Xialiang Yao provides a detailed review of Kweichow Moutai marketing strategies. The chapter discusses how understanding potential customers' emerging needs and habits is a primary objective for luxury companies. Kweichow Moutai, China's iconic liquor producer, has always held a leading position in the high-end market. However, after a staggering decline (by more than half) in China's total liquor production over the past six years (China Alcoholic Drinks Association, 2023), Moutai realised that this trend indicated a shift in consumer preferences, with the most affluent demographic, Millennials and Gen Zs, turning away from baijiu, the traditional Chinese distilled white spirit. Moutai's customers in the high-end market are mainly middle-aged and older adults, but the size of this group is gradually shrinking.

In Chapter 12, 'Authenticity as consistency: insights from micro-influencers partnerships with sustainable fashion brands', Giovanna Pegan and Marco Balzano examine the role of authenticity as consistency between an entity's internal values and external expressions in the strategic choices of social media influencers within the fashion industry regarding sustainability-focused collaborations. After a theoretical background, this chapter focuses on the perceptions of green micro-influencers directly involved in sustainable fashion brand partnerships operating on Instagram to understand how their internal values align with their external collaborations.

In Chapter 13, 'Virtual corporate social responsibility co-creation and consumer engagement', Ling Lin and Liya An discuss the emergence of virtual corporate social responsibility (CSR) co-creation as a transformative approach to engage consumers, particularly through digital platforms. They highlight the transition from traditional one-way CSR communication to two-way interactive engagement that involves stakeholders in meaningful ways. By examining case studies such as Alipay's Ant Forest initiative, the chapter illustrates how virtual CSR co-creation can effectively mobilise and sustain consumer engagement in environmental sustainability efforts. The chapter also discusses the theoretical underpinnings and practical applications of virtual CSR, and provides insights into how companies can leverage technology to foster collaborative value creation and address critical global challenges.

In Chapter 14, 'Leadership and digital transformation in the luxury brand industry', Samuel Osei-Nimo, Cindy Millman and Wajiha Kazim examine the influence of leadership on emerging workplace design driven by technological developments. The chapter also explores the monitoring, surveillance and automation strategies utilised by business organisations to improve the effectiveness of their marketing initiatives. Despite the well-documented evidence for the effectiveness, efficiency and sustainability of digital transformation of business organisations, it can have severe impacts on business stakeholders, such as customers, employees and society. This chapter focuses on the luxury and fashion industry and proposes approaches that leaders can utilise to implement and support digital transformation effectively.

In Chapter 15, 'Virtual corporate social responsibility and sustainable value creation', Abdullah Promise Opute, Xi Jiang and Jafar Ojra discuss how corporate social responsibility (CSR) is a core aspect of sustainability mechanisms. The chapter commences by providing a justification for the theoretical premise of the chapter. The foundation of fashion and sustainability, and CSR and its aspects, are explained. Virtual CSR (VCSR) and VCSR dialogue are introduced. The impacts of VCSR, such as value creation and its effects on organisational performance, are highlighted. This chapter offers relevant recommendations on strategising VCSR and optimising its utility for customer engagement and organisational performance impact.

In Chapter 16, 'Social media influencers: influencing sustainable practices in the fashion industry', Favour Ben and Wilson Ozuem examine how sustainability has become an important topic in the fashion industry in recent years, and how influencers are using this opportunity to advocate for, and promote, sustainable practices. Sustainable fashion influencers have become powerful figures influencing consumers and driving trends in a variety of industries, particularly the fashion industry.

Influencers have become increasingly significant with the growing popularity of social media platforms, such as Instagram, TikTok and Reddit. This chapter examines how social media influencers are influencing sustainable practices in the fashion industry.

In Chapter 17, 'Storytelling and the sustainability of fashion and luxury brands', Taiwo Fimihan Olajumoke and Sajad Rezaei examine storytelling and the sustainability of fashion and luxury brands. This chapter discusses issues with unidirectional marketing in relation to the evolution of digital tools. The roles of storytelling, digital content marketing and sustainable storytelling in the fashion and luxury brands industry are emphasised. The way forward for future sustainable practices of storytelling and digital marketing are highlighted.

In Chapter 18, 'CSR communication and luxury brands: themes for cultivating stakeholder-oriented communication on sustainability through social media', Fabrizio Mosca, Valentina Chiaudano and Brigida Morelli examine how luxury brands use social media to convey their corporate social responsibility (CSR) initiatives to discern whether the content emphasises tangible sustainability actions rather than promises. They reveal a notable trend among luxury brands towards integrated CSR communication on LinkedIn, which engages diverse stakeholders with content related to the preservation of the planet Earth, social inclusion and sustainable practices that include circular product design, upcycling recycling and innovations aimed at reducing environmental impacts.

In Chapter 19, 'Metaverse Fashion Ecosystem: a sustainable marketing perspective', Mostafa Mohamad, Fandi Omeish and Anna Tarabasz discuss the mechanism of building the Metaverse Fashion Ecosystem (MFE) as an alternative platform for sustainable marketing. MFE offers a more sustainable venue for fashion companies post-COVID-19, including Gucci, Burberry, Balenciaga and The Fabricant.

Part III: Strategies and Techniques

In Chapter 20, 'Chatbots and customer experience in luxury fashion', Isolde Ward-Lubbe and Steven Mbeya examine how the integration of chatbots within the luxury fashion industry has the potential to significantly enhance customer experiences and promote sustainable practices, which are crucial in this globally influential sector. Luxury in fashion is defined by its origins and evolving attributes, which emphasise high quality, exclusivity and superior artisanship Current trends in the industry highlight the increasing roles of technology and sustainability, which are driven largely by millennials' preference for digital interactions and ethical consumption. Millennials' attitudes towards luxury brands, which prioritise experiences and sustainability, shape their purchasing decisions.

In Chapter 21, 'More sustainability than digitalization: Prato and the global fashion supply chain', Daniela Toccafondi examines the flexibility and creativity in fashion collections over the years. One of the key elements of this model is the division of labour among a multitude of specialised small and medium-sized enterprises. For over a hundred years, it has leveraged the circular economy, embracing the motto 'reuse, reduce, recycle'. It thus has a well-established tradition of sustainability that is environmental and ethical. Few consumers are aware of this because communication in the area has been neglected for a long time. Now, new consumption models require more detailed information on materials and production processes.

In Chapter 22, 'Black swan events: mitigating disruption to a supply chain using blockchain and artificial intelligence', Gordon Bowen, Hamid Jahankhani and Imad Nawaz review how geopolitical situations, such as the Ukraine–Russia war, the Israel–Hamas conflict and pandemics, can disrupt supply chains, for example, the rerouting of oil tankers via South Africa to avoid the impact of the Israel–Hamas conflict. These events will probably occur again, but they are black swan events and difficult to predict. How can firms manage these events to minimise disruption to their supply chains? This chapter proposes that a blockchain architecture has the potential to build resilience in supply chains and give them the flexibility to withstand the challenges of black swan events.

In Chapter 23, 'Artificial intelligence and sustainability in fashion: a triple bottom line approach', Emily Rosa Shahaj discusses how artificial intelligence (AI) undergoes an arms race of investment and development. This chapter evaluates AI tools' impact on both the environment and various jobs within the fashion industry, as well as potential avenues for luxury fashion to leverage such tools to alleviate current financial burdens implicit within the medium of online retail. Beyond the hype and headlines, this chapter identifies where sustainability is and is not being discussed in regard to AI, as well as the inherent opportunities, risks and limitations involved with its uptake across a fashion business's operations.

In Chapter 24, 'Artificial intelligence: building sustainability in the implementation of SDGs', Gordon Bowen, Janakan Sothinathan, Richard Bowen, Deidre Bowen and Atul Sethi examine how sustainable development goals (SDGs) are necessary and recognised to bring benefits, such as sustainability, which could contribute to economic growth, reduce poverty and reduce inequalities. The implementation of SDGs is generally accepted as coherent and reasonable to many in society. However, the adoption of SDGs by society is hindered by economic situations and societal behaviour towards the implementation of SDGs. The aim of this chapter is to understand how economic circumstances and societal behaviour influence the implementation and sustainability of SDGs.

In Chapter 25, 'Kering's strategy for digital and sustainable transformation: twin transition through NFTs in the luxury industry', Stefania Masè and Elena Cedrola examine Kering's pioneering approach to integrating digital and sustainability strategies within the luxury industry. As an exemplar of the twin transition towards digital and sustainable futures, Kering leverages the synergistic potential of digitalisation and sustainability to propel economic, social and environmental progress. Through the lens of the triple bottom line framework, this chapter discusses how Kering's focus on profit, people and the planet guides its business practices and underscores a holistic view of sustainable business impact. Kering's journey from its foundational years to its contemporary status as a global luxury leader demonstrates strategic transformation and commitment to innovation, sustainability and digital excellence.

In Chapter 26, 'Elevating luxury brand digital engagement using chatbots', Nicole Cunningham examines how various industries have adapted to integrating chatbots into their digital platforms. However, the luxury brand industry has been reluctant to integrate chatbots due to the perception that chatbots would not offer the same level of personalisation as a human being; instead of offering chatbots, luxury brands offer live agent chats, which could result in frustrated customers. The luxury brand industry focuses on the concept of exclusivity, personalisation and a focused approach to engagement when customers enter luxury brand stores.

In Chapter 27, 'The role of blockchain in sustainable luxury fashion', Silvia Ranfagni Massimo Rosati and Michele Di Giura provide a detailed review on the relationships between some of the most popular concepts in the current industry landscape, namely supply chain, blockchain and sustainability; they explore how they intersect within the high fashion industry. First, the peculiarities of luxury fashion supply chains and the characteristics of a sustainable supply chain are analysed. Then, the main features, operating mechanisms, types and most popular areas of application of blockchain are highlighted to identify the positive and negative aspects of this innovation.

In Chapter 28, 'Certification standards and ecolabelling for sustainability and traceability in the textile supply chain', Leonardo Borsacchi examines the integration of certified management systems (MS) in fostering sustainable supply chain management within the textile industry. Certified MSs, such as ISO 9001 and ISO 14001, play a vital role in improving process efficiency, product quality and environmental performance. In addition, ecolabels like the EU Ecolabel and Global Organic Textile Standard build consumer trust by certifying compliance with stringent environmental standards.

Wilson Ozuem
University for the Creative Arts
Business School
Epsom, UK
wilson.ozuem@uca.ac.uk

Silvia Ranfagni
Department of Economics
and Business
Florence, Italy
silvia.ranfagni@unifi.it

Cindy Millman
University for the Creative Arts
Business School
Epsom, UK
cindy.millman@uca.ac.uk

References

Cherapanukorn, V., & Focken, K. (2014). Corporate social responsibility (CSR) and sustainability in Asian luxury hotels: Policies, practices and standards. *Asian Social Science, 10*(8), 198–209.

China Alcoholic Drinks Association. (2023). *Mid-year research report on China's Baijiu Market in 2023*. China Alcoholic Drinks Association. Available at https://www.sohu.com/a/687543862_121406416

Dao, V., Langella, I., & Carbo, J. (2011). From green to sustainability: Information Technology and an integrated sustainability framework. *The Journal of Strategic Information Systems, 20*(1), 63–79.

Ranfagni, S., & Ozuem, W. (2022). Luxury and sustainability: Technological pathways and potential opportunities. *Sustainability, 14*(9), 5209. https://doi.org/10.3390/su14095209

Contents

Notes on Contributors

Liya An a lecturer at Chengdu University of Information Technology, earned her Doctoral degree from the University of Wales Trinity Saint David, specialising in customer engagement and value co-creation.

Marco Balzano is a research fellow at the DEAMS, University of Trieste and a PhD candidate of Management attending a Double PhD Programme between the Ca' Foscari University of Venice and SKEMA Business School. He published in several international outlets including California Management Review, International Journal of Management Reviews, European Management Review, Technovation, IEEE Transactions on Engineering Management and Journal of Small Business Management. His main research interests deal with the study of serendipity, business strategy and technology innovation.

Favour Ben is a lecturer at Arden University. Her research interests lie at the intersection of fashion and generative AI, exploring how emerging technologies are shaping the future of the fashion industry. With a keen focus on innovation and leadership, Favour is committed to advancing academic understanding in these areas. She supervises student projects and is actively involved in academic research, contributing to discussions on technology-driven transformation. Favour is passionate about blending creativity with AI to drive new insights into both fashion and management.

Sara Bocci Benucci is a psychologist and she is currently a PhD student in psychology at the University of Florence. Her main research interest involves the study of the psychological processes and risk factors that could lead to the onset and maintenance of Problematic Social Network Sites Use. Moreover, she is interested in the development of prevention interventions for problematic behaviors related to internet use (e.g. gaming, online shopping, smartphone use) to promote more user well-being. This latter research interest combines with a more general interest in computer-mediated communication.

Leonardo Borsacchi holds a PhD in Commodity Sciences. He is a researcher and coordinator of the Circular Innovation and Sustainable Commodities research unit at ARCO - PIN, University of Florence. His research focuses on defining and implementing sustainability strategies for production processes and textile supply chains, integrated management systems and certifications, introducing circular innovation practices within organisations, and urban-level circular economy. He teaches 'Sustainability of Production Chains' and 'Circular Economy and Sustainable Human Development' at the School of Economics and Management, University of Florence.

Richard Bowen has worked at some of the largest and fastest growing technology companies and startups, including Amazon, Microsoft, Facebook and Instacart. He now plies his trade at Chime after working at Robomart, a Silicon Valley startup, as Interim Chief Operating Officer and now Board Member. Rich is also an early-stage startup advisor and mentor, investor, board member, research author and visiting lecturer, with over 15 years of industry diverse operations experience, with a balance of business experience and academia. Rich holds a first class, with honors BA in Business and Management and is a doctoral candidate.

Rich was recently nominated to attend Stanford University Executive Education Program, focused on the Emergence of Chief Operating Officers.

Deidre Bowen holds a master's in applied management (Henley Business School) with distinction, is a qualified solicitor and completed her degree at Oxford University. She is currently Director of Delivery at Mental Health UK, responsible for leading and developing all UK wide programmes. Her research interests are strategy, organisational culture, SMEs sustainability and leadership. More recently, Deidre has explored the impact of the pandemic on the mental health of both young people and adults. Deidre plays an active role in promoting women and leadership in business; she was a key-note speaker at an event held at Sheffield University.

Gordon Bowen is an associate professor in Management at Anglia Ruskin University and works as an associate lecturer at various universities and higher education institutions, including Warwick University, University of Gloucestershire, Northumbria University, Cumbria University, Regent's University London, Ulster University, University of Hertfordshire, University of Wales Trinity St. David and Grenoble Graduate Business School. His research interests are strategy, marketing, digital marketing and SMEs, and he supervises PhD and DBA students in these areas.

Elena Cedrola, PhD is the head of the Department of Economics and Law at the University of Macerata. At the same University she is a full professor and teaches International Management and Marketing. She has been a visiting scholar at Beijing Normal University, University Paris IV Sorbonne and Aix-Marseille University. Her research areas are international management and marketing for SMEs, with a focus on China. She has an extensive portfolio of intellectual contributions including publications in peer-reviewed journals, presentations and conferences. Her latest studies focus on the country-of-origin, the fashion industry, blockchain and gamification, the latter two being contextualised in corporate management and marketing strategies.

Valentina Chiaudano holds a PhD in Business and Management from the University of Turin, Italy. She is a research fellow and lecturer in marketing and sustainability management at the University of Turin, Italy. Her research interests include marketing and sustainability management applied to various industries focusing on luxury brand management. She applies her marketing and business management expertise by collaborating on consulting projects with a range of national and international organisations.

Nicole Cunningham is an associate professor in the Department of Marketing Management at the University of Johannesburg, South Africa. Her research focuses on consumer behaviour, particularly contemporary marketing trends, digital adoption and the luxury industry. Her work has been published in several journals, including the Journal of Consumer Behaviour, the Journal of International Retail and Distribution Management and the European Business Review. Prof Cunningham has presented at numerous conferences both locally and internationally. She supervises Masters and Doctoral students and has edited multiple textbooks used at various higher education institutions in South Africa.

Cristian Di Gesto, PhD in Psychology, is currently an adjunct professor of Social Psychology at the University of Florence and a research fellow at the University of Rome 'La Sapienza'. His research expertise encompasses persuasive communication, the relationships between attitudes, intentions and behaviors, intergroup dynamics, body image and social media influences and psychosocial well-being. He has authored numerous publications in both national and international journals in the fields of social and health psychology. He is a member of the European Association of Social Psychology, the European Health Psychology Society, the Italian Psychological Association and the Italian Society of Health Psychology.

Michele Di Giura holds a master's degree in Business Administration and Management from the University of Florence. He is a practitioner and an expert on sustainability, business ethics and corporate social responsibility. His recently work is entitled 'Supply Chain Sustainability and Blockchain: technological innovation at the service of luxury fashion'.

Silvia Frescucci holds a master's degree in Business Management and Marketing from the University of Florence, Italy. She is a product manager assistant at a pharmaceutical company. Her research interests are consumer experience in the social network commumities.

Samar Ghurab is currently a doctoral candidate at the University of Cumbria, United Kingdom, where she is pursuing a PhD in digital marketing. Her doctoral research explores the intersection of user-generated content and consumer brand engagement within the luxury fashion industry. Prior to her doctoral studies, Ghurab earned a Bachelor of Arts (Hons) in English Literature and Linguistics and a Master of Arts from the University of Westminster. She subsequently completed a Master of Science in Management at Queen Mary, University of London. Her academic background, combined with her practical experience, has equipped Ghurab with a unique perspective on the luxury fashion market. She has provided consultancy services to a range of small and medium-sized enterprises (SMEs) operating in the fashion sector in the Middle East, offering valuable insights into digital marketing strategies and consumer behaviour.

Marta Giovannetti, PhD is a researcher and lecturer in Marketing at the University of Macerata. She currently teaches Business Marketing for Innovation and Sustainable Business Management. She has several publications with international co-authors in many relevant international journals on BtoB marketing, including Industrial Marketing Management, Journal of Business and Industrial Marketing, Journal of Service Theory and Practice and others. Her qualitative and quantitative works deal with personal selling, sales management, sales technology, sales training, BtoB marketing, tourism marketing, fashion marketing, technology. Dr. Giovannetti has collaborated in various Erasmus+ projects related to education and training in sales, business, digital transformation and sustainability.

Hamid Jahankhani gained his PhD from the Queen Mary College, University of London. In 1999 he moved to the University of East London (UEL) to become the first professor of Information Security and Cyber Criminology at the university in 2010.

Hamid's principal research area for a number of years has been in the field of cybersecurity, information security and digital forensics. In partnership with the key industrial sectors, he has examined and established several innovative research projects that are of direct relevance to the needs of UK and European information security, digital forensics industries, Critical National Infrastructure and law enforcement agencies.

Caroline Jawad a social scientist at the Institute of Management and Health of the University of Wales Trinity Saint David, is dedicated to exploring business ethics and corporate responsibility, with a particular focus on consumer vulnerability and global supply chain ethics.

Xi Jiang is a doctoral researcher at the University of Wales Trinity Saint David, exploring consumer behaviour in the tourism industry. Also, she is a lecturer of Network and Nemia at Chengdu JinChen College in China. With many years of industrial experience in the tourism industry, her core research domain is consumer behaviour, with particular interest in understanding the influence of social media and cultural factors. She is also interested in understanding the role of technology on consumer behaviour, as well as entrepreneurship and SMEs.

Annette Kallevig is an associate professor of marketing communications at Kristiania University College in Oslo (Norway). Her research interest lies in the relationship between creativity and data in marketing communications in the digital era. Her work is inspired by 25 years of experience as a creative and strategic advisor in advertising and digital marketing in Norway and the United States. Her work has been featured at AMA and EMAC conferences and published in The Journal of Advertising research, in addition to book chapters.

Wajiha Kazim is a senior lecturer in Management at Nottingham Business School, Nottingham Trent University. Her research interests stem from a rich background in both research and practical experience, focusing on the impact of leadership and workplace factors on organisational behaviour. She conducts research across diverse contexts, emphasising the influence of leadership while considering the multi-level contextual demands involved. Wajiha's work is distinguished by its interdisciplinary approach, weaving together insights from higher education, the construction industry, and the luxury brands sector.

Ling Lin is a lecturer in Fujian Jiangxia University, China. She is also a doctoral candidate in Business Administration at University of Wales Trinity Saint David, focusing on digital marketing and corporate social responsibility. Her research explores the impact of virtual corporate social responsibility on consumer engagement, particularly in the context of service-dominant logic. In addition, she has experience in the logistics industry and contributes to her family's private business over 15 years. Dr. Liya An, a lecturer at Chengdu University of Information Technology, earned her doctoral degree from the same university, specialising in customer engagement and value co-creation.

Mei Kun (Vicky) Loi is a lecturer in Marketing at De Montfort University, UK. With a strong academic background in Hospitality and Tourism, she specialised in branding and digital strategies for the hotel sector. Her research interests focus on the intersection of sustainability and digital transformation, exploring innovative ways that enable organisations engage with ethical practices while maintaining a competitive edge. Vicky has contributed to academic journals and conferences, and her book chapter reflects her dedication to advancing corporate social responsibility communication in the luxury hotel sector. Currently, she is pursuing research on the transformative role of Artificial Intelligence in internal brand management.

Stefania Masè is an associate professor of Marketing at IPAG Business School, France. She earned her dual-degree PhD at Macerata University (Italy) and Sorbonne University (France), integrating managerial studies with aesthetic philosophy. Her research explores the intersection of marketing, aesthetics and consumer behavior, with a focus on luxury brands, digital services and people sustainability. A member of the STEP Project Global Consortium (https://spgcfb.org/), she also investigates family businesses. Her work appears in international journals and conferences. In 2020, she published her first book with Springer, Art & Business: Perspectives on Art-based Management.

Steven Mbeya is an emerging researcher who obtained his Master of Commerce degree in Marketing Management with distinction at the University of Johannesburg, South Africa. His research interest lies in the field of e-retailing, digital, applications of AI in marketing and data analytics. He has published as a co-author in peer-reviewed journals such as Journal of Financial Services Marketing and Future Business Journal including in conferences such as 16th International Business Conference (IBC) 2023 in Swakopmund, Namibia where his co-authored research paper was voted into top 6. He has been lecturer in sales and statistic tutor at UJ. Continuing his studies at Rennes School, he has obtained a specialization in Data Analytics, Intelligence and Security in France.

Vésma Kontere McQuillan is a fashion researcher, architect and professor at Kristiania University College in Oslo, Norway. Her academic work focuses on the interdisciplinary dialogue between architecture and fashion, examining how spatial design both influences and is influenced by fashion practices. McQuillan also serves as the Contributing Fashion Editor for FRAME Magazine in Amsterdam, bridging theory and practice to deepen the understanding of these interconnected fields.

Cindy Millman is a professor of Business Innovation, Director of Business School for the Creative Industries, University for the Creative Arts. Her doctoral studies and previous research projects influenced her interests in entrepreneurship behaviour, as well as creative education. She undertakes research in SMEs with particular interest in exploring all aspects of entrepreneurial behaviour, especially in the context of internationalisation, innovation and market orientation. With its cross-disciplinary and inter-disciplinary nature, Cindy's research triangulates findings from small business, higher education and the creative industries.

Mostafa Mohamad is a scholar and industry expert in Digital Transformation, AI for Business, FinTech, Digital Innovation, and Business Analytics. Before joining Zayed University, he had 20 years of academic experience at Manchester Business School, Newcastle Business School, Leeds Business School, and Salford Business School. Mo served as a director of PG programmes, a director of Admissions, and a deputy DBA director. He also led significant research funds for Virtual Reality, Machine Learning, Artificial Intelligence, FinTech and Technology transfer in the Energy, automotive, tourism & telecommunication sectors. He is an associate editor in Q1 journals in IS & Digital Marketing.

Brigida Morelli is a PhD student in Business and Management at the University of Turin, Department of Management (XXXVIII). Her research interests are the following: Strategic marketing, Stakeholder theory, Stakeholder approach, Stakeholder marketing, Company Responsibility, Sustainability and Marketing communication.

Fabrizio Mosca is a full professor of Corporate, Business Strategy and Marketing at University of Torino (Italy). He took a PhD at

Bocconi University. His research interests include Corporate and Business Strategy, Strategic Marketing with a focus on luxury markets. His most recent work focuses on CSR. He has published several books, papers in International Journals such as the *Journal of Business Research, Psychology and Marketing, Symphonia - Emerging Issues in Management* and *The Italian Journal of Marketing*. During his career he was invited as a *visiting professor* at University of Córdoba, Pompeu Fabra University in Barcellona, University Paris Nanterre, IUM Monaco.

Imad Nawaz is working as a deputy dean for the Business and Arts Design and Social Science Department at Northumbria University, London. Imad has worked in various academic, commercial and non-profit organisations in the UK and abroad. He is a human resource management practitioner and holds qualifications in the same area. Imad is also a graduate member of the Chartered Institute of Personnel Development (CIPD) and is associated with many other professional associations and networks in the UK and abroad. He also delivered various corporate trainings and undertook consultancies in the area of business, management and education in the UK and Middle Eastern region particularly Qatar and the United Arab Emirates.

Raye Ng is an associate professor of International Business at University of Cumbria. Raye read BA (Hons) Financial Economics, MA in Geographies of Globalisation and Development, and PhD (Corporate Culture). Raye has a Postgraduate Certificate in E-Learning, Postgraduate Certificate in Teaching and Learning in Higher Education. His academic interests include International Business, Marketing, Corporate Culture and Cross-Cultural Management. He is a senior fellow in Higher Education Academy and member of British Academy of Management.

Jafar Ojra is a senior lecturer of Accounting at Swansea University with over ten years of experience teaching undergraduate and postgraduate programmes. He has a multi-disciplinary research background, covering areas such as Accounting, Performance Measurement, Corporate Governance, Entrepreneurship and Marketing. Dr. Ojra's background includes diverse roles across various industries in both the UK and international settings.

Taiwo Olajumoke is a lecturer at Arden University. His research interests lie at the intersection of online brand communities, sustainability and luxury fashion brands. Olajumoke has authored and published several scholarly papers and presented his work at various international conferences. He is currently pursuing a PhD, focusing on the relationship between online brand communities and consumer post-purchase assessment within the tourism industry.

Fandi Omeish received his PhD from a top-ranked university in the world (Peking University) and master's degree in international marketing strategies from Hasselt University in Belgium. His research focuses on Tourism Marketing and Digital Marketing. Before joining PSUT, he was the Marketing and Public Relations director for the American University of Madaba and a Marketing Lecturer, providing students with the stepping stones of marketing. Moreover, he has practical experience working for an international advertising agency.

Abdullah Promise Opute is a researcher and freelance academic and management consultant with almost 20 years of professional experience in the academic industry. Dr. Abdullah Promise Opute is a visiting professor (Lecturer, PhD (DBA) Supervisor and Examiner) in several Management fields at UK and African Universities. He won 'Best Paper' award at the AM-Conference in 2007. Dr. Abdullah Promise Opute reviews for, and has published in top journals, e.g. Journal of Business and Industrial Marketing, International Journal of Entrepreneurship and Small Business, International Journal of Management Education, among others. His research interest includes inter-functional integration, relationship management, cross-cultural management, consumer behaviour, entrepreneurship and SMEs, strategic management accounting, etc.

Samuel Osei-Nimo is a senior lecturer in Management at Nottingham Business School, Nottingham Trent University. His research focuses on entrepreneurship in the creative sectors, including construction and fashion, with a particular interest in innovation, diversity, and addressing societal challenges. Samuel applies systems-thinking and information systems methodologies to explore power, knowledge and organisational dynamics. He is passionate about fostering inclusive growth and tackling complex socioeconomic issues within small businesses in these industries.

Wilson Ozuem is a professor of Digital Marketing & Innovation at the University for the Creative Arts, UK. His general area of expertise lies in digital marketing and fashion marketing, with a specific research focus on understanding the impacts of emerging computer-mediated marketing environments (CMMEs) on the fashion industry. Professor Ozuem has published in several leading journals, including Psychology & Marketing, European Journal of Marketing, Internet Research, Journal of Business Research, Information Technology & People, Journal of Advertising Research and many others.

Giovanna Pegan is an associate professor of Marketing and Management at the Department of Economics, Business, Mathematics, and Statistics of the University of Trieste (Italy). She currently coordinates the Master in Strategy and Business Consulting, where she teaches Consumer Behaviour and Business Communication. Her research interests focus on sustainable consumption, marketing communication and the effect of country of origin on international marketing strategies, with particular reference to the food and fashion industry. She has authored or co-authored numerous national and international book chapters, books and articles on these topics.

Silvia Ranfagni PhD, is a professor of Marketing at the Department of Economics and Management at the University of Florence (Italy).

Her research interests include innovation, internationalisation and brand management with special reference to the fashion and cultural industry. She has participated in international marketing conferences, and has published in national and international journals such as Journal of Fashion Marketing and Management, Management Decision, European Journal of Marketing, Journal of Consumer Behaviour, Journal of Business Research, Journal of Interactive Marketing and Journal of Psychology and Marketing.

Massimo Rosati is a senior lecturer in Business Economics and Management at the University of Florence, where he has held teaching and research roles since 2000. His expertise spans branding, distribution models, entrepreneurship and digital innovation. A member of SIM (Italian Marketing Society) and AIDEA (Italian Academy of Business Economics), Rosati has taught management and marketing at several US universities since 2014. In parallel with his academic work, he has served as a management consultant since 2000, holding executive roles in leading tourism companies and specialising in complex business management and digital marketing.

Sajad Rezaei is a senior lecturer in digital marketing at Worcester Business School, University of Worcester, UK. Dr. Rezaei's research focuses on the intersection of emerging technologies and usage, with a particular interest in how these technologies can be used for consumers' well-being, marketing, productivity and innovation. Dr. Rezaei's impactful work has been published in leading academic journals, including the *Journal of Business Research*, *Journal of Retailing and Consumer Services*, *Marketing Intelligence & Planning*, *Online Information Review* and *Computers in Human Behavior*. He is also a member of the editorial boards of several top academic journals in the field.

Atul Sethi has extensive experience in business and academia, with a total of 28 years in business and lecturing in education. His qualifications include BA Hons (Business Studies, Sussex University), MCIP (Masters in Chartered Institute of Personnel and Development, Sussex University), PGCE (Postgraduate Certificate in Education, Greenwich

University) and MA (Marketing, London Metropolitan University). Atul is a visiting lecturer for Strategy, Marketing & Business Research. His portfolio of clients includes Thames Valley University, Surrey University, Sussex University, London Metropolitan University, Ulster University (London Campus) and Roehampton University Business School. Alongside his lecturing profession, Atul has started up and is running a very successful property portfolio company based in Sussex, Surrey and Kent (UK).

Emily Rosa Shahaj, MA, FHEA leads the MA Digital Fashion course at the University for the Creative Arts in the UK. She holds an MA in Printed Textiles from the University for the Creative Arts and a BFA in Communications Design from Syracuse University. Bridging theory and creative practice as well as fashion and digital media, she previously worked in art direction and as a web3 fashion startup founder. Her interdisciplinary research interests include avatar clothing, identity expression in digital spaces, technology's implications for fashion sustainability and the posthumanities.

Janakan Sothinathan Senior lecturer in Business Management Faculty of Business and Law—University of Northumbria—London Campus. Module leader for the Postgraduate MSc Business with Strategic Management & Undergraduate BA (Hons) SME Business Strategy modules. I am also Involved in the administration of degree and postgraduate courses as well as responsible for organizing lectures and supervising seminars and tutorials, involved in the research and designing of new courses and materials and assessing students coursework and material.

My research and teaching interests are: international Business Strategic management, Strategic Management for Competitive Advantage, Strategic Project Management, SME Business Strategy Implementation and innovation & entrepreneurship.

Anna Tarabasz specialises in a wide range of areas of marketing, digital marketing, and e-commerce research. Her experience covers vital contexts in Poland, France, Kazakhstan, the United Arab Emirates,

Singapore, and Australia. She also has industry experience banking, automotive, and cosmetics industries. Serves as independent marketing & e-commerce consultant, keynote speaker, trainer, and business advisor for companies in MENA region (FMCG (Cosmetics, HoReCa, Agriculture), Manufacturing, Service, Transportation, Banking, and Consulting industries). Her research and publications in scopus-listed journals focus on Trends in Digital Marketing, Social Media Listening, SEO optimization & digital audit, eCommerce, and Generative AI in Academia.

Daniela Toccafondi has been an adjunct professor at the University of Florence (Italy). Her research interests are the local economy, the evolution of small and medium-sized in industrial districts. Starting from 2019 she has been President of Pin, Polo Universitario Città di Prato (Italy). She has published papers and books on the textile and fashion sustainability and on the Chinese community in the Prato district.

Isolde Ward-Lubbe is the head of the Department of Marketing Management at the University of Johannesburg (UJ). With more than a decade of experience in research, teaching and industry collaboration, she is dedicated to bridging the gap between academia and industry. Dr. Ward works closely with the Marketing Association of South Africa (MASA) to ensure students are future-ready and equipped for the workplace. Before joining UJ, she worked in London at KPMG and Mazars, where she was the head of UK Marketing Communications. Her expertise spans professional and financial services marketing and teaching strategic marketing, consumer behaviour and contemporary retailing. She has received several awards, including the SCiiS Excellence in Teaching Award (2022, 2019) and the Master's Supervision Award (2021).

Michelle Willis PhD, is a digital marketing lecturer at London Metropolitan University, UK. Her doctoral research focuses on customer loyalty and engagement within online brand communities. Her work examines emerging technologies, particularly the intersection of social networking sites and the development of marketing programmes, as well as online service failure and recovery strategies within the context of the millennial consumer generation. She has published numerous articles in journals such as Psychology & Marketing, Information Technology & People, and Internet Research. Her research has been presented at international conferences, including those organised by the American Marketing Association and the European Marketing Academy.

Xialiang Yao is a Doctor of Business Administration (DBA) candidate at the University of Wales Trinity Saint David and specialises in Strategic Management Accounting. She holds a bachelor's in Commerce (Accounting) and a master's in International Business from the University of South Australia, and has over 10 years of teaching experience in finance and accounting at Hunan Institute of Science and Technology. Her research bridges theory and practice and focuses on the impact of SMA techniques on corporate performance. Her interests include management accounting practices, corporate governance, technology integration in financial decision-making and accounting informatisation in emerging markets.

List of Figures

List of Tables

Part I

Foundations of Sustainable Digital Marketing

1

Postdigital Iconicity of Runways: Redefining Sustainability in High-End Fashion Marketing

Annette Kallevig and Vésma Kontere McQuillan

Introduction

The field of fashion studies is interdisciplinary by nature, combining diverse elements from various fields, methods, and approaches. Given that fashion research inherently involves integrating various disciplines, themes, methodologies, and perspectives spanning both theoretical frameworks and practical viewpoints, the contemporary fashion show emerges as a physical venue that serves as a digital marketing tool. In response, we propose combining fashion studies with marketing theory to redefine how brand values, such as sustainability, can be transmitted and extended through these iconic events.

Where luxury and fashion marketing in general is defined by exclusive, coveted, and iconic brands (Fionda & Moore, 2009), the most exclusive and iconic of all the elements that make up fashion marketing is perhaps the physical runway show presenting the coming collection (Pinchera &

A. Kallevig (✉) · V. K. McQuillan
Kristiania University of Applied Sciences, Oslo, Norway
e-mail: annette.kallevig@kristiania.no

W. Ozuem et al. (eds.), *Sustainable Digital Marketing for Fashion and Luxury Brands*,
https://doi.org/10.1007/978-3-031-82467-8_1

Rinallo, 2021). Access to front row seats has always been coveted. With fast fashion on the rise, presenting multiple collections annually, both the iconicity and exclusivity of the presentation of new collections are challenged. This high-volume fashion collection production with questionable ethical and environmental standards also threatens the social responsibility image of the fashion industry as a whole (Jestratijevic et al., 2024). High-end fashion brands distance themselves from sustainability perpetrators to maintain their status and retain the trust of their customers.

Luxury fashion shows are frequently treated as mere artful showcases of creativity, while in fact they present pivotal moments that can influence market and consumer behaviour, enhance brand loyalty, and drive sales. Integrating marketing theory into this discussion emphasises the role of fashion shows as strategic marketing tools. However, if the physical event is isolated and audited in terms of sustainability, these costly, temporary spectacles can be seen as wasteful extravaganzas not fit for modern sustainability requirements. Viewed from an extended postdigital perspective, the fashion show can be conceptualised as a multifaceted marketing campaign that leverages a brand's sustainability value proposition to a broader audience over time through a combination of physical and digital assets. Moreover, the digital dimension of postdigital runways allows for greater flexibility and creativity in presenting collections, potentially reducing the need for physical resources required for traditional show production. Brands can experiment with digital models, virtual reality experiences, and augmented reality fitting rooms to offer an immersive experience while emphasising their commitment to sustainability. Appeal does not need to rely on physical items but could use non-fungible tokens, for example (Azemi & Ozuem, 2023; McQuillan, 2024).

By blending digital and physical elements, a physical fashion show can also reduce its carbon footprint—less travel for attendees, reduced material waste from constructing temporary physical spaces, and the potential for a longer, more engaging digital lifespan for each show. This can amplify and support a brand's sustainability efforts, as digital platforms offer innovative ways to showcase eco-friendly practices and materials, engage with a global audience on sustainability issues, and foster a community around sustainable fashion.

Such an approach can significantly impact how brands strategise their presentations, focusing on creating immersive, interactive experiences that resonate with consumer values both on-site and online.

To succeed with a postdigital runway marketing strategy will require selecting and orchestrating a complex blend of assets with potentially conflicting goals, values, and identities. This leads us to ask: How can a luxury fashion show communicate a brand's sustainability profile and extend it postdigitally through digital influencers while retaining its marketplace iconicity?

Since the fashion show itself represents a stage in many layers with props and participants playing various roles within the same set, the theoretical framework of Erving Goffman (1959) regarding identity construction is applied to explore this phenomenon. First, we review how the high-end fashion show has evolved through various stages of iconicity and mediation, before this is aligned with the development of luxury fashion marketing towards the postdigital era and recent sustainability requirements. We then explore and discuss the dynamics as they interplay to create an extended fashion show experience, and how this can be used to extend sustainability efforts. Goffman's theory is explored as a tool for developing a collective brand identity, and a model for postdigital brand identity construction is proposed.

The aim of this article is twofold: first, to define the concept of a postdigital runway within the contexts of marketing theory and fashion studies, addressing a gap in the literature concerning fashion shows. We will primarily base this part on recent literature within fashion, consumerism, and cultural studies.

Second, we will discuss "postdigitality" as it pertains to the extended, mediated fashion show experience, and to what degree it can contribute to a sustainable brand identity and marketing strategy.

Theoretical Foundation and Context

Due to the multidisciplinary nature of this exploratory conceptual work, this section presents the history and theory behind each of the elements and phenomena that will be juxtaposed, converged, and discussed in the conceptual discussion.

The Runway as an Evolving Marketplace Icon

Fashion shows, traditionally the first scene to present new styles and collections, have evolved significantly since their inception in the second half of the nineteenth century. Originally practical demonstrations of clothing on living models, they gradually transformed into elaborate mannequin parades (Evans, 2001). Over nearly 170 years, as the fashion system changed, fashion shows morphed from exclusive events to extravagant spectacles celebrated during fashion weeks worldwide, and sometimes as standalone destination events in exotic geographical locations or unexpected venues.

Although the history of fashion shows is well-documented in fashion studies, the most defined framework for categorising their developmental stages is found within consumerism and cultural studies, which introduce the concept of the "marketplace icon" (Pinchera & Rinaldo, 2021). The term "marketplace icon" may need clarification within marketing and fashion studies. According to Ahir Gopaldas, "*Marketplace icons are brands, products, or services that are significant for their cultural meanings. Iconicity is about cultural significance rather than market share. Marketplace icons represent something novel or unusual about current times and are polarising, often celebrated by some and critiqued by others. They sustain iconicity through frequent media mentions and creative adaptations, transcending everyday consumption*" (Gopaldas, 2016).

Pinchera and Rinaldo (2021) categorised the industry's development into four distinct periods: Proto Iconicity (1850s–1950s), which marked the genesis and establishment of fashion as a cultural and social symbol; Challenged Iconicity (1950s–1970s), a period of questioning, experimentation, and breaking away from established norms; Mediated

Iconicity (1980s–2000s), characterised by the rise of mass media and global brands shaping public perception of fashion; and Digital Iconicity (2010s and beyond), where digital platforms, social media, and online retail transformed how fashion is consumed, shared and produced. While each era has contributed to the current fashion show experience, the latter is especially relevant to this chapter and is explored in more detail.

Digital Iconicity (2010s and Beyond)

Digital innovation, online platforms, social media, and the advent of online retail have dramatically changed how fashion is presented, consumed, and discussed since rich media has been transmitted digitally via the Internet. This transformation is evident through several key examples of the profound impact of these digital advancements on the fashion world. Fashion shows have become digital spectacles, accessible to global audiences, and integrated with social media to engage consumers directly. Shows are increasingly crafted with social media in mind, transforming into mediatised events—productions staged specifically for consumption online and on digital screens (Mendes, 2021). This period marks the shift towards a more democratised and interactive fashion culture.

Rebecca Halliday, in her comprehensive work "The Fashion Show Goes Live: Exclusive and Mediatised Performance", argues that the live stream of the "Plato's Atlantis" show in Paris on October 6, 2009, was one of the key moments in demonstrating the impact of social media on fashion. This show was live-streamed, drawing so many viewers that it caused a technical shutdown, mainly due to Lady Gaga's promotion of the event on Twitter (Halliday, 2022). This marked a turning point where social media began to transform the traditional setup of fashion shows, making them more accessible worldwide and blending the digital and physical aspects of fashion presentations.

Other pivotal moments at the intersection of fashion collections and social media were marked by the presence of fashion bloggers in the front row of Dolce & Gabbana's September 2009 collection, as well as the worldwide digital access to Burberry's September 2013 collection. The latter was live-streamed across 11 social networks, displayed on digital screens in its flagship store, and shown on outdoor screens in prominent locations worldwide, such as New York's Times Square. This approach allowed thousands of people to access the live event virtually through live streaming on their social media channels. A photo of the show's finale was retweeted 1200 times, and a video received 18,000 likes within a few hours on Instagram. These examples illustrate how social media have gradually redefined the approach to organising, running, and communicating fashion shows (Ozuem et al., 2008; Rocamora, 2017).

Now positioned at the nexus of diverse media streams involving brands, designers, models, traditional media, influencers, and consumers, this form of iconicity is increasingly developed outside the brand itself. Social media has introduced various changes to the fashion industry, prompting a re-evaluation of the enduring role of fashion shows as iconic elements within the marketplace (Pinchera & Rinallo, 2021).

Pandemic Disruption (2020–2022)

The COVID-19 pandemic accelerated or intensified the existing trend of mediatisation (Colucci & Pedroni, 2021; Ozuem et al., 2021). Government-enforced restrictions and widespread lockdowns drastically changed how people interacted, significantly affecting the social fashion industry. With physical socialising nearly impossible, fashion week events and other large fashion shows were either banned or heavily limited. The ability of social media creators to quickly adapt by creating new content at home and using their immediate surroundings became crucial in keeping the relationship between fashion brands and their audiences alive (Colucci & Peroni, 2021). Many fashion houses offered unique experiences by sending physical objects to spectators' homes in parallel with digital fashion presentations. For instance, J.W. Anderson's innovative "Show-in-a-Box" for Loewe, which included fabric samples, paper patterns, and other elements enabling recipients to engage interactively with the fashion show from home, exemplifies this. These physical items, widely shared and discussed on social media, symbolise the blend of physical and digital experiences that define contemporary fashion studies and history. The inclusion of a cardboard record player to play the event's soundtrack further bridged the physical and digital by providing an auditory layer to the experience (Linfante & Pompa, 2021). By distributing these curated material objects, brands maintained a tactile connexion with their audience, underscoring the importance of materiality even in a digitally dominated world. This method not only preserved but also enhanced the sensory experience of fashion, making it more personal and interactive. The ensuing social media engagement helped reach a wider audience, turning traditional viewers into active participants. It also highlighted the shift towards a more sustainable and consumer-involved approach to fashion, where both creation and consumption of fashion have become more democratised.

Being restricted to digital interaction accelerated digital fashion innovation in place of fashion shows by necessity and has had a vast impact on the physical fashion shows of today. By combining digital and physical resources, fashion shows have become immersive experiences that communicate on many levels. Live, tactile fashion events can include digital interactivity and virtual participation, creating an inclusive and innovative hybrid model. These truly integrated experiences also bring new opportunities for sustainable consumption and marketing (Mendes, 2021).

Luxury Fashion Marketing Extended

Before digital marketing, most marketing communication efforts were planned in campaign cycles, with each campaign usually spanning a few months. This corresponded well with the cyclical, seasonal planning of fashion collections. With digital channels, these cycles have been replaced with an always-on approach to marketing communication. While this creates an opportunity for the brand experience to always be available for consumption, it is demanding to plan for since the luxury fashion collections still arrive in cycles, creating a somewhat asynchronous relationship between the two. The fashion industry has increased the number and volume of collections for continual novelty marketing at the cost of decreased production sustainability (Long & Nasiry, 2022; Ozuem et al., 2023), which is not a viable option for luxury fashion brands without threatening their iconic and exclusive qualities. Instead, luxury fashion brands should harness the new digital transformational opportunities to amplify their branded, luxury experiences and extend the reach and lifetime of their marketing efforts in a seamless and holistic manner (Ranfagni & Ozuem, 2022). This agrees with the exclusive iconicity that defines these brand identities without compromising sustainable production and marketing communication.

Towards Postdigital Integration

At the beginning of the digital era, our physical and digital lives were separate entities, as was physical and digital marketing. Cyberspace was a separate and alternate reality parallel to the physical space we occupy, accessed only through desktop computers. Digital connectivity is now available at virtually all times through mobile devices, and the digital aspects of our lives have become increasingly integrated with our everyday physical activity. The term "postdigital" has been introduced to describe this hybrid construct. Although the use, definitions, and perspectives of the term vary greatly, postdigital is defined by the ubiquitous integration of digital technology in all aspects of our lives, extending beyond the digital (Taffel, 2016).

Postdigital evolution holds a user-centric perspective based on human technology adoption and is therefore a cross-disciplinary phenomenon that is as relevant to psychology as it is to marketing (Taffel, 2016). As consumers, we may move so seamlessly between digital and analogue spaces that we are frequently unaware of the distinction between channels, sometimes oblivious to which channels led us to an affinity towards a brand, or even a purchase, for better or for worse (Humayun & Belk, 2020).

The COVID-19 pandemic is likely to have radically accelerated postdigital evolution. When suddenly forced to interact purely digitally over extended periods during lockdown, organisations replaced physical services with digital ones at exceptional speed, and even the digitally reluctant were moved to increase their digital literacy at an unexpected pace. New innovations and broad digital literacy in society have made new and informed hybrid experiences possible (Ozuem et al., 2024; Silvestri, 2020).

From a postdigital marketing perspective, it is useful to identify digital and nondigital touchpoints throughout a customer journey and work to minimise friction between them for a smooth customer journey towards the desired marketing outcome (Heine & Berghaus, 2014).

Postdigital Fashion Marketing

In a fashion marketing context, a postdigital perspective offers new opportunities for impactful but temporary real-time events, such as fashion shows. For these typically costly and short-lived events, digital channels have provided an opportunity to significantly extend their lifespan and reach new audiences in channel-appropriate ways, thereby increasing cost-effectiveness (Mendes, 2021). Where mass media merely broadcast the events, postdigital marketing offers the opportunity to engage with audience members by providing timely and relevant extensions of the original content, thereby creating optimised customer journeys over time (Silvestri, 2020). This creates opportunities for extended, immersive experiences for broad audiences and increases their measurability towards direct sales through digital data collection.

For a unified brand presence across all channels, a creative integrated marketing communication approach is needed (Kallevig et al., 2022). Fashion shows are immersive experiences where the brand needs to be reflected in a complex combination of physical, non-physical, and digital aspects beyond marketing communication, with many specialists involved in the execution. A holistic, postdigital strategy is required to manage this new, extended experience.

Sustainable Marketing

Sustainability as a complex social construct has been widely interpreted as it has gained popularity as a business responsibility. A sustainable business or organisation generally implies corporate social responsibility (CSR). Within CSR, sustainability is generally agreed to refer to the ethical, environmental, and social responsibility of companies (Shu, 2023). Sustainability initiatives in all fields and industries are held up against the United Nations Sustainable Development Goals (SDGs) of 2015 (Sheth & Parvatiyar, 2021; *THE 17 GOALS | Sustainable Development*, n.d.). This ensures that all activities adhere to the holistic international standard of sustainability. The responsibility of marketing in terms of sustainable production and consumption has grown from a mere concern to a megatrend within marketing in the twenty-first century, as has the fashion industry. The industry has received much criticism regarding sustainability, with questionable practices in conflict with several of the UN SDGs. Many of the breaches of conduct are related to garment production, distribution, waste management, and exploitation of human capital, but more overarching fashion brand attributes, notably inspiring unnecessary consumption, have also been challenged. Greenwashing refers to the corporate practice of extensively communicating minor sustainability initiatives while other larger breaches of sustainability goals go unreported (Parguel et al., 2011). A recent longitudinal study confirms that greenwashing also prevails among luxury fashion brands and recommends external audits and governmental reporting requirements to improve transparency (Jestratijevic et al., 2022).

SDG 12, which specifically addresses responsible consumption and production, is particularly relevant to luxury fashion brands and products. The relationship between the luxury fashion industry and sustainability holds a paradoxical tension due to the diametrical differences between the two constructs (Shu, 2023). Where sustainability is characterised by restraint according to the need for the greater good, abundance and the use of scarce resources for personal consumption is a core driver of the luxury fashion industry. This has led Shu and other researchers to apply a paradoxical perspective when exploring this tension or friction as it applies to sustainability in fashion. It has been argued that luxury fashion, characterised by quality, exclusivity, and craftmanship by skilled labour, is the most sustainable segment within the fashion industry, while the coveted aspect of the products may inspire unnecessary consumption. The discussion of whether the luxury fashion industry in and of itself is sustainable is an interesting, multifaceted subject without a clear answer at present, and further research is required (Ranfagni & Ozuem, 2022).

Regardless of sustainability initiatives a brand undertakes to improve its CSR profile, the goal of promotional marketing of products is ultimately economic growth by way of production, so this must be balanced against responsible consumption to remain sustainable.

Sustainability of the Fashion Show

The fashion and fashion event industry, including fashion shows, is increasingly focusing on sustainability, and ISO standards play a crucial role in this effort. The International Organisation for Standardisation (ISO) is an independent, non-governmental organisation that develops and publishes standards (ISO, 2024). One relevant standard is ISO 20121, which is tailored for event sustainability management and provides a framework that aligns with the broader ISO principles of quality and efficiency. It integrates sustainability into event planning and execution, ensuring that fashion events are environmentally responsible, socially equitable, and economically efficient.

In McQuillan's architectural research, an in-depth analysis of fashion show design and production design revealed a significant trend: Specialised fashion show and event production firms dominated the design and execution of these events. A total of 78 fashion shows were examined to reveal the substantial influence of event production specialists such as Bureau Betak and La Mode en Image. In contrast, architectural firms such as PAF Atelier are emerging but still have a limited presence in this domain (McQuillan, 2024).

Specialised fashion show production companies are now essential in orchestrating and executing high-profile fashion events. These companies manage everything from conceptualisation, set design, lighting, music, and choreography to ensure a seamless and memorable experience, often in collaboration with independent artists, designers, or architectural companies. The most influential in the European context are Villa Eugénie, Bureau Betak, and La Mode en Images. The latter two have earned ISO 20121 certifications.

Among the entities studied, Bureau Betak and PAF Atelier have the most explicitly articulated sustainability strategies. Bureau Betak has implemented ten commandments linked to real-world actions executed before, during, and after each event production since 2020 (Bureau Betak, 2023). PAF Atelier, representing the architectural perspective, emphasises sustainable strategies in their work with fashion shows. In interviews with FRAME magazine, they stated, *"Our role will be to contribute to new solutions and help accelerate ideas, to rethink outdated codes and organisational principles, to integrate ideas of openness, social co-presence, and gender fluidity into the spaces we design"* (Kuitert, 2022). PAF Atelier's sustainability initiatives include creating a library of props that can be reused and transformed for different shows and renting building materials from a specialised company to reduce environmental impact (McQuillan, 2022).

Fashion show production and design companies employ various strategies that can be applied on both micro and macro levels to significantly enhance the sustainability of fashion show production. These strategies include the following:

Reusing materials: Reusing existing decor (furniture, props, artistic designs), renting stage elements, and reducing the necessity to build elements from scratch.

Upcycling and redistributing set decor: Giving a second life to materials and repurposing set components between shows.

Reducing waste and abolishing single-use plastics: Sorting and recycling materials that cannot be reused and selecting more sustainable materials where single-use items are unavoidable.

Green energy: Minimising fossil fuel use. When generators are necessary, priority is set on renewable biofuels (such as colza oil) instead of traditional fossil fuels, for example.

Reducing travel and supporting local economy and employment: Compensating for an event's carbon dioxide emissions by financing environmental projects that counteract those emissions or sequester carbon, and monitoring activity and compiling feedback to improve practices from one event to the next (Bureau Betak, 2023).

Digital awareness: Optimising the use of digital tools while being aware of their impact.

Mediated Fashion Marketing Evolution

Exclusive fashion brands have a history of being dependent on many stakeholders, including mediators outside the organisation. When the press became a part of the marketing communication mix, the dynamics of control over the brand image towards the mass market changed. The duality of the relationship where paid and earned media appeared in the same media outlets with various degrees of mediation has created notable tension (Colucci & Pedroni, 2021). An example would be a costly luxury fashion ad series opening a fashion magazine that also contains a critical editorial review of the latest runway show. Editorial reviews of the coming season's collection are still sought by the brands to add trustworthiness not attained by advertising. Gaining favourable reviews is an important factor in the marketing communication mix of luxury fashion brands.

As opposed to journalist reviews, which target mass media and are governed by editorial ethics, reviews shared by digital influencers are neither: They target more intimately, are perceived as peer-to-peer communication, and are frequently paid collaborations. In this relation, perceived authenticity of the influencer is key to the trust relationship with the consumer (Colucci & Pedroni, 2022; Jacobson & Harrison, 2022).

Where traditional celebrity influencers attain their fame from physical world accomplishments, the digital influencers of the past two decades have gained their status solely through online content creations (Leung et al., 2022). Digital fashion influencers are social media practitioners who wield substantial power as cultural intermediaries connecting consumers and brands (Pedroni, 2023). According to research by Colucci and Pedroni, some influencers have fabricated an image of authenticity for brands they collaborate with (2022). If such fabrication is revealed when collaborating on promoting sustainable efforts, the brand involved risks being labelled as greenwashing and jeopardising its brand value. Recent literature has proposed that congruency, authenticity, and trust are key components in successful online influencer marketing collaborations (Breves et al., 2019; Kallevig, 2024). This may be especially true when seeking to spread value-driven communication, such as sustainability.

Influencer culture has also been associated with encouraging excessive consumerism. Many influencers promote fast fashion, excessive purchasing, and lifestyle inflation, all of which are inherently at odds with sustainable consumption. A fundamental tension between the influencer business model and the goals of reduced consumption and waste has been identified (Jacobson & Harrison, 2022; Liu, 2022).

Content creators' activities tend to have a broader, long-term effect on a brand than direct promotional activities (Albuquerque et al., 2012). Digital influencers' presence and content creation from fashion shows represent an opportunity for extended reach and long-term effect for a brand message, including underlying value propositions such as sustainability. The precarious balance between paid partnerships, brand transparency, content creator autonomy, and inspiring sustainable consumption may be useful to bear in mind when designing for and catering to the extended experiences of influencers as mediators at fashion shows.

The Theory of Identity Construction

Erving Goffman's seminal work on identity construction (1959) theorises face-to-face interactions in real time, and what we convey about our true identity in these immediate interactions. A frontstage versus backstage metaphor of human identity is central to this theory. Since its conception, there has been much discussion about whether the theory of identity construction can be applied to mediated interaction, with several interesting perspectives on the effect of mediation (Rettie, 2009). Central elements to the discourse are whether the human interactions need to be direct vs. indirect, synchronous vs. asynchronous, physical vs. virtual, and temporal vs. permanent. Rettie's work shows how theories regarding face-to-face interaction can be applied and give meaning to mediated encounters, but that the dynamics may differ from that of a direct encounter. Synchronicity of communication is emphasised as a key factor, replacing synchronous physical presence in mediation.

In Rettie's research, the participants perceived a telephone conversation as if they were with the person they were talking to, illustrating how real-time mediation had become ubiquitous. New technology has greatly increased the opportunity for synchronous, mediated interactions since the publication of this study in 2009.

The key concept of gatherings in Goffman's work also becomes more complex in mediated encounters because an extended audience may have access to only one side of an encounter and interpret that half. This brings a duality to the interaction, where communication is sometimes adapted to both audiences by the performer (Rettie, 2009). An example would be answering only "yes" or "no" to a telephone caller to prevent listeners in the shared physical space from decoding the conversation. In this case, the performer administers two different frontstage "shows" simultaneously.

Media evolution since 2009 has not diminished the duality of transmission between intended and unintended audiences, but rather multiplied the effect. A digital adoption of Erving Goffman's theory of identity construction to the postdigital realm concludes that the physical world can become "backstage identity" and the digital "frontstage" for personalities primarily known through their online identity, such as digital influencers (Bullingham & Vasconcelos, 2013). Pre-COVID, this may have been only an academic discussion, but during the pandemic lockdowns, the general public became instantly aware of digital front- and backstage issues, and identity construction to make the backstage of our homes frontstage material became mainstream. We learned to stage our on-screen environment for conference calls, dressing what was visible on-screen differently than the off-screen parts. While most digital fashion influencers create their content in the real world, it is created specifically and carefully curated for digital consumption. This physical world becoming their curated, digital backstage is as evident in their livestreams as in the asynchronous content they produce.

A recent study regarding sustainable social media influencers extensively refers to Erving Goffman's theory (Jacobson & Harrison, 2022). In this study, the theory is applied to analyse social media influencers' portrayal of self on social media while engaging in marketing, a topic we will explore in more depth in the discussion.

With the fashion show itself holding the obvious, connexion to Goffman's stage metaphor both physically and conceptually, and the recent trend towards placing the digital influencer front row at the runway shows to convey its content and meaning onwards to a broader audience, has inspired combining these two disciplines to add a postdigital layer to the Goffman stage model.

Discussion

With this theoretical backdrop, we return to the initial question: How can a luxury fashion show communicate a brand's sustainability profile and extend it postdigitally through digital influencers while retaining its marketplace iconicity? Since the fashion show itself is concerned with identity construction for the brand, and the digital influencer is concerned with their own identity construction through their association with the brand, we explore the topic through the theory of identity construction (Goffman, 1959) seeking to find a path of transmission for the sustainability message through the various "stages" within the "set". We start with the physical backstage, where the sustainable initiatives of the brand are created and to be conveyed from.

Brand Backstage and Frontstage of a Fashion Show

In the context of a fashion show, the original, physical backstage of the show corresponds well to Goffman's backstage. Backstage is where all the preparations occur, such as dressing the models, planning choreography, and discussing strategies. The extended backstage also includes all the preparations that occur before and behind the show, as well as outside the physical backstage area, such as garment production. The fashion show backstage used to be unavailable to mainstream media. Although many of the "performers" are the same "actors" as frontstage, the dynamics and presentation of self are quite different in the backstage gathering and is usually more natural and open. While there is a social performance happening backstage, which can be seen as a type of frontstage for most actors, they collectively create the brand's backstage personality. In this setting, the group of performers can learn and agree on the brand's frontstage personality.

Goffman's theory, particularly his concepts of the "presentation of self" and the distinctions between "frontstage" and "backstage" areas, provides a rich framework for analysing how fashion shows can encapsulate and communicate sustainability. Conscientiously selecting fabrics and methods for the collection that are environmentally friendly and ethically sound is the first step for the fashion industry towards its sustainable symbolic output, so that what the public sees and interprets on the runway genuinely reflects sustainable practices. If the backstage processes of a fashion show incorporate sustainable strategies, such as using locally sourced materials, minimising transportation, and employing eco-friendly production methods, it can enhance the authenticity of the sustainability message and reinforce brand commitment to environmental and social responsibilities. Many important sustainable improvements a fashion brand can make backstage are invisible to the public, even when brought forward. Although we can argue that the frontstage becomes inherently more sustainable, it needs to be communicated forward by actors who bridge the back- and frontstage realms. Only then can the fashion show evolve from a mere spectacle to a meaningful conduit for promoting and instilling sustainable values within the industry and its audience.

Bringing Sustainability Forward

The runway represents the stage where fashion performance occurs. Models, designers, and their garments must all convey a desired image or brand identity to the audience. Every aspect of this presentation is carefully curated to influence perceptions, embody the brand's aesthetic, and engage the audience. The actors on this frontstage are not necessarily portraying their personal frontstage personality, but that of the brand. An example would be a model working fashion week, displaying a somewhat different front-stage personality for each collection she presents, drawing on her own unique assets and adapting them to the brand personality and show concept.

From Goffman's perspective, the fashion show can be seen not just as a display of new collections but also as a complex performance of identity and impression management. Each model's walk, the music, the lighting, and even the audience's reactions are part of a carefully orchestrated experience designed to convey a specific message and evoke particular feelings and responses, which Laing describes as the close connexion between fashion, dreaming, and desire (Laing, 2024). This highlights the performative aspects of fashion and how they are used to construct and communicate identity both on an individual and brand level. The collective brand personality can be value-based, so that the symbols and signage of an explicitly sustainable brand personality can be learned and conveyed through the actors, such as models, and even the structure of the event itself.

Drawing on the strategies delineated by Grose (2014), we can adapt their transformative approaches for fashion products to the context of a fashion show. These strategies not only improve the environmental footprint of the fashion industry but also position fashion shows as leaders in sustainability advocacy:

Materials selection: By choosing sustainable materials, fashion shows can significantly reduce their environmental impact. This involves selecting organic materials that avoid the use of pesticides, utilising recycled materials to decrease waste and incorporating innovative, eco-friendly materials that minimise environmental damage. Showcasing these choices during fashion shows educates the audience and sets a standard for industry practices. Highlighting fashion show environments made from these materials during the show can serve as a direct demonstration of the brand's commitment to sustainable practices.

Production techniques: Adopting environmentally friendly manufacturing processes is crucial. For fashion shows, promoting local manufacturing is particularly beneficial. This not only helps reduce transportation emissions but also supports local economies, contributing to a smaller overall carbon footprint. By integrating local artisans and suppliers into the production process, fashion shows can highlight regional craftsmanship and reduce logistical complexities associated with long-distance transportation.

Transparency and traceability: Increasing transparency in the supply chain is vital for building trust and accountability. Fashion shows provide a platform to showcase the origins of materials and the ethical practices involved in the production processes. This can be achieved by providing detailed backstories during the show, such as video segments or digital presentations that trace the journey of a garment from raw materials to the runway. Incorporating QR codes or interactive digital tags on garments that provide this information can engage the audience and encourage them to learn more about the sustainability efforts behind each piece is another option. The latter also provides a digital bridge to a site where the experience can be extended directly, for prolonged brand interaction or even sales.

Transparency Through the "Stages"

When sustainability initiatives backstage are reframed and emphasised for public consumption through multimedia communication frontstage, there is always a risk that the communication is perceived as greenwashing. In the pervasive media discussions about sustainable fashion, the topic often becomes diluted, struggling to capture the audience's attention effectively despite its significant implications. The dominance of pressing sustainability narratives over fashion's creative expression can lead to what is termed "green fatigue". Laing (2024) argues that the symbolic production of fashion is just as critical as its material production: thoughtfully considered material production will lead to sustainable symbolic production.

Both green fatigue and perceived greenwashing will not only diminish the intended effect and potentially increase scepticism towards sustainable fashion, but it can also damage the brand's iconicity. Lack of consistency in the level of sustainability throughout the experience can cause doubt in the authenticity of the initiatives. If, for example, a brand conveys sustainable fabric and production in the garments on the runway, then the show venue should signal the same sustainable material choice by avoiding unsustainable materials to avoid mixed signals regarding the authenticity of sustainability efforts. The sustainability initiatives of production companies such as Betak (Bureau Betak, 2023) should be aligned with those of the brand to ensure a holistic, sustainable experience. By communicating sustainability efforts and values through every aspect of production, a brand can avoid dissonance at the venue by securing not only its own sustainable production but also that of its suppliers.

Although brands within this sector tend to have high traceability in their supply chains to verify their exclusivity, few have complete sustainability in every part of their production process. As sustainability requirements change, being 100% sustainable is probably an impossible task. To influence the public towards positive change proactively, brands may need to communicate their sustainability efforts before they are successfully implemented. To avoid undesirable reveals of breaches of sustainability associated with greenwashing, a brand is well advised to also be transparent regarding ongoing sustainability initiatives. Presenting sustainability programme details at the show may detract from the immersive experience, which is about the collection, not the company. This information could be available on demand through the training of staff in the sustainability narrative and digitally through QR codes, for example. This use of postdigital opportunities makes complex, backstage information available without diminishing the creative experience of the fashion show.

Front Row and Digital Backstage

When digital influencers are invited front row at runway shows, they enter a real-world celebrity setting, which can be seen as part of the frontstage at the fashion event. While the front row invitation carries status and therefore physically brings them into a frontstage situation, their role carries a duality (Rettie, 2009). For most influencers, whose fame is derived from digital content creation, this is not their normal frontstage, and in Goffman's terms, they may not be familiar with the "sign equipment" of this "play" (Goffman, 1959). Their area of expertise is in turning physical experiences into digital content appropriate to their personal digital brand and their followers, and this is their primary goal here as well. From this perspective, the digital, mediated transmission from influencer to followers is the frontstage for the influencer as soon as content production takes place, and the fashion show as a whole becomes the digital backstage. For this reason, the areas outside the venues at the big fashion weeks have become street fashion shows of their own as influencers compete in the dressing game when attending the shows (Moore, 2022). The iconic display on the catwalk may be a small part of their lavish social narrative, where the primary iconicity promoted may well be their own.

Since digital influencers need to have autonomy to create authentic, trustworthy content, luxury brands should invite influencers to their shows not only based merely on mega-influencer status and metrics but also seek congruency with values and brand identity of the influencer (Kallevig, 2024). While digital content creation is increasingly catered to by the shows (Mendes, 2021), their selection criteria regarding influencers attending the shows are less known.

Given their power of influence, there is a vast potential for digital influencers to contribute positively to sustainability efforts or, conversely, to propagate unsustainable practices. Given their reach and impact, influencers who are genuinely committed to sustainability can serve as important allies in communicating sustainability goals and values. They can showcase sustainable living as both desirable and attainable, influence brands to adopt more sustainable practices due to consumer demand shifts, and act as role models by integrating sustainability deeply into their own lives and content. Influencers can use their platforms to educate their audiences about environmental issues and sustainable practices. This might include sharing information about recycling, waste reduction, or the impacts of overconsumption. Influencers can help foster a more environmentally conscious consumer base by demystifying complex sustainability topics. A challenge might be selective sustainability. An example would be an influencer promoting sustainable clothing while travelling extensively by plane between fashion weeks.

Fortunately, with the increased focus on sustainability, sustainable fashion social media influencers have been identified as a category of fashion influencers (Jacobson & Harrison, 2022). In their study, they identified three subgroups: Sustainable lifestyle influencers, sustainability influencers, and thrifting influencers. Because runway shows involve new products, thrifting influencers are naturally excluded as a likely match in this context. Where the sustainability influencer category may appear to provide a congruent match, Jacobsen and Harrison's research reveals a potential obstacle. Their category of sustainable fashion influencers has the greatest challenge in monetising their influencer status due to uncompromising ethics. Therefore, it is likely that they will experience ethical incongruency with the paradox of sustainability and luxury fashion marketing (Ranfagni & Ozuem, 2022; Shu, 2023). The best match for most luxury fashion brands is likely to be a sustainable lifestyle influencer. These influencers advocate sustainability as an integral part of their lives, but since they also share other lifestyle content, they were found to afford more flexibility in their commercial collaborations. This flexibility is useful for a fashion brand that wants to integrate the sustainability of its brand identity into its overall iconic presence, since these digital influencers can create various types of content, highlighting different aspects of a brand presentation.

Overall, the front-self of all digital sustainability influencers is accountable towards sustainable practices, which makes them a good match for a sustainable luxury fashion brand. Since the commercial potential of these influencers remains largely untapped, a sustainable luxury fashion brand is well advised to seek such collaborations, invite influential sustainable lifestyle influencers to the front row, and ensure that the show caters to their content calibration. A successful collaboration with such an influencer is likely to increase trust in the sustainability of a brand (Jacobson & Harrison, 2022).

Extended Digital Frontstage

With the rise of the postdigital fashion show, fashion brands have begun showing aspects of backstage, using transparency to change the perception of the formerly distant and elitist industry (Mendes, 2021). In the evolving landscape of fashion, particularly in a postdigital context, the traditional concepts of "backstage" and "frontstage" can be reimagined to align with the dual realities of physical and digital presentations. In this framework, the physical fashion show, often perceived as the main spectacle, shifts to function as the "backstage" area. This space, though central to the production, remains largely hidden from the broader, digital audience and is where raw, unedited preparation and execution occur. This includes orchestrating the physical event, but it also encompasses the wider operational and production tasks that are critical yet not visible to the online audience. Conversely, the "frontstage" now also includes the digital extension of the show—what the online audience experiences.

Sustainable practices such as selecting eco-friendly materials, employing energy-efficient production methods, and supporting local manufacturing are implemented in the extended brand backstage. When these efforts are engrained in the collection being displayed, the physical show acquires this backstage sustainability. The sustainable practices implemented behind the scenes can be projected onto the physical and digital frontstage, potentially influencing a global audience about the importance and feasibility of sustainability in fashion. This approach ensures that sustainability is woven through both the seen and unseen aspects of fashion shows, enhancing the industry's integrity and commitment to environmental stewardship.

The frontstage has expanded beyond the physical runway, extending into the digital realm. Here, the frontstage is not just about the live event anymore but also encompasses how the fashion show is represented online. Instagram, for example, serves as one of the digital frontstages where brands meticulously curate and showcase their images and narratives. Here they can project a refined, idealised version of their fashion show to a global audience, enhancing and sometimes overshadowing the physical event. This dynamic underscores the evolving nature of social interactions and identity management in the fashion industry, which is influenced by digital technology, social media platforms, and new mediators such as fashion influencers. According to Mendes (2021), the Instagram presentation is now as important as the formal presentation of the collection, as a way for the brand to extend the ephemeral event beyond the dissemination of "official" press images or through the vector of digital influencers, who act as intermediaries between brand and consumer.

Conclusion and Managerial Implications

Through this conceptual exploration, we conclude that Goffman's model is applicable to hybrid, postdigital identity creation, both on the individual and collective levels.

In a brand context, the teams that make up the back- and frontstage gatherings at a fashion show become part of a greater brand identity construction, in which also Goffman's theories can be applied. To visualise this, a conceptual model for sustainable brand identity construction is proposed (Fig. 1.1). Much like Goffman's theory of identity construction, some aspects of the identity can be purposely constructed to convey a certain image, while other aspects will shine through and show the true nature of the brand. The object of the model is to facilitate maintaining a congruent brand identity throughout marketing initiatives, in line with sustainability efforts and the iconic identity that the brand already has. In the case of a specific collection for a runway show, the conceptual model can also be applied at the campaign level.

Runway Marketing Redefined

Based on this theoretical exploration, we propose the following definition: A Postdigital runway show is a presentation and promotion of an upcoming fashion collection at a physical event, extended across space, time, and reach through seamlessly integrated and immersive multimedia experiences. Strategically positioned at the intersection of multiple media

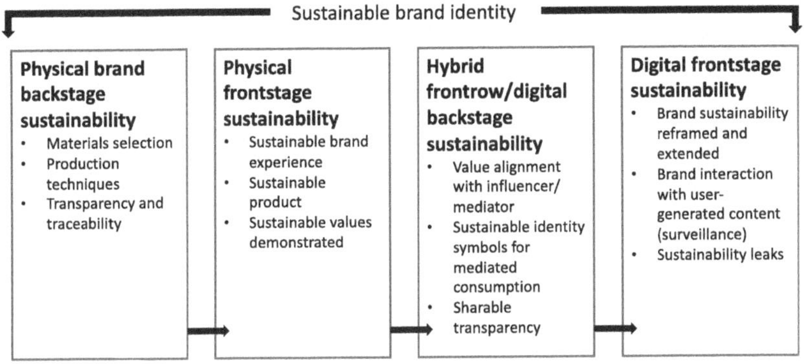

Fig. 1.1 Sustainable brand identity construction—A conceptual model

streams, it incorporates paid, owned, and earned contributions from brands, designers, models, traditional media, influencers, and consumers. This convergence enhances the event's influence, contributing to the iconic status of the runway and the fashion brand it represents.

"Sustainable Postdigital Iconicity" may be seen as a consecutive stage in the evolution of fashion show development to encapsulate the ongoing transformation within the industry. This approach not only recognises the immediate adaptations and innovations spurred by the COVID-19 pandemic but also anticipates the future trajectory towards sustainability and integrated experiences. By taking a human identity approach to the work, we facilitate aligning the various identities involved in the work, including the fashion influencers and their personal brands, to the fashion brand identity.

By embedding the proposed conceptual model in the fabric of their operations, fashion shows can transform into powerful platforms for promoting the sustainable practices of a brand. Not only can they demonstrate practical and effective ways to integrate environmentally conscious practices, but they can also influence the broader fashion industry and its consumers to adopt more sustainable behaviours. Such a proactive approach in fashion shows can lead to a ripple effect, encouraging all stakeholders in the value chain to prioritise sustainability.

To facilitate the maintenance of a sustainable yet iconic brand image through digital influencer mediation, we recommend the following steps:

- Develop a sustainable brand core. The foundation for a sustainable brand conveyed through a fashion show is a sustainable core. Material selection, production techniques, and traceability in line with UN sustainability goals must be aligned across the product, brand, and show production. Transparency is also advised regarding shortcomings to avoid greenwashing accusations.
- Project a sustainable brand personality. By holding the brand personality to the standards of Goffman's theory, construct a sustainable brand identity that encompasses the four stages discussed (Fig. 1.1). This will ensure a coherent brand personality and inherent sustainable values in all aspects of the project, including value alignment with collaborators.
- Stage the sustainable postdigital experience. The digital aspects of the postdigital iconic experience are integrated into the physical event, and awareness that the frontstage physical experience is backstage for digital influencer content creation should be planned. Immersive experiences, including those involving sustainability, should be readily available for exploration, adoption, and consumption by creative digital influencers. For a holistic perspective on this work, our conceptual model (Fig. 1.1) may be useful.
- Communicate sustainable iconicity. Sustainability should be communicated creatively in line with the brand personality to retain iconicity. A seamless postdigital experience at the show provides the opportunity to obtain more details regarding sustainability initiatives, thereby supporting rather than competing with the iconic presentation of the collection.
- Select influencers by congruent values. Luxury fashion brands that wish to convey sustainable values through influencers should select influencers not only by metrics and reach, but also actively seek those with a sustainability profile congruent with that of the brand.

By integrating these practices, the fashion show can transcend its traditional role as merely a site of aesthetic display and emerge as a powerful advocate for sustainability. This approach not only aligns with broader environmental goals but also enhances the authenticity and integrity of the fashion narrative, which in turn can strengthen brand iconicity.

References

Albuquerque, P., Pavlidis, P., Chatow, U., Chen, K. Y., & Jamal, Z. (2012). Evaluating promotional activities in an online two-sided market of user-generated content. *Marketing Science, 31*(3), 406–432. https://doi.org/10.1287/MKSC.1110.0685

Azemi, Y., & Ozuem, W. (2023). How does retargeting work for different Gen Z mobile users? *Journal of Advertising Research*, 2023-023. https://doi.org/10.2501/jar-2023-023

Breves, P. L., Liebers, N., Abt, M., & Kunze, A. (2019). The perceived fit between Instagram influencers and the endorsed brand: How influencer–brand fit affects source credibility and persuasive effectiveness. *Journal of Advertising Research, 59*(4), 440–454. https://doi.org/10.2501/JAR-2019-030

Bullingham, L., & Vasconcelos, A. C. (2013). 'The presentation of self in the online world': Goffman and the study of online identities. *Journal of Information Science, 39*(1), 101–112. https://doi.org/10.1177/0165551512470051

Bureau Betak. (2023). *BETTER BETAK: Sustainability Manifesto.* https://betterbetak.bureaubetak.com/

Colucci, M., & Pedroni, M. (2021). Mediatized fashion: State of the art and beyond. *ZoneModa Journal, 11*(1), III–XIV.

Colucci, M., & Pedroni, M. (2022). Got to be real: An investigation into the co-fabrication of authenticity by fashion companies and digital influencers. *Journal of Consumer Culture, 22*(4), 929–948.

Evans, C. (2001). The enchanted spectacle. *Fashion Theory, 5*(3), 271–310. https://doi.org/10.2752/136270401778960865

Fionda, A. M., & Moore, C. M. (2009). The anatomy of the luxury fashion brand. *Journal of Brand Management, 16*(5–6), 347–363. https://doi.org/10.1057/bm.2008.45

Goffman, E. (1959). *The presentation of self in everyday life* (First). Anchor Books (Random House).

Gopaldas, A. (2016). Therapy. *Consumption markets & culture, 19*(3), 264–268. https://doi.org/10.1080/10253866.2015.1096070

Grose, L. (2014). Fashion as material. In K. Fletcher & M. Tham (Eds.), *Handbook of sustainability and fashion* (pp. 223–233). Routledge.

Halliday, R. (2022). *The fashion show goes live: Exclusive and mediatized performance*. Bloomsbury Publishing.

Heine, K., & Berghaus, B. (2014). Luxury goes digital: How to tackle the digital luxury brand–consumer touchpoints. *Journal of Global Fashion Marketing, 5*(3), 223–234. https://doi.org/10.1080/20932685.2014.907606

Humayun, M., & Belk, R. (2020). The analogue diaries of postdigital consumption. *Journal of Marketing Management, 36*, 633–659. https://doi.org/10.1080/0267257X.2020.1724178

Jacobson, J., & Harrison, B. (2022). Sustainable fashion social media influencers and content creation calibration. *International Journal of Advertising, 41*(1), 150–177. https://doi.org/10.1080/02650487.2021.2000125

Jestratijevic, I., Uanhoro, J. O., & Creighton, R. (2022). To disclose or not to disclose? Fashion brands' strategies for transparency in sustainability reporting. *Journal of Fashion Marketing and Management, 26*(1), 36–50. https://doi.org/10.1108/JFMM-09-2020-0182

Jestratijevic, I., Uanhoro, J. O., & Rana, M. R. I. (2024). Transparency of sustainability disclosures among luxury and mass-market fashion brands: Longitudinal approach. *Journal of Cleaner Production, 436*, 140481. https://doi.org/10.1016/j.jclepro.2023.140481

Kallevig, A. (2024). The distributed creative brand image: Integrating digital influencer collaboration into omnichannel marketing communication. In W. Ozuem, S. Ranfagni, & M. Willis (Eds.), *Digital Transformation for Fashion and Luxury Brands* (pp. 249–270). Springer International Publishing. https://doi.org/10.1007/978-3-031-35589-9_12

Kallevig, A., Ozuem, W., Willis, M., Ranfagni, S., & Rovai, S. (2022). Managing creativity in the age of data-driven marketing communication: A model for agencies to improve their distribution and valuation of creativity. *Journal of Advertising Research, 63*(4), 301–320. https://doi.org/10.2501/JAR-2022-025

Kuitert, F. (2022). *Through 'constantly reinventing' themselves, the Paf Atelier team finds success in creative flexibility*. https://Frameweb.Com/Article/Work/through-Constantly-Reinventing-Themselves-the-Paf-Atelier-Team-Finds-Success-in-Creative-Flexibility (Accessed 22 May 2024).

Laing, M. (2024). Sustainability and the fashion media: Micro-utopia, social dreaming and hope in the margins. *Fashion Theory—Journal of Dress Body and Culture*, 1–24. https://doi.org/10.1080/1362704X.2024.2339937

Leung, F. F., Gu, F. F., & Palmatier, R. W. (2022). Online influencer marketing. *Journal of the Academy of Marketing Science, 50*(2), 226–251. https://doi.org/10.1007/S11747-021-00829-4

Linfante, V., & Pompa, C. (2021). Space, time and catwalks: Fashion shows as a multilayered communication channel. *ZoneModa Journal, 11*(1), 15–42. https://doi.org/10.6092/issn.2611-0563/13100

Liu, M. (2022). Determining the role of influencers' marketing initiatives on fast fashion industry sustainability: The mediating role of purchase intention. *Frontiers in Psychology, 13*, 940649. https://doi.org/10.3389/FPSYG.2022.940649/BIBTEX

Long, X., & Nasiry, J. (2022). Sustainability in the fast fashion industry. *Manufacturing and Service Operations Management, 24*(3), 1276–1293. https://doi.org/10.1287/msom.2021.1054

McQuillan, V. K. (2022). *At Lecavalier's AW22 show, rented and reused elements reflect long-term sustainability thinking*. https://Frameweb.Com/Article/Shows/at-Lecavaliers-Aw22-Show-Rented-and-Reused-Elements-Reflect-Long-Term-Sustainability-Thinking (Accessed 22 May 2024).

McQuillan, V. K. (2024). Rethinking fashion review with architectural fashion analysis method. *International Journal of Fashion Studies, 11*(1), 161–180. https://doi.org/10.1386/INFS_00110_1

Mendes, S. (2021). The instagrammability of the runway: Architecture, scenography, and the spatial turn in fashion communications. *Fashion Theory—Journal of Dress Body and Culture, 25*(3), 311–338. https://doi.org/10.1080/1362704X.2019.1629758

Moore, B. (2022). Paris runways lure new generation of groupies set on self-expression. *WWD*, 6–7.

Ozuem, W., Howell, K. E., & Lancaster, G. (2008). Communicating in the new interactive marketspace. *European Journal of Marketing, 42*(9/10), 1059–1083.

Ozuem, W., Ranfagni, S., Willis, M., Salvietti, G., & Howell, K. (2024). Exploring the relationship between chatbots, service failure recovery and customer loyalty: A frustration–aggression perspective. *Psychology and Marketing*. https://doi.org/10.1002/mar.22051

Ozuem, W., Willis, M., Ranfagni, S., Howell, K. E., & Rovai, S. (2023). Examining the role of social media influencers in service failure and recovery strategies: An empirical investigation of millennials' views. *Information Technology & People*. https://doi.org/10.1108/itp-05-2022-0371

Ozuem, W., Ranfagni, S., Willis, M., Rovai, S., & Howell, K. (2021). Exploring customers' responses to online service failure and recovery strategies during Covid-19 pandemic: An actor–network theory perspective. *Psychology & Marketing, 38*(9), 1440–1459.

Parguel, B., Benoît-Moreau, F., & Larceneux, F. (2011). How sustainability ratings might deter "greenwashing": A closer look at ethical corporate communication. *Journal of Business Ethics, 102*(1), 15–28. https://doi.org/10.1007/S10551-011-0901-2

Pedroni, M. (2023). Two decades of fashion blogging and influencing: A critical overview. *Fashion Theory—Journal of Dress Body and Culture, 27*(2), 237–268. https://doi.org/10.1080/1362704X.2021.2017213

Pinchera, V., & Rinallo, D. (2021). Marketplace icon: The fashion show. *Consumption, Markets and Culture, 24*(5), 479–491. https://doi.org/10.1080/10253866.2019.1703699

Ranfagni, S., & Ozuem, W. (2022). Luxury and sustainability: Technological pathways and potential opportunities. *Sustainability (Switzerland), 14*(9), 5209. https://doi.org/10.3390/SU14095209

Rettie, R. (2009). Mobile phone communication: Extending Goffman to mediated interaction. *Sociology, 43*(3), 421–438. https://doi.org/10.1177/0038038509103197

Rocamora, A. (2017). Mediatization and digital media in the field of fashion. *Fashion Theory, 21*(5), 505–522. https://doi.org/10.1080/1362704X.2016.1173349

Sheth, J. N., & Parvatiyar, A. (2021). Sustainable marketing: Market-driving, not market-driven. *Journal of Macromarketing, 1*, 150–165.

Shu, E. (2023). Behind the runway: Managing paradoxical tensions on sustainable luxury. *Environment, Development and Sustainability*, 1–13. https://doi.org/10.1007/S10668-023-04071-6

Silvestri, B. (2020). The future of fashion: How the quest for digitization and the use of artificial intelligence and extended reality will reshape the fashion industry after COVID-19. *ZoneModa Journal, 10*(2), 61–73. https://doi.org/10.6092/ISSN.2611-0563/11803

Taffel, S. (2016). Perspectives on the postdigital: Beyond rhetorics of progress and novelty. *Convergence, 22*(3), 324–338. https://doi.org/10.1177/1354856514567827

THE 17 GOALS|Sustainable Development. (n.d.). Retrieved March 25, 2024, from https://sdgs.un.org/goals

2

Online Brand Communities: Digitally Sustaining Fashion Brands' Sustainability

Michelle Willis

Defining Online Brand Communities

In today's digital ecosystem, online brand communities (OBCs) are a fundamental component of digital marketing. OBCs validate fashion and luxury brands' online image and foster or bind relationships between consumers and brands. An OBC is a type of brand community, which is created and managed online, in which the majority of community members' engagement and communications are conveyed through internet-mediated channels. The term "OBC" was derived from the term "brand community". Muniz and O'Guinn (2001, p. 412) introduced the term "brand community" to describe a "*specialized, non-geographically bound community, based on a structured set of social relationships among users of a brand*". This definition has become a common academic

M. Willis (✉)
Guildhall School of Business and Law, London Metropolitan University, London, UK
e-mail: m.willis@londonmet.ac.uk

W. Ozuem et al. (eds.), *Sustainable Digital Marketing for Fashion and Luxury Brands*,
https://doi.org/10.1007/978-3-031-82467-8_2

concept cited in a wide variety of brand community and OBC literature, which characterises the purpose of OBCs and users' motivations for joining and conducting interactive behaviours through OBCs. A brand's characteristics, values, and personalities are conspicuous factors that influence users' brand loyalty. It is the same brand image and identity factors that can motivate users to develop additional loyalty behaviours, such as becoming an OBC member to join a community of other like-minded loyal brand users. Ozuem and Willis (2022a, p. 5) commented that OBCs "*are not exclusive in regards to limited sign-up access, but in the sense of the nature that the brand represents*". This reflects similar arguments from other authors, including Albert et al. (2008) and Scaraboto et al. (2020), who associated consumers' conscious admiration for a brand, shared brand sentiments with other consumers, and willingness to commit to shared community activities dedicated to a brand as critical factors to determining groups of consumers as brand communities.

OBCs offer valuable and interconnectable resources and benefits to brands and their customers and followers. Both parties are able to publish, collect, and exchange information. Marketing practitioners of brands are able to collect relevant consumer market data on their customers' or followers' online engagement, and the brand sentiments displayed through the community's interactions. The information they collect is useful for marketing initiatives, including customer acquisition, retention, and loyalty campaigns, and other online community activities, such as community socialisation and gamification. OBCs enable customers and followers to form closer contact with brands, which can increase their attachment and long-term commitment to the brand. Customers with increased interpersonal contact with brands and like-minded community members are also given greater empowerment to participate in the community (Ozuem et al., 2024) and influence the brand sentiments reflected through OBCs. Customers as OBC members became creators of messages and other content that they voluntarily publish online, which is commonly referred to as user-generated content (UGC). They may also initiate online brand-related discussions that strengthen the binding of OBC members, promote the brand's image, and enhance the equity of the brand's image and identity among other members of the online audience; this increases a brand's potential competitive advantages through digital ecosystems. To further comprehend the value of OBCs, it is important to recognise several factors. First, the distinction between OBCs and other digital platforms is discussed in Sect. 2.2. Second, the co-created value elements of OBCs that influence the interface between fashion and luxury consumers and brands are described in Sect. 2.3. Third, is the significance of OBCs' dual role in sustaining brands' long-term online presence and in delivering sustainability marketing practices that establish and maintain the authenticity of fashion-related brands' sustainable practices. Section 2.4 of this chapter introduces the concept of sustainability marketing, which is associated with sustainability practices and messages. Sustainability is a factor external to fashion and luxury brands' environments, but it is relevant to engaging online audiences through their OBCs and to influencing brands' long-term sustainability.

Differentiating OBCs from Other Online Communities

OBCs have arguably emerged following various developments in, and disruptions to, digital platforms and communities that have influenced and changed the purposes and structures of OBCs for both customers and marketers. The following subsections discuss how OBCs emerged from traditional digital platforms, websites, and social media platforms, the impact OBCs had on these platforms, and the marketing factors that influenced fashion brands' continued adoption of OBCs.

Digital Platforms and Communities

In digital marketing, digital platforms can be described as electronic tools that utilise communication software that is channelled through desktop computers, mobile phones, and social and email systems. These systems enable users to directly access or communicate with other users through the communication features installed within the platform, which can range from textual-based to videotelephony-based exchanges. The level of communicated engagement and interactivity can vary within each digital platform depending on the purpose of the platform, the chosen communication features installed within the platform, and the users' intended usage of the platform.

Websites and Social Media Communities

Websites and social media pages are the most common form of digital platforms. A website often represents a fixed display of a brand, particularly the image, message, and positioning the brand aims to communicate to the audience. Brands use the pages of their website to attract audiences, to display relevant information to an audience, or to encourage the audience to conduct behaviours that would benefit a brand's profitability and online presence. Brands' websites can influence a degree of interactivity and engagement. Installed interactive media and immersive website designs emphasise a brand's intention to engage the audience and to offer users a consumption experience and extended value online (Chaffey & Ellis-Chadwick, 2019). Communication features, including comments sections, allow users to directly communicate through the website, whereas logo links for email and social media pages will probably transfer audiences to pages to initiate contact with other audience members outside the website platform. Users' intentions for engaging with the website arguably align with product-related or service-related information consumption, purchase intentions, and purchase experiences. For these reasons, users are unlikely to initiate in-depth personal interactions with other users through the website. Such interactions may be conducted when users consume or engage in communications to support product-related or service-related experiences. Social media is perceived as platforms that allow users to reach audiences in a significantly personal, interactive, and real-time manner. Unlike websites, which may limit users to uploading text-based comments or contacting service representatives through private communication systems, social media enables users to create and share content, also known as UGC, either to a general or specific social community through the digital platform.

Emergence of OBC Communities

OBCs are not explicitly categorised as a platform in the way websites and social media pages are categorised. OBCs can be described as digital spaces that can be facilitated through any selected digital platform or system, including websites and social media platforms. Unlike traditional websites or social media pages that are applied as networking sites, OBCs are used for multiple purposes, such as community and marketing initiatives, by users and brands. These two contrasting initiatives arguably reflect the purpose of OBCs: to engage brand customers, followers, and marketers in a dynamic space that can combine promotional and community exchange initiatives. A goods-dominant logic view of OBCs would consider them to be product information and display spaces, which can be accompanied by product development and innovation initiatives offered through user exchanges (Xie et al., 2024). From a service-dominant logic perspective, OBCs facilitate value experiences that are often facilitated through social exchanges between members, and between members and the brand (Wang et al., 2023). The latter reflects the practice of delivering online experiences and value to users that extend beyond the product purchase and consumption stages.

Brands can attract brand community members to their website for the purpose of consuming brand-related information. These websites usually contain structured information and page displays that are tailored to direct the audience's attention to specific factors and not to support social interactions between users. Furthermore, several brands limit direct communication features within their websites to maintain the purpose and positioning of the digital platform and the brand image that is represented through the website. Brands' websites are to some extent restricted because brands wish to direct consumers who intend to engage in interactive communications to platforms that are purposely set as social networking platforms, such as OBCs.

One of the core purposes of an OBC is to build a community of members and engage them with the attributes of the brand represented through the OBC space and the content created and shared through the digital space. Additionally, customers and followers of brands can use the digital space of an OBC to meet a community of individuals who reflect similar values and aspirations of a select brand. As a result, OBC members will arrange the majority of their exchanges around their brand consumption experiences, or engage with content or exchanges that reflect attributes of the selected brand, which may simultaneously lead to branded product displays within the community.

OBCs are often predominantly created with an open-access setting, which allows individuals to join and engage within OBCs free of access charges or social barriers; membership is subject to exclusivity based on the members' cognitive and affective reasoning. OBCs can attract various user segments from the online population. Ozuem et al. (2021a) categorised OBC users by their level of engagement and loyalty intentions; they concluded that some users reflect more passive forms of online engagement, and different levels of purchasing, brand advocacy, and loyalty to the brand. Users' loyalty to a brand can arguably indicate their possible motivations for engaging within OBCs. Users who are interested in product-specific enquiries are more likely to consume content uploaded to the OBC than actively participate in social exchanges with other members. Some users may briefly join OBCs without the intention to establish membership within the OBC. In contrast, users with a significant emotional attachment to a brand, and those who desire to be part of a community exclusive to the brand, are more likely to engage and actively participate within OBCs in the long term. The diverse characteristics of online users support the view that OBC membership is exclusive to members who identify value in joining a community dedicated to a particular brand of preference, a preference that they share with the community. Therefore, OBCs provide customers with an exclusive digital space to access brand-related information, experiences, and value, and they generate a loyal customer base for marketers to obtain first-party data to understand customer behaviour and preferences to guide engagement and loyalty strategies.

OBCs' Impact on Sustaining Brand Experience Digitally

Social communities have been essential for brands, not just for generating profitable sales but also for enabling marketers to maintain promotional and social contact with customers. In the digital social era, OBCs have continued to support a bridge between brands and customers under various economic and social circumstances. At the beginning of government-issued COVID-19 lockdowns across the globe, the user population of digital platforms increased and the essential social and marketing purposes of social media were extended, which disrupted the traditional online customer experience with fashion and luxury brands (Ozuem et al., 2021b). The worldwide population became reliant on social media, and other digital communications channels, as a means to maintain contact with family, peers, and other community networks. In addition, the population relied on digital platforms to continue their day-to-day and product and service consumption tasks. The lockdown restrictions revealed the extent of some fashion and luxury brands' preparedness for maintaining consumption experiences for customers through a fully digital environment. Some brands found that the digital platforms and systems they had utilised prior to the pandemic were insufficient to manage an increase in purchase demands and at the same time maintain social contact with customers. The International Monetary Fund found that the pandemic accelerated the adoption of technology and that it motivated companies and economies to facilitate more digital practices and policies to maintain business (Jaumotte et al., 2023).

Arguably, the global pandemic and other crisis situations highlighted the growing importance of establishing and maintaining OBCs for fashion and luxury brands. Although customers of various generations had been increasingly referring to websites to seek and obtain fashion products, and to social media for social contact and experiences, fashion and luxury brands faced challenges in reaching and engaging their target customers to conduct behaviours that would favour their marketing performance. Consumer communication behaviours towards brands, especially brands from the fashion and luxury industry, have influenced brands to shift from traditional digital communication platforms to channels with an omnipresence strategy. Fashion and luxury brands took the initiative to combine social media and website platforms and systems. This shift led to the extension of social networking sites to platforms for immersive purchasing and social experience for users, and it allowed marketers to promote and communicate brand messaging and products (Li et al., 2023), and monitor the engagement and interactivity of brand community customers and followers. Importantly, the implementation of OBCs that apply aspects of brand product experience and brand-based community engagement allowed the members of fashion and luxury OBCs to become important actors in establishing online experiences and value.

Value Co-creation Definition and Application

Value co-creation is a marketing strategy that promotes customers' active involvement in collaborative processes with brands and other target audiences (Ozuem & Willis, 2022a). Brands of various industries have adopted this strategy, for example, they invite consumers to actively contribute time, insights, ideas, and skills to product development and innovation initiatives (Nadeem & Salo, 2023). Early co-created contributions made by customers came in the form of feedback, reviews, and UGC in response to product and service initiatives proposed by marketers. This can be directly linked to the prioritisation of maintaining the value and equity of the products customers will consume, so marketers can reduce or avoid negative outcomes associated with defective product designs that impact consumption, as argued by goods-dominant logic. Yet, as digital technology became more advanced, digitally raised consumers were demanding more immersive and seamless experiences that enhanced purchasing and social consumption experiences with brands. The goods-dominant logic assumes that customers are passive individuals in marketing processes whose active role in creating value is restricted to consuming the end-product (Lusch et al., 2007). However, this view failed to take into account the importance of customer experience, and the dynamic impact customers' real-time and active exchanges could have on marketing processes. According to service-dominant logic, value is not perceived or determined until the customer has active experiences (Vargo & Lusch, 2008). Arguably, when value co-creation is limited to engaging the customer at later stages of the purchase and consumption experiences, brands can lose opportunities to adapt to customers' needs and wants, and to build customers' attachment to the brand earlier in the consumption experience before actual product purchases.

Recent digital experiences offered by fashion and luxury brands arguably provide evidence that customers' passive role has continued to decline and their active role has increased, particularly in the digital marketplace. The rise of augmented and artificial reality created more opportunities for product personalisation and enabled fashion and luxury customers to actively partake in creative processes for both products and consumption experiences. Tommy Hilfiger, in collaboration with IBM and The Fashion Institute of Technology (FIT) Infor Design and Tech Lab, invited FIT students to design a collection using IBM's artificial intelligence systems and product and pattern images prepared by Tommy Hilfiger. The campaign was both a reflection of providing product and experimental value to the audience and it allowed members of the audience to have personalised experiences. Additionally, marketers and retailers gained insights into how Millennial and Generation Z fashion consumers interact with digital experiences, and they could monitor trends and prospective market demands (Arthur, 2018). Other fashion brands, including Prada, Chanel, FILA, Glossier, and Off-White, partnered with game developers to connect with young audiences to give gamers the opportunity to personalise a character avatar, including facial, body, and clothing features. At the same time, users were able to participate in these experiences with social and peer groups, thus reflecting the role of the community in value co-creation. These initiatives reveal the significance of centralising the customer throughout co-creation processes. Although marketers are the key facilitators of customer experiences, value for customers is generated when they are allocated ownership of any part of the process. This, in turn, can enhance customers' affective motivation to further engage with brands and develop long-term loyalty intentions.

Value Co-creation and OBCs

Engaged OBC members are fundamental co-creators of OBC experiences (Kumar & Kaushal, 2023), and are central to forming and maintaining OBCs, and to sustaining brands' online market share. As OBCs reflect brand-related information and activities, community members and visitors become motivated to explore brands more deeply to determine the brand's value and authenticity, and to participate in community role behaviours. When addressing value co-creation within OBCs, fashion and luxury brands may apply various co-creation initiatives according to their intentions towards the members of their online community and their marketing goals. An example of these goals includes utilising OBCs to attract more members to the community to encounter and engage with brand-related information, which may prompt visitors to generate purchase intentions and become more permanent members of the community. Another goal could be to generate more content that explicitly reflects brand attributes through the digital space to encourage or enhance customer engagement and to influence other members' loyalty to the brand. With a wide range of goals and activities being applied within OBCs, it is essential for managers to determine the level and type of online interactivity of each segment of OBC community groups.

Online members' participation within OBCs differs, with some conducting more passive forms of engagement than others. This means that not all members within OBCs will actively contribute towards the application or development of value co-creation initiatives within OBCs. However, each member will be influenced by other members' online activities, including the expressions they display through UGC. The more active members within OBCs develop UGC which, along with content created and published by brands internally or externally to OBCs, can attract new members and motivate passive members to perform online behaviours, including viewing, clicking, and sharing of published content. These forms of participation are as equally important as the act of creating and uploading UGC. Even with these forms of passive participation, marketers are able to monitor and track online engagement behaviour and traffic, and analyse statistically the engagement impact of OBC content and activities.

Active participants within OBCs are very likely to reflect a perspective or insights that can contribute to shaping how other online users will perceive a brand's online image. However, within OBCs a variety of individuals' perspectives or sentiments towards a brand can be published and encountered. UGC can potentially contain positively and negatively worded comments or sentiments, which can influence the perspective of observing consumers (Ibrahim et al., 2017). OBC members who are highly attached to a brand, or harbour an intention to be a positive advocate for a specific brand, are very willing to express positive brand sentiments and engage in positive brand-related discussions. However, other online members within OBCs directly reflect negative sentiments or views towards a specified brand within the community. Such individuals could be anti-brand consumers or customers who had negative experiences with the brand. As many OBCs can be open-accessed, marketers are unable to prevent negative forms of UGC unless they explicitly select digital features that prevent users from creating and uploading UGC. OBC visitors who encounter UGC content or community activities that reflect the contrasting attitudes and behaviours of active members may face difficulty in establishing the credibility or authenticity of any brand-related message or activity (Ozuem et al., 2021c) or may develop an indifferent view of the brand.

As marketers observe how members within OBCs engage with each other, they can potentially identify a complex range of members with a diverse range of characteristics connected to their participation and loyalty intentions towards brands through OBCs. Many scholars of digital space community research have categorised online members according to their perspectives and sentiments towards companies, and the behaviours they intend to deliver through OBCs. Azemi et al. (2020) categorised online users by the level of negative severity they intended to display through their online negative word of mouth (lenient, moderate, or severe) when they experienced an ineffective service delivered by a provider. Ozuem et al. (2021b) proposed three types of online customers (blanders, empathisers, and churners) that emerge when marketplaces are impacted by external crises; each type responds with varying levels of expectations and commitment to the brand within specific situations. At least some of the listed customer segments are likely to emerge in OBCs during specific value co-creation activities, published marketing messages, and under dynamic external situations that impact fashion and luxury brands and their customers.

Each fashion and luxury brand will have customer segments with distinct personalities, values, and aspirations that differ from other brands' customer segments. However, varying online participation behaviours further segment these customers and affect others' online engagement and loyalty intentions within OBCs. This requires marketers to continuously observe and manage the ways in which active OBC members or visitors are affecting the brand image and attributes represented online. This will be vital to sustaining the impact of OBCs on customer engagement and loyalty, and to sustaining brands' online presence and positioning on a range of factors that are internal or external to the OBC.

Sustainable Marketing

Sustainability is a term that many consumers associate with brands' efforts or contributions to business-related practices that impact societies. When the term emerged, it was commonly associated with economic, social, and environmental-related issues and practices. Environmental issues influenced governments and companies to make changes to production and manufacturing processes and gave rise to the eco-friendly consumer. Sustainability eventually became a sub-category of marketing, known as sustainable marketing. The emerging marketing term raised fundamental questions concerning the need to understand its meaning and practice.

The University of Cambridge (2023) argued that sustainable marketing can be misinterpreted as an act of promoting eco-friendly products. The broader purpose of sustainable marketing is to act as a source of influence on audiences so that they aspire to positive attitudes and behaviours that serve the long-term well-being of societies; this can be achieved by strengthening the adoption or acceptance of sustainable behaviours, norms, and values. Kemper and Ballantine (2019) conceptualised three types of sustainability marketing: auxiliary, reformative, and transformative sustainability marketing. In practice, each of these reflect varying levels of sustainability promotion, from the production of sustainable products, to promoting institutional and perspective changes. The growing pressure from governmental policy and consumers' growing interest in sustainability have influenced companies to develop sustainable goals or practices as an initiative to engage with the environmentally concerned community and to differentiate themselves from competitors.

Scepticism of Online Consumers

As the sustainability movement began to inspire consumers to adapt their behaviours in favour of improving environmental and societal ecosystems, consumer scepticism towards brands became increasingly noticeable (Barreto, 2023). To maintain brand equity within the sustainability movement, many fashion and luxury brands took to promoting their values and efforts towards sustainability through marketing material. Their marketing material included commercialised product offers and scenarios, the testimonials of internal and external personnel, and publicly available reports that provided statistical representations of a brand's sustainability output. Consumers are continuously exposed to content that can trigger feelings of self-consciousness about their purchasing and lifestyle consumption, which can lead them to adapt their behaviours to obtain self-assurance (Sangwan et al., 2024). For example, they might engage in societal concerns towards sustainability or actively conduct ethical consumption. However, the social media era has provided online audiences with unprecedented access to information and online members that can either, or both, authenticate or contradict the sustainable values and efforts promoted by brands. Several fashion and luxury brands have taken to promoting messages or programmes that encourage consumers to participate, including "used clothes recycling or donation". However, reports by both mainstream media and UGC indicate pretences in fashion brands' sustainability marketing, and imply inconsistencies between a brand's business model and processes, and its external sustainability initiatives. This led to the emergence of website pages, social media communities, and mobile applications that were specifically created as community platforms for ethical fashion consumers. An example is Good On You—Ethical Fashion, which was created for the purpose of rating fashion brands' environmental and labour policies. Consequently, brands can face greenwashing accusations from the online consumer community, a domestic government's regulators, and international committees who set global sustainability standards. Additionally, an assigned status of greenwashing can have a negative impact on a brand's equity as consumers can become estranged from brands whose practices contradict their messages or from brands that do not conduct actual sustainable practices. It is for this reason that online communities on a wide range of digital platforms appeal to brands to "practice the preach" (Townsend, 2024) or to be held accountable for practices that do not align with sustainability goals.

Sustainability and OBCs

Digital platforms and spaces, including OBCs, are key components of brands' communication strategies for online presence, from channelling message cues in reference to sustainability, to building or maintaining their online equity and authenticity. Engaging with online audiences and communicating sustainability initiatives to online audiences can help establish connections between brands and consumers that lead to positive brand evaluations and image, purchasing intentions, and increased consumer advocacy (Azemi & Ozuem, 2023; Sarkar et al., 2023). The sustainability messages, values, and practices that fashion and luxury brands display through their OBCs can arguably be considered a reflection of their overall position and intentions towards sustainability, which influence the online audience's brand evaluations.

Gucci Equilibrium and H&M Group are departments of Gucci and H&M, respectively that specifically address and organise the two brands' investment and actions in relation to sustainability. Both brands communicate the partnership programmes they facilitate to address a range of environmental and social sustainability initiatives that concern stakeholders. These collaborations consist of various groups of stakeholders, including consumer community members, charity foundations, and government legislators, who actively participate in these partnership programmes. Gucci Equilibrium's platform provides information regarding Gucci's partnerships involving UNICEF and women's rights foundations, as well as Gucci's efforts to make its supply chain and craftsmanship processes environmentally and socially responsible. H&M promotes similar initiatives, including the H&M Move partnerships with Sport Without Borders, Zlatan Ibrahimovićs and Laureus Sport for Good, with the purpose of benefitting young consumers from vulnerable or marginalised backgrounds through sport. H&M's collaboration with the Ellen MacArthur Foundation is promoted as a partnership that intends to support the integration of sustainability efforts into H&M's business model, rather than sustainability playing a complementary role to business.

Both Gucci and H&M promote the importance of collaboration to address sustainability, which they attempt to signal through their OBCs on various platforms. This approach increases the reach of their sustainability messages and contributes to attracting OBC members, who can further associate with the brands' efforts, and it builds members' motivation to follow and share sustainability-specific information. This is arguably a passive, but impactful, form of a value co-creation initiative that centralises OBC members' efforts towards sustaining the equity of a brand through digital spaces and their promoted sustainable positioning.

OBC Members' Active Participation in Co-created Sustainability Initiatives

An OBC is arguably a representation of a brand's identity within a digital space, which signals brand attributes that audiences can potentially relate to. Identifiable brand attribute signals can influence an audience's sense of belonging within an OBC and motivate them to increase their consumption of future OBC content and activities. Consequently, consumers who are advocate followers of a brand, or of sustainability, can evaluate the brand as a party to admire or they could aspire to conduct behaviours that align with the brand's sustainability values. Ozuem and Willis (2022b) emphasised the importance of brands merging both the brand's and consumers' identities through OBCs to increase active participation within the digital spaces.

Consumers can become co-creators of sustainability equity and practices that can be associated with a brand through OBCs. This includes engaging OBC members in active participation in the co-creation process, rather than limiting them to passive information consumers. To achieve this, Ozuem and Willis (2022b) emphasised the practice of displaying relevant messages and content that appeals to target audiences who are more likely to conduct active behaviours in response to the content. In the context of sustainability, OBC content and activities should both influence customers' positive perspectives of the brand and of behaviours that benefit societies (Sarkar et al., 2023). This creates opportunities for brands to facilitate activities that encourage customers' active co-creation and participation in the sustainable practices the company promotes in contrast to simply sharing or commenting on displayed sustainability marketing content created by the brand.

Engaging Consumers and Advocates in Sustainability Initiatives

From a macro-perspective, fashion and luxury brands can facilitate departments dedicated to managing and promoting sustainability initiatives through their digital platforms. Yet, given the complex procedures of individual sustainability initiatives, not all stakeholders, particularly consumers, will have the direct opportunity to actively co-create value for the brand. Content displayed on brands' websites that describe sustainability initiatives may not encourage interactive engagement and the participation of each stakeholder. A particular strategy that can support active co-creation initiatives through OBCs is the celebration of consumers' and advocates' sustainability efforts. Common activities include fashion consumers promoting their individual consumption behaviours that benefit sustainability practices. Fashion consumers with sustainability interests may begin by consuming or creating UGC depicting the mending or alteration of clothes to extend the item's life-cycle, or their purchase and consumption of fashion items that are categorised as second-hand or pre-owned. Consumers with influencer intentions might apply this approach, which could lead to a fashion and luxury brand being referenced as part of their material. This content acts as a form of organic content that could create a description of the level of authenticity of the sustainability status of fashion and luxury branded products.

An example of another strategy to actively engage consumers and advocates in fashion and luxury brands' sustainability practices is Gucci Changemakers, which is part of Gucci Equilibrium's sustainable initiative. This programme aims to contribute to transforming and changing aspects of the fashion industry to benefit communities and the environment by supporting emerging students who aspire to actively contribute to sustainable initiatives. Stakeholders of Gucci Changemakers programme can potentially attract a range of consumer segments with an interest in the fashion industry; these segments may represent micro-social communities with an interest in a variety of sustainable initiatives. Successful applicants of the Gucci programme have the opportunity to become part of the content and message strategies signalled through Gucci's OBCs, which include content generated by Gucci's marketing team and UGC. This can be a long-term OBC initiative, as the same applicants may develop to become creators of content that addresses factors that the Changemakers programme represents. Additionally, the applicants, as representatives of their communities and generation, indirectly become influencers for the Gucci OBC and attract members to engage in the content and bond with other community members.

Fashion and sustainability advocates, who can be categorised as a type of influencer, can be engaged in fashion and luxury fashion brands' sustainability marketing campaigns. Several fashion-branded influencer campaigns can be noted, including Puma's "Voices of a Re:Generation" campaign, sustainable underwear brand Stripe & Stare's collaboration with Camille Charrière, and Izzy Manuel's, creator of #ImperfectSustyFashion30, collaboration with ritdye and Purdeys. Each of these campaigns applies different levels of active participation from the influencers they collaborate with, from endorsing or promoting the brand, to being actively involved in implementing sustainable practices within the brand's business models. What they have in common is their ability to extend the brand's sustainable message through their own social communities; thus, they extend fashion brands' digital spaces beyond the brands' own OBCs. This is critical not only for promoting sustainable values, but also for sustaining brands' long-term online presence and connections with a variety of online communities.

Conclusion and Managerial Implications

OBCs provide digital spaces for multiple purposes that can be beneficial for fashion and luxury brands' marketing strategies. They provide a specific digital space that allows brand followers and consumers to bond and engage with each other, and to consume brand-specific content and messages. Members within the brand-specific digital space of an OBC are more likely to engage with content and focus on the signalled attributes related to the brand, which increases their level of engagement within the OBC. This engagement can lead OBC members to conduct further positive behaviours towards the brand. From an analytical perspective, OBC members generate data on their direct online behaviours, including clicks, visit time durations, visits to other digital platforms connected through the OBC, and uploads of UGC. These can provide marketers with analytical insights into the overall engagement impact of their OBC content and activities. This will enable marketers to determine what potential content strategies, and online community interactions, will be most effective for specific marketing programmes, including customer purchase intentions, engagement and loyalty programmes, and recruitment of potential influencers and affiliate programmes.

As a digital space that facilitates purchasing and social networking-related exchanges, fashion and luxury brands must develop effective ways to utilise their OBC members as value co-creators. Some digital platforms, like websites and specific social media platforms, restrict the degree to which consumers are able to interact with, and actively contribute to, co-created initiatives. An OBC bridges the gap between transactional and social consumption, and its members are key to socially influencing other members to engage with OBC activities. OBCs will have segments of members that can generate UGC that displays identity attributes that reflect the brand's image; these attributes can include the brand's values in relation to sustainability. In identifying active members, fashion and luxury brands will be able to maintain active co-created contributions, which will enhance the perceived authenticity of the community from the perspective of observing consumers. It is important to centralise members who are positive advocates for the brand within marketing activities that have a significant impact on digitally sustaining the brand's image and values. Marketers must also monitor consumers, or influencers, outside their OBC, because they have the potential to extend the brand to other communities and to integrate other values and aspirations appealing to these communities into the brand's online identity. This will allow fashion and luxury brands to maintain their long-term sustainability within online communities that are subject to shifts in perspective and demands in regard to marketplaces and external ecosystems.

References

Albert, N., Merunka, D., & Valette-Florence, P. (2008). When consumers love their brands: Exploring the concept and its dimensions. *Journal of Business Research, 61*(10), 1062–1075.

Arthur, R. (2018). Artificial intelligence empowers designers in IBM, Tommy Hilfiger and FIT collaboration. *Forbes* [Online]. Available at https://www.forbes.com/sites/rachelarthur/2018/01/15/ai-ibm-tommy-hilfiger/ [Accessed 5 May 2024].

Azemi, Y., Ozuem, W., & Howell, K. E. (2020). The effects of online negative word-of-mouth on dissatisfied customers: A frustration–aggression perspective. *Psychology & Marketing, 37*(4), 564–577.

Azemi, Y., & Ozuem, W. (2023). How does retargeting work for different Gen Z mobile users? *Journal of Advertising Research*, 2023-023. https://doi.org/10.2501/jar-2023-023

Barreto, H. (2023). How to market sustainability while avoiding greenwashing. *Forbes* [Online] Available at https://www.forbes.com/sites/forbescontentmarketing/2023/09/14/how-to-market-sustainability-while-avoiding-greenwashing/ [Accessed 19 March 2024].

Chaffey, D., & Ellis-Chadwick, F. (2019). *Digital marketing*. Pearson.

Ibrahim, N., Wang, X., & Bourne, H. (2017). Exploring the effect of user engagement in online brand communities: Evidence from Twitter. *Computers in Human Behavior, 72*, 321–338.

Jaumotte, F., Oikonomou, M., Pizzinelli, C., & Tavares, M. M. (2023). How pandemic accelerated digital transformation in advanced economies. *International Monetary Fund* [Online]. Available at https://www.imf.org/en/Blogs/Articles/2023/03/21/how-pandemic-accelerated-digital-transformation-in-advanced-economies [Accessed: 5 May 2024].

Kemper, J. A., & Ballantine, P. W. (2019). What do we mean by sustainability marketing? *Journal of Marketing Management, 35*(3–4), 277–309.

Kumar, V., & Kaushal, V. (2023). Role of customer perceived brand ethicality in inducing engagement in online brand communities. *Journal of Retailing and Consumer Services, 71*, 103184.

Li, F., Larimo, J., & Leonidou, L. C. (2023). Social media in marketing research: Theoretical bases, methodological aspects, and thematic focus. *Psychology & Marketing, 40*(1), 124–145.

Lusch, R. F., Vargo, S. L., & O'Brien, M. (2007). Competing through service: Insights from service-dominant logic. *Journal of Retailing, 83*(1), 5–18.

Muniz, A., & O'Guinn, T. (2001). Brand community. *Journal of Consumer Research, 27*(4), 412–432.

Nadeem, W., & Salo, J. (2023). Does value co-creation matter? Assessing consumer responses in the sharing economy. *Information Technology & People, 37*(3), 1279–1304.

Ozuem, W., & Willis, M. (2022a). Introducing online brand communities. In *Digital marketing strategies for value co-creation.* Palgrave Macmillan. https://doi.org/10.1007/978-3-030-94444-5_1

Ozuem, W., & Willis, M. (2022b). Social identity and online brand communities. In *Digital marketing strategies for value co-creation.* Palgrave Macmillan. https://doi.org/10.1007/978-3-030-94444-5_5

Ozuem, W., Willis, M., Howell, K., Helal, G., Ranfagni, S., & Lancaster, G. (2021a). Effects of online brand communities on millennials' brand loyalty in the fashion industry. *Psychology & Marketing, 38*(5), 774–793.

Ozuem, W., Ranfagni, S., Willis, M., Rovai, S., & Howell, K. (2021b). Exploring customers' responses to online service failure and recovery strategies during Covid-19 pandemic: An actor–network theory perspective. *Psychology & Marketing, 38*(9), 1440–1459.

Ozuem, W., Willis, M., Howell, K., Lancaster, G., & Ng, R. (2021c). Determinants of online brand communities' and millennials' characteristics: A social influence perspective. *Psychology & Marketing, 38*(5), 794–818.

Ozuem, W., Willis, M., Howell, K., Ranfagni, S., & Rovai, S. (2024). Examining user-generated content, service failure recovery and customer–brand relationships: An exploration through commitment-trust theory. *Internet Research, 34*(3), 784–809.

Sangwan, V., Maity, M., Tripathi, S., & Chakraborty, A. (2024). From discomfort to desirable: The effect of embarrassment on prosocial consumption. *Psychology & Marketing* (in Press).

Sarkar, J. G., Sarkar, A., & Sreejesh, S. (2023). Developing responsible consumption behaviours through social media platforms: Sustainable brand practices as message cues. *Information Technology & People, 36*(2), 532–563.

Scaraboto, D., Almeida, S. O. D., & dos Santos Fleck, J. P. (2020). "No piracy talk": How online brand communities work to denormalize controversial gaming practices. *Internet Research, 30*(4), 1103–1122.

Townsend, S. (2024). Sustainability marketing just got tricky, and better. *Forbes* [Online]. Available at https://www.forbes.com/sites/solitairetownsend/2024/02/11/sustainability-marketing-just-got-tricky-and-better/ [Accessed: 19 March 2024].

University of Cambridge. (2023). *What is sustainable marketing?* [Online]. Available at https://www.cisl.cam.ac.uk/news/blog/what-sustainable-marketing#:~:text=Sustainable%20marketing%20is%20a%20purpose,for%20its%20impacts%20and%20opportunities. [Accessed: 19 March 2024].

Vargo, S. L., & Lusch, R. F. (2008). Service-dominant logic: Continuing the evolution. *Journal of the Academy of Marketing Science, 36*(1), 1–10.

Wang, K., Tai, J. C., & Hu, H. F. (2023). Role of brand engagement and co-creation experience in online brand community continuance: A service-dominant logic perspective. *Information Processing & Management, 60*(1), 103136.

Xie, X., Yu, L., Staniewski, M. W., & Ribeiro-Navarrete, S. (2024). Focus on yourself: The impact of users' self-focus orientation on NPD ideas' attention allocation in online innovation communities. *Technological Forecasting and Social Change, 201*, 123216.

3

Brand Building Using Digital Marketing Tools: Insight into an Innovative Hybrid Model

Silvia Ranfagni, Massimo Rosati, and Silvia Frescucci

Introduction

In an increasingly connected world, where the online channel plays a central role in people's daily lives, a brand's web presence takes on unprecedented strategic importance. A company's ability to stand out in a saturated market, attract and maintain the attention of consumers, and build a lasting relationship with them, depends to a large extent on its online visibility and the quality of interaction it manages to establish through various digital channels. In this context, online research tools emerge as indispensable allies for companies aiming to develop a brand, offering possibilities for analysis, understanding, and engagement with their audience (Ozuem et al., 2023; Ranfagni et al., 2023).

The chapter begins by defining what a brand is and its importance in today's landscape, then moves on to examine what it means to be an online brand today. It will discuss the challenges and opportunities

S. Ranfagni (✉) · M. Rosati · S. Frescucci
Department of Economics and Business, 50127 Florence, Italy
e-mail: silvia.ranfagni@unifi.it

W. Ozuem et al. (eds.), *Sustainable Digital Marketing for Fashion and Luxury Brands*,
https://doi.org/10.1007/978-3-031-82467-8_3

presented by the digital environment, looking at how the transition from traditional to digital has transformed branding strategies.

This chapter's empirical section focuses on the practical use of online analytical tools such as Google Trends, Pinterest Trends, SEMrush, Not Just Analytics, Keywords Everywhere, and Google Forms. When combined with traditional research methods (Aaker & Day, 1980), these tools give a full picture of the market, making it easier to come up with effective branding strategies for the Italian cosmetics industry. Through market analysis, identification of emerging trends, competitive analysis, and the creation of a new brand, it is shown how the strategic use of online research tools can facilitate market understanding, identification of target audiences, and formulation of branding strategies (Naeem et al., 2023). Further focus is placed on consumer feedback, collected through a traditional questionnaire conveyed online, to assess the alignment between brand values and audience expectations (Ranfagni et al., 2021). This chapter offers practical and theoretical guidance for brand development in the digital context, highlighting how choosing and integrating online research tools with traditional ones can make all the difference in building a successful new brand.

Branding and Competition in the Digital Environment

The primary function of marketing has perpetually been to generate value for both the customer and the company providing a product or service (Ferrero, 2013). However, at the core of value creation lies a pivotal element—an essence that marketing endeavours to cultivate—and this essence is none other than the brand identity (Baietti, 2000). Let us envision an entrepreneur from an SME or a marketing manager from a large corporation and explore the factors that would motivate a consumer to opt for our product or service over those offered by our competitors. The brand is that intangible, abstract entity that allows us to convey the message we want to transmit to the end consumer (Bertoli & Busacca, 2002; Busacca et al., 2022; Farquar, 1989; Keller et al., 2005). According to the American Marketing Association (AMA), brand is "*a name, term, sign, symbol or design, or a combination of these elements that is intended to identify the goods and services of a seller or group of sellers, differentiating them from those of competitors*". We are talking about a medium that goes beyond the identifying and distinctive sign of the company (Ferraresi, 2008), as it constitutes an intangible resource that contributes to consumer trust and consequently the relational capital of the company itself. Sometimes the brand is even more important than the product itself, in fact in recent years it is also defined by marketing experts as an element "facilitator of conversations", thanks to the use of digital technologies (Busacca et al., 2022). Furthermore, when integrating the online channel into a brand strategy, it is imperative to recognise that the internet harbours a substantially greater number of competitors compared to those found in the physical realm. According to Cardoni and Nurra (2022), Italian SMEs achieved a digital intensity of 60.3 per cent in 2021, surpassing the European average of approximately 56 per cent. However, further improvement is needed to reach the European target of 90 per cent by 2030. While the percentage of Italian companies with at least 10 employees selling online remains relatively low (18.4 per cent in 2020), it is comparable to the European average (23 per cent in 2020). Conversely, among larger companies with at least 250 employees, which are more active in the online sales market (44.5 per cent in 2020, up from 40.2 per cent in 2019), these are predominantly companies selling their products and services via the web, with the majority of their customers being other businesses (86.2 per cent). In addition, 72.4 per cent of the above businesses sell through their own websites or apps. Given that Italian companies are increasingly transitioning their operations online, it is important to recognise that this route is not always straightforward. Instead, it often conceals potential pitfalls that warrant investigation and understanding to prevent detrimental impacts on the brand image cultivated over time (Ranfagni & Rosati, 2023). The online channel presents a potent avenue for reaching fresh consumers and bolstering brand visibility (Ozuem et al., 2024a, 2024b). Nonetheless, as companies strive to adapt to the digital landscape, they are also presented with both challenges and opportunities to enhance their environmental, social, and economic sustainability (Sebastian et al., 2017). Digitalisation has the potential to promote green innovation and foster a more sustainable business landscape (Bednarčíková & Repiská, 2021) by driving significant improvements in sustainability across various business functions. Digital technologies, such as artificial intelligence, the Internet of Things, digital manufacturing, and blockchain, can enable more efficient resource utilisation, reduce waste, and mitigate the environmental impact of business operations (Bednarčíková & Repiská, 2021; Feroz et al., 2021). For example, the application of big data analytics in analysing waste disposal records can provide valuable insights to help businesses optimise their waste management practices and reduce their environmental footprint (Feroz et al., 2021).

However, the relationship between digitalisation and sustainability is not without its complexities. While digital technologies can unlock new opportunities for sustainable business practices, they can also introduce new challenges and unintended consequences (Schneider, 2019). For instance, the increased energy consumption associated with digital technologies, such as data centres and cryptocurrency mining, can have a significant carbon footprint, potentially offsetting the environmental benefits of other digital applications (Sun & He, 2023). To ensure that the digital transformation journey leads to a more sustainable future, businesses must carefully navigate the complex interplay between digitalisation and sustainability, leveraging the opportunities while addressing the challenges.

To develop a customised brand strategy, it is crucial to distinguish between the two primary types of online businesses: those that exist solely in the digital sphere and click-and-mortar enterprises, which integrate traditional physical operations with online channels (Ozuem & Ranfagni, 2021). While both can be seen as competitors, their business models are closely intertwined with the opportunities presented by the internet. Generally, brands that focus exclusively on the online channel tend to adopt strategies based on market or target differentiation rather than price differentiation; in contrast, click-and-mortar brands tend to directly develop new business processes. In any case, neither business formulation demonstrates superiority over the other (Koo et al., 2004). Typically, companies operating exclusively online tend to be newer establishments, while click-and-mortar businesses, having a longer history, initially established their presence through physical channels before integrating an online strategy. With the rise of the Internet and e-commerce, market dynamics have become increasingly complex. Initially, it appeared that traditional businesses would face challenges rendering them obsolete, as the Internet had lowered many entry barriers. However, click-and-mortar businesses have adeptly leveraged the Internet's advantages. In their study, Koo et al. (2004) explore the differences in competitiveness and performance between "fully online" firms and those using online channels as complements. They argue that Porter's (1985) model is applicable to all firms in the online marketplace, though each must consider industry type, market conditions, and organisational variables. In any scenario, irrespective of the selected market strategy within the online channel, it's crucial to consistently monitor tactics and adjust them according to demand trends to maximise business ROI. Still, the study does not show whether the difference between strategy and performance is because of how the online market is changing or because the researchers do not have enough experience to fully understand how things work. Nonetheless, it is notable that certain markets are still in their infancy and not entirely open to competition, rendering them challenging to grasp (Koo et al., 2004). What we know is certain to be important online is that trust and the positively perceived usefulness of a brand influence the *online brand experience.*

A number of academic studies have deepened our understanding of the multifaceted online brand experience. An influential study proposes a model that integrates marketing and information systems perspectives (Morgan-Thomas & Veloutsou, 2013). The study highlights the critical importance of the online brand experience for practitioners, despite the lack of academic attention. Focusing on search engines, the authors examine how the absence of direct sales allows for more immediate and personal brand experiences, emphasising the quality of experience and long-term user relationships. Beyond search engines, online brands emerge from technological advancements, embodying a heightened product identity that customers perceive as valuable and distinct. The subjective perceptions of information and experiences evoke a sense of brand personality and performance (Homburg et al., 2010).

Recent studies have further explored the multidimensional nature of the online brand experience. Pillarisetty & Mishra have identified four key dimensions: informativeness, entertainment, social presence, and sensory appeal, all of which influence e-satisfaction (Pillarisetty & Mishra, 2022). Moreover, the authors of a study on the "rediscovery" of brand experience dimensions using big data analysis propose a possible sixth dimension that incorporates sensory, affective, intellectual, behavioural, and social aspects (Oh et al., 2019; Ozuem et al., 2024a, 2024b). As the digital landscape continues to evolve, the importance of understanding and effectively managing the online brand experience cannot be overstated. Leading companies seek to build a strong base of loyal, profitable customers who are advocates for their products and services (Sinha & Ahuja, 2022). Given the vast number of customer interfaces, companies have to manage multiple channels, frontline employees, and customer segments. The key challenge is to create the right buying experiences at the right time in the right way for the right cost (Sinha & Ahuja, 2022). To complicate matters, customer expectations are constantly evolving, requiring companies to continuously innovate and adapt their brand experiences (Kharat et al., 2018).

Online contexts have emerged as information-rich, dynamic, and technologically innovative environments that present both opportunities and challenges for brands (Zi-yu, 2023). The virtual nature of these contexts is characterised by a lack of physical cues, which can increase the sense of intangibility and uncertainty for users (Xue et al., 2020).

However, these online environments also offer the possibility of interactivity and a brand experience, allowing customers to engage with the brand and other users. This continuous two-way interaction between the user and the brand is a critical resource for the brand's success, as online brands rely on repeated user engagement to generate revenue through advertising, licensing, subscriptions, and direct sales (Li et al., 2021; Martiyanti, 2023).

The online brand experience is a key consideration for companies, as it captures the individual's subjective and emotional response to the brand (Eigenraam et al., 2021). This can include factors related to the usability and functionality of the online brand, as well as more hedonistic experiences such as consumer enjoyment (Huseynov et al., 2020). Effective user experience design is a primary objective for companies seeking to create a successful online brand.

Individuals engage with brands online across a wide range of activities, including navigating websites, using mobile apps, participating in social media interactions, and more (Mondol et al., 2021). These diverse touchpoints can lead to a variety of customer behaviours and experiences, which have been extensively examined in the information systems literature (Pascucci et al., 2023). Researchers have investigated phenomena such as internet experience, online customer experience, and brand website experience to better understand how users perceive and interact with brands in digital environments (Morgan-Thomas & Veloutsou, 2013; Pillarisetty & Mishra, 2022; Rowley, 2004; Sinha & Ahuja, 2022).

A central issue for researchers in this field is understanding the conditions that are pivotal for the acceptance of technological products or services by users (Morgan-Thomas & Veloutsou, 2013; Ozuem et al., 2021; Pillarisetty & Mishra, 2022). Studies in information systems have typically addressed the outcomes of online brand experiences within theoretical frameworks that consider the role of factors such as informativeness, entertainment, social presence, and sensory appeal in shaping e-satisfaction and brand resonance (Pillarisetty & Mishra, 2022; Sinha & Ahuja, 2022). Morgan-Thomas and Veloutsou provide a model that emphasises the emotional aspect of the brand relationship and implements it with the dimension of technological acceptance in order to illustrate the consumer's experience of the brand online. Variables related to perceived usefulness and perceived ease of use are also present in the model: trust and brand reputation represent additional antecedent factors. The model's outcomes include both online brand experience and customer satisfaction, as well as their online relationship with the brand. When an online brand is not only a technology but also a product, and when technology users are also consumers, brand reputation can be a determinant of technology acceptance. The reputation of a brand offering is the collective perception of its relevance, which evolves over time through consumers' experiences with the brand (Lampignano, 2016). Brand evaluation plays a key role in the development of brand relationships, especially in the context of technology research, where reputation and image exert a strong influence on the perceived value and usefulness of technology. Brand familiarity and positive perceptions towards the brand are important predictors of trust because they mitigate concerns about privacy or security. Trust represents a multidimensional construct intrinsically linked to the concepts of uncertainty and risk. Due to the Internet's relatively recent emergence and the inherent "distance" in customer-business interactions, concerns regarding risk are amplified. The online environment requires high levels of trust as opposed to direct customer contact. Often, the reason customers refrain from interactions with brands online is that they do not have enough trust in relating to the brand in that context. In essence, trust positively influences conversion on the online channel and has the power to mitigate the uncertainty raised by privacy concerns.

What emerges is that a positive online brand experience occurs when the net value of good brand interactions exceeds the value of bad ones, so satisfaction is only a consequence of positive emotional and cognitive states of the online brand experience. This could lead to a person's intention to revisit the brand's website, and perhaps the intention to make a purchase again in the future.

The study's findings suggest two hypotheses: firstly, that online brand experience positively influences consumer behavioural intentions and satisfaction; and secondly, that behavioural intentions and satisfaction positively impact online brand relationships. Ultimately, it becomes evident that brand relationships are a significant outcome of the online brand experience. Over time, positive interactions with an online brand lead to more than immediate satisfaction as consumers establish relationships with the brands they interact with. We have already anticipated that a lasting relationship between customer and brand is essential for brand success. This study states that this is especially important for online channels and search engines.

In conclusion, to create a robust online brand, organisations must consider several key factors, including a strong digital presence, consistent messaging, and strategic use of social media (Cruz & Karatzas, 2019). Building a strong digital presence involves developing a visually appealing and user-friendly website that effectively showcases the brand's products, services, and values (Fayed, 2022). Consistent messaging across all online platforms, from the website to social media channels, helps reinforce the brand's identity and enhances recognition (Sinha & Ahuja,

2022). Furthermore, strategic utilisation of social media platforms allows organisations to actively engage with their target audience, foster relationships, and amplify their brand's reach and influence (Helal et al., 2018; Li et al., 2021). Successful online brands also leverage the power of emotional attachment, creating a sense of belonging and affinity between the brand and the consumer's digital self. By fostering disproportionately higher levels of emotional attachment, these brands are able to establish a deeper, more meaningful connection with their audience, which in turn can lead to increased loyalty, advocacy, and long-term business success (Sciarrino, 2014). In addition to the points discussed, another crucial aspect to consider when positioning a brand online is the comparison between online and offline brand loyalty (Danaher et al., 2003). Studies suggest that for well-established brands, brand loyalty is more pronounced in the digital landscape compared to the physical store environment (Amankwah-Amoah, 2018). This phenomenon may be attributed to consumers associating product quality with well-known brand names, which reduces perceived risk.

Branding and Digital Marketing

To be an online brand today entails tackling the challenges posed by the communication channels available to the brand, increasingly emphasising digital marketing (Berti, 2017; Martínez-López & López, 2021; Mocanu & Szakal, 2023). The emergence of new technologies has spurred fresh business opportunities for companies. Managing communication spaces, such as brand websites and social media, facilitates the attainment of business objectives. Consequently, for the establishment of a new brand, it becomes imperative to thoroughly analyse the data provided by these digital touchpoints (Davis & Longoria, 2003). Many companies have now proven the effectiveness and utility of digital marketing tools in achieving results, with the accessibility of content and speed of navigation emerging as critical factors in a brand's success. Additionally, word-of-mouth (WOM) marketing has emerged as a significant means of achieving success in the digital realm, as it is intricately tied to generating new leads for the brand. As website traffic surges, visibility proportionally increases, further solidifying the importance of WOM marketing in the digital landscape. Social media has not only facilitated communication between companies and millions of individuals, but it has also created fresh marketing prospects. Blogs serve as vital communication platforms in digital marketing, playing a pivotal role in boosting sales revenues, especially for products that customers can review and share personal experiences about. In conjunction with this, online reviews form a cornerstone of the comprehensive marketing strategy aimed at building a new brand. The findings of Bala and Verma's (2018) study reveal that communication spaces and digital tools wield significantly greater influence than their traditional counterparts. Currently, the internet stands out as the paramount tool for companies, and marketers who neglect its potential put themselves at a distinct disadvantage. Indeed, the internet is reshaping brands, pricing, distribution, and promotional strategies. Considering that, as Kotler and Keller (2010) assert, "*marketing is the social process through which individuals and groups fulfill their needs and desires by creating and exchanging products and value with others*", and given the growing trend of consumers utilising the online channel for product acquisition and exchange, it is logical for marketing research to transition to the online platform. This transition involves analysing web page content, advertising materials, and consumer feedback to enhance market research methodologies. The benefits that digital marketing can bring to consumers and, by extension, to new brands are many. Digital marketing has changed customers' buying behaviour, so companies that want to build their own online communication space have to cope with several changes. First, companies must ensure that consumers are always up-to-date on product or service news, as digital marketing technologies allow consumers to access information at any time and place. In addition to this, it is crucial to try to create more engagement, as consumers can interact with the company's various activities and can visit the website, read information about products or services, and make online purchases and provide feedback. Curating information about products or services becomes basic. Digital marketing provides consumers with clear information about their interests, reducing the potential for misinterpretations when interacting with salespeople in retail stores. The internet provides comprehensive product details, empowering customers to make informed purchasing decisions. Attention should then be directed towards comparing with other brands. With numerous companies leveraging digital marketing to promote their offerings, this presents customers with the greatest advantage: the ability to swiftly and affordably compare products or services from various providers (Dastane, 2020). Digital marketing enables users to browse websites and easily share product or service content with others, facilitating seamless information transfer and access (Pazhouheshfar et al., 2021). Another aspect to consider is that prices are consistently showcased via digital channels, enhancing transparency for customers. This allows the company to regularly adjust prices or provide special offers (Veleva & Tsvetanova, 2020). Finally, the convenience and speed of online transactions, facilitated by features such as one-click purchasing and mobile-friendly interfaces, have made it easier than ever for consumers to make impulse purchases (Ibrahim et al., 2023). In principle, brands can leverage numerous advantages due to the rapid pace inherent in the online channel; however, the challenge lies in the fact that traditional research tools alone may not consistently keep pace with and monitor these dynamic shifts.

Exploring Cosmetics: A Hybrid Approach Integrating Traditional and Online Search Tools

The theoretical background outlined above, coupled with our collaboration with an Italian web agency (Gruppo Co.) based in Florence, serves as an introduction to the case study of this chapter. The analysis of this case stems from an opportunity afforded to the agency's client within the cosmetics sector, enabling the exploitation of significant economies of scale. This strategic edge was transformed into the potential for birthing a new brand, a venture we are now poised to explore. Below (Table 3.1), we delineate the online research tools employed and their respective functions in facilitating empirical analysis.

Table 3.1 Online research tools employed in the research

Tool	Function in empirical analysis
Google Trends	Analysis of online consumer search trends, with geographic insight
Pinterest Trends	Analysis of consumer sources of inspiration, with insight into demographics interested in certain search trends
SEMrush	Research and analysis in the field of SEO and SEM in relation to the websites of potential competitors
Keywords Everywhere	Combined use of the two tools for analysing social media and related metrics, such as social community engagement
Not Just Analytics	
Google Forms	Construction of an online questionnaire to be administered to potential consumers of the new brand and collect their feedback

Source *Personal processing*

Using the tools mentioned above, we developed an analysis that was divided into three main parts. Table 3.2 provides a summary of the tools' application and results.

The initial phase of the analysis employed quantitative methods with the aim of providing a comprehensive market overview, with particular emphasis placed on understanding consumer preferences. The findings revealed a pronounced preference for utilising the online channel within the cosmetics sector, accompanied by a notable interest in skincare. Consequently, there was a discernible demand for specialised skincare products. According to existing literature, our research has identified that the primary target audience comprises women. However, we have also identified captivating niche markets for the new brand, including men aged 18–35 and older women in the menopausal age group. Our analysis also substantiated a significant interest in inclusivity, personalisation, and a growing demand for products featuring customised formulations and ingredients designed to target specific concerns.

In the second phase of the analysis, our attention shifted towards three potential competitors of the new brand: Miamo, Yepoda, and Dermalogica. For competitors, we conducted an in-depth analysis of their websites and primary social media platforms. Our findings highlighted a predominant focus within the cosmetics industry, particularly

Table 3.2 Empirical analysis

Phase	Methodology	Analysis	Tool	Achievements
1	Quantitative	Market Analysis	Online accredited sources	Industry overview Consumer purchasing criteria Consumer preferences
			Google Trends, Pinterest Trends, SEMrush	Market trends Emerging trends Market niches
2	Quali-quantitative	Analysis of potential competitors (Miamo, Yepoda, Derma-logica)	Google Trends	Analysis of search trends
			SEMrush	Online authority assessment and traffic analysis Study of web traffic and keywords Comparison with competitors and backlink analysis
			Google Ads, Meta	Examination of advertising strategies
			Proprietary Website	Analysis of website architecture

(continued)

Table 3.2 (continued)

Phase	Methodology	Analysis	Tool	Achievements
			Not Just Analytics, Keywords Every-where	Assessment of social media presence
			Website, social media	Unique brand value proposition
3	Qualitative	Analysis of feedback from potential consumers	Google Forms	Surveys of consumer habits Consumer values Personalisation factors Inclusiveness of brands Information and transparency of production methods

Source *Personal processing*

in skincare, on quality and personalisation. Communication channels consistently convey this emphasis, aiming to cultivate communities and provide tailored advice along with specialised products or services to consumers (Faraoni et al., 2015).

The final stage of the analysis involved crafting and administering a multiple-choice questionnaire to 127 potential consumers of the new brand.[1] This was done to assess the alignment between the values identified in the initial phases of empirical analysis and public perception, aiming to corroborate our findings. The questionnaire was meticulously structured based on insights from prior analysis phases, enabling us to pinpoint specific areas for investigation. This approach saved time and yielded highly precise feedback on consumer habits, values, personalisation, inclusivity, and product quality.

[1] Sample representing skincare product consumers, consisting of 80.2% women and 19.8% men, aged 18 to 55 years and older.

The hybrid analysis approach outlined, which combines online research tools with traditional methodologies, ultimately empowered the company to establish a new brand.[2] This underscores an innovative model that maximises the potential of research. In fact, by integrating new online research tools with traditional methods, brands gain access to real-time data on people's searches, discussions, and purchasing habits. This empowers them to swiftly discern emerging trends and adjust their marketing and communication strategies accordingly. Furthermore, the process simplifies and enhances target selection, especially through the capability to monitor and analyse online user behaviour. Brands can thereby construct intricate profiles of their ideal customers and employ this information to refine their identity development efforts with greater precision. Moreover, by leveraging social media and community listening, brands can receive direct feedback, enabling them to engage directly with their customers and gain valuable insights into sentiment regarding products and services. This fosters stronger connections with the brand. Finally, monitoring competitors through online research tools enables brands to refine their branding strategies: this information can be used to identify opportunities for differentiation and develop more effective competitive strategies. In particular, by leveraging online research tools such as web traffic analysis and keyword searches, companies can delve into their competitors' website optimisation strategies. This empowers them to glean insights for enhancing their search engine visibility and delivering a superior brand experience tailored to individual preferences and behaviours. It follows an increased engagement and enhances customer loyalty. In essence, emerging online search tools serve as invaluable allies when coupled with traditional search methods. They facilitate a paradigm shift in how brands comprehend, connect with, and engage their audiences, offering fresh avenues for growth and success.

[2] The brand's trademark has not been registered yet, therefore we are unable to disclose its name.

Conclusions

The conclusion of this chapter presents a comprehensive reflection on three pivotal concepts that have surfaced through the examination and real-world implementation of novel online research tools within the context of new brand development, particularly within the Italian cosmetics sector. These concepts form the cornerstone for grasping the significance of modern analytics tools in today's digital landscape and elucidate their combined influence, alongside traditional methodologies, artificial intelligence, and automation, on the strategic framework of branding practices. Moreover, this analysis underscores their profound impact on fostering creativity, enhancing operational efficiency, and nurturing human connections.

The first notable aspect revolves around the significant paradigm shift from traditional research tools to innovative digital tools. The widespread adoption of digital tools has profoundly transformed the landscape of market research. Traditional methods, such as paper surveys and physical focus groups, are increasingly giving way to innovative online research platforms that leverage big data analytics, artificial intelligence, and social listening capabilities. This paradigm shift not only enhances the speed and efficiency of data collection and analysis but also provides companies with a more granular understanding of consumer preferences and behaviours. The static nature of data gathered through traditional methods often fails to capture the rapid changes in consumer sentiments, whereas online research tools offer access to a continuous stream of real-time data. These digital tools, powered by advanced algorithms, excel at processing vast amounts of information, delivering profound insights and precise predictions that would otherwise remain elusive. This transition presents both opportunities and challenges, as companies must navigate the ethical implications of data usage while leveraging the insights to shape more effective products, services, and marketing campaigns. The implications of this shift extend beyond the realm of market research, as it directly influences decision-making within organisations (Guercini, 2023). By facilitating a deeper comprehension of consumer desires and requirements, online research tools empower companies to evolve their offerings more effectively, ensuring closer alignment with audience expectations.

The second relevant aspect emerging from the research is related to automation. The advent of automated online search tools has revolutionised the landscape of market research, empowering businesses of all scales to extract invaluable insights and make more informed strategic decisions. Automation, enabled by advanced algorithms and artificial intelligence, facilitates large-scale data collection and analysis that were previously unimaginable, acting as a catalyst for creativity and innovation (Schilling & Izzo, 2012). The proliferation of big data has significantly improved research scalability, making it equally applicable to niche surveys and expansive global analyses. Automated tools can identify patterns, correlations, and trends hidden within the data, providing deeper insights into consumer behaviour and market dynamics. This precision is crucial for understanding complex market changes and anticipating future developments, allowing companies to adapt quickly and remain competitive. Moreover, automated search tools can personalise the user experience in real-time, which is particularly relevant in the context of digital marketing and e-commerce. By leveraging past user behaviour, these tools can tailor interactions and create tailored experiences that resonate more effectively with individual needs and preferences, leading to increased engagement and conversions. In conclusion, the use of automated online search tools has changed things. It has allowed businesses to rely less on old methods and use data-driven insights to enhance their strategies.

The final concept explained in this chapter revolves around the theme of creativity intertwined with the use of novel online search tools and automation. Firstly, analyses indicate a beneficial synergy between human creativity and online search tools. The establishment of the new brand exemplifies how digital tools not only fail to impede creativity, but rather enhance it. By scrutinising emerging trends and tracking competitors, platforms like Google Trends, SEMrush, and Not Just Analytics offer invaluable insights that inform creative choices, spanning from name selection to brand identity definition. These tools do not supplant human creativity; instead, they augment it by furnishing a data foundation for generating innovative concepts aligned with market demands.

Secondly, creativity evolves into an informed process. Real-time data availability and comprehensive analysis empower aspiring brand creators to foster ideas that are imaginative and strategically aligned. Using these tools transforms creativity into a practice that combines imagination and precision, with concrete data on consumer preferences and behaviours supporting each creative decision. This method mitigates the risks linked to innovation and enhances the prospects of brand success in the market. Third, the creation of the new brand highlights how the use of online search tools and artificial intelligence can ensure the sustainability of creativity over time. These tools' ability to adapt and predict future market trends allows brands to stay relevant and anticipate changes in consumer tastes and preferences. Creativity, in this context, is not a bolt from the blue but an ongoing process of adaptation and innovation, driven by accurate data and predictive analytics.

In conclusion, the new brand development experience illustrates a landscape in which new online research tools and automation, in support of traditional tools, play a crucial role in the evolution of creativity in branding. With this new hybrid model, not only does it improve efficiency and accuracy in data collection, but it also enriches the creative process by providing an unprecedented understanding of consumer needs and expectations. Far from being a threat to creativity, the integration of these tools represents an opportunity to explore new frontiers, ensuring that the brand remains relevant, responsive, and resonant in a constantly evolving marketplace.

References

Aaker, D. A., & Day, G. S. (1980). *Marketing research: Private and public sector decisions*. Wiley & Sons.

Amankwah-Amoah, J. (2018). Global consolidation of industries and business failures: Insights from brick-and-mortar and online outlets. *International Journal of Comparative Management (IJCM), 1*(2), 185–185.

Baietti, I. (2000). Dalla brand identity alla site identity: l'influenza della comunicazione off line sulla site image e sulla brand image (accessed April

23, 2024). In J.-C. Andreani & U. Collesei (Eds.), *Proceedings of the 1st International Marketing Trends Conference, 24 November 2000, Venice, Italy*.
Bala, M., & Verma, D. (2018). A critical review of digital marketing. *International Journal of Management, IT & Engineering, 8*(10), 321–339.
Bednarčíková, D., & Repiská, R. (2021). Digital transformation in the context of the European Union and the use of digital technologies as a tool for business sustainability. In *SHS Web of Conferences*, 115, 01001. EDP Sciences. 1–11. https://doi.org/10.1051/shsconf/202111501001
Berti, D. (2017). *Digital marketing grammar for the contemporary economy*. Franco Cesati.
Bertoli, G., & Busacca, B. (2002). La misurazione della brand equity: La prospettiva delle relazioni. *Micro & Macro Marketing, 11*(3), 547–562.
Busacca, B., Bertoli, G., & Ostillio, M. C., (2022). *La marca: Costruzione, sviluppo, valutazione*. EGEA.
Cardoni, D., & Nurra, A. (2022). Imprese ed ICT. *Istituto Italiano di Statistica (ISTAT)*. Report number: 2021.
Cruz, A., & Karatzas, S. (2019). Developing an effective digital presence. *GBOE (Global Business and Organizational Excellence), 38*(2), 64–74.
Danaher, P. J., Wilson, I. W., & Davis, R. A. (2003). A comparison of online and offline consumer brand loyalty. *Marketing Science, 22*(4), 461–476.
Dastane, O. (2020). Impact of digital marketing on online purchase intention: Mediation effect of customer relationship management. *Journal of Asian Business Strategy, 10*(1), 142–158.
Davis, S., & Longoria, T. (2003). Harmonising your touch points. *Brand Packaging, 1*, 17–23.
Eigenraam, A. W., Eelen, J., & Verlegh, P. W. (2021). Let me entertain you? The importance of authenticity in online customer engagement. *Journal of Interactive Marketing, 54*(1), 53–68.
Farquar, P. H. (1989). Managing brand equity. *Journal of Marketing Research, 1*(3), 24–33.
Faraoni, M., Ranfagni S., & Crawford Camiciottoli, B., (2015). Il posizionamento competitivo del brand nelle online communities: un approccio interdisciplinare. In J.-C. Andreani & U. Collesei (Eds.), *Proceedings of the 14th international marketing trends conference, 22–24 January 2015, Venice, Italy.* 1–12. ISBN: 978-2-9532811-2-5.
Fayed, A. E. (2022). Tools to deliver an outstanding digital customer experience for B2C organizations in the age of uncertainty. *Research, Enlightment, Findings Accelerated Applications Development (REFAAD), 12*(6), 848–859.

Feroz, A. K., Zo, H., & Chiravuri, A. (2021). Digital transformation and environmental sustainability: A review and research agenda. *Multidisciplinary Digital Publishing Institute, 13*(3), 1530–1530.

Ferraresi, M. G., (2008). *I linguaggi della marca: breve storia, modelli, casi.* Carocci.

Ferrero, G. (2013). *Marketing e creazione del valore.* G. Giappichelli.

Guercini S. (2023). *Marketing automation and decision making. The role of heuristics and AI in marketing*. Edward Elgar Publishing.

Helal, G., Ozuem, W., & Lancaster, G. (2018). Social media brand perceptions of millennials. *International Journal of Retail & Distribution Management., 46*(10), 977–998.

Homburg, C., Klarmann, M., & Schmitt, J. (2010). Brand awareness in business markets: When is it related to firm performance? *International Journal of Research in Marketing, 27*(3), 201–212.

Huseynov, K., Pinto, D. C., Herter, M. M., & Rita, P. (2020). Rethinking emotions and destination experience: An extended model of goal-directed behavior. *Journal of Hospitality & Tourism Research, 44*(7), 1153–1177.

Ibrahim, N. A. N., Husseini, F., Aisyah, N., Camelia, N., Khazlyn, N., Faiz, W., & Kahar, N. (2023). Online shopping behaviour in youth: A systematic review of the factors influencing online shopping in young adults. *International Journal of Academic Research in Business and Social Sciences, 13*(2), 168–178.

Kharat, M. G., Chikhalkar, R. D., Jha, M. K., & Kharat, M. G. (2018). Brand experience: Development of the conceptual framework and critical research propositions. *International Journal of Management Concepts and Philosophy, 11*(3), 340–363.

Keller, K. L., Busacca, B., & Ostillio, M. C., (2005). *Gestione e sviluppo del brand*. EGEA.

Koo, C. M., Koh, C. E., & Nam, K. (2004). An examination of Porter's competitive strategies in electronic virtual markets: A comparison of two on-line business models. *International Journal of Electronic Commerce, 9*(1), 163–180.

Lampignano, S. P., (2016). *Digital reputation management. Come gestire, promuovere e difendere la propria reputazione online*. Maggioli.

Li, F., Larimo, J., & Leonidou, L. C. (2021). Social media marketing strategy: Definition, conceptualization, taxonomy, validation, and future agenda. *Journal of the Academy of Marketing Science, 49*(1), 51–70.

Martínez-López, F. J., & López, D. L. (eds.). (2021). *Advances in digital marketing and eCommerce: Second international conference, 2021.* Springer Nature.

Martiyanti, D. (2023). Does brand love make every consumer behave on social media? The role of personality traits and brand love on customer engagement behavior. *AMAR (Andalas Management Review), 6*(1), 14–38.

Mocanu, A. A., & Szakal, A. C. (2023). Digital marketing strategies: A comprehensive literature review. *Bulletin of the Transilvania University of Brasov. Series V: Economic Sciences, 16*(65), 37–44.

Mondol, E. P., Salman, N. A., Rahid, A. O., & Karim, A. M. (2021). Determinants of Consumer's Willingness to Purchase Online in Malaysia: The Role of GEN Z's Attitude. *International Journal of Academic Research in Business and Social Sciences, 11*(7), 368–385.

Morgan-Thomas, A., & Veloutsou, C. (2013). Beyond technology acceptance: Brand relationships and online brand experience. *Journal of Business Research, 66*(1), 21–27.

Naeem, M., Ozuem, W., Howell, K., & Ranfagni, S. (2023). A step-by-step process of thematic analysis to develop a conceptual model in qualitative research. *International Journal of Qualitative Methods, 22,* 1–28.

Oh, J., Connerton, T. P., & Kim, H. (2019). The rediscovery of brand experience dimensions with big data analysis: Building for a sustainable brand. *Sustainability, 11*(19), 5438, 1–21.

Ozuem, W., & Ranfagni, S. (2021). *The art of digital marketing for fashion and luxury brands.* Springer.

Ozuem, W., Ranfagni, S., Willis, M., Rovai, S., & Howell, K. (2021). Exploring customers' responses to online service failure and recovery strategies during Covid-19 pandemic: An actor–network theory perspective. *Psychology & Marketing, 38*(9), 1440–1459.

Ozuem, W., Willis, M., Howell, K., Ranfagni, S., & Rovai, S. (2023). Examining user-generated content, service failure recovery and customer–brand relationships: An exploration through commitment-trust theory. *Internet Research.* https://doi.org/10.1108/intr-07-2022-0580

Ozuem, W., Ranfagni, S., & Willis, M. (2024a). *Digital transformation for fashion and luxury brands.* Springer.

Ozuem, W., Ranfagni, S., Willis, M., Salvietti, G., & Howell, K. (2024). Exploring the relationship between chatbots, service failure recovery and customer loyalty: A frustration–aggression perspective. *Psychology and Marketing.* https://doi.org/10.1002/mar.22051

Pascucci, F., Savelli, E., & Gistri, G. (2023). How digital technologies reshape marketing: Evidence from a qualitative investigation. *Italian Journal of Marketing, 2023*(1), 27–58.

Pazhouheshfar, P., Biabani, H., & Behboudi, M. R. (2021). Interactive model of digital marketing in online service startups based on mobile commerce in modern sociology. *Iranian Journal of Educational Sociology.*, *4*(3), 81–91.

Pillarisetty, R., & Mishra, P. (2022). A review of AI (Artificial Intelligence) tools and customer experience in online fashion retail. *International Journal of E-Business Research (IJEBR), 18*(2), 1–12.

Porter, M. E. (1985). Technology and competitive advantage. *Journal of Business Strategy, 5*(3), 60–78.

Porter, M. E. (2011). *Competitive advantage of nations: Creating and sustaining superior performance*. Simon and Schuster.

Ranfagni, S., Faraoni, M., Zollo, L., & Vannucci, V. (2021). Combining online market research methods for investigating brand alignment: The case of Nespresso. *British Food Journal, 123*(13), 37–58.

Ranfagni, S., Rosati, M., & Veloutsou, C. (2023). Patchworking research paradigms to investigate the brand in virtual spaces. In *XX SIM conference, Florence, Italy, 20–21 October 2023.*

Ranfagni, S., & Rosati, M. (2023). Triangulating online brand reputation, brand image, and brand identity: An interdisciplinary research approach to design the pathways of online branding strategies in luxury hospitality. In R. Rialti, Z. Kvítková, & T. Makovník (Eds.), *Online reputation management in destination and hospitality: What we know* (pp. 213–235). Emerald Publishing Limited.

Rowley, J. (2004). Online branding. *Online Information Review, 28*(2), 131–138.

Schilling, M., & Izzo, F. (2012). *Gestione dell'innovazione*. The McGraw-Hill Companies.

Schneider, S. (2019). The impacts of digital technologies on innovating for sustainability. In N. Bocken, P. Ritala, L. Albareda, & R. Verburg (Eds.), *Innovation for sustainability* (pp. 415–433). Palgrave Macmillan.

Sciarrino, J. (2014). Leveraging the virtuous circle of brand and the extended self. *Journal of Marketing Theory and Practice, 22*(2), 147–148.

Sebastian, I. M., Ross, J. W., Beath, C. M., Mocker, M., Moloney, K., & Fonstad, N. O. (2017). How big old companies navigate digital transformation. *MIS Quarterly Executive, 16*(3), 197–213.

Sinha, N., & Ahuja, V. (2022). Increasing Brand Resonance by Improving Brand Salience-A Study of 5 Product Brands of Hul. *Management Dynamics, 12*(2), 81–91.

Sun, Y., & He, M. (2023). Does digital transformation promote green innovation? A micro-level perspective on the Solow Paradox. *Frontiers in Environmental Science, 11,* 1–21.

Veleva, S., & Tsvetanova, A. I. (2020). Characteristics of the digital marketing advantages and disadvantages. *IOP Conference Series: Materials Science and Engineering, 940*(012065), 1–9. https://doi.org/10.1088/1757-899X/940/1/012065

Xue, L., Parker, C., & Hart, C. (2020). How to design fashion retail's virtual reality platforms. *International Journal of Retail & Distribution Management, 48*(10), 1057–1076.

Zi-yu, W. (2023). Innovative research on digital new media in corporate brand communication. In *SHS Web of Conferences,* 170, 01013. EDP Sciences, 2–4. https://doi.org/10.1051/shsconf/202317001013

4

Fostering Meaningful Interactions Through User-Generated Content: Reshaping How Fashion Brands Interact with Consumers

Samar Ghurab and Raye Ng

Introduction and Context

The advent of Web 2.0 and the widespread adoption of social media platforms have brought about a notable transformation in the process of content generation. This transformation made it easier for users to produce content, which is known as user-generated content (UGC), and distribute it on digital platforms. The accessibility of user-generated material has expanded to encompass various stakeholders, including individual users and commercial entities, such as retailers and manufacturers. The process of making knowledge accessible to a wider audience has profoundly changed how information is spread and consumed. The emergence of Web 2.0 technology and social media platforms has provided individuals with unparalleled opportunities to articulate their thoughts, exchange personal narratives, and actively participate in virtual exchanges. As a result, there is a wide range of information created

S. Ghurab (✉) · R. Ng
London SW11 8BG, UK
e-mail: ghurabme@gmail.com

W. Ozuem et al. (eds.), *Sustainable Digital Marketing for Fashion and Luxury Brands*,
https://doi.org/10.1007/978-3-031-82467-8_4

by users, including personal blogs, social media posts, product evaluations, and multimedia content. Brands, specifically, have acknowledged the significance of UGC as a potent instrument for actively involving consumers and influencing brand image. By utilising UGC, retailers and manufacturers can access genuine, firsthand experiences that are shared by their customers. The material provided by users plays a significant role in providing social proof, which in turn can influence the purchasing choices of other consumers and bolster the legitimacy of consumer–brand relationships.

The significance of UGC in creating customer views and influencing decision-making is evident in diverse industries. Nevertheless, comprehending its subtleties necessitates a clear definition. Kaplan and Haenlein (2010) defined UGC as "online content generated by consumers" (p. 61). The comprehensive scope of this term embraces various types of material generated and disseminated by individuals on the internet. Prior research has provided support for this conceptualisation and emphasised the multifaceted characteristics of UGC, which encompasses written materials like online reviews and social media comments, visual media such as images and videos, and interactive forms like user-generated games and polls (Ozuem, Ranfagni et al., 2023). The Organisation for Economic Co-operation and Development (2007) described UGC as content that is created without following professional process, is publicly available on the internet, and exhibits a certain level of creative contribution. This statement recognises that UGC comprises both content created through technology-driven platforms and collaborative efforts by users with the intention of sharing it with other users. The definition also highlights the difference between the creation of professional content and the creation of content comprising impromptu, individual contributions made by users. Research corroborates this viewpoint and highlights the genuine and individualistic characteristics of UGC, which can bolster its legitimacy and impact on consumer conduct (Wang et al., 2019). It is crucial to acknowledge that platforms frequently offer their own interpretations of UGC in their terms of service. YouTube describes UGC as content that is developed and uploaded by an individual user on the YouTube platform (YouTube, 2023). This more limited definition highlights the particular circumstances and possession inside the platform itself. The significance of platform-specific definitions in the analysis of UGC is emphasised by research, as they influence the processes of content production, dissemination, and consumption within a specific online environment (Chen et al., 2018). Precise definitions of UGC are contingent upon the particular setting, research goals, and marketing strategy.

Previous scholarly works have examined many dimensions of UGC and their impact on consumers' purchase intentions in the context of social commerce. These dimensions, which include authenticity, informativeness, social influence, and engagement (Naeem & Ozuem, 2021; Smith et al., 2012), offer valuable perspectives on the diverse facets of UGC that influence consumer behaviour. Authenticity, informativeness, social influence, and engagement are each discussed in turn in the next section.

Authenticity, Informativeness, Social Influence, and Engagement

The concept of authenticity is a crucial aspect in the domain of UGC, as it pertains to the perceived truthfulness and reliability of the content under consideration. It refers to content that is impartial, unaltered, or not supported by commercial entities. Consumers are drawn to authentic UGC because it is viewed as transparent and aligns with the true experiences and opinions of other users. As a result, users are more likely to have higher confidence in, and actively participate in, content that they believe is genuine. The concept of authenticity plays a crucial role in shaping consumer behaviour and attitudes towards UGC (Karjaluoto et al., 2016). In today's world, which is characterised by an abundance of sponsored material and marketing communications, genuine UGC emerges as a prominent symbol of genuineness that offers people unadulterated perspectives and firsthand narratives. The genuineness of material promotes a feeling of trustworthiness and connection that enhances the relationship between authors of content and consumers (Kolar & Zabkar, 2010).

Furthermore, authenticity holds a greater importance than just consumer preferences; it serves as the foundation for the integrity and legitimacy of online communities and platforms. Genuine UGC cultivates an atmosphere of trust and mutual exchange, where users are encouraged to freely express their own experiences without apprehension of manipulation or exploitation. As a result, platforms that place a high value on authenticity tend to foster dynamic and actively involved communities; thus, they enable significant contacts and the flow of knowledge. Nevertheless, attaining genuineness in UGC presents difficulties, especially in an era characterised by widespread dissemination of false information and manipulation. Content providers and platform managers are faced with the challenge of striking a nuanced equilibrium between fostering genuineness and protecting against instances of misuse and deceit. To address these problems, it is important to establish strong verification procedures, transparent regulations for revealing information, and moderation tactics led by the community. These measures will create an environment where genuine UGC may flourish. Authenticity plays a fundamental role in UGC; it exerts influence on consumer views, cultivates trust, and supports the liveliness of online communities.

According to Zhou et al. (2023), by placing authenticity as a top priority, retailers could foster a digital environment that is distinguished by transparency, honesty, and authentic human interactions. The concept of informativeness, as it relates to UGC, refers to the degree to which the content provides consumers with meaningful and relevant information. This dimension pertains to the ability of UGC to offer valuable insights and pertinent information that assist consumers in making well-informed decisions. The role of informative UGC is crucial in empowering consumers by providing them with relevant information regarding different elements of products or services, such as product specifications, performance benchmarks, and usage suggestions. This type of content generally includes comprehensive explanations, evaluations, viewpoints, and personal accounts, which provide insights into the characteristics, advantages, and practical applications of a product. Informative UGC provides consumers with a full perspective that enables them to effectively evaluate offerings and make informed choices. The importance of informativeness is in its capacity to exert a favourable impact on consumer attitudes and intentions to make a purchase. Research conducted by Zhou et al. (2023) suggests that consumers are more likely to interact with UGC that provides valuable insights and practical recommendations. This type of UGC allows consumers to assess the appropriateness and quality of items or services. Furthermore, users' confidence and credibility are enhanced by informative UGC, because they view content creators as trustworthy providers of important information (Moore et al., 2021). Among the overwhelming number of options in the digital marketplace, informative UGC acts as a guiding light that provides consumers with clear guidance during the decision-making process.

Informativeness has a broader influence beyond individual purchasing choices; it enhances the general quality of online conversations and community involvement. Informative UGC supports a culture of knowledge sharing and expertise exchange. It establishes dynamic online communities where consumers may seek guidance, share insights, and work with those who share similar interests. To attain informativeness in UGC, content creators must prioritise the principles of accuracy, relevance, and clarity. Creators may optimise the informativeness of their content and maximise its influence on consumer decision-making by following best practices in content development, which include offering comprehensive explanations, supporting assertions with facts, and seeking constructive criticism. The provision of informative content is a fundamental aspect of successful UGC, as it empowers consumers to make well-informed choices and promotes active participation within virtual communities (Moore et al., 2021). By placing emphasis on the dissemination of valuable and pertinent information, stakeholders have the ability to harness the potential of UGC in order to enhance customer experiences and foster favourable results within the digital marketplace.

UGC exerts social influence by shaping users' views and actions through interpersonal interactions and peer endorsements. This dimension highlights the significant impact that UGC can have through its generation of engagement metrics, such as likes, shares, and comments, which can signal popularity and social validation, which in turn stimulate social influence. This influence is derived from the capacity of UGC to facilitate peer-to-peer communication and the exchange of recommendations within online communities. When UGC connects with viewers and generates significant levels of interaction, it communicates social validation and support, hence amplifying its persuasive influence. According to Willis (2021), consumers tend to regard content that garners extensive engagement as possessing greater credibility and trustworthiness, because it signifies the collective affirmation of their peers.

The impact of UGC goes beyond simple measures of popularity. It includes the shaping of social standards and the development of social identities (Ozuem et al., 2021). Consumers may exhibit a tendency to imitate the actions and inclinations of individuals within their social networks or online communities, which results in heightened openness to recommendations and endorsements driven by UGC. At the core of the social influence framework lies the significance of social proof; social proof refers to the psychological occurrence in which individuals rely on the acts and behaviours of others as indicators for their own decision-making processes. Within the domain of UGC, social proof is evident through the presence of engagement metrics, which act as compelling signs of the quality and relevance of the information. Consumers exhibit a propensity to conform with the beliefs and actions of their peers, especially when exposed to UGC that garners extensive social validation. The capacity of UGC to leverage social influence carries substantial consequences for consumer behaviour and marketing methods. Brands and content providers could utilise social validation as a means to magnify their messages and augment the credibility of their brand. Brands can leverage the social dynamics of UGC to promote favourable customer impressions and achieve desired outcomes, such as higher purchase intentions and brand loyalty, by actively encouraging genuine involvement and establishing online communities.

Engagement, an essential element of UGC, encompasses the level of contact and active participation that consumers demonstrate towards this content. It indicates the degree to which UGC attracts the interest of consumers and encourages active engagement, which would promote a dynamic and interactive connection between content providers and audiences. Engagement with UGC extends beyond simple consumption; it includes diverse interactive behaviours, such as commenting, sharing, and enjoying, and consumers may even generate their own material in response (Hollebeek et al., 2014). Engaging UGC fosters a sense of co-creation and community participation by promoting active user engagement, whether through direct interactions or contributions. Engagement is important because it can increase consumer participation with the brand or product mentioned in the UGC (Naeem & Ozuem, 2021). When individuals actively participate in UGC, they allocate their time and exert effort towards engaging with the content, thereby establishing a more profound affiliation with the brand or product. The increased level of involvement can have a favourable impact on consumer attitudes and actions, such as intentions to make a purchase and loyalty to a company. According to Ozuem et al. (2021), consumers' active engagement in UGC has the capacity to enhance the extent and influence of brand communications, because it frequently results in heightened visibility and virality. Engaging content that stimulates substantive conversations, encourages user-generated conversations, or motivates the creation of UGC has the potential to generate excitement and momentum within virtual communities, thereby augmenting brand visibility and significance. Engagement plays a pivotal role as a fundamental measure for assessing the efficacy and influence of UGC. By promoting active involvement and communication, UGC not only captivates audiences but also nurtures brand loyalty and stimulates consumer behaviour. Brands and content creators could utilise engagement as a strategic tool to establish stronger relationships with their audience, thereby exerting a significant impact on consumer perceptions and habits.

UGC: Insights into Evolving Cultural Norms, Trends, and Consumer Preferences

UGC has had a significant influence on customers' behaviour and their perceptions of brands in different industries in today's digital world. The luxury fashion industry is a noteworthy subject of analysis due to its ability to effectively manage a balance between exclusivity and accessibility within the contemporary era of social media and online communities (Jacobson & Harrison, 2022). The luxury apparel sector has historically been distinguished by its focus on exclusivity, meticulous artisanry, and cultural legacy. The democratisation of luxury brand access was facilitated by the emergence of digital platforms and social media, which allowed customers to actively engage in the generation and distribution of information. UGC has become widespread on platforms such as Instagram, TikTok, and Pinterest, with fashion bloggers, influencers, and ordinary users posting outfit-of-the-day photos. Recent research has brought attention to the increasing impact of UGC on customer buying behaviour in the luxury goods industry. A study conducted by Ozuem et al. (2021) revealed that individuals belonging to the millennial and Gen Z cohorts exhibit a significant preference for authenticity and peer endorsements when interacting with premium companies. UGC, because of its genuine and relatable nature, powerfully connects with these specific groups of people; it typically generates greater brand recognition and affinity compared to conventional marketing initiatives. The emergence of social commerce platforms has resulted in a convergence of content creation and shopping, thus facilitating a smooth integration of inspiration and transactional activities. Luxury fashion brands have strategically utilised UGC to establish immersive shopping experiences that facilitate consumers' exploration, sharing, and acquisition of products within a unified digital environment. The impact of UGC on customers' identity formation and luxury fashion firms' customer communication strategies is significant. In contrast to traditional advertising practices that frequently depict an idealised and aspirational image, UGC provides a more genuine and varied representation of brand experiences. Research has indicated that customers tend to regard user-generated material as possessing greater credibility and authenticity, and that it generates a sense of community and affiliation with the brand. Helal et al. (2018) conducted a study.

UGC facilitates the ability of luxury fashion firms to promptly adjust to evolving cultural norms and consumer preferences. Brands can acquire vital insights into developing trends and adjust their marketing strategy accordingly by monitoring social media conversations and actively engaging with their audience. The dynamic nature of this connection facilitates a collaborative process in which consumers are enabled to actively build the narrative of the brand through their participation. Nevertheless, the widespread creation of material by users presents difficulties for luxury fashion firms in terms of effectively managing their reputation and brand value. Although UGC provides genuine perspectives on consumer lives and preferences, it also presents the possibility of brand dilution and distortion. Research has underlined the necessity for businesses to achieve a harmonious equilibrium between cultivating UGC and upholding their luxury positioning. This underscores the significance of establishing explicit guidelines and implementing monitoring methods to uphold brand integrity.

Engagement and Community Building

The capacity of UGC to encourage customer interaction and community development is a significant catalyst within the luxury fashion sector. Social media platforms function as digital spaces for fashion enthusiasts; they provide fashion enthusiasts with opportunities to seek inspiration, exchange styling advice, and participate in conversations with those who share similar interests. Luxury brands can leverage UGC to develop devoted communities of brand advocates who have a strong personal investment in the brand's achievements. Prior research has demonstrated that UGC not only enhances user engagement but also fosters user involvement and collaborative development (Ozuem & Willis, 2022). Luxury fashion firms may enhance the influence of their customers and promote a feeling of inclusiveness and belonging by showcasing user-generated material on their official platforms. This collaborative approach not only strengthens customer loyalty but also acts as a catalyst for natural expansion, as contented consumers become advocates for the brand. In addition, the utilisation of UGC allows luxury fashion firms to access specialised groups and micro-influencers who possess substantial persuasive power inside their specific domains. Through establishing partnerships with these content creators, brands have the opportunity to effectively engage with specific audiences and foster genuine interaction by means of tailored narratives and genuine endorsements. The emergence of UGC has transformed the way the luxury fashion sector engages with consumers and conveys its brand identity. UGC plays a vital role in influencing consumer views and purchase decisions in the digital era. UGC encompasses brand awareness, affinity, community participation, and co-creation. Nevertheless, in this dynamic environment, luxury fashion businesses are faced with the challenge of finding an equilibrium between welcoming UGC and upholding the exclusivity and integrity of their brand. Luxury fashion firms may establish stronger connections with their audience and achieve sustainable success in a highly competitive environment by effectively harnessing the potential of UGC.

UGC Facilitates Collective Action

Access to the internet is now widespread, and content created by users has become a powerful and influential factor in defining the digital environment. UGC has grown since its inception in specialised online forums and is now prevalent on various social media platforms. UGC comprises a wide range of content that is generated and shared by individual users. However, understanding the complex and diverse characteristics of the digital domain is essential for both organisations and individuals. An examination of existing research offers several viewpoints on the manner in which companies and consumers use UGC. According to Kozinets (2010), UGC is seen as a collaborative platform that fosters a sense of community and belonging among users. Platforms such as Reddit and Wikipedia demonstrate this principle by enabling collective cooperation and collective generation of knowledge. Similarly, social media platforms also function as spaces for the exchange of collective experiences and viewpoints. According to Kaplan and Haenlein (2010), the process of collaborative content creation empowers users by providing them with a platform to express their opinions, which fosters a sense of ownership. Ozuem et al. (2021) examined the dynamics of online communities, specifically investigating how UGC promotes social relationships and enables collective action in digital environments. An alternative viewpoint considers UGC as a powerful marketing instrument that is a valuable resource for brands (Hennig-Thurau et al.,

2014). Businesses utilise the authenticity and wide reach of UGC for promotional purposes. They adopt tactics such as online reviews, influencer marketing, and user-generated advertising. UGC augments brand recognition and consumer confidence.

For several users, UGC functions as a customised platform for self-expression and the formation of one's identity. By exchanging photographs, videos, and viewpoints, people carefully shape their online identities and establish relationships with communities that share similar interests. This viewpoint highlights the emotional and social factors that motivate the development of UGC, with a focus on self-presentation and the need for social connection. Recent research, exemplified by the work of Ozuem et al. (2023a, 2023b), examines the psychological incentives that drive the creation of UGC and investigates its impact on individuals' self-esteem and sense of belonging. In view of this aspect of UGC, it is imperative that platforms place the utmost importance on user privacy and safety. This entails providing tools that promote responsible self-expression and serve as safeguards against online abuse.

Although the viewpoints of organisations and users are separate, they frequently overlap and mutually impact one another. When a user shares a product review, they may concurrently seek validation from the community and express their personal preferences. Brands could capitalise on this type of UGC by developing platforms that foster collaborative production, while also recognising individual motivations and upholding ethical marketing principles.

Emerging Challenges

Robust content moderation standards are required to address the emergence of deepfakes and misinformation while ensuring a balance between free expression and responsible content management. Furthermore, the possibility of data abuse and issues regarding user privacy necessitate careful deliberation. Transparency, appropriate data gathering techniques, and user agency in controlling their online identities should be given priority by businesses and platforms. Gaining a comprehensive understanding of the complex characteristics of UGC enables individuals and businesses to adeptly navigate this intricate terrain. A recognition of its capacity for fostering community, facilitating marketing efforts, and enabling self-expression enables conscientious and strategic involvement. In the ever-changing digital environment, it is crucial to prioritise ethical issues and the well-being of users in order to fully utilise the potential of user-generated material.

In the context of the highly interconnected digital environment, UGC holds a dominant position; it has a significant impact on consumer choices, which presents both advantages and disadvantages. Favourable online evaluations, social media content, and online forums function as influential brand proponents that magnify favourable encounters and cultivate confidence. Nevertheless, the occurrence of service failures can rapidly escalate into reputational harm and lead to negative feedback.

The fundamental pillars of effective service recovery are empathy and transparency. According to Azemi et al. (2020), it is advisable to refrain from employing generic apologies and defensiveness, and instead prioritise the offering of genuine acknowledgements of the customer's anger. The provision of tailored solutions that effectively address specific concerns with authentic empathy is of utmost importance, in conjunction with elucidation of the underlying causes and the tangible measures being implemented to resolve the matter. The use of a transparent strategy fosters trust, and showcases a dedication to acquiring knowledge from errors, which strongly appeals to consumers who prioritise genuineness and straightforward communication. It is imperative for businesses to proactively demonstrate the efficacy of service recovery. When customers openly acknowledge favourable results, these testimonials serve as potent instruments for cultivating trust and they demonstrate an enterprise's dedication to surpassing customers' expectations. By disseminating these instances of achievement across several channels, enterprises exhibit a commitment to ensuring consumer contentment, thereby enhancing brand allegiance inside the marketplace.

Maintaining a careful equilibrium between moderation and responsibility assumes the utmost importance within the domain of UGC management. Although it is crucial to screen for offensive language, offensive material, and false information, businesses must exercise caution to avoid suppressing authentic negative feedback. Establishing transparent contact with consumers fosters connections, but suppression undermines confidence. Achieving this equilibrium necessitates meticulous examination of ethical parameters and regulatory structures; this approach will help guarantee conscientious moderation methodologies that provide candid criticism while mitigating the risk of detrimental content. The advent of new technologies, such as artificial intelligence (AI), indicate promising prospects for UGC. Utilising AI-driven sentiment analysis, businesses may detect patterns of service failures and give priority to customer issues, thus facilitating pre-emptive action and tailored recovery initiatives. Furthermore, chatbots powered by AI have the capability to provide prompt assistance and resolution to clients encountering service-related problems, hence augmenting the process of recovery.

Harnessing the Power of UGC

At a time when customers are constantly bombarded with marketing messages, authenticity has become a highly valued asset. Traditional advertising formats frequently encounter difficulties in building confidence with customers who have developed a sense of caution towards refined and scripted campaigns. In contrast, UGC exhibits an intrinsic genuineness that profoundly connects with audiences. UGC, whether in the form of an honest product review provided by a fellow consumer or an unfiltered social media post demonstrating an authentic engagement with a business, emanates a reliability and authenticity that conventional advertising may find challenging to replicate. The authenticity of UGC is enhanced by the fact that it is usually produced by individuals who share genuine experiences without being influenced by marketing objectives or corporate communications. The potency of UGC resides in its genuine narrative. When contented customers utilise social media, review platforms, or other UGC outlets to express their favourable encounters with a company, they transcend the role of mere consumers and transform into brand champions. According to Karjaluoto et al. (2016), consumers who are sincerely satisfied with a particular product or service, or excited by it, can exert a significant level of influence over their peers and followers. The significance of their recommendations lies in their perceived impartiality and authenticity, which renders them highly valuable assets within a brand's marketing repertoire. By leveraging the influence of these natural brand champions, enterprises may enhance their outreach, access untapped demographics, and cultivate a network of devoted advocates who promote their brand.

One notable characteristic of UGC is its capacity to surpass conventional marketing limitations and access extensive networks of consumers who actively engage in the development and dissemination of content. UGC has the capacity to naturally disseminate on social media platforms, review sites, and online communities, in contrast to conventional advertising methods that depend on sponsored placements and targeted campaigns to reach certain audiences. According to Ma et al. (2015), when consumers actively participate in sharing and engaging with UGC, they assume the role of brand ambassadors; thus, they significantly expand the dissemination of branded content beyond the limitations of paid advertising alone. This process of organic diffusion not only serves to increase brand visibility but also fosters significant participant involvement as individuals engage with, and react to, information generated by their peers. The influence of user-generated material on enterprises' comprehension of consumers' preferences and product valuations is evident, and results in more precise estimations. According to Kwark et al. (2018), the phenomenon in question can be characterised as an enhancement in precision resulting from UGC. Furthermore, it is worth noting that UGC also exerts a more nuanced influence, because it tends to bring the estimations of rival companies into closer alignment. The accessibility of UGC to all firms is attributed to its public nature.

UGC not only provides promotional advantages but also presents a plethora of vital insights pertaining to customer behaviour, preferences, and attitudes. Through the surveillance and examination of UGC platforms, marketers can acquire a profounder comprehension of their intended demographic; useful observations can be made that guide the creation of products, marketing tactics, and customer service endeavours. Reviews, comments, and social media posts serve as a means of obtaining unadulterated feedback directly from consumers; this feedback provides immediate insights into consumers' preferences and aversions, and financial incentives. These data, which hold significant value, can be utilised to uncover patterns, identify specific areas that require enhancement, and optimise marketing communications in order to more effectively connect with consumers. One of the most attractive features of UGC from a marketing standpoint is its cost-efficiency. Contrary to conventional advertising, which typically necessitates significant financial resources for content creation and distribution, UGC can be generated and shared by consumers at minimal or no expense to the brand. Businesses can decrease their dependence on costly advertising campaigns and effectively reach and engage their target market by leveraging pre-existing content generated by their audience. In addition, the intrinsic authenticity and reliability of UGC frequently renders it more efficacious compared to conventional advertising, which results in a greater return on investment in relation to brand recognition, customer allegiance, and sales conversions.

The UGC Landscape Comes with Its Share of Challenges

In the contemporary era of digital technology, customers who are dissatisfied frequently resort to online platforms as a means to express their problems through unfavourable reviews and complaints, which have the capacity to damage the reputation of a brand. It is imperative for marketers to establish comprehensive plans that can promptly and proficiently handle adverse feedback, which would effectively minimise any possible harm to the brand's reputation and position in the market. This involves the timely addressing of customer problems as well as the implementation of proactive strategies to resolve the root causes and reinstate customer trust in the brand's offerings. In order to maintain brand integrity and cultivate an atmosphere of unrestricted expression, it is imperative to implement rigorous content filtering and quality control protocols. Marketers face a continuous struggle in maintaining a delicate equilibrium between eliminating offensive or unsuitable information and permitting authentic feedback to emerge. The successful identification and resolution of objectionable content, while maintaining the authenticity and diversity of user-generated contributions, necessitates the adoption of sophisticated content moderation rules and tools. The utilisation of UGC in marketing campaigns necessitates the careful management of intricate intellectual property dynamics and legal structures. In order to effectively utilise consumer-generated content, marketers must ensure that they have acquired the necessary rights and permissions, thereby upholding user ownership and complying with pertinent data protection legislation, such as the General Data Protection Regulation. This involves enacting explicit and open policies for the procurement and use of UGC, and developing procedures for gaining consent and resolving potential copyright violations.

The widespread existence of counterfeit reviews and influencer deception presents a substantial menace to the genuineness and trustworthiness of UGC. In order to effectively detect and prevent fraudulent tactics, marketers must have robust procedures and technologies. The proposed measures encompass the implementation of rigorous verification procedures for user-generated reviews and endorsements, alongside the utilisation of sophisticated analytics and machine learning algorithms to detect potentially fraudulent trends and anomalies. Marketers may ensure the integrity of their UGC efforts and maintain customer faith in the authenticity of UGC by being watchful and open.

Evaluating the influence and efficacy of UGC initiatives presents distinct difficulties, particularly in terms of clearly attributing conversions and revenues to such content. Marketers need to create advanced measurement frameworks and attribution models that can precisely evaluate the impact of UGC on marketing objectives and results. To effectively monitor and attribute conversions across several touchpoints and channels, it may be necessary to utilise sophisticated analytics tools, employ multi-touch attribution methodology, and employ customer journey mapping strategies. Marketers may enhance their strategies and allocate resources more efficiently by obtaining insights into the return on investment of UGC initiatives. This will enable them to maximise the impact of their UGC efforts.

Strategies for Successful UGC Integration

Although there are difficulties in using UGC, marketers can employ several strategic methods to properly utilise UGC, thus fully exploiting its potential as a potent marketing tool. These methods cover a range of proactive approaches that are designed to promote authentic participation, cultivate brand advocacy, and uphold integrity in UGC projects. By implementing these tactics, marketers can effectively traverse the intricacies of UGC management while leveraging the potential it offers for establishing genuine connections with their target audience. The establishment of explicit criteria for UGC contributions is of utmost importance in upholding uniformity and excellence, while also mitigating potential legal liabilities. It is imperative for marketers to establish clear guidelines around the definition of acceptable content and the utilisation of user inputs. This entails maintaining transparency in data gathering processes and gaining explicit consent from users when deemed required. By promoting transparency and upholding ethical principles, marketers have the ability to cultivate trust among content creators and consumers, so enhancing brand reputation and integrity.

The core of fostering positive UGC creation is centred around the creation of excellent customer experiences. It is imperative for marketers to give precedence to proactive customer service and swiftly attend to consumer issues in order to foster a culture characterised by satisfaction and loyalty. Through surpassing customer expectations and providing exceptional experiences, brands have the ability to naturally motivate consumers to share their great experiences via UGC. This, in turn, enhances brand advocacy and encourages a positive cycle of engagement. Interactive campaigns and contests are recognised as excellent strategies for promoting user engagement and fostering the generation of UGC. Marketers can encourage consumers to contribute UGC and promote meaningful engagement with the brand by creating compelling initiatives that align with brand values and objectives. Brands could leverage the creative capabilities of their audience to produce genuine and captivating content, which effectively connects with their intended demographic, by employing various strategies such as creative challenges, social media contests, and UGC campaigns. In order to cultivate favourable relationships with consumers, it is imperative to uphold an active online presence and actively interact with user-generated material in real time. It is imperative for marketers to adopt a proactive approach in monitoring online platforms for brand mentions and actively participate in both positive and negative UGC. Brands exhibit attention and responsiveness by immediately addressing comments, reviews, and inquiries, so cultivating a sense of community and trust among their audience (Ranfagni et al., 2016).

Engaging in partnerships with influencers that genuinely share brand values and effectively connect with the intended audience has the potential to enhance the effectiveness of UGC projects (Ozuem et al., 2023a, 2023b). When choosing influencers, marketers should give priority to authenticity and relevance, while also avoiding inauthentic collaborations or instances of influencer fraud that have the potential to harm trust in the brand. Marketers may effectively enhance UGC and expand brand reach by collaborating with influencers that sincerely endorse the brand and engage with their audience in an authentic manner. The utilisation of technological tools and analytics platforms is vital in order to acquire valuable insights into UGC trends, ascertain consumer preferences, and efficiently manage content moderation. AI-powered solutions can be utilised by marketers to assess UGC data, extract valuable insights, and then optimise content strategy. Furthermore, the utilisation of technology-driven moderation tools has the potential to optimise the content curation process and guarantee adherence to regulatory obligations, while upholding user privacy and data protection standards.

It is essential to considering UGC as a strategic approach to cultivate relationships with customers to achieve long-term success. Marketers should give priority to clear and open communication, cultivate authentic relationships, and allocate resources to establish an atmosphere where consumers feel appreciated and empowered to express their opinions. Through the establishment of enduring connections with their target audience, brands have the ability to foster a devoted community of brand advocates who actively participate in UGC activities and advocate for the brand's core principles and objectives. By employing these strategic methods, marketers may successfully overcome the difficulties linked to the use of UGC while taking use of its inherent advantages for increasing user involvement, strengthening brand loyalty, and cultivating genuine relationships with their target audience. Brands may fulfil their marketing objectives and promote sustainable growth in a digital context by promoting transparency, prioritising consumer experiences, and utilising technology-enabled insights to harness the power of UGC.

The Trajectory of UGC

The domain of UGC is characterised by continuous change that is influenced by rapid technological progress and consumers' evolving tastes. In the foreseeable future, there are several emerging trends that are expected to significantly impact the trajectory of UGC and exert a substantial influence on customer interaction tactics. The rise of AI-driven personalisation signifies the advent of a novel era characterised by highly personalised UGC experiences. By utilising advanced algorithms, AI systems have the capability to examine extensive collections of user data in order to identify individual interests, habits, and inclinations (Ozuem & Willis, 2022). AI-powered personalisation facilitates increased user engagement and improves the relevance of UGC interactions by customising content recommendations and responses based on individual users' attributes. This phenomenon highlights the necessity for fashion brands to allocate resources to AI-powered solutions in order to provide customised UGC experiences that deeply resonate with consumers at a detailed level. Furthermore, the use of blockchain technology holds the potential to completely transform the genuineness and reliability of UGC platforms. Blockchain technology provides unchangeable records that document and authenticate the origin of digital content, thereby addressing issues associated with fraudulent activities, plagiarism, and manipulation. Blockchain technology fosters confidence among consumers and content creators by promoting transparency and traceability throughout the whole lifecycle of content. Organisations could utilise blockchain technology in order to verify UGC, protect intellectual property rights, and cultivate an environment of responsibility and confidence within online communities.

Moreover, the increasing significance of micro-influencers signifies a fundamental change in the dynamics of influencer marketing. The increasing preference of consumers for relatable and real material has led to a significant rise in the influence exerted by everyday persons, commonly referred to as micro-influencers. Micro-influencers have relatively small yet dedicated followings. These individuals have a sincere connection with their audience, which fosters trust and credibility in their recommendations. Through collaboration with micro-influencers, brands may enhance the genuineness and extent of their UGC campaigns by utilising grassroots advocacy to magnify brand communication and stimulate interaction.

Conclusion

UGC serves as a unique platform for brands to establish deep connections with their consumer base, nurture long-lasting relationships, and promote continuous engagement in the long run. By acquiring a thorough understanding of the many types of interaction, strategically implementing adaptable strategies, and adopting a flexible attitude to changing patterns, brands may effectively utilise UGC in the modern digital environment. It is crucial to acknowledge that true engagement goes beyond simple measurements; it thrives by nurturing genuine relationships, fostering trust, and enabling customers to actively influence the brand story. In the current ever-changing digital environment, UGC acts as a powerful instrument for companies to genuinely engage with their audience on a more profound level. Brands possess the potential to access the genuine voices and experiences of their customers through various means, such as customer testimonials, social media interactions, or user-generated reviews. Brands may showcase their dedication to client satisfaction and cultivate a feeling of community around their products or services by actively listening to and interacting with UGC. The implementation of strategic response tactics is of utmost importance in effectively harnessing the complete potential of UGC. It is imperative for brands to adopt a proactive approach in answering customer feedback, resolving complaints, and enhancing positive sentiments. Brands may bolster client loyalty and bolster their reputation in the digital realm by exhibiting responsiveness and attentiveness towards UGC. It is crucial for brands aiming to optimise the influence of UGC to remain cognisant of developing trends and changes in customer behaviour. Brands must demonstrate agility and adaptability in their approach to UGC, whether it involves embracing new social media platforms, using emerging technologies, or capitalising on viral trends.

References

Azemi, Y., & Ozuem, W. (2023). How does retargeting work for different Gen Z mobile users? *Journal of Advertising Research*, 2023-023. https://doi.org/10.2501/jar-2023-023

Chen, T., Drennan, J., Andrews, L., & Hollebeek, L. D. (2018). User experience sharing: Understanding customer initiation of value co-creation in online communities. *European Journal of Marketing, 52*(5/6), 1154–1184.

Helal, G., Ozuem, W., & Lancaster, G. (2018). Social media brand perceptions of millennials. *International Journal of Retail & Distribution Management, 46*(10), 977–998.

Hollebeek, L., Glynn, M., & Brodie, R. (2014). Consumer brand engagement in social media: Conceptualization, scale development and validation. *Journal of Interactive Marketing, 28*(2), 149–165.

Jacobson, J., & Harrison, B. (2022). Sustainable fashion social media influencers and content creation calibration. *International Journal of Advertising, 41*(1), 150–177.

Kaplan, A. M., & Haenlein, M. (2010). Users of the world, unite! The challenges and opportunities of social media. *Business Horizons, 53*(1), 59–68.

Karjaluoto, H., Munnukka, J., & Kiuru, K. (2016). Brand love and positive word of mouth: The moderating effects of experience and price. *Journal of Product & Brand Management, 25*(6), 527–537.

Kolar, T., & Zabkar, V. (2010). A consumer-based model of authenticity: An oxymoron or the foundation of cultural heritage marketing? *Tourism Management, 31*(5), 652–664.

Kwark, Y., Chen, J., & Raghunathan, S. (2018). User-generated content and competing firms' product design. *Management Science, 64*(10), 4608–4628.

Ma, L., Sun, B., & Kekre, S. (2015). The squeaky wheel gets the grease. An empirical analysis of customer voice and firm intervention on Twitter. *Marketing Science, 34*(5), 627–664.

Moore, K., Buchmann, A., Mansson, M., & Fisher, D. (2021). Authenticity in tourism theory and experience. Practically indispensable and theoretically mischievous? *Annals of Tourism Research, 89*, 1–11.

Naeem, M., & Ozuem, W. (2021). Developing UGC social brand engagement model: Insights from diverse consumers. *Journal of Consumer Behaviour, 20*, 426–439.

Ozuem, W., Willis, M., Ranfagni, S., Howell, K., & Rovai, S. (2023a). Dynamics of user-generated content and service failure recovery: Evidence from millennials. *Qualitative Market Research, 26*(5), 600–631.

Ozuem, W., Willis, M., Ranfagni, S., Howell, K., & Rovai, S. (2023). Examining the role of social media influencers in service failure and recovery strategies: An empirical investigation of millennials' views. *Information Technology & People*, Vol. ahead-of-print No. ahead-of-print. https://doi.org/10.1108/ITP-05-2022-0371

Ranfagni, S., Crawford Camiciottoli, B., & Faraoni, M. (2016). How to measure alignment in perceptions of brand personality within online communities: Interdisciplinary insights. *Journal of Interactive Marketing, 35*, 70–85.

Smith, A. N., Fischer, E., & Yongjian, C. (2012). How does brand-related user-generated content differ across YouTube, Facebook, and Twitter? *Journal of Interactive Marketing, 26*(2), 102–111.

Wang, H. S., Noble, C. H., Dahl, D. W., & Park, S. (2019). Successfully communicating a cocreated innovation. *Journal of Marketing, 83*(4), 38–57.

Willis, M. (2021). Online brand communities and brand loyalty: Toward a social influence theory. In W. Ozuem & S. Ranfagni (Eds.), *The art of digital marketing for fashion and luxury brands: Marketspaces and marketplaces* (pp. 153–177). Palgrave.

Zhou, M., Lu, X., & Wang, B. (2023). Travel pictures authenticity in social media space. *Annals of Tourism Research, 101*, 103581.

5

Chinese Online Literature: Sustainability and Customers' Value Co-creation on an Online Brand Platform

Liya An, Ling Lin, and Caroline Jawad

Introduction and Overview

The virtual literary space in China has developed over a period of 20 years. It is described as spontaneous, fluid, open, and decentralized, and made up of a vast number of community members (Choi, 2023, p. 107). The popularity of Chinese online literature increased

L. An (✉)
The School of Foreign Languages, Chengdu University of Information Techonology, Chengdu, Sichuan, China
e-mail: 576861261@qq.com

L. Lin
The School of Foreign Languages, Fujian Jiangxia University, Fuzhou, Fujian, China
e-mail: 27558248@qq.com

C. Jawad
Swansea Business School, University of Wales, Trinity Saint David, Swansea, United Kingdom
e-mail: caroline.jawad@uwtsd.ac.uk

W. Ozuem et al. (eds.), *Sustainable Digital Marketing for Fashion and Luxury Brands*,
https://doi.org/10.1007/978-3-031-82467-8_5

with the introduction of literary websites, consumer-to-consumer self-publishing, and interactive platforms. According to recent data released by the Chinese Academy of Social Sciences (CASS), the market value of Chinese online literature reached 40.43 billion yuan (approximately £42.85 billion) by the end of 2023, which represented a 3.8% increase compared to the previous year. The industry also saw growth in the number of writers, published works, and readers. The number of writers surpassed 24 million, with 2.25 million new writers joining in 2023. The total number of works reached 36.2 million, an increase of 4.2 million from the previous year. Additionally, the number of users reached a total of 537 million (Yang, 2024), which represents a year-on-year increase of 9%.

Nevertheless, in the Western world, there is a lack of awareness about the existence of literature on the internet. When discussions in the West mention 'electronic literature', they typically refer to experimental, electronic, multimedia, and hypertext works that cannot be replicated on paper (Hockx, 2005). It should be noted that the Electronic Literature Organization, the only scholarly body in the USA dedicated solely to the investigation of literature produced for digital media, is a non-profit organization (Electronic Literature Organization, 2022).

However, Chinese internet literature is more than just a literary genre; it is a profitable business. Wang and Hockx (2022, p. 87) argued, 'The true characteristics of mainland Chinese internet literature lie not in the phenomenon itself but in its academic evaluation and its business model'. They also pointed out that Western scholarship on web literature is primarily concentrated on the most cutting-edge forms, such as hypertext and hypermedia. While this focus keeps researchers informed about the latest advances, it unfortunately overlooks the majority of literary works created by internet users (Hockx, 2005). Arguably, Chinese netizens' passion and endeavour in literary production is the bedrock of the commercialization of Chinese web fiction.

Chinese online literature is genuinely unique; it has novel elements and a strong focus on the interaction between authors and readers or producers and consumers. It is thus defined as 'written especially for publication in an interactive online context and meant to be read on-screen' (Hockx, 2015, p. 4). The *China Network Literature Development*

Report, released at the 2nd China Network Literature Summit Forum, refers to literary creators using the internet as a display platform and dissemination medium, and using text as a means of expression to create and publish literary works that internet users can pay for or read for free (Wang & Hockx, 2022).

Eagleton (2007) argued that traditional writers prioritize artistic autonomy and preserving the essence of literature; they focus on self-expression while readers focus on making sense of the text. In contrast, Chinese online writers must adeptly handle their online presence, collaborate with readers, and engage with website operators. They can achieve this by setting up a microblog account on Sina.com, the Chinese counterpart to Twitter, to bolster popularity, interact with readers, market their works, strengthen their personal brand, and participate in cultural dissemination. They prioritize real-time feedback from readers so they can adapt their style and content to align with readers' expectations and avoid any material that could be considered 'pornographic', which could potentially lead to being blacklisted (Feng, 2013, p. 22).

The earliest commercial literature websites in China, such as Qidian Chinese Network and Jinjiang Literature City, seized this special historical opportunity of 'democratization of content production', which allowed them to break through the traditional publishing industry's monopoly of the best-selling novel market and rise rapidly (CASS, 2024). Against the background of this industry practice, young people in China who read online literature, unlike those who read traditional print literature, are not passive consumers. Actors in Chinese web fiction do not presuppose that one actor (the company, the producer) creates value, embedded in tangible goods, and the other actor (the customer) usually consumes or destroys the value. Instead, a view has developed that all actors are involved in collective and reciprocal prosumption (production by consumers) of value (Fehrer & Vargo, 2022); this view highlights resource exchanges among actors and the way they co-create value (Maglio & Spohrer, 2008; Read et al., 2009), which is the core concept in service-dominant (S-D) logic. Actor–network theory can help us understand how relationships between actors are always evolving, especially with the help of digital platforms. These platforms are essential for businesses to collaborate with customers to co-create value (Ramaswamy & Ozcan, 2018).

Sustainability entails economic, social, environmental, and organizational dimensions (Ranfagni & Ozuem, 2022). Chinese online literature has an impact on various aspects of sustainability in the context of digital transition (Rosário & Dias, 2022). In economic sustainability, two key aspects are considered: one pertains to traditional financial performance, like cost reductions, while the other concerns the economic welfare of external stakeholders, which encompasses a widespread enhancement of economic well-being and living standards (Sheth et al., 2010). As mentioned earlier, Chinese internet literature is not just a literary genre but also a profitable business. This commercialization can be seen as part of a sustainable economic model where literary works are created, distributed, and consumed in a way that supports the livelihoods of authors, publishers, and other stakeholders in the digital economy (Pombinho et al., 2023). On the one hand, digital platforms have democratized the process of literary creation, allowing a multitude of writers to publish their work online. This has opened up new avenues for authors to earn a living through their writing; avenues supported by various monetization models such as pay-per-chapter, subscriptions, or advertising revenue (Myren-Svelstad, 2020). On the other hand, the interactive nature of the internet enables readers to engage directly with authors and literary works (Gupta et al., 2023). This engagement often takes the form of feedback, donations, or purchases of additional content; thus, creating a dynamic ecosystem where reader demand can directly influence the success of a literary work.

In the realm of social sustainability, the focus lies on enhancing the welfare of individuals and communities; social sustainability strives for an even distribution of human well-being that encompasses security, health, and education. This involves fostering an egalitarian society by addressing issues such as poverty, disparities in resource access, and unfair working conditions (Closs et al., 2010). The Chinese Literature Network and similar bodies play a role in fostering a community around digital literature, which can contribute to social sustainability by promoting cultural diversity, literacy, and access to literature. The democratization of literary production through the internet allows a broader range of voices to be heard (Feng, 2013); thus, it supports social inclusion and cultural sustainability. Arguably, these activities, emerging within Chinese web novel digital platforms supported by websites and networks, exemplify social sustainability in the digital era.

In terms of environmental sustainability, the OECD's (2012) *Environmental Outlook to 2050* highlighted the need for new models of development that are centred on human well-being and the interface with the natural environment. Digital transition, which includes the proliferation of internet literature, can contribute to environmental sustainability by reducing the need for paper-based books and the associated environmental impact of printing, transportation, and storage (Pombinho et al., 2023). Moreover, digital media allow for a more efficient distribution of literature, which could lead to a decrease in resource consumption and waste (Myren-Svelstad, 2020).

What Is the Chinese Online Literature Industry?

Online literature in the West is very marginal, with a specific audience and little cultural impact (Hockx, 2015; Tian, 2019). However, in China, online literature attracts a large proportion of the total population and is a mainstream culture (China Internet Network Information Center, 2024). China is home to the world's largest online community (Zhou, 2019).

The origin of consuming literature in China can be traced back to the centrally controlled system of cultural production introduced by the Chinese government, which restricted access to literature that was not considered politically sound or morally uplifting, such as fantasy, romance novels, or ghost stories (Ren & Montgomery, 2012, p. 118). Chinese web fiction, beginning in the early 1990s, stemmed from self-published amateur novels that could be accessed online within communities (Ren & Montgomery, 2012, p. 121). Hockx (2015) interpreted the commercialization of Chinese literature in the 1990s as a consequence of 'the withdrawal of state support for the literary system' and 'the relaxation of state control over publishing houses' (p. 27). With the emergence of internet technology, internet literature became a new label full of potential, one through which regular publishers, ambitious amateur writers, and IT businesses could collectively hype and market their cultural products (Kong, 2005, p. 180). Chinese online literature consisted primarily of original serialized novels written by amateur authors for peers and fandom within communities. Arguably, online literature began as a popular grassroots movement largely free of the commercial ambitions of its authors and website operators; however, as audiences grew, a demand for self-published online fiction was created and a formal online literature industry thus began to emerge (Ren & Montgomery, 2012).

In 2003, the freemium business model, which allows users to start for free and then pay for 'VIP content', revealed user-generated content's capacity for monetization (Ren & Montgomery, 2012, p. 122). The model provides a steady stream of revenue while also allowing for broad access to content. A recent advance in this field is the adoption of non-fungible tokens via a 'digital collectibles' platform introduced by Tencent Holdings (Feng, 2022). This new direction in Chinese online literature signifies a shift in its business model; a shift that introduces innovative ways to monetize digital assets and potentially enhance the economic sustainability of the online literature sector. Consequently, online literature has emerged as a key driver of the cultural and creative industries in China (Tian, 2019, p. 6).

In 2017, the world became aware of how profitable Chinese online literature was when a subsidiary platform of Tencent Holdings, China Literature Limited, the country's biggest online publisher, had a highly profitable initial public offering (i.e. shares were sold to the public for the first time). Thus, Chinese online literature exemplifies economic sustainability through the successful monetization of digital platforms.

In today's China, the social influence of online literature continues to grow. *The 53rd Statistical Report on China's Internet Development*, released by the China Internet Network Information Center (2024), showed that by the end of 2023, the number of internet users in China had reached 1.092 billion, an increase of 24.80 million compared to December 2022, with an internet penetration rate of 77.5%. Among them, the user base of online literature had reached 520 million, an increase of 27.83 million compared to December 2022, accounting for 47.6% of the overall internet users. In other words, nearly half of internet users in China are consumers of online literature.

Overseas Markets

According to the *Report on the Development of Chinese Online Literature*, released by CASS in 2024, the overseas influence of Chinese online literature continues to expand; the market size of online literature going abroad exceeded 40 billion yuan (approximately £4.39 billion). Taking Web Novel (起点国际) as an example, the overseas online reading platform of China Literature Limited (阅文集团), by the end of 2023, about 3800 translated works had been launched on the site, which was a 31% increase compared to 2022. Renowned China-based online literature companies, represented by Yuewen Group, have cooperated with nearly a hundred overseas publishing institutions, such as Penguin Random House, Amarin, and Libre, authorizing about 2000 works for digital publishing and physical book publishing around the world, including Japan, South Korea, Southeast Asia, Europe, and America.

By the end of 2023, Web Novel alone had cultivated about 410,000 overseas online writers, four times the number from the same period three years ago. These writers come from more than 100 countries and regions around the world; the top ten countries in terms of the number of online writers are the USA, the Philippines, India, Indonesia, Nigeria, the UK, Pakistan, Malaysia, Canada, and Australia. The overseas authors are from all walks of life, covering dozens of professions, such as teachers, doctors, accountants, college students, insurance brokers, restaurant waiters, computer engineers, and family business managers. CASS (2024) revealed that the post-2000 generation accounts for 42.3% of contracted authors of Web Novel, which was followed by the post-1995 generation that accounts for 27.2%. It is not difficult to see that Generation Z is the main force.

Looking at the reading situation, by the end of 2023, the number of overseas visiting users of web novels had exceeded 230 million, three times the number from the same period three years ago. These users come from more than 200 countries and regions around the world, with an average daily reading time of 90 minutes. Among them, the US has the largest number of users. The top five countries with the fastest user growth in 2023 are France, Tunisia, Greece, Zimbabwe, and South Africa. The age distribution of readers is similar to that of authors; young people are the main force of online literature reading. Generation Z accounts for nearly 80% of the registered users of Web Novel.

In 2022, the British Library included web novels from China in its Chinese bibliography for the first time (Yang, 2022), as reported both by *China Daily*, the largest English-language media group in China, and British media. These works total 16 online novels that cover more than 20 years of online literature from the early days to current classic works. Chinese online literature continuously extends its reach as a lively practice of mass participation and global customer co-creation, and as a manifestation of the originality of Chinese culture.

The phenomenon of Chinese online literature 'winning over' global readers is attracting increasing attention. Why are 230 million overseas readers moved by Chinese online literature? This is closely related to the close interaction between users and authors, and users and users, on the interactive platforms of Chinese online novels, as well as customers' co-creation of value within virtual fandom communities.

What Is Value?

Value perception varies across consumers due to their different demands and psychographic profiles (Verma, 2020, p. 158). The discussion of value and its definition can be traced back to Aristotle, who debated and argued two general meanings of value: use value and exchange value (Fleetwood, 1997, p. 732). Smith (2000, p. 31) explained that 'the things which have the greatest value in use have frequently little or no value in exchange; and on the contrary, those which have the greatest value in exchange have frequently little or no value in use'. Smith shifted his focus from value-in-use to value-in-exchange, that is, the monetary or nominal value (Vargo & Lusch, 2004). Zeithaml (1988) reported several different sorts of consumer's perceived value from the perspective of value-in-exchange: (1) value is about a low price; (2) value is about product quality; (3) value is about the benefit received from the product; and (4) value is about the consumer's overall assessment of certain products (pp. 13–14).

The focus of research into value-in-use in the post-industrialized and post-consumption era shifted from a firm's value offering to customer-derived value-in-use (Heinonen & Strandvik, 2020; Helkkula et al., 2012). S-D logic recognizes and emphasizes the independent role of customers as active value creators (Vargo & Lusch, 2004); the phenomenological nature of value (Edvardsson et al., 2011) is characterized by value-in-use (Vargo & Lusch, 2004). This conceptualization of the nature of value describes how value in the use of a service or a product increases the perceived well-being of customers (Grönroos, 2008). From the perspective of S-D logic, value is co-created through the interactions that take place between actors, as they make use of the resources at their disposal and incorporate these resources into their engagement activities, which ultimately results in value-in-use (Grönroos & Voima, 2012; Vargo & Lusch, 2008).

Apart from value-in-exchange and value-in-use, two additional categories of conceptualizations of value perception have emerged based on an investigation of prior literature: value-in-context and experiential value (Leclercq et al., 2016). Value-in-context emerged with the evolution of S-D logic and was integrated into service science (Akaka & Parry, 2019). Context, such as time, space, and resource availability, plays a crucial role in enabling actors to create value (Chandler & Vargo, 2011; Ng & Smith, 2012). This emphasizes the contextual nature of value creation; time, place, and network relationships are key variables in determining and co-creating value (Vargo et al., 2008). Additionally, value-in-context suggests that value can be derived from indirect resources, without the need for direct utilization of the offering.

The experiential perspective of value may include the aforementioned three value perceptions (Ozuem et al., 2024; Park & Ha, 2016). These value perceptions overlap but they can be differentiated by understanding the increase in customer-dominant service logic and the importance of value creation within practices and experiences affected by customers' own social contexts. Studies on consumer online behaviours have helped to identify the different values consumers develop from branded social media consumption experiences and engaging within online communities. For example, Carlson et al. (2018, 2019) proposed five specific categories of customers' perceptions of the value of engagement activities: (1) functional value, (2) socialization value, (3) emotional value, (4) innovativeness value, and (5) relationship building value. Thus, experiential value can be defined as 'an interactive relativistic preference experience, characterizing a subject's experience of interacting with a product or service' (Varshneya & Das, 2017, p. 49).

Ramaswamy and Ozcan (2018) proposed a more comprehensive perspective of value, known as 'value-in-interactional creation', which emphasizes the individual and experience-centric view of interactional value creation. It moves away from 'use' to 'interactional creation' and shifts the focus of value from activities to interactions. This conceptualization of value focuses on the 'jointness' of value creation; it emphasizes the interplay between the interactive agencies of actors and the networked structure of interactive system environments, which are enabled by technological platforms and digital technologies (Alexander et al., 2018; Hollebeek et al., 2018). In the context of Chinese online literature, the interactive features of digital platforms and online brand communities involved in literary websites play a crucial role in facilitating consumer value formation. This will be further elaborated in the following section that discusses online brand communities and actor–network theory.

In practice, the interactions taking place between consumer and author and between consumers and consumers of Chinese web novels create both value-in-experience and value-in-interaction for the community and its members as a whole. These interactions also serve as additional resources for customer engagement, and they provide continuous opportunities for value creation and co-creation among members on the digital platform.

Value Co-creation and Prosumers

The notion of value co-creation, based on S-D logic, is prominent in the marketing literature (Vargo & Lusch, 2008, 2011, 2012). According to S-D logic, all companies are merely service providers that can create value propositions; these value propositions function as a central cue for consumers to respond to engagement marketing and engage in value co-creation (Vargo & Lusch, 2008, 2016). Customers are considered to be proactive co-creators rather than passive receivers of value. Brands and customers are joint facilitators of the value co-creation process, which is achieved through the exchange of resources (Merz et al., 2018; Payne et al., 2008). Hence, the foundational principles of S-D logic rest on the idea that businesses cannot generate value in isolation, but can only propose value propositions; consumers are active participants in value creation (Vargo & Lusch, 2008, 2016).

The term prosumer/prosumption was coined by Toffler (1980). However, this concept was largely neglected until the twenty-first century when, with the advent of the digital era, the division between consumption and production faded away (Bhattacharyya et al., 2021; Ritzer, 2019) and resource integration and customer participation were emphasized. Prosumers co-create their own products in the consuming process; they display creativity and seek entertainment or opportunities to make monetary profits. However, in recent years, new insights into prosumers have emerged: prosumers create value for everyone in their community and share it globally (Dellaert, 2019; Kviat, 2021; Sugihartati et al., 2020). Through co-creation with brands or peers within fandom communities, they build a citizenship identity and form specific meanings. Through prosumption, individuals are able to evolve themselves and complete the establishment of their identity. Hence, prosumers are empowered, knowledgeable, and skilled consumers who use advanced digital technologies to cooperate and get involved in product design and usage, and they have a salient influence on their social networks within their communities (Shah et al., 2019).

Xie et al. (2008) noted that S-D logic has an affinity to and is consistent with the idea of prosumption. It is essential to note that prosumption shares similarities with S-D logic and co-creation since the consumer is characterized by their active engagement in the process of both producing and consuming the focal objects (Ritzer & Miles, 2018).

Consumers are empowered and thus evoke their creative capabilities through the co-production of the focal products they consume (Zeng & Mourali, 2021). These productions vary from media products (Chen, 2021; Maciel & Wallendorf, 2017) to cultural products and display prosumers' innovative competence (Moufahim et al., 2018; Sugihartati et al., 2020). Given prosumers' devotion and loyalty, they are willing to be helpful in publicizing the company and brand (Obiegbu et al., 2019). Often, these prosumer activities are motivated by co-creation; consumers gather in their communities (digital communities, in particular) to actively cooperate in the process of production, learning, and sharing related knowledge (Fox, 2018). In this sense, it is common for consumers to integrate their imagination, skills, or even professional knowledge to express their creativity through prosumption; they use digital technologies to share their productions with other peers within fandom communities (Chan et al., 2022; Obiegbu et al., 2019; Ozuem & Willis, 2022). In some cases, companies assemble consumers, such as leading clients, to yield new ideas and plans (Ng et al., 2021; Yang et al., 2011).

Prosumption functions as both a work and leisure means for utilitarian or hedonic purposes, for example, prosumers co-create content as a way to gain monetary profits or as a leisure activity to enhance their well-being (Chen, 2021; Das et al., 2018; Roberts & Cremin, 2019). Productive consumption can meet prosumers' needs for social communication and interaction (Chen, 2021; Fox, 2018). On the one hand, prosumers express themselves and share their productions with other peers through social networks and online brand communities (Ozuem & Willis, 2022; Planells, 2017), establishing new forms of social bonds and tie-strength (Eden, 2017; Hollebeek et al., 2021); on the other hand, productive consumption contributes to the construction of meaning, which helps to shape the identity of the consumer as an individual (Obiegbu et al., 2019).

Chinese Online Literature and Customer Value Co-creation

Western electronic literature is technology driven, whereas Chinese web fiction is community driven. Chinese online literature emphasizes its societal impact rather than its artistic and literary significance. Thus, Chinese online literary products are platform related and community oriented. Actor–network theory views human entities as being on the same level as non-human entities; this perspective is mirrored in Chinese online literature websites because human and non-human resources are inseparable.

In this modern age of connectivity, made possible by digitalization and technology, collaborative creation can take place in digital environments (Ozuem & Willis, 2021). These environments bring together objects, procedures, interfaces, and individuals to build systems and spaces on interactive digital platforms (Ramaswamy & Ozcan, 2018). Hence, Chinese web fiction must be discussed in terms of a digital platform that is underpinned by media/multimedia. Transmedia storytelling represents a process where integral elements of fiction get dispersed systematically across multiple delivery channels for the purpose of creating a unified and coordinated entertainment experience (Jenkins, 2016, 2020). Jenkins (2008) used the term 'transmedia narrative', or transmedia storytelling, to refer to a new aesthetic that has emerged as a result of media convergence. In the age of media convergence, consumer's experiential value depends not on a single text media but on value-in-interaction resulting from the active participation of their knowledge communities, which takes place on the interactive digital platform of literary websites.

Customer engagement with Chinese web fiction is tightly bound to platform-based interactive mechanisms that use multiple media, which can enhance the interaction between authors and readers and enrich the reading experience. For example, Qidian Reading, which is the official mobile app of the Qidian Chinese Network, has introduced specialized areas for characters. Users can express their affection for favourite characters by using 'likes', creating tags, and they can even produce derivative works. Features such as 'Chapter Comments', 'Easter Egg Chapters', and

'Bibliophile Community' facilitate author–reader interaction. All these features aim to involve customers more effectively by enhancing their interactive and co-creative experiences.

Take 'Chapter Comments' as an example, which is a popular feature on Qidian Reading. In any paragraph of a novel, readers can underline, comment, and engage in real-time discussions with others about the plot, urge for updates, support their favourite characters, and even initiate second-time creations. They can upload dubbing, videos, pictures, or self-made portraits of characters in the novel; gags or memes can spread to peers in the communities. According to the product team of Qidian Reading, online fiction readers place significant emphasis on interactivity. This approach helps readers establish a deeper connection with the work and it creates a more immersive experience (Lu, 2022).

As reported by *Jiemian News*, Qidian readers post over 150,000 comments daily in the 'Chapter Comments' section, with nearly 280,000 registered characters on the platform. The total number of 'likes' or 'hearts' has exceeded 100 million (Lu, 2022). In addition, authors can collaborate with readers to create additional content in the form of comics, videos, and more. By nurturing fan communities from the outset of a serialized work, Qidian strengthens the emotional bond between readers and the content. By using interactive mechanisms that connect authors, readers, and works, each individual contributes to the collaborative creation of online content.

According to China Literature's announcement of their 2023 interim results, artificial intelligence (AI), especially generative AI, will become a key part of China Literature's new medium to long-term business blueprint to improve efficiency and quality (China Literature, 2023). Arguably, the success of Qidian Reading owes much to customer engagement and co-creation, which sets Qidian Reading apart from other digital platforms.

Conclusion

S-D logic (Vargo & Lusch, 2004, 2008) and research supporting the notion of value co-creation argues that value resides not in the object of consumption but in the experience of consumption (Merz et al., 2018) and that value creation is embedded in personalized experiences (Prahalad & Ramaswamy, 2004). Customer value is described as 'an interactive relativistic preference experience, characterizing a subject's experience of interacting with a product or service' (Varshneya & Das, 2017, p. 49). In today's business landscape, stakeholders include both human and non-human elements, with digital platforms playing a key role in facilitating customer engagement and experience as well as enabling firms to co-create value with customers (Ramaswamy & Ozcan, 2018).

In addition, S-D logic asserts that consumers have the ability, resources, and conditions to assume more roles in corporate marketing and value creation, such as co-production, co-creation, value originality, and resource integration (Vargo & Lusch, 2008, 2016). Through resource integration in activities such as communication, relationship building, and skill improvement, value co-creation is enabled (Ballantyne & Varey, 2006). Rather than passively receiving the value that businesses try to convey, consumers now desire to engage in co-creating value (Sawhney et al., 2005). If this participatory nature is taken a step further, the 'producer–consumer' emerges, who fully presents value-in-interaction; this stresses the interplay between the interactive agencies of actors and the networked structure of interactive system environments, which are enabled by technological platforms and digital technologies.

The ability to innovate and adapt is crucial for economic sustainability (Hermundsdottir & Aspelund, 2021; Shelomentsev et al., 2021). Businesses need to be able to respond to changes in the market, technology, and customer preferences (MCDA CCG, Inc., 2023). In the context of S-D logic, this might involve developing new ways to engage consumers in the value creation process or leveraging technology to create new types of value. S-D logic emphasizes that customers are integral to the process of value creation. They are not just passive recipients of goods and services, but active participants in their creation and use (Fehrer & Vargo,

2022). This shift in perspective changes the traditional business model and allows for more sustainable economic growth. Businesses that can effectively engage consumers in the value creation process are likely to see increased customer loyalty, improved brand reputation, and, ultimately, higher profits (Iglesias et al., 2020). Furthermore, digital platforms play a crucial role in facilitating value co-creation between businesses and customers as well as between customers and customers. They provide a space where consumers can interact with businesses and each other; thus, contributing to the creation of value. These platforms also provide businesses with new ways to monetize their offerings (Tafesse & Dayan, 2023).

The transition towards value co-creation and digital platforms is fostering the emergence of sustainable business models that focus on generating value that is not only profitable but also beneficial to society and the environment (Vargo, 2021). Digital platforms, integral to value co-creation, promote inclusivity and accessibility (Fanea-Ivanovici & Pană, 2020); they enable a broader consumer base to engage in value creation within communities irrespective of their location or circumstances. Additionally, social sustainability entails ethical considerations regarding a company's actions (Chang & Ke, 2024). Within the S-D logic framework, this may involve ensuring fairness and transparency in the value creation process, as well as upholding respectful treatment of customers (Karpen et al., 2012; Williams & Aitken, 2011). The environmental dimension of sustainability is supported by the shift in focus from the consumption of physical goods to the experience of consumption, which can potentially reduce the environmental impact of consumption (Polat, 2022). Digital platforms play a key role in this by facilitating customer engagement and experience; thus, they enable firms to co-create value with customers without the need for physical products.

Chinese online literature stands as a prime example of sustainable business practices. With 80% of new users on Qidian belonging to the post-1995 generation (funstory.ai, 2023), commonly referred to as Generation Z, a discernible trend emerges of active engagement in collaborative web fiction creation within online fan communities. These virtual interactive platforms offer enthusiasts of web fiction the chance to initiate creative endeavours and generate value that transcends mere consumerism. Moreover, this highlights the pivotal role played by digital platforms and technology in this phenomenon, because interactive platforms are key agents in the creation of novel value. Chinese web fiction is thus perceived as a movement encompassing literary websites and their entire processes (Choi, 2023, p. 109), rather than solely focusing on individual works or products.

In summary, with implications for sustainability in terms of economic viability, social equity, and environmental conservation, the digital transition, including the shift to internet literature, offers opportunities to address sustainability challenges by promoting more responsible consumption patterns, supporting sustainable economic growth, and enhancing social well-being through increased access to cultural content.

References

Akaka, M. A., & Parry, G. (2019). Value-in-context: An exploration of the context of value and the value of context. In Maglio, C. A. Kieliszewski, J. C. Spohrer, & K. Lyons (Eds.), *Handbook of service science II* (pp. 457–477). Springer.

Alexander, M. J., Jaakkola, E., & Hollebeek, L. D. (2018). Zooming out: Actor engagement beyond the dyadic. *Journal of Service Management, 29*(3), 333–351.

Ballantyne, D., & Varey, R. J. (2006). Creating value-in-use through marketing interaction: The exchange logic of relating, communicating and knowing. *Marketing Theory, 6*(3), 335–348.

Bhattacharyya, J., Dash, M. K., Hewege, C., Balaji, M. S., & Lim, W. M. (2021). *Social and sustainability marketing: A casebook for reaching your socially responsible consumers through marketing science*. CRC Press.

Carlson, J., Rahman, M. M., Taylor, A., & Voola, R. (2019). Feel the VIBE: Examining value-in-the-brand-page-experience and its impact on satisfaction and customer engagement behaviours in mobile social media. *Journal of Retailing and Consumer Services, 46*, 149–162.

Carlson, J., Wyllie, J., Rahman, M. M., & Voola, R. (2018). Enhancing brand relationship performance through customer participation and value creation

in social media brand communities. *Journal of Retailing and Consumer Services, 50*, 333–341.
CASS. (2024). *Report on the development of Chinese online literature.* Retrieved from, http://casseng.cssn.cn/latestnews/202403/t20240311_5737746.shtml. Accessed 20 March 2024.
Chan, H., Zeng, K. J., & Yang, M. X. (2022). Review platforms as prosumer communities: Theory, practices and implications. *European Journal of Marketing, 56*(10), 2698–2720.
Chandler, J. D., & Vargo, S. L. (2011). Contextualization and value-in-context: How context frames exchange. *Marketing Theory, 11*(1), 35–49.
Chang, Y. L., & Ke, J. (2024). Socially responsible artificial intelligence empowered people analytics: A novel framework towards sustainability. *Human Resource Development Review, 23*(1), 88–120.
Chen, Z. T. (2021). Poetic prosumption of animation, comic, game and novel in a post-socialist China: A case of a popular video-sharing social media Bilibili as heterotopia. *Journal of Consumer Culture, 21*(2), 257–277.
China Literature. (2023). China literature announces 2023 interim results, 10th August. Retrieved from, https://ir.yuewen.com/en/press-releases.html. Accessed 20 March 2024.
China Internet Network Information Center. (2024). *The 53rd statistical report on China's Internet development*. Retrieved from, https://www.cnnic.net/n4/2024/0321/c208-10962.html. Accessed 3 April 2024.
Choi, J. Y. 崔宰溶 (2023).网络文学研究的原生理论 (*Vernacular theory of the study of Chinese web fiction*). Zhongguo wenlian chu ban she.
Das, G., Mukherjee, A., & Smith, R. J. (2018). The perfect fit: The moderating role of selling cues on hedonic and utilitarian product types. *Journal of Retailing, 94*(2), 203–216.
Dellaert, B. G. (2019). The consumer production journey: Marketing to consumers as co-producers in the sharing economy. *Journal of the Academy of Marketing Science, 47*(2), 238–254.
Eagleton, T. (2007). *How to read a poem.* Blackwell Publishing Ltd.
Eden, S. (2017). Blurring the boundaries: Prosumption, circularity and online sustainable consumption through Freecycle. *Journal of Consumer Culture, 17*(2), 265–285.
Edvardsson, B., Tronvoll, B., & Gruber, T. (2011). Expanding understanding of service exchange and value co-creation: A social construction approach. *Journal of the Academy of Marketing Science, 39*(2), 327–339.
Electronic Literature Organization. (2022). *ELO history.* Retrieved from https://eliterature.org/elo-history/. Accessed 21 February 2024.

Fanea-Ivanovici, M., & Pană, M. C. (2020). From culture to smart culture. How digital transformations enhance citizens' well-being through better cultural accessibility and inclusion. *IEEE Access, 8*, 37988–38000.

Fehrer, J. A., & Vargo, S. L. (2022). Service-dominant logic and service management 4.0. In B. Edvardsson & B. Tronvoll (Eds.), *The Palgrave handbook of service management* (pp. 85–106). Palgrave Macmillan.

Feng, J. (2013). *Romancing the Internet: Producing and consuming Chinese web romance*. Brill.

Feng, C. (2022, May 30). Tencent-backed online literature platform the latest Chinese firm to jump on NFT bandwagon. *South China Morning Post*. Retrieved from, https://www.scmp.com/tech/tech-trends/article/3179669/tencent-backed-online-literature-platform-latest-chinese-firm-jump. Accessed 24 February 2024.

Fleetwood, S. (1997). Aristotle in the 21st century. *Cambridge Journal of Economics, 21*(6), 729–744.

Fox, S. (2018). Domesticating artificial intelligence: Expanding human self-expression through applications of artificial intelligence in prosumption. *Journal of Consumer Culture, 18*(1), 169–183.

Funstory.ai. (2023, May 29). 中国网络文学 "出海" 作品达 16000 余部 (The number of Chinese online literature works "going global" has exceeded 16,000). Retrieved from, https://funstory.ai/2023/05/29/. Accessed 3 Mar 2024.

Grönroos, C. (2008). Service logic revisited: Who creates value? And who cocreates? *European Business Review, 20*(4), 298–314.

Grönroos, C., & Voima, P. (2012). Critical service logic: Making sense of value creation and co-creation. *Journal of the Academy of Marketing Science, 41*(2), 133–150.

Gupta, K., Kar, A. K., & Gupta, M. P. (2023). Internet of things and sustainability: A literature review. In *IFIP advances in information and communication technology* (pp. 35–45). Springer Nature Switzerland.

Heinonen, K., & Strandvik, T. (2020). Customer-dominant service logic. In E. Bridges & K. Fowler (Eds.), *The Routledge handbook of service research insights and ideas*. Routledge.

Helkkula, A., Kelleher, C., & Pihlström, M. (2012). Characterizing value as an experience: Implications for service researchers and managers. *Journal of Service Research, 15*(1), 59–75.

Hermundsdottir, F., & Aspelund, A. (2021). Sustainability innovations and firm competitiveness: A review. *Journal of Cleaner Production, 280*, 124715.

Hockx, M. (2005). Virtual Chinese literature: A comparative case study of online poetry communities. *The China Quarterly, 183*, 670–691.

Hockx, M. (2015). *Internet literature in China*. Columbia University Press.

Hollebeek, L. D., Jaakkola, E., & Alexander, M. (2018). Beyond the dyadic: Customer engagement in increasingly networked environments. *Journal of Service Management, 29*(3), 330–332.

Hollebeek, L. D., Sprott, D. E., & Brady, M. K. (2021). Rise of the machines? Customer engagement in automated service interactions. *Journal of Service Research, 24*(1), 3–8.

Iglesias, O., Markovic, S., Bagherzadeh, M., & Singh, J. J. (2020). Co-creation: A key link between corporate social responsibility, customer trust, and customer loyalty. *Journal of Business Ethics, 163*, 151–166.

Jenkins, H. (2008). *Convergence culture: Where old and new media collide*. NYU Press.

Karpen, I. O., Bove, L. L., & Lukas, B. A. (2012). Linking service-dominant logic and strategic business practice: A conceptual model of a service-dominant orientation. *Journal of Service Research, 15*(1), 21–38.

Kong, S. (2005). *Consuming literature: Best sellers and the commercialization of literary production in contemporary China*. Stanford University Press.

Kviat, A. (2021). Post-digital prosumption and the sharing economy of space: The pay-per-minute café. *Journal of Consumer Culture, 22*(3), 801–822.

Leclercq, T., Hammedi, W., & Poncin, I. (2016). Ten years of value cocreation: An integrative review. *Recherche Et Applications En Marketing (English Edition), 31*(3), 26–60.

Lu, K. Y. (陆柯言) (2022, May 15).阅文起点读书: 一家 20 岁的网文平台, 新增用户 6 成是 95 后 (Exclusive interview: Yuewen Qidian reading—A 20-year-old online literature platform, with 60% of new users born after 1995"). Retrieved from: https://m.jiemian.com/article/7467423.html. Accessed 10 February 2024.

Maciel, A. F., & Wallendorf, M. (2017). Taste engineering: An extended consumer model of cultural competence constitution. *Journal of Consumer Research, 43*(5), 726–746.

Maglio, P. P., & Spohrer, J. (2008). Fundamentals of service science. *Journal of the Academy of Marketing Science, 36*(1), 18–20.

MCDA CCG, Inc. (2023, 28 September). *The importance of adaptability in business*. Retrieved from, https://www.mcdaccginc.com/post/the-importance-of-adaptability-in-business?trk=article-ssr-frontend-pulse_little-text-block. Accessed 12 May 2024.

Merz, M. A., Zarantonello, L., & Grappi, S. (2018). How valuable are your customers in the brand value co-creation process? The development of a Customer Co-Creation Value (CCCV) scale. *Journal of Business Research, 82*, 79–89.

Moufahim, M., Wells, V., & Canniford, R. (2018). The consumption, politics and transformation of community. *Journal of Marketing Management, 34*(7–8), 557–568.

Myren-Svelstad, P. E. (2020). Sustainable literary competence: Connecting literature education to education for sustainability. *Humanities, 9*(4), 141. https://doi.org/10.3390/h9040141

Ng, I. C. L., & Smith, L. A. (2012). An integrative framework of value. In S. L. Vargo & R. F. Lusch (Eds.), *Special issue—Toward a better understanding of the role of value in markets and marketing, Review of marketing research* (Vol. 9, pp. 207–243). Emerald Group Publishing Limited.

Ng, S., Faraji-Rad, A., & Batra, R. (2021). Uncertainty evokes consumers' preference for brands incongruent with their global–local citizenship identity. *Journal of Marketing Research, 58*(2), 400–415.

Obiegbu, C. J., Larsen, G., & Ellis, N. (2019). Experiential brand loyalty: Towards an extended conceptualisation of consumer allegiance to brands. *Marketing Theory, 20*(3), 251–271.

OECD. (2012). *OECD environmental outlook to 2050: The consequences of inaction.* OECD Publishing.

Ozuem, W., & Willis, M. (2021). Online brand communities, customer participation and loyalty in the luxury fashion industry: Strategic insights. In W. Ozuem (Ed.), *The art of digital marketing for fashion and luxury brands: Marketspaces and marketplaces* (pp. 107–129). Palgrave Macmillan.

Ozuem, W., Ranfagni, S., Willis, M., Salvietti, G., & Howell, K. (2024). Exploring the relationship between chatbots, service failure recovery and customer loyalty: A frustration–aggression perspective. *Psychology and Marketing*. https://doi.org/10.1002/mar.22051

Ozuem, W., & Willis, M. (2022). *Digital marketing strategies for value co-creation.* Palgrave Macmillan.

Park, J., & Ha, S. (2016). Co-creation of service recovery: Utilitarian and hedonic value and post-recovery responses. *Journal of Retailing and Consumer Services, 28*, 310–316.

Payne, A. F., Storbacka, K., & Frow, P. (2008). Managing the co–creation of value. *Journal of the Academy of Marketing Science, 36*(1), 83–96.

Planells, A. J. (2017). Video games and the crowdfunding ideology: From the gamer-buyer to the prosumer-investor. *Journal of Consumer Culture, 17*(3), 620–638.

Polat, I. (2022). Environmental sustainability, value co-creation, and innovation in service industries with the lens of SD logic. In *Social customer relationship management (Social-CRM) in the Era of Web 4.0* (pp. 128–152). IGI Global.

Pombinho, M., Fialho, A., & Novas, J. (2023). Readability of sustainability reports: A bibliometric analysis and systematic literature review. *Sustainability, 16*(1), 260. https://doi.org/10.3390/su16010260

Prahalad, C., & Ramaswamy, V. (2004). Co-creation experiences: The next practice in value creation. *Journal of Interactive Marketing, 18*(3), 5–14.

Ramaswamy, V., & Ozcan, K. (2018). What is co-creation? An interactional creation framework and its implications for value creation. *Journal of Business Research, 84*, 196–205.

Ranfagni, S., & Ozuem, W. (2022). Luxury and sustainability: Technological pathways and potential opportunities. *Sustainability, 14*(9), 5209.

Read, S., Dew, N., Sarasvathy, S., Song, M., & Wiltbank, R. (2009). Marketing under uncertainty: The logic of an effectual approach. *Journal of Marketing, 73*(3), 1–18.

Ren, X., & Montgomery, L. (2012). Chinese online literature: Creative consumers and evolving business models. *Arts Marketing: An International Journal, 2*(2), 118–130.

Ritzer, G. (2019). Contemporary capitalism and the 'new' prosumer. In F. F. Wherry & I. Woodward (Eds.), *The Oxford handbook of consumption* (pp. 75–94). Oxford University Press.

Ritzer, G., & Miles, S. (2018). The changing nature of consumption and the intensification of McDonaldization in the digital age. *Journal of Consumer Culture, 19*(1), 3–20.

Roberts, J. M., & Cremin, C. (2019). Prosumer culture and the question of fetishism. *Journal of Consumer Culture, 19*(2), 213–230.

Rosário, A., & Dias, J. C. (2022, January 19). *Sustainability and the digital transition: A literature review*. Sustainability; MDPI AG. https://doi.org/10.20944/preprints202201.0283.v1

Sawhney, M., Verona, G., & Prandelli, E. (2005). Collaborating to create: The internet as a platform for customer engagement in product innovation. *Journal of Interactive Marketing, 19*, 4–17.

Shah, T. A., Khattak, M. N., Zolin, R., & Shah, S. Z. A. (2019). Psychological empowerment and employee attitudinal outcomes: The pivotal role of psychological capital. *Management Research Review, 42*(7), 797–817.

Shelomentsev, A. G., Goncharova, K. S., Stepnov, I. M., Kovalchuk, J. A., Lan, D. H., & Golov, R. S. (2021). Strategic innovation as a factor of adaptation of national economies to the development of global value chains. *Sustainability, 13*(17), 9765.

Smith, A. (2000). *The wealth of nations (1776).* The Modern Library.

Sugihartati, R., Suyanto, B., & Sirry, M. I. (2020). The shift from consumers to prosumers: Susceptibility of young adults to radicalization. *Social Sciences, 9*(4), 40.

Tafesse, W., & Dayan, M. (2023). Content creators' participation in the creator economy: Examining the effect of creators' content sharing frequency on user engagement behavior on digital platforms. *Journal of Retailing and Consumer Services, 73*, 103357.

Tian, X., et al. (2019). Fantasy is more believable: The shadow civil sphere in Chinese online fiction. In J. Alexander (Ed.), *The civil sphere in East Asia* (pp. 167–187). Cambridge University Press.

Vargo, S. L., & Lusch, R. F. (2011). It's all b2b... and beyond: toward a systems perspective of the market. *Industrial Marketing Management, 4*(2), 181–187.

Vargo, S. L. (2021). Beyond circularity—A service-dominant (s-d) logic perspective. *Circular Economy and Sustainability, 1*(1), 257–260.

Vargo, S. L., & Lusch, R. F. (2004). Evolving to a new dominant logic for marketing. *Journal of Marketing, 68*(1), 1–17.

Vargo, S. L., & Lusch, R. F. (2008). Service-dominant logic: Continuing the evolution. *Journal of the Academy of Marketing Science, 36*(1), 1–10.

Vargo, S. L., & Lusch, R. F. (2012). The nature and understanding of value: A service-dominant logic perspective. In S. L. Vargo & R. F. Lusch (Eds.), *Special issue—Toward a Better understanding of the role of value in markets and marketing* (pp. 1–12). Emerald Group Publishing Limited.

Vargo, S. L., & Lusch, R. F. (2016). Institutions and axioms: An extension and update of service-dominant logic. *Journal of the Academy of Marketing Science, 44*(1), 5–23.

Vargo, S. L., Maglio, P. P., & Akaka, M. A. (2008). On value and value co-creation: A service systems and service logic perspective. *European Management Journal, 26*(3), 145–152.

Varshneya, G., & Das, G. (2017). Experiential value: Multi-item scale development and validation. *Journal of Retailing and Consumer Services, 34*, 48–57.

Verma, S. (2020). Value co-creation through value-in-use experience: A netnographic approach. *South Asian Journal of Management, 27*(3), 156–175.

Wang, W. B. (王婉波), & Hockx, M. (2022). 中国网络文学的起源及其经典化 (The origin and classicization of Chinese online literature). *Yangzi River Academic, 4*, 86–96.

Williams, J., & Aitken, R. (2011). The service-dominant logic of marketing and marketing ethics. *Journal of Business Ethics, 102*(3), 439–454.

Xie, C., Bagozzi, R., & Troye, S. (2008). Trying to prosume: Toward a theory of consumers as co-creators of value. *Journal of the Academy of Marketing Science, 36*(1), 109–122.

Yang, Y. (2022, September 13). Chinese online novels now available at the British Library. *China Daily*. Retrieved from, https://www.chinadaily.com.cn/a/202209/13/WS632024a0a310fd2b29e7756b.html. Accessed 14 January 2024.

Yang, Y. (2024, March 2). Online literature industry continues to grow. *China Daily*. Retrieved from, http://english.cssn.cn/whats_new/reports/202403/t20240318_5739078.shtml Accessed 8 May 2024.

Yang, X., Ringberg, T., Mao, H., & Peracchio, L. A. (2011). The construal (in)compatibility effect: The moderating role of a creative mind-set. *Journal of Consumer Research, 38*(4), 681–696.

Zeithaml, V. A. (1988). Consumer perceptions of price, quality, and value: A means-end model and synthesis of evidence. *Journal of Marketing, 52*(3), 2–22.

Zeng, X., & Mourali, M. (2021). Consumers as creative agents: How required effort influences willingness to engage. *Psychology & Marketing, 38*(8), 1220–1237.

Zhou, C. (2019, October 21). China's youth are shaping internet culture at home and abroad amid censorship. *South China Morning Post*. Retrieved from, https://www.scmp.com/economy/china-economy/article/3033922/how-chinas-youth-are-shaping-internet-culture-home-and-abroad. Accessed 24 February 2024.

6

Social Media and Discursive Practices in the Global Fashion Industry

Samuel Osei-Nimo and Cindy Millman

Introduction

The fashion industry, often characterised by its fast-paced evolution and substantial influence on cultural and economic landscapes, is undergoing significant transformations after the COVID-19 pandemic (Casciani et al., 2022). This period of global upheaval has amplified the discourse around sustainability, particularly within luxury fashion firms. These discussions are about environmental responsibility and broader social and economic dimensions, positioning sustainability at the core of the industry's recovery and future resilience (Fletcher & Tham, 2015). This

S. Osei-Nimo (✉)
Nottingham Trent University, Nottingham NG1 4FQ, UK
e-mail: samuel.osei-nimo@ntu.ac.uk

C. Millman
University for the Creative Arts, Business School, Epsom KT18 5BE, UK
e-mail: cindy.millman@uca.ac.uk

W. Ozuem et al. (eds.), *Sustainable Digital Marketing for Fashion and Luxury Brands*,
https://doi.org/10.1007/978-3-031-82467-8_6

chapter explores the complex interplay between social media and discursive practices in the fashion industry, focusing on how these elements combine to drive the sustainability agenda in the post-pandemic world.

Social media integration in fashion has not only transformed the industry but also opened up new avenues for sustainability (Todeschini et al., 2017). Beyond their operational effects, these technologies act as powerful tools of knowledge and influence that can redefine the narratives and practices surrounding sustainable fashion. Through Michel Foucault's theories of power and discourse, this chapter delves into how social media platforms, in their transformational capacity, enable and shape the sustainability discourses within the fashion industry, offering practical insights for industry stakeholders.

Foucault's concept of power/knowledge offers a valuable framework for analysing how information circulated through digital means can construct and control perceptions and practices around sustainability (Foucault, 1977). Leclercq-Vandelannoitte (2011) argues that the main ideas of Foucault's philosophy can be applied to analyse the relationships between technology, discourse, discipline, control, subject, and identity within an organisation. That is, by redefining technology as a practice that affects our daily lives and is shaped by language and communication, this approach helps us better understand how communication shapes organisations.

Thus, through the Foucauldian lens, the study addresses the following research question: "*How does social media reshape the discursive practices related to sustainability in luxury fashion industry?*" This question explores the mechanisms through which social media platforms and interactions shape sustainability narratives and practices in the fashion industry, examining the changes in power relationships and regulatory environments that result from these technological influences.

Furthermore, we will focus on how social media platforms reshape how sustainability is communicated, implemented, and regulated in the fashion industry. Social media empowers designers and firms to innovate in eco-friendly practices by providing immediate feedback and engagement opportunities and enables consumers and regulators to critically engage with and influence the industry's sustainable initiatives (Strähle & Gräff, 2017). These platforms allow clear communication, enabling brands to share their sustainability efforts and challenges openly. This fosters a more informed and active consumer base, crucial for driving accountability and promoting genuinely sustainable practices within the fashion industry (Gondoputranto et al., 2024).

The chapter provides a comprehensive overview of these dynamics and highlights the critical role of social media in supporting sustainable practices and fundamentally transforming the discourses of sustainability in luxury fashion. This investigation contributes to a deeper understanding of the potential for digital tools to foster a more sustainable and equitable fashion industry in the post-pandemic era.

Theoretical Framework: Foucault's Theory of Power and Knowledge

In the contemporary discourses on sustainability within the fashion industry, Michel Foucault's theory of power and knowledge provides a critical lens for understanding how social media platforms shape and are shaped by societal narratives. Foucault's concept of power, distinct in its relational nature, posits that power is not merely repressive but also productive, embedded in a network of ongoing tensions and activities that influence human behaviour and societal norms (Foucault, 1977). This framework is pivotal for dissecting the roles that social media platforms play in constructing, spreading, and regulating sustainable practices in fashion.

Foucault's theory articulates that power and knowledge are not separate entities but are co-constitutive, influencing and reinforcing each other. According to Foucault, knowledge is not just a tool used by those in power but is itself a form of power. This interdependence implies that every power relationship is a nexus of knowledge systems, and every knowledge practice is bound by power relations (Foucault, 1982). Understanding this interplay is crucial for dissecting the mechanisms by which social media serves as a medium of power within the fashion industry.

In Foucault's terms, power is omnipresent and more about strategic relationships than possession. It is operational within social relationships and is both an effect and a cause of various social strategies (Foucault, 1977). In the context of social media platforms, specifically social media platforms, power manifests in how these technologies influence what is considered 'sustainable' in fashion. By controlling the flow of information, social media platforms can reinforce and challenge prevailing norms about sustainability.

Foucault asserts that discourse is central to the creation and dissemination of knowledge. Discourses are systems of representation that construct versions of truth, which are not merely reflections of reality but shape it (Rose et al., 2006). In the fashion industry, discourses around sustainability are profoundly shaped by social media narratives, affecting consumer perceptions and industry standards. Thus, discourses serve not just as passive carriers of meaning but as active influencers defining what is knowable and actionable.

In terms of the role of social media in fashion, platforms such as Instagram, Facebook, and Twitter serve as powerful mediums through which discourses of sustainability are crafted and disseminated. By promoting certain narratives over others, these platforms play a pivotal role in what Foucault would describe as the regime of truth, a system within which specific assertions are made authoritative, and others marginalised. This regime influences both public perception and the internal practices of fashion firms, guiding them on how sustainability should be understood and implemented (Leclercq-Vandelannoitte, 2011).

Sustainability in the fashion industry emerges as a set of practices and a discursive field where meanings are constantly negotiated and contested. Social media facilitates this by offering platforms for discourse generation and interaction, where diverse stakeholders such as consumers, companies, and regulators engage with and shape sustainability narratives. Hardy and Phillips (1999) suggest that diverse discourses around sustainability lead to 'discursive struggles', which significantly impact how stakeholders perceive and enact their environmental responsibilities.

The transformative potential of social media in reshaping discursive practices around sustainability in fashion is significant. By facilitating wider and more dynamic interactions than traditional media, social media platforms increase the visibility of sustainable practices and challenge existing power structures within the fashion industry (Boyd &

Holton, 2018). They even enable smaller brands to amplify their sustainability narratives, potentially shifting market dynamics in favour of more sustainable practices (Akram et al., 2022; De Perthuis & Findlay, 2019).

Thus, this study uses Foucault's theory of power and knowledge to reveal how social media platforms are not merely tools but integral to shaping the landscape of sustainable fashion. Through the lens of Foucault, we see that these technologies are instrumental in constructing new discourses and altering power relations, thereby influencing how sustainability is practised and how it is conceptualised within the fashion industry.

Social Media in the Fashion Industry

Social media integration within the fashion industry has marked a transformative era, reshaping the luxury sector's design, marketing, and consumer engagement approach. This evolution is pivotal in Industry 4.0, where social media platforms have fundamentally altered production processes and business models, allowing brands to meet the increasing demands for customisation and speed (Akram et al., 2022; Bertola & Teunissen, 2018).

The trajectory of social media in fashion began with platforms like Instagram and Facebook becoming integral to marketing strategies, enabling brands to engage in direct consumer interaction and build a brand story that resonates with a digital-savvy clientele (Behr, 2018). The impact of these platforms is profound, shifting the marketing paradigm from a one-to-many to a more personalised, one-to-one communication that emphasises consumer engagement and brand loyalty.

E-commerce and virtual showrooms have further digitised the consumer experience, offering convenience and a tailored shopping experience. Aiolfi and Sabbadin (2019) argue that the rise of online shopping platforms has compelled luxury fashion brands to rethink their retail strategies, integrating omnichannel approaches that blur the lines between physical and digital spaces. Wu et al. (2022) also cite virtual showrooms, augmented reality (AR) and virtual reality (VR) as examples of modern platforms that enhance consumer journeys by providing them with an immersive shopping experience that can replicate, and sometimes surpass, the tactile engagement offered by physical stores.

Social media has also emerged as a transformative tool for enhancing transparency and traceability in the fashion supply chain. By allowing for a secure and immutable record of transactions and product journeys, social media supports the authenticity claims of luxury brands, helping build consumer trust, a crucial element in the luxury market where provenance and authenticity are significant (Benstead et al., 2022). Moreover, social media facilitates the implementation of more sustainable practices by providing transparent records of a product's environmental impact, aligning with the increasing consumer demand for sustainable and ethically produced fashion items (Akbari & Hopkins, 2022). Additionally, Oguntegbe et al. (2023) reveal that social media analytics, coupled with blockchain technology, can enhance responsible management practices within the supply chain by ensuring that all steps are visible and verifiable.

The COVID-19 pandemic accelerated the adoption of social media technologies. As the crisis disrupted traditional retail and global supply chains, fashion brands were compelled to rapidly embrace digital solutions to mitigate the impact and cater to altered consumer behaviours, which leaned heavily towards online shopping and digital engagement (Berman, 2012). The pandemic highlighted the need for brands to be agile and digitally adept, making significant investments in digital infrastructure essential for survival and competitive advantage in the post-pandemic landscape (Casciani et al., 2022).

Furthermore, social media technologies sustained operations during the pandemic and pushed companies to innovate in their approach to market challenges. For example, the use of Artificial Intelligence (AI) to predict consumer trends and manage inventories became more prevalent, helping brands respond dynamically to fast-changing market conditions (Parida et al., 2019). Thus, the crisis served as a catalyst for a profound digital transformation in the fashion industry, which will continue evolving rapidly in the coming years.

The adoption of these technologies, however, is not without challenges. Issues related to cybersecurity, the digital divide between large and small firms, and the loss of certain types of jobs due to automation are concerns that the industry must address as it continues to integrate these digital tools (Manavalan & Jayakrishna, 2019). Moreover, Quiles-Soler et al. (2023) argue that the push towards more sustainable practices through digital means requires a balanced approach to ensure that technological advancements do not overshadow the core ethical values of sustainability but rather enhance transparency and accountability in fashion production and consumption.

Some researchers have also critically assessed the implementation of social media technologies in supply chains to respond to crises (Beheshti-Kashi, 2020; Oguntegbe et al., 2023). Ralston and Blackhurst (2020) caution that these technologies may fail to enhance capabilities, introduce inefficiencies, and incur unexpected costs without tactical deployment. This highlights the need for strategic planning to ensure that the integration of such technologies genuinely contributes to supply chain resilience.

Therefore, despite the challenges mentioned, it is evident that the introduction and increasing adoption of social media technologies have significantly transformed the luxury fashion industry. This transformation encompasses various aspects, including product design, supply chains, manufacturing, marketing, and sales. The industry's potential for further advancements and enhancements is vast as it continues to evolve under the influence of these technologies.

Discursive Practices and Sustainability

Sustainability in fashion encapsulates a complex array of practices aimed at reducing environmental impact and promoting ethical labour standards. Markkula and Moisander (2012) state that the discourses surrounding sustainable fashion frame the practices themselves and significantly influence consumer behaviour and industry standards. Thus, in the rapidly evolving fashion industry, sustainability has transitioned from a secondary issue to the primary strategy for numerous firms, especially those in the luxury sector.

The definition of sustainable practices within the fashion industry is broad and multi-faceted, addressing the lifecycle of garments from design to disposal (Islam et al., 2021). These practices include using environmentally friendly materials, reducing waste through cutting-edge production techniques, ensuring fair labour conditions, and promoting clothing longevity over 'disposability' (Gwilt & Rissanen, 2012). The approach towards sustainability in fashion is not just about environmentalism but also incorporates social and economic dimensions, aiming to achieve a comprehensive ethical framework.

The role of discourse in shaping sustainability is critical, as it influences how consumers and companies perceive and engage with sustainable practices (Genus, 2014). Urmínová and Kusá (2020) highlight the media's pivotal role in bridging sustainable fashion brands and the public. Through various platforms, from traditional print magazines to dynamic social media channels, media outlets have the power to highlight sustainable initiatives and educate the public about the importance of sustainability in fashion (Zhao et al., 2022). This promotion increases consumer awareness and sets a narrative that brands are expected to align with if they wish to be perceived as sustainable.

Consumer awareness and education are fundamentally tied to how effectively the discourses on sustainability are disseminated. Knowledge about the impacts of fashion consumption and the benefits of choosing sustainable products is crucial for fostering a culture of responsible consumption. Educational campaigns and transparency initiatives help demystify sustainability for consumers, empowering them to make informed choices. For example, Bernstein (2012) mentions that disclosing product origins, materials used, and manufacturing conditions can help consumers understand the real costs and benefits of their purchases, thus encouraging more mindful consumption behaviour.

Concerning the practical implementations of these discourses, several luxury fashion brands have successfully integrated sustainability into their business models and marketing strategies. A notable example is the campaign launched by Patagonia, a brand synonymous with environmental advocacy, which has utilised social media to amplify its sustainability message. The 'Don't Buy This Jacket' campaign, launched in 2011, remains a decisive case of how social media can drive sustainability discourses. By urging consumers to think critically about their consumption habits, Patagonia used its social media channels to spread the campaign's message, emphasising the importance of reducing consumption and promoting product longevity (Michel et al., 2019). This campaign strengthened Patagonia's reputation as an environmental leader and sparked widespread discussion about consumerism and sustainability in fashion (Thorisdottir & Johannsdottir, 2019).

Niinimäki (2013) cites another illustrative case of Adidas, which has made significant strides in integrating recycled materials into its products. Social media was pivotal in promoting this initiative, educating consumers about ocean pollution, and demonstrating how recycled materials can be transformed into high-quality products (Todeschini et al., 2017). Through platforms like Instagram and Twitter, Adidas engaged with consumers by sharing compelling stories and visuals about the recycling process and their products' environmental benefits, reinforcing their brand's commitment to sustainability (Niinimäki, 2013).

The cases from brands like Patagonia and Adidas' sustainability campaigns do more than promote individual products; they contribute to a broader narrative that challenges the fashion industry to reconsider its environmental impact and social responsibilities (Joy et al., 2012). These examples highlight how discourses on sustainability are not merely abstract ideals but are actively shaped and reshaped through real-world applications and consumer interactions.

Despite these positive developments, the sustainability discourse also faces challenges, such as the risk of greenwashing, where sustainability claims may not fully align with actual business practices (Adamkiewicz et al., 2022; Niinimäki, 2015). This discrepancy can lead to consumer scepticism and discursive confusion, undermining genuine efforts towards sustainability (Markkula & Moisander, 2012). Therefore, maintaining transparency and adhering to verifiable standards is crucial for the credibility and effectiveness of sustainability narratives.

Influencer collaborations and user-driven content have also significantly impacted fashion discourses, particularly in promoting sustainability. These influencers who command large social media followers can sway consumer perceptions and behaviours. For example, collaborations between luxury fashion brands and eco-conscious influencers have helped raise awareness about sustainable fashion practices. Pérez-Curiel et al. (2021) add that these influencers share content that highlights the environmental and ethical values of the brands they endorse, thereby influencing their followers to make more sustainable fashion choices.

One prominent example is the collaboration between the luxury fashion brand Stella McCartney and various environmental activists. Marcella-Hood (2023) mentions Stella McCartney's use of influencers to promote her sustainable collections has been instrumental in spreading awareness about the importance of eco-friendly fashion. Through Instagram posts, stories, and live sessions, influencers have communicated the brand's commitment to sustainability, reaching a wide audience and fostering a community of environmentally conscious consumers (Choi, 2020).

These examples demonstrate that social media campaigns are crucial in shaping fashion discourses and promoting sustainable practices. The Fashion Revolution campaign, for instance, uses the hashtag #WhoMadeMyClothes to encourage transparency in the fashion industry (Modi & Zhao, 2021). This campaign leverages social media to ask brands about their supply chains and labour practices, urging them to be more transparent and accountable (Kim & Kim, 2020). The widespread use of this hashtag on platforms like Twitter and Instagram has created a global conversation about the ethics of fashion production, pressuring brands to adopt more sustainable and ethical practices.

Similarly, Brydges et al. (2021) highlight that the #RewiringFashion campaign, initiated by a coalition of independent designers, retailers, and executives, calls for restructuring the fashion industry to prioritise sustainability and ethical practices. This campaign has gained significant traction through social media, promoting discussions about the need for systemic change in the fashion industry and advocating for a more sustainable future (Hsiao et al., 2020; Ozuem & Willis, 2022).

Furthermore, Vladimirova et al. (2024) emphasise the influence of user-driven content and community engagement on promoting sustainability in the fashion industry through social media platforms like Instagram and Pinterest. These platforms enable users to share their sustainable fashion choices, DIY projects, and upcycling ideas, inspiring others to adopt more sustainable practices and building a sense of community among like-minded individuals. For instance, the #SecondHandSeptember campaign encourages consumers to refrain from buying new clothes in September and instead focus on second-hand and vintage shopping. This campaign, widely promoted on social media, has garnered extensive participation and support, underscoring the environmental benefits of second-hand shopping and reducing the demand for fast fashion (Vladimirova et al., 2024).

Lastly, the prevailing discourses significantly impact sustainable practices in the fashion business, which has a crucial role in shaping consumer views and industry norms. Social media, along with targeted educational efforts, are vital in promoting these practices. At the same time, evidence and cases from luxury brands demonstrate the potential of sustainability to drive both business innovation and environmental stewardship. To advance the sustainability agenda in the global fashion industry, it is vital to understand the relationship between discursive practices and concrete actions (Markkula & Moisander, 2012).

Transforming Power Dynamics and Shaping Regulatory and Ethical Considerations in the Fashion Industry

The discussion above shows that social media platforms have redefined the fashion industry regarding discourses and approaches of both firms and consumers, significantly influencing power dynamics and introducing new ethical and regulatory challenges. These technologies have reconfigured traditional power structures through their various applications and prompted a need for comprehensive ethical oversight and regulatory frameworks.

The fashion industry has seen a profound transformation in how power dynamics plays out, thanks in part to the pervasive influence of social media. Platforms such as Instagram and Twitter have become instrumental in shaping consumer behaviour and brand strategies. Anjorin et al. (2024) highlights that social media marketing significantly impacts consumer behaviour in the retail industry by creating new channels for engagement and visibility, which is crucial for the fashion sector. This influence is evident in how brands utilise these platforms to promote sustainability and ethical practices.

Data analytics derived from social media interactions have become foundations for understanding and predicting consumer behaviour. Fashion companies leverage vast amounts of data from online interactions to tailor marketing strategies and optimise consumer engagement (Cabigiosu, 2020; Ozuem et al., 2021). While this enables better customer experiences and service personalisation, it also raises questions about consumer autonomy and the manipulative potential of targeted advertising, which can subtly influence fashion trends and consumer choices (Brydges et al., 2018).

From a Foucauldian perspective, power in the fashion industry is not only held by those who create the clothes but also by those who control the information about how and by whom these clothes are made and sold. Social media leaders and innovators, wielding significant influence, have redefined power structures within the industry. Godart (2014) points out that as technology becomes more intertwined with the fashion industry, it has the potential to either democratise or consolidate it among a few technologically savvy leaders. These leaders, by virtue of controlling digital platforms and tools, command substantial influence over both market trends and the operational aspects of fashion companies.

The ethical implications of AI and automation in fashion design and manufacturing are profound. AI systems, which help design patterns and predict trends, also pose risks of cultural appropriation and the dilution of artisanal elements that are often the hallmark of luxury fashion. Automation in manufacturing, while increasing efficiency, raises significant ethical questions regarding the displacement of workers and the ensuing social impact (Liu et al., 2023).

Furthermore, regulatory and ethical considerations have become increasingly prominent with the rise of social media. Data protection and privacy are paramount, as the fashion industry handles a significant amount of personal data through e-commerce and digital marketing (de Koning, 2019). The European General Data Protection Regulation (GDPR) and similar frameworks worldwide dictate stringent guidelines for data handling, imposing a legal imperative to protect consumer information. Leclercq-Vandelannoitte (2022) delves deeper into the fashion industry by emphasising the broader ethical implications of pervasive technology use in organisations, highlighting a Foucauldian perspective on the ethics of ubiquitous technology uses. This analysis is particularly relevant to our discussion, where we explore that the integration of social media which not only raises concerns about consumer data privacy, employee surveillance, but also technological 'ill-being'.

Corporate responsibility also plays a critical role in the industry as it goes beyond compliance with legal standards to embrace genuine accountability for their operations' social and environmental impacts (Thorisdottir & Johannsdottir, 2020). Arrigo (2013) mentions that this involves implementing sustainable practices that are transparently reported and actively engaging in ethical labour practices. Companies like Gap Inc. have exemplified this approach by integrating corporate social responsibility into their business models, addressing ethical concerns head-on (Arrigo, 2013; Ozuem et al., 2023a, 2023b).

As we consider the critical role of corporate responsibility in addressing ethical and environmental impacts within the fashion industry, it becomes clear that the evolving digital landscape also presents unique challenges and opportunities. This transition segues into our discussion on how social media has fundamentally altered the industry's discourses, reshaping interactions between brands, consumers, and other stakeholders and redefining the communication of values and practices on a global scale.

Discussion

Social media has profoundly reshaped discourse within the fashion industry, creating new platforms and means through which brands and consumers interact. The advent of digitalised technologies, particularly social media, has democratised fashion communication, enabling consumers to participate actively in brand narratives and discussions (Creevey et al., 2022). This shift has not only altered how fashion is marketed but also how its values and practices are communicated to a global audience.

As Akram et al. (2022) note, the integration of these technologies has brought both opportunities and challenges, facilitating greater engagement and customisation while also raising issues regarding data security and the authenticity of digital interactions. Holmqvist et al. (2020) further argue that luxury brands must navigate these digital forums carefully to maintain their exclusivity while engaging with a broader audience, highlighting a delicate balance between accessibility and maintaining traditional luxury values.

Sustainability in fashion has become increasingly critical, spurred by greater global awareness and consumer demand for ethical practices. However, as Gardetti and Larios-Francia (2023) discuss, the fashion industry still faces significant sustainability challenges, including the need to address its role in the ongoing civilisation crisis and to consider aspects of cultural legacy and decolonisation. These dimensions underscore the complexity of implementing truly sustainable practices that go beyond mere tokenism to embrace systemic changes. Calefato (2017) emphasises the need for the fashion industry to move from global standardisation to critical customisation, suggesting a more nuanced approach to sustainability that considers local contexts and cultural significance.

While digital interventions in sustainability are widely acknowledged for their potential to drive positive change within the fashion industry, they also bring significant limitations and unintended consequences that merit critical examination. For instance, Parguel et al. (2015) found that some companies exploit eco-labels in online advertising to appear more sustainable without making substantial environmental improvements. This practice, known as 'greenwashing', misleads consumers and dilutes the credibility of genuinely sustainable initiatives.

The rapid pace of technological advancement leads to a shorter lifespan for digital devices, resulting in significant e-waste challenges that contradict the sustainability goals of reducing environmental footprints (Ahmed, 2016; Azemi & Ozuem, 2023). These insights underscore the need for the fashion industry to critically evaluate the environmental impact of digital interventions and ensure these efforts genuinely contribute to sustainability rather than exacerbate existing issues.

Furthermore, while promoting sustainable practices, digital platforms can also be double-edged swords. Vanko and Zaušková (2019) highlight that social media can effectively raise public awareness of eco-innovations, yet it often leads to superficial engagement rather than profound, lasting behavioural change. Byrum (2019) similarly notes that social media campaigns aiming to influence eco-purchasing behaviour often rely on simplistic messages that may not fully convey the complexities of sustainable consumption, potentially leading to consumer fatigue or scepticism.

The implications for future research and practice in fashion are vast. The intersection of social media and sustainability presents extensive opportunities for exploration, particularly in understanding how these platforms can be leveraged to promote sustainable practices more effectively and inclusively (Yang et al., 2017). Researchers must investigate how social media can facilitate more substantial, impactful engagement with sustainability issues, potentially transforming consumer behaviour and industry standards (Mukendi et al., 2020; Ozuem et al. 2024). For example, Williams et al. (2014) discuss how new social media platforms can be utilised to foster green sustainability by creating interactive and engaging content that educates and motivates consumers towards more sustainable choices.

Additionally, there is a pressing need to examine the ethical dimensions of digitalisation in fashion, particularly how data is used and the potential consequences of AI and automation in design and production processes. Yeo et al. (2022) investigate the impact of AI-powered technologies on Instagrammers' purchase decisions, highlighting how these technologies influence consumer behaviour in the fashion and apparel industry. As the industry evolves, these areas will undoubtedly become critical focal points for both academic inquiry and practical implementation. Aligning technological advancements with ethical and sustainable practices will be essential for ensuring that digital interventions genuinely contribute to sustainability.

Conclusion

In conclusion, social media, discursive practices, and sustainability in the luxury fashion industry present a multi-faceted and transformative dynamic. The adoption of social media and networks has completely transformed how fashion firms communicate their sustainability efforts and engage with consumers. Through the Foucauldian lens, it becomes clear that power and knowledge are linked in a complex relationship, with social media platforms acting as powerful mediums that shape and regulate sustainability discourses.

Digital platforms such as Instagram, Facebook, and Twitter have democratised the fashion narrative, allowing for a broader and more interactive engagement between brands and consumers. This shift has facilitated disseminating sustainable practices, enabling brands to share their efforts transparently and foster a more informed and active consumer base. Campaigns by brands like Patagonia and Adidas demonstrate how social media can drive sustainability narratives and promote ethical consumer behaviour.

However, we have also highlighted significant challenges in this chapter. For instance, the potential for greenwashing and inadequate engagement with sustainability issues has been identified as a critical concern. The authenticity of sustainability claims and the need for verifiable standards are paramount to maintaining consumer trust and ensuring that sustainability efforts are genuine and impactful. Additionally, the ethical implications of social media usage, such as data privacy and the displacement of workers through automated marketing tools and customer service bots, necessitate careful consideration and regulatory oversight.

Another crucial aspect is the transformation of power dynamics within the fashion industry. Social media platforms have reconfigured traditional power structures, enabling smaller brands and eco-conscious influencers to amplify their voices and challenge established norms. This power shift can potentially foster more equitable and sustainable practices within the industry.

Therefore, future research and practice must continue to examine the relationship between social media and sustainability. Understanding how digital platforms can be leveraged to promote deeper and more meaningful engagement with sustainability issues is essential. Additionally, examining the ethical dimensions of digitalisation and ensuring that technological advancements align with sustainable and ethical practices will be critical for the industry's ongoing evolution.

In summary, this chapter has emphasised the transformative power of social media in creating and shaping sustainability discourses in the fashion industry. Social media platforms can play a pivotal role in promoting genuinely sustainable practices by fostering transparency, accountability, and active consumer engagement. However, addressing the challenges and ethical considerations related to these technologies is crucial for understanding their full potential in driving the sustainability agenda forward in the post-pandemic world.

References

Adamkiewicz, J., Kochańska, E., Adamkiewicz, I., & Łukasik, R. M. (2022). Greenwashing and sustainable fashion industry. *Current Opinion in Green and Sustainable Chemistry, 38*, 100710.

Ahmed, S. F. (2016). The global cost of electronic waste. *The Atlantic*. Available at https://www.theatlantic.com/technology/archive/2016/09/the-global-cost-of-electronic-waste/502019/ [Accessed 24 April 2024].

Aiolfi, S., & Sabbadin, E. (2019). Fashion and new luxury digital disruption: The new challenges of fashion between omnichannel and traditional retailing. *International Journal of Business and Management, 14*(8), 41–51.

Akbari, M., & Hopkins, J. L. (2022). Digital technologies as enablers of supply chain sustainability in an emerging economy. *Operations Management Research, 15*(3), 689–710.

Akram, S. V., Malik, P. K., Singh, R., Gehlot, A., Juyal, A., Ghafoor, K. Z., & Shrestha, S. (2022). Implementation of digitalized technologies for fashion industry 4.0: Opportunities and challenges. *Scientific Programming, 2022*.

Arrigo, E. (2013). Corporate responsibility management in fast fashion companies: the Gap Inc. case. *Journal of Fashion Marketing and Management: An International Journal, 17*(2), 175–189.

Azemi, Y., & Ozuem, W. (2023). How does retargeting work for different Gen Z mobile users? *Journal of Advertising Research*, 2023-023. https://doi.org/10.2501/jar-2023-023

Beheshti-Kashi, S. (2020). Development of a social media process model for fashion and apparel supply chain decisions. *Cyber-Physical Systems, 6*(2), 76–95.

Behr, O. (2018). Fashion 4.0–digital innovation in the fashion industry. *Journal of Technology and Innovation Management, 2*(1), 1–9.

Benstead, A. V., Mwesiumo, D., Moradlou, H., & Boffelli, A. (2022). Entering the world behind the clothes that we wear: Practical applications of blockchain technology. *Production Planning and Control*, 1–18.

Berman, S. J. (2012). Digital transformation: Opportunities to create new business models. *Strategy and Leadership, 40*(2), 16–24.

Bernstein, E. S. (2012). The transparency paradox: A role for privacy in organizational learning and operational control. *Administrative Science Quarterly, 57*(2), 181–216.

Bertola, P., & Teunissen, J. (2018). Fashion 4.0. Innovating fashion industry through digital transformation. *Research Journal of Textile and Apparel*, *22*(4), 352–369.

Boyd, R., & Holton, R. J. (2018). Technology, innovation, employment and power: Does robotics and artificial intelligence really mean social transformation? *Journal of Sociology, 54*(3), 331–345.

Brydges, T., Henninger, C. E., & Hanlon, M. (2022). Selling sustainability: Investigating how Swedish fashion brands communicate sustainability to consumers. *Sustainability: Science, Practice and Policy, 18*(1), 357–370.

Brydges, T., Hracs, B. J., & Lavanga, M. (2018). Evolution versus entrenchment: Debating the impact of digitization, democratization and diffusion in the global fashion industry. *International Journal of Fashion Studies, 5*(2), 365–372.

Byrum, K. (2019). "Hey friend, buy green": Social media use to influence eco-purchasing involvement. *Environmental Communication, 13*(2), 209–221.

Cabigiosu, A. (2020). Digitalization in the luxury fashion industry. *Springer International Publishing*.

Calefato, P. (2017). Sustainable luxury and fashion: From global standardisation to critical customisation. In *Sustainable Management of Luxury* (pp. 107–123).

Casciani, D., Chkanikova, O., & Pal, R. (2022). Exploring the nature of digital transformation in the fashion industry: Opportunities for supply chains, business models, and sustainability-oriented innovations. *Sustainability: Science, Practice and Policy, 18*(1), 773–795.

Creevey, D., Coughlan, J., & O'Connor, C. (2022). Social media and luxury: A systematic literature review. *International Journal of Management Reviews, 24*(1), 99–129.

Choi, A. (2020). Social comparison in fashion blogging:"Creative self" as the new genre in fashion communication. *Journal of Fashion Marketing and Management: An International.*

de Koning, M. (2019). Fashion and luxury product franchising in the European digital landscape. *Franchise Law Journal, 39*(2), 215–234.

De Perthuis, K., & Findlay, R. (2019). How fashion travels: The fashionable ideal in the age of Instagram. *Fashion Theory, 23*(2), 219–242.

Fletcher, K., & Tham, M. (eds.). (2015). *Routledge handbook of sustainability and fashion* (p. 15). Routledge.

Foucault, M. (1977). *Discipline and punish: The birth of the prison.* Pantheon Books.

Foucault, M. (1982).The subject and power. *Critical Inquiry, 8*(4), 777–795.

Gardetti, M. Á., & Larios-Francia, R. P. (2023). *Sustainability challenges in the fashion industry: Civilization crisis, decolonization, cultural legacy, and transitions.* Springer.

Genus, A. (2014). Governing sustainability: A discourse-institutional approach. *Sustainability, 6*(1), 283–305.

Godart, F. (2014). The power structure of the fashion industry: Fashion capitals, globalization and creativity. *International Journal of Fashion Studies, 1*(1), 39–55.

Gondoputranto, O., Raharja, G., Ratna, T., & Pebryani, N. (2024). The digital paradox when future and tradition co-exist contemporary fashion with augmented reality. *Archive-SR, 8*(1), 33–48.

Gwilt, A., & Rissanen, T. (2012). *Shaping sustainable fashion: Changing the way we make and use clothes.* Routledge.

Hardy, C., & Phillips, N. (1999). No joking matter: Discursive struggle in the Canadian refugee system. *Organization Studies, 20*, 1–24.

Holmqvist, J., Wirtz, J., & Fritze, M. P. (2020). Luxury in the digital age: A multi-actor service encounter perspective. *Journal of Business Research, 121*, 747–756.

Islam, M. M., Perry, P., & Gill, S. (2021). Mapping environmentally sustainable practices in textiles, apparel and fashion industries: A systematic literature review. *Journal of Fashion Marketing and Management: An International Journal, 25*(2), 331–353.

Joy, A., Sherry, J. F., Jr., Venkatesh, A., Wang, J., & Chan, R. (2012). Fast fashion, sustainability, and the ethical appeal of luxury brands. *Fashion Theory, 16*(3), 273–295.

Kim, K. H., & Kim, E. Y. (2020). Fashion marketing trends in social media and sustainability in fashion management. *Journal of Business Research, 117*, 508–509.

Leclercq-Vandelannoitte, A. (2011). Organizations as discursive constructions: A Foucauldian approach. *Organization Studies, 32*(9), 1247–1271.

Leclercq-Vandelannoitte, A. (2022). Is employee technological "ill-being" missing from corporate responsibility? The Foucauldian ethics of ubiquitous IT uses in organizations. In *Business and the Ethical Implications of Technology* (pp. 33–55). Springer Nature Switzerland.

Liu, N., Lin, J., Guo, S., & Shi, X. (2023). Fashion platform operations in the sharing economy with digital technologies: Recent development and real case studies. *Annals of Operations Research, 329*(1), 1175–1195.

Manavalan, E., & Jayakrishna, K. (2019). A review of Internet of Things (IoT) embedded sustainable supply chain for industry 4.0 requirements. *Computers and Industrial Engineering, 127*, 925–953.

Marcella-Hood, M. (2023). Augmenting sustainable fashion on Instagram. *Sustainability, 15*(4), 3609.

Markkula, A., & Moisander, J. (2012). Discursive confusion over sustainable consumption: A discursive perspective on the perplexity of marketplace knowledge. *Journal of Consumer Policy, 35*, 105–125.

Michel, G. M., Feori, M., Damhorst, M. L., Lee, Y. A., & Niehm, L. S. (2019). Stories we wear: Promoting sustainability practices with the case of Patagonia. *Family and Consumer Sciences Research Journal, 48*(2), 165–180.

Modi, D., & Zhao, L. (2021). Social media analysis of consumer opinion on apparel supply chain transparency. *Journal of Fashion Marketing and Management: An International Journal, 25*(3), 465–481.

Mukendi, A., Davies, I., Glozer, S., & McDonagh, P. (2020). Sustainable fashion: Current and future research directions. *European Journal of Marketing, 54*(11), 2873–2909.

Niinimäki, K. (2013). *Sustainable fashion: New approaches*. Aalto University.

Niinimäki, K. (2015). Ethical foundations in sustainable fashion. *Textiles and Clothing Sustainability, 1*(1), 1–11.

Oguntegbe, K. F., Di Paola, N., & Vona, R. (2023). Communicating responsible management and the role of blockchain technology: Social media analytics for the luxury fashion supply chain. *The TQM Journal, 35*(2), 446–469.

Ozuem, W., Ranfagni, S., Willis, M., Rovai, S., & Howell, K. (2021). Exploring customers' responses to online service failure and recovery strategies during Covid-19 pandemic: An actor–network theory perspective. *Psychology & Marketing, 38*(9), 1440–1459.

Ozuem, W., & Willis, M. (2022). *Digital marketing strategies for value co-creation : Models and approaches for online brand communities.* Palgrave Macmillan.

Ozuem, W., Willis, M., Ranfagni, S., Howell, K. E., & Rovai, S. (2023). Examining the role of social media influencers in service failure and recovery strategies: An empirical investigation of millennials' views. *Information Technology & People.* https://doi.org/10.1108/itp-05-2022-0371

Ozuem, W., Willis, M., Howell, K., Ranfagni, S., & Rovai, S. (2023). Examining user-generated content, service failure recovery and customer–brand relationships: An exploration through commitment-trust theory. *Internet Research.* https://doi.org/10.1108/intr-07-2022-0580

Parguel, B., Benoit-Moreau, F., & Russell, C. A. (2015). Can evoking nature in advertising mislead consumers? The power of 'executional greenwashing.' *International Journal of Advertising, 34*(1), 107–134.

Parida, V., Sjödin, D., & Reim, W. (2019). Reviewing literature on digitalization, business model innovation, and sustainable industry: Past achievements and future promises. *Sustainability, 11*(2), 391.

Quiles-Soler, C., Martínez-Sala, A. M., & Monserrat-Gauchi, J. (2023). Fashion industry's environmental policy: Social media and corporate website as vehicles for communicating corporate social responsibility. *Corporate Social Responsibility and Environmental Management, 30*(1), 180–191.

Ralston, P., & Blackhurst, J. (2020). Industry 4.0 and resilience in the supply chain: A driver of capability enhancement or capability loss? *International Journal of Production Research, 58*(16), 5006–5019.

Rose, N., O'Malley, P., & Valverde, M. (2006). Governmentality. *Annual Review of Law and Social Science, 2*, 83–104.

Strähle, J., & Gräff, C. (2017). The role of social media for a sustainable consumption. J. Strähle (Ed.), *Green fashion retail*, Springer Series in Fashion Business, 225–247.

Thorisdottir, T. S., & Johannsdottir, L. (2019). Sustainability within fashion business models: A systematic literature review. *Sustainability, 11*(8), 2233.

Thorisdottir, T. S., & Johannsdottir, L. (2020). Corporate social responsibility influencing sustainability within the fashion industry. A systematic review. *Sustainability, 12*(21), 9167.

Todeschini, B. V., Cortimiglia, M. N., Callegaro-de-Menezes, D., & Ghezzi, A. (2017). Innovative and sustainable business models in the fashion industry: Entrepreneurial drivers, opportunities, and challenges. *Business Horizons, 60*(6), 759–770.

Urmínová, M., & Kusá, A. (2020, September). Innovative approaches in marketing communication in sustainable fashion business. In *European Conference on Innovation and Entrepreneurship* (pp. 834–XIX). Academic Conferences International Limited.

Vanko, M., & Zaušková, A. (2019, September). Raising public awareness of eco-innovations through social media. In *European Conference on Innovation and Entrepreneurship* (pp. 1076–XXVIII). Academic Conferences International Limited.

Vladimirova, K., Henninger, C. E., Alosaimi, S. I., Brydges, T., Choopani, H., Hanlon, M., ... , & Zhou, S. (2024). Exploring the influence of social media on sustainable fashion consumption: A systematic literature review and future research agenda. *Journal of Global Fashion Marketing, 15*(2), 181–202.

Williams, K. C., Page, R. A., & Petrosky, A. R. (2014). Green sustainability and new social media. *Journal of Strategic Innovation and Sustainability, 9*.

Wu, J., Joo, B. R., Sina, A. S., Song, S., & Whang, C. H. (2022). Personalizing 3D virtual fashion stores: An action research approach to modularity development. *International Journal of Retail and Distribution Management, 50*(3), 342–360.

Yang, Y., Han, H., & Lee, P. K. (2017). An exploratory study of the mechanism of sustainable value creation in the luxury fashion industry. *Sustainability, 9*(4), 483.

Yeo, S. F., Tan, C. L., Kumar, A., Tan, K. H., & Wong, J. K. (2022). Investigating the impact of AI-powered technologies on Instagrammers' purchase decisions in digitalization era—A study of the fashion and apparel industry. *Technological Forecasting and Social Change, 177*, 121551.

Zhao, L., Lee, S. H., Li, M., & Sun, P. (2022). The use of social media to promote sustainable fashion and benefit communications: A data-mining approach. *Sustainability, 14*(3), 1178.

7

Luxury Hotels' Corporate Social Responsibility Communications and Online Brand Communities

Mei Kun (Vicky) Loi

Introduction

In an era marked by increasing environmental consciousness and social responsibility, sustainability has emerged as a defining factor in luxury hospitality. Luxury hotels have become increasingly more socially and ethically responsible. They have committed to balancing the issue of positively contributing to social causes while maintaining the skill, quality and exclusivity of their products (Kunz et al., 2020; Osburg et al., 2021); In particular, the luxury hotel sector is embracing the concept of corporate social responsibility (CSR) as a form of sustainability (Cherapanukorn & Focken, 2014; Pereira et al., 2021).

The original version of the chapter has been revised: The author name has been updated. A correction to this chapter can be found at
https://doi.org/10.1007/978-3-031-82467-8_29

M. K. (Vicky) Loi (✉)
De Montfort University, Leicester, UK
e-mail: vicky.loi@dmu.ac.uk

W. Ozuem et al. (eds.), *Sustainable Digital Marketing for Fashion and Luxury Brands*,
https://doi.org/10.1007/978-3-031-82467-8_7

Consumers nowadays demand information about organisation's CSR activities. Within this context, the generation of messages related to CSR activities is a key element in CSR communication. Corporate communication of CSR is defined as 'communication that is designed and distributed by the company itself about its CSR efforts' (Morsing, 2006). Most communication activities in this domain have focused on the creation of CSR reports or their distribution among shareholders in annual meetings or via websites. New media, such as social media, provide further channels for corporate CSR communication (Aguirre et al., 2023). Hotel guests are now able to participate, share and collaborate on social media, which may increase consumer engagement with luxury hotels (Kang et al., 2015). The benefits of increased engagement include higher levels of satisfaction, trust, loyalty and brand relationship quality (So et al., 2016). The importance of online brand communities (OBCs) has been widely accepted in an era where establishing long-term relations with customers is vital for business success. With this in mind, the communication of CSR messages through luxury hotel OBCs could increase consumer engagement because OBCs make it easy for hotel guests (existing and potential) to share messages with each other and other stakeholders.

Insufficient attention has been paid to hotel OBCs hosted on social media (Touni et al., 2020). Previous studies have investigated the relationship between CSR and hotels' financial performance (Babajee et al., 2022), CSR and brand equity (Kang & Namkung, 2018), CSR and service quality evaluation (Albus & Ro, 2017), CSR and brand positioning, customer loyalty and intention to visit (Akbari et al., 2020, 2021; Latif et al., 2020); however, little attention has been paid to CSR communication via OBCs on social media in the hospitality industry (Kucukusta et al., 2019). In particular, there is a lack of research into consumer engagement with luxury hotel CSR communications on OBCs on social media. Consequently, the aim of this chapter is to explore luxury hotel CSR communications on OBCs on social media and the level of consumer engagement. The objectives of the chapter are:

1. To identify which CSR practices were communicated by luxury hotel in OBCs.

2. To evaluate the level of consumer engagement with CSR communications on OBCs.

This chapter contributes to the CSR communication and luxury hospitality literature. First, it highlights the role of OBCs in luxury hotels' dissemination of CSR information. Second, the chapter approaches consumer engagement in the CSR domain. The next part of the chapter will review the key concepts. The results of the exploration of luxury hotel CSR communications via OBCs and the level of consumer engagement with CSR communications are presented and then discussed. The results and discussion are followed by a conclusion in which theoretical and managerial implications are addressed. The chapter closes with a section on the study's limitations and future research directions.

Defining CSR

In the early 1960s, CSR was seen as synonymous with an organisation's voluntary and philanthropic activities aimed at alleviating social ills or benefiting a disadvantaged group; these activities went above and beyond meeting their economic and legal obligations (Meehan et al., 2006). Since then, the definition of CSR has evolved. OECD (2001) defined CSR as business's contribution to sustainable development and emphasised that corporate behaviour must not only ensure returns to shareholders, wages to employees and products and service to customers, it must also respond to societal and environmental concerns. In the same vein, the European Commission (2011) defined CSR as 'the responsibility of enterprises for their impacts on society'. Companies can become socially responsible by integrating social, environmental, ethical, human rights and consumer concerns into their business operations and by collaborating with their stakeholders, such as workers, communities and society. One of the most adopted definitions of CSR was proposed by the World Business Council for Sustainable Development (WBCSD), which stated that 'CSR is the continuing commitment by business to behave ethically and contribute to economic development while improving the quality of life of the workforce and their families as well as the local community and society at large' (WBCSD, 1999). Although the above definitions of CSR vary, economic, environmental and social responsibility are seen as three key aspects of CSR activities. Today, CSR is seen as a core business activity that can transform a company's business model and its operations (De Grobois, 2012).

As one of the key sectors in the tourism industry, the hotel sector plays an important role in supporting the social and economic development of the destination where it operates, for instance, through job creation, increased tax revenue and accelerating leisure and business travel. However, the hotel sector is also characterised by its high consumption of natural resources that have an impact on the social and economic environment. For instance, hotels consume energy, water, food, paper, linen, laundry, stationery, cleaning materials and other resources, which contribute to climate change, air and noise pollution, biodiversity loss and waste generation. Given that many hotels are situated in major cities, often close to cultural or natural heritage attractions, they receive large numbers of tourists; thus, hotels increase the ecological footprint. The hotel industry is also seen as having an impact on local communities through their occupation of space and use of infrastructure.

The growing interest in sustainable development, and the resulting pressure from the media and governments, and growing awareness in society in general and tourists in particular, is forcing many hotels to increasingly implement CSR practices. The major CSR activities adopted by the hotel sector lie in the environment, community, employees and supply chain (Cherapanukorn & Focken, 2014). Environment-related CSR practices typically involve addressing water and energy efficiency and conservation, climate change and greenhouse gas emissions, waste management and recycling, biodiversity and the protection of natural resources and environmentally responsible sourcing. Communities-related CSR practices involve working with local communities and employing local people. Employee-related CSR practices include initiatives on workforce diversity, equitable benefits and career advancement. Supply chained-related CSR activities usually entail the sourcing of local products. In addition, some international hotel chains develop stand-alone pronouncements while many other hotels create partnerships or CSR alliances (Cherapanukorn & Focken, 2014).

CSR and the Luxury Hotel Sector

Luxury hospitality has the third-largest market share in the global luxury market, followed by luxury cars and personal luxury goods (Statista, 2023). The debate about the compatibility between CSR and the luxury sector is ongoing (Hu et al., 2023). For instance, a study by Achabou and Dekhili (2013) found that CSR can impact customer perceptions about the quality of luxury products, because of concerns that recycled materials might bring inferior quality. The research of Barber and Deale (2014) and Peng and Chen (2019) likewise found that consumers hesitate to visit luxury hotels that implement environmentally friendly initiatives because they are concerned that these initiatives may reduce the comfort of the luxury experience. By contrast, Janssen et al. (2014) argued that if luxury goods elicit perceptions of scarcity and ephemerality through their offering, and consumers perceive a match between luxury and CSR, then it will lead to positive evaluations. Similarly, Kapferer (2010) argued that sustainability can be compatible with luxury because both concepts place an emphasis on rarity.

Despite a high level of comfort, service and exclusivity are still key elements for luxury hospitality; many luxury hotels are committing to sustainability and integrating it into their strategic plan (Abdou et al., 2020). For example, the Four Seasons Hotels and Resorts reported its commitment to sustainability as follows: 'Through our Environmental, Social and Governance (ESG) program, *Four Seasons for Good,* we seek to preserve and regenerate the beautiful places in which we operate, and leave a positive, enduring impact on your communities. Our *Four Seasons for Good* Program is centered around two pillars: Planet (environmental impact) and People (social impact). Each pillar is supported by specific activities and objectives, with a close eye to how our efforts will contribute to the achievement of United Nation's Sustainable Development Goals (SDGs)' (Four Seasons, 2024). Similarly, The Ritz Carlton Hotel, part of Marriott International, stated that 'With our size and scale, we have a global responsibility and a unique opportunity to be a force for good. Guided by our 2025 Sustainability and Social Impact Goals, as well as the UN Sustainable Development Goals, we commit to creating positive and sustainable impact wherever we do business' (Marriott

International, 2024). To realise sustainable aims, for instance, the Ritz Hotel London ensures that all procured electricity comes from renewable sources, labelled as 'green' energy. Additionally, to minimise water consumption, the hotel has implemented various measures including the installation of slow-flow showerheads, pressure-reducing systems and systems to measure flush volume.

CSR Communication

Although it is important that luxury hotels practice their commitments to CSR, what CSR practices are communicated by the hotels is also important otherwise stakeholders would rarely know about them (Öberseder et al., 2013). Therefore, CSR communications are of the utmost importance. If the communications are managed successfully, the hotel will be rewarded with higher consumer awareness of CSR, with strong and mostly positive reactions from stakeholders, and higher brand equity (Andreu et al., 2015; Wang et al., 2021). Moreover, it is essential to minimise any deviations between the hotel's CSR communications and business practices disclosed by other sources, as they can have a negative impact on the hotel in terms of image, reputation and sales.

Today, CSR communications can be disseminated through various sources, such as CSR reports, CSR advertising on television or in magazines, public relations, corporate websites and social media. In the context of the online environment, although corporate websites are among the most common and important online communication tools (Du & Vieira, 2012; Wong et al., 2015), it is noteworthy that social media is increasingly used for CSR communication (Ettinger et al., 2018).

OBCs in Social Media

The popularity of virtual communities has exploded rapidly because of social media's user-friendly interface applications that support interactivity. This has led to intense academic interest in OBCs. An OBC is a distinct type of virtual community that is unrestricted by geographical boundaries and marked by common identities and traditions (Muniz & O'Guinn, 2001; Ozuem et al., 2021). Jang et al. (2008, p. 57) described OBCs as 'specialised, non-geographically bound communities, based upon social relationships among admirers of a brand in cyberspace'. An example of an OBC is the Nike enthusiast community, which is found on niketalk.com. OBCs can be a separate website, they can also be formed within Google Groups or created within social networking sites (SNSs). Another type of OBC is an OBC hosted by a firm on a SNS, for example, Lego's official Instagram account. Brands have become highly interested in organising consumers in their own OBCs on SNSs to harness the potential of consumers in value co-creation (Manchanda et al., 2015). For instance, previous studies have demonstrated that members of firm-hosted OBCs are ideal collaborators for companies in a variety of areas, such as product knowledge diffusion (Thompson & Sinha, 2008), product innovation (Füller et al., 2008) and word-of-mouth marketing (Kozinets, 2010). The interaction between consumer and brand or between consumer and consumer in OBCs could be regarded as a 'social activity similar to the process of socialisation' (Wu & Fang, 2010). It therefore extends dialogue within consumer engagement.

Consumer Engagement

Consumer engagement has been defined as 'a user-initiated action' (Gluck, 2012, p. 8) that leads to a co-creation of value among community participants (Brodie et al., 2013; Vivek, 2009). Hollebeek (2011) viewed engagement as a multidimensional concept that comprises emotional (feelings), cognitive (thoughts) and behavioural (actions) aspects. Similar descriptions can be seen in other research, for example, Dessart et al. (2015) and Lima et al. (2019). It is worth noting that the terms consumer engagement, customer engagement and brand engagement are often used interchangeably. There is also a lack of agreement over the conceptual domain of consumer engagement (Lima et al., 2019). Nevertheless, the focal point of consumer engagement mostly relates to brands, products and services, as well as brand communities and communications.

In the hotel sector, firm-hosted OBCs on SNSs, such as Facebook, enable hotels to not only deliver their CSR messages and stories to hotel guests and engage them in dialogue (Lee et al., 2019; Ozuem & Willis, 2024) but also enable hotel guests to express their opinions on CSR activities. In this context, consumer engagement with hotel CSR communications on hotel-hosted OBCs is a form of electronic word-of-mouth behaviour given that hotel guests receive, create or share information about a hotel's CSR activities. Examples of online behavioural engagement with hotel-hosted OBCs are actions such as liking, commenting and sharing (Sicilia et al., 2020). On YouTube, such engagement is manifested through actions such as liking, disliking, commenting, sharing and uploading videos (Khan, 2017).

Results and Discussion

The aim of the chapter is to explore CSR communications on OBCs in social media and the level of consumer engagement with CSR communications within the luxury hotel sector. The dimensions of supply chain, community, employees and environment, which are based on the CSR framework proposed by Cherapanukorn and Focken (2014), were used to assess luxury hotels' CSR communications. The five Scottish luxury hotels considered in this chapter were found to engage in limited communication on their own OBCs about their CSR practices: only 8% of the sample posts were related to CSR (see Fig. 7.1) and the majority of the posts were marketing-oriented posts.

The finding suggests that hotel-hosted OBCs may not be a primary channel for communicating CSR practices in the luxury hotel sector. The finding supports the argument of De Grosbois (2012) that corporations have been slow to adapt their CSR efforts to the contemporary media landscape. This is rather disappointing. OBCs could serve as an additional channel for hotels to communicate their CSR practices directly to guests; an OBC is a free and firm-controlled platform and it is able to foster a sense of connection and loyalty between a hotel and its guests. If this finding is representative, then it would suggest that luxury hotels

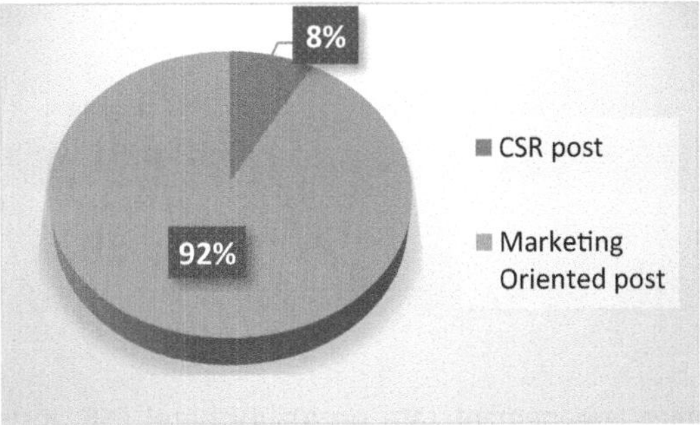

Fig. 7.1 Total luxury hotel CSR posts rate on Facebook in 2023 (CSR, corporate social responsibility)

are missing the opportunity to harness the platform to promote, educate and influence their guests about their CSR practices.

In spite of the above, another finding showed that all of the sampled luxury hotels included at least two references to CSR dimensions on Facebook; the majority of them focused on communicating supply chain and community dimensions of CSR (see Table 7.1).

The supply chain was predominantly highlighted on luxury hotel OBCs, with hotel suppliers given prominent mentions. Specifically, the use of local produce, trusted and transparent suppliers and responsible sourcing were the CSR activities that were emphasised on hotel-hosted OBCs. This finding is consistent with Cherapanukorn and Focken (2014) who stated that luxury hotel CSR activities are mostly related to the use of locally sourced products. The supply chain dimension of

Table 7.1 Luxury hotel CSR dimensions and number of relevant posts on Facebook

	Hotel A	Hotel B	Hotel C	Hotel D	Hotel E	Total
Environment	1	0	3	0	2	6
Community	4	1	7	1	0	13
Employees	0	0	3	2	0	5
Supply chain	0	5	4	5	6	20

CSR, corporate social responsibility

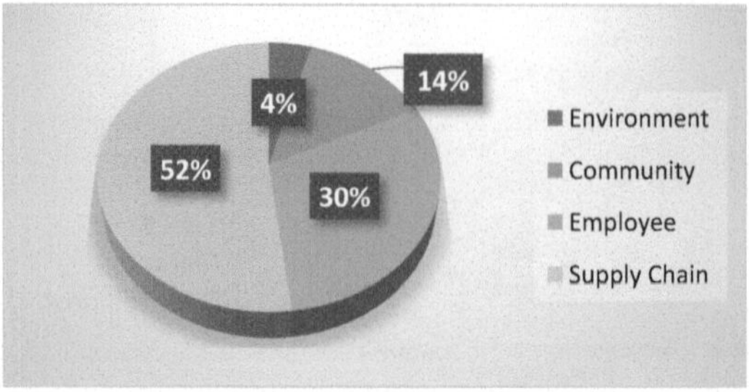

Fig. 7.2 Consumer engagement rate on luxury hotel CSR posts on Facebook (CSR, corporate social responsibility)

CSR was also the dimension that most engaged the hotel guests, with 52% of engagement featuring this CSR dimension (see Fig. 7.2).

In most cases, the engagement was concerned with food. The importance of food, something that is a personal concern and physically affects consumers, could be a core factor influencing hotel guests' assessment of CSR and purchasing decisions (Ettinger et al., 2018). The result therefore highlighted that it was important for luxury hotels to continue to strongly communicate CSR efforts concerned with the sustainable local sourcing of food. Such efforts might attract more guests by emphasising quality and authenticity. It is important to note that a hotel's relations with guests/customers and with investors in the supply chain dimension, according to Cherapanukorn and Focken's (2014) CSR framework, are not considered CSR activities given that CSR activities are discretionary (Koler & Lee, 2005). To explain, a hotel's relations with its guests are clearly aimed at delivering a positive customer experience, including efforts to maintain customer satisfaction and manage customer relationships. Similarly, investors' expectations in terms of financial returns should not fall into CSR activities (Cherapanukorn & Focken, 2014).

The community dimension of CSR was frequently communicated by the sample of luxury hotels. The key CSR activities in relation to the community dimension were: supporting charities; fund raising; education, such as supporting men's mental health and menopause; supporting the LGBT community; and supporting local communities during the cost-of-living crisis by offering a complimentary desk and W-Fi free of charge.

This finding is consistent with Cherapanukorn and Focken (2014) who stated that luxury hotel CSR activities are mostly related to the community. However, very few consumers (14%) engaged with this dimension (see Fig. 7.2). The results suggest that luxury hotel guests may prioritise other CSR activities that directly impact them, for instance employees over community. Hotel guests might not prioritise community because they may not see the immediate benefits of community activities to their own experience at luxury hotels, whereas employees might be considered in terms of personalised services. Hotel guests' lack of awareness of the community-focused CSR activities undertaken by a luxury hotel could be another reason (Lee et al., 2016). If a luxury hotel is dedicated to community work, then it is crucial that the hotel communicates this accordingly.

The CSR activities related to employees were mainly related to employee communications, for instance, having a diverse workforce. The CSR dimension of employees was not communicated strongly in the sample (see Table 7.1). The results corroborate the findings of Ettinger et al. (2018) and Cherapanukorn and Focken (2014). However, there was higher consumer engagement with this dimension, with 30% of engagement featuring the dimension (see Fig. 7.2). The majority of engagement in this context concerned public recognition postings in relation to the Hotelier of the Year and the youngest Indian chef ever to receive a Michelin star. This finding is not surprising as both stories could be seen as reinforcing the high quality and exclusivity of the luxury hotel sector.

Surprisingly, the environment dimension of CSR was not communicated strongly by the luxury hotels and only 4% of consumer engagement was linked to this CSR dimension (see Fig. 7.2). The environmental activities were focused on managing air pollution, for example, improving air quality by having plants in hotel rooms, and highlighted the gain of a green certificate. This finding is not consistent with the CSR communications of hotels globally because the environment is a primary focus of their CSR efforts. One possible explanation for this might be that the primary audience for luxury hotels prioritises comfort, exclusivity and premium service over environmental concerns (Barber &

Deale, 2014; Peng & Chen, 2019); hotels might focus their communication efforts on what they believe their audience values most. The finding may suggest that luxury hotels still face challenges in effectively communicating their environmentally friendly practices while offering a high level of luxury services. Balancing these two aspects remains a challenge given that an emphasis on environmental sustainability might dilute their luxury image or shift attention from the luxurious experiences they offer. The low consumer engagement with this dimension suggests that luxury hotel guests may prioritise other aspects of CSR, for instance, in this study the supply chain and employee dimensions.

Conclusion

CSR communication has become an important field of study in corporate communications (Yang et al., 2020). This chapter contributes to the existing body of knowledge; in particular, the chapter provides fresh evidence about the ways in which some luxury hotels communicate their CSR on OBCs and the extent of consumer engagement. The findings reveal that majority of the communications between the sample of luxury hotels and their hotel guests is marketing oriented. CSR communications are minimal and account for only 8% of the total posts in OBCs. This may imply that these luxury hotels in Scotland have underestimated the power of their own OBCs on social media. The chapter also advances understanding of one of the CSR dimensions (i.e., supply chain) by emphasising the significance of national supplier relations (e.g., Scotland) and food quality in the luxury hotel sector. In addition, the chapter provides valuable insights for luxury hotel managers by highlighting the relevance of specific CSR dimensions and the level of consumer engagement with hotel-hosted OBCs. It is recommended that luxury hotels should align their CSR practices with their communications on their own OBCs on social media to develop awareness and understanding of CSR practices. The alignment can improve the visibility of their CSR efforts and make it easier for hotel guests to understand how luxury hotels contribute to addressing the pressing issues of the environment. Furthermore, given social media serves not only as a communication tool but also as an engagement tool, hotel managers can take full advantage of their hotel-hosted OBCs on social media to inspire highly engaged customers and turn them into their brand advocates (Touni et al., 2020). For example, Marriott International has established a dedicated team tasked with engaging customers by monitoring their interactions, particularly positive posts. The team extends tokens of appreciation, such as gifts or discounts, to highly engaged customers as a gesture of gratitude.

Limitations and Future Research Directions

Despite the meaningful findings, the chapter has several limitations. The study is based on five luxury hotels in Scotland and is not necessarily representative of the whole of Scotland. Future research might investigate more luxury hotels for authentication. The sample of the luxury hotels' CSR communications on their own OBCs was based on the period from 1 January to 31 December 2023; therefore, the findings cannot be generalised to all CSR communications in other periods. However, the findings and conclusions are still relevant to an understanding of luxury hotel CSR communications in OBCs. The study was limited to the use of one social media platform (i.e., Facebook). Future research might use more social media platforms, such as Instagram and YouTube, for further authentication. Consumer engagement in this chapter was measured based on the total number of hotel guests' 'liking/loving', 'commenting' and 'sharing' the CSR posts from the selected hotels' Facebook brand pages. The details of individual consumers' comments on CSR posts were not considered or analysed. Future research might examine this form of engagement to better understand hotel guests' reactions to a luxury hotel's CSR posts.

References

Abdou, A. H., Hassan, T. H., & El Dief, M. M. (2020). A description of green hotel practices and their role in achieving sustainable development. *Sustainability, 12*(22), 9624.

Achabou, M. A., & Dekhili, S. (2013). Luxury and sustainable development: Is there a match? *Journal of Business Research, 66*(10), 1896–1903.

Aguirre, C., Ruiz de Maya, S., Palazón Vidal, M., & Rodríguez, A. (2023). Consumer motivations for engaging with corporate social responsibility on social media. *Spanish Journal of Marketing-ESIC, 27*(2), 202–220.

Akbari, M., Mehrali, M., SeyyedAmiri, N., Rezaei, N., & Pourjam, A. (2020). Corporate social responsibility, customer loyalty and brand positioning. *Social Responsibility Journal, 16*(5), 671–689.

Akbari, M., Nazarian, A., Foroudi, P., Seyyed Amiri, N., & Ezatabadipoor, E. (2021). How corporate social responsibility contributes to strengthening brand loyalty, hotel positioning and intention to revisit? *Current Issues in Tourism, 24*(13), 1897–1917.

Albus, H., & Ro, H. (2017). Corporate social responsibility: The effect of green practices in a service recovery. *Journal of Hospitality & Tourism Research, 41*(1), 41–65.

Andreu, L., Casado-Díaz, A. B., & Mattila, A. S. (2015). Effects of message appeal and service type in CSR communication strategies. *Journal of Business Research, 68*(7), 1488–1495.

Babajee, R. B., Seetanah, B., Nunkoo, R., & Gopy-Ramdhany, N. (2022). Corporate social responsibility and hotel financial performance. *Journal of Hospitality Marketing & Management, 31*(2), 226–246.

Barber, N. A., & Deale, C. (2014). Tapping mindfulness to shape hotel guests' sustainable behavior. *Cornell Hospitality Quarterly, 55*(1), 100–114.

Brodie, R. J., Ilic, A., Juric, B., & Hollebeek, L. (2013). Consumer engagement in a virtual brand community: An exploratory analysis. *Journal of Business Research, 66*(1), 105–114.

Cherapanukorn, V., & Focken, K. (2014). Corporate social responsibility (CSR) and sustainability in Asian luxury hotels: Policies, practices and standards. *Asian Social Science, 10*(8), 198–209.

De Grosbois, D. (2012). Corporate social responsibility reporting by the global hotel industry: Commitment, initiatives and performance. *International Journal of Hospitality Management, 31*(3), 896–905.

Dessart, L., Veloutsou, C., & Morgan-Thomas, A. (2015). Consumer engagement in online brand communities: A social media perspective. *Journal of Product & Brand Management, 24*(1), 28–42.

Du, S., & Vieira, E. T. (2012). Striving for legitimacy through corporate social responsibility: Insights from oil companies. *Journal of Business Ethics, 110*, 413–427.

Ettinger, A., Grabner-Kräuter, S., & Terlutter, R. (2018). Online CSR communication in the hotel industry: Evidence from small hotels. *International Journal of Hospitality Management, 68*, 94–104.

European Commission. (2011). *Corporate sustainability and responsibility.* Available at https://single-market-economy.ec.europa.eu/industry/sustainability/corporate-sustainability-and-responsibility_en [Accessed 25 March 2024].

Four Seasons. (2024). *Four seasons for good.* Available at https://www.fourseasons.com/landing-pages/corporate/esg/ [Accessed 15 April 2024].

Füller, J., Matzler, K., & Hoppe, M. (2008). Brand community members as a source of innovation. *Journal of Product Innovation Management, 25*(6), 608–619.

Gluck, M. (2012). *IAB digital ad engagement whitepaper: An industry overview and reconceptualization.* IAB. Available at https://www.iab.com/insights/iab-digital-ad-engagement-whitepaper-anindustry-overview-and-reconceptualization/ [Accessed 12 September 2019].

Hollebeek, L. D. (2011). Demystifying customer brand engagement: Exploring the loyalty nexus. *Journal of Marketing Management, 27*(7–8), 785–807.

Hu, J., López-Bonilla, L. M., & López-Bonilla, J. M. (2023). CSR perceptions and brand attitudes in Chinese luxury hospitality: The moderating effect of ads vs. Media Reports. *Sustainability, 15*(9), 7689.

Marriott Internation. (2024). *Serve 360. Doing good in every direction.* Available at https://serve360.marriott.com/ [Accessed 20 April 2024].

Jang, H., Olfman, L., Ko, I., Koh, J., & Kim, K. (2008). The influence of on-line brand community characteristics on community commitment and brand loyalty. *International Journal of Electronic Commerce, 12*(3), 57–80.

Janssen, C., Vanhamme, J., Lindgreen, A., & Lefebvre, C. (2014). The Catch-22 of responsible luxury: Effects of luxury product characteristics on consumers' perception of fit with corporate social responsibility. *Journal of Business Ethics, 119*, 45–57.

Kang, J. W., & Namkung, Y. (2018). The effect of corporate social responsibility on brand equity and the moderating role of ethical consumerism: The case of Starbucks. *Journal of Hospitality & Tourism Research, 42*(7), 1130–1151.

Kang, J., Tang, L., & Fiore, A. M. (2015). Restaurant brand pages on Facebook: Do active member participation and monetary sales promotions matter? *International Journal of Contemporary Hospitality Management, 27*(7), 1662–1684.

Kapferer, J. N. (2010). All that glitters is not green: The challenge of sustainable luxury. *European Business Review, 2*(4), 40–45.

Khan, M. L. (2017). Social media engagement: What motivates user participation and consumption on YouTube? *Computers in Human Behavior, 66*, 236–247.

Koler, P., & Lee, N. (2005). *Corporate social responsibility*. John Wiley & Sons.

Kozinets, R. V. (2010). *Netnography: Doing ethnographic research online*. Sage.

Kucukusta, D., Perelygina, M., & Lam, W. S. (2019). CSR communication strategies and stakeholder engagement of upscale hotels in social media. *International Journal of Contemporary Hospitality Management, 31*(5), 2129–2148.

Kunz, J., May, S., & Schmidt, H. J. (2020). Sustainable luxury: Current status and perspectives for future research. *Business Research, 13*, 541–601.

Latif, K. F., Pérez, A., & Sahibzada, U. F. (2020). Corporate social responsibility (CSR) and customer loyalty in the hotel industry: A cross-country study. *International Journal of Hospitality Management, 89*, 102565.

Lee, H., Jai, T. M., & Li, X. (2016). Guests' perceptions of green hotel practices and management responses on TripAdvisor. *Journal of Hospitality and Tourism Technology, 7*(2), 182–199.

Lee, S. Y., Zhang, W., & Abitbol, A. (2019). What makes CSR communication lead to CSR participation? Testing the mediating effects of CSR associations, CSR credibility, and organization–public relationships. *Journal of Business Ethics, 157*, 413–429.

Lima, V. M., Irigaray, H. A. R., & Lourenco, C. (2019). Consumer engagement on social media: Insights from a virtual brand community. *Qualitative Market Research: An International Journal, 22*(1), 14–32.

Manchanda, P., Packard, G., & Pattabhiramaiah, A. (2015). Social dollars: The economic impact of customer participation in a firm-sponsored online customer community. *Marketing Science, 34*(3), 367–387.

Meehan, J., Meehan, K., & Richards, A. (2006). Corporate social responsibility: The 3C-SR model. *International Journal of Social Economics, 33*(5/6), 386–398.

Morsing, M. (2006). Corporate social responsibility as strategic auto-communication: On the role of external stakeholders for member identification. *Business Ethics: A European Review, 15*, 171–182.

Muniz Jr., A. M., & O'guinn, T. C. (2001). Brand community. *Journal of Consumer Research, 27*(4), 412–432.

Öberseder, M., Schlegelmilch, B. B., & Murphy, P. E. (2013). CSR practices and consumer perceptions. *Journal of Business Research, 66*(10), 1839–1851.

OECD. (2001). *Corporate social responsibility*. OECD iLibrary. Available at https://www.oecd-ilibrary.org/governance/corporate-social-responsibility_9789264194854-en [Accessed 25 March 2024].

Osburg, V. S., Davies, I., Yoganathan, V., & McLeay, F. (2021). Perspectives, opportunities and tensions in ethical and sustainable luxury: Introduction to the thematic symposium. *Journal of Business Ethics, 169*, 201–210.

Ozuem, W., & Willis, M. (2024). Artificial intelligence and predictive analytics: Towards a Praxis of personalised shopping experiences. In W. Ozuem, S. Ranfagni, M. Willis (Eds.), Digital transformation for fashion and luxury brands. Palgrave Macmillan.

Ozuem, W., Willis, M., Howell, K., Helal, G., Ranfagni, S., & Lancaster, G. (2021). Effects of online brand communities on millennials' brand loyalty in the fashion industry. *Psychology & Marketing, 38*(5), 774–793.

Peng, N., & Chen, A. (2019). Luxury hotels going green—The antecedents and consequences of consumer hesitation. *Journal of Sustainable Tourism.*

Pereira, V., Silva, G. M., & Dias, Á. (2021). Sustainability practices in hospitality: Case study of a luxury hotel in Arrábida Natural Park. *Sustainability, 13*(6), 3164.

Sicilia, M., Palazón, M., & López, M. (2020). Intentional vs. unintentional influences of social media friends. *Electronic Commerce Research and Applications, 42*, 100979.

So, K. K. F., King, C., Sparks, B. A., & Wang, Y. (2016). Enhancing customer relationships with retail service brands: The role of customer engagement. *Journal of Service Management, 27*(2), 170–193.

Statista. (2023). *Value of various global luxury markets in 2022, by market type.* Statista. Available at https://www.statista.com/statistics/246115/value-of-various-global-luxury-markets-by-market-type/ [Accessed 12 April 2024].

Thompson, S. A., & Sinha, R. K. (2008). Brand communities and new product adoption: The influence and limits of oppositional loyalty. *Journal of Marketing, 72*(6), 65–80.

Touni, R., Kim, W. G., Choi, H. M., & Ali, M. A. (2020). Antecedents and an outcome of customer engagement with hotel brand community on Facebook. *Journal of Hospitality & Tourism Research, 44*(2), 278–299.

Vivek, S. D. (2009). *A scale of consumer engagement* (PhD thesis). The University of Alabama.

Wang, S., Liao, Y. K., Wu, W. Y., & Le, K. B. H. (2021). The role of corporate social responsibility perceptions in brand equity, brand credibility, brand reputation, and purchase intentions. *Sustainability, 13*(21), 11975.
Wong, E., Leung, R., & Law, R. (2015). How effective are Asian hotels in communicating CSR efforts through the property websites? The case of Hong Kong. In *Information and communication technologies in tourism 2015: Proceedings of the international conference in Lugano, Switzerland, February 3–6, 2015* (pp. 651–663). Springer International Publishing.
World Business Council for Sustainable Development. (1999). Corporate social responsibility: Meeting Changing expectations, Switzerland.
Wu, S. C., & Fang, W. (2010). The effect of consumer-to-consumer interactions on idea generation in virtual brand community relationships. *Technovation, 30*(11–12), 570–581.
Yang, J., Basile, K., & Letourneau, O. (2020). The impact of social media platform selection on effectively communicating about corporate social responsibility. *Journal of Marketing Communications, 26*(1), 65–87.

8

Persuasive Communication and Emotional Appeals: The Contribution of Psychology

Sara Bocci Benucci and Cristian Di Gesto

Introduction

In the domain of luxury marketing, the use of persuasive communication plays a crucial role in shaping the success and efficacy of campaigns targeted at attracting consumers (Huang et al., 2018). This chapter aims to analyze persuasive communication and its significance within the context of luxury brands, with a particular emphasis on emotional appeals. Subsequently, the discourse will delve into the subject of emerging emotional trends, particularly examining eco-anxiety and its importance in communicating sustainability, while paying special attention to the utilization of social networks for disseminating companies' sustainability values and initiatives.

S. Bocci Benucci (✉) · C. Di Gesto
Department of Experimental and Clinical Medicine, University of Florence, Florence, Italy
e-mail: sara.boccibenucci@unifi.it

C. Di Gesto
Department of Psychology, Sapienza University of Rome, Rome, Italy

W. Ozuem et al. (eds.), *Sustainable Digital Marketing for Fashion and Luxury Brands*,
https://doi.org/10.1007/978-3-031-82467-8_8

Scholars have defined persuasion in different ways. According to communication scholars, persuasion involves "a communication process in which the communicator seeks to elicit a desired response from the receiver (Andersen, 1971, p. 6)". It is also described as "a conscious attempt by one individual to change the attitudes, beliefs, or behavior of another individual or group of individuals through the transmission of a message (Bettinghaus & Cody, 1987, p. 3)". Furthermore, persuasion is seen as "a symbolic activity whose purpose is to affect the internalization or voluntary acceptance of new cognitive states or patterns of overt behavior through the exchange of messages (Smith, 1982, p. 7)". Lastly, it is defined as "a successful intentional effort at influencing another's mental state through communication in a circumstance where the ersuade has some measure of freedom (O'Keefe, 2016, p. 4)". Boiling down the main components into one unified perspective, persuasion can be defined as a symbolic process in which communicators try to convince other people to change their own attitudes or behaviors regarding an issue through the transmission of a message in an atmosphere of free choice. There are five components of the scientific definition of persuasion (Perloff, 2021).

1. *Persuasion Is a Symbolic Process.* Persuasion is a gradual process that involves multiple steps and actively engages the audience. It is more akin to teaching than a boxing match, where persuaders guide individuals toward a solution by helping them understand why a particular position is the best (Perloff, 2021). Symbolism plays a crucial role in persuasion, with symbols such as words, nonverbal signs, and images carrying rich psychological and cultural meanings (Coski, 2005). The interpretation of symbols can vary greatly among different audiences.
2. *Persuasion Involves an Attempt to Influence.* Although persuasion can be powerful, it does not always guarantee success in influencing attitudes or behavior. Just as businesses may fail soon after opening, persuasive communications also face the risk of not reaching their target audiences effectively. However, persuasion involves a deliberate attempt to influence another person's attitudes or behaviors, with the persuaders aiming to induce a change and possessing

a degree of awareness regarding their objective. It is essential to differentiate persuasion from overall social influence, as persuasion entails purposeful communication directed at impacting the recipient (Perloff, 2021).

3. *People Persuade Themselves.* A common misconception about persuasion is that persuaders manipulate individuals into doing things they do not genuinely want to do by overwhelming them with arguments or verbal tactics (Johnson & Boynton, 2010). However, the reality is that individuals ultimately persuade themselves to alter their attitudes or behaviors. Communicators present arguments and create opportunities, but individuals themselves decide whether to accept or reject the persuasion. Persuasion cannot be forced upon people; instead, it involves activating their desire and demonstrating the rationale behind the ideas presented (Watkins, 2001). Individuals have the power to transform their own lives by changing their mindset, and by practicing self-persuasion (Johnson & Boynton, 2010).
4. *Persuasion Involves the Transmission of a Message.* Persuasion encompasses a wide range of messages, whether conveyed verbally or nonverbally, through various channels such as interpersonal interactions, mass media, or social networking platforms. These messages can be rational or emotional, containing arguments or simple cues that prompt individuals to alter their attitudes. Beyond traditional realms like advertising and political campaigns, messages from sources such as news media and artistic expressions significantly impact attitudes and beliefs (McCombs & Reynolds, 2002). Hence, these communication forms straddle the line between persuasion and broader social influence, delivering nuanced and multifaceted messages that have the potential to significantly shape worldviews (Perloff, 2021).
5. *Persuasion Requires Free Choice.* Self-persuasion plays a crucial role in successful influence, requiring individuals to have the freedom to modify their behavior or follow their own desires within a communication context (Perloff, 2021). There exist over 200 definitions of freedom, making it challenging to precisely differentiate between coercion and persuasion. A suggested criterion for freedom is the ability to act differently from what a persuader proposes or to critically evaluate one's choices in a given situation (Smythe, 1999). These

considerations highlight the nuanced nature of freedom and the relative constraints that influence individuals' decisions and behaviors (Perloff, 2021).

Emotional Appeals in Persuasive Communication

Emotions represent intricate phenomena. An emotion entails a cognitive evaluation of a situation, a physiological arousal, a subjective array of feelings, the motivation to behave in a particular manner, and a motor or facial expression (Nabi, 2015). Considering the emotional foundations of attitudes, emotions inevitably play a role in the design of communications aimed at altering attitudes. In contrast to positive emotions, such as pride, fear spurs individuals into action (Perloff, 2021).

As Stefanile (2011) reminisces, the origins of the scientific exploration of persuasion can be traced back to the 1930s; during the 1940s–1950s, the Yale school group headed by Carl Hovland emerged as a pivotal reference point. Even in the present day, despite significant shifts in theoretical stances over time, a considerable portion of the findings and insights stemming from the "school" are regarded as a cornerstone for the advancement of effective communications.

Emotions serve as potent drivers of human conduct, frequently influencing decision-making processes and responses to persuasive communications. When employed strategically, emotional appeals can elevate the effectiveness of persuasive communication by establishing a profound connection with the audience. Emotions such as fear, joy, anger, sadness, and empathy can evoke distinct reactions and mold perceptions. There are different types of emotional appeals, including (Alhabash et al., 2013):

- *Fear Appeals*: fear appeals leverage the emotion of fear to motivate individuals to take action or change their behavior. By highlighting potential risks and consequences, fear appeals aim to persuade individuals to adopt a recommended course of action to avoid negative outcomes.

- *Guilt Appeals*: guilt appeals aim to evoke feelings of compassion, understanding, empathy, and solidarity with others. By highlighting shared experiences or struggles, guilt appeals can foster a sense of connection and empathy, making the message more relatable and persuasive.
- *Humor Appeals*: humor appeals use comedy, wit, or amusement to evoke positive emotions and capture audience attention. Humor can enhance message recall, likability, and receptivity, making it a popular choice in advertising and marketing campaigns.
- *Emotional Stories*: narratives and storytelling are powerful tools for evoking emotions and engaging audiences. Emotional stories can create empathy, evoke nostalgia, or inspire action by connecting with the audience on a personal and emotional level.

Throughout history, fear appeals have been subject to scientific scrutiny and are deemed as fundamental in the realm of persuasive messaging, serving as the basis for all other types of appeals (Ruiter et al., 2014). The central aim of these messages is to encourage individuals to prioritize self-care by advocating for healthy behaviors (Stefanile, 2011). Since its inception, fear-based communication has typically been organized to provide two types of information: threat and recommendation. The threat aims to induce a fear response by presenting a serious danger, a severe consequence to which the recipient is vulnerable. The second information—sometimes implicit—offers behavioral recommendations to prevent the risk, emphasizing its protective efficacy and ease of implementation (Ruiter et al., 2014). For nearly six decades, this form of persuasive communication has been extensively employed in health promotion interventions and campaigns, addressing a wide range of socially pertinent threats, with its efficacy being thoroughly examined. This focus has also spurred a multitude of studies and research endeavors (e.g., Halkjelsvik & Rise, 2015; Zhang Meadows, 2020) aimed at assessing the effectiveness of interventions geared toward fostering protective and healthy behaviors. Despite the use of emotional appeals has been largely adopted in psychological fields, more often emotional appeals are used in the field of marketing and advertising (Yousef et al., 2023).

Persuasive Communication Has Gone Digital

Digital technology has changed the nature of persuasion in several key aspects (Ghofrani, 2024). It has increased complexity, blurring lines among information, entertainment, and influence. Contemporary technologies make it possible for people to alter the content of persuasive messages, giving messages meanings they did not have, and that the original communicator did not intend (Mateus, 2021).The Internet has democratized persuasive discourse, creating a mechanism by which regular citizens, possessing nothing more than a cheap video camera can have a significant impact on an election, a public debate, a business controversy, or any other form of public issue (Bakir et al., 2019). Social media blurs these boundaries even more. It also is changing the topography of persuasion (Ghofrani, 2024). Many persuasions now occur online—via tweets, posts, hashtags, and emojis—rather than face-to-face. Contemporary social media persuasive message effects are unique in that they: (a) can involve simple catchphrases; (b) diffuse more quickly and widely than previous technologies; (c) enable others to participate in meaning conferral; and (d) are capable of mobilizing individuals across national boundaries (Perloff, 2021).

Persuasive Communication-Based Campaigns and Luxury: What Link?

Persuasive communication has long been a cornerstone in the design and implementation of marketing campaigns across various industries (Huang et al., 2018). In the realm of luxury branding, where exclusivity, sophistication, and aspiration play significant roles, the use of persuasive communication strategies becomes even more crucial (Díaz et al., 2016). Over the years, there has been a notable shift from traditional marketing campaigns to more contemporary approaches, especially through the utilization of social media platforms (Huang et al., 2018; Ozuem et al., 2023a, 2023b).

The evolution of marketing campaigns within the luxury sector has seen a transition from conventional print advertisements and television commercials to more targeted and interactive strategies on social media platforms. This shift has been largely driven by changes in consumer behavior, with audiences increasingly turning to social media channels for product discovery, peer recommendations, and brand engagement (Alavi et al., 2021).

The decision to buy a product is influenced by the initial positioning of the product and its branding in the consumer's perception. In today's consumer culture, characterized by mass-produced goods at affordable prices, there has emerged a demand for products that embody the essence of design: luxury items (Akgün et al., 2013).

Luxury brands excel in employing persuasive communication strategies to captivate their audience and cultivate a robust brand presence. Among the most powerful tools at their disposal are storytelling and emotional appeals. Emotional branding leverages the emotional resonance and sentiments evoked by advertisements in consumers (Kim & Sullivan, 2019). By evoking profound emotions like love, nostalgia, empathy, pride, shame, and anger, emotional branding fosters a deep emotional bond between the consumer and the endorsed product, influencing purchase decisions even when the product carries a premium price tag (Akgün et al., 2013). Luxury goods, acting as status symbols linked with sensations of pride and allure, remain highly coveted despite their prices surpassing their intrinsic value (Kim & Sullivan, 2019).

By weaving intricate narratives that resonate with their target demographic, luxury brands can evoke emotions, curiosity, and a sense of exclusivity among consumers. Fashion luxury brands like Chanel and Louis Vuitton are renowned for their campaigns that transport viewers into a world of opulence and refinement, creating a desire to be part of that exclusive narrative (Alavi et al., 2021).

Emotions are at the core of consumer behavior, especially within the luxury industry where purchases are often driven by aspirations, status, and self-expression (Akgün et al., 2013; Ozuem et al., 2021).

In the digital era characterized by the prevalence of social media, social proof has emerged as a pivotal catalyst of consumer behavior. Luxury brands harness social influence by showcasing endorsements from celebrities, influencers, and contented customers in their marketing initiatives (Gurzki et al., 2019). Through affiliations with thought leaders and trendsetters, luxury brands bolster their credibility and broaden their appeal to a wider demographic, utilizing the influence of social validation to fortify their brand identity and interact with consumers on a more intimate level (Alavi et al., 2021). Exclusivity and scarcity are fundamental principles that underpin the allure of luxury brands (Roncha & Montecchi, 2017). By emphasizing limited edition products, exclusive events, and bespoke services, luxury campaigns convey a sense of rarity and luxury that elevates the perceived value of their offerings. This emphasis on exclusivity and scarcity not only drives demand and creates a sense of urgency among consumers but also enhances the prestige and desirability of the brand in the eyes of the consumer (Gurzki et al., 2019).

Social Media Campaigns for Luxury Brands

Traditional media channels have provided luxury brands with a robust platform to exhibit their products and principles. However, they encounter obstacles in a progressively digital and fragmented media environment. The emergence of social media, influencer marketing, and online platforms has revolutionized consumer-brand interactions and content consumption, presenting fresh hurdles for luxury marketers striving to uphold relevance and exclusivity (Godey et al., 2016). Social media campaigns offer luxury brands a unique opportunity to connect with their target audience on a more personal and engaging level. By leveraging the visual appeal and storytelling capabilities of platforms like Instagram, Facebook, and Pinterest, luxury brands can craft narratives that resonate with consumers' desires for status, elegance, and exclusivity (Vinerean & Opreana, 2019). Furthermore, social media campaigns allow luxury brands to create immersive experiences that go beyond mere product promotion. Through influencer partnerships, behind-the-scenes content, and interactive features, brands can cultivate a sense of community and belonging among their followers, fostering brand loyalty and advocacy (Godey et al., 2016).

Upon examining the transition from conventional marketing campaigns to social media campaigns in the luxury sector, it is apparent that persuasive communication continues to be fundamental to effective brand messaging. The capacity to customize content to align with the preferences and aspirations of the target demographic, all while preserving an air of exclusivity and desirability, is crucial in attracting the interest and fostering the loyalty of luxury consumers in the contemporary digital realm. By harnessing the influence of social media as a medium for compelling storytelling, luxury brands can persist in captivating and motivating their audiences in a marketing environment that is constantly evolving (Pentina et al., 2018). Furthermore, the effectiveness of traditional media campaigns in reaching younger, digitally-savvy consumers remains a pressing concern for luxury brands. As millennials and Gen Z consumers gravitate toward digital platforms for information and inspiration, luxury marketers are tasked with finding innovative ways to integrate traditional media channels with digital strategies to create a cohesive and engaging brand experience (Savić et al., 2019). Among the strategies that persuasive communication predominantly employs to leverage attitude and behavior change, appeals to emotions stand out as particularly effective (Savić et al., 2019).

Emotional Branding and Luxury

Emotional branding entails establishing and fostering emotional ties between a brand and its clientele. It transcends rational features and practical advantages to evoke emotions, attitudes, and perceptions that strike a chord with consumers on a personal level (Keller, 2016). When consumers form emotional attachments to a brand, they are more likely to engage with the brand, advocate for it, and establish long-term relationships (Keller, 2016; Ozuem & Willis, 2022).

In the contemporary landscape, luxury has transcended its purely economic connotations to become predominantly an emotional construct. Luxury goods are often synonymous with a focus on superior quality, although it is important to note that not all high-quality products qualify as luxury items, and vice versa. The association with a luxury brand does not automatically guarantee exceptional quality, underscoring the diversity within the realm of luxury brands (Savić et al., 2019).

The pillars of emotional branding rest upon four fundamental tenets: proximity, sensory experiences, imagination, and vision (Gobé et al., 2006). *Proximity* entails establishing a deep connection with consumers that is intimate and personalized, reflecting a profound respect for their individual preferences and providing sensory encounters that resonate with their desires. By offering consumers *sensory experiences* that evoke longing through tastes, captivating sounds, hypnotic colors, tactile shapes, and alluring scents, brands can foster a sense of continual closeness that nurtures preference and engenders brand loyalty (Ozuem et al. 2024; Savić et al., 2019).

Imagination has evolved from a desirable quality to an imperative in brand creation. Embracing an imaginative approach across product design, packaging, retail environments, advertising, and website aesthetics opens up new avenues for brands to surpass consumer expectations and capture their hearts in innovative ways. Design serves as a conduit for brands to communicate essential messages that foster enduring connections between manufacturers and end-users.

Vision emerges as a critical driver for long-term brand success, mandating a strategic positioning that supports adaptability and innovation. A clear and robust vision is indispensable for brands seeking to navigate market complexities and cultivate lasting consumer relationships. In the realm of fashion product design, the interplay between product adaptation and creation is pivotal, with the fusion of these processes representing a common practice in the industry (Savić et al., 2019).

The shifting consumer demographics, shaped by factors such as the rise of ethnic markets, generational changes, and the growing impact of women in modern society, highlight the fluidity of consumer behavior (Savić et al., 2019). Design emerges as the primary channel through which brands showcase their identity, allowing them to communicate powerful messages that form lasting connections between producers, retailers, and consumers.

Luxury brands utilize various emotional appeals to connect with consumers and communicate their brand values effectively. These appeals may include:

1. *Prestige and Exclusivity*: by leveraging feelings of exclusivity, status, and prestige to appeal to high-end consumers who seek unique and elite experiences (Vigneron & Johnson, 2004).
2. *Aspiration and Lifestyle*: by creating aspirational lifestyles and associating the brand with desirable qualities and values that consumers aspire to embody (Kapferer & Bastien, 2009).
3. *Sensory Appeal*: luxury brands engage consumers' senses through visually appealing advertisements, luxurious packaging, and immersive brand experiences that evoke positive emotions and sensory pleasures (Hultén, 2011).
4. *Storytelling and Heritage*: emotional branding in luxury often involves storytelling that highlights the brand's heritage, craftsmanship, and traditions, creating an emotional connection with consumers based on nostalgia and authenticity (Vigneron & Johnson, 2004).

The Ten Commandments of Emotional Branding

The essence of emotional branding lies in establishing partnerships and fostering communication. Evoking authentic emotions signifies a substantial commitment to a brand, symbolizing a promise to consumers and granting them the opportunity to engage deeply with the brand's universe. To strengthen relationships, foster intimacy, and embrace consumers as collaborators, proactive initiatives are essential. Numerous companies cultivate emotional connections with consumers by sparking creativity and providing glimpses into new realms: for instance, Gucci through sensual sophistication, Vogue through allure, and others. The efficacy of such strategies is evident as individuals respond emotionally to their encounters, projecting their emotional values onto the objects surrounding them (Savić et al., 2019). Given the apparent success of these approaches, evoking the appropriate emotions can be deemed the most valuable asset of a brand. Branding serves as a conduit between the provider and the recipient, between authority and liberty, with its core rooted in trust and dialogue (Savić et al., 2019). Gobé's tenets of emotional branding delineate the fundamental disparities between traditional brand awareness and the emotional depth required for a brand to gain favor (Gobé et al., 2006):

1. *Transitioning from consumers to individuals*—Consumers make purchases, while individuals lead lives. Consumers are often viewed as adversaries, necessitating combat or strategic maneuvers to conquer them. A more effective approach entails a collaborative mindset founded on relationships and mutual esteem, where every party emerges as a victor.
2. *Shifting from products to experiences*—Products address needs, whereas experiences cater to desires. A shopping experience should offer something extraordinary, creating lasting memories and forging emotional connections that transcend mere necessity. Attributes like adventurous spirit, curiosity, and the pursuit of novel encounters are gaining precedence over familiarity.
3. *Progressing from honesty to trust*—Honesty is anticipated, while trust is personal and alluring, needing to be earned. For a brand to resonate with customers, trust must be engendered. Some companies opting for no-questions-asked returns signify a significant stride in earning customer trust.
4. *Evolving from quality to preference*—Sales are increasingly driven not solely by quality, but by preference. Success hinges on the priority a brand holds in a consumer's hierarchy of choices. The consumer's ranking of a brand in their preferences determines its fate.
5. *Advancing from ubiquity to aspiration*—Popularity does not equate to affection. To make a brand desirable, it must convey a message that resonates with buyers' aspirations.
6. *Distinguishing between identity and physiognomy*—Identity denotes recognition, while physiognomy encompasses character, charisma,

and exclusivity, traits that inspire admiration and a desire to possess a particular brand.

7. *Emphasizing emotion over function*—A product's function pertains to its practical, external attributes, while its emotional appeal relates to the experiential pleasure derived from using it. The sensory experience carries significant market value.
8. *Prioritizing emotional presence over ubiquity*—Emotional presence is palpable, unlike omnipresence, which is merely visible. Strategies focused on brand omnipresence typically emphasize quantity over quality. A quality-oriented approach involves cultivating innovative methods to foster genuine, enduring relationships.
9. *Emphasizing dialogue over communication*—Consumers seek more than just information; they desire opportunities to exchange viewpoints. Digital platforms, public relations, brand presence, and promotional activities are more effective in engaging with customers through dialogue rather than mere product advertisement.
10. *Elevating connection over service*—While service drives sales, connection fosters recognition. Establishing connections entails understanding buyers' identities and demonstrating appreciation for them.

In today's landscape, luxury brands have extended their presence into mainstream consumer markets. However, it is essential to recognize that brands go through lifecycles. What is deemed luxurious today may not maintain its appeal in the future. The future trajectory of a brand relies on its resonance in a particular era and its ability to uphold the foundational values that initially bestowed luxury status upon it. Additionally, consumers make daily brand choices based on the emotional significance and quality provided (Savić et al., 2019). Excessive ubiquity poses a significant challenge to luxury branding, as consumers can quickly become fatigued and seek fresh, exclusive alternatives. Ultimately, a brand's essence is rooted in the authenticity and significance it embodies. Brands can establish genuine, intimate emotional connections with consumers, as evidenced by Hermes, where demand often surpasses supply, resulting in waiting lists for their products (Savić et al., 2019).

Branding Identity Toward Sustainability

In recent years, there has been a growing emphasis on sustainability in business practices. As the world faces environmental challenges such as climate change and resource depletion, consumers are becoming more conscious of the impact of their purchasing decisions. Companies that prioritize sustainability not only contribute to a better future for the planet but also build a stronger connection with their customers who share these values (Melewar et al., 2020).

When it comes to branding identity, integrating sustainability values can be a powerful way to differentiate a company in the market. By making sustainability a core part of the brand identity, a company can communicate its commitment to environmental and social responsibility. This not only attracts like-minded customers but also helps to foster a positive reputation in the marketplace.

There are several ways in which companies can incorporate sustainability values into their branding identity (Alakkas et al., 2022; Melewar et al., 2020).

1. *Mission and Vision Statements:* companies can clearly articulate their commitment to sustainability in their mission and vision statements. These statements should reflect the company's values and goals related to environmental and social impact.
2. *Logo and Visual Identity:* incorporating elements that symbolize sustainability, such as green colors, nature-inspired designs, or symbols of eco-friendliness, can visually communicate the company's commitment to sustainability.
3. *Product Packaging and Messaging:* using eco-friendly materials for packaging and labeling products with messages about sustainability practices can help to reinforce the company's values with customers.
4. *Marketing and Communication:* companies can leverage their sustainability initiatives in marketing campaigns and communication strategies. Sharing stories about sustainability efforts, partnerships with environmental organizations, or carbon footprint reduction can engage customers and build brand loyalty.

5. *Corporate Social Responsibility (CSR) Initiatives:* Engaging in meaningful CSR programs that benefit the environment and society can further demonstrate the company's commitment to sustainability.

By integrating sustainability values into the branding identity, a company not only differentiates itself in the market but also contributes to a more sustainable future. Customers are increasingly looking to support companies that align with their values, and by prioritizing sustainability, companies can build a strong and loyal customer base while making a positive impact on the world.

New Emotional Trends: The Case of Eco-anxiety and Its Role in Communicating Sustainability

In recent years, scholars started to discuss about emerging phenomenon called *eco-emotions* (Böhm, 2003) which refers to emotional experiences significantly related to the climate crisis (Pihkala, 2022). Even research on the taxonomy of climate emotions (for a review see Pihkala, 2022) reported the high plethora of eco-emotions that could emerge in several populations, the present paragraph will focus on exploring the conceptualization of eco-anxiety and how this eco-emotion could lead individuals to behave in a pro-environmental way. Additionally, a short focus on which types of eco-emotional appeals luxury brands could adopt to communicate their sustainability values will be discussed.

Eco-anxiety is a complex and multifaceted phenomenon that encompasses significant distress related to the ecological crisis. It should be viewed as a meaningful indication that an individual cares about the well-being of the planet, rather than as a problem (Clayton & Karazsia, 2020). Building on this perspective, some scholars have proposed that eco-anxiety can be understood as a type of practical anxiety, which can be described as the anxiety experienced when confronted with a new or challenging decision (Kurth, 2016; Kurth & Pihkala, 2022;

Pihkala, 2019). As far as every emotion has adaptive functions, practical anxiety serves the individual to attune to challenges and uncertainty related to the situation and, secondly, it prompts to minimize risks and get the required information for taking the best decision. Research using experimental design showed that individual experiencing practical anxiety about new or challenging issues made more informed decisions compared to individuals experiencing anger (Valentino et al., 2008). Linked to this, advertisements that enhance eco-anxiety could, on one side, bring the consumer to get more information about how to put in act pro-environmental behaviors, including supporting companies that operate sustainably; on the other side, could help the company to share their sustainable values to reach out to an audience that shares its values. Cross-sectional research on the link between eco-anxiety and pro-environmental attitudes showed that higher eco-anxiety correlates with higher efforts to become more informed about environmental threats (Hmielowski et al., 2019), as well as with declared support for pro-environmental policies and actions (Goldberg et al., 2021). Since cross-sectional design does not give the possibility to make causal inferences, research using an experimental design takes a step forward enlightening that provoking eco-anxiety alone is not enough to influence the behavior, but appealing to consumers' self-interests while promoting environmental benefits (Ginsberg & Bloom, 2004) could lead the individual to engage in a more cognitive engagement with the issue, which in turn predicts more pro-environmental attitudes and behaviors, rather than focusing only on the environmental concern. For instance, an experiment conducted by Fernando et al. (2016) showed that situational involvement is a significant predictor of attitudes in the context of green advertising. Situational involvement with the message is defined as an engagement with the content of the message which is temporary, evoked by external stimuli and goal-directed (Richins & Bloch, 1986). Companies promoting green values in their advertisements should not target their campaigns only on *eco-friendly consumers* (i.e., those with a more enduring ego-involvement with the message; Petty & Cacioppo, 1986) to avoid falling into the phenomenon termed *green marketing myopia* (Ginsberg & Bloom, 2004). Moreover, in line with previous research studying the application of fear appeals in green marketing communications suggests that fear appeals that leave the audience with a sense of hope, empowerment, or self-efficacy and the communication is sensitive to contexts seem particularly effective in promoting pro-environmental attitudes and behaviors (Nabi et al., 2018; Witte & Allen, 2000).

It is important to note that to date, there are no studies available in the literature that tested fear appeals based on eco-anxiety for fashion luxury brands. In the realm of fashion advertising, Pickett-Baker and Ozaki (2008) suggest that companies should shed the light on benefits of buying eco-friendly clothes. In addition, a study conducted in the United States found that the primary factor that consumers referred to be a drive for their purchasing behavior is the positive perception of the quality of the product displayed in the advertisement (Song & Kim, 2018). Finally, the perception of personal relevance (Celsi et al., 1992) seems to have a role in predicting positive attitudes toward the brand as well as the intention to purchase, also in fashion advertising (Kang et al., 2013).

Conclusions

Nowadays, social networks are part of the new media in which brands can promote their products through a more effective communication of their values and emotions. Social networks are defined as "virtual communities where users can create individual public profiles, interact with real-life friends, and meet other people based on shared interests" (Kuss & Griffiths, 2011, p. 3529).

In the last several years, social networks also become a space for companies to create a stronger bond with their audience (i.e., create a *community*), as well as new media for advertising products and services. Because of the way they are designed, companies can create their business profiles on social networks and use them as a more direct way to interact with their audience and facilitate consumer decision-making (Pentina et al., 2018). Furthermore, as individuals engage with the brand through social media platforms, their attitudes toward the brand and emotional attachment are both influenced and affected (McAlexander et al., 2002). Correspondingly, the increasing consciousness among consumers regarding environmental concerns and the consequences of corporate decisions on the environment, particularly within the fashion industry, prompt consumers to urge companies to prioritize sustainability and integrate it into their core practices (Kim & Hall, 2015).

In the realm of social network marketing, there has been an increasing interest in the concepts of *electronic Word-Of-Mouth* (eWOM; Cho et al., 2014). Linked to this, brands started to advertise their efforts for being more sustainable as well as sharing their sustainability values (Han et al., 2017) not only to increase sales, but also with the aim of gaining more popularity, visibility, credibility, and greater acceptance (Cho et al., 2014). It is important to note that according to Kagawa's (2007) recommendations, to promote a successful sustainability marketing campaign, brands need to understand that consumers' perception of sustainable actions comprises several dimensions, including environmental, social, economic, and cultural aspects and choices. A recent research on depicting sustainable fashion companies through image-based social networks emphasized that fashion brands can share their sustainability values through images and those photos that create more digital engagement are linked to the dimensions of environmental sustainability, rather than fashion-centric content; nevertheless, as the authors' underline, it is important to implement a social media strategy that transparently inform the consumer on business practices to avoid of evoking in the consumer the feeling being in front of a green-washing practice, also by giving the importance to the other dimensions of sustainability (Milanesi et al., 2022).

As of now, while research on how luxury brands can successfully promote sustainability is still relatively new, some findings show promise. For instance, an experiment conducted by Septianto et al. (2021) showed the efficacy of using pride and gratitude emotional appeals in increasing sharing intentions for sustainable luxury brand campaigns. Moreover, taking a step forward, pride appeals demonstrate their efficacy in broadcasting eWOM, while narrowcasting eWOM was more elicitated by gratitude appeal. This research enhances how specific emotional appeals can overcome potential barriers in advertising sustainable luxury through social networks.

In conclusion, social networks hold significant potential for sustainable luxury campaigns to achieve various objectives, provided that companies prioritize transparency, adopt a multidimensional approach to sustainability, and employ the most suitable emotional appeal aligned with the campaign's objectives.

References

Akgün, A. E., Koçoğlu, İ, & İmamoğlu, S. Z. (2013). An emerging consumer experience: Emotional branding. *Procedia-Social and Behavioral Sciences, 99*, 503–508.

Alakkas, A. A., Vivek, Paul, M., Nabi, M. K., & Khan, M. A. (2022). Corporate social responsibility and firm-based brand equity: The moderating effect of marketing communication and brand identity. *Sustainability*, *14*(10), 6033.

Alavi, S., Kocher, B., Dörfer, S., & Habel, J. (2021). The role of salesperson communication in luxury selling. *Journal of Personal Selling & Sales Management, 41*(4), 301–315.

Alhabash, S., McAlister, A. R., Hagerstrom, A., Quilliam, E. T., Rifon, N. J., & Richards, J. I. (2013). Between likes and shares: Effects of emotional appeal and virality on the persuasiveness of anticyberbullying messages on Facebook. *Cyberpsychology, Behavior, and Social Networking, 16*(3), 175–182.

Andersen, K. (1971). *Persuasion: Theory and practice.* Allyn & Bacon.

Bakir, V., Herring, E., Miller, D., & Robinson, P. (2019). Organized persuasive communication: A new conceptual framework for research on public relations, propaganda and promotional culture. *Critical Sociology, 45*(3), 311–328.

Bettinghaus, E. P., & Cody, M. J. (1987). *Persuasive communication* (4th ed.). Holt, Rinehart & Winston.

Böhm, G. (2003). Emotional reactions to environmental risks: Consequentialist versus ethical evaluation. *Journal of Environmental Psychology, 23*(2), 199–212.

Celsi, R. L., Chow, S., Olson, J. C., & Walker, B. A. (1992). The construct validity of intrinsic sources of personal relevance: An intraindividual source of felt involvement. *Journal of Business Research, 25*, 165–185.

Cho, S., Huh, J., & Faber, R. J. (2014). The influence of sender trust and advertiser trust on multistage effects of viral advertising. *Journal of Advertising, 43*(1), 100–114.
Clayton, S., & Karazsia, B. T. (2020). Development and validation of a measure of climate change anxiety. *Journal of Environmental Psychology, 69*, 101434.
Coski, J. M. (2005). *The Confederate battle flag: America's most embattled emblem.* Belknap Press of Harvard University Press.
Díaz, E., Martín-Consuegra, D., & Estelami, H. (2016). A persuasive-based latent class segmentation analysis of luxury brand websites. *Electronic Commerce Research, 16*, 401–424.
Fernando, A. G., Sivakumaran, B., & Suganthi, L. (2016). Message involvement and attitude towards green advertisements. *Marketing Intelligence and Planning, 34*(6).
Ghofrani, T. (2024). The impact of new media technologies on persuasive communication in the time of global crisis. *International Journal of Technology Management, 94*(3–4), 419–435.
Ginsberg, J. M., & Bloom, P. N. (2004). Choosing the right green-marketing strategy. *MIT Sloan Management Review, 46*(1), 79–84.
Gobé, M., Gligorijević, M., & Gligorijević, V. (2006). *Emocionalno brendiranje: Nova paradigma povezivanja brendova i ljudi.* Mass Media International.
Godey, B., Manthiou, A., Pederzoli, D., Rokka, J., Aiello, G., Donvito, R., & Singh, R. (2016). Social media marketing efforts of luxury brands: Influence on brand equity and consumer behavior. *Journal of Business Research, 69*(12), 5833–5841.
Goldberg, M. H., Gustafson, A., Ballew, M. T., Rosenthal, S. A., & Leiserowitz, A. (2021). Identifying the most important predictors of support for climate policy in the United States. *Behavioural Public Policy, 5*(4), 480–502.
Gurzki, H., Schlatter, N., & Woisetschläger, D. M. (2019). Crafting extraordinary stories: Decoding luxury brand communications. *Journal of Advertising, 48*(4), 401–414.
Halkjelsvik, T., & Rise, J. (2015). Disgust in fear appeal anti-smoking advertisements: The effects on attitudes and abstinence motivation. *Drugs: Education, Prevention and Policy, 22*(4), 362–369.
Han, J., Seo, Y., & Ko, E. (2017). Staging luxury experiences for understanding sustainable fashion consumption: A balance theory application. *Journal of Business Research, 74*, 162–167.

Hmielowski, J. D., Donaway, R., & Wang, M. Y. (2019). Environmental risk information seeking: The differential roles of anxiety and hopelessness. *Environmental Communication, 13*(7), 894–908.

Huang, R., Ha, S., & Kim, S. H. (2018). Narrative persuasion in social media: An empirical study of luxury brand advertising. *Journal of Research in Interactive Marketing, 12*(3), 274–292.

Hultén, B. (2011). Sensory marketing: The multi-sensory brand-experience concept. *European Business Review, 23*(3), 256–273.

Johnson, B. T., & Boynton, M. H. (2010). Putting attitudes in their place: Behavioral prediction in the face of competing variables. In J. P. Forgas, J. Cooper, & W. D. Crano (Eds.), *The psychology of attitudes and attitude change* (pp. 19–38). Psychology Press.

Kagawa, F. (2007). Dissonance in students' perceptions of sustainable development and sustainability. *International Journal of Sustainability in Higher Education, 8*(3), 317–338.

Kang, J., Liu, C., & Kim, S. H. (2013). Environmentally sustainable textile and apparel consumption: The role of consumer knowledge, perceived consumer effectiveness and perceived personal relevance. *International Journal of Consumer Studies, 37*(4), 442–452.

Kapferer, J. N., & Bastien, V. (2009). The specificity of luxury management: Turning marketing upside down. *Journal of Brand Management, 16*(5), 311–322.

Keller, K. L. (2016). Reflections on customer-based brand equity: Perspectives, progress, and priorities. *AMS Review, 6*, 1–16.

Kim, H. S., & Hall, M. L. (2015). Green brand strategies in the fashion industry: Leveraging connections of the consumer, brand, and environmental sustainability. *Sustainable Fashion Supply Chain Management: From Sourcing to Retailing*, 31–45.

Kim, Y. K., & Sullivan, P. (2019). Emotional branding speaks to consumers' heart: The case of fashion brands. *Fashion and Textiles, 6*(1), 1–16.

Kurth, C. (2016). Anxiety, normative uncertainty, and social regulation. *Biology and Philosophy, 31*(1), 1–21.

Kurth, C., & Pihkala, P. (2022). Eco-anxiety: What it is and why it matters. *Frontiers in Psychology, 13*, 981814.

Kuss, D. J., & Griffiths, M. D. (2011). Online social networking and addiction—A review of the psychological literature. *International Journal of Environmental Research and Public Health, 8*(9), 3528–3552.

Mateus, S. (2021). Welcome to media rhetoric-where human persuasion and technological means collide. *Southern Communication Journal, 86*(2), 165–174.

McAlexander, J. H., Schouten, J. W., & Koenig, H. F. (2002). Building brand community. *Journal of Marketing, 66*(1), 38–54.

McCombs, M., & Reynolds, A. (2002). News influence on our pictures of the world. In J. Bryant & D. Zillmann (Eds.), *Media effects: Advances in theory and research* (2nd ed., pp. 1–18). Lawrence Erlbaum Associates.

Melewar, T., Foroudi, P., & Jin, Z. (2020). Corporate branding, identity, image and reputation: Current and future trends, developments and challenges. *Journal of Business Research, 117*, 672–674.

Milanesi, M., Kyrdoda, Y., & Runfola, A. (2022). How do you depict sustainability? An analysis of images posted on Instagram by sustainable fashion companies. *Journal of Global Fashion Marketing, 13*(2), 101–115.

Nabi, R. L. (2015). Emotional flow in persuasive health messages. *Health Communication, 30*(2), 114–124.

Nabi, R. L., Gustafson, A., & Jensen, R. (2018). Framing climate change: Exploring the role of emotion in generating advocacy behavior. *Science Communication, 40*(4), 442–468.

O'Keefe, D. J. (2016). Persuasion: *Theory and research* (3rd ed.). Sage.

Ozuem, W., Ranfagni, S., Willis, M., Rovai, S., & Howell, K. (2021). Exploring customers' responses to online service failure and recovery strategies during Covid-19 pandemic: An actor–network theory perspective. *Psychology & Marketing, 38*(9), 1440–1459.

Ozuem, W., & Willis, M. (2022). *Digital marketing strategies for value co-creation: Models and approaches for online brand communities.* Palgrave Macmillan.

Ozuem, W., Willis, M., Ranfagni, S., Howell, K. E., & Rovai, S. (2023a). Examining the role of social media influencers in service failure and recovery strategies: an empirical investigation of millennials' views. *Information Technology & People*. https://doi.org/10.1108/itp-05-2022-0371

Ozuem, W., Willis, M., Howell, K., Ranfagni, S., & Rovai, S. (2023b). Examining user-generated content, service failure recovery and customer–brand relationships: An exploration through commitment-trust theory. *Internet Research*. https://doi.org/10.1108/intr-07-2022-0580

Pentina, I., Guilloux, V., & Micu, A. C. (2018). Exploring social media engagement behaviors in the context of luxury brands. *Journal of Advertising, 47*(1), 55–69.

Perloff, R. M. (2021). *The dynamics of political communication: Media and Politics in a Aigital Age*. Routledge.
Petty, R. E., & Cacioppo, J. T. (1986). *The elaboration likelihood model of persuasion* (pp. 1–24). Springer.
Pickett-Baker, J., & Ozaki, R. (2008). Pro-environmental products: Marketing influence on consumer purchase decision. *Journal of Consumer Marketing, 25*, 281–293.
Pihkala, P. (2019). *Climate anxiety: A report*. MIELI Mental Health Finland, Helsinki.
Pihkala, P. (2022). Toward a taxonomy of climate emotions. *Frontiers in Climate, 3*, 738154.
Richins, M. L., & Bloch, P. H. (1986). After the new wears off: The temporal context of product involvement. *Journal of Consumer Research, 13*(2), 280–285.
Roncha, A., & Montecchi, M. (2017). The underpinning strategies leading to high value perception of luxury fashion brands. *IUP Journal of Brand Management, 14*(3), 7–21.
Ruiter, R. A., Kessels, L. T., Peters, G. J. Y., & Kok, G. (2014). Sixty years of fear appeal research: Current state of the evidence. *International Journal of Psychology, 49*(2), 63–70.
Savić, M., Perić, N., & Frfulanović, Š. (2019). Emotional branding of luxury goods. *Middle-East Journal of Scientific Research, 27*(6), 494–499.
Septianto, F., Seo, Y., & Errmann, A. C. (2021). Distinct effects of pride and gratitude appeals on sustainable luxury brands. *Journal of Business Ethics, 169*, 211–224.
Smith, M. J. (1982). *Persuasion and human action: A review and critique of social influence theories*. Wadsworth.
Smythe, T. W. (1999). Moral responsibility. *Journal of Value Inquiry, 33*, 493–506.
Song, S. Y., & Kim, Y. K. (2018). A human-centered approach to green apparel advertising decision tree predictive modeling of consumer choice. *Sustainability, 10*, 3688.
Stefanile, C. (2011). *Fear Appeals in psicologia della salute*. In: A. Pazzagli, P. Vanni, S. Casale, D. Vanni (Eds.), Psicologia: Storia e Clinica. Omaggio a Saulo Sirigatti (pp. 241–250). Fondazione Giorgio Ronchi.
Valentino, N. A., Hutchings, V. L., Banks, A. J., & Davis, A. K. (2008). Is a worried citizen a good citizen? Emotions, political information seeking, and learning via the Internet. *Political Psychology, 29*(2), 247–273.

Vigneron, F., & Johnson, L. W. (2004). Measuring perceptions of brand luxury. *Journal of Brand Management, 11*(6), 484–550.

Vinerean, S., & Opreana, A. (2019). Social media marketing efforts of luxury brands on Instagram. *Expert Journal of Marketing, 7*(2), 144–152.

Watkins, M. (2001). In practice: Principles of persuasion. *Negotiation Journal, 17*(2), 115–137.

Witte, K., & Allen, M. (2000). A meta-analysis of fear appeals: Implications for effective public health campaigns. *Health Education & Behavior, 27*(5), 591–615.

Yousef, M., Rundle-Thiele, S., & Dietrich, T. (2023). Advertising appeals effectiveness: a systematic literature review. *Health Promotion International, 38*(4), daab204.

Zhang Meadows, C. (2020). The effects of fear appeals and message format on promoting skin cancer prevention behaviors among college students. *Societies, 10*(1), 21.

Part II

Scope and Application

9

Digital Fashion in the Metaverse and Innovation for Sustainability in Fashion

Marta Giovannetti and Elena Cedrola

Introduction

In recent years we have witnessed significant environmental changes affecting the fashion industry. From economic and political instability, to digital transformation, we have also seen the pandemic and its consequences on consumption at a global level impact or modify fashion industry practices (Janmark et al., 2024). Among the consumer shifts, McKinsey (Amed et al., 2023) identifies trends such as: the return of the importance of tourism; the growth of the luxury sector; the importance of leisure activities and open spaces translated in terms of demand for athleisure; the increasingly large rather than generative artificial intelligence; the strain for companies of balancing tradition, innovation and

M. Giovannetti (✉) · E. Cedrola
Department of Economics and Law, University of Macerata, Macerata, Italy
e-mail: marta.giovannetti@unimc.it

E. Cedrola
e-mail: elena.cedrola@unimc.it

W. Ozuem et al. (eds.), *Sustainable Digital Marketing for Fashion and Luxury Brands*,
https://doi.org/10.1007/978-3-031-82467-8_9

scale; the transformation of supply chains through trust and transparency, and the ever-increasing role of sustainability. With regard to sustainability, up to 80% of a product's environmental impact is determined in the design phase, followed by the materials and dyes being used. Although there are still many international regulations to consider, these will become increasingly standardised and stringent, as will the digital passport, which collects and shares information. Surveys of executives' opinions also seem to indicate that companies will prepare to face these challenges not so much by implementing cost containment strategies, but rather by increasing sales that will be underpinned by new pricing and promotion strategies, rather than volume increases (Amed et al., 2023; Ozuem et al., 2024).

In this context, the metaverse offers many opportunities for fashion brands to expand their audience, especially among younger users. The first step taken by fashion brands in the metaverse has been to create digital apparel for users' digital identities, i.e. avatars, and events such as fashion shows, games, and brand experiences (Cedrola & Giovannetti, 2024). These include Gucci and Stella McCartney, entering Roblox with digital clothes and accessories in 2021, or Decentraland Fashion Week which boasted more than 60 brands including Estée Lauder, Tommy Hilfiger, Dolce & Gabbana, and Forever 21. The above are just some examples of a wide range of practices being established in the fashion industry by innovative, pioneering brands, to be present in novel digital environments, offer sales opportunities to additional users through innovative and immersive e-commerce, and reinforce brand awareness and reputation. This is also to take advantage of seemingly relevant and promising trends such as gaming, which as a form of entertainment is attracting consumers—young people especially—on a global scale (Panhans et al., 2021).

The main motivations for companies to experiment and implement projects on digital assets include: the desire to attract a new customer base; the manifestation of creativity and innovation; the generation of marketing/PR, and also experimentation with future-proofing concepts and collections (The Business of Fashion, 2021). According to a study by Morgan Stanley, the market for digital fashion and luxury brands is expected to reach $50 billion USD by 2030, with most of the growth coming from NFTs[1] and social gaming. In fact, these two areas are expected to grow the industry's total addressable market and EBIT[2] by more than 10% and 25% respectively over the next eight years. Soft luxury products such as ready-to-wear, leather goods and shoes are expected to be the main growth markets (Statista, 2023a).

A promising new direction for creativity and fashion design is digital software applications for 3D garment creation, which realistically simulates garments and accelerate physical production, as done by Clo3D and Browzwear (Wetherell et al., 2023). The design and marketing of purely digital fashion products are also finding their way through the use of NFT. In 2021, for instance, RTFKT studios, a purely digital shoe company that merges the worlds of fashion and gaming within the NFT scene, launched its first collection of artistic sneakers, which sold out in no time. After this resounding success, RTFKT studios was purchased by Nike.[3]

With thousands of NFTs already created and millions of dollars already traded on the market, this looks like just the beginning. Despite the metaverse's early problems—such as concerns about the quality of graphics, the limitations of data streaming, and the inability to move assets across the metaverse's various co-existing spaces—the opportunities it presents are attractive to brands, as the metaverse opens up new ways for them to engage customers and create communities (Zając & Jordan-Kulczyk, 2022).

Additionally, in the metaverse, user-created content enables monetisation in game-based virtual worlds. In 2023, in particular, there were an estimated 250 million monthly active users on Fortnite,[4] 202 million

[1] NFT (non-fungible token) is a unique digital identifier. It certifies the ownership and authenticity of a specific digital asset, such as art, music, or other digital files.

[2] The acronym "EBIT" stands for Earnings Before Interest and Taxes. It is a widely used measure in calculating a company's cash flow, highlighting its profitability before accounting for financial charges and taxes.

[3] Founded in 2020 by Benoit Pagotto, Chris Le, and Steven Vasilev, RTFKT pioneers the use of Web3 technology, Non-Fungible Tokens (NFTs), blockchain, and augmented reality to create unique virtual sneakers and collectibles. https://rtfkt.com/.

[4] Fortnite is an online video game and game platform developed by Epic Games. It was released in 2017 and has become a cultural phenomenon. https://fortnite.gg/player-count; https://www.businessofapps.com/data/fortnite-statistics/.

on Roblox,[5] and 172 on Minecraft[6] (Statista, 2023b). Notably, Roblox and Minecraft are classified as open systems where users can play but also create and contribute to the world ecosystem with environments, objects, and character accessories. These circumstances highlight the fact that business opportunities for companies that initially saw the metaverse as a new immersive and interactive digital channel—to engage users, create brand experiences, interact, and sell digital products—can also be associated with the typical aspects of digital business models and open innovation.

Recent surveys have also found that participation in metaverse environments and experiences enhances creativity and imagination (37%) and provides opportunities for self-expression (27%) (Rejoult, 2022). While Web 1.0 permitted the flow of information from one user to another, and Web 2.0 focused on connecting individuals and creating a sharing economy, Web 3.0 allows these connections to be explored on a more participatory level; consumers can now become prosumers who co-create the offer they are buying, not only for product customisation but also for the creation of digital fashion items, and digital experiences in the metaverse and gaming world (Ozuem et al., 2023a, 2023b; Rejoult, 2022).

We are also seeing consumers move away from fast fashion and towards sustainability in the industry. Fashion companies need to address this new trend, which is becoming increasingly relevant and widespread, especially among the younger generation. Therefore, they need to rethink and reshape their designs and production according to new sustainable paradigms, limiting their carbon footprint and having a proactive impact in terms of environmental, social, and economic sustainability. All this while continuing to produce new, stylish collections for the market.

[5] Roblox is an online game platform and game creation system developed by Roblox Corporation. It allows users to program and play games created by themselves or other users. https://www.roblox.com/.

[6] Minecraft is a 3D sandbox game created by Swedish game developer Markus "Notch" Persson. It is maintained by Mojang Studios, which is part of Xbox Game Studios, itself a division of Microsoft. The game revolves around blocks, creatures, and community interaction. https://www.minecraft.net/en-us/article/what-minecraft.

These new approaches and the push towards increasingly digital fashion were fostered by the 2020–2021 global pandemic, which dramatically affected global supply chains and reinforced the shift towards digitalisation for fashion company processes and their interaction with consumers. All these drivers pushed even more in the direction of digital fashion in all its possible facets and applications, aligning the supply chain.

Since digital fashion, and digital artwork in general, involves relatively little cost and few resources—essentially, a laptop, software, and the availability of an Internet connection—we expect the metaverse to offer more and more opportunities for even small designers to produce and gain visibility, to access a huge and even more empowered potential market than was the case with social media 15 years ago (Ozuem et al., 2021; Zając & Jordan-Kulczyk, 2022).

Moreover, among the more important trends that are spreading among consumers, we also find a desire to be involved and participate in experiences, design activities, and the customisation of offerings to meet their tastes and needs (Wetherell et al., 2023). Additionally, consumers are now increasingly paying attention to sustainability when purchasing fashion items. This suggests that the fashion industry needs to respond to this demand by providing sustainable products and services and communicating its responsible values (Abbate et al., 2024).

According to recent studies, clothing that exists only in the digital world is far more environmentally friendly than its physical equivalent, generating 97% less CO2 and using around 3300 litres of water per garment. In addition to this, working with digital samples in design, development, modelling, sampling and marketing before their physical versions go into production can reduce a brand's carbon footprint by up to 30%, drastically cutting the overall environmental impact of a fashion item's entire lifecycle, and shortening time to market by 40% (Ozuem & Willis, 2022; Zając & Jordan-Kulczyk, 2022). Moreover, at the point of sale, digital garment models can alleviate problems associated with overproduction, which is commonly seen as a key obstacle in today's fashion business (Rejoult, 2022).

This chapter not only looks at the latest developments and emerging trends in the fashion market in terms of consumer needs, it also examines the dynamics, technologies and interactions implemented by the different companies in this sector. The goal is specifically to highlight aspects in which the metaverse has a place, along with all the technologies that are fundamental, related or tangential to it, in order to understand how these can help or emphasise the consumption and use experience from a sustainable perspective. Moreover, this chapter will set out the way companies can use these technologies to maximise their research and innovation capacities, minimising the consumption of resources, waste, and emissions, and making it possible to adapt to the demands of consumers and operators in the supply chain and ultimately, to perform better in terms of innovation and economics. The following paragraphs illustrate some business cases and the relevant literature and concludes with some ideas for research and management.

Metaverse and Application Areas in Business

Notable metaverses based on blockchains include Minecraft, Roblox, Sandbox, Decentraland, and Somnium (Periyasamy & Periyasami, 2023). In these spaces, cryptocurrencies such as Bitcoin or Ethereum are often integrated into new blockchain railroads, creating a mechanism that facilitates the transport of digital data while also conferring ownership of same. In the worlds of the metaverse, it is possible to perform various activities, such as acting, learning, shopping, trading, and moving between the different spaces there.

As recently highlighted by McKinsey (Hazan et al., 2022), one of the main activities implemented in the metaverse is gaming, followed by immersive retail, entertainment, sports, and educational experiences. However, there are also less well-known applications with potential impact and diffusion, such as: virtual employee training and team collaboration using avatars; virtual prototyping in manufacturing and construction, or virtual showroom displays for products such as cars (Hazan et al., 2022).

Companies operating in the metaverse are demonstrating their potential by attracting investment and forging collaborations, agreements and alliances with prominent brands around the world. In 2021, metaverse-related companies are expected to have raised more than $10 billion USD, more than double the amount raised in the previous year. In the past 12 months, Fortnite creator Epic Games not only raised $3 billion USD to fund its long-term vision for the metaverse, but also announced a partnership with LEGO to build a metaverse for children. There is a lot of potential in the metaverse, and it seems that one of the key changes on the management side is a more consumer-led approach to brand marketing and engagement. The shift towards individual content creators is evident in the rise of influencer marketing (+50% between 2017 and 2022) on social platforms such as WeChat and Pinduoduo in China, and YouTube, TikTok, and Instagram in the Western world. This circumstance only increases the growth of the metaverse in terms of value and diffusion, thanks to the innovative and engaging experiences that are likely to come from these user-creators (Hazan et al., 2022).

Among the fashion brands, Balenciaga was already active in the metaverse in 2021, having launched its seasonal collection via a gaming app in autumn 2021, and collaborated with Fortnite to develop a series of "skins" for the game's characters. Balenciaga then dedicated a business unit to the metaverse to explore potential opportunities (Rejoult, 2022). Another brand active in the fashion metaverse is Dolce and Gabbana, which released a nine-piece digital clothing collection in September 2021, available for purchase in Ethereum, one of the metaverse cryptocurrencies. The company's first NFT collection was subsequently auctioned off for around $6 million USD (Rejoult, 2022). Gucci produced a limited-edition series of CryptoJanky NFT in collaboration with SUPERPLASTIC, a leading manufacturer of toys, vinyl action figures and digital collectibles with kawaii imagery and a loyal following of fans ready to spend on the digital creations of the two brands. The creations of the SUPERGUCCI collection synthesised Superplastic's toy characters and Alessandro Michele's poetic bucolic vision, launched in two drops and were met with great success (Giano, 2022). These brands have created digital collections—or their real-world equivalents—to make themselves known to potential young consumers, offer brand experiences, but also to experiment with digital fashion and VR. Perhaps the most innovative aspect of this is the possibility to create digital clothing, which is very popular among designers, influencers, environmentalists, and fashionistas (Rejoult, 2022).

Digital fashion could be used by customers in many ways, such as in virtual worlds, games, or as a simple overlay on photographs. Customers will be able to try on as many outfits as they like from the digital inventory in their own homes: anytime, anywhere, without the need or desire to buy them in real life, which provides many opportunities for interaction, play and ultimately, potential sales (Rejoult, 2022). These digital-to-physical (D2P) and physical-to-digital (P2D) technologies also provide a test bed and serve as a platform for manufacturing in the real world. Data integration in this context will also lead to Industry 4.0 or Fashion 4.0, and digital fashion items will be increasingly associated with NFTs (Periyasamy & Periyasami, 2023). Forward-thinking companies understand that the benefits of having a presence on a metaverse platform go beyond immediate revenue: these platforms also offer the opportunity for companies to use virtual marketing that translates into physical sales.

In November 2021, Nike launched "Nikeland", its own digital space on Roblox, where visitors can play simulated sports games, wear Nike clothing, and create their own mini-games. Nikeland also features a virtual lab that showcases shoe prototypes, allowing people to try on shoes virtually before real-world production begins. In its first five months of operation, it attracted 6.7 million visitors from 224 countries (Zając & Jordan-Kulczyk, 2022). Nike is also investing not only in the metaverse, but in many emerging technologies in order to reap the benefits and advantages of each in its supply chain. In fact, Nike has created patents for cryptographic digital assets to secure their retail products on the blockchain (Andon & Pham, 2021). They have also partnered with RTFTK and cryptokicks internet of adaptive apparel footwear (IoAAF) in 2021, as well as developing intelligent electronic shoes (IES) in 2019 (Nike Inc., 2019). Nike also acquired the digitally native brand RTFKT, and the first release of Nike x RTFKT NFT fashion items was worth $250 million USD, representing two-thirds of the total value of NFTs sold in 2022 (Zając & Jordan-Kulczyk, 2022).

Fashion industry leaders are aware of the potential of the metaverse, especially due to the large number and global distribution of platform users and the versatility of the experiences and fashion items that can be produced and sold on these platforms, whether linked to real-life fashion or not. Fashion companies that have already designed skins for metaverse avatars are H&M, Wrangler, Levi Strauss & Co., Louis Vuitton, Fendi, Dior, Givenchy, Kenzo, Prada, PUMA, Under Armour, and Dolce & Gabbana. On Fortnite, Balenciaga offers seasonal collections and Nike sells simulated Air Jordans that can be obtained by completing challenges. Burberry started a collaboration with Mythical Games and released skins for the game Blankos Block Party (Zając & Jordan-Kulczyk, 2022).

Some brands have gone beyond creating fashion items in the metaverse to develop their own worlds, in particular the worlds of Vans and Gucci on Roblox, which have had some success. In particular, Vans Shoes has created "Vans World", where users can dress their own avatar with Vans clothing and accessories in an environment that simulates skateboard parks. Meanwhile, Gucci launched "Gucci Garden" in May 2021 to celebrate the company's 100th anniversary, giving event participants blank avatars to collect virtual clothes and accessories as they moved through a simulated floral environment representing the brand's values and aesthetic. The experience was intended to be temporary and was indeed shut down after two weeks, having attracted numerous visitors from around the world. A year later, Gucci unveiled "Gucci Town", a space reminiscent of Milan's Brera district, with three different spaces: the Modal collection showroom; the fashion show, and the suitcase game, the first Home product in a running game set in an airport terminal. Other brands subsequently entered the metaverse with their own spaces, such as Louis Vuitton, Givenchy, Kenzo, Tommy Hilfiger, Ralph Lauren, American Outfitters, Timberland, Forever 21, PUMA and Adidas (Cedrola et al., 2024). Despite the significant activity and increasing investments of fashion brands in the metaverse, and the share of clothes and items created by fashion houses, we have found that they do not dominate the market share of the metaverse digital fashion in this world full of stimuli and user-generated content. For example, in Fortnite, branded skins by Balenciaga, Nike, and Moncler currently represent less than 1%

of all outfits available, while in Roblox, the combined number of Gucci, Ralph Lauren, and Tommy Hilfiger items is less than 100, compared to the hundreds of thousands of skins available in the shop (Zając & Jordan-Kulczyk, 2022). Moreover, due to the creative nature of metaverse users and to openness to players' creations, there is an also enormous quantity of counterfeit luxury items in the metaverse, reproducing the problem of counterfeiting with non-original branded products online too. For example, unauthorised luxury products have been spotted for sale on virtual platforms like Roblox, including unauthorised Chanel blazers and Cartier "love bracelets".[7]

Furthermore, these digital-to-physical (D2P) and physical-to-digital (P2D) technologies offer platforming for use in manufacturing in the real world, while data integration in this context will lead to Industry 4.0 or Fashion 4.0 (Periyasamy & Periyasami, 2023). Another distinctive instance of the pragmatic applications of non-fungible tokens concerns the digital fashion domain.

In this context, the fashion brand Fabricant[8] released the Iridescence Dress in 2019, which was the first dress to be exclusively digital and use blockchain technology. Its initial sales value was $9500 USD, but was destined to grow, since this was a collectible, a unique piece. Similarly, an RTFKT-designed digital jacket was sold at an online auction in 2022, achieving a price of over $125,000 (Periyasamy & Periyasami, 2023).

Various fashion labels that are already very active in the metaverse, including LVMH, Dior, Hermès and Marc Jacobs, together with Gucci and Burberry have considered or already launched NFTs attached to their real products. In fact, NFTs allow real purchases to be tracked using blockchain technology. Not only does this allow product authenticity to be certified, but it also facilitates accountability and traceability for logistics, customer service, and possible disposal or resell, extending the product's life cycle (Raman & Edwin Raj, 2021).

[7] https://www.marks-clerk.com/insights/articles/fashion-disputes-in-the-metaverse/.

[8] https://www.thefabricant.com/about—From their Manifesto: "We're building a new fashion industry that belongs to creators, one where we remove history's gatekeepers and create a new economy where our financial rewards are finally equal to our talent".

Fashion R&D, Technology and the Metaverse: The State of the Art

Researchers see the metaverse from a range of angles, and it is important to share their views in order to emphasise the aspects that this idea—as well as the technology ecosystem—creates and makes possible, outside of the domain of business and marketing literature. The metaverse is an ecosystem that consists of technology, identity, participation, socialisation, experience, and norms, as seen through the lens of social structure (Chen et al., 2024). Moreover, the metaverse might be viewed as a "new type of digital economy" from an Internet technology standpoint (Bai, 2022). A plethora of metaverse applications have also emerged in the fields of cognitive interaction, business, industry, education, culture, and the digital economy (Zhao et al., 2022).

With the emergence of the metaverse and its establishment as a mainstream term, companies are presented with a wide range of new opportunities for innovation in technology and business models. While definitions may vary, the metaverse has been described as "a massively scaled and interoperable network of real-time rendered 3D virtual worlds that can be experienced synchronously and persistently by an effectively unlimited number of users" (Zabel et al., 2023). The attributes of the metaverse are: continuity (or persistence) of identity and objects; a shared environment; the use of avatars (or embodied selves); synchronisation; being three-dimensional (or virtual); interoperability, and an interactive, immersive, and social user experience (Kim, 2021; Kraus et al., 2023). The metaverse is an environment based on a number of emerging technologies, such as: virtual reality (VR); artificial intelligence; blockchain; non-fungible tokens (NFTs), and the Internet of Things (Zabel et al., 2023).

As the main body of digital cultural industry development, metaverse companies play a crucial role in driving industry transformation, fostering cultural industry modernisation, and facilitating digital innovation. To date, research on the metaverse is mainly concerned with conceptualisation, potential applications in gaming, film and media production, education and business (Jaung, 2022; Thomas et al., 2023), acceptance of the metaverse and factors that can influence it. However, research on the innovative efficiency of companies in the metaverse is very scarce. Government subsidies and incentives are the subject of the study by Chen et al. (2024). This issue is critical, as research and innovation are crucial to the competitive advantage of companies that focus on the technological frontier and metaverse.

The metaverse may have the potential to expand technological development and product innovation opportunities, thanks to the inclusion of customer-led development and co-creation routines. However, Zabel et al. (2023) show that this direction may often face problems of accessibility to these technologies and resources, depending on the size of the company. This is because larger companies often invest resources in exploring/experimenting with the metaverse, while smaller companies face resource constraints and opportunity costs. As a result, while larger firms invest substantial resources and formalise their innovation activities in these sectors, smaller firms facing resource constraints may engage in sensing activities and bricolage behaviour, and short-term actionability over long-term strategy. Furthermore, the authors summarise the main challenges in reaching new customers. For BtoC firms the priority is to estimate demand, while for BtoB firms the main challenges are to predict demand for some of the multiple use cases in the metaverse and to estimate the willingness to pay for these innovations (Zabel et al., 2023). In any case, the metaverse is an ecosystem, a concept, and a space for strategic and operational manoeuvring for companies. There is currently no evidence of successful collaborations between users and companies in the field of research and innovation, although all the conditions for this to happen seem to be in place (Linde et al., 2021), especially in the fashion industry.

Sayem (2022) maps out four main themes of innovation in digital fashion in the academic literature: Digital design and e-prototyping; Digital business and promotion; Digital human and metaverse, and Digital apparel and smart e-technology. Särmäkari and Vänskä (2021) hypothesise that tomorrow's fashion designers will be "cyborg designers 4.0", comparing physical and digital craftsmen, such as generative garment design using machine learning (ML) and artificial intelligence (AI)-assisted fashion sketching. This is consistent with the direction of design and the development of pure digital garments as tradable assets in the NFT era of fashion design, which has implications for both business and fashion design education. Moreover, Chakraborty et al. (2021), propose a deep learning approach to train machines in automatic print defect detection for real deployment in the textile printing industry, facilitating the digitalisation of the full cycle of fashion product development. There is also still room for further implementation of the integration of Artificial Intelligence (AI) in textile process control in the near future.

Additionally, three-dimensional (3D) printing technology is a direct approach to efficiently converting a digital entity into a physical one, particularly in the design and prototyping of fashion accessories (Sayem, 2022). The lines between physical and digital design are becoming increasingly blurred, as evidenced by the development of 3D fashion design software for the construction of digital design tools in both industrial and educational applications. These programs, like Clo3D or Browzwear, have the ability to create digital representations of fashion companies that are more realistic, imaginative, and intricate than ever before. This may help fashion firms reach new heights and benefit from many advantages across their value chains, because they facilitate communication with potential customers as well as brand suppliers, improving accuracy and speed, and minimising waste generated by extensive sampling, as well as saving labour and resources (Wetherell et al., 2023).

The repetition of the "design-evaluation-adjustment" phases through physical prototypes is both time- and resource-intensive. Consuming materials, generating waste, and having a negative impact on the environment. This means that prototyping and the creation of innovative fashion designs are delicate processes and particularly sensitive to sustainability considerations (Wang et al., 2023). As a result, an interdisciplinary field called "garment e-MC" (e-mass customisation) is gaining more attention for its approach, which involves fabrics, styles, and human body shapes to synthesise them through the use of virtual reality (VR), optimisation, and problem-solving techniques like machine learning (ML) and many more.

Conclusions

Business and research are now looking to the metaverse as a driver for fashion companies and to issues of innovation, technology, design improvement, openness and collaboration with external stakeholders, current and potential customers, and content creators both on the metaverse and beyond. The metaverse makes it possible to reach otherwise unattainable customer segments with global potential and to capitalise on trends such as active user participation—especially in gaming experiences and immersive virtual realities. It can also boost networking by bringing expertise and the necessary collaboration with strategic partners and network nodes from a competitive, technological, and creative point of view. This advanced way of working with digitalisation, not only in the interaction phase with the customer, but also in the design, creation, and distribution phase, through blockchain technology, NFTs, and other related computational technologies to generative and computational artificial intelligence, is increasingly seen as leading to significant competitive advantages for larger and smaller fashion companies.

Although the priority in the fashion industry appears to be for manufacturing, design, operations, safety and testing, there is significant room for growth—especially in the metaverse—in the areas of marketing, product placement, product demos, product testing and try-on, enhanced virtual and physical shopping, and brand experience (Azemi & Ozuem, 2023; Rejoult, 2022). From this point of view, new technologies related to the metaverse, and its manifestation offer various opportunities for intervention and innovation. In particular, with the application of blockchain technologies and digital fashion it would be possible not only to integrate requests from consumers-users-designers, but also to co-design with supply chain partners, anticipating problems, optimising design and innovation processes, and limiting the use of materials, samples and waste.

Therefore, the metaverse can act as much more than the ultimate platform for reaching consumers, and for how its interactive and immersive potential can serve as a test bed for physical and digital fashion house collections and items. Fashion will be increasingly permeated by consumer demand for stimuli and a seamless experience between online and offline, and technologies will continue to drive this direction, even in the face of consumers' increasing focus on sustainability. These circumstances create huge opportunities for all players in the fashion supply chain in terms of competitiveness and technology.

Finally, some key statements are provided for the continuation of the research and indications for fashion companies, detailed below.

- Future studies could analyse and propose theoretical frameworks that summarise the contribution of the metaverse as a platform and as a technological ecosystem to the fashion supply chain.
- Businesses should make the best use of the metaverse as an ecosystem of technologies not only for the management of operations, sales and customer experience, but also to exploit areas such as R&D, innovation and logistics, strengthen relationships in the supply chain, and maximise returns and opportunities from technological investments, thanks to the technology-sustainability combination. This can boost competitive advantage, thanks to a strategic approach towards the metaverse, entailing customer experience technologies, blockchain, and VR for design, implementation and customer testing, ML and AI for problem solving and optimisation, all of which can be used to the full with BtoB applications.
- Businesses should benefit from the ever-increasing customer willingness to participate and be involved in fashion brands. These are aspects to leverage not only in terms of marketing but also in innovation, R&D and ICT, in an open innovation logic.
- The impact of the metaverse on sustainability will need to be explored in terms of technology, servers, and emissions. It must also be examined in positive terms, such as the lack of waste, reduced emissions and errors, and in general, the investments that can lead to competitiveness and greater collaboration between companies in the metaverse, technological partners, established and emerging fashion brands.
- Businesses should use the metaverse from a sustainable perspective, also considering the possible applications for internal and external stakeholders. These can include training and welfare of employees and onboarding of candidates; the creation of collaborations and partnerships with cultural institutions and local authorities for the promotion

of culture and community; the promotion of healthy, sustainable lifestyles, characterised by diversity, equity and inclusion (DEI) for employees, customers, and stakeholders.

Thus, the use of the metaverse in business has a very promising future. Would you wear it? This question, which until now fashion brands answered with market research, which in any case did not shelter them from inventory, can now be answered in new ways. This applies especially to younger populations who—at least on paper—pay more attention to the future of the planet they live on.

References

Abbate, S., Centobelli, P., Cerchione, R., et al. (2024). Sustainability trends and gaps in the textile, apparel and fashion industries. *Environment, Development and Sustainability, 26*, 2837–2864. https://doi.org/10.1007/s10668-022-02887-2

Amed, I., Balchandani, A., Barrelet, D., Berg, A., D'Auria, G., Rölkens, F., & Starzynska, E. (2023, November). *The state of fashion 2024, McKinsey.* Retrieved May 29, 2024, at The State of Fashion 2024 report | McKinsey

Azemi, Y., & Ozuem, W. (2023). How does retargeting work for different Gen Z mobile users? *Journal of Advertising Research*, 2023-023. https://doi.org/10.2501/jar-2023-023

Cedrola, E., & Giovannetti, M. (2024). Fashion and gamification. *Digital transformation for fashion and luxury brands: Theory and practice* (pp. 423–442). Springer International Publishing.

Cedrola, E., Kulaga, B., & Pomi, G. L. (2024). Blockchain: technology transforming the fashion industry. *Digital transformation for fashion and luxury brands: Theory and practice* (pp. 27–46). Springer International Publishing.

Chakraborty, S., Moore, M., & Parrillo-Chapman, L. (2021). Automatic defect detection for fabric printing using a deep convolutional neural network. *International Journal of Fashion Design, Technology and Education.* https://doi.org/10.1080/17543266.2021.1925355

Chen, L., Xiaohan, X., Weidong, H., & Weiwei, Z. (2024). The evaluation of innovation efficiency and analysis of government subsidies influence—Evidence from China's metaverse listed companies. *Technological Forecasting & Social Change, 201*, 123213.

Giano, A. (2022). Gli NFT sono il futuro della moda? Secondo Gucci, sì. *Vogue World Paris.* Retrieved June 07, 2024, at Gucci Vault presenta la collaborazione con SUPERPLASTIC | Vogue Italia

Hazan, E., Kelly, G., Khan, H., Spillecke, D., & Yee, L. (2022, May). *Marketing in the metaverse: An opportunity for innovation and experimentation.* McKinsey Quarterly. Retrieved May 27, 2024, at https://www.mckinsey.com/capabilities/growth-marketing-and-sales/our-insights/marketing-in-the-metaverse-an-opportunity-for-innovation-and-experimentation

Janmark, J., Marcos, I., & Wiener, E. (2024). *Sustainable style: How fashion can afford and accelerate decarbonisation.* Retrieved June 17, 2024, at https://www.mckinsey.com/industries/retail/our-insights/sustainable-style-how-fashion-can-afford-and-accelerate-decarbonization/

Jaung, W. (2022). Digital forest recreation in the metaverse: Opportunities and challenges. *Technological Forecasting and Social Change, 185*, 122090. https://doi.org/10.1016/j.techfore.2022.122090

Kim, J. (2021). Advertising in the metaverse: Research agenda. *Journal of Interactive Advertising, 21*(3), 141–144. https://doi.org/10.1080/15252019.2021.2001273

Kraus, S., Kumar, S., Lim, W. M., Kaur, J., Sharma, A., & Schiavone, F. (2023). From moon landing to metaverse: Tracing the evolution of technological forecasting and social change. *Technological Forecasting and Social Change, 189*, 122381. https://doi.org/10.1016/j.techfore.2023.122381

Linde, L., Sjödin, D., Parida, V., & Wincent, J. (2021). Dynamic capabilities for ecosystem orchestration A capability-based framework for smart city innovation initiatives. *Technological Forecasting and Social Change, 166*, 120614.

Ozuem, W., Ranfagni, S., Willis, M., Rovai, S., & Howell, K. (2021). Exploring customers' responses to online service failure and recovery strategies during Covid-19 pandemic: An actor–network theory perspective. *Psychology & Marketing, 38*(9), 1440–1459.

Ozuem, W., & Willis, M. (2022). *Digital marketing strategies for value co-creation: Models and approaches for online brand communities.* Palgrave Macmillan.

Ozuem, W., Willis, M., Ranfagni, S., Howell, K. E., & Rovai, S. (2023). Examining the role of social media influencers in service failure and recovery strategies: An empirical investigation of millennials' views. *Information Technology & People*. https://doi.org/10.1108/itp-05-2022-0371

Ozuem, W., Willis, M., Howell, K., Ranfagni, S., & Rovai, S. (2023). Examining user-generated content, service failure recovery and customer–brand relationships: An exploration through commitment-trust theory. *Internet Research*. https://doi.org/10.1108/intr-07-2022-0580

Panhans, D., Joniškis, P., Tamer, F., & Saunier F. (2021, December). *Gaming & esports: Media's next paradigm SHIFT*. Business Consulting Group. Retrieved May 29, 2024, at Gaming & Esports Sector Is The Next Frontier for Media | BCG

Periyasamy, A. P., & Periyasami, S. (2023). Rise of digital fashion and metaverse: Influence on sustainability. *Digital Economy and Sustainable Development, 1*(16), https://doi.org/10.1007/s44265-023-00016-z

Raman, R., & Raj, B. E. (2021). The world of NFTs (non-fungible tokens): The future of blockchain and asset ownership. In *Enabling blockchain technology for secure networking and communications* (pp. 89–108). IGI Global.

Rejoult. (2022). Comprehensive overview on metaverse. Retrieved May 29, 2024, at https://rejolut.com/blog/a-comprehensive-overview-on-metaverse/

Särmäkari, N., & Vänskä, A. (2021). 'Just hit a button!'—Fashion 4.0 designers as cyborgs, experimenting and designing with generative algorithms. *International Journal of Fashion Design, Technology and Education*. https://doi.org/10.1080/17543266.2021.1991005

Sayem, A. S. M. (2022). Digital fashion innovations for the real world and metaverse. *International Journal of Fashion Design, Technology and Education, 15*(2), 139–141.

Statista. (2023a). *Luxury goods—Worldwide*. Retrieved May 29, 2024, at Luxury Goods - Worldwide | Statista Market Forecast

Statista. (2023b). *Metaverse: Market data & analysis Market Insights report, Statista Marketing Insight*. Retrieved May 29, 2024, at Metaverse: market data & analysis | Statista

The Business of Fashion. (2021). The State of Fashion 2021 Report: Finding Promise in Perilous Times|BoF. Retrieved May 29,2024, at http://businessoffashion.com/

Thomas, N. J., Baral, R., Crocco, O. S., & Mohanan, S. (2023). A framework for gamification in the metaverse era: How designers envision gameful experience. *Technological Forecasting and Social Change, 193*, 122544.

Wang, Z., Tao, X., Zeng, X., Xing, Y., Xu, Z., & Bruniaux, P. (2023). Design of customized garments towards sustainable fashion using 3D Digital simulation and machine learning-supported human–product interactions. *International Journal of Computational Intelligence Systems, 16*, https://doi.org/10.1007/s44196-023-00189-7

Wetherell, S. V., Nicholson, T. R., & James, A. M. (2023). Utilising 3D fashion design software to enable remanufacturing in sportswear. *International Journal of Fashion Design, Technology and Education*, 1–11. https://doi.org/10.1080/17543266.2023.2277254

Zabel, C., O'Brien, D., & Natzel, J. (2023). Sensing the Metaverse: The microfoundations of complementor firms' dynamic sensing capabilities in emerging-technology ecosystems. *Technological Forecasting & Social Change, 192*, 122562.

Zając, O., & Jordan-Kulczyk, K. (2022). *Metaverse sustainability in fashion. Opportunity or threat?* Boston Consulting Group. Retrieved May 29, 2024, at https://www.bcg.com/publications/2022/rise-of-metaverse-fashion-and-sustainability-impact similarities and machine learning-supported [illegible] product interactions. [illegible] *Journal of Consumer* [illegible] https://doi.org/10.1007/s41236-023-00189 [illegible]

[illegible]

10

Social Media Influencers: Transition from Fast Fashion to Slow Sustainable Causes

Wilson Ozuem and Michelle Willis

Introduction

Social media influencers (SMIs) are associated with marketing strategies designed to facilitate collaborations between brands and influencers with the intention of promoting products or services and encouraging audiences to communicate to build customer engagement with brands. SMIs foster digital lifestyles and skills to become opinion leaders who inspire individuals to adopt behaviours and perspectives in accordance with the influencer's (Kim & Chakraborty, 2024). Fashion SMIs and brands exchange support to maintain their market sustainability. Fashion brands offer SMIs monetary incentives, including sponsorships, and

W. Ozuem (✉)
Business School, University for the Creative Arts, Epsom, UK
e-mail: wilson.ozuem@uca.ac.uk

M. Willis
Guildhall School of Business and Law, London Metropolitan University, London, UK
e-mail: m.willis@londonmet.ac.uk

W. Ozuem et al. (eds.), *Sustainable Digital Marketing for Fashion and Luxury Brands*,
https://doi.org/10.1007/978-3-031-82467-8_10

ambassadorship benefits that give them a platform of market status and influence. In return, fashion SMIs offer brands platforms and digital spaces to place their products, promote giveaways and other forms of digital campaigns (Ozuem & Willis, 2022), and give them access to micro- and mega-communities to extend their market reach.

Fashion brands continue to invest significantly in SMIs from a variety of influencer backgrounds, from personality presenters and designers, to social fashion influencers. Hugo Boss partnered with Senegalese Italian influencer Khaby Lame under a $450,000 contract to feature in their rebrand campaign, co-design a collection, and attend the 2022 Milan Fashion Week (The Business of Fashion, 2024). Yet, despite the growing investment in the influencer industry, its sustainability is threatened by social resistance and criticism of SMIs involved in marketing campaigns. According to the Business of Fashion (2024), 65% of consumers had become less reliant on fashion influencers prior to 2024. With the emerging trend of AI-generated systems, digital audiences are debating the authenticity and originality of SMIs and the sponsorship status that accompanies SMI content. Consequently, fashion brands have had to pay more attention to attracting followers through organic means. This includes attracting fashion SMIs who feel relatable and authentic to the audience, as well as providing fashion SMIs with creative control and value that extend beyond financial incentives. To achieve this requires critical awareness of how fashion SMIs maintain their digital sustainability, the criteria online audiences apply to authenticate SMIs, and the goals and motivations of fashion SMIs that affect their presence and performance in the social marketplace of the fashion industry. The following chapter sections examine these factors and the impact they have on fashion brands' digital sustainability.

Determining Fashion SMIs' Sustainable Influence

Following influencers is one of the most common activities that social media users engage in as part of the time they spend online and consuming digital content. Yet in the digital environments where significant numbers of influencers populate the online user community, SMIs compete to retain their audiences' attention in an effort to continue obtaining the financial and social benefits from follower counts and traffic.

The fashion industry comprises SMIs of diverse demographic and psychographic backgrounds who are further segmented by the roles they play for the fashion industry and social media community. SMIs are further categorised by their follower count: the smallest generated for nano-influencers (1000 to 10,000) and the largest and most wide-reaching generated by mega- or celeb-influencers (500,000 or more). Social media has made online community presence more attainable to audiences and extended the marketing role beyond firm-based personnel; this had led to the need for a more comprehensive identification and characterisation of influencers to determine their potential to sustain their SMI status and fashion brands' online presence and value propositions.

The process of determining fashion SMIs' digital sustainability performance involves applying the criteria that followers use to characterise SMIs and consideration of the personal attributes associated with influencers that determine their role and delivery within the online fashion community. Masuda et al. (2022) argued that while influencers determine their personal attributes, it is the followers' evaluation that determines the persuasion of a fashion SMI's portrayal and the messages they attempt to communicate to their audience. However, although followers' characterisation of SMIs is the major factor determining SMIs' level of influence, SMIs' personal attributes act as important signals that support followers' assessments of an influencer's degree of engagement that indicates their potential to be sustainable influencers in digital environments. Personal attributes are attitudes, character traits, and physical characteristics that can personalise or differentiate fashion SMIs from each other;

personal attributes are examined in Sect. 11.4, which defines the types of SMIs specific to the fashion industry and their social media practices. The criteria that followers use to characterise SMIs include their ability to engage, and their perceived expertise and trustworthiness. These factors act as antecedents that influence followers' evaluation and characterisation of SMIs and can be generally applied to all types of fashion SMIs and the content they develop. Although there is an extended list of criteria used by followers to characterise fashion SMIs, this chapter narrows these down to five critical factors that reflect essential practices and qualities portrayed by SMIs to obtain an impactful count of followers and engage them in their social media activities.

Five Critical Factors that Followers Use to Characterise Fashion SMIs

Engaging Content

SMIs are most associated with the term "content creators", which refers to the act of creating digital media content and sharing the content on digital platforms. Although the term "content creators" is associated with SMIs' content-producing activities, it has led to misconceptions concerning the difference between influencers and creators. The main goal of influencers is to engage and build communities, whereas creators might develop their content without intending to develop a SMI status or following. Creators develop content through various formats, such as photography or videography, writing, storytelling, poetry, and other forms of artistry, for personal leisure, creative expression, or as part of their job profession; their content can be classified as professionally created.

Creative content practices can coexist with the social media practices of fashion SMIs, but the level of media and creativity richness they apply is subject to the activity they are promoting through their influencer channels. For example, a fashion SMI showcasing their day-to-day lifestyle and consumption might use basic content creation tools and features, particularly templates created and provided by social media platforms, with an informal approach to developing and distributing the content. In contrast, a SMI's attendance at an important event, a specified outfit selection, styling, or review, or involvement with a sponsor, may require more critical research, planning, and content format selection. Although fashion SMIs are not expected to specialise in content creation or develop content that embeds rich media, they are expected to develop content that is impactful on audience engagement and keeps their followers' focus away from other fashion SMIs.

Responsible Content

Fashion SMIs are able to offer their distinct voice and perspectives through their content that can either centre on their personal lifestyle or a broad fashion category. Some of this content can influence purchasing behaviours towards specific fashion branded products or influence consumption behaviours and attitudes to various fashion brand segments. Social media has made the fashion industry more accessible and provided more opportunities to distribute informative and entertaining content. However, social concerns related to social media activities and the user community create additional factors that influencer marketers and fashion SMIs need to accommodate in their content planning and creation. SMIs are expected to take responsibility for their day-to-day social media activities. Responsibility also applies to the extent of ethical obligations that SMIs uphold when planning their content creation and promotion for online audiences.

Ozuem et al. (2023) examined the extent to which SMIs can be held responsible for any negative experiences that social media users had with a product or brand previously endorsed by the SMI. Examples include content that contains inaccurate product disclosure that may lead followers to experience bodily harm or financial losses from fashion-related products. Users may assign blame to the SMI if they fail to address or justify the incidents that impacted the followers, especially if there was a transactional exchange between followers, brands, and SMIs. This assignment of responsibility also extends to the social impact of fashion SMIs' content. In an effort to showcase hedonic lifestyles, fashion

SMIs promote content or messages that could potentially be harmful to audiences, such as body image and lifestyle dissatisfaction, or undermine efforts to overturn external issues or barriers, such as environmental sustainability, or other consumption behaviours of the fashion industry that have a negative impact on communities. Therefore, as fashion SMIs harbour a level of influence over their audience, the behaviours and attitudes that emerge from their online activity and community are likely to be associated directly with the SMI's voiced perspectives and behaviours.

Authenticity

The rich media and messages reflected in SMIs' content are not critical to sustaining fashion SMIs' long-term influence over their follower community. Even the most professional and rich-looking content does not guarantee that social media users will respond favourably to the fashion SMI. Although the reasons why many social media users resist content created and facilitated by fashion SMIs vary for each social media user, there are two main reasons. The first is online users' general habit of spontaneously scrolling through social media platforms, which reduces their attention to specific fashion SMIs. The second reason is users' interpretation of the SMI as an online source. The first reason is linked with continuous adaptability, as users may gradually increase their attention to individual fashion SMIs following repeated encounters. In contrast, the second reason entails a more complex understanding of users' responses and behaviours towards fashion SMIs, as it is coupled with users' immediate scrolling behaviours and their spontaneous and mixed evaluation of the encountered fashion SMI.

A user who encounters a fashion SMI may instinctively conduct an evaluation to determine the fashion SMI's credibility and authenticity. Although the practices of establishing credibility and authenticity are interdependent, they are affected by different personal attributes of fashion SMIs. A user identifies an influencer as credible when they are able to establish that the information the influencer provides is trustworthy and believable (Melnychuk et al., 2024). Whereas a user perceives an influencer to be authentic when they perceive the influencer to be genuine and true to the personal attributes they reflect through online content and activities (Ozuem et al., 2023). A fashion SMI's motivation for conducting their online activities can also signal their authenticity. For example, if a fashion SMI indicates a significant personal interest in the fashion industry or other related topics, then their audience may perceive the SMI to be authentic. However, if the audience perceives a lack of personal interest in a fashion SMI's content, then the audience may assign ulterior motives to the SMI, such as seeking only to gain more followers and a higher online status or to gain financial incentives provided by influencer sponsorship programmes. Given the increasing legal requirements that necessitate influencer posts to include #ad or #sponsored, SMIs' transparency and authenticity are constantly threatened by public criticism. Although the followers of fashion SMIs value and appreciate the status of influencers that distinguishes them from other online users, a fashion SMI's authenticity remains a critical factor that could impact their digital sustainability and how followers will evaluate their digital content.

Community Management and Giving

In cultivating a community of followers, the influencer's role as a content creator or facilitator extends to managing relationships and engagement with their audience. Social media users develop the habit of repeatedly viewing the same content and other visiting behaviours that gradually motivate them to become followers to specific fashion SMIs. This is achieved when influencers ensure that the content of their social media activity engages the audience and reflects attributes that indicate they are responsible influencers. Eventually, online users build a sense of assurance that the fashion SMI is both credible and authentic. These characteristics cause followers to consider fashion SMIs as individual people, rather than passive virtual agents, which enables them to develop a sense of intimacy and form pseudo-friendships with SMIs (Hwang & Zhang, 2018).

A pseudo-connection stabilises contact between individuals, although the individuals may never meet in person or even exchange direct messages with each other. This is a common occurrence between followers and fashion SMIs, especially for mega-influencers or celebrity influencers. A report by HubSpot indicated that 80% of brands' marketers recruit content creators or influencers with less than 100,000 followers, with the remaining continuing to recruit mega-influencers or celebrity influencers who attract roughly 1 million followers (Iskiev, 2023). According to an article by American business magazine, *Forbes*, influencers with a smaller follower audience have higher credibility associated with their online content and messages because their content and messages are tailored to the interests of their niche audience (Belsky, 2024). As a result, several fashion brands have taken to targeting nano-influencers (1000 to 10,000 followers) or micro-influencers (10,000 to 100,000 followers) for their effective audience targeting and engagement, as well as the personal attributes their audiences associate with nano-SMIs' and micro-SMIs' content.

A fashion SMI is responsible for communicating and managing the responses of their audience throughout their content creation and implementation. However, authentic pseudo-relationships are formed when SMIs demonstrate their acknowledgement of, and engagement with, the responses generated by their audience. This includes replying to questions directed to them and addressing discussions occurring between groups of their followers. It is expected that followers will also contribute by responding to comments posted by audience members, but this is dependent on the SMI's prior commitment to fostering valuable connections with their followers at the early stages of their social media activities.

Fashion SMIs' management responsibilities also extend to the manner in which they give back to their community of followers. Arguably, although fashion SMIs can display significant efforts and dedication to develop their influencer career, it is the engagement and positive support generated by the followers they attract that determines the effective sustainability of their status, activities, and influence. For these reasons, as fashion SMIs grow in the influencer community and attract financial and social benefits, they may develop a sense of obligation to return favourable rewards to their followers. This can range from creating and delivering exclusive content or giveaways to their entire follower community, or creating shout-outs or exclusive gift-giving to specific individual followers. Each fashion SMI will conduct different levels of community giving activities depending on their activities, sponsorship agreements, and their resources and financial positioning. However, all fashion SMIs are required to effectively monitor and manage their community to maintain their sustainable presence in the online marketspace and influencer community.

Professionalism

Despite the skills, knowledge, and experience that fashion SMIs can readily bring to initiate their influencer career, a key critical factor that has a significant impact on SMIs' sustainability is their professional or unprofessional behaviour and conduct. This factor builds on the previous discussion of fashion SMIs' development of responsible and authentic content directed towards their community. However, professionalism extends beyond SMIs' personal attributes and content, which are specific to their fashion and social media activities, to include their commitments to employee contract arrangements and their conduct towards stakeholder groups, industries, and other relevant parties in the macro-level environment.

In an effort to maintain their own professional image, and maintain effective work ethics, fashion brands seeking to recruit fashion SMIs set clear requirements and standards under contract agreements for influencer programmes. This requires fashion SMIs to maintain professional interview and negotiation skills, as well as a commitment to upholding contractual agreements, which are commonly expected across multiple industries. Influencer programmes are a form of human resource investment, as well as a marketing investment, therefore fashion brands will expect prospective influencers to conduct themselves in a professional manner to ensure both financial and social returns from the contractual arrangements. Like any job interview, influencer recruiters will take note of the personal attributes that signal an individual's professionalism, work ethic, and willingness to work in a team. Recruiters' criteria for influencer employment will vary depending on the brand and the requirements aligning with the intended influencer programme. Some may target influencers because of the perceived fit between the brand and fashion image attributes of the SMI, while others may select an SMI based on their ability to stand out, advocate, or be an outspoken member of their online community. Beyond the desired personal attributes, recruiters would consider the manner in which an influencer would conduct themselves when engaging with their followers as they promote and review a brand. Although a fashion SMI would be expected to provide honest and authentic reviews through their content, their choice of words and product display can have an impact on the image of the brand. Thus, the selection of fashion SMIs will come with criteria linked to professionalism when sponsored arrangements are involved.

Even for non-sponsored social media activities, fashion SMIs need to display professionalism in their social media arrangements, expressed messages, and the actions they perform outside their influencer activities. The fashion industry has faced criticism concerning their association with attitudes and behaviours perceived as toxic to society, as well as unprofessional, such as racism, which resulted in calls by online users to hold influencers and brands accountable for such conduct (Lawson, 2021). Consequently, fashion SMIs can become the subject of various debatable topics, some of which benefit SMIs' digital sustainability, but others less so. Fashion SMIs are also categorised as key players in sustainability practices connected to the fashion industry, which causes them to become a central topic of online discussions. Such online discussions bring audiences' attention to how SMIs respond to these discussions. Some SMIs may choose to remain silent, while others may actively engage. Whichever pathway the SMI chooses, they have to critically consider the manner in which they engage in the discussion and prepare for multiple responses from the wider audience that might lack professionalism.

Types of Fashion SMIs

Generally, SMIs can be defined and categorised by their number of followers and the content genre they create and publish on their social media platforms. While follower count, content, and the critical factors previously discussed relate to all SMIs, fashion SMIs can be further distinguished by fashion business models, the occupation the influencer holds within the fashion industry, and the relationship the influencer has with fashion brands. This section identifies four categories of SMIs that represent varying occupations and influencer roles in the fashion industry, and the types and level of engagement they conduct through social media.

Presenters and Designers as Fashion SMIs

Since the mid-2000s, fashion brands have been relying on a range of digital platforms and technologies (Ozuem et al., 2024) to promote their upcoming collections, present highlights of significant events, and provide audiences with access to the lifestyle and values of celebrity fashion designers and presenters. For this reason, social media management has evolved into an extra activity for presenters and as an alternative career pathway for fashion designers who have evolved into fashion influencers. Presenter individuals may have worked for reality television, either as contestants or as presenters of the show, and gradually developed a following that would attract fashion sponsorship deals or discussions around the presenter's fashion lifestyle. Trinny Woodall, before she became a mega-influencer with over one million followers, began her career providing a weekly style guide for *The Daily Telegraph* and became a co-host and fashion advisor for five series of the BBC's *What Not to Wear* programme.

Designers may have begun their career by learning textile and design skills with the intention to work for fashion brands or develop their own clothing line. Some began their careers working as models, or as interns with existing fashion brand designers, or as personalised stylists for influential individuals, before advancing to become independent fashion designers and brand owners. Over time, in an effort to market themselves to prospective audiences, these designers develop their social media profiles and content to inform audiences of their designs and to promote existing users' consumption of their designs to build their online follower community.

Early fashion designers, like Victoria Beckham, Donatella Versace, and Tom Ford, would have relied on traditional marketing displays of fashion, including catwalk events, and magazine and newspaper tactics. These same designers would gradually develop their social media platforms; thus, enabling their fans to develop closer connections with them as individuals and follow the work they contribute to the industry. More recently discovered designers, who made their debut in the late 2000s, like Sohee Park and Nigel Xavier, arranged their social platforms to generate viral exposure of their collections in their early career as independent designers. In particular, Park's first collection, "The Girl in Full Bloom", was intended to be displayed at an official show, which was cancelled due to the COVID-19 pandemic. Park released pictures of her floral-styled pieces through Instagram, which enabled her designs to go viral on social media during the global pandemic. Gradually, her designs were published on fashion magazine covers and editorials, and her pieces were worn by a variety of celebrities, including Ariana Grande and Gemma Chan. Xavier achieved public recognition as the winner of the Netflix reality show and fashion design competition series, *Next in Fashion*, winning $200,000, and a place to launch his collection on Rent the Runway (Kessler, 2023). During the competition, the number of Xavier's Instagram followers doubled, which led him to become a mega-influencer within the fashion industry and design for musician clients.

Fast and Luxury Fashion SMIs

Individuals in the fast and luxury category of fashion SMIs often create and publish on social media to initiate their influencer activities, which they do as a hobby alongside their educational or work commitments, or as an intended long-term career. As the category implies, SMIs may choose to associate their influencer content with a particular fashion style category, including casual or formal wear, which can be generally narrowed down to the fast or luxury sector. Fast and luxury fashion brands represent different characteristics related to perceived quality, price, level of perceived inclusivity to target audiences, production levels, and adaptability to market trends (Azemi & Ozuem, 2023; Yoo, 2023). The common factor that bridges these two fashion categories is the similarity between the social media behaviours influencers conduct to represent the clothing, accessories, and brands of the fast and luxury sector. Consumers of both these fashion categories can be frequent purchasers of their products, and consumers of brand-related information and events. This gives fast and luxury fashion SMIs opportunities to develop regular and real-time content that enables them to continue building or maintaining their follower community.

Fast Fashion SMIs

A fast fashion SMI centres the majority of their content on frequent fashion, accessories, and make-up purchases. Fast fashion has a shorter lifecycle compared to luxury fashion, and it changes quickly when new trends and demands emerge in the consumer market. Fast fashion also comes with prices considered very affordable compared to luxury brands' prices (Joung, 2014), which prompts customers to conduct regular purchases for a variety of products and adapt their wardrobe to match new fashion market trends. For fast fashion SMIs, this means they need to develop content that regularly displays their consumption of new fashion products and styles to sustain the attention of their online audience. This content would emphasise fast fashion-specific factors, including disclosures of newest and specific styles, and promotional information, such as price affordability. As the fast fashion industry strongly aligns with the aim to provide consumers with a variety of choices at different price points, the SMI may concentrate less on discussing the personal attributes of brands or on displaying a commitment towards a particular brand. Some fast fashion SMIs develop content in which they wear the styles and products of two different fashion brands separately, with the intention to directly compare the two brands' product offers. Other SMIs may develop content that is specific to a fashion brand or combine multiple brands when arranging their styles. In the maturity stage of their social media activities, fast fashion SMIs may gradually increase their focus on specific brands if they engage in specific affiliate programmes or attract sponsorship deals from fashion brands. However, they will continue to create and present content that presents new styles and product purchases as part of their main social media activities.

Luxury Fashion SMIs

Luxury fashion SMIs create and distribute social media content to an extent similar to fast fashion SMIs, but orientate their content around factors specific to the luxury sector. Luxury fashion is perceived as having an extended seasonal lifecycle, and to harbour attributes that reflect premium product quality, rarity, heritage, artistry, high pricing, and exclusivity to specific customer segments (Amatulli et al., 2021). Although marketers of luxury brands develop content to signal their products and visually display attributes of the brand, they consider how their audience will react to communications related to product promotions. To maintain favourable brand impressions, luxury brands recruit fashion SMIs to advocate the qualities and attributes of their products. Luxury fashion SMIs value the personal experiences and social status luxury brands bring to them, which they channel through their social media activities. Like the luxury brands they wear, they critically consider the manner in which they display and discuss the products they consume. They provide their followers with exclusive information and close access to products they directly purchased or were gifted by brands, and communicate their real-time engagement with the branded products. Additionally, luxury fashion SMIs display their day-to-day activities; they make subtle disclosures of events or venues they are attending that align with their selected outfits or personal attributes associated with a luxury brand. This gives audiences the opportunity to be part of personal luxury experiences and it increases recognition of brands through the luxury fashion SMI's posted content.

Slow Fashion SMIs

Slow fashion SMIs are a sub-category of influencers who develop content specific to portraying or discussing sustainability issues and practices on social media. Sustainable fashion encompasses several factors, including financial and environmental concerns about clothing production, the social and working well-being of textile workers and communities, and the consumption cycles and recycling economy of fashion pieces. The definition and characteristics of sustainable fashion are often applied to the "slow fashion" category (Jacobson & Harrison, 2022). Slow fashion acts as a philosophy that alerts people to various stakeholders and macro-environment factors impacted by the fashion industry (Pookulangara & Shephard, 2013). It is also the implementation of sustainable practices by fashion designers and companies, such as localising production and selling, applying fairness and equal treatment to their labour forces, and developing environmentally and socially responsible clothing products. Consumers can contribute by adjusting their consumption habits, such as purchasing newly created sustainable fashion products or selling and repurchasing existing fashion products, which is aligned to the pre-owned or second-hand fashion categories.

This category of fashion gave rise to SMIs who create content portraying their perspectives of, and commitments to, sustainable fashion practices. In a similar manner to luxury fashion SMIs, slow fashion SMIs frequently incorporate aspects of their day-to-day life into their content, such as narrating their experience with sustainable fashion consumption habits and their usage of fashion products marketed as sustainable. SMIs within the slow fashion category vary in terms of sustainability commitment and discussions and can generally be categorised into three groups: sustainable lifestyle influencers, sustainable influencers, and thrifting influencers (Jacobson & Harrison, 2022). Sustainable lifestyle influencers portray themselves as being influenced by sustainability trends inspired by sustainable influencers (Jacobson & Harrison, 2022). They generally engage in various topics of discussion in their social media content to intimate sustainability or how they aspire to become more sustainable, as well as to attract wider audiences with different interests connected to sustainability. In contrast, sustainable influencers display significant commitment and passion towards sustainability fashion. They directly commit to living a sustainable lifestyle and attempt to educate and encourage their audiences to adopt similar practices in the long term. Thrifting influencers display engagement with sustainable fashion practices that motivate consumers to comply for the financial benefits. These SMIs display habits such as second-hand or pre-owned selling and purchasing, partnering with companies including fast fashion companies that appeal to low-budget customers, or providing creative tips or life-hacks that allow consumers to experience social and financial benefits of fashion. Each of the three groups attracts positive engagement and criticism from prospective audiences, who, like them, have varying ideas about the appropriate level of applying sustainability to their fashion consumption and varying commitment to sustainability. Thus, slow-fashion SMIs will vary the levels of their discussions about sustainability according to their intended audience.

Social Fashion SMIs

Social fashion SMIs are a sub-category of SMIs that can be combined with any of the previous fashion categories, particularly fashion presenter and designers, and luxury and slow fashion SMIs. These SMIs develop and share content specific to portraying or discussing social and cultural issues and practices linked to social fashion. Social fashion is related to the consideration of physical clothing designs, signs, and symbols that reflect social and cultural meanings and positions. Throughout the twenty-first century, fashion companies and designers have been criticised for underrepresenting or misrepresenting consumer groups of various ages, body shapes and sizes, physical disabilities, gender identities, sexual orientation, and racial and cultural attributes. Discussions on fashion brands' and designers' ethical behaviour towards product designs and marketing messages have centred on the beauty standards and norms set by the fashion industry, and the portrayal of social groups by fashion companies, designers, and media channels, which have led to some groups being marginalised both financially and socially.

For every social group, there are different factors that contribute to the unequal or unfair treatment they experience from the fashion industry on a micro- and macro-environmental scale and the initiatives that social fashion SMIs take to confront these issues. For example, fashion consumers of various body types and sizes have often had limited access to all-size inclusive clothes; this limits their ability to experience a wide range of styles and products promoted by fashion influencers who may fit the ideal body image that fashion designers develop their products for. Some fashion brands and designers took the initiative to ensure their collections could be inclusive for various sizes, but faced a challenge in gaining consumers' trust and confidence. This gave rise to the plus size influencers, also labelled as curve influencers, who act as both formal and informal ambassadors in an effort to build trust and confidence between fashion brands and audiences. Plus size influencers demonstrate ways in which fashion products can be worn and styled according to the wearer's body shape and size. Similar actions have been taken by members of the feminist and LGBTQIA+ communities who advocate for clothing representation that resists social conventions related to the fashion industry, and to normalise the inclusion of clothing styles to wider audience segments (McCann, 2017; Saha et al., 2021).

Social movements developed to resist institutional barriers and actions that marginalised individuals of racial and cultural groups across the globe gave rise to fashion designers whose collections were inspired by their cultural heritage and values. Between July 2022 and April 2023, the UK-based Victoria and Albert Museum organised an exhibition presenting African fashions. The event showcased pieces inspired by past and current textile artistry of various regions of Africa. It was attended by designers representative of African communities, including haute couture fashion designer Imane Ayissi and Nigerian stylist and creative director of IAMISIGO, Bubu Ogisi (Victoria & Albert Museum, n.d.). Denesuliné and Canadian fashion designer, Sage Paul, integrated themes of family, sovereignty, resistance for balance, as well as symbols, styles, and images of indigenous heritage into her collections. At a TEDx Talk 2020, she expressed concerns of dominating beauty norms and standards accepted by Western audiences, and cultural appropriation behaviours conducted through exploitation of non-Western nations' cultures to develop and profit from fashion trends without crediting or including representative members of those cultures (TEDx Talks, 2020). She uses her platform to support other creative designers of Indigenous heritage and to sustain their traditional practices in fashion. Like several fashion designers across the globe, Ayissi, Ogisi, and Paul attracted followers to their online communities. However their follower count ranges from 2000 to 50,000 across their social media platforms, which effectively makes them a nano- or micro-influencer. This arguably reflects their intention to focus their influence on audiences with an interest in fashion and causes they are dedicated to, which indicates that social fashion SMIs can have a significant impact on social movements regardless of the volume of their follower community.

Fashion SMIs' Collaborations with Fashion Brands

A significant volume of collaborations are expected to occur between fashion brands and retailers and fashion SMIs that contribute to achieving marketing investment returns in terms of brand awareness, market share, and product sales. The diverse population of SMIs attracted to the fashion industry has led to the generation of social media content that draws fashion consumers' attention to various fashion brands and retailers; thus, contributing to their long-term sustainability. Each collaboration reflects different goals and returns based on the relationship between the fashion SMI and the brand. Notable fashion SMI collaboration programmes can be identified through the social media marketing content of ASOS and Clothing Cider, who seek to employ a wide range of SMIs to enhance their reach to micro-communities. Other companies have advanced their influencer collaborations by actively engaging them in their marketing sustainability initiatives; these company examples are discussed in the next subsections.

Micro-influencer Programmes: ASOS and Clothing Cider

Online fashion retailers' brands like ASOS (www.asosplc.com/) and Shop Cider (www.shopcider.com/) have been key drivers in shifting the usage of sponsored social media posts, to building networks of sponsored influencers to increase the reach and engagement of fashion customers. As well as targeting mega-influencers, these two brands have predominantly targeted nano- and micro-influencers to enhance the organic traffic and engagement of online audiences to achieve a global market share within the online fashion industry. ASOS and Clothing Cider offer SMIs sponsorship and affiliation programmes in an effort to motivate them to participate in marketing strategies to influence consumers' perspectives; ASOS and Clothing Cider do this because consumers can have negative sentiments towards traditional methods of advertising, which are often perceived as impersonal and commercially motivated. With the backing of these programmes, fast fashion SMIs are able to generate organic user traffic towards online platforms for fashion brands, which increases potential sales and word of mouth by fashion consumers. With micro-influencers, companies like ASOS and Clothing Cider have a greater possibility of engaging a range of niche communities with content that is personal or targeted towards the micro-audience and reducing the perceived generalisation of fashion marketing messages and offers.

ASOS's influencers can be identified by the hashtag #AsSeenOnMe, and Shop Cider's influencers can be noted through the hashtags #shopcider, #cidergang, and #cidercurve. Prospective ASOS influencers can sign up to affiliate programmes organised by affiliate agents partnered with ASOS. ASOS affiliate programmes allow influencers to target either global markets or localised markets, including the UK, USA, New Zealand, Australia, Malaysia, China, Singapore, Thailand, and India. Each programme offers different levels of commissions that allow influencers to earn between 0.5 and 6% from successfully leading new and existing customers to purchase branded products they promoted. Additionally, ASOS implemented the ASOS Insiders programme in an effort to recruit key individuals who reflect individual styles and identities, and who exude authentic passion, have a knowledge of fashion, and exert a genuine influence on their audience or community. Shop Cider, in addition to directly sponsoring influencers' social media content, offers CiderGang, a gifted collaboration programme where influencers receive free product samples in exchange for promoting their products. Shop Cider also promotes the #cidercurve ambassador programme, which invites influencers to promote and enhance online shopping experiences with products that are size inclusive.

"Voices of a Re:Generation"—Andrew Burgess and Puma

Sustainability is a fundamental part of the fashion industry; however, not all fashion brands are able to effectively appeal to their target audience solely using their in-housed marketing efforts to promote their sustainability efforts and achieve long-term sustainability. These brands have adopted collaboration strategies by recruiting fashion SMIs to directly participate in both the promotion and practices of their brand's sustainable initiatives.

US upcycler Andrew Burgess is a slow fashion SMI known for his content depicting his creations of new clothes using second-hand materials through his TikTok channel @wandythemaker. While generally categorised as a sustainable influencer, Burgess's content fundamentally focuses on designing clothing that appeals to consumers of the retro sports market using unused or damaged textile material (Bauck, 2021). Burgess owns a small clothing product range, which is custom made using second-hand quilt material, sold under the brand name VIVID VISIONS (https://vividvisions.shop/). Sport and casual wear company Puma launched a campaign titled, "Voices of a Re:Generation", and invited four individuals with creative, fashion, and influencer backgrounds to assist in actively implementing sustainable innovations to enhance Puma's sustainability initiatives (Fibre2Fashion, 2023). As one of the invited influencers, Burgess created a sport wear collection using Puma's recycled polyester RE:FIBRE fabric with a blend of futuristic fashion and retro sport designs. In an interview, Burgess commented that his collections were inspired by the need to combine futuristic aspirations with Puma's past and present brand concepts and designs as an initiative to allow them to advance further into the future (Puma, 2024). This collaboration reflects attempts to achieve key sustainable practices not only for the slow fashion industry, but for long-term sustainability for clothing and fashion brands. The decision to recruit young aspiring fashion SMIs implies that Puma's goal is to extend their appeal to the younger demographic audience by projecting styles that appeal to them and environmental sustainability values.

Simons IFWTO x Edito Collection

Fashion SMIs who also work as designers, entrepreneurs, and as official spokespersons within the fashion industry have the potential to influence others and to attract industry players to participate in fashion events and collaborations. Sage Paul, the previously discussed social fashion SMI, is an example of an influencer who used her platform to attract and facilitate Indigenous designers from Canada to official events, including showcases commencing during the Milan Fashion Week (Allaire, 2023). Paul's aim was to build networks between artists, prospective international buyers and traders, and media agents to enable Indigenous designers to benefit through business opportunities and to expand knowledge of the artistry and designer culture of the designers' communities.

Collaborative efforts between social fashion SMIs and fashion designers, who rely on their social media platforms to portray their activities, optimise their level of search mentions and user traffic generation. These efforts increase the possibility of their content becoming noticed by fashion brands and retailers, who often seek fashion designers and SMIs for future business and marketing ventures and investments. Simons, a Canadian fashion retailer based in Quebec City, showcased a clothing line that highlighted the works of designers from a variety of Indigenous communities in a collaborative project based around the Indigenous Fashion Week Toronto (IFWTO) titled the IFWTO x Edito collection (Droganes, 2020). This collaboration specifically highlights the significance of SMIs using their platform to support social movements that impact the relevant social groups. Furthermore, the collaboration specifically addresses the importance of implementing social-related fashion collaborations effectively and responsibly by ensuring that relevant social groups are key contributors to the communications and that fashion brands and retailers retain their marketing and digital sustainability authentically and ethically.

Conclusion and Managerial Implications

Fashion brands' investments in SMIs will continue to remain important for digital sustainability, and fashion SMIs will continue to convey fashion brands' sustainable practices. However, criticism of influencers' conduct and the financial incentives provided by brands signifies that influencers will be required or expected to develop beyond having a platform to distribute content to qualify as SMIs for fashion brands. The profile and character of each SMI will vary according to their interests and target audience; each will be required to reflect a degree of authenticity to increase engagement generated through their content. An increase in the number of visible sponsorship disclaimers displayed alongside the content of fashion SMIs can negatively impact audiences' evaluation of a fashion SMI's content, despite the requirement for brands and influencers to signal legal and ethical practices in their digital marketing. Sponsored tags next to content can cause audiences to perceive marketing attempts to persuade purchasing acquisitions. Individuals with such reactions may have had a negative experience following a purchase inspired by an influencer campaign, thus making them susceptible to negative perceptions of sponsored content.

Yet sponsored content is not limited to purchase or promotion communications, it can include social publications, like influencers' daily lives through vlogs, content aiming to answer follower-published questions, the sharing of consumption experiences and advice, and the encouragement of community challenges. Such content can also include mentions of fashion brands without disrupting the original narrative of the SMI's content. Such approaches are commonly associated with organic or unpaid content, which can be utilised in sponsored content to increase the perceived naturalness of the fashion SMI and the brand collaboration. SMIs' effective achievement of the discussed five critical factors that followers use to characterise SMIs will be pivotal to enhancing online audiences' positive perception of online content created as part of a collaboration between fashion SMIs and brands. Ensuring that a fashion SMI reflects the ability to engage and acts responsibly and professionally towards their online communities and influencer obligations will enhance their digital sustainability beyond implemented digital marketing campaigns. In circumstances where fashion brands are associated with a negative message by online audiences, the pre-created equity of fashion SMIs could be a key foundation on which to maintain fashion brands' positive online presence, and it could potentially increase positive responses and evaluations with little reliance on further paid or sponsored marketing communications.

References

Allaire, C. (2023). How Sage Paul is bringing indigenous talent to Milan fashion week. *Vogue* [Online]. Available at https://www.vogue.com/article/sage-paul-indigenous-designers-milan-fashion-week [Accessed 10 March 2024].

Amatulli, C., De Angelis, M., Sestino, A., & Guido, G. (2021). *Omnichannel shopping experiences for fast fashion and luxury brands: An exploratory study.* In F. Mosca, C. Casalegno, & R. Gallo (Eds.), *Developing successful global strategies for marketing luxury brands* (pp. 22–43). IGI Global.

Azemi, Y., & Ozuem, W. (2023). How does retargeting work for different Gen Z mobile users? *Journal of Advertising Research*, 2023-023. https://doi.org/10.2501/jar-2023-023

Bauck, A. (2021). TikTok is shaping how Gen Z sees 'sustainable' fashion. *Financial Times* [Online]. Available at https://www.ft.com/content/9d0cb6ba-5303-410b-bd5d-78b9ac3010a0 [Accessed 6 March 2024].

Belsky, I. (2024). Four ways to level up your influencer marketing in 2024. *Forbes* [Online]. Available at https://www.forbes.com/sites/forbestechcouncil/2024/01/31/five-ways-to-level-up-your-influencer-marketing-in-2024/ [Accessed 6 March 2024].

Droganes, C. (2020). Canadian retailer simons unveils indigenous design platform. *Women's Wear Daily* [Online]. Available at https://wwd.com/feature/canadian-retailer-simons-indigenous-design-platform-1203630322/ [Accessed 10 March 2024].

Fibre2Fashion. (2023). Puma launches 'Voices of a Re:Generation' initiative. *Fashion Network* [Online]. Available at https://uk.fashionnetwork.com/news/Puma-launches-voices-of-a-re-generation-initiative,1504572.html [Accessed 10 March 2024].

Hwang, K., & Zhang, Q. (2018). Influence of parasocial relationship between digital celebrities and their followers on followers' purchase and electronic word-of-mouth intentions, and persuasion knowledge. *Computers in Human Behavior, 87*, 155–173.

Iskiev, M. (2023). *HubSpot's 2023 social media marketing report* [Data from 1000+ Global Marketers]. HubSpot [Online]. Available at https://blog.hubspot.com/marketing/hubspot-blog-social-media-marketing-report?hubs_content=blog.hubspot.com%2Fmarketing%2Finfluencer-platforms&hubs_content-cta=social%20media%20trends%20survey [Accessed 8 March 2024].

Jacobson, J., & Harrison, B. (2022). Sustainable fashion social media influencers and content creation calibration. *International Journal of Advertising, 41*(1), 150–177.

Joung, H. M. (2014). Fast-fashion consumers' post-purchase behaviours. *International Journal of Retail & Distribution Management, 42*(8), 688–697.

Kessler, A. (2023). Why the next in fashion winner is worthy of every bit of hype. *British Vogue* [Online]. Available at https://www.vogue.co.uk/fashion/article/next-in-fashion-season-2-winner-nigel-xavier [Accessed 8 March 2024].

Kim, H. M., & Chakraborty, S. (2024). Exploring the diffusion of digital fashion and influencers' social roles in the Metaverse: An analysis of Twitter hashtag networks. *Internet Research, 34*(1), 107–128.

Lawson, C. E. (2021). Skin deep: Callout strategies, influencers, and racism in the online beauty community. *New Media & Society, 23*(3), 596–612.

Masuda, H., Han, S. H., & Lee, J. (2022). Impacts of influencer attributes on purchase intentions in social media influencer marketing: Mediating roles of characterizations. *Technological Forecasting and Social Change, 174*, 121246.

McCann, H. (2017). *Queering femininity: Sexuality, feminism and the politics of presentation.* Routledge.

Melnychuk, H.-A., Arasli, H., & Nevzat, R. (2024). How to engage and attract virtual influencers' followers: a new non-human approach in the age of influencer marketing. *Marketing Intelligence & Planning* (in press).

Ozuem, W., Ranfagni, S., Willis, M., Salvietti, G., & Howell, K. (2024). Exploring the relationship between chatbots, service failure recovery and customer loyalty: A frustration–aggression perspective. *Psychology & Marketing* (in press).

Ozuem, W., & Willis, M. (2022). Influencer marketing. In *Digital marketing strategies for value co-creation.* Palgrave Macmillan. https://doi.org/10.1007/978-3-030-94444-5_10

Ozuem, W., Willis, M., Ranfagni, S., Howell, K., & Rovai, S. (2023). Examining the role of social media influencers in service failure and recovery strategies: An empirical investigation of millennials' views. *Information Technology & People* (in press).

Pookulangara, S., & Shephard, A. (2013). Slow fashion movement: Understanding consumer perceptions—An exploratory study. *Journal of Retailing and Consumer Services, 20*(2), 200–206.

Puma. (2024). *Puma X Vivid vision by Andrew Burgess: A textile-to-textile fashion experiment.* [Online]. Available at https://about.puma.com/en/newsroom/news/puma-x-vivid-visions-andrew-burgess-textile-textile-fashion-experiment [Accessed 10 March 2024].

Saha, I., Akanksha, & Basu, D. (2021). *Androgynous fashion from the concept to consumers: An empirical study.* In A. Chakrabarti, R. Poovaiah, P. Bokil & V. Kant (Eds.), *Design for tomorrow*—Volume 1. ICoRD 2021. Smart Innovation, Systems and Technologies (vol. 221). Singapore.

TEDx Talks. (2020). *Your clothes are the most political choice you make every day, Sage Paul, TEDxToronto* [Online]. Available at https://www.youtube.com/watch?v=TYJVK13RVo8 [Accessed 5 March 2024].

The Business of Fashion. (2024). *The year ahead: The alluring new face of influencer marketing.* [Online] Available at https://www.businessoffashion.com/articles/marketing-pr/the-state-of-fashion-2024-report-influencer-marketing-brand-partnerships-content-creators/ [Accessed 13 March 2024].

Victoria & Albert Museum. (n.d.). *About the Africa fashion exhibition* [Online]. Available at https://www.vam.ac.uk/articles/about-the-africa-fashion-exhibition [Accessed 5 March 2024].

Yoo, J. J. (2023). Visual strategies of luxury and fast fashion brands on Instagram and their effects on user engagement. *Journal of Retailing and Consumer Services, 75*, 103517.

11

Repositioning of Chinese Luxury Spirit: Kweichow Moutai

Xialiang Yao

Introduction

The environment of luxury is continually evolving while the characteristics of consumers are changing. Understanding potential customers' emerging needs and habits is a primary objective for luxury companies. Kweichow Moutai, China's iconic liquor producer, has always held a leading position in the high-end market. However, after a staggering decline (by more than half) in China's total liquor production over the past six years (CADA, 2023), Moutai realised that this trend indicated a shift in consumer preferences, with the most affluent demographic, Millennials and Gen Zs, turning away from baijiu, the traditional

X. Yao (✉)
School of Economics and Management, Hunan Institute of Science and Technology, Yueyang, Hunan, China
e-mail: 12012022@hnist.edu.cn

W. Ozuem et al. (eds.), *Sustainable Digital Marketing for Fashion and Luxury Brands*,
https://doi.org/10.1007/978-3-031-82467-8_11

Chinese distilled white spirit.[1] Moutai's customers in the high-end market are mainly middle-aged and older adults, but the size of this group is gradually shrinking. With the rise of the younger generations, Moutai needed to find ways to appeal to this consumer group and reposition its strategy to enhance brand sustainability.

To expand its reach among younger consumers, Moutai embarked on a series of co-branding initiatives, which started in 2022, to change brand awareness. One of the most influential and widespread on social media was "Jiangxiang Latte" (baijiu flavoured coffee), which was co-branded with Luckin (a Chinese coffee chain). The popularity of this innovative drink shows that co-branding can bridge the generation gap and revitalise brand perception; this approach paves the way for continued relevance and success in a highly competitive consumer market. Brand collaboration was just one part of Moutai's repositioning strategy. Knowing the profound impact online social networks (OSNs) have on the post-80s and 90s generations, Moutai not only increased its exposure on various social media platforms, but also relaunched its e-commerce business with the "iMoutai" digital marketing app to broaden its online brand community (OBC) for long-term growth. Through marketing and strategic deployment, Moutai has gradually transformed its brand image and built a new brand relationship with the younger generations.

One of the objectives of this chapter is to explore how traditional high-end brands can build brand relationships with younger generations. A recent luxury global consumer report revealed that the personal luxury goods market among younger generations (Millennials and Gen Z) witnessed a remarkable surge in value, and this remarkable growth trajectory is projected to continue, with forecasts indicating that the market will double in size by 2026 (BCG & Altagamma, 2023). Consequently, attracting and retaining Millennial and Gen Z consumers has

[1] Baijiu has often been directly translated as "white spirit", sometimes called "Chinese wine" or "Chinese spirit". It is a type of distilled spirit produced using traditional Chinese techniques and has long needed an official English name. To better promote baijiu in the international market, the China Alcoholic Drinks Association adopted "Chinese Baijiu" as its official English name in 2017 and has used it widely in different contexts. The name was officially changed in 2019 as part of the "Terminology of the Baijiu Industry" revision. With the efforts and promotion of academics, the term "Chinese Baijiu" is gradually gaining recognition among international industry experts and consumers.

become paramount for luxury brands across diverse categories to ensure continued success and growth.

The Concept of Luxury

Even though definitions of "luxury", "luxury brand" and "luxury marketing" are not provided in the dictionary of the American Marketing Association, scholars across diverse fields maintain that grasping the concept of "luxury brands" remains of paramount importance (Ko et al., 2019). The concept of "luxury" was pointed out to be relative in nature (Mortelmans, 2005) and it changes over time (Cristini et al., 2017). These characteristics have led to a lack of clarity in defining, operationalising and measuring luxury (Miller & Mills, 2012). Moreover, Godey et al. (2012) claimed that although the concept of luxury is not subjective by nature, its definition and measurement are highly subjective. Thus, researchers have been calling for a more precise definition of luxury marketing (Berthon et al., 2009) and luxury brands (Ko et al., 2019).

Ko et al. (2019) proposed that a definition of luxury brand that captures the concept should meet three conditions: be based on a sound conceptual foundation, be broadly applicable to all categories of luxury brands and measurable in an operationalised way. Building on these conditions, Ko et al. (2019, p. 406) proposed that:

> A luxury brand is a branded product or service that consumers perceive to: 1) be high quality; 2) offer authentic value via desired benefits, whether functional or emotional; 3) have a prestigious image within the market built on qualities such as artisanship, craftsmanship, or service quality; 4) be worthy of commanding a premium price; and 5) be capable of inspiring a deep connection, or resonance, with the consumer.

Therefore, in addition to its high value in terms of money and quality, luxury exhibits a range of other attributes like emotion, originality, innovation and elite communication (Giachino et al., 2021). The expenditure on, or possession of, a luxury product can go far beyond its physical equivalent and take on a symbolic dimension (Kapferer, 2015). Perceptions and definitions of luxury are dynamic and evolve with societal trends and cultural shifts. As consumer demographics and behaviours change, a large portion of purchasing activity is shifting to online channels. It is crucial for luxury brands to recognise and adapt to these trends in order to remain competitive in a rapidly changing market.

Moutai's Brand Heritage

In relation to the concepts and attributes of luxury brands presented in the previous section, Moutai possesses five features that assure its luxurious status: (a) cultural significance, (b) global visibility, (c) uniqueness and rarity, (d) high price and (e) investment value.

Steeped in Chinese tradition, Moutai boasts a remarkable history that stretches back centuries (Li & Wu, 2024). In addition to being a famous brand, it is deeply embedded in Chinese culture and has become a highlight of significant celebrations. Beyond that, its frequent use in state banquets and diplomatic events further enhances its recognition and reputation for prestige on the international stage (Liu, 2021).

Other than the cultural significance, its traditional production methods also contribute to its rarity (Ren & Wu, 2024). Its distinctive flavour comes from a unique brewing process and techniques that UNESCO recognised as "intangible cultural heritage" (Zhang & Zhang, 2021). Moutai liquor is produced under rigorous quality control measures and processes and is subject to limited production capacity (Xinhuanet, 2023). The scarcity of authentic Moutai liquor contributes to its exclusivity and makes it highly sought-after by collectors and connoisseurs. Moutai liquor commands a premium price, with an official retail price of approximately RMB 1499 per bottle. However, market prices often surpass this figure due to high demand and scarcity (Ma & Chen, 2022). Collectors and investors view Moutai liquor as an asset with significant appreciation potential (Ma & Chen, 2022). Over time, rare varieties can experience substantial value increases, which makes them an appealing investment opportunity.

Moutai's Challenges

Despite Moutai's long history of high brand awareness, the brand does not have as much of a presence in the younger demographic compared to middle-aged and older adults who are more influenced by the traditional Chinese drinking culture (Wang, 2024). Young people seem to have little interest in traditional liquor. According to the "Alcohol Industry Development and Competitive Situation Analysis Report in China 2023–2024" (iiMedia Research, 2023), a detailed and professional report on the alcohol industry and its consumer market, the primary consumer base for alcoholic beverages in China is exhibiting a gradual trend towards younger demographics. The report forecasts that this trend will continue to drive new changes in the liquor market. The research data in the report showed that in 2023, the highest proportion of Chinese alcohol consumers was in the 31 to 40 age group, accounting for 49.78%, followed by the 18–30 age group, accounting for 39.13%. Analysts of the report believe that the consumption patterns and values of younger consumers exhibit personalised and diverse characteristics. These new generational consumer traits will drive the liquor industry to undergo transformations in brand building, product development, value proposition shaping, marketing strategies and innovative promotion to cater to the preferences of Millennial and Gen Z consumers (iiMedia Research, 2023). This view coincides with what Smith and Brower (2012) have previously argued: generational differences in values and consumption patterns can influence corporate strategic choices.

Despite being a frontrunner in China's liquor industry, Moutai shares the challenge of shifting consumer demographics and behaviours with other baijiu companies and luxury brands. According to the "Mid-Year Research Report on China's Baijiu Market in 2023" issued by the China Alcoholic Drinks Association (2023), the consumption of baijiu has undergone significant structural differentiation due to the economic environment and consumer sentiment. The liquor industry and market are entering a new round of adjustment and are expected to exhibit a slow growth trend.

Since 2023, leading liquor firms have begun to expand their product portfolios into lower-tier markets; thus, further squeezing the survival space of small and medium-sized enterprises (SMEs). From a market structure perspective, sales and growth rates of high-end baijiu brands have weakened; they have failed to match the performance of the same period in 2022. Additionally, due to slow market turnover and high inventory levels, both first- and second-tier baijiu prices have experienced varying degrees of decline. Taking Moutai as an example, during the 2023 Spring Festival, the prices of mainstream products fell by around 200 yuan compared to the same period in the previous year.

The traditional liquor industry has transitioned from a phase of incremental growth to stock competition. From a production perspective, since the industry's revival in 2016, the rapid expansion of high-quality production capacity among leading enterprises has accelerated the elimination of SMEs and outdated production capacities.

The Chinese baijiu industry has witnessed a significant consolidation phase that has been characterised by a decline in the number of baijiu enterprises and their annual outputs. From 2018 to 2022, according to iiMedia Research (2023), the number of baijiu enterprises above scale (industrial legal entities with annual revenue of 20 million yuan and above) nationwide decreased by 33% (from 1445 to 963). This consolidation trend is further reflected in the substantial decline in total output. From 2016 to 2022, the output of baijiu enterprises above scale nationwide plummeted by 50% (from 135.8 million kilolitres to 67.1 million). These figures underscore the mounting pressure of oversupply in the whole industry.

For the year 2023, Chinese consumers' preference for beer, wine, baijiu and imported spirits was 73.68%, 67.57%, 59.17% and 33.43%, respectively. As a representative of baijiu, Moutai started to realise that young people today prefer beer and different types of wine. Baijiu is connected with traditional Chinese drinking culture, such as toasting, social bonding and drinking manners at the table, which is not popular among many of today's young people (Wang, 2020; Zhao, 2014). Even Jiang Xiaobai, a baijiu brand that targets young people that used to be popular and was quite successful in marketing for a time, is no longer able to retain its consumer base, and sales continue to decline (Jiemian, 2021; Sina, 2022).

For many years, there has been a saying in the industry: "Young people don't drink baijiu". Since its inception in 2011, Jiang Xiaobai targeted its products at the younger generation. In catering itself to the likes of young people from product design to consumption scenarios, it has been differentiating itself from traditional liquor brands. According to Tao Shiquan, the founder of Jiang Xiaobai: "It's not that young people don't like to drink baijiu, but that traditional liquor has abandoned young people in terms of products and brands" (Sina, 2022, para. 8). However, in 2020, its market share plummeted from 20% at its peak to 0.5% in less than a year (Sina, 2022).

Although the decline in sales of Jiang Xiaobai had a certain relationship with the epidemic, according to Wu (Sina, 2022) the company had only focused on developing offline channels and began its online sales deployment after 2020. Unfortunately, it was too late by then, as the company's failure to cultivate a strong OBC ultimately resulted in its inability to sustain its already low customer engagement and retention during the epidemic. This shows that choosing a distribution strategy is also a challenge for the liquor industry that cannot be ignored. The current external environment makes it impossible for brands in the luxury sector to remain confined to a single distribution channel (Giachino et al., 2021). The integration of online sales with shops and social media is strategically crucial for these brands (Kim, 2019).

As Ding Xiongjun, Chairman of the Moutai Group, commented, "Capture the youth, and you capture the future of Moutai" (Guan & Song, 2023, p. 36). To achieve this, Moutai took a two-pronged approach: it built online channels and brand communities while actively transforming its brand image. To enhance its appeal to younger generations, Moutai quickly bound itself to their favourite products, such as ice cream, milk tea and chocolate, opening up a series of diversified explorations. Yet, of all the co-branding attempts, "Jiangxiang Latte" had the biggest impact. This is undoubtedly closely related to Luckin's expertise in utilising social media and understanding how to increase online and offline exposure.

Luckin's Solutions

In less than a decade since opening its first store in October 2017, this young brand has emerged as one of China's largest coffee chains (Ren & Wu, 2024). Luckin Coffee has gone from rapid expansion to being among China's leading coffee chains. Its achievements show that it has succeeded in its strategic choices and marketing techniques. According to Ren and Wu (2024), Luckin's strengths include precise brand positioning, rapid product updates and proactive marketing strategies.

Luckin's brand positioning is characterised by its emphasis on style, convenience and value for money (Ren & Wu, 2024). Accurate brand positioning has helped the company gain a better foothold in the market. Luckin Coffee's primary clientele comprises young professionals and students residing in urban areas. These individuals are characterised by aesthetic sensibilities and their pursuit of trendy lifestyles, which Luckin strives to match through shop design, brand identity and product offerings. To provide consumers with a more convenient purchase experience, most of Luckin's shops are located in commercial districts, office buildings and shopping malls. The company also opened an online ordering and delivery service, which allows consumers to order their products with mobile phones without waiting in line. Moreover, Luckin's beverages are priced at an average of 16 yuan per cup, with weekly discounts offering cups for as low as 9.9 yuan. These prices are significantly lower compared to those of Starbucks and other international chain brands.

To sustainably engage consumers and create heat, Luckin launches new products much faster than other beverage brands. In 2021, Luckin launched about 100 new products per year, producing an average of 2.2 per week, a growth rate far outpacing its competitors (Tencent, 2022). Starbucks launched 38 new products in the same year, with a weekly frequency of 0.7 new products. Even though Luckin launched only 55 new products in 2022, this was higher than that of other chain beverage brands in the Chinese domestic market (Tencent, 2022). According to Ren and Wu (2024), the market success of this brand depends on its continued product innovation.

Before launching new products, Luckin generates online buzz and engages consumers through social media activities. These activities aim to pique consumer interest and anticipation for the upcoming product release. For instance, Luckin uses Weibo, a popular Chinese microblogging platform, to interact with consumers by offering free coffee samples to those who follow and share their posts about the new product.

These strengths made Luckin a perfect partner for Moutai to collaborate with to establish a new relationship with younger generations.

Generational Differences in Consumption Patterns

Generational theorists suggest that a generational cohort can influence consumption behaviours (Giachino et al., 2021); therefore, there is a growing interest in analysing industries through the lens of different generations (Chen & Shoemaker, 2014). Four generational cohorts are often considered: baby boomers (1940–1959), Gen X (1960–1979), Gen Y/Millennials (1980–1994) and Gen Z (1995–2010). On the other hand, Chinese generational studies on consumer behaviour typically categorise consumers into cohorts based on their birth decades (Zhu, 2024), such as the post-80 s generation, which refers to individuals born between 1980 and 1989. This classification is also widely used in marketing practices, such as promotion targeting strategy choice. According to Wen and Cai (2019), from the perspective of macro consumer groups and micro consumer behaviour, the post-80s and post-90s generations have become the leading force in China's luxury consumer groups.

Based on D'Arpizio and Levato's (2014) research on worldwide luxury consumers, as the country with the third largest consumer base and the second highest spending, China has the biggest market for luxury consumption, while it is also a self-contained and dynamic market with very diverse consumer characteristics. As the detachment of young consumers, especially the post-80s and post-90s generations, poses a concern for future consumption in the liquor market (Li & Wu, 2024), baijiu companies are starting to reposition their strategy by targeting consumers born after 1980 (i.e., Gen Y and Gen Z).

Marketers often lump Millennials in with Gen Z consumers, although they are alike they have different needs and hold different perspectives (Fromm, 2023). Gen Y, or Millennials, are considered the first generation to use digital tools (Helal et al., 2018). Taking Millennials in the US as an example, according to an investigation by the Pew Research Center (Bialik & Fry, 2019), Millennials bring more racial and ethnic diversity to their society, and Millennial women, like the women of Gen X, are more likely to participate in the US workforce compared to previous generations. On top of that, Millennials are delaying or forgoing marriage and are proving slightly slower to start their own families. Millennials grew up in a period of heightened environmental concern and are therefore potentially sensitive to environmental issues (Straughan & Roberts, 1999). Other than being eco-aware, Eastman and Iyer (2021, p. 567) claim that Millennials are "socially motivated, needing success, achievement and closer peer bonds". Being the most educated, Millennials have strong curiosity and are eager to learn (Bright Horizons, 2021). Their beliefs, values and purchasing decisions have influenced companies' strategies, such as their approach to sustainability (Smith & Brower, 2012).

The youngest generation, Gen Z, represents the first digital native generation and is crucial for the future of many industries. Gen Z represents a significant portion of the market, has money to spend and has significantly changed how companies buy and choose products (Giachino et al., 2021). Like Millennials, Gen Zs are also concerned about environmental issues and they are more likely to demand that brands demonstrate a commitment to sustainability (Fromm, 2023). Being the first generation to live in a digital environment, Gen Z is accustomed to a constant flow of information and is adept at distinguishing between real content and false marketing messages. Fromm (2023) also suggested that they prefer to connect with brands that honestly present themselves and transparently communicate their values. Analysing the relationship between the luxury industry and young generations is crucial to identify their potential impact (Gazzola et al., 2020). By prioritising authenticity, brands can build trust and make genuine connections with Gen Z consumers, which would ultimately lead to more effective marketing efforts.

According to Deloitte's global survey series (2023, 2024) on Millennials and Gen Z, the two generations share some common characteristics that are likely to influence their consumer behaviour. First, financial stress is a major issue for both generations. The high cost of living has become the social issue they are most concerned about, with unemployment and climate change coming in second and third (Deloitte, 2023). It was reported that 32% of Gen Y and 30% of Gen Z feel financially insecure, with more than half of these groups living "paycheck to paycheck" (Deloitte, 2024). Nonetheless, faced with uncertainties in their own countries, many feel that while they are unable to influence the overall direction of their own country, they do have power to effect social change on challenges like climate change.

Similar attributes are found in the Chinese context, for example, post-90s individuals exhibit the highest proportion of engagement in green and low-carbon consumption practices out of all the generations (Zhu, 2024). Specifically, 68.7% of them reported frequently purchasing green and low-carbon products, while 58.0% and 55.0% indicated frequently adopting low-carbon practices in product usage and disposal, respectively. Among the post-80s generation, green and low-carbon consumption practices have witnessed a significant increase compared to the post-70s generation and post-60s generation. This growth is particularly evident in areas like waste classification and unused goods disposal.

With growing awareness of sustainability, the concept of luxury has also changed (Giachino et al., 2021). Accordingly, luxury brands need to constantly respond to these changes, not only to take on their social responsibility for the environment, but also to put sustainability into practice in a transparent way (Kong et al., 2021), rather than hyping it up. Transparency can increase trust, which eventually enhances word of mouth (WOM) and electronic-WOM of the brand (Katz et al., 2017).

Another characteristic of Gen Y and Gen Z consumers is that their lives are significantly influenced by OSNs. They have adapted to, and appreciate, the interactive nature of OSNs; they participate in a variety of online activities, such as sharing information and keeping in touch with friends (Xu & Pratt, 2018). The use of OSNs permeates all aspects of people's lives. Take travel, for example, Gen Y and Gen Z rely heavily on OSNs to gather travel information and they often read user-generated content before making travel-related purchases (Xu & Pratt, 2018). The proportion of Gen Y users making online travel arrangements has been increasing: it reached 65% in 2008 (Jones & Fox, 2009). With the rise of social media influencers (SMIs), Xu and Pratt (2018) found that the congruence between perceived images of SMIs and ideal self-images of Gen Y consumers could positively impact regional tourism. These studies reveal the extent to which the younger generation utilises digital platforms for communication and information sharing, particularly their reliance on information from social networks when deciding to make a consumption experience.

Therefore, in addition to actively embracing the values of the younger generations, such as sustainability, luxury brands are also experimenting with online channels and cultivating OBCs to retain young potential clients (Kong et al., 2021). In providing media content, social networking and community engagement, OBCs are able to attract and sustain ties and connections between brands and their customers (Ozuem & Willis, 2022). "In a world disoriented by a global pandemic and embracing e-commerce like never before", digital engagement has become a crucial strategy for marketers to differentiate their brands online (Cioban, 2021, para. 1).

Consumer Behaviour Shifts in the Baijiu Industry

The drinking habits of younger generations exhibit a significant divergence from those of their predecessors; this has created a noticeable age gap among Moutai's consumers (Li & Wu, 2024). Traditionally, baijiu has been associated with social gatherings, business interactions and fostering interpersonal relationships. However, as China's economy has developed and lifestyles have modernised, this "alcohol table culture" has faced criticism from younger generations who increasingly favour a "dining table culture" and health-conscious eating habits.

This generational shift in drinking preferences has led to a decline in baijiu's appeal among younger consumers; younger consumers gravitate towards alternative alcoholic beverages such as wine and cocktails (iiMedia Research, 2023). Additionally, the high price and perceived social status associated with premium baijiu brands like Moutai have created a sense of pressure and exclusivity, which has further alienated younger consumers (Azemi & Ozuem, 2023; Li & Wu, 2024). As a result, the consumption of Moutai is concentrated among older generations, which has created a distinct age gap within its consumer base. According to Roland Berger's report (2016), the post-80s and post-90s generations (Gen Y and Gen Z) comprise only 26% of the baijiu market. This divergence in consumer preferences poses a potential challenge for the future of baijiu consumption.

Traditionally associated with male consumers, baijiu brands have overlooked the significant potential of the female consumer market. The rise of the "she economy" in recent years highlights the growing purchasing power of women. According to a report (Sina, 2021) from 1919, a leading Chinese platform of liquor retail, the proportion of female consumers has experienced a remarkable surge from 4.79 to 19.02% between 2017 and 2021, with an average annual growth rate of 64.48%. The growing presence of young female consumers in the liquor market has further motivated manufacturers of traditionally distilled spirits to cater to this particular demographic.

In today's digital age, technology and social media have empowered customers with a wealth of information and a wider range of choices (Ozuem & Willis, 2022). This has led to a heightened focus on customer experience, as it plays a crucial role in influencing purchasing decisions. As mentioned in the previous section, sustainability is growing as a new form of cultural capital, which according to Kim and Oh (2022) can influence the luxury consumption of materialistic individuals. Individuals with new high cultural capital are transforming into ethical and conscious consumers (Carfagna et al., 2014). As sustainability becomes increasingly important in luxury consumption, many brands (e.g., fashion) are utilising sustainable practices to drive product purchases and enhance brand reputation (Achabou & Dekhili, 2013). In order to change the image of the Moutai brand among these potential consumers, Moutai has also taken an active role in its social responsibility as a leading company by proactively disclosing its sustainability programme. In their latest environmental, social and governance report, Moutai disclosed their efforts and short-term goals in the following four areas: combating climate change, green operations, water resource management and protecting the environment (Kweichow Moutai Co. Ltd., 2023).

Success Through Brand Collaboration

Luxury brands are continuing to seek ways to meet the challenges of volatile and competing markets, sustainability and dealing with shifting consumer perceptions. Collaboration and partnership have become pivotal for sustained success (Bwambale, 2023). One example would be the collaboration between Louis Vuitton and Supreme, which embodies the convergence of high-end luxury and urban culture that reaches a wider, younger demographic (Yu et al., 2020).

To boost in-store traffic and sales, retailers tend to collaborate with manufacturer brands in product promotion (Nguyen et al., 2020). This brand collaboration or co-branding, according to Chang (2009, p.77) and quoted by Mitchell and Balabanis (2021), is "a marketing arrangement to utilise multiple brand names on a single product or service". While numerous business case studies have demonstrated the effectiveness of brand collaborations in expanding brand reach and driving sales (Mitchell & Balabanis, 2021), not all collaborations have yielded significant revenue gains for both parties. Moreover, the value generated through co-branding often exhibits an asymmetrical distribution between collaborators (Nguyen et al., 2020). Selecting the right partner is essential to the success of a collaboration (Mitchell & Balabanis, 2021), and issues like the image fit of parent brands, the brand strength of the retailer, and the fit of product categories cannot be neglected when considering brand collaboration (Banerjee & Drollinger, 2017).

Previous co-branding research indicated that the effect of fit is a significant factor influencing successful co-branding (Mitchell & Balabanis, 2021). In brand collaboration, fit is defined as the level of psychological alignment between two product categories, brands or retailers and "perceived" fit is typically valued in the context (Uggla, 2004). In co-branding initiatives, two established brands join forces and act as the "parent brands" of the collaboration. A successful partnership hinges on a solid fit between these parent brands, as they are often combined to leverage each other's positive image and create a more appealing offering (Mitchell & Balabanis, 2021; Ozuem & Willis, 2024).

Mitchell and Balabanis (2021) explained that co-branding introduces a new dimension of fit beyond the traditional focus on image compatibility between parent brands. While ensuring a strong image fit between parent brands remains important, co-branding success also hinges on the fit between the parent brands' retail categories and the new co-branded product category. Assuming two parent brands collaborate, a fashion brand and a car manufacturer, the critical question is whether the image of fashion aligns well with the car itself (new co-branded product category). This category fit is distinct from the traditional focus on image similarity between the two parent brands.

When choosing a co-branding partner, functional and image fit represent independent dimensions and are not always correlated, so they should be investigated separately (Banerjee & Drollinger, 2017). Furthermore, the match of brand strength within a collaboration is also a crucial factor. Dahlén and Lange (2005) suggested that the strengths of brand collaboration typically enhanced the weaker parent's brands in the case of non-retail product brands.

Moutai's Diversified Co-branding Strategy

At the first anniversary celebration of Moutai Ice Cream, the Chairman of the Group revealed that the company will intensify its efforts to develop products such as liquor-filled chocolate, liquor-containing drinks, popsicles and soft ice cream, with the aim to establish a product matrix characterised by diverse types, varying price points and distinctive features (Guan & Song, 2023). Moutai's strategic layout shows that they are trying to bring their wine and food into people's lives.

Since embarking on a diversified co-branding strategy, Moutai has partnered with a variety of brands from different industries, in addition to young brands like Luckin, to expand its consumer base and redefine its brand image. This approach has yielded remarkable results: it attracted

Table 11.1 Moutai's co-branding strategy (2022–2023)

Date	Co-branding Partner	Product/Initiative	Target audience
May 2022	Mengniu Ice Cream	Moutai Ice Cream	Younger consumers, particularly females
September 4, 2023	Luckin Coffee	"Jiangxiang Latte"	Students, White-collar commuters
September 16, 2023	Dove	Moutai Chocolate	Gift-givers, Chocolate enthusiasts
September 17, 2023	Alibaba's Fliggy	"Feitian Moutai Night"	Luxury travellers, business executives
November 20, 2023	MOJT	"Kweichow" Series of Jiuxiang Cocktails	Cocktail enthusiasts, Baijiu aficionados

younger consumers and enhanced the brand's appeal beyond its traditional target market. Table 11.1 summarises the co-branding initiatives of Moutai in the past two years.

As revealed in Table 11.1, Moutai's co-branding initiatives span various industries, including ice cream, coffee, chocolate, hospitality and cocktails. The target audiences encompass younger consumers, urban office workers, gift-givers, luxury travellers and cocktail enthusiasts. The pricing strategy varies across partnerships and caters to a wide spectrum of consumer segments. The co-branding efforts have effectively enhanced the accessibility of the brand, redefined its image and expanded its consumer base. Behind each of these co-branding initiatives lies Moutai's own strategic logic: audience diversification, price accessibility and expanded distribution channels.

Moutai's co-branding strategy embraces cultural contrasts and targets diverse audiences. For instance, the collaboration with Luckin Coffee caters to students and white-collar commuters, while the partnership with Mengniu Ice Cream targets a younger female demographic. This approach broadens the brand's appeal beyond its traditional base of older male consumers. Moutai's co-branding efforts extend beyond domestic collaborations and reach international markets. The partnership with Dove, a global brand, showcases Moutai's intention to introduce Chinese baijiu culture to a broader international audience. Moutai has strategically reduced its product prices through co-branding; thus, making its offerings more accessible to a broader range of consumers, particularly younger generations. These products include the 59 yuan "Moutai Ice Cream", 29 yuan "Moutai Petite Pops", 19 yuan "Jiangxiang Latte" and 20 yuan alcohol-filled chocolate. By collaborating with fast-moving consumer goods (FMCG) brands, Moutai has gained access to a broader range of distribution channels, which increases its visibility and reach among consumers. This co-branding action series has opened up new avenues for engagement with younger consumers who frequent FMCG product channels.

Jiangxiang Latte: A Strategic Partnership with Luckin

Strategically partnering with Luckin, Moutai officially introduced and promoted the new product on various social media platforms. With the slogan "How hot is this collaboration? 53 degrees!" the product started selling for 19 yuan on 4 September 2023. Featuring Moutai branding and packaging, this innovative drink quickly took social media by storm and generated widespread interest and discussion on a variety of platforms. The bold fusion of two distinct beverage cultures, the traditional baijiu culture of Moutai and the modern coffee experience of Luckin, was a risky step for the luxury brand. Surprisingly, this unique product captured consumers' attention and stimulated coffee lovers' and baijiu enthusiasts' curiosity and interest.

Strategic Significance of Moutai–Luckin Collaboration

This partnership marks Moutai's strategic expansion into a new consumer segment, a market with tremendous growth potential and a young consumer base. Moutai can leverage Luckin's extensive distribution network and brand awareness to build new brand relationships with a broader audience and younger generation of consumers.

Based on the sales figures of the new product, the co-branding is undoubtedly a win–win situation for both parent brands (Wang, 2024). The partnership with Moutai provides an opportunity for Luckin to enhance its brand image and appeal to a more discerning consumer base. Thus, in addition to rapidly growing daily sales in the short term, more importantly, by partnering with an established premium liquor brand, Luckin is reaping medium- to long-term benefits from this co-branding campaign, such as increasing its brand awareness and attracting consumers who are looking for a premium, unique coffee experience.

Social Media Buzz and Consumer Engagement

The launch of Jiangxiang Latte generated a massive response on social media platforms, with netizens sharing experiences, opinions and creative content related to the product. Such online engagement has fuelled consumer interest and sparked discussions about blending the flavours of baijiu and coffee. Luckin has always been a brand that carries its own level of conversation on various social media platforms. As such, this new product quickly attracted a lot of social media buzz even before it was officially sold. With a packaging design that resembles Moutai's iconic logo, this latte generated feverish debate upon its launch. Many companies and organisations even used it as a team-building activity during the time the product was first launched.

The initiative not only boosted the sales of drinks in stores but also led to a rise in Kweichow Moutai's stock price. While the introduction of coffee products is unlikely to have a significant impact on Moutai's financial performance directly, its foray into the coffee sector, following its ice cream venture, holds significant symbolic importance, as coffee is a more frequently consumed beverage and more closely aligned with the lifestyles of younger consumers. Moving forward, Moutai plans to introduce more alcohol-infused products to the market.

Building Relationships

Over the past 25 years, businesses have increasingly recognised brands as valuable assets as investment in advertising and brand equity has increased (Hazan et al., 2021). As awareness increases, brands become an intangible asset that improves their relationship with potential and existing customers (Ozuem & Willis, 2022). Positive brand emotions and experiences can lead customers to conform to norms and influence their behaviour and reactions (You et al., 2021). Marketing practitioners believe that the relationship between consumers and brands can sometimes be likened to a human relationship, with passionate brands providing both functional needs and emotional value.

When discussing brand relationships, normative behaviour refers to customers' actions, such as purchasing and generating WOM messages, and their willingness to provide for another. In this context, two types of relationships that affect consumers' normative behaviour are identified: exchange and communal social relationships (Ozuem & Willis, 2022). Exchange relationships involve individuals expecting resources or benefits from a brand, while communal relationships do not expect immediate returns of specific benefits and conduct less monitoring and comparison of contributions (Clark & Mils, 1993). Customers with a loyalty mindset desire a return of value and may be less willing to express sentiments (Ozuem & Willis, 2022). They focus on a brand's performance, competencies and fair value. Their willingness to return positive feedback depends on the brand meeting these conditions. Obligation in brand relationships means customers engage immediately but may not be committed to contributing further. On the other hand, communal relationships emerge from increased customer trust that often arises from the development of brand knowledge and satisfactory experiences. Customers with communal relationships respond with reciprocating benefits, often out of appreciation rather than obligation. When brands display appreciation, customers will reciprocate and participate in online activities that favour the brand and maintain a positive relationship with the brand.

Affected by the pandemic, many traditional liquor enterprises are starting to consider and evaluate their brand relationships with their existing and potential consumers (Li & Wu, 2024). They realise that in establishing their relationship with young generations, they need to enhance consumer engagement in OBCs, which, according to Ozuem and Willis (2022), is influenced by their trust and familiarity with a brand. A high-quality brand relationship reflects a customer's commitment, passion and connection to the brand; it ensures stability throughout their lifecycle. Low engagement indicates low trust, experience or attachment, which reduces the quality of the brand relationship and results in low psychological attachment to the brand and OBC and to moderate WOM messages.

Moutai therefore is actively deploying online communities and trading platforms while transforming its image. iMoutai app, the digital marketing platform of the company, attracted millions of people on its first day of online trial on 31 March 2022 and topped the Apple App Store free list on the same day. The number of users exceeded 10 million in 19 days (Suo, 2023).

Redefining Brand Perception

Moutai's diversified co-branding strategy has successfully changed young consumers' perceptions of the brand. By offering affordable co-branded products, Moutai challenged its traditional reputation as a high-priced brand and made it more accessible to young consumers on a budget. The co-branding initiative increased the accessibility of Moutai's products. By having 11,133 stores across 29 provinces and 291 cities (36Kr, 2023), Luckin makes Jiangxiang Latte available in places of everyday consumption, such as neighbourhood shopping centres. This fosters a sense of familiarity and intimacy among young consumers. A diverse range of co-branded products and partnerships injected vigour and modernity into the Moutai brand. This resonates with young consumers who seek brands that align with their modern lifestyles. While collaborating with popular brands to break into new markets is certainly a crucial step, establishing an online platform is the cornerstone of Moutai's strategic transformation. Since its launch nearly a year ago, official data shows that as of 30 March 2023, "iMoutai" has accumulated over 37.92 million registered users, with an average daily active user base of nearly 5 million and a cumulative sales volume of nearly 21 billion yuan (Suo, 2023).

Conclusion and Future Outlook

Moutai's diversified co-branding strategy has proved to be a huge success: expanding its consumer base, redefining its brand image and positioning it as a vibrant, approachable brand for younger generations. This approach is a valuable case study for brands seeking to expand their reach, increase brand awareness and connect with changing consumer preferences. Changing consumer demographics and the untapped potential of female consumers present challenges and opportunities for the liquor industry. To adapt to these changes, baijiu producers should consider product innovation, market repositioning and brand repositioning. They should develop liquor products that cater to the preferences of younger consumers, including low alcohol content options and innovative packaging designs and flavours that appeal to a wider audience. In addition, producers should develop targeted marketing campaigns that resonate with younger generations and female consumers and highlight the social, cultural and personal benefits of modern liquor consumption. In the face of a rapidly changing consumer environment, traditional Chinese liquor producers must reimagine their brand positioning. These brands must move beyond the traditional "banquet culture" and its inherently male-centred associations to a more inclusive and lifestyle-oriented approach that resonates with modern values and consumer preferences.

References

36Kr. (2023). *Luckin coffee's store expansion strategy: Slowing down in lower-tier cities, regaining ground in Tier 2 and above*. Available at https://36kr.com/p/2387624919906566. Accessed 25 April 2024.

Achabou, M. A., & Dekhili, S. (2013). Luxury and sustainable development: Is there a match? *Journal of Business Research, 66*(10), 1896–1903.

Azemi, Y., & Ozuem, W. (2023). How does retargeting work for different Gen Z mobile users? *Journal of Advertising Research*, 2023-023. https://doi.org/10.2501/jar-2023-023

Banerjee, A., & Drollinger, T. (2017). Store within a store: Matched versus mismatched image perceptions. *Journal of Retailing and Consumer Services, 36*, 53–61. https://doi.org/10.1016/j.jretconser.2017.01.002

BCG and Altagamma. (2023). *True-luxury global consumer insight 2023.* Available at https://web-assets.bcg.com/d7/7b/ac47bd5c4f018aa58d0449b96590/bcgxaltagamma-true-luxury-global-consumer-insight-2023-final4.pdf. Accessed 25 April 2024.

Berthon, P., Pitt, L., Parent, M., & Berthon, J. P. (2009). Aesthetics and ephemerality: Observing and preserving the luxury brand. *California Management Review, 52*(1), 45–66.

Bialik, K., & Fry, R. (2019). *Millennial life: How young adulthood today compares with prior generations.* Pew Research Center. Available at https://www.pewresearch.org/social-trends/2019/02/14/Millennial-life-how-young-adulthood-today-compares-with-prior-generations-2/. Accessed 22 May 2024.

Bright Horizons. (2021). *Millennials are highly educated but still eager to learn.* Available at https://www.brighthorizons.com/resources/Blog/Millennials-educated-eager-learn. Accessed 22 May 2024.

Bwambale, F. (2023). Strategic marketing in the luxury goods industry. *Journal of Strategic Marketing Practice, 1*(1), 30–39.

Carfagna, L. B., Dubois, E. A., Fitzmaurice, C., Ouimette, M. Y., Schor, J. B., Willis, M., & Laidley, T. (2014). An emerging eco-habitus: The reconfiguration of high cultural capital practices among ethical consumers. *Journal of Consumer Culture, 14*(2), 158–178.

Chang, W. L. (2009). Roadmap of co-branding positions and strategies. *The Journal of American Academy of Business, 15*(1), 77–84.

Chen, S. C., & Shoemaker, S. (2014). Age and cohort effects: The American senior tourism market. *Annals of Tourism Research, 48*, 58–75.

China Alcoholic Drinks Association. (2023). *Mid-year research report on China's Baijiu market in 2023.* China Alcoholic Drinks Association. Available at https://www.sohu.com/a/687543862_121406416. Accessed 25 April 2024.

Cioban, J. (2021). *Customer engagement in 2021: Create dialogue, not 'personalisation'*. Forbes. Available at https://www.forbes.com/sites/forbesagencycouncil/2021/01/29/customer-engagement-in-2021-create-dialogue-not-personalization/?sh=3e82cb9f2e62. Accessed 25 April 2024.

Clark, M. S., & Mils, J. (1993). The difference between communal and exchange relationships: What it is and is not. *Personality and Social Psychology Bulletin, 19*(6), 684–691.

Cristini, H., Kauppinen-Räisänen, H., Barthod-Prothade, M., & Woodside, A. (2017). Toward a general theory of luxury: Advancing from workbench definitions and theoretical transformations. *Journal of Business Research, 70*, 101–107.

D'Arpizio, C., & Levato, F. (2014). *Lens on the worldwide luxury consumer*. Bain Company.

Dahlén, M., & Lange, F. (2005). Advertising weak and strong brands: Who gains? *Psychology & Marketing, 22*(6), 473–488. https://doi.org/10.1002/mar.20069

Deloitte. (2023). *Gen Z and millennial survey waves of change: Acknowledging progress, confronting setbacks*. Available at https://www.deloitte.com/content/dam/assets-shared/legacy/docs/deloitte-2023-genz-Millennial-survey.pdf?dl=1. Accessed 20 May 2024.

Deloitte. (2024). *Gen Z and millennial survey living and working with purpose in a transforming world*. Available at https://www.deloitte.com/content/dam/assets-shared/docs/campaigns/2024/deloitte-2024-genz-Millennial-survey.pdf?dlva=1. Accessed 20 May 2024.

Eastman, J. K., & Iyer, R. (2021). Understanding the ecologically conscious behaviors of status motivated Millennials. *Journal of Consumer Marketing*, 38(5), 565–575. Available at https://doi.org/10.1108/jcm-02-2020-3652

Fromm, J. (2023, August 4). *Millennials Vs. Gen Z: How CMOs can use key drivers*. Forbes. Available at https://www.forbes.com/sites/jefffromm/2023/08/04/Millennials-vs-gen-z-how-cmos-can-use-key-drivers/. Accessed 20 May 2024.

Gazzola, P., Pavione, E., Pezzetti, R., & Grechi, D. (2020). Trends in the fashion industry. The perception of sustainability and circular economy: A gender/generation quantitative approach. *Sustainability, 12*(7), 2809.

Giachino, C., Bertoldi, B., & Bargoni, A. (2021). Generations' attitudes and behaviours in the luxury sector. In *Developing successful global strategies for marketing luxury brands* (pp. 214–229). IGI Global. Available at https://doi.org/10.4018/978-1-7998-5882-9.ch012

Godey, B., et al. (2012). Brand and country-of-origin effect on consumers' decision to purchase luxury products. *Journal of Business Research, 65*(10), 1461–1470.

Guan, J., & Song, Z. (2023). Marketing considerations of Moutai Luckin co-branding. *Enterprise Management, 11*, 36–38. CNKI:SUN:QIGL.0.2023-11-017.

Hazan, E., Smit, P. S., Woetzel, A. J., Biljana Cvetanovski, S., Mekala Krishnan, L., & Gregg, B. (2021). *Getting tangible about intangible: The future of growth and productivity?* McKinsey Global Institute. Available at http://dln.jaipuria.ac.in:8080/jspui/bitstream/123456789/14247/1/Getting-tangible-about-intangibles-the-future-of-growth-and-productivity.pdf. Accessed 20 April 2024.

Helal, G., Ozuem, W., & Lancaster, G. (2018). Social media brand perceptions of Millennials. *International Journal of Retail & Distribution Management, 46*(10), 977–998.

iiMedia Research. (2023). *Alcohol industry development and competitive situation analysis report in China 2023–2024*. Available at https://www.iimedia.cn/c400/93080.html. Accessed 20 April 2024.

Jiemian. (2021). *Chongqing Jiang Xiaobai on the hot search again, behind the hustle and bustle, sales decline, listing a mystery*. Available at https://m.jiemian.com/article/6841322.html. Accessed 23 April 2024.

Jones, S., & Fox, S. (2009). *Generations online in 2009*. Available at https://faithformationlearningexchange.net/uploads/5/2/4/6/5246709/generations_online_in_2009_-_pew.pdf. Accessed 15 May 2024.

Kapferer, J. N. (2015). *Kapferer on luxury: How luxury brands can grow yet remain rare*. Kogan Page Publishers.

Katz, E., Lazarsfeld, P. F., & Roper, E. (2017). *Personal influence: The part played by people in the flow of mass communications*. Routledge.

Kim, J. (2019). Luxury fashion goods ownership and collecting behavior in an omni-channel retail environment: Empirical findings from affluent consumers in the US. *Research Journal of Textile and Apparel, 23*(3), 212–231.

Kim, Y., & Oh, K. W. (2022). The effect of materialism and impression management purchase motivation on purchase intention for luxury athleisure products: the moderating effect of sustainability. *Journal of Product and Brand Management, 31*(8), 1222–1234. https://doi.org/10.1108/jpbm-07-2021-3578

Ko, E., Costello, J. P., & Taylor, C. R. (2019). What is a luxury brand? A new definition and review of the literature. *Journal of Business Research, 99*, 405–413. https://doi.org/10.1016/j.jbusres.2017.08.023

Kong, H. M., Witmaier, A., & Ko, E. (2021). Sustainability and social media communication: How consumers respond to marketing efforts of luxury and non-luxury fashion brands. *Journal of Business Research, 131*, 640–651. https://doi.org/10.1016/j.jbusres.2020.08.021

Kweichow Moutai Co. Ltd. (2023). *Environmental, social and governance report 2023*. Available at https://book.yunzhan365.com/xtqxl/oubn/mobile/index.html. Accessed 8 May 2024.

Li, T., & Wu, Y. (2024). Differentiated co-branding communication under Moutai brand rejuvenation. *Old Brand Marketing, 05*, 10–12.

Liu, Y. (2021). International competitiveness analysis and suggestions of Guizhou Moutai. *Industrial Innovation Research, 07*, 97–99.

Ma, G., & Chen, X. (2022). Research on the investment value of Moutai. *Co-Operative Economics and Technology, 07*, 72–74. https://doi.org/10.13665/j.cnki.hzjjykj.2022.07.012

Miller, K. W., & Mills, M. K. (2012). Contributing clarity by examining brand luxury in the fashion market. *Journal of Business Research, 65*(10), 1471–1479.

Mitchell, V. W., & Balabanis, G. (2021). The role of brand strength, type, image and product-category fit in retail brand collaborations. *Journal of Retailing and Consumer Services, 60*, 102445. https://doi.org/10.1016/j.jretconser.2021.102445

Mortelmans, D. (2005). Sign values in processes of distinction: The concept of luxury. *Semiotica, 2005*(157), 497–520.

Nguyen, C., Romaniuk, J., Cohen, J., & Faulkner, M. (2020). When retailers and manufacturers advertise together; examining the effect of co-operative advertising on ad reach and memorability. *Journal of Retailing and Consumer Services, 55*, 102080. https://doi.org/10.1016/j.jretconser.2020.102080

Ozuem, W., & Willis, M. (2024). Artificial intelligence and predictive analytics: Towards a praxis of personalised shopping experiences. In W. Ozuem, S. Ranfagni, & M. Willis (Eds.), Digital transformation for fashion and luxury brands. Palgrave Macmillan.

Ozuem, W., Willis, M. (2022). *Digital marketing strategies for value co-creation.* Palgrave Macmillan. https://doi.org/10.1007/978-3-030-94444-5_7

Ren, J., & Wu, S. (2024). Exploring the cooperation mode between emerging and established brands–Taking Luckin Coffee as an example. *Green Packaging, 03*, 160–163. https://doi.org/10.19362/j.cnki.cn10-1400/tb.2024.03.034

Roland Berger. (2016). *The revolution in alcohol consumption brought about by young consumers.* Available at https://www.rolandberger.com/publications/publication_pdf/young_drinkers_fuelling_development_of_new_alcoholic_beverage_categories_and_brands_0909.pdf. Accessed 20 April 2024.

Sina. (2021). *1919: Female user liquor purchase big data.* Available at https://finance.sina.com.cn/tech/2021-03-08/doc-ikkntiak6275542.shtml. Accessed 25 April 2024.

Sina. (2022). *Jiang Xiaobai falls off the "small wine" altar*. Available at https://finance.sina.cn/chanjing/gsxw/2022-12-20/detail-imxxiayr7306693.d.html?from=wap. Accessed 23 April 2024.

Smith, K. T., & Brower, T. R. (2012). Longitudinal study of green marketing strategies that influence Millennials. *Journal of Strategic Marketing, 20*(6), 535–551.

Straughan, R. D., & Roberts, J. A. (1999). Environmental segmentation alternatives: A look at green consumer behavior in the new millennium. *Journal of Consumer Marketing, 16*(6), 558–575.

Suo, W. (2023). *Digital economy watch|The underlying logic of digital marketing reinvented from iMoutai*. Available at http://www.news.cn/enterprise/20230330/a3724123187a4bc187466af7c178ea9d/c.html. Accessed 8 May 2024.

Tencent. (2022). *Luckin Coffee's "emergence" and "survival" mystery*. Available at https://new.qq.com/rain/a/20221108A03SI400. Accessed 23 April 2024.

Uggla, H. (2004). The brand association base: A conceptual model for leveraging partner brand equity. *The Journal of Brand Management, 12*(2), 105. https://doi.org/10.1057/palgrave.bm.2540208

Wang, G. Q. (2020). Reflections on the sustainable development of China's liquor industry. *Modern Enterprise, 04*, 43–44.

Wang, M. X. (2024). Brand co-branding co-operative marketing strategy to help enterprises transform and break the situation—Take Kweichow Moutai and Luckin Coffee co-branding as an example. *Mall Modernisation, 08*, 46–48. https://doi.org/10.14013/j.cnki.scxdh.2024.08.052

Wen, J. D., & Cai, Z. Q. (2019). Research on differences in luxury goods purchasing behaviour of heterogeneous consumer groups—An empirical analysis based on CHFS data. *Research on Financial Issues, 09*, 128–136. https://doi.org/10.19654/j.cnki.cjwtyj.2019.09.016

Xinhuanet. (2023). *Through the years, let perseverance become faith: China's most trusted food companies put on the list, Moutai topped the list for a while*. Available at http://www.news.cn/enterprise/20230709/86118c36514542709266c95acbb7b85f/c.html. Accessed 23 April 2024.

Xu (Rinka), X., & Pratt, S. (2018). Social media influencers as endorsers to promote travel destinations: An application of self-congruence theory to the Chinese Generation Y. *Journal of Travel & Tourism Marketing, 35*(7), 958–972. https://doi.org/10.1080/10548408.2018.1468851

You, Y., He, Y., Chen, Q., & Hu, M. (2021). The interplay between brand relationship norms and ease of sharing on electronic word-of-mouth and willingness to pay. *Information & Management, 58*(2), 103410.

Yu, Y., Rothenberg, L., & Moore, M. (2020). Exploring young consumer's decision-making for luxury co-branding combinations. *International Journal of Retail & Distribution Management* (ahead-of-print). https://doi.org/10.1108/ijrdm-12-2019-0399

Zhang, Y., & Zhang, C. (2021). From China to the world: The rise of Moutai, a national brand. *International Brand Watch, 30*, 27–33.

Zhao, F. (2014). *Research on the sustainable development of China's Baijiu industry* (Dissertation, Graduate School of the Chinese Academy of Social Sciences). PhD. https://kns.cnki.net/kcms2/article/abstract?v=5UWSsHjGZiECRuSguBaETUQVE-BNB2z0UcPWa51zVHhsDNTM3bl3Qs6-RBZjlVcQS5n6maxyZwGll6-FmMKSLJZO-2HF-cxXh7BFE36au_XLPDT_gYn4CEZ9L_1SDkfs_QzfEZkJw9R7W3kwOMwWJg==uniplatform=NZKPTlanguage=CHS

Zhu, D. (2024). Research on green and low carbon consumption of middle income group and youth group—Empirical analysis based on different consumption segments and consumption areas. *Social Science Series*, 1–12.

12

Authenticity as Consistency: Insights from Micro-influencers Partnerships with Sustainable Fashion Brands

Giovanna Pegan and Marco Balzano

Introduction

In contemporary business environments, authenticity is in high demand, particularly as markets become more transparent and consumers more discerning (Balzano & Vianelli, 2022; Bartsch et al., 2022; Lehman et al., 2019). Still, the construct of authenticity is blurred and multi-faceted (Fritz et al., 2017; Morhart et al., 2015). Indeed, a recent review pointed out that there exist three fundamental but distinct perspectives on authenticity: authenticity as conformity of an entity to the norms of its social category, authenticity as a connection between an entity and a person, place, or time as claimed, and authenticity as consistency between an entity's internal values and its external expressions

This study stems from the Authors' involvement in the Research Project of National Interest (PRIN 2022): 'Communicating sustainable supply chain practices of companies in a digital environment' (National Coordinator, Prof. Guercini).

G. Pegan (✉) · M. Balzano
DEAMS Department, University of Trieste, Trieste, Italy
e-mail: giovanna.pegan@deams.units.it

W. Ozuem et al. (eds.), *Sustainable Digital Marketing for Fashion and Luxury Brands*,
https://doi.org/10.1007/978-3-031-82467-8_12

(Lehman et al., 2019). This latter perspective (which from now on we will refer to as 'authenticity as consistency') underscores the relevance for organizations to embody authenticity in every business decision, action, and communication, making it a central element of brand trust and customer loyalty (Nunes et al., 2021). Authenticity as consistency in an organization fosters trust among its stakeholders, including employees, customers, and partners. When there is alignment between an organization's states and practices, stakeholders are more likely to trust it (Södergren, 2021).

In this perspective, authenticity as consistency pertains to many aspects of organizational life, such as addressing sustainability issues (Bulmer et al., 2024; Wallach & Popovich, 2023), thus ensuring that commitments to environmental and social responsibility are genuinely reflected in business decisions and actions. To pursue sustainability, firms must operate under triple responsibility, including social, environmental, and economic dimensions, the so-called CSR (Guercini & Ranfagni, 2013; Wilson, 2015). Consumers and stakeholders are growing more attentive to the importance of sustainable business operations, often holding firms and respective brands accountable when they fall short of sustainability standards.

Amid a widespread crisis of trust, there is a demanding expectation for firms to demonstrate both moral and business integrity through concrete actions (Mirzaei et al., 2022). Those brands that actively contribute to improving global conditions are increasingly recognized and supported by consumers (Kotler & Sarkar, 2020). In order not to see their CSR efforts thwarted, brands, now more than ever considered key players in the pursuit of the SDGs set by the 2030 Agenda, need to build a system of trusting relationships with their key stakeholders, primarily consumers, by conveying messages and choosing communication channels that ensure proper decoding by consumers (Kim et al., 2021; Pegan et al., 2020; Sheth et al., 2011).

Over the years, scholars predominantly examined sustainability issues from a consumer perspective (e.g., Acuti et al., 2022; Hanss & Böhm, 2012; McDonald & Oates, 2006), while relatively less attention has been devoted to the business perspective (e.g., Bansal & DesJardine, 2014; De Giacomo & Bleischwitz, 2020). In other words, few studies investigated how business actors perceive sustainability and how they deal with it. Still, understanding how corporations interpret and implement sustainability strategies is critical for assessing the efficacy of these approaches at the organizational level. Furthermore, examining the motivations, challenges, and outcomes businesses face in adopting sustainability practices can offer insights into the effective implementation of such strategies.

Among the various business actors, social media influencers (SMI) represent a unique category whose role in sustainability is gaining increasing attention (Masuda et al., 2022; Pittman & Abell, 2021). Their influence on consumer behaviors and their ability to shape public opinion makes them highly effective in promoting sustainable practices (Freberg et al., 2011). Influencers can communicate sustainability-oriented messages by leveraging digital platforms, directly affecting consumer choices, and encouraging businesses to adopt more sustainable practices (Confetto et al., 2023). As such, studying the role of social media influencers in sustainability efforts provides a nuanced understanding of how such business actors engage with and influence the broader sustainability agenda.

Specifically, SMIs are defined as users who can influence others on social media platforms and serve as a new form of independent third-party endorsers (Freberg et al., 2011). SMIs have made a significant difference in the social media marketing landscape, with brand marketers moving away from the use of traditional celebrities to SMIs for brand endorsement (Cheung et al., 2022; Masuda et al., 2022). Recent research indicates that SMI marketing is nearly seven times more impactful than traditional marketing efforts in effectively reaching and convincing consumers (Ye et al., 2021). SMI content can be perceived as more genuine than brands' content creation (Torres et al., 2019). SMIs possess the unique ability to reach and engage large audiences through their social media platforms. They have cultivated followers who trust their opinions and recommendations, making them influential endorsers and trendsetters. This engagement level is quantitatively and qualitatively impactful, as influencers often foster a sense of community and personal connection with their followers. Secondly, influencers are adept at creating content that resonates with their audience's preferences and values, enhancing the relatability and appeal of the brands they endorse (Pegan & Verginella, 2024). Their content is often perceived as more genuine and less commercial than traditional advertising, which can lead to higher levels of consumer trust and loyalty towards the brand. Moreover, SMIs actively shape brand narratives and consumer perceptions through interactions and storytelling. This ability to influence public perception makes them critical to brand image management, particularly when public relations crises can arise and spread rapidly online (Torres et al., 2019). The strategic collaboration with SMIs allows firms to precisely target specific demographics and market segments (Ibáñez-Sánchez et al., 2022). Influencers often have well-defined audience niches, potentially implying that firms can engage with particular groups more effectively than through broad-spectrum traditional media channels. Surprisingly, despite their proven influence and the critical role of authenticity in their operations, little attention has been paid to how authenticity—and particularly authenticity as consistency—guides SMIs' choices when collaborating on sustainability-focused projects.

Against this backdrop, this chapter aims to explore how authenticity as consistency can shape SMIs' choices of collaboration with fashion brands on sustainability issues. To this end, the chapter begins with a theoretical background analyzing the construct of authenticity as consistency and its role as a driver in strategic collaborations. It then focuses on sustainable collaborations and social media influencers. To offer a concrete contribution, the chapter enriches the theoretical background by analyzing the perception of a specific category of specialized SMIs, green micro-influencers (Pittman & Abell, 2021), operating on Instagram. Listening to the experience of twenty green micro-influencers who declare themselves in their profiles as fashion sustainability-oriented provided a nuanced picture of how authenticity as consistency informs and actively guides their selection of brand partnerships in the fashion industry. Most of these green micro-influencers seek brand partnerships whose sustainability practices are well-established and align with their personal and public personas, ensuring a genuine representation of shared values and fostering consistency between their internal and external expressions. The chapter concludes by discussing managerial implications and outlining concluding remarks, hence setting the ground for future avenues of research.

Theoretical Background

Authenticity as Consistency

Scholars noted that there exist three distinct perspectives on authenticity: authenticity as conformity, authenticity as connection, and authenticity as consistency (Lehman et al., 2019). These perspectives shape perceptions and behaviors in business contexts, including marketing management. Authenticity as conformity means adhering to the norms and expectations of a particular social category or industry standard (e.g., Glynn & Lounsbury, 2005; Gunawan et al., 2020). Authenticity as connection means establishing a genuine link between the entity and a specific person, place, or tradition (e.g., Kim et al., 2016; Newman & Dhar, 2014; Ozuem et al., 2024).

Authenticity as consistency means 'consistency between an entity's internal values and its external expressions' (Lehman et al., 2019, p. 1). As such, this underscores the relevance of consistent messaging and behavior that aligns with the brand's core values (Harter, 2002; Kernis & Goldman, 2006). This consistency strengthens consumer trust and loyalty, as customers are more likely to support brands that genuinely practice what they previously stated.

In business environments, this latter perspective of authenticity underpins the trust and reliability perceived by stakeholders (Lehman et al., 2019). Indeed, consistency between a firm's stated values and its actual practices builds enhanced credibility and establishes a foundation for partnerships and business collaborations. This perspective views authenticity as a fundamental aspect of integrity and genuine character in a business context (Beverland, 2005; Södergren, 2021).

Authenticity as consistency can shape corporate governance and ethics. It encourages businesses to align their strategies with their core values, ensuring that their operations and external communications reflect these principles authentically (Mazutis & Slawinski, 2015). Businesses perceived as authentic are likely to enjoy a more robust reputation, increased consumer trust, and, consequently, positive performance outcomes (Alhouti et al., 2016). As framed, authenticity as consistency can thus be particularly salient in sustainability and CSR. In this domain, consistency encourages business actors to initiate and sustain meaningful partnerships that advance their sustainability goals. Such partnerships, often built around shared values and commitments to environmental and social governance principles, require a foundation of trust and alignment underpinned by consistent, authentic behavior, as discussed below.

Consistency as a Driver in Strategic Collaborations

Strategic collaborations, particularly those centered on CSR, are integral in enhancing the impact of business practices towards societal goals (Peloza & Falkenberg, 2009). These collaborations involve multiple entities, including businesses, non-governmental organizations (NGOs), and occasionally governmental agencies, working together to address complex social, environmental, and economic challenges. Strategic collaborations range from focused contributions between a single firm and an NGO to complex networks involving multiple firms and NGOs addressing broad societal issues. In this view, strategic collaborations represent a critical mechanism through which organizations can amplify their sustainable impact, access new markets, and share resources effectively (Ozuem et al., 2023; Scandelius & Cohen, 2016; Thorne et al., 2017).

The focus on shared values and objectives fosters a cooperative environment conducive to tackling grand challenges while mitigating the risks associated with 'greenwashing,' where firms claim more environmentally friendly practices than they perform, which can severely damage reputational capital (Lyon & Maxwell, 2011). Moreover, the integrity of strategic collaborations in CSR and sustainability initiatives can be enhanced through transparent communication and the integration of feedback mechanisms. Transparency in operations and decision-making processes allows for greater accountability and can facilitate the engagement of a broader range of stakeholders in meaningful dialogue, thereby enriching collaborative efforts (Servaes & Tamayo, 2013).

Furthermore, authenticity, as consistency, in strategic collaborations enhances the collaborating entities' reputations and contributes to a more significant corporate responsibility narrative and sustainable development narrative (Murray et al., 2010). This narrative, in turn, shapes consumer perceptions and behaviors, influencing regulatory policies and guiding the future of corporate strategies towards more sustainable and ethically sound practices. The narrative engages public perception, laying a foundation for more informed and supportive consumer behavior. To this end, the bridge from corporate actions to consumer perceptions is built on the integrity and authenticity of these narratives (Huang & Guo, 2021), which can significantly enhance the impact of sustainability initiatives.

Sustainable Collaborations and Social Media Influencers

Among the various business actors, SMIs are occupying an increasingly central position in the firms' communication strategies, also in the context of sustainability and CSR issues (Cheng et al., 2024; Kent & Taylor, 2016). This shift reflects broader societal trends, where digital platforms have become critical arenas for public discourse and consumer engagement. SMIs are vital in modern marketing (Masuda et al., 2022), operating as business actors who can influence through their digital followings on platforms like Instagram, YouTube, Twitter, and TikTok. Their influence stems primarily from their perceived authenticity and the trust they establish with their followers (Kim et al., 2021). As 'opinion leaders' (Casaló et al., 2020), SMIs can uniquely shape perceptions, attitudes, and behaviors through their endorsements and the narratives they craft in their content. This influential capacity makes them valuable in firms' marketing strategies, where they act as connectors between brands and consumers, offering a personalized and engaging approach to brand communication. Furthermore, SMIs are adept at targeting niche markets or specific demographic segments, enabling brands to launch targeted marketing campaigns more likely to resonate with and impact the intended audience effectively (Ibáñez-Sánchez et al., 2022; Ozuem & Willis, 2022). Integrating SMIs in sustainability initiatives is significant, as their ability to shape opinions and behaviors can be instrumental in promoting sustainable practices.

In this context, SMIs serve as intermediaries who facilitate a two-way communication stream, aligning brand messages with the values and expectations of their followers. This alignment supports the effective communication of sustainability-related decisions and actions by firms, where consumer skepticism often challenges corporate claims of responsible practices (Skarmeas & Leonidou, 2013). Furthermore, the credibility of SMIs hinges on their authenticity and the perceived consistency between their personal brand and the endorsed sustainability initiatives (Ibáñez-Sánchez et al., 2022). This consistency enhances trust among the audience, making the influencer's endorsements more effective.

As outlined above, several studies focused on the role of firms' and SMIs' authenticity as consistency in affecting consumers' perceptions (e.g., Belanche et al., 2021; Breves et al., 2019; Zhao et al., 2024). On the other hand, much less attention has been devoted to exploring how SMIs value authenticity as consistency in their partnerships and strategic collaborations for sustainability-related ends.

Still, filling this research gap could be valuable for multiple reasons. First, exploring how SMIs value authenticity in their partnerships and strategic collaborations is functional to understand the integrity of their endorsements. If SMIs selectively collaborate with brands that reflect their genuine values and commitments, their endorsements will likely be more persuasive and resonate more deeply with their followers. This selective alignment could enhance the effectiveness of sustainability campaigns, as followers may perceive these efforts as more genuine and not merely as corporate greenwashing. Second, examining the consistency of SMIs in their partnerships can reveal the long-term impact of their influence on consumer behavior towards sustainability. If influencers consistently support sustainability initiatives across their partnerships and content creation, they can help foster a sustained consumer movement towards environmentally friendly and socially responsible products and practices. Third, analyzing how SMIs frame authenticity as consistency can provide valuable insights for developing guidelines for ethical influencer partnerships and strategic collaborations. This could lead to more consistent sustainability marketing practices, aligning corporate strategies more closely with societal values and expectations.

How Does Authenticity as Consistency Shape SMI-Brand Partnerships?

Evidence from the Voice of Green Micro-influencers in the dynamics of collaboration with Fashion brands

The fashion industry, which significantly impacts environmental and social aspects, makes sustainability a central concern both for firms and consumers (Kim & Kim, 2020). The risk of being perceived as a green-washed fashion brand is high, even in the presence of a real commitment to sustainability on the part of important global players in the sector. This risk challenges fashion companies to select marketing communication sources and channels capable of credibly communicating their CSR efforts, especially to the final market (Pegan et al., 2020; Sheth et al., 2011). Thus, fashion brands-SMIs collaborations' dynamics become more strategically relevant than in other industries. According to Kotler et al. (2021), the success of so-called fashion influencers depends on a fortunate alchemy that leads to the credibility of the source, which, in turn, is a function of the authoritativeness and attractiveness of social media influencers. Using these actors as a communication tool for brands represents a semantic shortcut aimed at increasing public goodwill to stimulate their intention to purchase fashion brands (Kotler et al., 2021, Verginella & Pegan, 2024). Therefore, sustainability-oriented collaborations between SMI and sustainable fashion brands are highly relevant in enhancing the credibility of fashion brands' sustainability communication, fostering more sustainable consumption styles.

Instagram is the primary platform for the influencers involved, leveraging its visual nature and vast user base to promote sustainability in fashion (De Veirman et al., 2017). In particular, we gathered qualitative data[1] on twenty[2] green micro-influencers (Pittman & Abell, 2021) who typically specialize in advocating for sustainable fashion practices, ranging from promoting sustainable brands to raising awareness about the environmental and social impacts of the fashion industry. This type of influencer typically exhibits a follower count ranging from 10,000 to 100,000, and it seems reasonable to argue that they are highly interested in maintaining a closer, authentic relationship with their audience, which is crucial for topics that require trust and personal commitment, such as sustainability issues. Their content often includes sustainable fashion tips, eco-friendly lifestyle choices, and partnerships with brands prioritizing ethical practices. Beyond the micro-influencer classification, the other criteria that guided our respondents' selection are reported as follows. First, the quality and consistency of content related to sustainability in fashion were considered. SMIs need to regularly produce content that not only promotes sustainable practices but is also able to engage the audience on environmental issues. They also had to show a clear commitment in this direction, as often manifested in their bios on Instagram. Moreover, the ability of SMI to affect consumer behavior towards more sustainable fashion choices was a key factor. This involves looking at past partnerships and qualitatively assessing the effectiveness of these collaborations in promoting sustainable products or practices. Another criterion consisted of meeting the experience-based requirement

[1] We follow the methodological procedures of narrative inquiry research (e.g., Josselson, 2011; Riessman, 2008; Balzano & Vianelli, 2022; Bloom et al., 2020) to explore authenticity in influencer marketing and sustainability in the fashion industry. The researchers followed five phases: attending, telling, transcribing, analyzing, and reading. Participants were chosen for their authentic engagement with sustainability issues on social media, and interviews were designed to encourage open conversation. The transcribing phase focused on preserving the authenticity of each influencer's voice. The average duration of the interviews was approximately 30–60 minutes. This variation in duration allowed for flexibility to delve deeper into specific topics as needed.

[2] In total, 88 influencers were initially contacted for participation in the study. Out of these, 20 influencers responded and agreed to participate in the study. The average age of the interviewed people was about 34 years old, and the sample consisted of 6 males and 14 females. Furthermore, influencers exhibited diverse demographic backgrounds and different areas of the fashion industry, thus ensuring a broad spectrum of perspectives within the study. To guarantee confidentiality, each participant was allocated a unique identifier (e.g., I1, I2, etc.), which we refer to when providing quotes in the text.

of multiple completed or ongoing collaborations with one or more firms in the fashion industry.

The Role of Authenticity as Consistency in the Selection of Green Micro-influencers Collaboration Choices

The desire to pursue authenticity as consistency in internal values and beliefs and external expressions in the search phase of a new partnership with a brand emerges clearly from the voices of the twenty green micro-influencers interviewed. Firstly, in the first steps of identifying a new partnership, several SMIs explain how consistency with one's values and beliefs related to sustainability is key from the start. For example, I20 states: '*To choose a new partnership, I evaluate carefully if the company is in line with my values because for me, first of all, it is important to collaborate with brands with the same values and beliefs as me.*' Similarly, I2 emphasizes how: '*I have always loved being authentic, being consistent, especially on issues such as sustainability, consistent with my ideals; tastes change quickly, while ideals remain, and if they change, they do so much slower and more difficult.*' The same two respondents emphasize how this desire to maintain authenticity as consistency with one's internal values can be translated into rejecting from the outset the proposal of a new collaboration with a brand: '*In the absence of this consistency, it* was *therefore spontaneous to refuse collaborations with realities that could not reflect these ideals of mine.*' While I20 emphasizes how a strong selection is necessary from the first contacts: '*When I am contacted, and it often happens, if they are not sustainable and vegan, I immediately discard them. For example, when I am asked to sponsor products on Amazon, I disregard it as e-commerce to incentivize people to buy.*' Similar statements emerge from I19: '*I only do collaborations that I believe in and are consistent with myself and my beliefs on sustainability principles. I reject many collaborations because they involve companies or products that align with my values.*'

In some cases, the search for authenticity can result in an attitude of the influencer that is rigid and not open to new collaborations, as in the case of I1: '*In general, I distrust and wonder whether I would ever do a collaboration related to sustainability issues with a company that has never communicated efforts in this sense before, and makes choices that are not sustainable. The reason why I would not do it is that I might be criticized or I might be criticized, or I might be pointed at as an opportunist. Also, I have worked hard to build a reputation and do not want to take a minute to ruin it. So I am cautious in my selection.*'

In this specific domain of collaborations, the pursuit of authenticity as consistency in terms of external expression is highly dependent on the perceived authenticity of the brand to be promoted by an SMI. For a green micro-influencer to decide to start a collaboration by including sustainability-related content of a new brand, this brand must be credible and trustworthy. To this end, it is crucial that behind the brand, there is, first and foremost, a product that reflects specific characteristics and meets sustainability principles, albeit with different nuances. In recounting their experiences, I17 and I12 respectively emphasize the importance of consistency between the country of manufacture and the country of the brand: '*I favor the selection of partners who make made-in-Italy production choices; I choose partners who have decided not to internationalize production in other countries, despite the increase in turnover.*' The importance of the product reflecting different principles of sustainability is expressed in varying detail by both respondent I20: '*First of all, the product itself: what the product is, where it is made, what materials it is made from, the quality it offers, and then I also look at whether they have a certain type of packaging*'; and by respondent I7: '*Definitely the product they want to promote must have sustainability criteria.*' Respondent I14 broadens the perspective by emphasizing the importance for the product to be promoted in terms of content to be accessible, both in terms of price and distribution, for people: '*In my opinion, it has to be sustainable on several fronts, to allow for a lower impact on the environment. It has to be something usable and easy for my community to find; I think that the accessibility of the product is, in a way, a sign of its sustainability. I also feel uncomfortable offering something that costs a lot or is not easily found.*' The issue of brand authenticity in terms of consistency with the values it embodies and communicates in its external expression is fundamental when selecting partners to collaborate with. For example, I4 states: '*When choosing a new partnership, the brand must be 100% sustainable; this means that it cannot be at risk of greenwashing or take controversial actions concerning sustainability.*' Similarly, I9 states: '*You have to understand if their communication is genuine or greenwashing. If all elements make me think that brand is sustainable (...).*'

The search for this consistency, both internally and externally, can lead a green micro-influencer to personally test the sustainability of a specific brand's product and its usefulness before starting the collaboration, as I14 explains: '*As a person, I have in mind the kind of brand I would like to collaborate with, which I find in line with my values and which I find useful for my followers(...). Before starting a collaboration, however, I usually ask to use the product at least a few times to test it personally. I never do closed-box collaborations.*' I11 also emphasizes that the choice of a potential collaboration with a brand is the result of a careful evaluation beforehand and that the actual choice only falls on those brands that guarantee authenticity in the sense of coherence with internal values and then external expression: '*I choose collaborations carefully, selecting only the alternative that I believe in, that I have tested beforehand and that I like.*' The importance that the search for authenticity is, however, accompanied by the personal pleasure that a micro-influencer feels towards a product to be promoted in her content also emerges from I4: '*In the selection of collaborations, however, the fact that I liked the product was also fundamental, I never recommend products and brands to my followers that I do* not like.'

In the selection phase of a potential collaboration between a green micro-influencer and a brand, authenticity, understood as the search for consistency with personal values (self-concept and self-presentation), represents a fundamental driver, albeit with some nuances. The search for this consistency is also essential because it is reflected in the external expression (self-presentation) the micro-influencer conveys to her followers. For this reason, a potential brand partnership must be chosen after analyzing how authentically sustainable the brand to be promoted is. In order to be a credible and trustworthy source of sustainability issues towards followers, a green micro-influencer must incorporate content related to brands that it personally perceives to be just as authentic about sustainability issues.

The Role of Authenticity as Consistency in the First Step of Green Micro-influencers Collaboration Brand Choices

The search for authenticity that allows a green micro-influencer to be consistent with its sustainability-oriented values and to communicate them externally coherently through the choices of brand partnerships intensifies when the collaboration is to be finalized. At this stage, presenting oneself to one's audience of followers as a credible source of sustainability-related messages requires a commitment to scrupulously ascertain that the brand with which one is collaborating is authentically sustainable and honest. For I2: '*To accept a collaboration, I do not just hear the word "sustainability" in their presentation; every time, I thoroughly research their overall reality to see if they are committed or if it is just greenwashing.*' Such selectivity requires a strong commitment of the green micro-influencer in gathering information, as in the case of I7: '*I accept very few collaborations because when you have the ethical responsibility of conveying such a message, and nowadays sustainability is overused, I make a rigorous selection. Before starting a collaboration, I must ensure no greenwashing behind the brand/company communication. I, therefore, make sure that it is not just a façade but that the brand is genuinely committed to sustainability through concrete actions. This is because those who follow me believe in me, so it is not worth the risk; it is much better to be genuine and sincere with your audience because it pays off in time.*'

In other cases, there may be more tolerance of the company's behavior as long as there is transparency and a willingness to change course, as I6 states: '*There must be objective parameters such as certifications or the absence of any particular scandal; or the certainty that you as a company have decided to learn from that possible scandal and change completely and then talk about it honestly, without filters.*' From the various voices, it emerges how important it is that the company with which the collaboration should begin is transparent and willing to document its commitment to sustainability objectively. This commitment may concern brands or even broader projects involving the company. For example, I18 says: '*We usually ask for material specific to the product, service, or project they want me to discuss rather than various insights. Additional material can be interesting when deciding whether or not to collaborate.*' I2 and I8, respectively, mention the critical theme of company ethics, which must translate into openness and transparency concerning the activities carried out with the various stakeholders: '*The company ethics (I have had the opportunity to visit the office and participate in events involving employees and you can immediately perceive when the working climate is healthy and when it is not), their approach to the product and the relationship they establish with suppliers*'; '*when the brand allows you to tell about the company, it allows you to enter inside the company and show the production process.*' The importance of the degree of openness of the company to show the actions carried out for sustainability is fundamental to encourage the start of a collaboration, as underlined by I18: '*The moment the brand is willing to share information and asks me if I can also go to them and show their reality, so if there is openness and transparency, the willingness to share. These are things that encourage my willingness to collaborate.*' Since it is a vocation that goes beyond the mere goal of short-term gain, sometimes it is about promoting content with a broader mission of spreading a sustainable culture. For example, I15 states: '*I always try to have a function, where possible, formative in that I like to teach others certain subjects or tips. So, if this possibility exists, I prefer a broader project than pure advertising.*'

Similarly, I6 admits that to retain its authenticity, it aims to initiate collaborations with educational purposes to bring about a fundamental change in society: '*The situation I prefer is when, in agreement with the company, I produce editorial content, hence popularising. Because if there is no real understanding of the concept, of the sense of urgency, but you make that specific choice based on my advice and that is it (and that is, unfortunately, content that works damn well on social media), the change lasts overnight.*'

Seeking and safeguarding authenticity as consistency in internal values and external expression concerning sustainability issues for a micro-influencer is crucial to safeguarding the credibility of one's content. I18 explains it clearly: '*You must be consistent because otherwise you get slaughtered. You have the pressure of the community's judgment. If you want to look at it another way, it becomes credibility. That is why I choose to start collaborations with those brands that can make me appear, or rather, resonate in a way consistent with my message. Otherwise, credibility collapses.*' The personal and authentic vocation for the sustainability of a micro-influencer is also a reason for demonstrating how collaboration for marketing purposes, as in the case of sponsors, can be based on conveying helpful content to improve consumption styles beyond market trends. Some respondents affirmed this with different nuances, such as I2: '*I started collaborating with them five years ago when there was minimal talk (at least in Italy) about sustainability; it was not a current or hot topic. Nevertheless, it was already essential to me; therefore, it was nice to show how promotional activities through influencer marketing could coexist with virtuous realities.*' For I4, the maturing of genuinely sustainable personal values led to the birth of effective collaborations: '*More than market trends, my path was essential to me, the moment I came into contact with this world and realized the seriousness of the situation, of how animals are treated, I approached these realities from which I no longer disregard. So, even if the market trend had not gone that way, I would have known them and chosen them because it is a personal choice based on sustainability principles.*' In some cases, to save the coherence of the self-concept, these micro-influencers choose to promote content related to smaller brands as I5 states: '*Authenticity is seen more when they are niche products, or if they are products that would compete with others from big brands and then the collaboration could make a difference. So, it is crucial that my collaboration can have some impact on my community.*'

On the contrary, some agree to be less biased with the big brands and act as an intermediary to offer a second chance to those who are trying to make up for the scandal and its impact, as I6 states: '*With Nike, I agreed because they were friendly and open: this is the way you work, this is the truth, I mean you are telling the truth. We are trying to align. Moreover, do something for the domain. We have arrived because nobody on this planet is 100 percent sustainable. However, we are working on it and would be happy if you would say we are working on it.*'

In this perspective of greater openness, some influencers believe that preserving one's authenticity as a coherence should not stand in the way of starting collaborations with companies embarking on a path of change and improvement to become more sustainable. For example, respondent I9: '*I try to communicate what they do well because 100 percent sustainable you cannot have it... However, you have to start somewhere. So it is useless, in my opinion, to keep saying that certain things are not going well because you have to try to see the things that are going well, hoping that the things that are not going well will also work over time. For example, I am against the fast fashion model, but if one of those brands does something well, it is right to point it out to encourage others, too (...) So, I am open.*'

The search for a personal authenticity transmitted and nurtured within brand collaborations is the basis for beginning the partnership between green micro-influencers and brands. At this stage, the accessibility of documentary sources that certify and testify to the brand's authenticity in terms of sustainability is essential to safeguard the credibility of the influencer's content. Similar to consumer experience, these actors fear falling into the trap of greenwashing that would ruin their image and reputation, destroying the relationship of trust built with their followers.

The Role of Authenticity as Consistency in Reinforcing Green Micro-influencers Brand Collaboration

In the perspective of long-term relationship consolidation, the perception that a micro-influencer has of being able to maintain and nurture authenticity concerning both self-concept and self-presentation is driven by a relationship of mutual trust and transparency of the company, as I3 explains: '*We have also established a relationship of trust, of esteem; the companies I continue to collaborate with have seen the results, and so many have stayed over the years.*' Similarly, I10 states that '*very often they give me access to documents that are generally only available to some. So trust, but above all, have the privilege of seeing for yourself whether what is being communicated in terms of sustainability by the company and its brand is authentic.*' Community feedback, however, is essential to feed the virtuous circle of self-concept and self-presentation through collaborations based on the principles of sustainability, as I18 states: '*What reinforces my commitment to collaborations with sustainable brands is the feedback from people, when the content goes online and reaches people who did not know the brand or who know the brand and liked it.*'

For several of the green micro-influencers interviewed, safeguarding authenticity as consistency in a long-term collaboration means deciding on the content the influencer wants to promote with freedom without restrictions or censorship by the sponsoring brand. For example, I2 states: '*Feeling that there was trust in me and wanting to give me total freedom in communicating was essential for us to continue collaborating.*' Freedom to manage content, even if there is *still mediation*, is the experience of I3: 'The *fact that they leave me complete freedom in the content; even if there is still mediation in the final realization of the work; the company has to leave me autonomy in managing the content because we influencers know what our community is and what it wants.*' Even for those who are already celebrities, as in the case of I19, it is fundamental to have: '*The freedom to decide how to communicate, as I am also a TV personality who has been talking about these topics for years; if brands contact me they know well that they cannot tell me what I have to do or say, but that I will decide according to my thoughts and knowledge.*' For I7, internal consistency with one's values and beliefs becomes a self-selection for the relationship in place: '*Many companies know the philosophy and ethics you have and try to get you to propose your idea. This is because many companies have realized there is often no need to impose something on the person you choose to use to promote your company. After all, the person knows well what they need.*'

In some cases, the collaboration may be less successful to the point of breakdown. The community can become the needle of the scales to understand whether or not it deserves to continue a collaboration begun after a perhaps initially less rigorous selection, as told by I20's experience: '*I care a lot what my community thinks because I see it as a kind of tribe. For example, in the past, I collaborated with Oceansapart, which is a small quantity of greenwashing because it is a company that makes sportswear out of recycled synthetic fibers. However, they offer new clothes and patterns and lines every week. Because a girl pointed out to me that we cannot fill our wardrobe with a thousand models, I did a check, and she was right. I decided to end the collaboration.*' The green micro-influencer believes that it is essential, however, that a learning process is set in motion whereby the company with which one might start collaborating is willing to improve its path towards sustainability by accepting her advice: '*whether or not they accept specific advice from me, for example, Bulk, has reduced much plastic in its packaging which is now almost 100% sustainable and has included organic things.*' Managing authenticity as consistency in green micro-influencer brand collaborations requires that the partnership is consolidated over the long term due to the consonance of intentions and values based on sustainability between influencers and brands.

Discussion and Conclusions

The experiences of the green micro-influencers reveal how the concept of authenticity, as consistency between their sustainability values and the external expression in the content they promote, is a critical driver in influencing the dynamics of their collaborations with brands in the fashion sector. From the gained insights, it emerges how their awareness that SMIs represent a source of authentic communication and the need to mitigate the typical risks of brand encroachment in their content drives them to select potential new brand collaborations carefully (Audrezet et al., 2020). Selection often occurs only after personal information gathering and evaluation based on documents, personal product tests, and company visits to understand potential collaborators' organizational climate. Respondents' voices emphasize the importance of shared values and goals among partners in the perspective of sustainable collaboration to mitigate the risk associated with the phenomenon of 'greenwashing' that can seriously damage reputation (Lyon & Maxwell, 2011; Ozuem et al., 2021) in the eyes of their communities. Trust, credibility, and transparency activate and nurture collaborative efforts with brands that transfer into the downstream relationship with the community of followers. In other words, their function as strategic intermediaries facilitating two-way communication by aligning brand content with followers' values and expectations (Kim et al., 2021; Pegan & Verginella, 2024) reaches its peak here: the credibility of these micro-influencers hinges on their authenticity and the perceived consistency between their personal brand and the endorsed sustainability initiatives related to a brand (Ibáñez-Sánchez et al., 2022). This consistency enhances trust among the audience, making the influencer's endorsements more effective. These testimonies emphasize how authenticity as an internal (self-concept) and external (self-presentation) consistency of the green micro-influencer based on long-term solid collaborations with sustainable brands enhance their ability to influence consumers, shifting followers towards more sustainable behavior and habits. Although there are nuances in the stories, several micro-influencers stated how the desire to act consistently with their beliefs and values makes them selective and careful in their choice of collaborations; further, they tend to prioritize the educational and informative aspect of their influencer function over the commercial one. In this way, these micro-influencers can better cope with the tension arising from the commercial opportunities and keep their self-authenticity intact and consistent with their beliefs (Audrezet et al., 2020). Collaboration can trigger a virtuous circle of learning sustainable practices between influencers, brands, and followers if the brand pursues the same goals of authenticity as consistency in its internal and external expressions (Lehman et al., 2019). The unity of values and intentions allows the company involved in the partnership to increase the credibility of its commitment to the SDGs and not to see its efforts thwarted among consumers who are often skeptical and fearful of falling into the trap of greenwashing (Pegan et al., 2020; Sheth et al., 2011) above all in the fashion sector. Suppose a brand consistently presents itself concerning the sustainability values it declares and its actions (Kotler & Sarkar, 2020). In that case, it can attract strategic collaborations with these green micro-influencers who, thanks to being micro, are perceived as more reliable and credible in the eyes of the consumer in conveying sustainability-related content (Pittman & Abell, 2021). At the same time, the company that aims to communicate its commitment to sustainability on digital channels effectively should be equally selective in seeking strategic collaborations with potential new partners. Mutual selectivity can facilitate a collaborative dynamic based on the desire for authenticity and consistency, fostering partner satisfaction.

Overall, this chapter contributes to the extant literature in several ways. Firstly, it delineates how authenticity as consistency shapes influencers' strategic collaborations. Secondly, the analysis of the perception of SMIs highlights the nuanced role of micro-influencers, who often serve as more credible sources of sustainability advocacy than their macro counterparts due to their perceived closeness with their followers. Thirdly, it underscores the potential of authentic collaborations to enhance fashion brand sustainability narratives in a way that resonates more profoundly with consumers. In practical terms, these insights deepen our understanding of influencer marketing dynamics and offer actionable strategies for brands seeking to leverage influencer partnerships for enhanced sustainability outcomes. Specifically, the study suggests that brands, and in particular fashion brands, that aim to communicate their CSR efforts effectively to be perceived as brand activists (Kotler & Sarkar, 2020) should prioritize transparency and genuine sustainability practices to attract collaboration with micro-influencers authentically aligned with their mission. Additionally, it highlights the importance of influencers' partner selection to maintain their authenticity, which is crucial for sustaining SMIs' influence and trustworthiness among followers.

Considering both the theoretical and managerial relevance of the phenomenon of authenticity in strategic collaborations and its declination between sustainable collaborations and SMIs, future research should first replicate the study by listening to the narratives of managers of sustainable fashion brands collaborating with this type of influencers in order to understand their challenges in managing authenticity in the same collaborations. Secondly, it would be helpful to analyze through the nethnography method the perceptions of the followers of these specific micro-influencers to obtain a complete picture of the experience of this authenticity and how it influences their attitudes and behaviors concerning sustainable choices. By cross-referencing the perceptions of the three main stakeholder categories, new opportunities, and research questions could arise on authenticity management on both the business and consumer sides in an ever-changing digital world.

References

Acuti, D., Pizzetti, M., & Dolnicar, S. (2022). When sustainability backfires: A review on the unintended negative side-effects of product and service sustainability on consumer behavior. *Psychology & Marketing, 39*(10), 1933–1945.

Alhouti, S., Johnson, C. M., & Holloway, B. B. (2016). Corporate social responsibility authenticity: Investigating its antecedents and outcomes. *Journal of Business Research, 69*(3), 1242–1249.

Audrezet A., de Kerviler, G., & Moulard, J. D. (2020, September). Authenticity under threat: When social media influencers need to go beyond self-presentation, *Journal of Business Research, 117*, 557–569.

Balzano, M., & Vianelli, D. (2022). What contributes to locavorism as a consumer ideology? *British Food Journal, 124*(13), 460–477.

Bansal, P., & DesJardine, M. R. (2014). Business sustainability: It is about time. *Strategic Organization, 12*(1), 70–78.

Bartsch, F., Zeugner-Roth, K. P., & Katsikeas, C. S. (2022). Consumer authenticity seeking: Conceptualization, measurement, and contingent effects. *Journal of the Academy of Marketing Science,* 1–28.

Belanche, D., Casaló, L. V., Flavián, M., & Ibáñez-Sánchez, S. (2021). Building influencers' credibility on Instagram: Effects on followers' attitudes and behavioral responses toward the influencer. *Journal of Retailing and Consumer Services, 61*, 102585.

Beverland, M. B. (2005). Crafting brand authenticity: The case of luxury wines. *Journal of Management Studies, 42*(5), 1003–1029.

Bloom, J., Dorsett, P., & McLennan, V. (2020). Vocational rehabilitation to empower consumers following newly acquired spinal cord injury. *Journal of Vocational Behavior, 53*(1), 131–144.

Breves, P., Liebers, N., Abt, M., & Kunze, A. (2019). The perceived fit between instagram influencers and the endorsed brand: How influencer-brand fit affects source credibility and persuasive effectiveness. *Journal of Advertising Research, 59*, 440–454.

Bulmer, S., Palakshappa, N., Dodds, S., & Harper, S. (2024). Sustainability, brand authenticity, and Instagram messaging. *Journal of Business Research, 175*, 114547.

Casaló, L. V., Flavián, C., & Ibáñez-Sánchez, S. (2020). Influencers on Instagram: Antecedents and consequences of opinion leadership. *Journal of Business Research, 117*, 510–519.

Cheng, Y., Hung-Baesecke, C. J. F., & Chen, Y. R. R. (2024). Social media influencer effects on CSR communication: The role of influencer leadership in opinion and taste. *International Journal of Business Communication, 61*(2), 336–359.

Cheung, M. L., Leung, W. K., Aw, E. C. X., & Koay, K. Y. (2022). "I follow what you post!": The role of social media influencers' content characteristics in consumers' online brand-related activities (COBRAs). *Journal of Retailing and Consumer Services, 66*, 102940.

Confetto, M. G., Covucci, C., Addeo, F., & Normando, M. (2023). Sustainability advocacy antecedents: How social media content influences sustainable behaviors among Generation Z. *Journal of Consumer Marketing, 40*(6), 758–774.

De Giacomo, M. R., & Bleischwitz, R. (2020). Business models for environmental sustainability: Contemporary shortcomings and some perspectives. *Business Strategy and the Environment, 29*(8), 3352–3369.

De Veirman, M., Cauberghe, V., & Hudders, L. (2017). Marketing through Instagram influencers: The impact of number of followers and product divergence on brand attitude. *International Journal of Advertising, 36*(5), 798–828.

Zhao, X., Zhu, Z., Shan, M., Cao, R., & Chen, H. A. (2024). "Informer" or "entertainers": The effect of social media influencers on consumers' green consumption. *Journal of Retailing and Consumer Services*, 77, 103647.

Freberg, K., Graham, K., McGaughey, K., & Freberg, L. A. (2011). Who are the social media influencers? A study of public perceptions of personality. *Public Relations Review, 37*(1), 90–92.

Fritz, K., Schoenmueller, V., & Bruhn, M. (2017). Authenticity in branding–exploring antecedents and consequences of brand authenticity. *European Journal of Marketing, 51*(2), 324–348.

Glynn, M. A., & Lounsbury, M. (2005). From the critics' corner: Logic blending, discursive change and authenticity in a cultural production system. *Journal of Management Studies, 42*(5), 1031–1055.

Guercini, S., & Ranfagni, S. (2013). Sustainability and luxury: The Italian case of a supply chain based on native wools. *Journal of Corporate Citizenship, 52*, 76–89.

Gunawan, S., Budiarsi, S. Y., & Hartini, S. (2020). Authenticity as a corporate social responsibility platform for building customer loyalty. *Cogent Business & Management, 7*(1), 1775023.

Hanss, D., & Böhm, G. (2012). Sustainability is seen from the perspective of consumers. *International Journal of Consumer Studies, 36*(6), 678–687.

Harter, S. (2002). Authenticity. In C. R. Snyder & S. Lopez (Eds.), *Handbook of positive psychology* (pp. 382–394). Oxford University Press.

Huang, C., & Guo, R. (2021). The effect of a green brand story on perceived brand authenticity and brand trust: The role of narrative rhetoric. *Journal of Brand Management, 28*, 60–76.

Ibáñez-Sánchez, S., Flavián, M., Casaló, L. V., & Belanche, D. (2022). Influencers and brands successful collaborations: A mutual reinforcement to promote products and services on social media. *Journal of Marketing Communications, 28*(5), 469–486.

Josselson, R. (2011). Narrative research: Constructing, deconstructing and reconstructing story. In F. J. Wertz, K. Charmaz, L. M. McMullen, R. Josselson & R. Anderson (Eds.), *Five ways of doing qualitative analysis.* Guilford Press.

Kent, M. L., & Taylor, M. (2016). From Homo Economicus to Homo dialogicus: Rethinking social media use in CSR communication. *Public Relations Review, 42*(1), 60–67.

Kernis, M. H., & Goldman, B. M. (2006). A multicomponent conceptualization of authenticity: *Theory and research. Advances in Experimental Social Psychology, 38*, 283–357.

Kim, E., Duffy, M., & Thorson, E. (2021). Under the influence: Social media influencers' impact on response to corporate reputation advertising. *Journal of Advertising, 50*(2), 119–138.

Kim, J. E., Lloyd, S., & Cervellon, M. C. (2016). Narrative-transportation storylines in luxury brand advertising: Motivating consumer engagement. *Journal of Business Research, 69*(1), 304–313.

Kim, K. H., & Kim, E. Y. (2020). Fashion marketing trends in social media and sustainability in fashion management. *Journal of Business Research, 117*, 508–509.

Kotler, P., & Sarkar, C. (2020). *Brand activism: From purpose to action.* Idea Bite Press.

Kotler, P., Pozzoli, R., & Stigliano, G. (2021). *On life fashion.* Hoepli.

Lehman, D. W., O'Connor, K., Kovács, B., & Newman, G. E. (2019). Authenticity. *Academy of Management Annals, 13*(1), 1–42.

Lyon, T. P., & Maxwell, J. W. (2011). Greenwash: Corporate environmental disclosure under threat of audit. *Journal of Economics & Management Strategy, 20*(1), 3–41.

Masuda, H., Han, S. H., & Lee, J. (2022). Impacts of influencer attributes on purchase intentions in social media influencer marketing: Mediating roles of characterizations. *Technological Forecasting and Social Change, 174*, 121246.

Mazutis, D. D., & Slawinski, N. (2015). Reconnecting business and society: Perceptions of authenticity in corporate social responsibility. *Journal of Business Ethics, 131*, 137–150.

McDonald, S., & Oates, C. J. (2006). Sustainability: Consumer perceptions and marketing strategies. *Business Strategy and the Environment, 15*(3), 157–170.

Mirzaei, A., Wilkie, D. C., & Siuki, H. (2022). Woke brand activism authenticity or the lack of it. *Journal of Business Research, 139*, 1–12.

Morhart, F., Malär, L., Guèvremont, A., Girardin, F., & Grohmann, B. (2015). Brand authenticity: An integrative framework and measurement scale. *Journal of Consumer Psychology, 25*(2), 200–218.

Murray, A., Haynes, K., & Hudson, L. J. (2010). Collaborating to achieve corporate social responsibility and sustainability? Possibilities and problems. *Sustainability Accounting, Management and Policy Journal, 1*(2), 161–177.

Newman, G. E., & Dhar, R. (2014). Authenticity is contagious: Brand essence and the source of production. *Journal of Marketing Research, 51*(3), 371–386.

Nunes, J. C., Ordanini, A., & Giambastiani, G. (2021). The concept of authenticity: What it means to consumers. *Journal of Marketing, 85*(4), 1–20.

Ozuem, W., Ranfagni, S., Willis, M., Rovai, S., & Howell, K. (2021). Exploring customers' responses to online service failure and recovery strategies during Covid-19 pandemic: An actor–network theory perspective. *Psychology & Marketing, 38*(9), 1440–1459.

Ozuem, W., Ranfagni, S., Willis, M., Salvietti, G., & Howell, K. (2024). Exploring the relationship between chatbots, service failure recovery and customer loyalty: A frustration–aggression perspective. *Psychology and Marketing*. https://doi.org/10.1002/mar.22051

Ozuem, W., & Willis, M. (2022). *Digital marketing strategies for value co-creation: Models and approaches for online brand communities*. Palgrave Macmillan.

Ozuem, W., Willis, M., Ranfagni, S., Howell, K. E., & Rovai, S. (2023). Examining the role of social media influencers in service failure and recovery strategies: An empirical investigation of millennials' views. *Information Technology & People*. https://doi.org/10.1108/itp-05-2022-0371

Pegan, G., Schoier, G., & de Luca, P. (2020). The importance of consumer perception of corporate social responsibility to meet the need for sustainable consumption: Challenges in the sportswear sector. In C. Silvestri, M.

Piccarozzi, & B. Aquilani (Eds.), *Customer satisfaction and sustainability initiatives in the fourth industrial revolution* (pp. 212–235). IGI Global.

Pegan, G., & Verginella, C. (2024). Influencer marketing and consumer behaviour: Insights into the 7 effectiveness of fashion influencers' sponsored content on Instagram. In W. Ozuem, S. Ranfagni, & M. Willis (Eds.), *Digital transformation for fashion and luxury brands*. Palgrave Macmillan.

Peloza, J., & Falkenberg, L. (2009). The role of collaboration in achieving corporate social responsibility objectives. *California Management Review, 51*(3), 95–113.

Pittman, M., & Abell, A. (2021). More trust in fewer followers: Diverging effects of popularity metrics and green orientation social media influencers. *Journal of Interactive Marketing, 56*, 70–82.

Riessman, C. K. (2008). *Narrative methods for the human sciences*. Sage.

Scandelius, C., & Cohen, G. (2016). Achieving collaboration with diverse stakeholders—The role of strategic ambiguity in CSR communication. *Journal of Business Research, 69*(9), 3487–3499.

Servaes, H., & Tamayo, A. (2013). The impact of corporate social responsibility on firm value: The role of customer awareness. *Management Science, 59*(5), 1045–1061.

Sheth, J. N., Sethia, N. K., & Srinivas, S. (2011). Mindful consumption: A customer-centric approach to sustainability. *Journal of the Academy of Marketing Science*, 39, 21–39.

Skarmeas, D., & Leonidou, C. N. (2013). When consumers doubt, watch out! The role of CSR skepticism. *Journal of Business Research, 66*(10), 1831–1838.

Södergren, J. (2021). Brand authenticity: 25 years of research. *International Journal of Consumer Studies, 45*(4), 645–663.

Thorne, L., Mahoney, L. S., Gregory, K., & Convery, S. (2017). A comparison of Canadian and US CSR strategic alliances, CSR reporting, and CSR performance: Insights into implicit–explicit CSR. *Journal of Business Ethics*, 143, 85–98.

Torres, P., Augusto, M., & Matos, M. (2019). Antecedents and outcomes of digital influencer endorsement: An exploratory study. *Psychology & Marketing, 36*(12), 1267–1276.

Wallach, K. A., & Popovich, D. (2023). When big is less than small: Why dominant brands lack authenticity in their sustainability initiatives. *Journal of Business Research, 158*, 113694.

Wilson, J. P. (2015). The triple bottom line: Undertaking an economic, social, and environmental retail sustainability strategy. *International Journal of Retail & Distribution Management, 43*(4/5), 432–447.

Ye, G., Hudders, L., De Jans, S., & De Veirman, M. (2021). The value of influencer marketing for business: A bibliometric analysis and managerial implications. *Journal of Advertising, 50*(2), 160–178.

13

Virtual Corporate Social Responsibility Co-creation and Consumer Engagement

Ling Lin and Liya An

Introduction

In the modern business landscape, corporate social responsibility (CSR) has evolved from a mere philanthropic endeavour to an integral component of business strategy that encompasses social and environmental considerations (Gond & Moon, 2011). The digital revolution has further reshaped CSR; it has paved the way for virtual CSR co-creation, which engages consumers through digital platforms in a more interactive and participatory manner (Capriotti, 2011; Coombs & Holladay, 2015). This chapter examines the theoretical and practical aspects of virtual CSR co-creation, highlighting its transformative potential in fostering consumer engagement (CE) and collaborative value creation.

L. Lin (✉)
Fujian Jiangxia University, Fuzhou, Fujian, China
e-mail: 27558248@qq.com

L. An
Chengdu University of Information Technology, Chengdu, Sichuan, China
e-mail: 576861261@qq.com

W. Ozuem et al. (eds.), *Sustainable Digital Marketing for Fashion and Luxury Brands*,
https://doi.org/10.1007/978-3-031-82467-8_13

The concept of CSR has been described as a "chameleon concept" due to its adaptability and the wide range of perspectives it encompasses (Gond & Moon, 2011; Ozuem et al., 2014; Sarkar & Searcy, 2016). Traditional CSR, often characterised by one-way communication from businesses to stakeholders, has been critiqued for its lack of transparency and potential to foster scepticism among consumers (Pope & Wæraas, 2016). In contrast, virtual CSR co-creation represents a shift towards two-way, interactive engagement that involves stakeholders in meaningful ways, thereby enhancing the impact and visibility of CSR initiatives (Du & Vieira, 2012; Iglesias et al., 2020).

Virtual CSR co-creation leverages digital technologies to reshape the CSR landscape; it offers innovative tools for companies to engage consumers and create shared value (Cho et al., 2017; Jeong et al., 2013). The success of initiatives like Alipay's Ant Forest illustrates the potential of virtual CSR to drive social and environmental outcomes, and it emphasises the importance of ongoing engagement and interactive relationships with consumers (Jurietti et al., 2017).

This chapter provides a comprehensive overview of the evolution of CSR, the transition from one-way to two-way value creation and the mechanisms and benefits of virtual CSR co-creation. It aims to offer valuable insights for both scholars and practitioners interested in the future of CSR in the digital age, with a focus on the millennial generation who are known for their tech-savviness and strong responses to CSR (Anderson et al., 2018; Azami et al., 2018; Luger et al., 2022).

Understanding the theoretical underpinnings of virtual CSR co-creation is crucial. Value co-creation theory has evolved from a goods-dominant logic to a service-dominant logic (SDL), which emphasises the interactive and collaborative nature of value creation between enterprises and consumers (Vargo & Lusch, 2004). Building on this, service logic (SL) further refines the understanding of value creation by highlighting the customer's central role in the process (Grönroos & Gummerus, 2014). The service science perspective extends this understanding by studying service systems and their configurations to advance the design and scaling of service systems for business and societal purposes (Maglio & Spohrer, 2008). The service ecosystem perspective also considers the interdependent network of actors and resources that facilitate value creation (Vargo et al., 2015). As the economy shifts towards service-oriented models, virtual CSR co-creation emerges as an extension of value co-creation as well as a strategic approach for companies to engage with consumers, particularly millennials, in addressing social and environmental challenges. This chapter explores the potential of virtual CSR co-creation as a strategic tool for engaging consumers and driving positive social change, which sets the stage for a deeper exploration of its theoretical foundations and practical applications.

CSR: Beyond One-Way Value Creation

CSR is an umbrella term that encompasses a wide range of perspectives, concepts and approaches. Gond and Moon (2011) used the term "chameleon concept" to capture the wide range of perspectives of CSR, which has evolved over a long and varied period to adapt to challenging realities and contexts, and this trend is still ongoing.

One-Way Value Creation—CSR Research Evolution

Howard R. Bowen, in 1953, recognising the significant influence wielded by large corporations and their impact on society, proposed the establishment of a distinct set of principles to guide corporations in fulfilling their social responsibilities; Bowen's concept of the social responsibility of business evolved into CSR. In the 1960s, scholars' participation in the study of CSR increased (Davis, 1960; Frederick, 1960; McGuire, 1963; Walton, 1967). The scholars reached a consensus to widen the scope of CSR to include corporate philanthropy, stewardship principles and business ethics. Others held sceptical opinions of the broadening of CSR and intimated that a firm's responsibility should be limited to shareholders' profit maximisation (Friedman, 1962, 1970; Levitt, 1958). The pyramid model proposed by Carroll in 1979 offered an arguably first unified CSR definition: "The social responsibility of business encompasses the economic, legal, ethical, and discretionary expectations that society has of organisations at a given point in time" (Carroll, 1979, p. 500). The belief that businesses exist only to generate economic profit evolved to include serving society. In the 2000s, the CSR agenda resurged due in no small part to corporate irresponsibility and ethical scandals (e.g. Enron, WorldCom, Tyco, Global Crossing, BP).

Traditionally, corporations always played the role of enactors, and CSR reports, websites, advertisements, public relations and social media were seen as channels through which corporations communicated CSR. However, CSR communication is planned and executed by professionals who have resources and expertise that are not readily available to stakeholders, such as consumers (Morsing & Schultz, 2006). The CSR communication dilemma arises because consumers know little about a corporation's CSR effort in reality although they claim to know more about it (Sen et al., 2006). As a result, consumers tend to react negatively towards corporations making too much effort to communicate CSR, which can lead to a boomerang effect, including consumer scepticism (Mantovani et al., 2017) and CSR weariness or fatigue (Crane & Matten, 2013) if the CSR communication does not create consumer awareness and identification (Porter & Donthu, 2008); consumer scepticism arises because consumers incline towards associating opacity in CSR reports with corporate hypocrisy or greenwashing (Pope & Wæraas, 2016), which can undermine organisational credibility (Devin, 2016).

Carroll and Shabana (2010) subsequently recognised that economic and legal obligations represent the traditional social agreement between business and society, whereas ethical and philanthropic duties signify a more advanced social pact between business and society. Porter and Kramer (2011) developed the concept of creating shared value (CSV) to call for a change in business strategies. The CSV concept represents one of the key turns in CSR evolution because it emphasised creating value for long-term success rather than narrowly viewed business purposes (Latapí Agudelo et al., 2019). Many globally well-known companies persevere in integrating complex context issues, such as reducing their environment footprint and cultivating needed talent (Heslin & Ochoa, 2008), into their strategic CSR policies based on their belief in the significance of shared value. CSV differs from philanthropic responsibility, which is at the top level of Carroll's CSR Pyramid (Carroll, 2016), because philanthropic responsibility normally does not generate financial return for enterprises. Corporations who believe in creating shared value show their concerns and integrate social and global issues into their core business to create new opportunities for growth and then generate a return for the company. In other words, CSV and philanthropic responsibility actually stem from a different perspective on the roles that corporations play within their social context. Porter and Kramer (2011) suggested that enterprises should take the initiative to create value for society and themselves, meet the needs of stakeholders and solve social problems during their communications and interactions with stakeholders; this was the first time that researchers combined the concept of shared value with CSR.

Two-Way Value Creation Diverges from One-Way Value Creation

In today's business landscape, the traditional approach of one-way value creation, where companies unilaterally decide on products and strategies, is increasingly being replaced by a two-way value creation model. This new paradigm involves active collaboration and communication between companies and their stakeholders, which fosters mutual benefits and innovation. Two-way value creation recognises the importance of engaging with both internal and external stakeholders; it allows stakeholders to contribute to the decision-making process and co-create value alongside the company.

Howe (2006) introduced and explained the concept of crowdsourcing, which embodies two-way value creation by involving users in the decision-making processes of an enterprise. Through crowdsourcing, users help co-create and redefine products, services and values; thus, crowdsourcing extends the innovation boundaries of enterprises by leveraging external resources and capabilities. Luxury and fashion brands, such as Burberry and Gucci, have adopted this model in their CSR initiatives. For example, Burberry's "Art of the Trench" campaign invited customers to share photos of themselves wearing Burberry trench coats, which were then featured on Burberry's website and social media platforms. This not only engaged customers directly in the brand's marketing efforts but also allowed them to contribute to the brand's identity and values. Similarly, Gucci has leveraged digital platforms to engage with its audience by inviting platform users to participate in design contests and share their interpretations of the brand's iconic items; in this way, Gucci fosters a collaborative and innovative environment. Crowdsourcing can be regarded as a category of co-creation operating on the Internet, on social media or mobile apps and it plays a crucial role in raising awareness and engagement in a company's CSR initiatives.

Furthermore, Morsing and Schultz (2006) emphasised the need for stakeholder communication to diverge from "inform" to "response" and then to "involve". They argued that enterprises should be conscious of the necessity to engage with internal and external stakeholders proactively in both "sensegiving" and "sensemaking" CSR communication processes to ensure that CSR is interactive and participatory. Gond et al. (2013) suggested that CSR research should explore ways for businesses to create value beneficial both to themselves and society. Schultz et al. (2013) critiqued traditional CSR views that focused solely on improving corporate reputation and financial performance or emphasised the societal impacts of corporations and their role in norm setting. They introduced the communicative view of CSR that highlights the importance of communication dynamics within complex networked societies, which significantly impact CSR management and structure. This perspective has led companies to evolve their CSR strategies into an organisational mindset that encompasses strategic integration and interactive communication, as noted by Walter (2014). Additionally, research by Nwagbara and Reid (2013) highlighted the importance of effective communication between policymakers and organisations in the successful planning, implementation and evaluation of CSR initiatives. They stressed that engaging users in the institutionalisation of CSR and aligning their internal and external motivations with CSR strategies foster deeper connections and mutual understanding, as discussed by Rademacher and Remus (2014) and Sheehy (2015). Madsen and Rodgers (2014) opined that stakeholders' appreciation of CSR efforts hinges on their awareness of specific actions the company has taken.

Elving et al. (2015) argued for diverse forms of communication (persuasive, informative, aspirational and participatory CSR communication) to mediate CSR concerns and achieve mutual understanding. Recent studies by Lee et al. (2019) and Kim (2019) have increasingly viewed CSR as a form of communication or discourse that focuses on stakeholder engagement within complex and dynamic networks (Guthey & Morsing, 2014; Qi et al., 2021; Schultz et al., 2013). This perspective supports the idea that CSR is "a moving target" that requires continuous adaptation to stakeholders' evolving expectations. Thus, fostering a two-way symmetrical CSR dialogue, involving idea generation, feedback reception and encouraging user participation, is crucial for maintaining relevance and CSV in today's interconnected business environment (Tu et al., 2020).

Value Co-creation in CSR Development

Bhattacharya et al. (2009), along with Sang and Han (2023), stressed that understanding stakeholders' perceptions and evaluations of CSR activities is crucial for creating value through CSR. The success of CSR efforts largely hinges on the involvement of customers and other stakeholders. The ability of a business to meet stakeholder expectations and sustain positive relationships is essential for the ongoing sustainable development of CSR. Value co-creation in CSR goes beyond traditional approaches by focusing on collaboration, inclusivity and collective impact; it aims to foster significant change collectively. Examples of CSR value co-creation include the Prada Re-Nylon Project, H&M Conscious Foundation and the Burberry Regeneration Fund. Ant Forest stands out as a prime example of virtual CSR in China. Launched by Alibaba in 2016 as an environmental initiative, by August 2022 it had motivated 650 million people to adopt eco-friendly consumption habits, which resulted in the planting of over 400 million trees and facilitated a reduction in carbon emissions of 26 million tons. While some virtual CSR co-creation projects like Ant Forest have successfully achieved sustainable development and generated positive social impacts, others have seen a decline. The critical factor for success in these initiatives is maintaining ongoing engagement and building enduring interactive relationships with consumers (Jurietti et al., 2017).

Virtual CSR Co-creation

With the rise of the digital era, every industry has adapted its marketing strategies through "Internet plus", which has led to significant changes in traditional CSR activities. These activities are increasingly moving online, leveraging cutting-edge web technology and the strength of social media, thus spawning numerous virtual CSR marketing methods. Research highlights that social media provides powerful, versatile and effective channels for CSR communication (Capriotti, 2011; Coombs & Holladay, 2015; Cho et al., 2017; Jeong et al., 2013). They enable two-way balanced interactions with stakeholders through idea sharing, feedback collection and engagement solicitation (Tu et al., 2020). Moreover, social media stakeholders, who also serve as a credible third-party source of CSR information, play a significant role in diminishing public scepticism towards CSR (Du & Vieira, 2012; Tomaselli et al., 2019). Consequently, companies can avoid overt self-promotion and reduce costs (de Oliveira & Carraro, 2021) as the business landscape progressively evolves into a multistakeholder community.

Virtual CSR co-creation represents a novel and effective approach for companies to engage in social responsibility initiatives in the modern age. Unlike traditional CSR activities, which are solely conducted by companies (de Oliveira & Carraro, 2021), virtual CSR targets a broader audience and encourages greater participation from users (Okazaki et al., 2020; Zhou et al., 2023). This method allows users to customise CSR initiatives according to their preferences, thereby fostering more active engagement on new media platforms (Tomaselli et al., 2019; Yoon, 2017).

This exploration of virtual CSR co-creation contributes to addressing gaps in the study of CSR. Virtual CSR co-creation represents a shift from traditional CSR engagement due to advancements in technology that enable enhanced network building and content sharing (see Table 13.1).

Table 13.1 Evolution of CSR and marketing approaches in the digital age

CSR Initiative	Tradition engagement	Digital/Virtual co-creation
CSR activities	**Traditional CSR Reporting** Typically involves companies issuing annual reports detailing their CSR activities and impact. This is often a one-way communication channel (e.g. ESG reports, Annual CSR reports)	**Collaborative CSR Projects** Involve stakeholders in the creation and implementation of CSR initiatives, leveraging social media for engagement and participation (e.g. Crowdsourced sustainability initiatives: Prada Re-Nylon Project; H&M Conscious Foundation; Burberry's Regeneration Fund; Alibaba Ant Forest)
Marketing efforts	**Conventional Advertising** Focuses on promoting products through traditional media channels, often without direct consumer interaction (e.g. TV, print and billboard ads)	**Interactive Consumer Campaigns** Encourage consumers to participate in brand-related activities, such as creating and sharing content on social platforms (e.g. User-generated content on social media)

Traditional CSR engagement focuses on addressing the social and environmental interests of stakeholders, which is less of a concern for traditional marketing programmes. Both online brand communities and virtual CSR co-creation leverage social media to foster communication with consumers and key stakeholders. However, organisations that actively engage their stakeholders, especially consumers, in co-creating value through social and environmental initiatives achieve successful virtual CSR co-creation (Korschun & Du, 2013; Zhou et al., 2023), also known as online (Fan et al., 2019) or digital CSR co-creation (Khattak & Yousaf, 2022; Okazaki et al., 2020).

Traditional CSR and Virtual CSR Co-creation

Virtual CSR co-creation revolutionises traditional CSR communication strategies and introduces several key changes (see Table 13.2): First, it transforms the role of users. Under the traditional CSR model, users are passive recipients with little participation or empowerment. Virtual CSR co-creation redefines users as designers and implementers, enhancing their understanding of, and engagement in, CSR, and bestowing them with a sense of ownership. Second, it alters the mode of communication. Traditional CSR communication is typically one-way and static, often resulting in a lack of interaction and feedback, which makes it difficult for companies to grasp user perspectives or address key social issues. Virtual CSR co-creation, however, establishes two-way symmetric communication that allows companies to receive timely feedback and better understand and address CSR-related social issues. Third, it addresses motivation scepticism. Traditional one-way CSR communication often lacks transparency, which leads to scepticism among users about corporate motives and suspicions of greenwashing or corporate hypocrisy (Pope & Wæraas, 2016). Virtual CSR co-creation's visible and transparent processes help diminish such scepticism and foster greater user engagement and more precise CSR implementation (Ilieva-Koleva & Dobreva, 2021). Fourth, it diversifies participation methods. Unlike traditional CSR, which typically involves purchasing products or charitable giving, virtual CSR co-creation includes modes like experiential, interactive, collaborative and gamified co-creation. This allows users to actively participate as partners in designing and implementing CSR initiatives or engage in gamified activities that have real-world environmental impacts. Fifth, it changes the nature of resource contributions. In virtual CSR co-creation, user participation extends beyond financial contributions to include time, cognitive resources and emotional investment. This fosters a deeper connection and identification with the company's CSR efforts, which enhances users' willingness to participate consistently.

These shifts between traditional CSR communications and virtual CSR co-creation highlight the evolution in how companies and users interact in relation to social responsibility initiatives.

Table 13.2 Key differences between virtual corporate social responsibility (CSR) activities and traditional CSR activities

Main differences	Traditional CSR	Virtual CSR co-creation
Roles	Enterprises are dominators Stakeholders are passive recipients	Stakeholders to engage proactively in CSR activities planning and implementation
Interaction	One-way	Two-way timely
Form of participation	Transactional co-creation: donation, volunteerism	Gamified, interactive and experiential co-creation
Channel	Offline	Online and offline integration, based on online participation
Resource contribution	Money oriented	Cognitive, emotional involvement
Model	"good-money" charity model	"interactive" co-creation model
Process management	Single behaviour with low transparency	Affordance, continuous positive feedback
Perspective	Social responsibility	Social value co-creation
Theory	Stakeholder theory, CSR theory	Value co-creation theory; stakeholder theory, CSR theory
Value creation subject	Enterprises	Enterprises and stakeholders
Value creation approach	Fulfil CSR	Enterprises and key stakeholders interact and participate together
Time and space	Limited	Unlimited
Stakeholder engagement	Low customer viscosity, less active, low implementation accuracy	High customer viscosity, more active, high implementation accuracy

Perspectives on Emerging Virtual CSR

Morsing and Schultz (2006) pointed out that if companies wanted to enhance their efforts in establishing legitimacy, foster a positive reputation and develop enduring stakeholder relationships, they needed to broaden stakeholder roles from merely informing and responding to actively involving stakeholders in corporate CSR communication strategies. CSR dialogue is regarded as a co-created mutual understanding between the company and its users (Johnson-Cramer et al., 2017). This dialogic communication provides users with insights necessary for their social roles in the CSR process. It clarifies the outcomes that dialogic communication can bring to the company, such as building company–user relationships, discovering common meanings, reducing conflicts, enhancing trust, encouraging participatory decision-making and promoting economic and social welfare (Payne & Calton, 2017).

Korschun and Du (2013) first proposed the burgeoning concept of virtual CSR; they drew on the use of social media to assess the benefits and risks for businesses initiating virtual CSR dialogues and developed a research framework that focused on how users identify with enterprises through recognition and expectations in the virtual CSR co-creation process. Jurietti et al. (2017) employed a case study of Unilever's Sustainable Living Lab to empirically validate Korschun and Du's (2013) theoretical framework. They discovered that the qualities of virtual CSR dialogue play a crucial role in facilitating value co-creation between consumers and companies (O'Brien et al., 2018; Soutar, 2017).

Virtual CSR co-creation is inseparable from the support of a co-creation platform. The rapid development of Internet technology has given birth to various social media platforms, such as Weibo, WeChat, Twitter and Facebook, which provide two-way dialogue and interaction among customers, and between customers and enterprises. This collaboration offers the opportunity to create or modify CSR strategies and programmes through social media to better meet stakeholder expectations. Sutton (2016) applied examples of fashion brands (H&M, TOMS and SAP) to propose that social media, with its interactive and social characteristics, is capable of offering CSR communication tremendous chances to push corporations to be viewed as open and transparent entities and facilitate the co-creation value of sustainability through engaging with consumers. Okazaki et al. (2020) claimed that virtual CSR is capable of the creation of consumer-centric CSR programmes that encourage consumers to proactively interact with brands to co-create value through informal partnerships. Consumers are encouraged to take part in, or create, corporate CSR activities and two-way interaction on the online platform or social media is emphasised.

This chapter categorises existing research on virtual CSR co-creation into five perspectives.

Motivational perspective. Some scholars mainly focus on the motives of virtual CSR co-creation. Okazaki et al. (2020) claimed that the most likely driver for customers co-creating with brands lies in their pursuit of socially sustainable and responsible activities through easy to use, convenient and efficient social media channels in the context of virtual CSR co-creation. Cheng and Kodono (2022) found that users had instinctive, responsible and cost avoidance motivations to participate in virtual CSR co-creation activities, which had a positive influence on users' brand attitude towards the company.

Psychological perspective. Other scholars deemed that customers' reactions to CSR activities usually involved underlying psychological mechanisms. Zhang et al. (2023) empirically proved that there were underlying psychological mechanisms in the relationship between digital social responsibility and customer engagement, which was mediated by affective commitment and moderated by gamification affordance. Fan et al. (2017a, 2017b) discussed the psychological mechanism of consumers' participation in social enterprise responsibility co-creation in virtual communities and its impact on virtual community identity based on social presence theory. Fan et al. (2017a, 2017b) used the Ant Forest project launched by Alipay and the WeRun Donation project launched by Tencent as examples to define virtual CSR co-creation and verify that it has a positive impact on consumer identification from consumers' psychological ownership perspective. Liu et al. (2020) took Ant Forest as an example of a virtual CSR co-creation activity to explore the underlying mechanism of the impact of CSR-corporate ability on consumers' continuous intention to participate in a virtual CSR co-creation activity from the consumers' personal characteristics perspective. Sun et al. (2022) explored whether the experience value gained by a user during the virtual co-creation process would lead to green consumption. Liu and Deng (2019) tested the impact of different interaction routes of virtual CSR co-creation and consumer characteristics on consumer psychological cognition. They found that an experiential route of virtual CSR co-creation activities influenced independent consumers more while a structural route in virtual CSR co-creation impacted interdependent consumers more. Deng (2022) further examined the impact of virtual CSR co-creation on different types of interactive routes on consumer identity and found that the experiential route of virtual CSR co-creation has stronger effects on consumer identity than the structural route of virtual CSR co-creation. Perceived CSR was originally proposed by Lichtenstein et al. (2004) who deemed that customers' overall perceptions of an enterprise and its CSR activities are based on the implementation of CSR activities and a psychological cognition is formed by understanding the content of CSR activities.

From a cognitive psychological perspective, Liu (2014) coded and divided perceived CSR into interest perception, emotional perception and expectation consistency; Liu (2014) explored the mechanisms of these different types of perceptions of CSR on participative willingness in virtual CSR co-creation. Zhang and Wang (2022) empirically proved the reliability and validity of this classification. Interest perception encompasses the degree to which customers perceive information control, social gains and enhanced self-esteem, all of which relate to their own interests. Emotional perception refers to the pleasure and emotional utility that customers derive from CSR activities. Expectation consistency pertains to the alignment between customers' values and anticipated outcomes of these activities. Customer psychological empowerment, which includes right to choose, and right to know and influence power, acts as a mediating factor in how perception of CSR impact intentions to participate. Fan et al. (2019), based on self-determination theory, divided virtual CSR co-creation into three basic psychological needs: a sense of competence, autonomy and relatedness; they tested their impact on consumer attitude.

Relational perspective. The relationship between social value co-creators (users, enterprises) has an important impact on the co-creation effect. Focusing on the theories of value co-creation and social entrepreneurship, Jiao and Fan (2019) defined the essence of social responsibility co-creation in virtual enterprises and constructed a theoretical analytical framework for customer–enterprise social value co-creation. Their research identified three types of virtual CSR co-creation:

transactional, collaborative and gamified virtual CSR co-creation. Transactional co-creation means that customers, as a party to market transactions, participate actively by purchasing a company's products or services to get involved with CSR activities, such as Timberland's "carbon footprint" label, DiDi's "Love mileage" and Taobao store's "public welfare baby". Collaborative co-creation means that customers, as partners of enterprises, jointly complete the design, organisation and implementation of CSR activities with enterprises and share responsibility identity, such as YumChina's "One Yuan Donation" programme (YumChina, 2019) and Sesame Credit's "Unmanned Station" (Zhang & Jiang, 2017). Gamified virtual CSR co-creation considers customers to be game players who participate in game-related CSR activities developed by enterprises, such as Alipay's "Ant Forest" and Deutsche Telekom's "Treasure Hunt at Sea". In follow-up research, some scholars divided virtual CSR co-creation into experimental co-creation and interactive co-creation (Luo et al., 2021).

Interactive process perspective. Scholars classified virtual CSR co-creation based on different routes of interactivity. Storbacka et al. (2016) divided virtual CSR co-creation into three types based on the interaction level difference between consumers and enterprises: enterprise-led value co-creation, consumer-led value co-creation and interactive value co-creation. Black and Veloutsou (2017) claimed that virtual CSR co-creation depends on interactions among consumers, brand and brand communities. Identity co-creation is generated through the communication of CSR co-creation behaviour between consumers and enterprises. Jiao and Fan (2019) suggested that the aim of CSR is to create social value and defined the co-creation of customer–enterprise social value as a behaviour where customers and enterprises jointly participate in CSR activities. More recent studies have expanded on these insights by highlighting the nuanced interactions in virtual CSR co-creation. Xu et al. (2022) and Zhou et al. (2023) demonstrated that gamified CSR activities in virtual environments enhance continuous CE and identification with the brand. Moreover, Zhao et al. (2023) emphasised the role of virtual reality in CSR communication by showing that immersive experiences can increase consumers' mental health awareness-related CSR messages. These studies provide valuable insights into the complex dynamics between virtual CSR co-creation activities and consumers, and they highlight the importance of aligning CSR initiatives with consumers' self-construals.

Consumer Engagement (CE)

Customer engagement and CE, while often used interchangeably, represent distinct aspects of interaction with a brand. Customer engagement specifically refers to the relationships and interactions a business cultivates with its existing customers, which focus on enhancing customer experience, loyalty and retention through personalised marketing, loyalty programmes and excellent customer service (Harrigan et al., 2018; Hollebeek et al., 2019). In contrast, CE encompasses interactions with both current customers and potential consumers, including those who have not yet made a purchase. This broader engagement aims to build brand awareness, shape brand perceptions and foster a strong community around the brand through social media, content marketing and public relations efforts (Bazi et al., 2023). While customer engagement metrics often include customer satisfaction scores, repeat purchase rates and customer lifetime value (Pansari & Kumar, 2017), CE metrics encompass social media interactions, website traffic and brand sentiment analysis (Morgan-Thomas et al., 2020). Strategically, customer engagement aims to deepen relationships with existing customers to increase profitability, whereas CE seeks to attract and involve a broader audience to enhance overall brand presence (Rather, 2020). This distinction underscores the need for brands to tailor their engagement strategies to effectively address both specific customer needs and the broader market audience. Therefore, this chapter focuses on CE rather than customer engagement.

CE is a concept that continues to grow in popularity and attract extensive research (Lim et al., 2022), for example, the Marketing Science Institute (2018, 2020) included CE in their priority list from 2018 to 2022. CE involves consumers' interactions and involvement with a brand or organisation that moves beyond simple awareness to foster deeper connections and participation (Brodie et al., 2011). Although the conceptualisation of engagement remains contested (Alexander et al., 2018; Brodie et al., 2013, 2019; Chahal et al., 2020; Grewal et al., 2017; Kumar et al., 2019; Obilo et al., 2021), researchers classify CE as either unidimensional or multidimensional in academic and business settings, as indicated in Table 13.3. This suggests that CE can encompass diverse viewpoints that capture the "nature of interaction" displayed by consumers. It also allows for the derivation of marketing strategies that either promote desired or deter undesired consumer behaviours in various specific situational contexts (Roy et al., 2018) across different industries and sectors (Lim et al., 2022).

CE in the CSR Context

The concept of CE has gained significant attention in the field of CSR. Bowden (2009) defined engagement as a component of a company's CSR efforts, while Morsing and Schultz (2006, p. 323) characterised it as the communication related to an organisation's "ethical and socially responsible initiatives". In the context of CSR, engagement is particularly important as it reflects customers' emotional connection with, and active participation in, a company's socially responsible activities (Hollebeek et al., 2014). CE, in the CSR context, refers to the active participation and emotional investment of consumers in a company's CSR activities, which can manifest through various forms, such as electronic word of mouth (WOM), social media interactions and other collaborative efforts.

One of the key findings from recent studies is that CE in CSR is influenced by the perceived interactivity of CSR campaigns (Lee et al., 2021). Interactivity, in this regard, refers to the extent to which consumers feel involved in the decision-making process and are able to influence the outcomes of CSR initiatives. Companies that successfully implement participatory CSR campaigns, which invite consumers to participate in solving social issues, have been found to foster higher levels of CE (Lee et al., 2021). This increased engagement not only raises awareness about CSR initiatives but also strengthens consumer–brand relationships and enhances brand image (Kim, 2019).

Table 13.3 An absence of agreement regarding the conceptualisation and operationalisation of consumer engagement

Article	Construct	Dimensions
Van Doorn et al. (2010)	Multidimensional	Valence, modality, scope, nature of impact and customer goals
So et al. (2014, 2016)	Multidimensional	Identification, attention, absorption, enthusiasm and interaction
Hollebeek et al. (2016)	Multidimensional (SDL)	Operant resources (including cognitive, emotional, behavioural and social knowledge and skills) and operand resources (e.g. equipment)
Pham and Avnet (2009), Higgins and Scholer (2009), Verhoef et al. (2010), Javornik and Mandelli (2012), Cambra-Fierro et al. (2013), Verleye et al. (2014), Jaakkola and Alexander (2014), Ashley and Tuten (2015), Kumar and Pansari (2016), Harmeling et al. (2017), Roy et al. (2018), Beckers et al. (2018), Harrigan et al. (2018), Obilo et al. (2021)	Unidimensional	Behaviour
Vivek et al. (2012)	Multidimensional	Cognitive, behavioural, emotional, social and other dimensions
Cheung et al. (2021), Calder et al. (2016), So et al. (2016), Pansari and Kumar (2016), Alvarez-Milan et al. (2018)	Multidimensional	Psychology and behaviour

(continued)

Table 13.3 (continued)

Article	Construct	Dimensions
Brodie (2011), Glynn and Brodie (2014), Hollebeek (2011), Hollebeek et al. (2014), Ozuem and Willis (2021)	Multidimensional	Cognition, emotion (affect), conation (behaviour)
Obilo et al. (2021)	Unidimensional	Behaviour (content engagement, consumer co-creation, consumer advocacy and negative engagement)

Moreover, the role of social media in facilitating CE in CSR cannot be overstated. Social media platforms provide an interactive and accessible space for consumers to express their opinions, share information and engage in dialogue with companies about their CSR practices (del Mar García-de los Salmones et al., 2021; Okazaki et al., 2020). A study by Chomvilailuk and Butcher (2018) highlighted the impact of strategic CSR marketing communications on CE; it showed that consumers who perceive a community value in CSR initiatives are more likely to engage in positive WOM, thus enhancing the effectiveness of CSR campaigns.

However, CE in CSR is not uniform across all demographics. Cultural differences significantly influence the extent to which consumers engage with CSR communication. A cross-cultural study by Chu et al. (2020) revealed that Chinese consumers' engagement with CSR communication in social media is stronger than that of their American counterparts. This suggests that companies should consider cultural nuances when developing their CSR strategies and communications to ensure they resonate with the local consumer base.

The Millennial Generation

Generation Y, also known as the millennial generation and echo boomers, represents a tech-savvy cohort born between the early 1980s and 2000s (Chuah et al., 2017; Ng et al., 2010; Sethi et al., 2018). Millennials are named due to their proximity to the new millennium and their upbringing in the digital age (Smith & Nichols, 2015). They exhibit a multidimensional identity with varying age classifications (Howe & Strauss, 2000; Flecha-Ortíz et al., 2021; Moreno et al., 2017; Pew Research Center, 2021). These individuals matured during an era marked by the rise of social media, the decline of traditional values and globalisation (Bento et al., 2018). Scholars and practitioners recognise them as tech-savvy, socially conscious and active social media users. In today's youth-oriented society, millennials are the most tech-fluent generation; they seamlessly integrate social media into their everyday communication, social interactions, online purchasing and information sharing (Celi, 2019). They constitute the largest population in the social media market, so millennials are crucial target audiences that business managers must actively engage with and cultivate (Soares et al., 2017). According to Bargoni et al. (2023), demographics could significantly impact consumers' online behaviours. Specifically, age, as one of the five consumer characteristics, is provisionally considered due to the belief that younger generations may hold distinct value systems compared to older generations (Lissitsa & Kol, 2021).

Unlike other generations, millennials exhibit strong responses to CSR that emphasise social, cultural and environmental consciousness. Anderson et al. (2018) highlighted that CSR significantly impacts their purchase decisions, for example, millennials are willing to pay more for products from socially responsible companies. Given their substantial purchasing power, further investigation of this consumer group is crucial (Azami et al., 2018). To influence their decisions positively, marketers should explore their values. Fridays for Future, one of the global environmental youth movements, demonstrates that millennials recognise societal impacts and feels a personal responsibility to create change (Boon et al., 2020). Formánková et al. (2019) proposed that CSR is an essential aspect of millennials' lives, and they are highly conscious of CSR. Millennials were increasingly educated about sustainability when they were students, and they have a strong understanding of fundamental ecological and sustainability principles and actively engage in environmentally responsible consumption practices (Frey, 2018).

Relevance of Millennials to Brand Engagement

Virtual CSR co-creation initiatives have been particularly effective in engaging millennial consumers who value authenticity, transparency and social responsibility (Deloitte, 2024). For example, the Ant Forest initiative by Alipay has significantly engaged millennial (Generation Y) consumers in China and beyond; thus, showcasing a successful model of virtual CSR co-creation (Yang et al., 2018). Ant Forest, launched by Alipay under the Alibaba Group, incentivises users to undertake eco-friendly activities, such as green commuting and paperless transactions, which are tracked and rewarded with virtual green energy points. These points can be used to grow virtual trees, which correspond to real trees planted in desertified areas once enough points are accumulated. Several studies and reports highlight the demographic engagement of Ant Forest and note that a substantial portion of its user base belongs to Generation Y (Tong & Sun, 2022; Yang et al., 2018). This group is particularly motivated by the gamified, interactive nature of the platform, which aligns well with their tech-savvy and socially conscious characteristics. The platform's success in mobilising over 650 million users to plant over 400 million trees and create 31 nature reserves is a testament to its appeal and effectiveness. By successfully engaging a diverse and large user base, Ant Forest demonstrates how digital platforms can facilitate significant contributions to environmental goals that align with Sustainable Development Goal 13: urgent action against climate change. The project's collaborative model, involving multiple stakeholders like non-governmental organisations and local communities, further enriches the co-creation experience and ensures a broad impact.

Value Co-creation Theory

Despite its frequent appearance in academic literature, value co-creation remains one of the most elusive concepts to grasp in marketing and management (Grönroos, 2008). The value co-creation process is unclear due to its individualistic evaluation characteristics without apparent starts, contents and ends. Before 2000, it primarily occurred within the realm of co-production rather than marketing, as corporations prioritised transactions involving commodities and services to align with a product-centric approach (Payne et al., 2009). The traditional perspective of goods-dominant logic sees enterprises and consumers as the primary and ultimate beneficiaries in the value chain, and it relies on tangible commodities for value creation. Enterprises are seen as the sole creators of value and responsible for delivering value, meeting consumer needs and managing products, services and marketing efforts while consumers are viewed merely as recipients of value without shouldering any relevant responsibility (Miller et al., 2002). The value transfers from enterprises to consumers as a one-way link within the value chain (Normann & Ramirez, 1993). Enterprises as service providers make consumers "better off" by increasing their well-being, on the other hand, they may also make them "worse off" (Grönroos & Voima, 2013), for instance, a product or service that did not live up to consumers' expectations, inadequate refund policies or an unfavourable impression caused by poorly crafted marketing messages.

The emergence of the co-production viewpoint redefines the role of consumers in the value chain. Consumers are seen as active contributors to value creation, participating within the confines of the enterprises' operations. However, the essence of co-production still remains firm-centric. The concept of value co-production firstly clarified the consumer as the value co-creator; it was thought that customer and enterprise jointly create and re-create value in the value chain. On this basis, Prahalad and Ramaswamy (2000, 2004) went a step further and proposed the concept of value co-creation by acknowledging customers as co-creators of value alongside an enterprise. It emphasises the interactive nature of value creation, which occurs through ongoing exchanges between customers and an enterprise. Value co-creation not only transforms the linear mode of value creation into an interactive, mutually beneficial one but also redefines the notion of value from short-term transaction to long-term value-in-use.

SDL Perspective

Since 2000, marketers have acknowledged the significance of intangible assets, including services and relationships. This recognition has led to a shift in marketing from a goods-dominant logic to a SDL, which offers a framework explaining value creation through interactions among actors. This logic transcends the traditional goods-dominant perspective by focusing on the process of serving rather than the output of products (Vargo & Lusch, 2004). SDL emphasises that value is "phenomenological" and "contextual" (Vargo & Lusch, 2008) and extends beyond a mere bundle of products and services exchanged for a price. It should be "experienced" by customers who transit from role of "co-producer" to "co-creator" in an ongoing process. As co-creators, customers are able to give their views on product design procedures and delivery processes to enhance enterprises' capabilities to satisfy customers' wants and needs (Lusch & Vargo, 2006).

SL Perspective

Grönroos and Gummerus (2014) extended the value co-creation theory to SL, which shares both similarities and differences with SDL. Both SL and SDL serve the common purpose of recognising the significance of service and the interaction between service providers and customers. A consensus on the meaning of "service" was reached in terms of the implicit application of resources (skills, knowledge) in value creation. Although value-in-use represents a core value concept in both SL and SDL, it is only determined and influenced by a goods logic in SDL articles, whereas it is both determined and created by the user for the user in SL; in other words, SL emphasises that value is experientially and contextually determined by the customer, thus making the customer the central driver of the value creation process. SL offers a distinct analytical perspective that examines the roles of various actors within the value creation process in more depth (Grönroos, 2011). In contrast, SDL's metaphorical use of co-creation can lead to a broad and unspecified understanding of the value creation process, which potentially limits the managerial applicability of the concept. SL, with its clear distinction between direct and indirect interactions, provides a more analytical framework for understanding and leveraging value co-creation in marketing practices (Grönroos & Voima, 2013).

Grönroos (2008) mentioned the value facilitation model and the value fulfilment model. In the former, customers are value creators during their consumption while suppliers play the roles of value facilitators by offering needed resources without interfaces between them. In the latter, suppliers, when adopting a SL and generating interfaces with customers, can actively participate in customers' consumption processes and expand their role beyond mere value facilitation, and effectively become value co-creators. Grönroos (2011) disagreed with Vargo and Lusch's (2008, p. 6) view that "enterprises...... cannot create/deliver value independently" and posited a value-in-use creation model consisting of a production process and value creation process. Enterprises take charge of, and play roles of, value facilitators to offer resources that customers need without direct interaction in the production process; customers engaged in the production process without direct interaction will lead to customers' independent value creation. In turn, customers are mainly in charge of the value creation process to generate real value; direct interaction exists between enterprise and customer, which forms a platform that could make value co-creation possible and in which interaction quality is fundamental. It should be noted that the two processes in reality will not always be linear but in different sequences sometimes, which means customers could actively develop new resources as co-developer at the start of the whole process, thus providing enterprises with chances to co-create value with customers in a value creation process before the production process begins.

The transition from a goods-dominant logic to a SDL, as proposed by SDL, is further refined by SL's focus on the analytical and managerial aspects of value creation. SL offers a more nuanced understanding of the customer's role in value creation and provides a framework for firms to engage in value co-creation through direct interactions, thus transforming marketing strategies and practices.

Service Science Logic Perspective

Service science, an interdisciplinary field, has emerged to address the complexities of service innovation and value co-creation in the modern economy. At its core, service science is the study of service systems, which are dynamic configurations of people, technology, value propositions and shared information that interact to co-create value (Maglio & Spohrer, 2008). The philosophical foundation of service science is often attributed to SDL. SDL emphasises the role of the customer as a co-creator of value, which challenges the traditional linear model of value creation and suggests a more collaborative and interactive process. SL, while closely related to SDL, offers a more nuanced and analytical approach to understanding service systems. SL focuses on the customer's role in value creation and the provider's role as a facilitator of that process (Grönroos, 2011). It suggests that value is not merely co-created but is primarily created by the customer through their use of resources in their own service processes (Grönroos, 2011). This view aligns with the idea that service systems are configurations that enable value co-creation, where the provider's role is to enhance the customer's ability to create value.

Service science, informed by SDL and SL, seeks to categorise and explain the various types of service systems and how they interact and evolve. It aims to apply scientific understanding to advance the design and scaling of service systems for business and societal purposes (Maglio & Spohrer, 2008). The study of service systems focuses on value-creation configurations involving people, technology and value propositions. It recognises the crucial role of technology in enabling value co-creation on a larger scale (Saarijärvi et al., 2013). It is particularly relevant in the context of complex business-to-business services, such as information technology (IT) outsourcing, where the provider and client co-develop a unique service system through shared information and risk (Maglio & Spohrer, 2008). By embracing SDL and SL, service science provides a framework for analysing and enhancing the collaborative processes that characterise modern service exchanges. As the economy continues to shift towards service-oriented models, the principles of service science will be increasingly important for businesses seeking to innovate and improve their service offerings.

Service Ecosystem and Value Co-creation

The service ecosystem perspective extends value co-creation by considering the interdependent network of actors and resources that facilitate value creation (Lusch & Nambisan, 2015) embedded in a wider social system (Edvardsson et al., 2011). Service ecosystems are complex, self-adjusting systems where value co-creation occurs through the interaction of various actors (Vargo et al., 2008) who are connected by shared institutional logic (Lusch & Nambisan, 2015; Vargo & Lusch, 2016). This perspective aligns with the principles of service science, which seeks to understand the underlying mechanisms and structures that support service provision and innovation (Spohrer & Maglio, 2008). Value co-creation in service ecosystems is facilitated by the collaborative efforts of these actors, who together form a network of resource integrators (Vargo & Lusch, 2008). The service ecosystem perspective complements service science by emphasising the interconnectedness of service systems and the role of institutional arrangements in enabling value co-creation (Vargo et al., 2015). It is also congruent with SDL in its emphasis on the collaborative nature of value creation and the importance of actor-to-actor interactions (Vargo & Lusch, 2011). Value co-creation from a service ecosystems perspective extends the dyadic orientation in SDL to dynamic network system orientation.

The mechanisms of value co-creation in service ecosystems involve the integration of resources, the application of specialised competences and the influence of institutional arrangements (Edvardsson et al., 2011). These mechanisms are supported by IT, which enables the coordination and collaboration necessary for value co-creation (Lusch & Nambisan, 2015). The role of IT is dual as both an operand resource, facilitating the process, and an operant resource, initiating and shaping value co-creation (Ordanini & Rubera, 2010).

The service ecosystem perspective on value co-creation offers a holistic understanding of the complex interplay between actors, resources and institutions in the creation of value. This perspective is closely linked to both service science and SDL and provides a comprehensive framework for researchers and practitioners to explore and enhance value creation processes.

In summary, value co-creation involves a collaborative process where users, enterprises, suppliers and other stakeholders actively participate in creating products, services and experiences. This joint effort is characterised by ongoing, dynamic communication and cooperation, which leads to the continuous creation of value. It is essentially based on the value proposition of interaction between the user and the enterprise and the behaviour of participation; it is through dialogue and communication with the user, that an enterprise understands and satisfies a user's value needs, while users and other stakeholders provide physical and non-physical resources to support the enterprise in becoming value co-creators (Wu & Guo, 2022). Value co-creation not only promotes the development of new products, cost savings and increased financial returns, but also enhances the relationship between the firm and its stakeholders, and non-financial gains, such as increased satisfaction and positive WOM communication behaviours (Zhang et al., 2015). With the Internet era and the boost of social media technology, value co-creation between enterprises and users has not been confined to traditional physical operations or limited by physical space, it has gradually developed into the virtual space through social media, and the concept of virtual value co-creation has become increasingly popular (Zhang et al., 2022). Based on the various perspectives on value co-creation, virtual CSR co-creation is an application and theoretical extension of the theory of value co-creation in the field of CSR. And the value co-creation from the latest service ecosystem perspective happens to coincide with the United Nations Industrial Development Organization's (2024, para. 1) definition of CSR: "a management concept whereby companies integrate social and environmental concerns in their business operations and interactions with their stakeholders". By integrating these perspectives, we can develop a more nuanced understanding of how virtual CSR co-creation enables multiple actors, including service providers and consumers who play the equal important role in the value co-creation process, to collaboratively create value and address social and environmental concerns through dynamic interactions among a network of relationships.

Conclusion and Future Research Direction

In conclusion, virtual CSR co-creation represents a promising approach for companies to engage consumers, particularly millennials, in collaboratively addressing social and environmental challenges. By leveraging digital technologies and social media platforms, virtual CSR co-creation initiatives enable companies to foster two-way communication, transparency and value co-creation with their stakeholders. As millennials increasingly prioritise CSR and authentic brand relationships, virtual CSR co-creation can serve as a powerful tool for building brand loyalty and driving positive social change.

Future research could explore the long-term impacts of virtual CSR co-creation on consumer attitudes, behaviours and brand relationships. Additionally, studies could investigate the organisational factors that facilitate or hinder the successful implementation of virtual CSR co-creation initiatives, as well as the potential challenges and risks associated with this approach. By further examining the dynamics of virtual CSR co-creation, researchers and practitioners can develop more effective strategies for engaging consumers and promoting sustainable business practices in the digital age.

References

Alexander, M. J., Jaakkola, E., & Hollebeek, L. D. (2018). Zooming out: Actor engagement beyond the dyadic. *Journal of Service Management, 29*(3), 333–351.

Anderson, R. L., Dahlquist, S. H., & Garver, M. S. (2018). Millennials' purchasing response to CSR behaviour. *Marketing Management Journal, 28*(1).

Ashley, C., & Tuten, T. (2015). Creative strategies in social media marketing: An exploratory study of branded social content and consumer engagement. *Psychology & Marketing, 32*(1), 15–27. https://doi.org/10.1002/mar.20761

Azami, N., Bathmanathan, V., & Rajadurai, J. (2018). Understanding Generation Y Green purchasing decision in Malaysia. *Global Business and Management Research, 10*(3), 1010–1024.

Bargoni, A., Kliestik, T., Jabeen, F., & Santoro, G. (2023). Family firms' characteristics and consumer behaviour: An enquiry into millennials' purchase intention in the online channel. *Journal of Business Research, 156*, 113462.

Bazi, S., Filieri, R., & Gorton, M. (2023). Social media content aesthetic quality and customer engagement: The mediating role of entertainment and impacts on brand love and loyalty. *Journal of Business Research, 160*, 113778.

Beckers, S. F., Van Doorn, J., & Verhoef, P. C. (2018). Good, better, engaged? The effect of company-initiated customer engagement behavior on shareholder value. *Journal of the Academy of Marketing Science, 46*, 366–383.

Bento, M., Martinez, L. M., & Martinez, L. F. (2018). Brand engagement and search for brands on social media: Comparing Generations X and Y in Portugal. *Journal of Retailing and Consumer Services, 43*, 234–241. https://doi.org/10.1016/j.jretconser.2018.04.003

Bhattacharya, C. B., Korschun, D., & Sen, S. (2009). Strengthening stakeholder-company relationships through mutually beneficial corporate social responsibility initiatives. *Journal of Business Ethics, 85*(2), 257–272.

Black, I., & Veloutsou, C. (2017). Working consumers: Co-creation of brand identity, consumer identity and brand community identity. *Journal of Business Research, 70*, 416–429. https://doi.org/10.1016/j.jbusres.2016.07.012

Boon, L. K., Fern, Y. S., & Chee, L. H. (2020). Generation Y's purchase intention towards natural skincare products: A PLS-SEM analysis. *Global Business and Management Research, 12*(1), 61–77.

Bowden, J. L. H. (2009). The process of customer engagement: A conceptual framework. *Journal of Marketing Theory and Practice, 17*(1), 63–74. https://doi.org/10.2753/MTP1069-6679170105

Brodie, R. J., Fehrer, J. A., Jaakkola, E., & Conduit, J. (2019). Actor engagement in networks: Defining the conceptual domain. *Journal of Service Research, 22*(2), 173–188. https://doi.org/10.1177/1094670519827385

Brodie, R. J., Hollebeek, L. D., Jurić, B., & Ilić, A. (2011). Customer engagement: Conceptual domain, fundamental propositions, and implications for research. *Journal of Service Research, 14*(3), 252–271.

Brodie, R. J., Ilic, A., Juric, B., & Hollebeek, L. (2013). Consumer engagement in a virtual brand community: An exploratory analysis. *Journal of Business Research, 66*(1), 105–114.

Calder, B. J., Malthouse, E. C., & Schaedel, U. (2009). An experimental study of the relationship between online engagement and advertising effectiveness. *Journal of Interactive Marketing, 23*(4), 321–331.
Cambra-Fierro, J. J., Melero-Polo, I., & Vázquez-Carrasco, R. (2013). Customer engagement: Innovation in non-technical marketing processes. *Innovation, 15*(3), 326–336.
Capriotti, P. (2011). Communicating corporate social responsibility through the Internet and social media. In Ø. Ihlen, J. L. Bartlett, & S. May (Eds.), *The handbook of communication and corporate social responsibility* (pp. 358–378). John Wiley & Sons.
Carroll, A. B., & Shabana, K. M. (2010). The business case for corporate social responsibility: A review of concepts, research and practice. *International Journal of Management Reviews, 12*(1), 85–105. https://doi.org/10.1111/j.1468-2370.2009.00275.x
Carroll, A. B. (2016). Carroll's pyramid of CSR: Taking another look. *International Journal of Corporate Social Responsibility, 1*(3). https://doi.org/10.1186/s40991-016-0004-6
Carroll, A. B. (1979). A three-dimensional conceptual model of corporate performance. *Academy of Management Review, 4*(4), 497–505.
Celi, C. (2019). Millennials or Digital Natives: Consuming and producing news from activism. *Journal of Applied Business and Economics, 21*(9).
Chahal, H., Wirtz, J., & Verma, A. (2020). Social media brand engagement: Dimensions, drivers and consequences. *Journal of Consumer Marketing, 37*(2), 191–204.
Chan, K. W., & Li, S. Y. (2010). Understanding consumer-to-consumer interactions in virtual communities: The salience of reciprocity. *Journal of Business Research, 63*(9–10), 1033–1040.
Cheng, H., & Kodono, Y. (2022). The motivation behind participation in virtual CSR co-creation by Chinese post-90s: A case study of ant forest. *Journal of Advanced Computational Intelligence and Intelligent Informatics, 26*(4), 549–554.
Cheung, M. L., Pires, G. D., Rosenberger, P. J., Leung, W. K. S., & Salehhuddin Sharipudin, M.-N. (2021). The role of consumer-consumer interaction and consumer-brand interaction in driving consumer-brand engagement and behavioral intentions. *Journal of Retailing and Consumer Services, 61*, 102574–. https://doi.org/10.1016/j.jretconser.2021.102574

Cho, M., Furey, L. D., & Mohr, T. (2017). Communicating Corporate social responsibility on social media: Strategies, stakeholders, and public engagement on corporate Facebook. *Business and Professional Communication Quarterly, 80*(1), 52–69. https://doi.org/10.1177/2329490616663708

Chomvilailuk, R., & Butcher, K. (2018). The impact of strategic CSR marketing communications on customer engagement. *Marketing Intelligence and Planning, 36*(7), 764–777.

Chu, S.-C., Chen, H.-T., & Gan, C. (2020). Consumers' engagement with corporate social responsibility (CSR) communication in social media: Evidence from China and the United States. *Journal of Business Research, 110*, 260–271.

Chuah, S. H.-W., et al. (2017). What drives Gen Y loyalty? Understanding the mediated moderating roles of switching costs and alternative attractiveness in the value-satisfaction-loyalty chain. *Journal of Retailing and Consumer services, 36*, 124–136. https://doi.org/10.1016/j.jretconser.2017.01.010

Coombs, W. T., & Holladay, S. J. (2015). Two-minute drill: Video games and social media to advance CSR. In A. Adi, G. Grigore, & D. Crowther (Eds.), *Corporate social responsibility in the digital age* (1st ed.). Emerald.

Crane, A., & Matten, D. (2013). *The top 5 CSR trends for 2013*. Available at https://craneandmatten.blogspot.com/2013/01/the-top-5-csr-trends-for-2013.html. (Accessed 1 May 2024).

Davis, K. (1960). Can business afford to ignore social responsibilities? *California Management Review, 2*(3), 70–76. https://doi.org/10.2307/41166246

de Oliveira, E. C., & Carraro, N. C. (2021). Corporate social responsibility: Study in companies in the State of Sao Paulo. *International Journal of Management Science and Business Administration, 7*(3), 46–57.

del Mar García-de los Salmones, M., Herrero, A., & Martínez, P. (2021). Determinants of electronic word-of-mouth on social networking sites about negative news on CSR. *Journal of Business Ethics, 171*(3), 583–597. https://doi.org/10.1007/s10551-020-04466-9

Deloitte. (2024). *Gen Z and millennial survey*. https://www.deloitte.com/content/dam/assets-shared/docs/campaigns/2024/deloitte-2024-genz-millennial-survey.pdf?dlva=1. (Accessed 12 May 2024).

Deng, W. X. (2022). *Research on the impact mechanism of virtual CSR co-creation on consumer identity*. Master's Thesis. Chongqing University of Posts and Telecommunications.

Devin, B. (2016). Half-truths and dirty secrets: Omissions in CSR communication. *Public Relations Review, 42*(1), 226–228. https://doi.org/10.1016/j.pubrev.2015.09.004

Du, S., & Vieira, E. T. (2012). Striving for legitimacy through corporate social responsibility: Insights from oil companies. *Journal of Business Ethics, 110*, 413–427. https://doi.org/10.1007/s10551-012-1490-4

Edvardsson, B., Tronvoll, B., & Gruber, T. (2011). Expanding understanding of service exchange and value co-creation: A social construction approach. *Journal of the Academy of Marketing Science, 39*(2), 327–339. https://doi.org/10.1007/s11747-010-0200-y

Elving, W. J. L., Golob, U., Podnar, K., Ellerup-Nielsen, A., & Thomson, C. (2015). The bad, the ugly and the good: New challenges for CSR communication. *Corporate Communications, 20*(2), 118–127. https://doi.org/10.1108/CCIJ-02-2015-0006

Fan, S., Tian, Z., & Hu, X. (2017). Research on consumer participation behaviors in virtual CSR co-creation from the perspective of psychological ownership [in Chinese]. *Chinese Journal of Management, 14*(3). https://doi.org/10.3969/j.issn.1672-884x.2017.03.010

Fan, S., Du, P., Tian, Z., & Cheng, S. (2017). The impact of virtual cocreation in the context of "Internet plus public interest' [in Chinese]. *Macroeconomics*, 166–183. https://doi.org/10.16304/j.cnki.11-3952/f.2017.07.016

Fan, S., Tian, Z. L., & Zhang, L. J. (2019). Research on the impact of the psychological needs on consumer attitude in the virtual CSR co-creation [in Chinese]. *Chinese Journal of Management, 16*(6), 883. http://manu68.magtech.com.cn/Jwk_glxb/EN/

Fan, J., Jiao, J., & Lin, P. (2020). Influence of virtual CSR gamification design elements on customers' continuance intention of participating in social value co-creation: The mediation effect of psychological benefit. *Asia Pacific Journal of Marketing and Logistics, 32*(6), 1305–1326.

Flecha-Ortíz, J. et al. (2021). Millennials & snapchat: Self-expression through its use and its influence on purchase motivation. *Journal of Business Research*, 125, 798–805. https://doi.org/10.1016/j.jbusres.2019.03.005

Formánková, S. et al. (2019). Millennials' awareness and approach to social responsibility and investment—Case study of the Czech Republic. *Sustainability (Basel, Switzerland), 11*(2), 504. https://doi.org/10.3390/su11020504

Frederick, W. C. (1960). The growing concern over business responsibility. *California Management Review, 2*(4), 54–61. https://doi.org/10.2307/41165405

Frey, W. H. (2018). The millennial generation: A demographic bridge to America's diverse future. *Brookings Metropolitan Policy Program*. https://www.brookings.edu/wp-content/uploads/2018/01/2018-jan_brookings-metro_millennials-a-demographic-bridge-to-americas-diverse-future.pdf
Friedman, M. (1970, September 13). The social responsibility of business is to increase its profits. *New York Times Magazine*, 32–33, 122–126.
Friedman, M. (1962). *Capitalism and freedom*. University of Chicago Press.
Gond, J. P., Bowen, H. R., & Bowen, P. G. (2013). Introduction to the new edition. In *Social responsibilities of the businessman* (pp. ix–xvi). University of Iowa Press. https://doi.org/10.2307/j.ctt20q1w8f.4
Gond, J. P., & Moon, J. (2011). Corporate social responsibility in retrospect and prospect: Exploring the life-cycle of an essentially contested concept. *ICCSR Research Paper Series, 59*, 1–40.
Grewal, D., Roggeveen, A. L., Sisodia, R., & Nordfält, J. (2017). Enhancing customer engagement through consciousness. *Journal of Retailing, 93*(1), 55–64.
Grönroos, C. (2008). Service logic revisited: Who creates value? And who co-creates? *European Business Review, 20*(4), 298–314. https://doi.org/10.1108/09555340810886585
Grönroos, C. (2011). Value co-creation in service logic: A critical analysis. *Marketing Theory, 11*(3), 279–301. https://doi.org/10.1177/1470593111408177
Grönroos, C., & Voima, P. (2013). Critical service logic: Making sense of value creation and co-creation. *Journal of the Academy of Marketing Science, 41*(2), 133–150. https://doi.org/10.1007/s11747-012-0308-3
Grönroos, C., & Gummerus, J. (2014). The service revolution and its marketing implications: Service logic vs service-dominant logic. *Managing Service Quality, 24*(3), 206–229.
Guthey, E., & Morsing, M. (2014). CSR and the mediated emergence of strategic ambiguity. *Journal of Business Ethics, 120*, 555–569.
Harmeling, C. M., Moffett, J. W., Arnold, M. J., & Carlson, B. D. (2017). Toward a theory of customer engagement marketing. *Journal of the Academy of Marketing Science, 45*, 312–335.
Harrigan, P., Evers, U., Miles, M. P., & Daly, T. (2018). Customer engagement and the relationship between involvement, engagement, self-brand connection and brand usage intent. *Journal of Business Research, 88*, 388–396.
Heslin, P. A., & Ochoa, J. D. (2008). Understanding and developing strategic corporate social responsibility. *Organizational Dynamics, 37*, 125–144.

Higgins, E. T., & Scholer, A. A. (2009). Engaging the consumer: The science and art of the value creation process. *Journal of Consumer Psychology, 19*(2), 100–114.

Hollebeek, L. D., Srivastava, R. K., & Chen, T. (2019). S-D logic–informed customer engagement: Integrative framework, revised fundamental propositions, and application to CRM. *Journal of the Academy of Marketing Science, 47*(1), 161–185. https://doi.org/10.1007/s11747-016-0494-5

Hollebeek, L. (2011). Exploring customer brand engagement: Definition and themes. *Journal of Strategic Marketing, 19*(7), 555–573.

Hollebeek, L. D., Conduit, J., & Brodie, R. J. (2016). Strategic drivers, anticipated and unanticipated outcomes of customer engagement. *Journal of Marketing Management, 32*(5–6), 393–398.

Hollebeek, L. D., Glynn, M. S., & Brodie, R. J. (2014). Consumer brand engagement in social media: Conceptualization, scale development and validation. *Journal of Interactive Marketing, 28*(2), 149–165.

Howe, N., & Strauss, W. (2000). *Millennials rising: The next great generation.* Vintage.

Howe, J. (2006). The rise of crowdsourcing. *Wired Magazine, 14*(6), 176–183.

Iglesias, O., Markovic, S., Bagherzadeh, M., & Singh, J. J. (2018). Co-creation: A key link between corporate social responsibility, customer trust, and customer loyalty. *Journal of Business Ethics, 163*(1), 151–166. https://doi.org/10.1007/s10551-018-4015-y

Ilieva-Koleva, D., & Dobreva, J. (2021). Social entrepreneurship as a form of social responsibility in Bulgaria. *International Journal of Operations Management, 1*(3), 25–31.

Jaakkola, E., & Alexander, M. (2014). The role of customer engagement behavior in value co-creation: A service system perspective. *Journal of Service Research, 17*(3), 247–261.

Javornik, A., & Mandelli, A. (2012). Behavioural perspectives of customer engagement: An exploratory study of customer engagement with three Swiss FMCG brands. *Journal of Database Marketing & Customer Strategy Management, 19*, 300–310.

Jeong, H. J., Paek, H.-J., & Lee, M. (2013). Corporate social responsibility effects on social network sites. *Journal of Business Research, 66*(10), 1889–1895. https://doi.org/10.1016/j.jbusres.2013.02.010

Jiao, J. N., & Fan, J. (2019). A literature review and prospects of customer-enterprise social value co-creation. *Foreign Economics and Management, 41*(02), 72–83.

Johnson-Cramer, M. E., Berman, S. L., & Post, J. E. (2017). Re-examining the concept of 'stakeholder management'. In J. Andriof et al. (Eds.), *Unfolding stakeholder thinking 2* (pp. 145–161). Routledge.

Jurietti, E., Mandelli, A., & Fudurić, M. (2017). How do virtual corporate social responsibility dialogs generate value? A case study of The Unilever Sustainable Living Lab. *Corporate Social-Responsibility and Environmental Management, 24*(5), 357–367.

Khattak, A., & Yousaf, Z. (2022). Digital social responsibility towards corporate social responsibility and strategic performance of Hi-Tech SMEs: Customer engagement as a mediator. *Sustainability (Basel, Switzerland), 14*(1), 131. https://doi.org/10.3390/su14010131

Kim, S. (2019). The process model of corporate social responsibility (CSR) communication: CSR communication and its relationship with consumers' CSR knowledge, trust, and corporate reputation perception. *Journal of Business Ethics, 154*(4), 1143–1159. https://doi.org/10.1007/s10551-017-3433-6

Korschun, D., & Du, S. (2013). How virtual corporate social responsibility dialogs generate value: A framework and propositions. *Journal of Business Research, 66*(9), 1494–1504.

Kramer, M. R., & Porter, M. (2011). *Creating shared value* (Vol. 17). FSG.

Kumar, V., & Pansari, A. (2016). Competitive advantage through engagement. *Journal of Marketing Research, 53*(4), 497–514.

Kumar, V., Rajan, B., Gupta, S., et al. (2019). 'Customer engagement in service. *Journal of the Academic Marketing Science, 47*, 138–160. https://doi.org/10.1007/s11747-017-0565-2

Latapí Agudelo, M. A., Jóhannsdóttir, L., & Davídsdóttir, B. (2019). A literature review of the history and evolution of corporate social responsibility. *International Journal of Corporate Social Responsibility, 4*(1), 1–23.

Lee, S. Y., Kim, Y., & Kim, Y. (2021). Engaging consumers with corporate social responsibility campaigns: The roles of interactivity, psychological empowerment, and identification. *Journal of Business Research, 134*, 507–517.

Lee, S. Y., Zhang, W., & Abitbol, A. (2019). What makes CSR communication lead to CSR participation? Testing the mediating effects of CSR associations, CSR credibility, and organization-public relationships. *Journal of Business Ethics, 157*(2), 413–429. https://doi.org/10.1007/s10551-017-3609-0

Levitt, T. (1958). The dangers of social responsibility. *Harvard Business Review, 36*, 41–50.

Lichtenstein, D. R., Drumwright, M. E., & Braig, B. M. (2004). The effect of corporate social responsibility on customer donations to corporate-supported nonprofits. *Journal of Marketing, 68*(4), 16–32. https://doi.org/10.1509/jmkg.68.4.16.42726

Lim, W. M., Rasul, T., Kumar, S., & Ala, M. (2022). Past, present, and future of customer engagement. *Journal of Business Research, 140*, 439–458.

Lissitsa, S., & Kol, O. (2021). Four generational cohorts and hedonic m-shopping: Association between personality traits and purchase intention. *Electronic Commerce Research, 21*, 545–570. https://doi.org/10.1007/s10660-019-09381-4

Liu, J. H. (2014). *The inherent mechanism of consumer reactions to corporate social responsibility.* Doctoral Dissertations. University of Shang Dong.

Liu, X. P., Deng, W. X., & Yang, Y. (2019). Research on the influence mechanism of virtual CSR co-creation on consumer identity. *WHICEB 2019 Proceedings*, 14. https://aisel.aisnet.org/whiceb2019/14

Liu, X. P., & Deng, W. X. (2019). Research on the mechanism of virtual CSR co-creation on consumer identity-the regulating role of self-construal [in Chinese]. *Soft Science, 33*(12), 139–144. https://doi.org/10.13956/j.ss.1001-8409.2019.12.22

Liu, X., Yang, Y., & Chen, S. (2020). Consumers' continuance intention for participation in virtual corporate social responsibility cocreation activities: Self-construal and flow. *Social behavior and personality, 48*(4), 1–11. https://doi.org/10.2224/sbp.9027

Luger, M., Hofer, K. M., & Floh, A. (2022). Support for corporate social responsibility among generation Y consumers in advanced versus emerging markets. *International Business Review, 31*(2), 101903.

Luo et al. (2021). Literature review and prospects of virtual CSR co-creation [in Chinese]. *Soft Science, 35*(09), 112–116, 130. https://doi.org/10.13956/j.ss.1001-8409.2021.09.17. Available at Literature Review and Prospects of Virtual CSR Co-creation - CNKI

Lusch, R. F., & Vargo, S. L. (2006). Service-dominant logic as a foundation for a general theory. In R. F. Lusch & S. L. Vargo (Eds.), *The service-dominant logic of marketing: Dialog, debate, and directions* (p. 406). M.E. Sharpe.

Lusch, R. F., & Nambisan, S. (2015). Service innovation. *MIS Quarterly, 39*(1), 155–176.

Lusch, R. F., & Vargo, S. L. (2014). *The service-dominant logic of marketing: Dialog, debate, and directions.* Routledge.

Madsen, P. M., & Rodgers, Z. J. (2015). Looking good by doing good: The antecedents and consequences of stakeholder attention to corporate disaster relief. *Strategic Management Journal, 36*(5), 776–794.

Maglio, P. P., & Spohrer, J. (2008). Fundamentals of service science. *Journal of the Academy of Marketing Science, 36*, 18–20.

Mantovani, D., de Andrade, L. M., & Negrão, A. (2017). How motivations for CSR and consumer-brand social distance influence consumers to adopt pro-social behaviour. *Journal of Retailing and Consumer Services, 36*, 156–163. https://doi.org/10.1016/j.jretconser.2017.01.009

Marketing Science Institute. (2018, May 13). Research priorities 2018–2020. *MSI at the ARF*. Available at https://www.msi.org/articles/marketers-top-challenges-2018-2020-research-priorities

Marketing Science Institute. (2020, May 7). MSI announces 2020–22 research priorities. *MSI at the ARF*. Available at https://www.msi.org/articles/2020-22-msi-research-priorities-outline-marketers-top-concerns/

McGuire, J. W. (1963). *Business and society*. McGraw Hill.

Miller, D., Hope, Q., Eisenstat, R., Foote, N., & Galbraith, J. (2002). The problem of solutions: Balancing clients and capabilities. *Business horizons, 45*(2), 3–12. https://doi.org/10.1016/S0007-6813(02)00181-7

Moreno, F. M., Lafuente, J. G., Carreón, F. Á., & Moreno, S. M. (2017). The characterization of the millennials and their buying behavior. *International Journal of Marketing Studies, 9*(5), 135–144.

Morgan-Thomas, A., Dessart, L., & Veloutsou, C. (2020). Digital ecosystem and consumer engagement: A socio-technical perspective. *Journal of Business Research, 121*, 713–723. https://doi.org/10.1016/j.jbusres.2020.03.042

Morsing, M., & Schultz, M. (2006). Corporate social responsibility communication: Stakeholder information, response and involvement strategies. *Business Ethics (Oxford, England), 15*(4), 323–338. https://doi.org/10.1111/j.1467-8608.2006.00460.x

Ng, E. S. W., Schweitzer, L., & Lyons, S. T. (2010). New generation, great expectations: A field study of the millennial generation. *Journal of Business and Psychology, 25*(2), 281–292. https://doi.org/10.1007/s10869-010-9159-4

Normann, R., & Ramirez, R. (1993). From value chain to value constellation: Designing interactive strategy. *Harvard Business Review, 71*(4), 65–77.

Nwagbara, U., & Reid, P. (2013). Corporate social responsibility communication in the age of new media: Towards the logic of sustainability communication. *Revista De Management Comparat International, 14*(3), 400.

O'Brien, I. M., Jarvis, W., Soutar, G., & Ouschan, R. (2018). Co-creating a CSR strategy with customers to deliver greater value. In M. Brueckner, R. Spencer, & M. Paull (Eds.), *Disciplining the undisciplined? Perspectives from business, society and politics on responsible citizenship, corporate social responsibility and sustainability* (pp. 89–107). Springer, Cham. https://doi.org/10.1007/978-3-319-71449-3

Obilo, O. O., Chefor, E., & Saleh, A. (2021). Revisiting the consumer brand engagement concept. *Journal of Business Research, 126*, 634–643. https://doi.org/10.1016/j.jbusres.2019.12.023

Okazaki, S., Plangger, K., West, D., & Menéndez, H. D. (2020). Exploring digital corporate social responsibility communications on Twitter. *Journal of Business Research, 117*, 675–682. https://doi.org/10.1016/j.jbusres.2019.09.006

Ordanini, A., & Rubera, G. (2010). How does the application of an IT service innovation affect firm performance? A theoretical framework and empirical analysis on e-commerce. *Information and Management, 47*(1), 60–67.

Ozuem, W., & Willis, M. (2021). *Digital marketing strategies for value co-creation: Models and approaches for online brand communities.* Palgrave Macmillan. https://doi.org/10.1007/978-3-030-94444-5

Ozuem, W., Howell, K., & Lancaster, G. (2014). Corporate social responsibility: Towards a context-specific perspective in developing countries. *Social Responsibility Journal, 10*(3), 399–415.

Pansari, A., & Kumar, V. (2017). Customer engagement: The construct, antecedents, and consequences. *Journal of the Academy of Marketing Science, 45*, 294–311.

Payne, S. L., & Calton, J. M. (2017). Towards a managerial practice of stakeholder engagement: Developing multi-stakeholder learning dialogues. In J. Andriof et al. (Eds.), *Unfolding stakeholder thinking* (pp. 121–135). Routledge.

Payne, A., Storbacka, K., Frow, P., & Knox, S. (2009). Co-creating brands: Diagnosing and designing the relationship experience. *Journal of Business Research, 62*(3), 379–389.

Pew Research Center. (2021). Gen Z, millennials stand out for climate change activism, social media engagement with issue. Available at https://www.pewresearch.org/science/2021/05/26/gen-z-millennials-stand-out-for-climate-change-activism-social-media-engagement-with-issue/. (Accessed 24 May 2024).

Pham, M. T., & Avnet, T. (2009). Rethinking regulatory engagement theory. *Journal of Consumer Psychology, 19*(2), 115–123.

Pope, S., & Wæraas, A. (2016). CSR-Washing is rare: A conceptual framework, literature review, and critique. *Journal of Business Ethics, 137*(1), 173–193. https://doi.org/10.1007/s10551-015-2546-z

Porter, C. E., & Donthu, N. (2008). Cultivating trust and harvesting value in virtual communities. *Management Science, 54*(1), 113–128. https://doi.org/10.1287/mnsc.1070.0765

Prahalad, C. K., & Ramaswamy, V. (2000). Co-opting customer competence. *Harvard Business Review, 78*(1), 79–90.

Prahalad, C. K., & Ramaswamy, V. (2004). Co-creating unique value with customers. *Strategy & Leadership, 32*(3), 4–9.

Qi, L. Y., Wang, Y., & Lv, Z. G. (2021). Research on the evolution of corporate social responsibility based on organisational sense-making theory and institutional theory [in Chinese]. *Management Review, 33*(01), 215–218, 241.

Rademacher, L., & Remus, N. (2014). Correlating leadership style, communication strategy and management fashion: An approach to describing the drivers and settings of CSR institutionalization. In R. Tench, W. Sun, & B. Jones (Eds.), *Communicating corporate social responsibility: Perspectives and practice* (pp. 81–110). Emerald Group Publishing Limited.

Rather, R. A. (2020). Customer experience and engagement in tourism destinations: The experiential marketing perspective. *Journal of Travel & Tourism Marketing, 37*(1), 15–32.

Roy, S. K., Balaji, M. S., Soutar, G., Lassar, W. M., & Roy, R. (2018). Customer engagement behavior in individualistic and collectivistic markets. *Journal of Business Research, 86*, 281–290.

Saarijärvi, H., Kannan, P. K., & Kuusela, H. (2013). Value co-creation: Theoretical approaches and practical implications. *European Business Review, 25*(1), 6–19. https://doi.org/10.1108/09555341311287718

Sang, Y., & Han, E. (2023). A win-win way for corporate and stakeholders to achieve sustainable development: Corporate social responsibility value co-creation scale development and validation. *Corporate Social-Responsibility and Environmental Management, 30*(3), 1177–1190. https://doi.org/10.1002/csr.2412

Sarkar, S., & Searcy, C. (2016). 'Zeitgeist or chameleon? A Quantitative Analysis of CSR Definitions. *Journal of Cleaner Production, 135*, 1423–1435.

Schultz, F., Castelló, I., & Morsing, M. (2013). The construction of corporate social responsibility in network societies: A communication view. *Journal of Business Ethics, 115*, 681–692.

Sen, S., Bhattacharya, C. B., & Korschun, D. (2006). The role of corporate social responsibility in strengthening multiple stakeholder relationships: A field experiment. *Journal of the Academy of Marketing Science, 34*(2), 158–166.

Sethi, R. S., Kaur, J., & Wadera, D. (2018). Purchase intention survey of millennials towards online fashion stores. *Academy of Marketing Studies Journal, 22*(1), 1–16.

Sheehy, B. (2015). Defining CSR: Problems and solutions. *Journal of Business Ethics, 131*(3), 625–648. https://doi.org/10.1007/s10551-014-2281-x

Smith, T. J., & Nichols, T. (2015). Understanding the millennial generation. *Journal of Business Diversity, 15*(1), 39.

So, K. K. F., King, C., Sparks, B. A., & Wang, Y. (2016). The role of customer engagement in building consumer loyalty to tourism brands. *Journal of Travel Research, 55*(1), 64–78.

Soares, R. R. et al. (2017). Why are Generation Y consumers the most likely to complain and repurchase? *Journal of service management, 28*(3), 520–540. https://doi.org/10.1108/JOSM-08-2015-0256

Soutar, G. N. (2017). Virtual corporate social responsibility dialog: Seeking a gap between proposed concepts and actual practices. In S. Diehl, M. Karmasin, B. Mueller, & R. Terlutter (Eds.), *Handbook of integrated CSR communication* (pp. 225–245). Springer International Publishing.

Spohrer, J., & Maglio, P. P. (2008). The emergence of service science: Toward systematic service innovations to accelerate co-creation of value. *Production and Operations Management, 17*(3), 238–246.

Storbacka, K., Brodie, R. J., Böhmann, T., Maglio, P. P., & Nenonen, S. (2016). Actor engagement as a microfoundation for value co-creation. *Journal of Business Research, 69*(8), 3008–3017.

Sun, C. W., Obrenovic, B., & Li, H. T. (2022). Influence of virtual CSR co-creation on the purchase intention of green products under the heterogeneity of experience value. *Sustainability (Basel, Switzerland), 14*(20), 13617. https://doi.org/10.3390/su142013617

Sutton, J. (2016). *Why social media and sustainability should go hand in hand.* Available at https://www.triplepundit.com/story/2016/why-social-media-and-sustainability-should-go-hand-hand/25341. (Accessed 29 May 2023).

Tomaselli, G., Melia, M., Garg, L., Gupta, V., Xuereb, P. A., & Buttigieg, S. C. (2019). Digital and traditional tools for communicating corporate social responsibility: A literature review. In Information Resource Management Association (Ed.), *Corporate social responsibility: Concepts, methodologies, tools, and applications* (pp. 679–696). IGI Global. https://doi.org/10.4018/978-1-5225-6192-7.ch036

Tong, T., & Sun, P. (2022). From "national tree planting" to "carbon accounts": Ant Forest's platformisation and youth discourse strategies. *China Youth Studies*. Available at 从"全民义务植树"到"碳账户":蚂蚁森林的平台化与青年话语策略反思 (qq.com). (Accessed 24 May 2024).

Tu, K., Yang, X. C., Su, X., & Ou, X. C. (2020). The influence of supplier user's role stress on continuous value co-creation behavior in the sharing economy: A mediated moderation model [in Chinese]. *Nankai Business Review, 23*(06), 88–98.

United Nations Industrial Development Organization. (2024). *Progress by innovation*. Available at https://www.unido.org/our-focus-advancing-economic-competitiveness-competitive-trade-capacities-and-corporate-responsibility-corporate-social-responsibility-market-integration/what-csr. (Accessed 25 May 2024).

Van Doorn, J., Lemon, K. N., Mittal, V., Nass, S., Pick, D., Pirner, P., & Verhoef, P. C. (2010). Customer engagement behavior: Theoretical foundations and research directions. *Journal of Service Research, 13*(3), 253–266.

Vargo, S. L., & Lusch, R. F. (2016). Institutions and axioms: An extension and update of service-dominant logic. *Journal of the Academy of Marketing Science, 44*(1), 5–23. https://doi.org/10.1007/s11747-015-0456-3

Vargo, S. L., & Lusch, R. F. (2004). Evolving to a new dominant logic for marketing. *Journal of Marketing, 68*(1), 1–17.

Vargo, S. L., & Lusch, R. F. (2008). Service-dominant logic: Continuing the evolution. *Journal of the Academy of Marketing Science, 36*, 1–10.

Vargo, S. L., & Lusch, R. F. (2011). It's all B2B… and beyond: Toward a systems perspective of the market. *Industrial Marketing Management, 40*(2), 181–187.

Vargo, S. L., Maglio, P. P., & Akaka, M. A. (2008). On value and value co-creation: A service systems and service logic perspective. *European Management Journal, 26*(3), 145–152.

Vargo, S. L., Wieland, H., & Akaka, M. A. (2015). Innovation through institutionalization: A service ecosystems perspective. *Industrial Marketing Management, 44*, 63–72.

Verhoef, P. C., Reinartz, W. J., & Krafft, M. (2010). Customer engagement as a new perspective in customer management. *Journal of Service Research, 13*(3), 247–252.

Verleye, K., Gemmel, P., & Rangarajan, D. (2014). Managing engagement behaviours in a network of customers and stakeholders: Evidence from the nursing home sector. *Journal of Service Research, 17*(1), 68–84.

Vivek, S. D., Beatty, S. E., & Morgan, R. M. (2012). Customer engagement: Exploring customer relationships beyond purchase. *Journal of Marketing Theory and Practice, 20*(2), 122–146.

Walter, B. L. (2014). Corporate social responsibility communication: Towards a phase model of strategic planning. In R. Tench, W. Sun, & B. Jones (Eds.), *Communicating corporate social responsibility: Perspectives and practice (Critical Studies on Corporate Responsibility, Governance and Sustainability)* (Vol. 6, pp. 59–79). Emerald Group Publishing Limited, Leeds. https://doi.org/10.1108/S2043-9059(2014)0000006022

Walton, C. C. (1967). *Corporate social responsibilities*. Wadsworth Publishing Company.

Wu, Z. X., & Guo, T. T. (2022). The influencing mechanism of interactive route on consumers' participation willingness of virtual CSR value co-creation [in Chinese]. *Journal of Central University of Finance and Economics, 08*, 119–128. https://doi.org/10.19681/j.cnki.jcufe.2022.08.003

Xu, J., Du, H. S., Shen, K. N., & Zhang, D. (2022). How gamification drives consumer citizenship behaviour: The role of perceived gamification affordances. *International Journal of Information Management, 64*, 102477.

Yang, Z., et al. (2018). Switching to green lifestyles: Behavior change of ant forest users. *International Journal of Environmental Research and Public Health, 15*(9), 1819. https://doi.org/10.3390/ijerph15091819

Yoon, H. S. (2017). *Doing good while playing: The effects of corporate social responsibility gamification on consumer response*. Doctoral Dissertation. University of Texas at Austin.

YumChina. (2019). *Yum China to Harness its 200 Million loyalty program members to boost its signature one Yuan donation program*. Available at https://www.yumchina.com/newDetail/1?id=303. (Accessed 24 May 2024).

Zhang, W., & Jiang, Q. Y. (2017). *Six-step action towards social value co-creation: Frontiers of CSR strategy practices* [in Chinese]. Social Science Academic Press (China).

Zhang, H., Jiang, Y. J., Lu, Y. B., & Deng, Z. H. (2022). Customer co-creation experience value empowered by social media: The multi-dimensional structure and multi-level influence effect [in Chinese]. *Journal of Management World*, (02), 150–168, 10–17. Available at Customer Co-creation Experience Value Empowered by Social Media:The Multi-dimensional Structure and Multi-level Influence Effect - CNKI

Zhang, X., Wan, J., & Jin, Y. (2023). Exploring the outcomes of customer engagement in DSR: The role of affective commitment and gamification affordance. *Sustainability (Basel, Switzerland), 15*(6), 5037. https://doi.org/10.3390/su15065037

Zhang, D. P., Lin, M. F., Chen, X. Y., & Zhang, F. L. (2015). Research on the customer innovation on referral intention: The mediating role of psychological ownership [in Chinese]. *Management Review, 27*(12), 131–140. https://doi.org/10.14120/j.cnki.cn11-5057/f.2015.12.013

Zhang, J. M., & Wang, H. (2022). The influencing factors on the willingness to participate in virtual corporate social responsibility co-creation. *Science Research Management, 43*(8), 90.

Zhao, W., Cheng, Y., & Lee, Y.-I. (2023). Exploring 360-degree virtual reality videos for CSR communication: An integrated model of perceived control, telepresence, and consumer behavioral intentions. *Computers in Human Behavior*, 144. https://doi.org/10.1016/j.chb.2023.107736

Zhou, F., Lin, Y., & Mou, J. (2023). Unpacking the effect of gamified virtual CSR cocreated on users' pro-environmental behavior: A holistic view of gamification affordance. *Technology in Society, 73*, 102228.

14

Leadership and Digital Transformation in the Luxury Brand Industry

Samuel Osei-Nimo, Cindy Millman, and Wajiha Kazim

Introduction

In the contemporary business landscape, the rapid pace of technological advancements has precipitated profound changes in workplace design, marketing strategies, and overall operational modalities (Phakamach et al., 2023; Schneider & Kokshagina, 2021). Particularly within the luxury and fashion industry, these changes herald a new era where digital transformation becomes not just a strategic option but a requisite for survival and growth. At the heart of this transformation lies the pivotal role of leadership in navigating the complexities and challenges posed by

S. Osei-Nimo (✉) · W. Kazim
Nottingham Trent University, Nottingham, UK
e-mail: samuel.osei-nimo@ntu.ac.uk

W. Kazim
e-mail: wajiha.kazim@ntu.ac.uk

C. Millman
University for the Creative Arts, Business School, Epsom, UK
e-mail: cindy.millman@uca.ac.uk

W. Ozuem et al. (eds.), *Sustainable Digital Marketing for Fashion and Luxury Brands*,
https://doi.org/10.1007/978-3-031-82467-8_14

the integration of technology into every facet of business operations. This chapter delves into the nuanced dynamics of how leadership influences the emerging workplace design driven by technological developments and examines the monitoring, surveillance, and automation strategies employed by business organisations to enhance the effectiveness of their marketing initiatives.

The landscape of the luxury and fashion industry is uniquely positioned to reflect the broader implications of digital transformation. Nevertheless, Holmqvist et al. (2020) contend that luxury firms frequently display reluctance in embracing technology-driven multi-actor interactions at the client interface. Given its fast-paced nature and the premium placed on brand image and customer experience, the sector serves as an illustrative case study for understanding the multifaceted impact of technology on business practices. The transition towards digital platforms, online retail, and automated processes has not only redefined the parameters of competition but has also raised critical questions regarding the sustainability, efficiency, and ethical considerations of such transformations (Azemi & Ozuem, 2023; Kapferer & Bastien, 2012; Todeschini et al., 2017).

Leadership, in this context, emerges as a critical determinant of the successful adoption and implementation of digital technologies. The ability of leaders to envision a digital future, communicate a clear strategy, and foster an organisational culture receptive to change is paramount. Moreover, leaders are tasked with balancing the pursuit of technological innovation with the implications for stakeholders, including customers, employees, and society at large. As such, the role of leadership extends beyond mere administrative functions to encompass a broader responsibility towards ethical and sustainable business practices (Avolio & Mhatre, 2012). Although an increasing number of organisations and their leadership are enthusiastic about adopting digitalisation (Breidbach et al., 2016), the luxury industry has been reluctant to accept it. This phenomenon is comprehensible because luxury firms flourish by emphasising their historical background (Kapferer & Bastien, 2012) and typically exhibit caution towards any change.

The integration of monitoring, surveillance, and automation technologies presents both opportunities and challenges for businesses in the luxury and fashion sectors. On the one hand, these technologies can significantly enhance the effectiveness of marketing initiatives, offering insights into consumer behaviour, optimising operational efficiency, and personalising the customer experience. On the other hand, the pervasive nature of such technologies raises pertinent concerns regarding privacy, data security, and the potential for intrusive surveillance (Coll, 2014; Zuboff, 2019). Thus, leaders must navigate the delicate balance between leveraging technology for business gains and upholding ethical standards and stakeholder trust.

Despite the well-documented benefits of digital transformation, including enhanced efficiency, competitiveness, and innovation, its implications extend far beyond the operational domain. The digital transformation journey can profoundly affect business stakeholders, with customers, employees, and society at large facing the brunt of its adverse impacts. Issues such as job displacement due to automation, erosion of privacy, and the digital divide underscore the need for a holistic and considerate approach to digital transformation in the luxury brand market (Schmidt et al., 2022; Schwab, 2017).

This chapter aims to explore these intricate dynamics by posing the following research question: *How can leaders in the luxury and fashion industry effectively implement and support digital transformation while mitigating its adverse impacts on stakeholders?*

To address this question, the chapter will first provide an overview of the current technological trends shaping workplace design and marketing strategies within the luxury and fashion industry. Subsequently, it will examine the role of leadership in steering digital transformation efforts, focusing on strategies for monitoring, surveillance, and automation. Finally, the chapter will propose approaches for leaders to navigate digital transformation's ethical and societal implications, ensuring a balance between innovation and stakeholder well-being.

The Landscape of Digital Transformation in the Luxury and Fashion Industry

Enhancing the discourse on the evolving landscape of digital transformation in the luxury fashion industry requires a deeper dive into how technological advancements are reshaping traditional models, consumer engagement, and sustainability practices (Ranfagni & Ozuem, 2022; Rathi et al., 2022). The integration of digital technologies is transforming operational efficiencies and redefining the consumer experience and brand engagement strategies within the luxury fashion sector.

The digital era has ushered in a new paradigm for luxury fashion brands, compelling them to integrate digital technologies across all facets of their operations. From design and production to marketing and sales, digital tools are becoming indispensable. For instance, Rayna and Striukova (2016) highlight 3D printing as revolutionising product development by enabling rapid prototyping and customisation. Similarly, AI-driven analytics provide insights into consumer behaviour, optimise inventory management, and personalised marketing efforts (Davenport et al., 2020).

A recent study by Statista (2024) predicts that the luxury fashion market in the United Kingdom expects an anticipated growth, with an annual rate of 1.76% extending from 2024 through 2028 (compound annual growth rate 2024–2028), indicating a vibrant future for the sector. This upward trajectory reflects the resilience and dynamism of the luxury fashion industry and sets the stage for exploring the transformative impact of digital innovation within this prestigious market.

Luceri and Martinelli (2022) assert that sustainability is gaining importance in consumer decision-making as consumers demonstrate a readiness to pay a higher price for environmentally friendly products. Similarly, executives in the fashion industry around the globe have identified environmental sustainability as the foremost challenge confronting the sector in 2020 (Business of Fashion, 2020). This consensus among fashion leaders underscores the critical importance of environmental sustainability as the predominant hurdle for the industry presently.

With regard to consumer engagement and e-commerce, luxury fashion has become a critical channel, expanding the market reach and providing consumers with an accessible platform to engage with brands. Social media and influencer marketing have further transformed the landscape, enabling direct communication and engagement with target audiences. Brands are leveraging AR and VR to offer virtual try-ons and immersive experiences, enhancing the online shopping experience and bridging the gap between physical and digital realms (Pantano & Priporas, 2016).

Rathore (2019) emphasises Gucci's digital transformation as a groundbreaking development in the luxury apparel industry. By adopting creative marketing methods such as social media interaction and digital storytelling, Gucci has greatly improved its brand appeal and customer involvement. This technique has modernised its image and strengthened its position as a leader in the luxury sector.

Furthermore, Javornik et al. (2021) explore how luxury brands, particularly Burberry, employ augmented reality (AR) to enhance customer experiences, aligning with the evolving expectations of luxury consumers. Burberry's AR initiative exemplifies the dual-edged nature of digital transformation, offering personalised, immersive experiences that strengthen consumer engagement and brand perception. However, this approach necessitates balancing innovation with maintaining the brand's luxury essence, highlighting the challenge of integrating digital technologies without compromising exclusivity.

Todeschini et al. (2017) highlight how sustainability has become pivotal in the digital transformation of the luxury fashion industry. Luxury brands are increasingly adopting innovative and sustainable business models to address both environmental concerns and consumer demands. This shift presents entrepreneurial opportunities to redefine luxury in the digital age, yet it also poses significant challenges in balancing traditional luxury values with sustainability imperatives. The move towards sustainability underscores a transformative period in the luxury market, where innovation is key to maintaining relevance and competitive edge. Further emphasising the importance of sustainability, Kapferer and Michaut-Denizeau (2020) discuss how luxury brands must integrate ethical practices and sustainability into their core strategy to meet the new luxury consumer expectations, thereby ensuring a sustainable future for the luxury sector.

Hennigs et al. (2015) underscore the transformative role of data analytics and artificial intelligence (AI) in crafting personalised luxury fashion experiences, pivotal for aligning with consumer expectations in the digital age. These technologies enable brands to discern and cater to individual preferences, reinforcing luxury's core values of exclusivity and uniqueness. However, this personalisation must be balanced carefully to preserve luxury's inherent allure against the backdrop of digital omnipresence. Kapferer and Michaut-Denizeau (2014) reinforce this, highlighting the risk of diluting luxury's essence with excessive digitalisation. Thus, judicious application of data insights is essential for sustaining luxury's appeal and market position.

Nonetheless, Mekonnen and Larner (2021) argue that when executed thoughtfully, digital initiatives can amplify a brand's narrative and connection with consumers, turning potential challenges into opportunities to reinforce brand exclusivity and allure. This emphasises how luxury fashion has transitioned from a crisis response to a strategic strength, further emphasising the critical role of data analytics and AI.

Jin and Shin (2021) mentioned that there is a significant amount of research on sustainability in the luxury fashion market. This research covers a wide range of topics, such as sustainable business models (Stål & Corvellec, 2018; Thorisdottir & Johannsdottir, 2019), consumer behaviour towards sustainable apparel purchase (Dhir et al., 2021), and emerging approaches to achieve sustainability, such as blockchain technology (Bullón Pérez et al., 2020). Jin and Shin (ibid.) also add that in academia, researchers have investigated various aspects of manufacturing, including factory productivity levels (Bheda et al., 2003), the implementation of technologies such as robotics (Michelini & Razzoli, 2013) and radio frequency identification (Nayak et al., 2015), and the adoption of technology by manufacturers (Varukolu & Park-Poaps, 2009).

Holmqvist et al. (2020) argue that too often, luxury brands mistake digitisation for just a retail channel and use technology mainly to advertise and operate an online store without paying sufficient attention to the multi-actor experience. They add that discourse on the digital transformation within the luxury brand sector emphasises the necessity for these brands to evolve in response to the changing dynamics of service encounters. This transformation is critical to maintain the essence of luxury that is inherent to these brands. Thus, the adaptation strategies proposed can enable luxury brands to navigate the challenges of digital transformation without compromising their unique luxury characteristics.

On the other hand, De Angelis et al. (2017) touch upon a significant challenge in the digital transformation of the luxury fashion industry: the perceived incompatibility between luxury and sustainability. Luxury, often associated with excess and narcissism, seems at odds with the principles of sustainability, which advocate for altruism and moderation. This dichotomy presents a hurdle for luxury brands striving to integrate sustainable practices into their operations and narratives, particularly in an era where digital platforms amplify every corporate move.

Furthermore, maintaining exclusivity while embracing digital platforms poses a significant challenge for luxury brands. Blasco-Arcas et al. (2016) and Baker et al. (2018) highlight the difficulty in preserving an aura of exclusivity in the digital age, which explains why brands like Chanel had hesitated to sell their luxury fashion online by 2020, prioritising the exclusivity and unique brand experience offered by their physical boutiques.

Consequently, it is argued that leadership is crucial in merging sustainability with the luxury fashion market, guiding innovation and integrating sustainability into core values (Pedersen et al., 2018). This requires a delicate balance, ensuring that digital transformation aligns with both luxury exclusivity and the imperative for sustainability. Luxury brands can leverage appropriate leadership approaches to redefine the narrative, demonstrating the compatibility of luxury and sustainability in the digital age and addressing ethical practices and consumer transparency demands (Burawat, 2019; Rzyczycki, 2023).

The Role of Leadership in Digital Transformation

In the late twentieth century, the fashion supply chain, marked by cost pressures and the shift towards outsourcing and lean production, transformed traditional hierarchical structures into horizontal, network-based organisations (Bertola & Teunissen, 2018; Varra, 2021). This significant shift underscores the need for new leadership strategies to navigate the complexities of digital transformation in the luxury brand industry, ensuring both efficiency and stakeholder consideration.

Schmid and Dowling (2020) argue that leadership styles and company culture play a significant role in how well modern technologies are implemented and perceived in organisations and beyond. They argue that leadership's role in digital adoption in an industry increases autonomy and motivation. At the same time, this technology also enables managers to monitor their subordinates more closely and can heighten the expectation of constant availability. Schmid and Auburger (2020) add that this leads to a lack of control and demotivation for the employee, thus confirming the importance of the role of leadership in mediating technology and employee motivation.

The effective management of employee perceptions towards new technologies is a crucial aspect of leadership, particularly during the intricate process of digital transformation within organisations in the context of emerging workplace designs driven by technological advancements. Research indicates that the way technologies are perceived by employees significantly influences whether they view these innovations as opportunities or threats (Cascio & Montealegre, 2016; Parker & Grote, 2022; Schmid & Dowling, 2020). Eden et al. (2010) also introduce the concept of 'means efficacy,' illustrating how belief in the utility of a tool can enhance an individual's sense of efficacy and productivity.

Carmignani and Zammori (2015) suggest that the increasing use of new technologies and globalisation have made it difficult to satisfy customers in the luxury brand industry. To remain competitive in a rapidly evolving market, businesses are encouraged to re-evaluate their business models and implement changes from a strategic to an operational level (Cozzolino et al., 2018). Turner and Myerson's (1998) research on physical and cultural transformations in the workspace can act as powerful levers for organisational change and is particularly relevant for discussion on leadership in the luxury brand sector, where the fusion of tradition with innovation forms the cornerstone of brand identity.

The digital transformation of the luxury brand market requires a leadership approach that not only drives innovation and change but also ensures these advancements align with ethical practices and sustain the core values of luxury (Tekic & Koroteev, 2019). In the context of the luxury brand industry, Schiuma et al. (2024) argue that the intersection of ethical leadership and digital transformation is pivotal, especially when considering sustainability initiatives. They explain that the context of digital leadership is relevant here because it offers luxury brands the opportunity to leverage technology to address ethical concerns while maintaining profitability and brand prestige.

Ethical leadership in the luxury brand industry is characterised by a commitment to sustainable practices that go beyond compliance to benefit the environment and society genuinely. Schiuma et al. (2024) assert that transformative leaders prioritise sustainable values to generate enduring effects. The industry, often considered the pinnacle of quality and exclusivity, faces a significant paradox in the digital age, particularly under the pressures of increased consumer demand for more goods at every price point. As detailed by Arrington (2017), this demand exacerbates ethical problems, creating a tension between consumerism and the need for sustainable practices. As the industry continues to grapple with the demands of modern consumerism, leaders must harness digital transformation strategically to foster sustainable practices, maintain ethical standards, and ultimately redefine the parameters of luxury in a consumer-driven market (Arrington, 2017; Ozuem et al., 2021).

Furthermore, in the luxury brand industry, the evolution towards digital transformation has necessitated a re-evaluation of leadership roles and strategies to merge traditional luxury with innovative technologies effectively. The transformation from hierarchical structures to network-based organisations, as noted by Rackwitz et al. (2021) and Rios (2016), illustrates the need for leaders who can navigate the complexities of digital environments while maintaining the core values and exclusivity inherent to luxury brands.

Leadership in this context has evolved beyond traditional management to become a pivotal element in steering the digital transformation agenda. Schmid and Dowling (2020) emphasise the critical role of leadership styles and company culture in influencing how technological innovations are implemented and perceived within organisations. Leaders are now expected to facilitate a culture where digital tools are seen as enhancers of productivity and creativity rather than threats to existing workflows (Schneider & Kokshagina, 2021).

Moreover, the introduction of digital tools has shifted the dynamics of workplace autonomy and surveillance. While digital platforms can increase transparency and enhance monitoring capabilities, they also raise concerns regarding privacy and constant availability, potentially leading to employee demotivation (Schmid & Auburger, 2020). Effective leaders must balance these aspects by fostering an environment where technology serves as a facilitator for improved work conditions and employee satisfaction.

The challenge extends to customer relations and market competition. As Carmignani and Zammori (2015) highlight, globalisation and digital advancements have intensified customer expectations. Cozzolino et al. (2018) further suggest that businesses need to adapt their strategies from the top down to stay competitive. In the luxury sector, this involves integrating digital innovations in a way that respects and enhances the traditional values of craftsmanship and exclusivity.

Turner and Myerson (1998) argue that physical and cultural transformations within workplaces can be significant levers for organisational change. For luxury brands, this means redesigning workspaces not only to integrate new technologies but also to reflect the brand's heritage and ethos, thus supporting a seamless blend of tradition and innovation.

The role of ethical leadership becomes even more crucial in this context. Tekic and Koroteev (2019) note that leadership in digital transformation must align with ethical practices to sustain the luxury brand's core values. Schiuma et al. (2024) reinforce this by discussing how ethical leadership can drive sustainability initiatives within the digital transformation framework. This approach not only addresses the ethical dilemmas posed by increased consumer demands but also positions the brand favourably in a market where consumers increasingly value sustainability (Arrington, 2017).

Thus, as luxury brands face the imperative of digital transformation, leadership must evolve to meet these new challenges. Leaders in the luxury brand industry are tasked with a complex role that involves driving innovation and digital integration while ensuring that these advancements reinforce, rather than undermining, the brand's luxury status and ethical commitments. The future of luxury branding in the digital age depends significantly on leaders who can skilfully navigate these waters, ensuring that the industry not only survives but thrives by turning potential challenges into opportunities for growth and enhanced customer engagement.

Monitoring, Surveillance, and Automation Strategies

In the luxury and fashion industry, the integration of monitoring, surveillance, and automation strategies has become increasingly prevalent as brands seek to enhance their marketing effectiveness. These strategies are primarily driven by advancements in technology, including the use of Artificial Intelligence (AI), big data analytics, and digital platforms that transform customer experiences and operational efficiency in the fashion industry (Mohiuddin Babu et al., 2022; Ozuem et al., 2024). However, the application of these technologies raises significant ethical considerations that necessitate a re-evaluation of leadership practices within the industry to balance innovation with the protection of stakeholder interests.

With the implementation of advanced technologies, the fashion industry has embraced a variety of digital tools to streamline operations and engage consumers more effectively. For instance, Radio Frequency Identification (RFID) technology, as discussed by Nayak et al. (2015), offers substantial improvements in inventory management and customer service. It enables companies to track items in real time and reduce losses from stock inaccuracies. This technology not only boosts efficiency but also enhances the customer shopping experience by ensuring product availability and speeding up the checkout process.

Similarly, Akram et al. (2022) explore the broader implications of Industry 4.0 for fashion, highlighting how automation and data analytics can radically transform production processes and consumer interaction. These technologies enable fashion brands to respond more swiftly to market trends and consumer preferences, thereby aligning product offerings more closely with demand and reducing waste.

However, as these advancements continue to integrate deeply into business operations, ethical considerations and privacy concerns become increasingly important. Ethical leadership becomes crucial in overseeing their deployment as these technologies collect and analyse vast amounts of consumer data. Fuchs (2011) and Aradau and Blanke (2018) discuss the potential privacy issues arising from such data-intensive practices. They emphasise the importance of maintaining a balance between leveraging data for business insights and respecting individual privacy rights, suggesting that transparent data practices and robust security measures are essential to maintaining consumer trust.

The AI-led ethical digital transformation framework proposed by Saurabh et al. (2022) further supports this, recommending that ethical considerations be integrated into the digital transformation process. Leaders in the luxury fashion industry must ensure that initiatives such as AI and machine learning algorithms adhere to ethical standards that prevent biases and protect consumer data from misuse.

Luxury brands such as Burberry and Gucci have moved beyond theoretical applications to real-world implementations and consumer engagement and have effectively utilised these technologies not just for operational efficiency but also to create enriched consumer experiences. For example, Burberry's use of AI in customer service provides personalised shopping experiences through chatbots and tailored recommendations (Econsultancy, 2019; Ozuem et al., 2023). This not only improves customer satisfaction but also drives higher sales volumes.

Moreover, Deloitte's 2019 Holiday Survey illustrates that consumers value brands that use technology to understand their individual needs and preferences. The report highlights how emotion-driven engagement, facilitated by digital tools, can significantly enhance consumer loyalty and brand reputation (Deloitte Digital, 2019).

While the benefits are considerable, the challenges of implementing these technologies are not trivial. As noted by McCormick et al. (2014)

and Huynh (2021), the rapid evolution of digital tools requires continuous learning and adaptation within organisations. Leaders must foster a culture of innovation and agility that can respond to technological advancements while ensuring ethical practices are not compromised.

Subsequently, monitoring, surveillance, and automation strategies, when guided by ethical and transformative leadership, can significantly enhance the marketing and operational capabilities of luxury fashion brands. However, the successful implementation of these technologies requires a careful balance between innovation and the safeguarding of stakeholder interests, particularly in areas related to consumer privacy and data security. As the industry continues to evolve, leadership will play a critical role in ensuring these technologies are used responsibly and sustainably.

Proposing Leadership Strategies for Effective Digital Transformation

In the luxury and fashion industry, effective leadership is paramount in steering any brand through the complex and dynamic process of digital transformation (Cabigiosu, 2020; Schiuma et al., 2024). This transformation demands not only the adoption of new technologies but also a profound cultural shift within the organisation that champions continuous improvement and embraces ethical and inclusive practices.

First of all, leaders in this field must create a culture that values continuous innovation and adaptation. They need to instil a mindset where ongoing improvement is preferred over traditional stability, as suggested by Bharadwaj et al. (2013). This involves embedding innovation into the daily operational ethos and encouraging teams to seek out and implement improvements constantly. By setting clear expectations, providing the necessary tools and training, and rewarding innovation and risk-taking appropriately, leaders can cultivate an environment ripe for transformation. Moreover, Cabigiosu (2020), the luxury industry has eagerly embraced innovation and the future, eschewing the aura of sacredness and uniqueness that it had, up until then, defined it.

Secondly, Hess et al. (2016) cite experimentation as another crucial element, stressing that leaders should actively promote experimentation within their teams to discover what works best in real-world applications. This could involve testing new digital marketing tools or experimenting with different e-commerce platforms to enhance the user experience. Maintaining a flexible approach to failure is crucial, as it can be a valuable learning opportunity instead of a setback. Hess et al. (2016) use the example of Burberry's strategic experimentation with new digital marketing tools and e-commerce platforms, where the luxury fashion brand embarked on a digital-first transformation in 2006. This included the pioneering use of social media platforms, live streaming of fashion shows, and the integration of customer experiences across digital and physical spaces by 2010. Burberry's approach demonstrates the importance of maintaining a flexible attitude towards failure, viewing each setback as a learning opportunity to refine strategies and enhance user engagement.

Thirdly, Kane et al. (2015) point out that, in the context of digital transformation in the luxury brand industry, adaptability is also crucial in highlighting the importance of fostering an organisational culture that is open to change. Leaders must work to dismantle any existing resistance by clearly communicating the benefits of digital strategies and aligning them with the organisation's broader goals (Sainger, 2018). Cabigiosu (2020) also cites Burberry's embraced digital and social media innovations under Angela Ahrendts' leadership, which led them to become an early adopter of digital and social media platforms. This push rejuvenated the luxury brand and enabled them to connect with a younger, more digital-savvy audience. This move, Cabigiosu adds, demonstrated a significant shift in organisational culture towards embracing new technologies and strategies, which was essential for the brand's continued relevance and success in the digital age.

Nonetheless, Westerman et al. (2014) stress the need for organisations to pay attention to significant ethical issues, particularly related to consumer data privacy and sustainable practices. Schiuma et al. (2024) urge leaders to ensure that their digital strategies uphold ethical standards and contribute positively to societal well-being. Vial (2021) also suggests that leaders should prioritise transparency and maintain open communication with all stakeholders about how data is collected, used, and protected. A notable example that supports the idea of luxury brands using blockchain technology to enhance transparency in their supply chains, thereby ensuring product authenticity and promoting responsible management practices, a notable example is LVMH (Moët Hennessy Louis Vuitton).

LVMH, in collaboration with ConsenSys and Microsoft, launched the AURA blockchain platform. According to Thanasi-Boçe et al. (2022), this initiative was designed to provide consumers with a full traceability and authenticity history of luxury products, from raw materials to point of sale, all the way to second-hand markets. The AURA blockchain technology helps combat counterfeiting, ensure traceability, and enhance the transparency of the entire production and distribution process. Thus, this initiative not only enhances consumer trust but also establishes a stronger foundation for sustainability in the luxury fashion industry by ensuring products are sourced responsibly and ethically (Ozuem & Willis, 2022; Thanasi-Boçe et al., 2022).

Finally, Rialti and Filieri (2024) highlight the need for organisations in the luxury fashion industry to embrace agile leadership in digital transformation projects. Greineder and Leicht (2020) explore how agile leadership approaches align with transformational and ethical principles, emphasising the importance of adaptability and visionary guidance in driving organisational change. They argue that agile leaders, much like transformational leaders, inspire innovation and flexibility, which are crucial for navigating the complexities of modern business environments effectively.

Agile leaders are able to respond quickly to changes in the market and adjust strategies as necessary. This involves fostering a culture that values innovation, flexibility, and continuous learning. Under CEO Michael Burke's leadership, Louis Vuitton exemplifies agile leadership in the luxury fashion industry, a concept emphasised by Rialti and Filieri (2024). During the COVID-19 pandemic, Louis Vuitton rapidly adapted its strategies to boost its digital presence. Initiatives like virtual tours and augmented reality experiences allowed customers to interact with products and the brand story safely from their homes. This agile response to shifting market conditions and consumer preferences showcases how effectively integrating digital transformation processes can maintain high levels of customer engagement even during uncertain times.

Riedmeier and Kreuzer (2022) explain that this demonstrates the effective application of agile leadership in managing the dynamics of co-creation, and digital integration aligns and illustrates how luxury brands must be flexible, forward-thinking, and open to innovation to navigate the challenges and opportunities of digital transformation. Agile leadership is crucial in such contexts as it ensures that the co-creation process remains dynamic and responsive, enabling continuous improvement and fostering a culture of flexibility and collaborative innovation (Sjödin et al., 2020).

In summary, digital transformation in the luxury and fashion industry presents numerous challenges and opportunities. Leaders who can foster a culture of innovation, uphold ethical practices, and engage inclusively with stakeholders are more likely to navigate their organisations through this complex landscape successfully. These leadership strategies provide a robust framework for future leaders aiming to leverage digital transformation effectively while maintaining the core values of luxury and fashion brands.

Conclusion

This chapter has comprehensively explored the crucial role of leadership in steering the digital transformation within the luxury and fashion industry. As the industry stands on the cusp of technological innovation and integration, the findings underscore the necessity for agile, visionary leadership capable of navigating these complex transformations. Leaders are not only orchestrators of change but also custodians of brand integrity and stakeholder trust in an increasingly digital marketplace.

Revisiting our research question on effective leadership strategies in digital transformation, it is clear that successful leaders are those who can envision a future where technology enhances traditional luxury values without compromising them. Leadership in this context involves more than just adopting new technologies; it requires fostering a culture that values continuous learning, flexibility, and innovation. The examples discussed, from Burberry's digital initiatives to Louis Vuitton's agile responses during the COVID-19 pandemic, highlight how proactive, responsive leadership can leverage digital tools to maintain customer engagement and drive brand growth.

Looking ahead, the future of leadership in the luxury and fashion industry will undoubtedly be shaped by its ability to adapt to the evolving technological landscape. As digital technologies continue to advance, leaders must remain vigilant and adaptable, ready to harness innovations that can deliver genuine value to consumers while safeguarding ethical standards and sustainable practices. The integration of advanced technologies such as AI, blockchain, and augmented reality into everyday business practices offers unprecedented opportunities for enhancing customer experiences and operational efficiencies. However, this also introduces challenges, particularly in terms of privacy, data security, and the ethical use of technology.

In conclusion, it is evident that sustaining innovation and ethical considerations in the luxury and fashion brand industry highlights a dual imperative. On the one hand, leaders must drive innovation to stay competitive in a fast-paced market; on the other, they must ensure that their strategies respect both people and the planet. This balance is crucial for maintaining the luxury essence, characterised by exclusivity and responsibility towards societal values. As digital transformation becomes more widespread, the luxury fashion industry is at an impasse where leadership decisions will determine the trajectory of brands in terms of market success and ethical stewardship.

References

Akram, S. V., Malik, P. K., Singh, R., Gehlot, A., Juyal, A., Ghafoor, K. Z., & Shrestha, S. (2022). Implementation of digitalized technologies for fashion industry 4.0: Opportunities and challenges. *Scientific Programming, 2022.*

Aradau, C., & Blanke, T. (2018). Governing others: Anomaly and the algorithmic subject of security. *European Journal of International Security, 3*(1), 1–21.

Arrington, D. W. (2017). Ethical and sustainable luxury: The paradox of consumerism and caring. *Fashion, Style and Popular Culture, 4*(3), 277–285.

Avolio, B. J., & Mhatre, K. H. (2011). Advances in theory and research on authentic leadership.

Avolio, B. J., & Mhatre, K. H. (2012). (2011). Advances in theory and research on authentic leadership. In K. S. Cameron & G. M. Spreitzer (Eds.), *The Oxford handbook of positive organizational scholarship* (pp. 773–783). Oxford University Press.

Azemi, Y., & Ozuem, W. (2023). How does retargeting work for different Gen Z mobile users? *Journal of Advertising Research*, 2023-023. https://doi.org/10.2501/jar-2023-023

Baker, J., Ashill, N., Amer, N., & Diab, E. (2018). The internet dilemma: An exploratory study of luxury firms' usage of internet-based technologies. *Journal of Retailing and Consumer Services, 41*, 37–47.

Bertola, P., & Teunissen, J. (2018). Fashion 4.0. Innovating fashion industry through digital transformation. *Research Journal of Textile and Apparel, 22*(4), 352–369.

Bharadwaj, A., El Sawy, O. A., Pavlou, P. A., & Venkatraman, N. V. (2013). Digital business strategy: Toward a next generation of insights. *MIS Quarterly, 37*(2), 471–482.

Bheda, R., Narag, A. S., & Singla, M. L. (2003). Apparel manufacturing: A strategy for productivity improvement. *Journal of Fashion Marketing and Management, 7*(1), 12–22.

Blasco-Arcas, L., Holmqvist, J., & Vignolles, A. (2016). Brand contamination in social media: Consumers' negative influence on luxury brand perceptions—A structured abstract. In *Rediscovering the essentiality of marketing: Proceedings of the 2015 academy of marketing science (AMS) world marketing congress* (pp. 265–269). Springer International Publishing.

Breidbach, C. F., Antons, D., & Salge, T. O. (2016). Seamless service? On the role and impact of service orchestrators in human-centred service systems. *Journal of Service Research, 19*(4), 458–476.

Bullón Pérez, J. J., Queiruga-Dios, A., Gayoso, V., & Martín del Rey, Á. (2020). Traceability of ready-to-wear clothing through blockchain technology. *Sustainability, 12*(18), 7491.

Burawat, P. (2019). The relationships among transformational leadership, sustainable leadership, lean manufacturing and sustainability performance in Thai SMEs manufacturing industry. *International Journal of Quality and Reliability Management, 36*(6), 1014–1036.

Business of Fashion. (2020). *The state of fashion 2020.* McKinsey and Company.

Cabigiosu, A. (2020). *Digitalization in the luxury fashion industry*. Springer International Publishing.

Camuffo, A. (2003). Transforming industrial districts: Large firms and small business networks in the Italian eyewear industry. *Industry and Innovation, 10*(4), 377–401.

Carmignani, G., & Zammori, F. (2015). Lean thinking in the luxury-fashion market: Evidences from an extensive industrial project. *International Journal of Retail and Distribution Management, 43*(10/11), 988–1012.

Cascio, W. F., & Montealegre, R. (2016). How technology is changing work and organizations. *Annual Review of Organizational Psychology and Organizational Behavior, 3*, 349–375.

Coll, S. (2014). Power, knowledge, and the subjects of privacy: Understanding privacy as the ally of surveillance. *Information, Communication and Society, 17*(10), 1250–1263.

Cozzolino, A., Verona, G., & Rothaermel, F. T. (2018). Unpacking the disruption process: New technology, business models, and incumbent adaptation. *Journal of Management Studies, 55*(7), 1166–1202.

Davenport, T. H., Guha, A., Grewal, D., & Bressgott, T. (2020). How artificial intelligence will change the future of marketing. *Journal of the Academy of Marketing Science, 48*(1), 24–42.

De Angelis, M., Adıgüzel, F., & Amatulli, C. (2017). The role of design similarity in consumers' evaluation of new green products: An investigation of luxury fashion brands. *Journal of Cleaner Production, 141*, 1515–1527.

Deloitte Digital. (2019). *Exploring the value of emotion-driven engagement*. [Online] Available at https://www.deloittedigital.com/us/en/blog-list/2019/driving-brand-loyalty-with-emotion.html [Accessed 15 March 2024].

Dhir, A., Sadiq, M., Talwar, S., Sakashita, M., & Kaur, P. (2021). Why do retail consumers buy green apparel? A knowledge-attitude-behaviour-context perspective. *Journal of Retailing and Consumer Services, 59*, 102398.

Econsultancy. (2019). 2019 digital trends report. [Online] Available at https://econsultancy.com/reports/2019-digitaltrends/ [Accessed 15 March 2024].

Fuchs, C. (2011). Towards an alternative concept of privacy. *Journal of Information, Communication and Ethics in Society, 9*(4), 220–237.

Greineder, M., & Leicht, N. (2020). Agile leadership—A comparison of agile leadership styles. *BLED 2020 Proceedings*. 24.

Hess, T., Matt, C., Benlian, A., & Wiesböck, F. (2016). Options for formulating a digital transformation strategy. *MIS Quarterly Executive, 15*(2), 123–137.

Holmqvist, J., Wirtz, J., & Fritze, M. P. (2020). Luxury in the digital age: A multi-actor service encounter perspective. *Journal of Business Research, 121*, 747–756.

Huynh, P. H. (2021). Enabling circular business models in the fashion industry: The role of digital innovation. *International Journal of Productivity and Performance Management, 71*(3), 870–895.

Javornik, A., Duffy, K., Rokka, J., Scholz, J., Nobbs, K., Motala, A., & Goldenberg, A. (2021). Strategic approaches to augmented reality deployment by luxury brands. *Journal of Business Research, 136*, 284–292.

Jin, B. E., & Shin, D. C. (2021). The power of 4th industrial revolution in the fashion industry: What, why, and how has the industry changed? *Fashion and Textiles, 8*(1), 31.

Kane, G. C., Palmer, D., Phillips, A. N., Kiron, D., & Buckley, N. (2015). Strategy, not technology, drives digital transformation. *MIT Sloan Management Review*.

Kapferer, J. N., & Bastien, V. (2012). *The luxury strategy: Break the rules of marketing to build luxury brands*. Kogan Page Publishers.

Kapferer, J. N., & Michaut-Denizeau, A. (2014). Is luxury compatible with sustainability? Luxury consumers' viewpoint. *Journal of Brand Management, 21*(1), 1–22.

Luceri, B., & Martinelli, E. (2022). *Managing sustainability: Perspectives from retailing and services*. Springer.

McCormick, H., Cartwright, J., Perry, P., Barnes, L., Lynch, S., & Ball, G. (2014). Fashion retailing–past, present and future. *Textile Progress, 46*(3), 227–321.

Mekonnen, A., & Larner, L. (2021). Digital marketing in luxury fashion: From crisis to strength. *The art of digital marketing for fashion and luxury brands: Marketspaces and marketplaces* (pp. 199–219).

Michelini, R. C., & Razzoli, R. P. (2013). Robotics in clothes manufacture. *International Journal of Mechanical Engineering and Applications, 1*, 17–27.

Mohiuddin Babu, M., Akter, S., Rahman, M., Billah, M. M., & Hack-Polay, D. (2022). The role of artificial intelligence in shaping the future of Agile fashion industry. *Production Planning & Control*, 1–15.

Nayak, R., Singh, A., Padhye, R., & Wang, L. (2015). RFID in textile and clothing manufacturing: Technology and challenges. *Fashion and Textiles, 2*(9), 1–16.

Ozuem, W., Ranfagni, S., Willis, M., Salvietti, G., & Howell, K. (2024). Exploring the relationship between chatbots, service failure recovery and customer loyalty: A frustration–aggression perspective. *Psychology and Marketing*. https://doi.org/10.1002/mar.22051

Ozuem, W., Willis, M., Ranfagni, S., Howell, K. E., & Rovai, S. (2023). Examining the role of social media influencers in service failure and recovery strategies: An empirical investigation of millennials' views. *Information Technology & People*. https://doi.org/10.1108/itp-05-2022-0371

Ozuem, W., Ranfagni, S., Willis, M., Rovai, S., & Howell, K. (2021). Exploring customers' responses to online service failure and recovery strategies during Covid-19 pandemic: An actor–network theory perspective. *Psychology & Marketing, 38*(9), 1440–1459.

Ozuem, W., & Willis, M. (2022). *Digital marketing strategies for value co-creation: Models and approaches for online brand communities*. Palgrave Macmillan.

Pantano, E., & Priporas, C. V. (2016). The effect of mobile retailing on consumers' purchasing experiences: A dynamic perspective. *Computers in Human Behavior, 61*, 548–555.

Parker, S. K., & Grote, G. (2022). Automation, algorithms, and beyond: Why work design matters more than ever in a digital world. *Applied Psychology, 71*(4), 1171–1204.

Pedersen, E. R. G., Gwozdz, W., & Hvass, K. K. (2018). Exploring the relationship between business model innovation, corporate sustainability, and organisational values within the fashion industry. *Journal of Business Ethics, 149*, 267–284.

Phakamach, P., Panjarattanakorn, D., & Onsampant, S. (2023). Conceptualization and development of digital leadership to drive corporate digital transformation for sustainable success. *International Journal of Educational Communications and Technology, 3*(2), 27–39.

Rackwitz, M., Hustedt, T., & Hammerschmid, G. (2021). Digital transformation: From hierarchy to network-based collaboration? The case of the German "Online Access Act"/Digitale Transformation: Von Hierarchie zu netzwerkbasierter Zusammenarbeit? Das Onlinezugangsgesetz in Deutschland. *dms–der moderne staat–Zeitschrift für Public Policy, Recht und Management*, *14*(1), 13–14.

Ranfagni, S., & Ozuem, W. (2022). Luxury and sustainability: Technological pathways and potential opportunities. *Sustainability, 14*(9), 5209.

Rathi, R., Garg, R., Kataria, A., & Chhikara, R. (2022). Evolution of luxury marketing landscape: A bibliometric analysis and future directions. *Journal of Brand Management, 29*(3), 241–257.

Rathore, B. (2019). Chic strategies: Revolutionizing the industry through innovative fashion marketing. *International Journal of New Media Studies: International Peer Reviewed Scholarly Indexed Journal, 6*(2), 23–33.

Rayna, T., & Striukova, L. (2016). From rapid prototyping to home fabrication: How 3D printing is changing the small-scale manufacturing landscape. *Technological Forecasting and Social Change, 102*, 214–224.

Rialti, R., & Filieri, R. (2024). Leaders, let's get agile! Observing agile leadership in successful digital transformation projects. *Business Horizons.*

Rios, A. E. (2016). The impact of the digital revolution in the development of market and communication strategies for the luxury sector (fashion luxury). *Central European Business Review, 5*(2), 17–36.

Rzyczycki, A. (2023). Sustainability in the fashion industry. *Journal of Multidisciplinary Research, 15*(1), 33–39.

Sainger, G. (2018). Leadership in digital age: A study on the role of leader in this era of digital transformation. *International Journal on Leadership, 6*(1), 1.

Saurabh, K., Arora, R., Rani, N., Mishra, D., & Ramkumar, M. (2022). AI led ethical digital transformation: Framework, research and managerial implications. *Journal of Information, Communication and Ethics in Society, 20*(2), 229–256.

Schiuma, G., Santarsiero, F., Carlucci, D., & Jarrarb, Y. (2024). Transformative leadership competencies for organizational digital transformation. *Business Horizons.* https://doi.org/10.1016/j.bushor.2024.04.004

Schmid, Y., & Auburger, J. (2020). Implementing workplace technologies: A motivation-oriented approach. In *Human interaction and emerging technologies: Proceedings of the 1st international conference on human interaction and emerging technologies (IHIET 2019), August 22–24, 2019, Nice, France* (pp. 53–58). Springer International Publishing.

Schmid, Y., & Dowling, M. (2020). New work: New motivation? A comprehensive literature review on the impact of workplace technologies. *Management Review Quarterly*, 1–28.

Schmitt, R., Rossi, A., & Bensoussan, A. (2022). *Omni-personal Luxury: How to Transform Your Luxury Business for the Digital Age*. Palgrave Macmillan.

Schneider, S., & Kokshagina, O. (2021). Digital transformation: What we have learned (thus far) and what is next. *Creativity and Innovation Management, 30*(2), 384–411.

Schwab, K. (2017). *The fourth industrial revolution*. Crown Currency.
Sjödin, D., Parida, V., Kohtamäki, M., & Wincent, J. (2020). An agile co-creation process for digital servitization: A micro-service innovation approach. *Journal of Business Research, 112*, 478–491.
Stål, H. I., & Corvellec, H. (2018). A decoupling perspective on circular business model implementation: Illustrations from Swedish apparel. *Journal of Cleaner Production, 171*, 630–643.
Tekic, Z., & Koroteev, D. (2019). From disruptively digital to proudly analog: A holistic typology of digital transformation strategies. *Business Horizons, 62*(6), 683–693.
Thanasi-Boçe, M., AL-Issa, N., & Ali, O. (2022). Combating luxury counterfeiting through blockchain technology. In *Blockchain technologies in the textile and fashion industry* (pp. 1–16). Springer Nature Singapore.
Thorisdottir, T. S., & Johannsdottir, L. (2019). Sustainability within fashion business models: A systematic literature review. *Sustainability, 11*(8), 2233.
Todeschini, B. V., Cortimiglia, M. N., Callegaro-de-Menezes, D., & Ghezzi, A. (2017). Innovative and sustainable business models in the fashion industry: Entrepreneurial drivers, opportunities, and challenges. *Business Horizons, 60*(6), 759–770.
Turner, G., & Myerson, J. (1998). *New workspace, new culture: Office design as a catalyst for change*. Gower Publishing, Ltd.
Varukolu, V., & Park-Poaps, H. (2009). Technology adoption by apparel manufacturers in Tirupur town, India. *Journal of Fashion Marketing and Management, 13*(2), 201–214.
Vial, G. (2021). Understanding digital transformation: A review and a research agenda. *Journal of Management Studies, 58*(1), 115–144.
Westerman, G., Bonnet, D., McAfee, A. (2014). Leading digital: Turning technology into business transformation. *Harvard Business Press*.
Zuboff, S. (2019). *The age of surveillance capitalism: The fight for a human future at the new frontier of power*. Public Affairs.

15

Virtual Corporate Social Responsibility and Sustainable Value Creation

Abdullah Promise Opute, Xi Jiang, and Jafar Ojra

Introduction

The importance of sustainability-driven practices is gaining significant attention in the academic domain and it is recognised by other organisations, including international bodies such as the United Nations (UN). As far back as 1987, the UN emphasised the need for sustainability-focused practices that narrow the poverty gap. Sustainability-oriented practices should be embraced to ensure equity and the ability of future generations to meet their own needs (UN World Commission on Environment and Development, 1987). Over three decades on, sustainability remains a critical topic. Organisations are increasingly recognising the pertinence to them of embracing operational strategies that align with

A. Promise Opute (✉) · X. Jiang
University of Wales Trinity Saint David, Lampeter SA48 7ED, UK
e-mail: a.opute@uwtsd.ac.uk

J. Ojra
Swansea University, Swansea, UK

W. Ozuem et al. (eds.), *Sustainable Digital Marketing for Fashion and Luxury Brands*,
https://doi.org/10.1007/978-3-031-82467-8_15

sustainability goals (e.g., Abbate et al., 2023; López et al., 2023). Understandably, scholars have increasingly advocated for more research effort towards enhancing sustainability knowledge (e.g., Abbate et al., 2023; Chan et al., 2020; Dzhengiz et al., 2023a; Kunz et al., 2020; López et al., 2023). As documented by recent literature, the after-effects of the COVID-19 pandemic have further accentuated the need for a sustainability orientation (e.g., Ozuem et al., 2024a; Shirvanimoghaddam et al., 2020).

Inspired by the aforementioned advocacy, this chapter seeks to contribute to sustainability knowledge development. To do that, we draw from literature that not only underlines the relevance of a sustainability focus in the fashion sector but also calls for efforts to enhance this premise (e.g., Dzhengiz et al., 2023b; López et al., 2023). The production and consumption of fashion have increased in the past few decades and led to increasing global incomes (Abbate et al., 2023). The textile and fashion industry is reported to be worth 2% of the world's GDP and provides employment for millions of people globally; it is considered critical in the UN's Sustainable Development Goals (SDGs) as well as the European Commission's Green Deal (Thakker & Sun, 2023). However, the industry is criticised on sustainability grounds because it is one of the largest polluters globally: it accounts for more than 1.2 billion metric tons of greenhouse gas emissions, 22 million tons of microfibres, and 21 billion tonnes of waste (SDG Watch Austria, 2020; The United Nations Sustainable Development Goals, 2022). Consequently, this industry is increasingly under scrutiny from the perspective of corporate social responsibility (CSR). This is a critical research premise; firms aiming to compete effectively in the post-COVID-19 era need to ensure genuine CSR practices as consumers are increasingly keeping a close eye on the activities of firms in this regard (Opute et al., 2022a). Recognising the increasing impact of digital evolution on organisational dynamics in general and marketing dynamics in particular (Opute et al., 2022b; Ozuem et al., 2023), this chapter responds to calls for research (e.g., Kunz et al., 2020; Nie et al., 2023) and considers virtual CSR (VCSR), particularly in the fashion industry.

This chapter is organised in the following order. First, "fashion and sustainability" is explained to enable a better understanding of fashion's sustainability features. Then, CSR and VCSR are explained to provide a clear path towards an understanding of these terms and the impacts of VCSR dialogues, including value creation. The chapter concludes with relevant recommendations to enable firms in the fashion industry to organise their marketing strategy towards maximising the corporate success impact of their VCSR initiatives.

Fashion and Sustainability

As documented in the UN World Commission on Environment and Development (1987) report, "Our Common Future", on sustainability:

> Humanity has the ability to make development sustainable to ensure that it meets the needs of the present without compromising the ability of future generations to meet their own needs. …….. Technology and social organisation can be both managed and improved to make way for a new era of economic growth. The Commission believes that widespread poverty is no longer inevitable. Poverty is not only an evil in itself, but sustainable development requires meeting the basic needs of all and extending to all the opportunity to fulfil their aspirations for a better life. A world in which poverty is endemic will always be prone to ecological and other catastrophes. (pp. 24–25)

Furthermore, the report underlines that a new era of economic growth for nations should be ensured with a focus on assuring that the poor get a fair share of the resources for sustaining that growth. Nearly 40 years on, achieving equity in that regard remains a challenge, as major sustainability issues are reported in the fashion industry. Using the caption sustainable fashion, Aakko and Koskennurmi (2013) described an endeavour that links sustainable development and fashion. For the fashion supply chain, sustainability is a sensitive issue due to its characteristics of high resource use and manufacturing delocalisation to low-cost countries that, in most cases, have lenient environmental and social concerns policies (De Brito et al., 2008). In their book *Going Global: The Textile and Apparel Industry*, Kunz and Garner (2011) categorised core sustainability elements that included environmental, social, and business elements. Building on the work of Kunz and Garner (2011), Gupta (2019) emphasised that sustainability in the fashion industry extends beyond basic legal compliance and reflects aspects of codes of conduct, ethics, and standards that guide the operations of companies. According to other literature (Entwistle & Slater, 2014), the most critical sustainability concerns in the fashion industry relate to the environment, cost of production and consumption practices regarding natural resources (e.g., air and water), sourcing costs and distribution-related costs, high water usage, over-consumption of fast fashion by the masses, and fashion-related landfill waste.

For example, environmental perspectives point to waste, toxic chemicals, and air pollution as major environmental issues in the fashion industry (e.g., Colucci et al., 2020; Da Giau et al., 2020). On the other hand, social perspectives on the fashion industry identify severe labour-related concerns (e.g., Koeksal et al., 2017; Pedersen et al., 2018). For example, Pedersen et al. (2018) and Koeksal et al. (2017) emphasised child labour, poor salaries, and labour-intensive occupational hazards. Insights from China (Cooke & He, 2010) point to relatively low labour pay-off and poor human rights awareness among Chinese textile manufacturing suppliers. Similar evidence has been reported about H&M's exploitation of developing countries, like Bangladesh, Morocco, and poor locations in China, to produce their products while ignoring human rights guidelines (Chan et al., 2020). Human Rights Now (2015) reported that manufacturing suppliers located in China do not commit to CSR and it noted three core concerns: factory workplace insecurity, inadequate compensation for the overtime worked, and workers are not allowed to freely express their opinions. Table 15.1 documents the UN's SDGs in relation to the textile and fashion industry.

Increasingly, consumers are conscious of these sustainability concerns and are pushing back on fashion and luxury brands companies (e.g., Gupta, 2019; Thakker & Sun, 2023). Also, social bodies and governments are lending their voice to pressure fashion companies to implement corporate sustainability initiatives (Abbate et al., 2023; Aguinis & Glavas, 2012).

Companies are therefore forced to respond with appropriate measures to meet consumers' and other stakeholders' concerns. It is important that

Table 15.1 Sustainable Development Goals and their measures (adopted from Thakker and Sun [2023])

Sustainable development goals	Measures
Goal 1: No poverty	• To raise farmers of cotton, hemp, flax, bamboo trees, and others above the poverty line • To raise textile factory workers above the poverty line
Goal 2: Zero hunger	• To provide free food to textile factory workers, their children, and families • To fulfil corporate social responsibilities that eliminate hunger
Goal 3: Good health and well-being	• Phasing out hazardous substances utilised in the growing and processing of textiles • Textile sectors ought to mandatorily follow health and safety regulations
Goal 4: Quality education	• To educate fashion farmers on sustainable farming such as crop rotation and herbal fertilisers to prevent soil depletion and increase the harvest • To educate garment workers about their privileges to wages, work conditions, holidays, perks, and working hours
Goal 5: Gender equality	• Fairtrade practice • No child worker • Work equivalent wage payment
Goal 6: Clean water and sanitation	• Fresh drinking water and hygiene facilities for fashion factory workers • Water recycling plants at textiles' wet processing units • Zero discharge of wastewater by textile colouring units into chief sources of water, namely oceans, rivers, lakes, and streams
Goal 7: Clean energy	• Textile units to follow the principles of green chemistry for their processing • Textile mills to install solar energy plants

(continued)

Table 15.1 (continued)

Sustainable development goals	Measures
Goal 8: Decent work and economic growth	• Health and safety at work including mental, physical, emotional, and financial security • Respectable wage allocation to fashion workshop workers • Circular economy
Goal 9: Industry, innovation, and infrastructure	• Need for safe infrastructure at the textile production site • Innovation in textiles and fashion to abide by sustainable development goals • Focus on slow industrialisation for a slow fashion cycle
Goal 10: Reduced inequalities	• Control inflation in the textile sectors across the nations • Reduce inequality to BIPOC due to fast fashion landfills
Goal 11: Sustainable cities and communities	• BIPOC communities' upliftment at textile dumping grounds in Africa • Corporate social responsibility for sustainable cities and communities
Goal 12: Responsible production and consumption	• Designers and manufacturers should utilise biodegradable materials only • Consumer awareness to buy less and enjoy more to prevent overflowing landfills • Manufacturers ought to avoid over-sourcing, over-processing, and over-production
Goal 13: Climate action	• Ozone depletion, smog formation, greenhouse effect, and global warming due to textile industries and fast fashion • Reduce carbon footprints from textile emissions and address the climate emergency

(continued)

Table 15.1 (continued)

Sustainable development goals	Measures
Goal 14: Life below water	• A wastewater treatment plant is a must at each textile manufacturing and processing unit • Protect aquatic biota from synthetic toxic chemicals and microfibres
Goal 15: Life on land	• Landfills due to textile wastes ought to be addressed at once • Plant trees twice the amount of consumption by the textile sector
Goal 16: Peace, justice, and strong institutions	• Textiles factories and fashion brands to ensure commitment and investment in circularity programmes and transparent business • Mandatorily adapt to fair trade business models to eliminate child abuse and corruption in the textile sector
Goal 17: Partnerships for the goals	• Textile manufacturers, designers, consumers, traders, and investors are required to work collaboratively • Global partnership to address, commit, and report on sustainable development goals followed by textile sectors

BIPOC, Black, Indigenous, and people of colour

companies behave ethically to form a positive image that would impact their relationship with customers and other stakeholders (Kethan & Basha, 2022). Ethical behaviour would not only shape customer perceptions but also boost the long-term success of businesses by meeting customer needs and ensuring quality products and services. Reinforcing that positive impact, Rabeson et al. (2022) emphasised that companies prioritising ethical practices gain a competitive edge by fostering strong relationships with the community, employees, and the environment. As noted in more recent literature, since the COVID-19 pandemic several global fashion corporations have focused more on environmental sustainability (e.g., Lahbib et al., 2023; López et al., 2023).

Since the last decade, there has been increasing awareness of climate change implications as well as the implications of rising greenhouse gas emissions for people's health and the planet's health (Habib et al., 2021). Scholars highlight the initiatives taken by companies to respond to environmental concerns. For example, Brennan et al. (2013) investigated the response initiatives of the Chinese manufacturing industry to criticisms from Greenpeace on environmental pollution and adoption of toxic chemicals. Caniato et al. (2012) indicated that in their drive to reflect environmental responsibility, fashion retailers are prioritising suppliers who are transparent about fabric sourcing and the environmental impacts of their production. Pointing to further response initiatives, Chan et al. (2020) advised that fashion brands could create sustainable product design, recycling, and waste reduction.

Virtual CSR (VCSR)

VCSR literature is a relatively new and developing domain; hence, this chapter draws significantly from the general discourse on CSR. The discourse here is structured along three themes:

1. definition and aspects of CSR,
2. VCSR and VCSR practices, and
3. VCSR dialogues and value creation.

CSR: Definition and Aspects

As captured in recent literature (Kunz et al., 2020, p. 542): "Challenges, like climate change, declining natural diversity, scarce water and food supply, and social imbalances, have prompted scholars to concentrate more attention on corporate social responsibility (CSR) and sustainable activities". Thus, organisations must recognise the obligation on their part to be more conscious and aware of the climatic, natural diversity, water and food, and social structure implications of their operational activities. Organisations therefore must embrace initiatives that reflect corporate social awareness, and ensure that sustainability[1] aspects and the aspirations of individual stakeholder groups are not neglected.

Emphasising the importance of an evaluation approach that considers the specific stakeholders of a firm, prior literature (Carroll, 1979) stated that CSR includes economic, legal, ethical, and discretional aspects. Lending their voice to CSR conceptualisation, Chan et al. (2020) underlined that "CSR is an issue which goes beyond the laws and is consistent with international norms of behaviour" (p. 2). As one of the safeguards for international norms of behaviour, the European Commission offers the most commonly adopted definition (Chan et al., 2020, p. 2) and proposes that CSR is "a concept whereby companies integrate social and environmental concerns in their business operations and in their interaction with their stakeholders on a voluntary basis" (European Commission, 2001, p. 6). The European Commission's definition clearly pinpoints two core aspects of CSR: social and environmental.

The former relates to "a variety of forms and points of focus, ranging from corporate support for training and educating adults and youth in local communities, to nationwide programs helping welfare recipients get jobs and to globally focused efforts providing aid to developing countries" (Hess et al., 2002, p. 110). Thus, the social aspect of CSR emphasises elements relating to how society is being affected and how activities could be steered more towards enhancing workers' benefits and welfare (e.g., Chan et al., 2020; Koeksal et al., 2018). In the latter, the focus is on eliminating and minimising the negative consequences arising from production processes and business practices (e.g., Chan et al., 2020; European Commission, 2001). This CSR element, which is grounded on an ecological foundation, relates to aspects on pollution reduction, adopting measures that preserve natural resources, and ensuring environmentally friendly design (e.g., Abbate et al., 2023; Chan et al., 2020; Dzhengiz et al., 2023b). As noted by Chan et al. (2020), environmentally friendly initiatives can be implemented across all supply change stages from manufacturing to retailing.

[1] Being related concepts, CSR and sustainability are often used interchangeably (Pelikánová et al., 2021; Thorisdottir & Johannsdottir, 2020).

VCSR and VCSR Practices

Overall, reviewed sustainability literature (e.g., Korschun & Du, 2013; Kunz et al., 2020; Nie et al., 2023) identified four core aspects that should be considered in understanding VCSR: social, economic, technological, and environmental. There are several sustainability challenges across supply chain points (Colucci & Vecchi, 2021), and these could be tackled by strategically utilising digital enabling technologies (Abbate et al., 2023).

In the past, it was a common practice that companies provided social responsibility reports as a way of evidencing their CSR awareness (Cai, 2022). This CSR communication practice enabled companies to communicate relevant CSR information to stakeholders and gain some understanding of how its CSR practices are recognised in the outside world (Cai, 2022). However, the more technology evolves, the more its marketing implications intensify (e.g., Opute et al., 2020, 2022b). Technological evolution has propelled digital initiatives and social media (SM) options that are increasingly shaping operational strategies for organisations as well as consumers (e.g., Enyinda et al., 2021; Opute et al., 2022b; Ozuem et al., 2024b).

SM is widely viewed as a vital platform for implementing customer interaction strategies and improving company communication through CSR initiatives (Cai, 2022). Digital devices and SM channels, such as WhatsApp, LinkedIn, Weibo, and WeChat, are leveraged by companies to engage with customers, make sales, and project their image to both customers and other stakeholders (Cai, 2022; Enyinda et al., 2021). According to the literature, the fashion industry embraces SM to promote its CSR initiatives in its direct engagement with consumers (Cai, 2022). Consumers' followership behaviours, such as liking, commenting, and knowledge sharing within a virtual community, can drive the disclosure process, influence CSR disclosure, and gain acknowledgement among stakeholders (Arrigo et al., 2022). Additionally, fashion brands can engage with their followers on SM platforms to capture the emotions and sentiments expressed through commenting, sharing, and liking (Ozuem et al., 2024a, 2024b, 2024c; Vrontis et al.,

2021), as well as leverage popular SM platforms such as Instagram, Facebook, and TikTok to effectively convey their CSR activities and interact with their intended consumers (Castillo-Abdul et al., 2024).

According to the literature (Guo et al., 2019), firms utilise SM for CSR implementation and to explore their relationship with customers and other stakeholders, in order to boost their reputation (e.g., Zhou et al., 2021). It has also been noted that companies could utilise SM platforms to draw closer to their customers (e.g., Enyinda et al., 2021; Ozuem et al., 2023), and brands can utilise SM more effectively to increase awareness and provide education to customers regarding environmental sustainability (Kardos et al., 2019). Further related insights suggest that SM technologies could enable companies to engage with stakeholders, if effectively utilised (Nasr et al., 2024).

VCSR dialogues are used to proactively engage stakeholders in CSR activities (Cai, 2022). VCSR dialogues are exchanges that take place between corporations and stakeholders using social media platforms (Okazaki et al., 2020) to design and implement CSR processes. SM platforms can be utilised to involve stakeholders in collaboratively developing VCSR initiatives in the fashion industry (Sun et al., 2022); if VCSR dialogues are effectively coordinated, then a value-generating impact of VCSR can be achieved (Arrigo et al., 2022; Korschun & Du, 2013).

To determine the most effective methods and standards for VCSR communication, researchers have analysed how global corporations engage in VCSR communication (Cheng et al., 2022). The Ant Forest brand community utilises the cause-related marketing concept of “Internet+ public welfare” to effectively encourage user engagement in CSR initiatives, which is referred to as “virtual CSR co-creation” (Cheng & Kodono, 2022). Nie et al. (2023) developed a theoretical model that examines the influence of self-expansion and consumer engagement on consumers’ continuous participation in VCSR co-creation.

VCSR, Value Creation and Impact on Firm Performance

To compete effectively, organisations are now giving due consideration to commercial details when making business decisions (Opute et al., 2022a). Consumers are becoming more conscious of socio-environmental sustainability issues, and that impacts their preference formation when buying products or services (e.g., Dwivedi et al., 2021). In the contemporary market landscape, constituent aspects of the aforementioned commercial details include social and environmental issues that relate to organisations (Cheng et al., 2022). In that operational orientation, organisations would need to embrace ethical guidelines and values that promote positive community and stakeholder interactions related to their CSR activities (Cai, 2022). The popularisation and application of SM have triggered CSR communication changes (Cai, 2022). VCSR is a strategic instrument that allows firms to meet their social duties and motivate customer loyalty (Nie et al., 2023). Firms that adapt to changes in the environment will more effectively achieve value creation-driven CSR (Cai, 2022). Callery (2024) sought to understand the strategic motivations for CSR and pointed to profitability and legitimacy. Instrumental to achieving value creation through CSR is the use of SM platforms (e.g., Cai, 2022; Zhou et al., 2021) and critical CSR value creation paths, which would include cultural construction, social capital accumulation, and reputation promotion (e.g., Cai, 2022).

Consumers are more likely to have a positive view of companies when they are actively involved in CSR campaigns, as they would perceive the company's motives as serving not only its corporate needs but also those of the public (Lee et al., 2021). The effect of such interactions between consumers and the company, and the resulting positive feeling, would be greater intention to purchase the company's products/services (Park & Kim, 2022). The literature lends support to this viewpoint, for example, Kethan and Basha (2022) suggested that ethical behaviour by supplier companies enables positive image and reputation, which impact relationships with customers and partners. In addition, Rabeson et al. (2022) argued that companies prioritising ethical practices gain a strategic edge by fostering strong relationships with the community, employees, and other stakeholders. Kethan and Basha (2022) further added that ethical behaviour not only shapes customer perceptions but also contributes to the long-term success of businesses by meeting customer needs and maintaining excellence in products and services. Also, in a study of the role of SM in CSR behaviour in the fashion industry, Baltezarević and Baltezarević (2020) argued that increased comprehension of corporate philanthropy, as a manifestation of socially responsible conduct, enables market positioning, boosts market share, improves company reputation and employee satisfaction, and fosters a sense of unity within the company and in society at large.

Thus, businesses utilise online community platforms to engage different stakeholders in interacting with CSR operations to achieve VCSR co-creation (Cai, 2022; Korschun & Du, 2013). Whether VCSR co-creation is indeed achieved hinges on several factors. For example, in a framework that examines the creation of corporate value through community identity and CSR expectations, Korschun and Du (2013) found that two factors influence the value achieved through VCSR dialogue: the characteristics of the dialogue platform, such as media richness and self-presentation, and the characteristics of the dialogue interaction, such as autonomy and exclusivity.

Recommendations

Competing effectively in the modern-day marketing landscape is becoming increasingly challenging as the market becomes increasingly globalised (Opute, 2022) and customers are not only conscious of the market's options (Opute, 2020) and readily exploit them in their purchase decision making (Opute et al., 2022a, 2022b) but also conscious of the sustainability behaviour (or non-compliance) of organisations (e.g., Cai, 2022; McKinsey & Company, 2021). As the pressure on fashion manufacturers to remain competitive and respond effectively to customers' demands intensifies (Kunz et al., 2020), fashion manufacturers need to ensure they have an operational marketing strategy that recognises the utility of CSR initiatives as a means of engaging with customers and utilising their emotional input to profitably satisfy their customers. As underlined by Willersdorf et al. (2020), shifting economic, consumer, and societal trends brings challenges as well as opportunities for brands. A committed effort by brands to rethink their value chain and ensure environmentally and ethically conscious operations would be a critical step towards addressing consumers' interest in sustainability. Fashion brand manufacturers need to strategically organise their VCSR efforts to change the narratives of exploitation and disregard of ecological implications for the society in the sector to positive stories of accountability, equity, care, and maintenance and restoration of ecological environment.

The disruptive impact of the COVID-19 pandemic intensified not only the significance of the technological evolution to marketing (e.g., Opute et al., 2020, 2022b) but also the awakening to sustainability-driven digital marketing and innovation in the fashion sector (e.g., Lahbib et al., 2023; López et al., 2023; Palm, 2023). To compete effectively in the post-COVID-19 era, fashion brand firms need to ensure they have a marketing strategy that utilises technology enablement to engage with modern-day customers and other stakeholders in a market dispensation that is technology shaped. As underlined in recent literature (e.g., Opute et al., 2020, 2022a, 2022b), consumers are not only increasingly becoming technology savvy but leveraging technology enablement to socialise and process product (and services) consumption decision making. To compete effectively therefore, firms need to incorporate technology-based channels into their sustainability design and implementation. Critical for effective competition is a marketing strategy that leverages such technology-based channels to engage effectively with consumers.

To optimise the gains of such engagement with consumers, fashion companies need to ensure that they clearly define and communicate their VCSR goals and ensure alignment with the needs and values of stakeholders. Fashion companies could also disclose their VCSR activities and prompt feedback from stakeholders. They could augment these engagement options by incorporating VCSR into their business strategy and demonstrate the value impact of VCSR to the company and society at large. As commented by Willersdorf et al. (2020), the year 2020 will be remembered as one of turmoil, as well as one of change (hopefully).

Opute et al. (2020) offered a guide for marketers in the post-COVID-19 era: retailers and marketers in general would need to optimally embrace technology-enabled marketing to engage effectively with customers and offer them desired value for money. Connecting to these marketing logics, this chapter recommends that marketers of fashion brands in their VCSR initiatives should ensure a comprehensive technology-enabled marketing strategy that also responds to the increasing demand for diversity, equity, and inclusivity in marketing (e.g., Opute et al., 2022a, 2022b; Willersdorf et al., 2020).

References

Aakko, M., & Koskennurmi-Sivonen, R. (2013). Designing sustainable fashion: Possibilities and challenges. *Research Journal of Textile and Apparel, 17*(1), 13–22.

Abbat, S., Centobelli, P., Cerchione, R., Nadeem, S. P., & Riccio, E. (2023). Sustainability trends and gaps in the textile, apparel and fashion industries. *Environment, Development and Sustainability.* https://doi.org/10.1007/s10668-022-02887-2

Aguinis, H., & Glavas, A. (2012). What we know and don't know about corporate social responsibility: A review and research agenda. *Journal of Management, 38*(4), 932–968.

Arrigo, E., Di Vaio, A., Hassan, R., & Palladino, R. (2022). Followership behavior and corporate social responsibility disclosure: Analysis and implications for sustainability research. *Journal of Cleaner Production, 360*, 132151.

Baltezarević, R., & Baltezarević, I. (2020). The role of social media in corporate social responsibility—Fashion industry confronting the challenges of the modern age. *(Media Dialogues) Medijski dijalozi, 35*(13), UDK: 316.774.

Brennan, N. M., Merkl-Davies, D. M., & Beelitz, A. (2013). Dialogism in corporate social responsibility communications: Conceptualising verbal interaction between organisations and their audiences. *Journal of Business Ethics, 115*(4), 665–679.

Cai, M. (2022). Influence of social media on corporate communication social responsibility under entrepreneurial psychology. *Frontiers in Psychology, 13*, 870373.

Callery, P. J. (2024). Strategic motivations for corporate social responsibility: Profitability or legitimacy? *Journal of Business Economics*. https://doi.org/10.1007/s11573-024-01193-9

Caniato, F., Caridi, M., Crippa, L., & Moretto, A. (2012). Environmental sustainability in fashion supply chains: An exploratory case based research. *International Journal of Production Economics, 135*(2), 659–670.

Carroll, A. B. (1979). A three-dimensional conceptual model of corporate performance. *Academy of Management Review, 4*(4), 497–505.

Castillo-Abdul, B., Ortega Fernandez, E., & Romero-Rodriguez, L. M. (2024). Corporate social responsibility communication of male luxury fashion brands: Analysis on Instagram, Facebook and TikTok. *Management Decision, 62*(2), 471–491.

Chan, H. L., Wei, X., Guo, S., & Leung, W. H. (2020). Corporate social responsibility (CSR) in fashion supply chains: A multi-methodological study. *Transportation Research Part E: Logistics and Transportation Review, 142*, 102063.

Cheng, Y., Wang, Y., & Pan, F. (2022). The impact of CSR perceptions on employees' turnover intention during the COVID-19 crisis in China. *International Journal of Environmental Research and Public Health, 19*(14), 8297. https://doi.org/10.3390/ijerph19148297

Colucci, M., & Vecchi, A. (2021). Close the loop: Evidence on the implementation of the circular economy from the Italian fashion industry. *Business Strategy and the Environment*, Wiley Blackwell, *30*(2), 856–873.

De Brito, M. P., Carbone, V., & Blanquart, C. M. (2008). Towards a sustainable fashion retail supply chain in Europe: Organisation and performance. *International Journal of Production Economics, 114*(2), 534–553.

Dwivedi, Y. K., Ismagilova, E., Rana, N. P., & Raman, R. (2021). Social media adoption, usage and impact in Business-To-Business (B2B) context: A state-of-the-art literature review. *Information Systems Frontiers*, 1–23.

Dzhengiz, T., Riandita, A., & Broström, A. (2023b). Configurations of sustainability-oriented textile partnerships. *Business Strategy and the Environment*, 1–21. https://doi.org/10.1002/bse.3372

Dzhengiz, T., Haukkala, T., & Sahimaa, O. (2023a). (Un)Sustainable transitions towards fast and ultra-fast fashion. *Fashion and Textiles, 10*(1), 19.

Entwistle, J., & Slater, D. (2014). Reassembling the cultural: Fashion models, brands and the meaning of 'culture' after ANT. *Journal of Cultural Economy, 7*(2), 161–177.

Enyinda, C., Opute, A. P., Fadahunsi, A., & Mbah, C. (2021). Marketing-sales-service interface and social media marketing influence on B2B sales process. *Journal of Business & Industrial Marketing, 36*(6), 990–1009.

European Commission. (2001). *Green paper: Promoting a European framework for corporate social responsibility*. Available at http://europa.eu/rapid/press-release_DOC-01-9_en.pdf (Accessed 9 May 2024).

Guo, B., Pérez-Castrillo, D., & Toldrà-Simats, A. (2019). Firms' innovation strategy under the shadow of analyst coverage. *Journal of Financial Economics, 131*(2019), 456–483.

Gupta, P. (2019). Top management team heterogeneity, corporate social responsibility disclosure and financial performance. *American Journal of Industrial and Business Management, 9*(04), 1076.

Habib, R., White, K., Hardisty, D. J., & Zhao, J. (2021). Shifting consumer behavior to address climate change. *Current Opinion in Psychology, 42*, 108–113. https://doi.org/10.1016/j.copsyc.2021.04.007

Hess, D., Rogovsky, N., & Dunfee, T. W. (2002). The next wave of corporate community involvement: Corporate social initiatives. *California Management Review., 44*(2), 110–125.

Kardos, M., Gabor, M. R., & Cristache, N. (2019). Green marketing's roles in sustainability and ecopreneurship. Case study: Green packaging's impact on Romanian young consumers' environmental responsibility. *Sustainability, 11*(3), 873.

Kethan, M., & Basha, M. (2022). Relationship of ethical sales behaviour with customer loyalty, trust and commitment: A study with special reference to retail store in Mysore City. *East Asian Journal of Multidisciplinary Research, 1*(7), 1365–1376.

Koeksal, D., Straehle, J., Mueller, M., & Freise, M. (2017). Social sustainable supply chain management in the textile and apparel industry—A literature review. *Sustainability*. https://doi.org/10.3390/su9010100

Korschun, D., & Du, S. (2013). How virtual corporate social responsibility dialogs generate value: A framework and propositions. *Journal of Business Research, 66*, 1494–1504.

Kunz, G. I., & Garner, M. B. (2011). *Going global: The textile and apparel industry*. Fairchild Books.

Kunz, J., May, S., & Schmidt, H. J. (2020). Sustainable luxury: Current status and perspectives for future research. *Business Research, 13*(2), 541–601.

Lahbib, O., Kessous, A., & Valette-Florence, P. (2023). Toward a better understanding of the phenomenon of ambivalence in the endorsement of sustainable luxury. *Décisions Marketing, 110*(2), 217–246.

López, B., Rangel-Pérez, C., & Fernández, M. (2023). Sustainable strategies in the luxury business to increase efficiency in reducing carbon footprint. *Journal of Business Research, 157*, 113607.

Nasr, A. K., Rashidirad, M., Yoganathan, V., & Sadaghiani, A. S. (2024). CSR marketing through social media and contextual effects on stakeholder engagement: A multinational cross-industry analysis. *Information Systems Frontiers, 26*, 987–1004.

Nie, J., Wang, X., & Yang, C. (2023). The influence of self-expansion and consumer engagement on consumers' continuous participation in virtual corporate social responsibility co-creation. *Behavioural Science, 13*, 545. https://doi.org/10.3390/bs13070545

Okazaki, S., Plangger, K., West, D., & Menéndez, H. D. (2020). Exploring digital corporate social responsibility communications on Twitter. *Journal of Business Research, 117*, 675–682.

Opute, A. P., Iwu, C. G., Adeola, O., Mugobo, V., Okeke-Uzodike, O. E., Fagbola, S., & Jaiyeoba, O. (2020). The Covid-19-pandemic and implications for businesses: Innovative retail marketing viewpoint. *Retail Marketing Review*, 16, SE.

Opute, A. P. (2020). Teamwork and customer service (Chapter 14). In R. O. Hinson, A. Ogechi, T. R. Lituchi, & A. F. O. Amartey (Eds.), *Customer service management: A strategic and operational perspective*. Taylor and Francis.

Opute, A. P., Kalu, I. K., Chukwuma-Nwuba, E. O., Ojra, J. and Iwu, C. G. (2022b). Technology and marketing: Understanding the interface and Post-Covid-19 implications. In A. Gbadamosi (Ed.), *Critical perspectives on diversity, equity and inclusion in marketing* (pp. 208–220). IGI Global Publishers. https://doi.org/10.4018/978-1-6684-3590-8.ch012

Opute, A. P., Jawad, C., & Jiang, X. (2022a). Marketing: Cultural identity implications and inclusion concept. In A. Gbadamosi (Ed.), *Critical perspectives on diversity, equity and inclusion in marketing* (pp. 61–74). IGI Global Publishers. https://doi.org/10.4018/978-1-6684-3590-8.ch004

Opute, A. P. (2022). Virtual teams: The New Work Norm for the Post Covid-19 Era. In O. Adeola, J. N. Edeh, R. E. Hinson, & F. Netswera (Eds.), *Digital service delivery in Africa*. Palgrave Studies of Marketing in Emerging Economies. Palgrave Macmillan, Cham. https://doi.org/10.1007/978-3-030-83909-3_13

Ozuem, W., Ranfagni, S., Willis, M., Salvietti, G., & Howell, K. (2024). Exploring the relationship between chatbots, service failure recovery and customer loyalty: A frustration–aggression perspective. *Psychology and Marketing*. https://doi.org/10.1002/mar.22051

Ozuem, W., Ranfagni, S., & Millman, C. (2024a). *Call for chapters—Sustainable digital marketing strategies for fashion and luxury brands: Theory and practice*. Palgrave.

Ozuem, W., Ranfagni, S., & Willis, M. (2024b). *Digital transformation for fashion and luxury brands: Theory and practice*. Macmillan.

Ozuem, W., Willis, M., Ranfagni, S., Howell, K., & Rovai, S. (2023). Examining the role of social media influencers in service failure and recovery strategies: An empirical investigation of millennials' views. *Information Technology and People*. https://doi.org/10.1108/ITP-05-2022-0371

Palm, C. (2023). Sustainable fashion: To define, or not to define, that is not the question. *Sustainability: Science Practice and Policy, 19*(1), 2261342. https://doi.org/10.1080/15487733.2023.2261342

Park, H., & Kim, S. Y. (2022). Consumer empowerment in corporate social responsibility: The effect of participatory CSR on company admiration and word-of-mouth communications. *Corporate Communications: An International Journal, 27*(2), 346–367.

Pedersen, E. R. G., Gwozdz, W., & Hvass, K. K. (2018). Exploring the relationship between business model innovation, corporate sustainability, and organisational values within the fashion industry. *Journal of Business Ethics, 149*(2), 267–284.

Pelikánová, R., MacGregor, R., & Cernek, M. (2021). New trends in codes of ethics: Czech business ethics preferences by the dawn of Covid-19. *Oeconomia Copernicana, 12*(4), 973–1009.

Rabeson, L., Paraschiv, C., Bertrandias, L., & Chenavaz, R. (2022). Couple ethical purchase behavior and joint decision making: Understanding the interaction process and the dynamics of influence. *Sustainability, 14*(13), 8105.

Shirvanimoghaddam, K., Motamed, B., Ramakrishna, S., & Naebe, M. (2020). Death by waste: Fashion and textile circular economy case. *Science of the Total Environment, 718*, 137317. https://doi.org/10.1016/j.scitotenv.2020.137317

Thakker, A. M., & Sun, D. (2023). Sustainable development goals for textiles and fashion. *Environmental Science and Pollution Research*, 30, 101989–102009. https://doi.org/10.1007/s11356-023-29453-1

Thorisdottir, T. S., & Johannsdottir, L. (2020). Corporate social responsibility influencing sustainability within the fashion industry. A systematic review. *Sustainability, 12*(21), 9167.

UN World Commission on Environment and Development. (1987). *Our common future: Report of the world commission on environment and development*. UN Document A/42/427.

Willersdorf, S., Hazan, J., Ricci, G., Prénaud, A., Bianchi, F., Seara, J., & Yang, V. (2020). *A new era and a new look for luxury*. BCG Global. United Nations World Commission on Environment and Development.

Zhou, J., Ye, S., Lan, W., & Jiang, Y. (2021). The effect of social media on corporate violations: Evidence from Weibo posts in China. *International Review of Finance, 21*(3), 966–988. https://doi.org/10.1111/irfi.12309

16

Social Media Influencers: Influencing Sustainable Practices in the Fashion Industry

Favour Ben and Wilson Ozuem

Introduction

Given the variety of definitions and perspectives surrounding the term influencer, it is necessary to examine it to ascertain the exact meaning of influencer marketing. An influencer is a third party who has a significant amount of influence over a brand's image and potential customers; influencers shape customers' purchasing decisions (Belanche et al., 2021). Influencer marketing started with celebrity endorsements and has since evolved to include a wide range of social media personalities, bloggers, and content creators. Influencer marketing in today's digital landscape has become a critical strategy for reaching and engaging audiences authentically and non-intrusively; influencer marketing stands out

F. Ben (✉)
Arden University, London, UK
e-mail: fben@arden.ac.uk

W. Ozuem
University for the Creative Arts, Business School, Epsom, UK
e-mail: wilson.ozuem@uca.ac.uk

W. Ozuem et al. (eds.), *Sustainable Digital Marketing for Fashion and Luxury Brands*,
https://doi.org/10.1007/978-3-031-82467-8_16

among the overwhelming 'digital noise' (Afifah, 2024). Digital noise is the excessive and overwhelming amount of information or content available in the digital ecosystem. This includes messages, advertisements, alerts, and other content that online users encounter while browsing the internet or using various digital platforms. In the context of influencer marketing, digital noise refers to the huge volume of content available online, which can make it difficult for brands to stand out and reach their target audience effectively. Online users are constantly confronted with the challenge of sorting and processing information in the online space, which can often be overwhelming; this can result in a loss of interest in engagement or physical interaction with the environment (Firth, 2019). The aim of adopting an influencer marketing strategy is to break through this digital noise by leveraging the popularity of several individuals with a significant online presence to promote products or services; the individuals are usually paid a fee or compensated based on their niche and relevance to the adopter's objectives (Ridge, 2023). Although influencer marketing can be effective in cutting through the noise and reaching consumers, it must be executed thoughtfully to avoid adding to existing noise. By observing audience preferences, personalizing approaches, ensuring relevance, and choosing the right channels, brands can drive successful influencer marketing campaigns that resonate with their target audience (Azemi & Ozuem, 2023; Ridge, 2023). Influencer marketing has a pronounced effect on brand engagement because it fosters authentic connections between brands and their target audience. By incorporating an influencer strategy, brands can significantly increase their reach and build a more loyal customer base. This then leads to an increase in sales, for example, recent studies showed that influencer recommendations have a higher impact on purchase decisions compared to traditional advertising methods like print ads and billboards (Shan et al., 2019).

Influencers have revolutionized word of mouth (WOM) marketing in the digital era and elevated it to electronic WOM (eWOM). They make use of authenticity, trust, and peer-to-peer influence and harness the power of social media and content creation to reach a larger audience; they provide a more sophisticated means of establishing a connection between brands and prospective clients (Verma & Yadav, 2021). As we look to the future, it is evident that influencer marketing will continue to evolve and diversify across platforms, embrace new media formats, and engage with niche audiences. The focus will shift towards authenticity, transparency, and value-driven content to align with the changing expectations of consumers (Ozuem et al., 2023). The integration of artificial intelligence (AI) and data-driven insights will enable a more targeted approach, which will maximize the impact of virtual influencer partnerships not necessarily human influencers. Therefore, future trends in influencer marketing are poised to be dynamic and influential in shaping the digital landscape (Vidani, 2021).

The Role of Social Media Influencers in Shaping Consumer Behaviour

The rise of social media influencers (SMIs) can be traced back to the early 2000s; it began as a hobby for everyday people but has since grown into a full-fledged career with various diversifications. SMIs differ from traditional celebrities, such as actors, politicians, singers, and thought leaders, who have built their brand through their work or career (Joshi et al., 2023). With the introduction of new platforms and the push for in-app shopping on socials, influencers are becoming the entire marketing funnel for several brands; these brands leverage SMIs as an awareness strategy and a purchase driver.

A recent study revealed that the market value of global influencer marketing stood at US$21.1 billion in 2023 (Dencheva, 2023), which is triple the value of 2019. The emergence of online platforms that make collaboration and partnership more profitable has opened the doors of influencer marketing to creators (Dencheva, 2023). SMIs have been perceived as online opinion leaders or market mavens in a chosen field or industry; they can arguably impact, positively or negatively, customers' personalities, attitudes, and identities (De Castro et al., 2021; Ozuem et al., 2021). They achieve this by adopting different content tactics, such as blogs, podcasts, and forums. They use the power of the web to appraise the virtues of products/services or brands and to criticize unfavoured ones.

SMIs sometimes have a large following on various digital platforms, such as Instagram, X (formerly Twitter), Snapchat, YouTube, and TikTok (Zeljko et al., 2018), where they actively engage their audience by regularly sharing content relevant to their niche or target market. They influence their followers' opinions, behaviours, and purchasing decisions due to their credibility, expertise, and relatability. SMIs carve out a niche for themselves online by understanding the platform's algorithms and employing effective content strategies (Bastrygina & Lim, 2023).

SMIs have a significant impact on consumer behaviour by influencing purchasing decisions, fostering trust, driving sales, shaping brand engagement, and impacting brand perception (Belanche et al., 2021). Their ability to communicate directly with consumers, provide valuable recommendations, and build communities has made influencer marketing an effective strategy for brands to reach their target audience and positively influence consumer behaviour. In today's competitive digital landscape, leveraging the influence of SMIs can effectively drive brand awareness, engagement, and, ultimately, consumer purchasing decisions (Joshi et al., 2023).

Parasocial interaction (PSI) is a psychological phenomenon in which people form one-sided emotional connections with media personalities via mediated communication channels like television (Jacobson & Harrison, 2021). With the rise of social media, the concept of PSI has expanded to include online-mediated relationships with SMIs. SMIs address their audiences personally and share content that encourages continued engagement, which leads to positive associations and wishful identification with the influencer. Despite the lack of real-life interaction, followers of SMIs feel a sense of intimacy and connection with the SMIs. Followers form emotional attachments with SMIs and even model their behaviour on SMIs due to the type of content they share (Jacobson & Harrison, 2021). Although PSIs are characterized by a perceived intimacy between influencers and their followers, a significant drawback of PSI for SMIs is the possibility of developing shallow and one-sided relationships with their followers. It may be harmful to both parties if followers develop irrational expectations and attachments to the influencer because of the perceived intimacy (Ozuem et al., 2024; Zhang &

Mac, 2023). These irrational expectations can put influencers under pressure to maintain a specific persona or image, which can result in them presenting an inauthentic version of themselves. This lack of authenticity can undermine an influencer's credibility and followers' trust, which could lead to a drop in engagement and potentially negative outcomes (Paolo et al., 2023). Before engaging influencers, brands should understand an influencer's target audience and establish clear objectives; brands should select an influencer who shares the brand's values to ensure authenticity in the partnership, and monitor campaign performance. By following these steps, brands can improve their influencer marketing strategies, establish genuine connections with their target audience, and achieve successful influencer collaborations (Ozuem et al., 2023).

Types of SMIs

SMIs have an enormous impact on customer engagement and brand perception; they are becoming vital brand partners in closing the gap between brands and consumers (Ozuem et al., 2023). SMIs are excellent at creating relevance, building trust, and influencing cultural trends. Through the utilization of influencers' storytelling skills and emotional connection, brands can establish genuine bonds with their intended audience (Jignesh & Das, 2021). SMIs are classified into several types based on their number of followers, content niche, and focus. Influencers may also specialize in specific topics such as fashion, beauty, travel, fitness, technology, parenting, food, gaming, pets, LGBTQ+ , and environmental issues. Each type works with brands that are relevant to their niche, which creates a variety of opportunities for influencer marketing. The social media landscape is evolving, and new influencer types may emerge over time (Angraini, 2023).

Nano-influencers: The number of followers for these SMIs ranges from 1000 to 10,000, which is far fewer followers in comparison to others, but their impact is substantial due to their intimately connected audience. Nano-influencers develop deep bonds, establish a sincere rapport, and cultivate trust with their followers. When it comes to influencer marketing for brands, nano-influencers are crucial and have advantages such as consumer trust, high levels of expertise, likeability, informative value, and entertainment value (Wibawa et al., 2021). Additionally, because of their bridging role in social networks, nano-influencers are useful for interacting with online communities supporting causes and promoting goods linked to those causes. Likewise, nano-influencers have the potential to increase brand equity, revenue, and presence in relevant sectors, especially target markets like the fashion sector, through promotional offers, reviews, recommendations, ratings, and educational content. The nature of the product being advertised and the level of customer interest are two factors that determine the effectiveness of nano-influencers (Himelboim & Golan, 2022). Their content is often personal and relatable, which leads to higher engagement rates. While engagement can be high, nano-influencers' overall reach is inherently small, which limits the number of people they can influence. For luxury products, celebrities may be less effective than nano-influencers. In contrast, celebrity endorsements outperform nano-influencers for products with low customer interest (Park et al., 2021). Lastly, because of their smaller audience sizes and the lack of readily available data analytics, measuring the return on investment from collaborations with nano-influencers can be difficult (Wibawa et al., 2021).

Micro-influencers: These individuals have 10,000 to 50,000 followers and are often experts in a specific niche, such as beauty, sustainable fashion, travel photography, or vegan baking. Because of their small audience, they can engage with followers more personally, and foster a sense of community and trust. This authenticity appeals to audiences who are growing weary of overly polished and potentially inauthentic content from mega-influencers. This trust can lead to greater brand loyalty and advocacy (Ehlers, 2022). In comparison to collaboration with mega-influencers, micro-influencers have less reach, limited brand recognition, the possibility of less genuine engagement, increased workload, niche limitations, and limited influence on the perception of industries. Despite these challenges, working with micro-influencers can help brands engage niche audiences authentically and cost-effectively. When incorporating micro-influencers into marketing strategies, brands must carefully weigh the potential benefits against the drawbacks. Working with micro-influencers is frequently more affordable for brands than working with mega-influencers. Micro-influencers are therefore a wise choice for new ventures, smaller companies, or focused marketing campaigns (Ailion, 2021).

Macro-influencers: These SMIs' target groups range from 50,000 to 500,000 followers and create a balance between reach and engagement. One advantage of macro-influencers is that they have a wide reach and can connect with more people who can become potential or existing customers. Working with well-known macro-influencers can significantly boost a brand's credibility, as they are often perceived as thought leaders or trendsetters in their respective fields; thus, they lend prestige and authority to the brands they endorse. However, because influencers with a large following focus on a more diversified and media-dependent audience when creating their content, the audience associated with them is more generalized and the product analysis that macro-influencers provide is not as personal or as in-depth as micro-influencers' analyses. What sets macro-influencers' marketing efforts apart is their emphasis on community building, interactions within platforms, and targeting niche markets, as opposed to the commercially oriented mainstream strategies that underpin celebrity influencers with larger numbers of followers (Kalemi, 2022).

Unlike micro-influencers, macro-influencers have access to a far wider range of potential customers and have power over product promotion, trendsetting, and brand awareness during a campaign. They are experts in their field and can be valuable partners for brands looking to reach specific demographics or interests. Working with macro-influencers can expose brands to oversaturation as influencer marketing becomes more popular. With so many brands seeking similar collaborations, the market can become saturated, which would reduce the uniqueness and effectiveness of campaigns (Zalani, 2022).

Mega-influencers: These SMIs have millions of followers and wield enormous influence across multiple demographics. Mega-influencers are perceived as experts in their field, they are widely known, and often build their audience through the content they post on social media. Mega-influencers are the highest-ranking category of SMIs (Fligler, 2023). They include celebrities and individuals who have amassed a significant online presence. Collaborating with mega-influencers can significantly impact a brand's success due to their extensive reach and influence over a large audience. Working with mega-influencers in brand marketing offers significant benefits such as enhanced visibility, immediate brand credibility, driving sales, impactful engagement, and effective content performance (Fligler, 2023). Leveraging the reach and influence of mega-influencers can greatly enhance a brand's reputation, expand its audience reach, and drive success in the competitive digital marketing landscape. Although their reach is unparalleled, their connection with individual followers may be compromised due to the size of their audience. They can be categorised into facets like lifestyle, gaming, and sustainability (Zalani, 2022).

In general, influencers are essential to contemporary branding because they act as storytellers, brand ambassadors, and designers of genuine brand marketing campaigns. Understanding the differences between each type of influencer is critical for brands looking to maximize influencer marketing effectiveness. Choosing the right type of influencer based on campaign objectives, target audience demographics, budget considerations, and industry alignment can significantly impact the success of influencer marketing initiatives in terms of brand awareness, engagement, and sales growth.

Sustainability and the Fashion Industry

The concept of sustainability refers to meeting current needs without jeopardizing future generations' ability to meet their own (Deloitte, 2023a, 2023b). The three pillars of sustainability, or the 3Ps, are people, planet, and profit. This means that for something to be sustainable, it must be beneficial to people, not harmful to the environment, and profitable enough to allow businesses and the economy to grow (Miller, 2020). The need to create a sustainable future is particularly pressing for the fashion industry as the world's population is expected to reach 9 billion by 2030. Fashion consumption and waste are on the rise, and global temperatures are rising year after year (United Nations, 2022).

The fashion industry is a major polluter: it is responsible for 10% of global carbon emissions and 20% of wastewater, which is more than aviation and shipping combined. This has led to calls from ethical consumers for sustainability in fashion to help keep the world safe (Stallard, 2022). Sustainable fashion is also known as slow fashion and is the antithesis of fast fashion. Slow fashion is a movement aimed at reducing the fashion industry's negative impact on the environment and people (Chomsky, 2023). It is about making conscious choices throughout the entire fashion lifecycle, from the materials used to the way clothes are produced, worn, and disposed of.

The global fast fashion market, worth more than US$106 billion in 2022, is expected to increase significantly in the coming years. The fashion industry, while glamorous and trendsetting, has come under fire for its environmental impact and ethical concerns. However, a growing movement is pushing for sustainable practices that prioritize both style and environmental consciousness. Sustainable practices in the fashion industry (see Table 16.1) entail implementing strategies and processes aimed at reducing the negative environmental and social impacts of clothing, accessory production, distribution, and disposal (Yang et al., 2017).

SMIs and Sustainable Practices

SMIs can play a key role in encouraging sustainable practices in the luxury fashion industry by shaping consumer behaviour and perceptions of sustainable fashion. Studies have shown that non-sponsored SMI posts are perceived as more convincing and authentic, and they lead to higher intention and engagement in sustainable fashion consumption (Haines et al., 2023). Furthermore, the sustainable fashion tribe's use of social media networks enables them to inform and reach a large audience within their community of like-minded individuals; members of this community encourage one another to explore deeper ethical and ecological fashion consumption by sharing their journeys, struggles, and triumphs as they embrace a more conscious approach to fashion on their channels (Klaus et al., 2023). This has prompted luxury brands to

Table 16.1 Examples of sustainable practices in the fashion industry

Sustainable practices in the fashion industry	Examples
Use of eco-friendly materials	– Organic cotton: sustainable and resource-efficient fibres – Pesticide-free cultivation: hemp, linen, tencel, modal
Ethical manufacturing	– Fair labour practices: safe working conditions and fair wages – Local sourcing: reducing the carbon footprint – Transparent supply chains: providing visibility in the entire supply chain
Circular fashion economy	– Recycling: using recycled materials for fabric production – Upcycling: repurposing discarded clothing items – Clothing take-back programmes: facilitating the return and recycling of old items (Srividya et al., 2024)
Reducing environmental impact	– Water conservation: efficient manufacturing processes and dyeing techniques – Energy efficiency: using renewable energy – Zero-waste design: minimizing fabric waste during production
Slow fashion	– Quality over quantity: encouraging investment in durable, high-quality pieces – Timeless design: focusing on enduring styles
Innovation and technology	– 3D printing: creating customizable and efficient designs – Digital prototyping: minimizing waste with digital models – Smart textiles: incorporating technology for enhanced functionality
Educating consumers	– Awareness campaigns: educating consumers about the impact of their choices – Promoting sustainable lifestyles

(continued)

Table 16.1 (continued)

Sustainable practices in the fashion industry	Examples
Certifications and standards	– Fair trade certification: ensuring fair wages and ethical practices – Global Organic Textile Standard: certifying organic textiles
Collaborations and partnerships	– Industry collaboration: addressing sustainability challenges collectively – Partnerships with innovators for cutting-edge practices
Continuous improvement and accountability	– Setting targets: establishing and sharing sustainability goals – Regular audits: ensuring adherence to commitments (Zhang et al., 2021)

recognize the significance of sustainability and incorporate it into their communication and reporting practices (Di Leo et al., 2023).

However, transforming the fashion industry requires the collective effort of consumers, brands, and policymakers. Previous studies claimed that green or sustainable influencers can become new policy endorsers for policymaking by actively promoting sustainability to achieve the Sustainable Development Goals (SDGs) in 2030 (Yıldırım, 2021). The focus is on SDG-12, which emphasizes sustainable consumption and production. Influencers are seen as instrumental in raising awareness and fostering a sense of responsibility among consumers. Collaboration between influencers and policymakers is considered essential for the long-term achievement of the 2030 SDGs, because collaboration provides a unique avenue to address environmental, economic, and social issues (United Nations, 2023). Luxury brands must embrace sustainability to remain relevant; understanding online audiences' attitudes, perceptions, and views of sustainable luxury is key to achieving this (Hauth et al., 2023). Luxury brands need to adopt and focus on a sustainability strategy to remain relevant, which starts with understanding how online audiences see sustainable luxury. However, there are challenges to be faced, such as the cost of sustainable materials, greenwashing, and maintaining ethical practices in complex supply chains

(Hauth et al., 2023). Even with these challenges, increasing awareness and new solutions give hope for a future where fashion is both eco-friendly and socially responsible. SMIs are crucial in promoting and shaping sustainable fashion trends in the industry (Kapoor et al., 2022).

Sustainable fashion influencers have emerged as a major trend in the fashion industry. Customers are increasingly beginning to recognize and value these influencers as they promote moral and eco-friendly fashion choices. Sustainable fashion influencers use their platforms to promote sustainable fashion brands, educate their followers about the negative consequences of fast fashion, and provide tips for conscious consumerism. This shift towards sustainability is being driven by a growing awareness of the fashion industry's environmental and social impact. Consumers are increasingly aware of the harm caused by fast fashion, and, as a result, they are looking for alternatives and turning to sustainable fashion influencers for advice and inspiration. Sustainable fashion influencers encourage the adoption of sustainable fashion practices such as upcycling, thrifting, and repurposing (Jacobson & Harrison, 2021). They are not typical trendsetters; they are educators, advocates, and changemakers who strategically collaborate with fashion brands to create, communicate campaigns, and lead projects that amplify change (Jacobson & Harrison, 2021). They deconstruct fast fashion's glossy façade and reveal the harsh realities of its production cycle. They tell stories about ethical alternatives and highlight sustainable brands, fair trade practices, and the benefits of buying second-hand.

As the industry invests in new marketing approaches, social media ads, and influencer marketing, it is suggested that consumer opinions and shopping habits may significantly change with the emergence of sustainable SMIs, such as lifestyle sustainable influencers and thrifting sustainable influencers (Jacobson & Harrison, 2021).

Lifestyle sustainable influencers can shift the narrative and conversation towards a more positive, solution-focused outlook by focusing on content relevant to their daily lifestyle and ethical clothing sourcing. The interactive and visually appealing nature of social media and digital marketing will broaden the potential audience and impact of sustainability initiatives. The content of influencer-led initiatives is more likely to be shared and go viral by leveraging the visual and social aspects of digital platforms; this content will increase lifestyle sustainable influencers' visibility, promote positive lifestyle messages and behaviours, and ultimately inspire more genuine engagement from the public. Each influencer will need to balance content direction, ethics, and making money for themselves. However, due to their commitment to sustainability, they are likely to remain true to their principles (Environmental Audit Committee, 2019).

According to Forbes, the real stars in influencer marketing are those who have fostered a deep connection with their audience that allows for effective communication and the facilitation of positive actions (Bringé, 2021). The success of influencer-led sustainability initiatives, particularly within the thrifting space, hinges on establishing an authentic and meaningful connection between content creators and their audience. Thrifting influencers, who have dedicated time to building their social media presence and connect genuinely with followers, are recognized as influential figures in the sustainability landscape (Environmental Audit Committee, 2019). Unlike celebrity influencers, these influencers collaborate extensively with sustainable and non-sustainable non-governmental organizations (NGOs) in the fashion industry, and enhance their engagement and communication capabilities. Thrifting influencers play a pivotal role in inspiring genuine lifestyle changes through initiatives like do-it-yourself (DIY) projects, collaborations with thrifting stores, and engagement with sustainable and non-sustainable fashion households to encourage followers to adopt sustainable practices. For instance, the promotion of brands offering less expensive upcycled items or items made from recycled materials aligns well with the preferences of thrifting influencers' followers. This approach not only promotes sustainable fashion but also encourages meaningful lifestyle changes among their engaged and environmentally conscious audience (United Nations, 2024).

Engaging the public on a personal level is just as vital as changing policies and implementing large-scale social reforms to address the deep-rooted causes of environmental and social problems. Small changes to a person's lifestyle can collectively have big impacts on the environment, so campaigns focused on facilitating and promoting these changes are highly valuable; these collective changes emphasize the role of a sustainable fashion influencer. Influencer-led campaigns offer a different kind of two-way communication than static public information campaigns. They do this by using generative content to showcase an everyday lifestyle, thrifting, styling, and potential collaborations, which help to articulate and encourage positive lifestyle messages. By providing visual and relatable examples of how individual actions can make a difference, such as through vlogs or blog entries that document personal sustainability challenges, audiences are much more likely to be inspired and motivated, and this can foster a sense of collective action.

Measuring the success of influencer-led sustainability initiatives is crucial for evaluating impact and refining strategies. Dencheva (2023) reported that 19% of marketers cited social media traffic increase as the best-performing metric of influencers' impact, while 11% mentioned that a lifting of brand metrics was the most effectively delivered metric. However, certain metrics are necessary to track success, such as engagement metrics that track likes, comments, shares, and saves on social media platforms, and provide insight into how well-received an influencer's content is by the target audience for a fashion brand. Another example of this type of metric involves tracking increases in website traffic before, during, and after the campaign using tools such as Google Analytics. This helps identify the source of traffic originating from influencer posts for brands. Conversion rates are crucial for any brand, and tracking specific actions like buying, subscribing to newsletters, or participating in sustainability projects can help gauge the effect and degree of audience engagement to know the impact on brands. Finally, data on sales peaks from previous periods can be compared with the campaign period to reveal the effect of a campaign on consumer behaviour and purchase choices (DeLane, 2023).

SMIs and Credibility Theory

SMIs are omnipresent occupiers of digital real estate across various web domains; they cut across different industries like fashion, beauty, electronics, and automobiles (Riedl et al., 2023). Amid their curated feeds and sponsored posts, it is crucial to understand how they garner trust and influence (Goanta & Ranchordas, 2019). SMIs, who have developed their online character and credibility, can influence their audience to purchase products through eWOM virality (Musa et al., 2023). However, it is important to note that the influencer's trustworthiness and appropriateness impact the way recipients respond to promotions.

Studies have found that consumers are becoming more responsive to sustainable fashion, with increasing engagement on relevant YouTube videos (Haines et al., 2023). Hill and Qesja (2022) investigated how consumers' purchase intentions are impacted by the popularity of SMIs; they considered the moderating influence of the influencer's perceived motive. Several researchers have discussed the credibility theory of SMIs, which is a theoretical framework that examines the relationship between SMIs' credibility and followers' intentions to buy recommended brands, and the threads of trust that connect brands, influencers, and the target audience. This theory indicates that influencers can help the fashion industry have a brighter, more sustainable future by prioritizing authenticity, transparency, and meaningful collaborations (Joshi et al., 2023) that contribute to their persuasiveness and trustworthiness in the digital media context. Trustworthiness is one of the key factors that improve persuasiveness and credibility, influencer–customer harmony, attitudes, and behavioural responses to products and services. The credibility theory of SMIs has some implications for marketing and advertising due to the direct and significant effect of credibility on brand equity and consumer satisfaction (Li & Peng, 2021). Łaszkiewicz and Kalińska-Kula (2023) emphasized the significance of influencer credibility in shaping brand attitudes, purchase intentions, and acceptance of virtual influencers in marketing and advertising strategies, because influencers lacking credibility could attract criticism of brands. An influencers' credibility plays a significant role in shaping followers' intentions to purchase recommended brands (Shoukat et al., 2023).

Threads of Credibility

The credibility theory of SMIs identifies three key aspects that influence the way in which audiences perceive and trust influencers: expertise, trustworthiness, and attractiveness. These three aspects are now discussed.

Expertise: Expertise involves SMIs being open about their experiences, opinions, and collaborations with brands, including the disclosure of sponsored content and avoiding misinformation. Displaying their true personality and values in their content allows followers to connect with them on a more personal level and perceive them as genuine. Furthermore, SMIs can demonstrate how the products or services they promote fit into their own lives and experiences. Practical applications are emphasized while avoiding unrealistic portrayals (Walter, 2023). Expert SMIs showcase their knowledge and experience in a specific niche, such as sustainable fashion, which builds authority.

Trustworthiness: Trustworthiness is an attribute that reflects the perceived goodness of an SMI. Trustworthiness encompasses characteristics such as honesty, believability, reliability, authenticity, and transparency, which are of high importance to preserve credibility and noteworthiness. Trustworthiness also includes maintaining a consistent message, values, and overall image by demonstrating reliability and dependability, which leads to a positive reputation. SMIs should avoid controversial behaviour or opinions that could harm their reputation and undermine trust in their target audience. SMIs should consciously strive for authentic connections with their audience, respond to comments and messages, and cultivate a sense of community. This shows that they value and care about their followers' opinions. Influencers who disclose sponsorships, avoid exaggerated claims, and share personal struggles are said to build strong connections with their followers. An example would be Venetia La Manna (@venetialamanna) on TikTok who is known for her witty, honest 'Recipe for Disaster' series that exposes fast fashion issues (Paolo et al., 2023).

Attractiveness: Physical attractiveness is not always the only factor; followers are also influenced over time by an influencer's sincere passion and message alignment. Hipster-style content producers make their stories accessible to the general public by leveraging relatable experiences to encourage conscious consumption; they align their values and tenets with the preferences of their audience and the companies they work with. This ensures that brand alliances are genuine and appealing to their fan base and that the content they offer is accurate, consistent, and in keeping with the overall theme and goals of the platform. Relating these beliefs or experiences to one another strengthens bonds and amplifies the impact of influencers who appear 'like us'. Instagram content producers advertise pre-owned and vintage fashion to a community passionate about slower, mindful consumption (Paolo et al., 2023).

By combining different elements like expertise, authenticity, trustworthiness, and alignment, SMIs can create a strong foundation of trust with their followers. It is important to note that trust-building is an ongoing effort and needs constant attention from the influencer. The importance of each element varies based on the influencer's niche and target audience. Social media algorithms and the changing online landscape also influence people's perceptions of an influencer's trustworthiness.

Brands that partner with credible influencers who align with their values can amplify their message and reach engaged audiences; however, brands need to collaborate with influencers who genuinely understand the brand objectives and partner with those who regularly generate excellent content to showcase their knowledge of the industry. Engaged influencers create content that demonstrates openness and sincerity, and they have a reputation for driving active participation in their community. Brands need to make sure that they are in sync with the audience by selecting influencers whose ideals are shared by the intended audience and the brand (Forbes, 2021).

Fast fashion's greenwashing and the constant pressure to consume, even within the sustainable realm, call into question the foundation of trust. In addition, there are concerns about accessibility and potential exclusion within the movement. Despite these challenges, credibility theory promotes responsible engagement with SMIs in the fashion industry. By focusing on authenticity, transparency, and ethical partnerships, influencers can continue to weave a brighter, more sustainable future for fashion; a future that is carefully measured one thread at a time (Erkan & Evans, 2016). Credibility theory helps us understand how influencers build trust and credibility. Recognizing the significance of expertise, authenticity, trustworthiness, and alignment allows influencers to form stronger connections with their audience and be more effective overall. Understanding these threads allows brands and audiences to navigate the landscape more effectively.

Challenges Faced by SMIs in Promoting Sustainability

Sustainability influencers are weaving a thread of conscious change in the fashion industry, but the thread might get snagged. Promoting sustainability through social media, especially for millennials and Gen Zers, presents a unique set of challenges, including navigating greenwashing and fostering accessibility. With the rise of influencer marketing, people are becoming more sceptical of influencers and their motivations (Khamis et al., 2017). Many influencers are perceived to be promoting products or causes for financial gain rather than genuine concern about sustainability. A lack of authenticity can damage influencer credibility, which would make it difficult for them to effectively promote sustainability. Another challenge is ensuring that influencers and products are compatible. The commercial nature of influencer partnerships presents several challenges to their effectiveness in advocating for sustainable practices (Ki et al., 2020).

Influencers and audiences are aware of greenwashing; distinguishing genuine efforts from greenwashing can be a complex process (Adamkiewicz et al., 2022). If brands present misleading images, then it makes it difficult for influencers to choose ethical partners without jeopardizing their credibility. To establish credibility, SMIs must decipher claims, research supply chains, and demand transparency, all of which are time-consuming activities (Bertola & Colombi, 2024). SMIs must support initiatives that promote genuine environmental stewardship over superficial marketing tactics. Regulators worldwide are working to prevent misleading marketing practices by safeguarding consumers from greenwashing in the fashion industry. To that end, they are creating guidelines to guarantee accountability and transparency in environmental claims made by brands (Tonti, 2022).

Promoting new, sustainable collections may appear positive, but it can contribute to an overconsumption mindset. Influencers walk a fine line when they encourage conscious choices while avoiding perpetuating the 'buy more' narrative.

Repair, DIY, and second-hand options should all be emphasized equally (Ge, 2024), especially since sustainable options frequently come at a premium that creates an exclusivity barrier. Influencers may feel stuck promoting options that are out of reach for many of their followers, which could alienate segments of their audience and create the perception of elitism. It is critical to strike a balance between showcasing aspirational pieces and highlighting more affordable alternatives (Ge, 2024). Many SMIs try to build welcoming communities/followers that reflect diverse identities, body types, and socioeconomic backgrounds. Partnering with diverse voices, amplifying marginalized narratives, and promoting affordability are critical steps that demonstrate the value of online communities. This collective effort can be used to establish the tangible impact of their efforts while finding ways to measure progress, celebrate wins, and stay motivated despite the inevitable obstacles and slow pace of change (La Rosa & Johnson Jorgensen, 2021).

Furthermore, the constant pressure from brand sponsorship for influencer analytics, such as clicks, likes, impressions, subscribers, and followers, can alter SMIs' genuine intentions to drive home their sustainability message (Goanta & Ranchordas, 2019); for example, the sponsorship might require algorithms prioritizing sensational content, such as catchphrase clickbait, and too detailed discussions of complex issues concerning sustainability in the fashion industry. Balancing engaging content with informative, critical narratives is a challenge for financially struggling SMIs.

Despite these challenges, sustainability influencers remain crucial agents of change. By fostering transparency, prioritizing ethical partnerships, advocating for accessibility, and offering diverse perspectives, the complexities of the industry can be eradicated, and sustainability influencers can inspire a collective shift towards a more responsible future for fashion. Every thread woven with genuine intention brings us closer to a greener future (Zhou et al., 2020).

The Future Landscape of Sustainable Fashion Influencers

The future landscape of sustainable fashion influencers is expected to evolve with trends emphasizing diversity, authenticity, AI, and transparency, as sustainable fashion is becoming increasingly complex and crucial. Sustainable fashion influencers will play a multifaceted role in supporting the fashion industry. Aside from promoting eco-friendly brands and styles, influencers will expand their role of promoting expertise by becoming investigative voices: they will unpack complex supply chains, expose greenwashing tactics, advocate for ethical labour practices, and educate consumers about the reuse of fashion materials for example (Vladimirova et al., 2023). SMIs will become collaborative changemakers who bridge the gap between brands, consumers, and prospective sustainable NGOs to foster the co-creation of sustainable solutions (Mukendi et al., 2020). Ethical brands will foster partnerships with sustainable influencers, develop capsule collections based on influencer input, or collaborate to organize educational workshops. Sustainability should not be a privilege; it should be inclusive, representing diverse body types, ethnicities, and socioeconomic backgrounds. The influencer movement can promote accessible sustainable options and advocate for fair pricing.

Influencers will use augmented reality and virtual reality to present eco-friendly apparel, which will cut down on the need for real samples and lessen the environmental effect (Bringé, 2021). Furthermore, influencers could transparently use blockchain technology to track and verify the ethical sourcing of materials. They will take a direct approach to the problem of overconsumption. Influencers will support slow fashion, encourage quality over quantity, and celebrate 'make do and mend' methods that transcend individual platforms. They will also cultivate online and physical communities that unite like-minded people to promote mindful consumption (Vladimirova et al., 2023). These communities will offer a forum for information exchange, teamwork on projects, and assistance for the sustainable fashion movement.

Concluding Remarks

As consumers become more conscious of, and involved in, sustainable fashion, the landscape of influencers in sustainable fashion is changing. Customers are looking for answers as they grow more conscious of the issues facing the fashion industry (Haines et al., 2023). Instagram has emerged as a key social media channel for conversations about, and experiences with, sustainable fashion (Marcella-Hood, 2023). Hashtags like #SustainableFashion are being actively used by Instagram content creators, such as vintage enthusiasts, designers, makers, and brands, to share proactive and targeted content about sustainable fashion solutions (Lee & Weder, 2021). Furthermore, consumers are becoming more conscious of sustainability in the fashion industry thanks to the influence of SMIs who support sustainable fashion and encourage shopping with sustainable values (Kapoor et al., 2022).

In conclusion, influencers have the potential to significantly impact the direction of sustainable fashion by advocating for reform in the industry, fostering authenticity and transparency, and educating the public. More diversity in the influencer market, a focus on circular fashion, partnerships with eco-friendly companies, creative content formats, and the use of technology to increase transparency are some of the trends that are predicted. Influencers should empower customers to make sustainable decisions, broaden their advocacy beyond fashion, and support an all-encompassing approach to sustainable living.

References

Adamkiewicz, J., Kochanska, E., Adamkiewicz, I., & Łukasik, R. M. (2022). Greenwashing and sustainable fashion industry. *Current Opinion in Green and Sustainable Chemistry*, [online] *38*(100710). https://doi.org/10.1016/j.cogsc.2022.100710

Afifah, N. (2024). Influencer marketing strategies and the use of Ai technology in enhancing brand awareness: A case study in the fashion industry. *Journal of Economic, Business and Accounting (COSTING)*, [online] *7*(2), 3058–3066. https://doi.org/10.31539/costing.v7i2.8723

Ailion, J. (2021). *4 Types of Influencers—The full list*. [online] *MOBURST*. https://www.moburst.com/blog/types-of-influencers/ [Accessed 27 Feb 2024].

Angraini, N. (2023). Social media marketing influencer: Literature review on promotional strategies using the influence of social media celebrities. *International Journal of Economic Research and Financial Accounting (IJERFA)*, *1*(4). https://doi.org/10.55227/ijerfa.v1i4.42

Azemi, Y., & Ozuem, W. (2023). How does retargeting work for different Gen Z mobile users? *Journal of Advertising Research*, 2023-023. https://doi.org/10.2501/jar-2023-023

Bastrygina, T., & Lim, W. (2023). Foundations of consumer engagement with social media influencers. *International Journal of Web Based Communities, 19*(2/3), 222–242. https://doi.org/10.1504/ijwbc.2023.131410

Belanche, D., Casaló, L. V., Flavián, M., & Sánchez, S. I. (2021). Understanding influencer marketing: The role of congruence between influencers, products and consumers. *Journal of Business Research*, [online] *132*(132), 186–195. https://doi.org/10.1016/j.jbusres.2021.03.067

Bertola, P., & Colombi, C. (2024). Can fashion be sustainable? Trajectories of change in organizational, products and processes, and socio-cultural contexts. *Sustainability: Science, Practice and Policy*, *20*(1). https://doi.org/10.1080/15487733.2024.2312682

Bringé, A. (2021). The digitization of the fashion industry and what it means for brands. [online] *Forbes*. https://www.forbes.com/sites/forbescommunicationscouncil/2021/07/29/the-digitization-of-the-fashion-industry-and-what-it-means-for-brands/ [Accessed 1 Mar 2024].

De Castro, C. A., O'Reilly, I., & Carthy, A. (2021). Social media influencers (SMIs) in context: A literature review. *Journal of Marketing Management*, [online] *9*(2), 59–71. https://doi.org/10.15640/jmm.v9n2a9

Chomsky, R. (2023). *What is slow fashion? A guide to sustainable style*. [online] Sustainable Review. https://sustainablereview.com/what-is-slow-fashion-a-guide-to-sustainable-style/

DeLane, J. (2023). Measuring long-term influencer marketing brand impact. [online] *Digital Delane*. https://digitaldelane.com/influencer-marketing-measurement [Accessed 29 Feb 2024].

Deloitte. (2023b). *The sustainable consumer 2023*. [online] Deloitte. https://www2.deloitte.com/uk/en/pages/consumer-business/articles/sustainable-consumer.html [Accessed 6 Mar 2024].

Deloitte. (2023a). *The Deloitte Global 2023 Gen Z and Millennial Survey*. [online] Deloitte. https://www.deloitte.com/global/en/issues/work/content/genzmillennialsurvey.html [Accessed 7 Mar 2024].

Dencheva, V. (2023). *Influencer marketing worldwide*. [online] Statista. https://www.statista.com/topics/2496/influence-marketing/#topicOverview [Accessed 24 Jan 2024].

Di Leo, A., Sfodera, F., Cucari, N., Mattia, G., & Dezi, L. (2023). Sustainability reporting practices: An explorative analysis of luxury fashion Brands. *Management Decision, 61*(5). https://doi.org/10.1108/md-02-2022-0142

Ehlers, K. (2022). Council post: Micro-influencers: When smaller is better. [online] *Forbes*. https://www.forbes.com/sites/forbesagencycouncil/2021/06/02/micro-influencers-when-smaller-is-better/?sh=58d29898539b [Accessed 6 Mar 2024].

Environmental Audit Committee. (2019). *Fixing fashion: Clothing consumption and sustainability*. [online] https://publications.parliament.uk/pa/cm201719/cmselect/cmenvaud/1952/1952.pdf [Accessed 6 Mar 2024].

Erkan, I., & Evans, C. (2016). The influence of eWOM in social media on consumers' purchase intentions: An extended approach to information adoption. *Computers in Human Behavior, 61*(1), 47–55. https://doi.org/10.1016/j.chb.2016.03.003

Firth, J. (2019). The 'online brain': How the internet may be changing our cognition. *World Psychiatry*, [online] *18*(2), 119–129. https://doi.org/10.1002/wps.20617

Fligler, L. (2023). *6 benefits of influencer marketing for 2023*. [online] YellowHead. https://www.yellowhead.com/blog/benefits-of-influencer-marketing/

Forbes. (2021, July 20). How to engage with influencers and form strong partnerships: 12 expert tips. [online] *Forbes*. https://www.forbes.com/sites/forbesagencycouncil/2021/07/20/how-to-reach-out-to-and-partner-with-with-right-influencers-12-tips/

Ge, J. (2024). Influencers marketing and its impacts on sustainable fashion consumption among Generation Z. *Journal of Soft Computing and Decision Analytics*, [online] *2*(1), 118–143. https://doi.org/10.31181/jscda21202438

Goanta, C., & Ranchordas, S. (2019). The regulation of social media influencers: An introduction. *SSRN Electronic Journal*. https://doi.org/10.2139/ssrn.3457197

Haines, S., Fares, O. H., Mohan, M., & Lee, S. H. (Mark) (2023). Social media fashion influencer eWOM communications: Understanding the trajectory of sustainable fashion conversations on YouTube fashion Haul videos. *Journal of Fashion Marketing and Management: An International Journal*, *27*(6). https://doi.org/10.1108/jfmm-02-2022-0029

Hauth, C., Palm, C., Eisner, C., & Hamid, H. (2023). Sustainable fashion on social media. *Kiel Journal of Consumer Studies, 1*(1), 32–38. https://doi.org/10.38071/2022-00862-4

Hill, S. R., & Qesja, B. (2022). Social media influencer popularity and authenticity perception in the travel industry. *The Service Industries Journal, 43*(5–6), 1–23. https://doi.org/10.1080/02642069.2022.2149740

Himelboim, I., & Golan, G. J. (2022). A Social network approach to social media influencers on Instagram: The strength of being a nano-influencer in cause communities. *Journal of Interactive Advertising, 23*(1), 1–13. https://doi.org/10.1080/15252019.2022.2139653

Jacobson, J., & Harrison, B. (2021). Sustainable fashion social media influencers and content creation calibration. *International Journal of Advertising*, [online] *41*(1), 150–177. https://doi.org/10.1080/02650487.2021.2000125 [Accessed 24 Jan 2024].

Jignesh, V., & Das, S. G. (2021). A review on evolution of social media influencer marketing: Reflection on consumer behaviour and consumer's decision-making process. *Turkish Online Journal of Qualitative Inquiry, 12*(9), 314–327.

Joshi, Y., Lim, W. M., Jagani, K., & Kumar, S. (2023). Social media influencer marketing: Foundations, trends, and ways forward. *Electronic Commerce Research*. [online] https://doi.org/10.1007/s10660-023-09719-z [Accessed 28 Jan 2024].

Kalemi, E. (2022). *Micro Vs macro influencers: Who's best for your brand?* [online] Publer's Blog. https://publer.io/blog/micro-vs-macro-influencers/ [Accessed 6 Mar 2024].

Kapoor, P. S., Tagore, A., & Dua, S. (2022). Social media influencer promoted sustainable fashion: Effects of sponsorship and benefit association. *Journal of Promotion Management, 29*(3), 1–30. https://doi.org/10.1080/10496491.2022.2163034

Khamis, S., Ang, L., & Welling, R. (2017). Self-branding, 'Micro-celebrity' and the Rise of Social Media Influencers. *Celebrity Studies, 8*(2), 1–18.

Ki, C., Park, S., & Ha-Brookshire, J. E. (2020). Toward a circular economy: Understanding consumers' moral stance on corporations' and individuals' responsibilities in creating a circular fashion economy. *Business Strategy and the Environment, 30*(2). https://doi.org/10.1002/bse.2675

Klaus, P., Manthiou, A., & Luong, V. H. (2023). Sustainability in luxury: Insights from Twitter activities. *Journal of Strategic Marketing*, 1–18. https://doi.org/10.1080/0965254x.2022.2160874

La Rosa, A., & Johnson Jorgensen, J. (2021). Influences on consumer engagement with sustainability and the purchase intention of apparel products. *Sustainability, 13*(19), 10655. https://doi.org/10.3390/su131910655

Łaszkiewicz, A., & Kalińska-Kula, M. (2023). Virtual influencers as an emerging marketing theory: A systematic literature review. *International Journal of Consumer Studies*. [online] https://doi.org/10.1111/ijcs.12956

Lee, E., & Weder, F. (2021). Framing sustainable fashion concepts on social media. An analysis of #slowfashionaustralia Instagram posts and post-COVID visions of the future. *Sustainability, 13*(17). https://doi.org/10.3390/su13179976

Li, Y., & Peng, Y. (2021). Influencer marketing: Purchase intention and its antecedents. *Marketing Intelligence & Planning*, [online] *39*(7), 960–978. https://doi.org/10.1108/mip-04-2021-0104

Marcella-Hood, M. (2023). Augmenting Sustainable Fashion on Instagram. *Sustainability*, [online] *15*(4), p. 3609. https://doi.org/10.3390/su15043609

Miller, K. (2020). *The triple bottom line: What it is & why it's important*. [online] Harvard Business School Online. https://online.hbs.edu/blog/post/what-is-the-triple-bottom-line [Accessed 7 Mar 2024].

Mukendi, A., Davies, I., Glozer, S., & McDonagh, P. (2020). Sustainable fashion: Current and future research directions. *European Journal of Marketing*, [online] *54*(11), 2873–2909. https://doi.org/10.1108/ejm-02-2019-0132

Musa, A. H., Baharuddin, F. N., Antara, P. M., Idris, A. R., Selamat, S. M., & Abedin, N. F. Z. (2023). Agent trustworthiness, electronic word of mouth (eWoM) and social media influencer roles in purchasing insurance: A conceptual paper. *International Journal of Academic Research in Business and Social Sciences,* [online] *13*(3), 917–922. https://doi.org/10.6007/ijarbss/v13-i3/16682

Ozuem, W., Ranfagni, S., Willis, M., Rovai, S., & Howell, K. (2021). Exploring customers' responses to online service failure and recovery strategies during Covid-19 pandemic: An actor–network theory perspective. *Psychology & Marketing, 38*(9), 1440–1459.

Ozuem, W., Ranfagni, S., Willis, M., Salvietti, G., & Howell, K. (2024). Exploring the relationship between chatbots, service failure recovery and customer loyalty: A frustration–aggression perspective. *Psychology and Marketing*. https://doi.org/10.1002/mar.22051

Ozuem, W., Willis, M., Ranfagni, S., Howell, K., & Rovai, S. (2023). Examining the role of social media influencers in service failure and recovery strategies: An empirical investigation of millennials' views. *Information Technology & People*. https://doi.org/10.1108/itp-05-2022-0371

Paolo, J., Molano, R., Garcia, J., Jose Bayson, A., & Igarza Cruz, M. (2023). Parasocial relationships and social media interactions: Building brand credibility and loyalty. *Spanish Journal of Marketing—ESIC, 28*(1), 21. https://doi.org/10.1108/sjme-09-2022-0190

Park, J., Lee, J. M., Xiong, V. Y., Septianto, F., & Seo, Y. (2021). David and Goliath: When and why micro-influencers are more persuasive than mega-influencers. *Journal of Advertising, 50*(5), 584–602. https://doi.org/10.1080/00913367.2021.1980470

Ridge, B. V. (2023). *Understanding noise marketing: Strategies and implications for brand visibility*. [online] Medium Multimedia Agencia De Marketing Digital. https://www.mediummultimedia.com/en/marketing-usa/what-is-noise-marketing/ [Accessed 6 Mar 2024].

Riedl, M., Lukito, J., & Woolley, S. (2023). Political influencers on social media: An introduction. *Social Media and Society, 9*(2), 205630512311779–205630512311779. https://doi.org/10.1177/20563051231177938

Shan, Y., Chen, K.-J., & Lin, J.-S. (Elaine). (2019). When social media influencers endorse brands: The effects of self-influencer congruence, parasocial identification, and perceived endorser motive. *International Journal of Advertising*, [online] *39*(5), 590–610. https://doi.org/10.1080/02650487.2019.1678322

Shoukat, M. H., Selem, K. M., & Asim Shah, S. (2023). How does social media influencer credibility blow the promotional horn? A dual mediation model. *Journal of Relationship Marketing*, [online] 172–201. https://doi.org/10.1080/15332667.2023.2197767

Srividya, N., Atiq, R., & Volety, N. S. (2024). Qualitative research on responsible consumption concerning apparel. *Cleaner and Responsible Consumption*, [online] *12*, 100178. https://doi.org/10.1016/j.clrc.2024.100178

Stallard, E. (2022, July 29). Fast fashion: How clothes are linked to climate change. *BBC News*. [online] https://www.bbc.co.uk/news/science-environment-60382624

Tonti, L. (2022). Fashion brands grapple with greenwashing: 'It's not a human right to say something is sustainable'. [online] *The Guardian*. https://www.theguardian.com/fashion/2022/nov/19/fashion-brands-grapple-with-greenwashing-its-not-a-human-right-to-say-something-is-sustainable [Accessed 24 Feb 2024].

United Nations. (2022). *World population to reach 8 billion this year, as growth rate slows*. [online] UN News. https://news.un.org/en/story/2022/07/1122272

United Nations. (2023). *Goal 12|Ensure sustainable consumption and production patterns*. [online] United Nations. https://sdgs.un.org/goals/goal12 [Accessed 28 Jan 2024].

United Nations. (2024). *Sustainable fashion communication strategy sustainable fashion*. [online] https://wedocs.unep.org/bitstream/handle/20.500.11822/41076/Sustainable_Fashion_Strategy.pdf?sequence=3 [Accessed 7 Mar 2024].

Verma, S., & Yadav, N. (2021). Past, present, and future of electronic word of mouth (EWOM). *Journal of Interactive Marketing, 53*(1), 111–128. https://doi.org/10.1016/j.intmar.2020.07.001

Vidani, J. (2021). A review on evolution of social media influencer marketing: Reflection on consumer behavior and consumer's decision-making process. *Turkish Online Journal of Qualitative Inquiry (TOJQI)*. [online] https://www.academia.edu/51368470/A_Review_on_Evolution_of_Social_Media_Influencer_Marketing_Reflection_on_Consumer_Behavior_and_Consumers_Decision_Making_Process?ri_id=2880772 [Accessed 15 Feb 2024].

Vladimirova, K., Henninger, C. E., Alosaimi, S., Brydges, T., Choopani, H., Hanlon, M., Iran, S., McCormick, H., & Zhou, S. (2023). Exploring the influence of social media on sustainable fashion consumption: A systematic literature review and future research agenda. *Journal of Global*

Fashion Marketing, [online] 1–22. https://doi.org/10.1080/20932685.2023.2237978

Walter, Y. (2023). leveraging social media for explosive brand growth. [online] *Forbes*. https://www.forbes.com/sites/forbesbusinesscouncil/2023/08/22/leveraging-social-media-for-explosive-brand-growth/ [Accessed 7 Mar 2024].

Wibawa, R. C., Pratiwi, C. P., & Larasati, H. (2021). *The role of nano influencers through Instagram as an effective digital marketing strategy*. [online] Semantic Scholar. https://www.semanticscholar.org/paper/The-Role-of-Nano-Influencers-Through-Instagram-as-Wibawa-Pratiwi/0a7eadbedfd9c9cf5b802d356987bd624c04ddb1 [Accessed 1 Mar 2024].

Yang, S., Song, Y., & Tong, S. (2017). Sustainable retailing in the fashion industry: A systematic literature review. *Sustainability*, [online] *9*(7), 1266. https://doi.org/10.3390/su9071266

Yıldırım, S. (2021). Do green women influencers spur sustainable consumption patterns? Descriptive evidences from social media influencers. *Ecofeminism and Climate Change, 2*(4), 198–210. https://doi.org/10.1108/efcc-02-2021-0003

Zalani, R. (2022). *26 types of influencers you need to know [with examples]|Kynship*. [online] www.kynship.co.https://www.kynship.co/blog/types-of-influencers [Accessed 27 Feb 2024].

Zeljko, D., Jakovic, B., & Strugar, I. (2018). New methods of online advertising: Social media influencers. *Proceedings of the 29th International DAAAM Symposium 2018*, [online] 0041. https://doi.org/10.2507/29th.daaam.proceedings.006

Zhang, W., Chintagunta, P. K., & Kalwani, M. U. (2021). EXPRESS: Social-media, influencers, and adoption of an eco-friendly product: Field experiment evidence from rural China. *Journal of Marketing, 85*(3), 10–27. https://doi.org/10.1177/0022242920985784

Zhang, Y., & Mac, L. (2023). Social media influencers: The formation and effects of affective factors during online interactions. *International Journal of Consumer Studies, 47*(5), 1824–1837. https://doi.org/10.1111/ijcs.12957

Zhou, S., Barnes, L., McCormick, H., & Blazquez Cano, M. (2020). Social media influencers' narrative strategies to create eWOM: A theoretical contribution. *International Journal of Information Management*, [online] *59*, 102293. https://doi.org/10.1016/j.ijinfomgt.2020.102293

17

Storytelling and the Sustainability of Fashion and Luxury Brands

Taiwo Olajumoke and Sajad Rezaei

Introduction

The relevance and importance of the storytelling revolution is accelerating in pace in the twenty-first century. Businesses, organisations, and industries are increasingly dependent on the internet, networking, media, and digital platforms to support their growth, to create a market, to dominate the market, and to win the market in a highly competitive, saturated market environment. The adaptation, adoption, application, and integration of internet technology as an integral part of the business planning process are no longer problematic, but there is some concern about how digital paradigms, such as storytelling, could be most successfully and sustainably positioned to fit the needs of a business. At present, the impressive advancement of storytelling has significantly

T. Olajumoke (✉) · S. Rezaei
University of Worcester St John's, Worcester, UK
e-mail: olahanjummy@yahoo.co.uk

T. Olajumoke
Arden University, Coventry, UK

W. Ozuem et al. (eds.), *Sustainable Digital Marketing for Fashion and Luxury Brands*,
https://doi.org/10.1007/978-3-031-82467-8_17

transformed approaches to communication and the platforms on which consumers and organisations interact. Hence, it is essential for scholars, researchers, and marketing executives to understand the concepts and the latest trends in the marketing environment, including the growing use of storytelling in luxury and fashion brands marketing. The adaptation, adoption, and application of storytelling concepts by consumers and luxury and fashion brands have drastically improved researchers', business gurus', and scholars' understanding, knowledge, and perceptions of the use of social media platforms in the luxury and fashion sector (Boerman, 2020; Liu et al., 2021; Naeem & Ozuem, 2021; Ozuem et al., 2024a, 2024b). If customers are unaware of an organisation's brands, then producing the best brand in the world is insignificant and meaningless. An organisation needs to work out how to identify the right strategy and right position to fit its need to sell its brands, and this is where storytelling comes in. Storytelling has emerged as a way for brands to reach consumers and spread brand-related information while simultaneously receiving valuable comments, texts, information, suggestions, and ideas from customers.

The role of storytelling in the luxury and fashion industry cannot be overlooked. Storytelling is essential at all levels of operations and activities of luxury and fashion systems, including logistics and supply chain management, from a brand's initial development through to its launch and commercialisation. Fashion and luxury are relevant to different designer levels, labels, trademarks, logos, symbols, signs, textures, colours, mass market, and more. Luxury and fashion have become a global business with different multifaceted structures that operate to reach customers of luxury and fashion brands or those who just buy clothing as a necessity of everyday life. Storytelling is an avenue of marketing that brings buyers and sellers together to strike bargains and transact goods and services in exchange for money through the means of electronic and interactive digital technologies, such as online platforms and social networks. However, the prime objective of storytelling is to create awareness and to invite, inform, persuade, and motivate customers to engage with brands, with the aim to generate sales and return on investment. Storytelling is acknowledged as an essential digital paradigm for maintaining sustainable communications and interactions that can impact the behaviour, attitudes, and experiences of customers (Dessart & Standaert, 2023).

In this phase of the evolution of storytelling, luxury and fashion organisations that are unaware of, or not quite incorporating, this innovative paradigm and digital tools to engage their customers could risk being left behind in the digital marketing revolution. More and more luxury and fashion brands are exploring how they can better utilise storytelling and tools, rather than ignoring the concepts and process. Storytelling can be perceived as sensitive, emotional, and intellectual content that management of marketing operations can tailor to appeal to customers (Krysanova & Shevchenko, 2021; Ozuem et al., 2024a, 2024b). The innovation of storytelling has been acknowledged by scholars and researchers because of its advantages in the marketing of fashion brands or products (Ledin & Machin, 2020).

Chaffey and Ellis-Chadwick (2012) introduced a generic digital marketing strategy and development process. Fashion and luxury brands can review generic strategies and concepts of digital marketing practice to uncover the important factors essential to foster vital and useful digital content marketing (DCM) and storytelling. The integration of digital marketing has paved the way for retailers of fashion and luxury brands to establish useful platforms; it has provided them with a golden opportunity to distinguish their offerings in a highly competitive market environment by establishing new digital approaches to DCM, storytelling, and sustainability.

Issues with Unidirectional Marketing

The evolution of digital tools, such as digitalised TV, networking, and mobile devices, has paved a way for vibrant opportunities to empower a new approach to establishing market segmentation and virtual targeting of customers (Kartajaya et al., 2019). These new opportunities enable organisations to effectively define offers for different customers and improve their management systems. The digital transformation of communications allowed the customisation of communication channels and the unconstrained dissemination of information and content. Therefore, marketing strategies acquired a new look, new ideas, and innovative concepts that established a transformation in consumer behaviour and perceptions. Hence, the digital evolution is neither a new marketing paradigm nor strategic tools, techniques, and tactics but rather a multifaceted system of people and connections with technologies; this indicates that organisations can utilise transversal strategies to comprehend customer needs, requirements, expectations, and satisfaction via an immediate and direct channel to customers (Kietzmann & Pitt, 2020; Ozuem & Willis, 2024).

The approach and system of marketing are fairer than they were due to the spreading of customers' opinions, facts, and thoughts. The use of traditional media to market brands has declined as the digital evolution has spread and reached consumers. Marketing organisations and firms have attempted to cut costs due to the recession, including marketing costs. Hence, companies, businesses, and firms started to develop their means of digital marketing by establishing omnichannel retailing strategies to override their traditional methods of marketing (Ozuem et al., 2017). In addition, customers are choosing different channels and media to purchase their brands, such as tablets, social medial platforms, computers, and mobile devices, and in the process initiating purchase transactions that establish different marketing channels options for customers.

Storytelling and social media, in conjunction with customer behaviour, have played a decisive role in fabricating new value in the world of marketing innovation. Digital technologies enable quick and simple access to, and consumption of, online content and useful information. Thus, consumers' opinions and their desire for information are becoming broader. Traditional models of marketing are now almost out of date. Therefore, professional marketers and executive business managers must mainly focus on how to become information suppliers and they should be aware that they are dealing with new types of customers due to innovation in the marketing world. Consumers are now the centre of attention; thereby, businesses are required to establish platforms that meet consumers' expectations. The digital revolution is a game changer in the world of marketing because it enables businesses to influence perceptions of products and services, opinions, and designs;

this influence arises from an in-depth knowledge of the market environment and the gathering of innovative ideas that enhance businesses' digital marketing strategies.

The Role of Storytelling

Storytelling, a digital marketing paradigm for luxury and fashion brands, has become a new topic of study in the field of marketing. Scholars and academic researchers have examined, classified, and assessed the antecedents and consequences of the actions of inspired consumers who participate in any form of online communication with brands. The media of marketing have transformed from traditional methods to digital platforms. However, the processes, procedures, tactics, techniques, and strategies of spreading the word remain unchanged. Consumer-generated content is a public dissemination of brand-related information. Storytelling is undoubtedly a sustainable means of effective communication. Through a brand's story, connections between society, online brand communities, and forums can be established that recognise the uniqueness and the symbolic nature of the narrated event. Businesses find it easier to educate and orientate customers about a brand through the use of the narrative storyline of storytelling, which is generated from the point of view of the brand of interest. For instance, Jimmy Choo is one of first luxury shoe brands in the luxury and fashion brands industry to apply the concept of storytelling; Jimmy Choo's DCM appeared on Facebook, Twitter, and Foursquare platforms as a 'Your Choo Stories' campaign where consumers could share their experiences of brands. At this juncture, storytelling and content marketing digital strategies are broadly used as a marketing tactic and approach.

Consumer-generated content enables businesses to create stories. Fashion and luxury brands solicit customers for storylines to establish a contextualised model of customer experiences that can be shared by society, online brand communities, and platforms. Hence, the co-creation model of consumer narratives is a digital marketing paradigm that fits the purpose of marketing luxury and fashion brands. Businesses can engage with customers in the co-creation of luxury and fashion brand images. Customer decisions, preferences, and choices tend to be influenced by storytelling irrespective of the digital revolution and transformations (Wagner, 2024). The storytelling concept is a key digital marketing and mobile strategy; it is associated with marketing events, social media platforms, and business exhibitions that are visible to the public who can share their storylines and history. The storytelling paradigm is used to persuade customers to join the brand's journey on digital platforms through digital communities, social networks, blogs, and online brand communities. It aims to integrate customers into a brand's communications to create and establish viral marketing across social networks to connect with relevant customers and make them part of the business brand world in the process. To achieve the predetermined marketing objectives of an organisation, brands may influence and determine the distinctive characteristics of the storytelling paradigm (Dessart & Standaert, 2023).

Unconventionally, detailed research and definitive explanations have not been provided on research gaps on consumers' attitudes and behaviour with respect to sustainability. However, customers who are aware of sustainability concepts are more likely to be interested in purchasing sustainable brands or products. Therefore, the fashion and luxury industry can utilise sustainability concepts as leverage when developing strategic communication plans, tactics, and policies. The growing pressure to meet sustainability prerequisites and necessities have stimulated various organisations to embark on sustainability plans and programmes, and to coordinate and assess developments, progression, and the consequences and results of their actions in the value chain context (Shashi et al., 2021). The issues of development and progression in relation to sustainability in the fashion and luxury industry have received significant and critical attention in the academic and theoretical literature. The practices and framework of sustainability have been accepted to reduce negative environmental effects in order to attain a competitive advantage and a modest reward of bundles of benefits (de Oliveira et al., 2022). Undeniably, businesses have come to understand the importance of sustainability and have tried to resolve the issues between abrupt economic development, the urgency of climate change, eco-friendly practices, and health problems by embracing the practices and concepts of corporate social responsibility.

Digital Content Marketing (DCM)

Marketing aims to identify, anticipate, and satisfy customer requirements profitably. DCM aims to attract consumers by producing novel content that informs consumers about services. In an effort to establish sustainable marketing content, researchers, academic writers, scholars, and practitioners are intensively and aggressively researching content marketing to improve their knowledge and understanding of its tools, concepts, and practices, and the consequences of using DCM (Greussing & Boomgaarden, 2019; Lorente-Paramo et al., 2020). However, most of the studies in this regard focus on consumer motivation, behavioural concepts, the online content service providers, and organisations' computer-generated digital content (Cheng et al., 2021; Kumar & Reinartz, 2016). Thus, issues regarding content marketing were not acknowledged in contemporary or recent literature but some scholars and practitioners were eager to explore them (Ho et al., 2020). However, previous research produced insights and a theoretical framework to explore the significance of content marketing, storytelling, and sustainability in relation to fashion and luxury brands. Studies considered how DCM could foster relationships and brand engagement (Azemi & Ozuem, 2023; Taiminen & Ranaweera, 2019).

The evolution of innovative digital marketing has had a significant effect on consumer consumption, marketing operations, and purchase decision-making processes globally. DCM is a notable digital marketing strategy in today's business marketing operations. DCM tends to drive customer engagement, communication, and interaction with specific brands at different levels that fit the purpose of consumers (Lievonen et al., 2023). DCM tends to meet customers' requirements, expectations, and needs compared to other marketing methods because it gives access to appropriate brand-related content that gives consumers added value. DCM adds value that inspires consumers and leads to customer acquisition, loyalty, retention, brand awareness, engagement, and interaction.

The present literature and studies on DCM reveal that marketers consider payment for digital content as a product or see DCM as the embodiment of value added that is embedded in digital products or brands. DCM enables advanced sales through marketing communication tools and interfaces, and it impacts customer behaviours (Bu et al., 2021). Producing social media content that is tailored to a customer's motivation to participate in, and engage with, social media poses challenges to businesses. However, there are limited or partial studies on the motivation that drives engagement in the sharing of digital content on platforms (Sabermajidi et al., 2020). There is a lack of research on the role of DCM and on defining various dimensions and scopes of DCM, which could support standard and complete implementation of DCM. Also, research on the impacts and development of DCM emerged from developed countries of the world. Markets are unique and customers conduct different behaviours in different countries of the world; hence, it is in the interest of the academic community to establish related studies in developing countries as this will help to establish a complete picture of DCM and enrich the literature in the field of DCM. There are few studies that provide a theoretical and practical framework for exploring the complexity of DCM and its impacts on customers.

Current research acknowledges DCM as one of the essential paradigms or strategies in the context of digital marketing that many organisations depend on (Mathew & Soliman, 2021). Thus, DCM is acknowledged as a strategy which businesses use to communicate and interact online with their target consumers through the publication of their marketing content (Hasani et al., 2023). DCM enables organisations, companies, and firms to create relevant digital content that is mainly targeted at existing and potential customers; DCM enables prospective customers to engage or participate in digital content creation and sharing with other members on the platform. As a result of digital evolution, customers are able to provide relevant information by themselves; for this reason, customers are not reliant on any classical advertising information for information about a product or brand. Hence, traditional formats and techniques no longer appeal to digital customers. Arguably, customer-oriented digital content is more active; for this reason, organisations should pay more attention to customers' problems and concerns about content (Terho et al., 2022).

Sustainability and the fashion and luxury market were perceived as non-compatible variables or concepts. This view was based on the belief that fashion and luxury brand products or goods were not essential items and sustainability would not improve an organisation's sales and marketing activities. However, customers of fashion and luxury brands with high purchasing profiles are now paying more attention to environmental issues. Changes are taking place in the realm of fashion and luxury brands in response to the hot topics and important concepts, ideas, and opinions emerging from the field of sustainability (Karaosman et al., 2020; Kunz et al., 2020). Not only does the sustainability of fashion and luxury brands depend on the effectiveness of organisation management in the planning and the processing of operations and the production cycle but also on the features and the reliability of the sources that secure the quality of the raw materials for the manufacturing process. It has been evident that large luxury brands are progressing in the advancement, development, and the implementation of sustainability practices; however, scholars propose that over-communication of sustainability practices could eventually diminish the prestige of luxury and fashions brands (Athwal et al., 2019). In general, luxury and fashion brands have increasingly integrated green practices and concepts of sustainability into their mode of operations, practices, and activities (Kang & Sung, 2022). However, there is a need for luxury and fashion brands to work on societal and environmental practices tailored to sustainability while also maintaining their exclusive branding; this need can exert lots of pressure on organisations or firms as sustainability concepts require brand values that are associated with equality, universalism, and the principles of individuality and self-indulgence.

Sustainable Storytelling and DCM

Research studies have shown that in the past the fashion and luxury industry did not pay much attention to sustainability. Thus, it is the responsibility of the fashion and luxury brand industry to continue to improve its quality of sustainability in the light of the criticism it previously received. Sustainable products, brands, production, and consumption can be achieved broadly and not only with the general and usual considerations applied to fast-moving consumer goods but also across different industries and sectors. For instance, quite a few fashion and luxury firms have a huge significant after-market, so that product use can be extended over a long period of time. Effective communication practices linked with relevant strategies that show or address issues of sustainability have widened the scope and the capacity of sustainability communication processes. For instance, four major strategies have been identified among the top ten noticeably sustainable luxury and fashion brands: the silent activist strategy, re-orientation strategy, elite activist strategy, and capitalist strategy. Firms communicate and disseminate their sustainability values and efforts to positively strengthen their corporate identity.

Fashion and luxury brands are connected with appeal, superficiality, and ostentation but the sustainability concept is associated with humanity, philanthropy, moderation, and integrity. There are some contradictory concepts between sustainability and luxury, but luxury and fashion brands have cultivated the habit of advertising their sustainability to augment the evaluation of brands. Luxury and fashion brand customers tend to give priority to brand quality compared to sustainability concepts. However, the motivations of the sensitivities of customers of luxury brands to the sustainability of luxury brands differ across generations (Kapferer & Michaut-Denizeau, 2020). Thus, customer responses and reactions to sustainability vary and cut across the categories, nature, and forms of luxury brands. Some customers consider and/or question the transparency of sustainability disclosures; Jestratijevic et al. (2020) reported that the transparency of supply chain disclosures was higher among mass-market fashion brands than luxury fashion brands.

Some fashion and luxury brands are dedicated to environmental initiatives and apply digital tools and paradigms, such as artificial intelligence, to enhance their innovative transition (Tomojzer, 2023). It is essential and vital that fashion and luxury brands consider storytelling, which impacts the behaviour, attitudes, intentions, and immersive experience of customers, to enable sustainability.

Conclusion

The luxury and fashion industry has spread across borders globally, and its supply chain and marketing of products or brands remain complex and multifaceted in operations. The sustainability implemented by major luxury and fashion companies shows that firms can improve their ability and capabilities to maintain the standard and quality of environmental practices. Sustainability and digital marketing strategies play a key role in the promotion of products, brands, and corporate image, especially the effective promotion of the cultural shift to sustainable narratives, storylines, storytelling, and content marketing and effective collaboration between companies in the process of selling brands or products (Woodside & Fine, 2019). Recent research shows that sustainability and strategic digital marketing are centred on brands, their environmental footprint, the brand or product chain, effective digital marketing strategies, the lifecycle of the brand or product, the corporate governance of internal policies, regulations, stakeholders, and processes to accomplish a company's objectives. The concept of sustainability has become an essential part of fashion and luxury brands, including the retailers and the buyers (Winston, 2016). There are contradictions between sustainability and fashion and luxury brands, but these have become a tactic in promoting and establishing practices of sustainability, such as elements of durability, quality, high standard, and rarity.

Ineffective environmental and social management of conflicts of interest or problems could reduce the competitiveness of companies. However, luxury and fashion brands are trying to implement sustainability practices in an effort to be perceived as more ethical and sustainable by their stakeholders, including their customers. Previous studies in the field of digital marketing have examined, explored, and investigated the fashion and accessories context. However, representations of the luxury and fashion industry differ and require further study. Future research should explore and examine innovative digital marketing in other industries.

References

Athwal, N., Wells, V. K., Carrigan, M., & Henninger, C. E. (2019). Sustainable luxury marketing: A synthesis and research agenda. *International Journal of Management Reviews, 21*(4), 405–426.

Azemi, Y., & Ozuem, W. (2023). How does retargeting work for different Gen Z mobile users? *Journal of Advertising Research*, 2023-023. https://doi.org/10.2501/jar-2023-023

Boerman, S. C. (2020). The effects of the standardized Instagram disclosure for micro-and meso-influencers. *Computers in Human Behavior, 103*, 199–207.

Bu, Y., Parkinson, J., & Thaichon, P. (2021). Digital content marketing as a catalyst for e-WOM in food tourism. *Australasian Marketing Journal, 29*(2), 142–154.

Chaffey, D., & Ellis-Chadwick, F. (2012). *Digital marketing: Strategy, implementation and practice*. Pearson Education Ltd.

Cheng, M., Liu, J., Qi, J., & Wan, F. (2021). Differential effects of firm generated content on consumer digital engagement and firm performance: An outside-in perspective. *Industrial Marketing Management, 98*, 41–58.

de Oliveira, L. G., Miranda, F. G., & de Paula Dias, M. A. (2022). Sustainable practices in slow and fast fashion stores: What does the customer perceive? *Cleaner Engineering and Technology, 6*, 100413.

Dessart, L., & Standaert, W. (2023). Strategic storytelling in the age of sustainability. *Business Horizons, 66*(3), 371–385.

Greussing, E., & Boomgaarden, H. G. (2019). Simply bells and whistles? Cognitive effects of visual aesthetics in digital long forms. *Digital Journalism, 7*(2), 273–293.

Hasani, V. V., Zeqiri, J., Todorovik, T., Jaziri, D., & Toska, A. (2023). Digital content marketing and EWOM: A mediational serial approach. *Business Systems Research: International Journal of the Society for Advancing Innovation and Research in Economy, 14*(2), 24–43.

Ho, J., Pang, C., & Choy, C. (2020). Content marketing capability building: A conceptual framework. *Journal of Research in Interactive Marketing, 14*(1), 133–151.

Jestratijevic, I., Rudd, N. A., & Uanhoro, J. (2020). Transparency of sustainability disclosures among luxury and mass-market fashion brands. *Journal of Global Fashion Marketing, 11*(2), 99–116.

Kang, E. Y., & Sung, Y. H. (2022). Luxury and sustainability: The role of message appeals and objectivity on luxury brands' green corporate social responsibility. *Journal of Marketing Communications, 28*(3), 291–312.

Kapferer, J. N., & Michaut-Denizeau, A. (2020). Are millennials really more sensitive to sustainable luxury? A cross-generational international comparison of sustainability consciousness when buying luxury. *Journal of Brand Management, 27*, 35–47.

Karaosman, H., Perry, P., Brun, A., & Morales-Alonso, G. (2020). Behind the runway: Extending sustainability in luxury fashion supply chains. *Journal of Business Research, 117*, 652–663.

Kartajaya, H., Kotler, P., & Hooi, D. H. (2019). Marketing 4.0: Moving from traditional to digital. In D. H. Hooi, P. Kotler, & H. Kartajaya (Eds.), *Asian competitors: Marketing for competitiveness in the age of digital consumers* (pp. 99–123). PTE Ltd.

Kietzmann, J., & Pitt, L. F. (2020). Computerized content analysis of online data–opportunities for marketing scholars and practitioners. *European Journal of Marketing, 54*(3), 473–477.

Krysanova, T., & Shevchenko, I. (2021). Conceptual blending in multimodal construction of negative emotions in film. In *Text-image-music: Crossing the borders: Intermedial conversations on the poetics of verbal, visual and musical texts in honour of Prof. Elzbieta Chrzanowska-Kluczewska* (pp. 357–371).

Kumar, V., & Reinartz, W. (2016). Creating enduring customer value. *Journal of Marketing, 80*(6), 36–68.

Kunz, J., May, S., & Schmidt, H. J. (2020). Sustainable luxury: Current status and perspectives for future research. *Business Research, 13*, 541–601.

Ledin, P., & Machin, D. (2020). Replacing actual political activism with ethical shopping: The case of Oatly. *Discourse, Context & Media, 34*, 100344.

Lievonen, M., Bowden, J., & Luoma-aho, V. (2023). Towards a typology of negative engagement behavior in social media. *The Service Industries Journal, 43*(3–4), 238–259.

Liu, X., Shin, H., & Burns, A. C. (2021). Examining the impact of luxury brand's social media marketing on customer engagement: Using big data analytics and natural language processing. *Journal of Business Research, 125*, 815–826.

Lorente-Paramo, A. J., Hernández-García, Á., & Chaparro-Pelaez, J. (2020). Influence of cultural dimensions on promotional e-mail effectiveness. *Technological Forecasting and Social Change, 150*, 119788.

Mathew, V., & Soliman, M. (2021). Does digital content marketing affect tourism consumer behavior? An extension of technology acceptance model. *Journal of Consumer Behaviour, 20*(1), 61–75.

Naeem, M., & Ozuem, W. (2021). Developing UGC social brand engagement model: Insights from diverse consumers. *Journal of Consumer Behaviour, 20*(2), 426–439.

Ozuem, W., Ranfagni, S., Willis, M., Salvietti, G., & Howell, K. (2024). Exploring the relationship between chatbots, service failure recovery and customer loyalty: A frustration–aggression perspective. *Psychology and Marketing*. https://doi.org/10.1002/mar.22051

Ozuem, W., & Willis, M. (2024). Artificial intelligence and predictive analytics: Towards a praxis of personalised shopping experiences. In W. Ozuem, S. Ranfagni, & M. Willis (Eds.), *Digital transformation for fashion and luxury brands*. Palgrave Macmillan.

Ozuem, W., Patel, A., Howell, K. E., & Lancaster, G. (2017). An exploration of consumers' response to online service recovery initiatives. *International Journal of Market Research, 59*(1), 97–115.

Ozuem, W., Willis, M., Ranfagni, S., Howell, K., & Rovai, S. (2024b). Examining the role of social media influencers in service failure and recovery strategies: An empirical investigation of millennials' views. *Information Technology & People, 37*(5), 2035–2068.

Sabermajidi, N., Valaei, N., Balaji, M. S., & Goh, S. K. (2020). Measuring brand-related content in social media: A socialization theory perspective. *Information Technology & People, 33*(4), 1281–1302.

Shashi, Centobelli, P., Cerchione, R., & Mittal, A. (2021). Managing sustainability in luxury industry to pursue circular economy strategies. *Business Strategy and the Environment, 30*(1), 432–462.

Taiminen, K., & Ranaweera, C. (2019). Fostering brand engagement and value laden trusted B2B relationships through digital content marketing: The role of brand's helpfulness. *European Journal of Marketing, 53*(9), 1759–1781.

Terho, H., Mero, J., Siutla, L., & Jaakkola, E. (2022). Digital content marketing in business markets: Activities, consequences, and contingencies along the customer journey. *Industrial Marketing Management, 105*, 294–310.

Tomojzer, M. (2023). *Implementing software as a service: The impact of modernizing traditional reporting tools from Deloitte's perspective*. Master's thesis, Universidade NOVA de Lisboa, Portugal.

Wagner, L. (2024). How can storytelling with sustainability claims benefits the luxury industry?

Winston, A. (2016). Luxury brands can no longer ignore sustainability. *Harvard Business Review, 8*(2), 1–3.

Woodside, A. G., & Fine, M. B. (2019). Sustainable fashion themes in luxury brand storytelling: The sustainability fashion research grid. *Journal of Global Fashion Marketing, 10*(2), 111–128.

18

CSR Communication and Luxury Brands: Themes for Cultivating Stakeholder-Oriented Communication on Sustainability Through Social Media

Fabrizio Mosca, Valentina Chiaudano, and Brigida Morelli

Introduction

In the contemporary era, the concept of sustainability has gained a notable degree of prominence. There is a growing consensus among the general public that businesses which pursue profit at any cost, while simultaneously failing to address the negative impacts of their activities on society and the environment, are acting in a socially and environmentally irresponsible manner (Latapí Agudelo et al., 2019). Consequently, a business model that is exclusively focused on creating value for shareholders is no longer deemed to be an acceptable approach. In contrast, there is a pervasive conviction that businesses must augment their commitments to sustainable development by considering the well-being of all their stakeholders (Freeman & Dmytriyev, 2017).

Despite the increasing acceptance of this sustainable orientation, even within the luxury sector, luxury companies face significant challenges

F. Mosca (✉) · V. Chiaudano · B. Morelli
University of Turin, 10128 Torino, Italy
e-mail: fabrizio.mosca@unito.it

W. Ozuem et al. (eds.), *Sustainable Digital Marketing for Fashion and Luxury Brands*,
https://doi.org/10.1007/978-3-031-82467-8_18

in meeting their environmental and social responsibilities. The concepts of luxury and sustainability have traditionally been perceived as incompatible due to their contrasting foundations. Luxury has historically been associated with excess, hedonism, and ostentation, whereas sustainability emphasizes altruism, sobriety, ethics, and moderation (Achabou & Dekhili, 2013). For years, scholars have attempted to reconcile these concepts, ultimately concluding that luxury, due to its emphasis on the quality of materials, artisanal production processes, scarcity, and uniqueness, is inherently sustainable. This is demonstrated by concrete sustainable commitments from luxury companies that have initiated the integration of sustainability into their business models, thereby creating positive value for the planet and overall well-being (Di Leo et al., 2023). For example, many luxury companies today prioritize the selection of reduced-impact materials and the sourcing of materials in a responsible manner. They focus on reducing emissions, promoting diversity and gender equality, and preserving traditional craftsmanship, all while providing employees with supportive work environment.

While in recent times the skepticism about the compatibility of luxury and sustainability has largely been overcome, some scholars argue that challenges persist in understanding how effectively luxury brands communicate their sustainability initiatives (Athwal et al., 2019; Kunz et al., 2020; Ozuem et al., 2024; Rathi et al., 2022). Luxury companies are aware that sustainability messages may have adverse effects on stakeholders. If they are perceived to be inconsistent with the brand's professed values, this could lead to skepticism and mistrust among stakeholders, ultimately harming the brand's reputation (Sthapita et al., 2017; Torelli et al., 2012). As a result, luxury brands are inclined to under-communicate their sustainability initiatives to prevent accusations of greenwashing.

To address the sustainability communication challenges, Civera et al. (2018) propose the model of "integrated CSR communication." This approach entails an integrated logic for sustainable communication, whereby companies present concrete CSR achievements (integrated outputs), communicating about sustainability performance in products, production processes, and other aspects related to the business model. Specifically, integrated CSR communication ensures that the company's social responsibility commitments, encompassing its mission, vision, and goals, are aligned with its actual CSR performance. The greater the alignment between sustainability commitments and CSR performance, the greater the likelihood of the company generating social value and fostering a robust reputation (Werther & Chandler, 2006).

By employing the integrated CSR communication concept proposed by Civera et al. (2018), our chapter contributes to the literature on CSR communication in the luxury market by examining the sustainable communication of luxury brands on social media (Athwal et al., 2019; Kunz et al., 2020; Rathi et al., 2022). In particular, this study aims to explore whether luxury communication on social media places an emphasis on integrated CSR principles, with a focus on tangible sustainability achievements as opposed to mere promises. In this endeavor, we examine sustainability-related content posted on Facebook, Instagram, TikTok, and LinkedIn with the aim of adopting a perspective that is not exclusively customer-centric. In examining sustainable performance, it is evident that companies prioritize disseminating information to a diverse array of stakeholders, including current and prospective employees, non-governmental organizations (NGOs), and other parties with an interest in the company's activities.

The structure of our chapter is as follows. First, we provide an overview of the link between luxury and sustainability, exploring the reasons that support their compatibility. Next, we discuss the challenges relate to online sustainability communication and examine the current channels utilized in the luxury industry to communicate about sustainability. Finally, we analyze how luxury brands convey their sustainability communication across various social media platforms.

Bridging the Gap Between Luxury and Sustainability

Sustainable development has become essential for companies across all sectors. Businesses are increasingly focusing on responsible procurement of raw materials, conserving rare resources, minimizing pollution during production, maintaining high standards, respecting workers' rights, and implementing recycling processes. This shift is evident even in the luxury industry, which has often been criticized for its slow response in following a sustainable path (Chevalier & Mazzalovo, 2020). Criticisms in the luxury sector are less about ecological impact and more about supply chain transparency, particularly regarding precious stones or animal skins, animal treatment, and working conditions (Kapferer, 2010).

The luxury sector's initial hesitation to embrace sustainability stemmed from skepticism about the compatibility of luxury and sustainability. Even scholars were uncertain whether to include sustainability in luxury brand management discussions. The so-called luxury-sustainability paradox highlighted the perceived conflict between luxury and sustainability (Achabou & Dekhili, 2013; Cervellon & Shammas, 2013; Torelli et al., 2012; Wong & Dhanesh, 2016). Some authors argued that luxury, associated with excess and social distinction, inherently conflicts with sustainability's principles of equality and frugality. Frequent greenwashing scandals in the luxury sector reinforced this perceived incongruence.

However, this skepticism has waned over time, and literature has shifted from examining the incongruence between luxury and sustainability to exploring their alignment. The literature suggests there is no fundamental conflict between luxury and sustainability, as these concepts are inherently compatible (Chevalier & Mazzalovo, 2020). Given that sustainability is defined as "development that can meet the needs of the present without preventing future generations from doing the same," there is no reason luxury companies cannot adhere to this principle.

Joy et al. (2012) argue that the durability and quality of luxury goods demonstrate the connection between luxury and sustainability. Authentic luxury rejects the "disposable" nature typical of fast fashion, where economies of scale and planned obsolescence dominate. Instead, authentic luxury emphasizes the longevity of its products, making them naturally more sustainable. Moreover, using natural materials is central to the identity of luxury brands. Materials such as linen, silk, cotton, cashmere, wood, and precious stones are integral to certain brands and typically require less energy to produce compared to synthetic materials. Importantly, these natural materials are recyclable. Producing with natural materials often means keeping production local to maintain the country-of-origin factor, which reduces CO2 emissions compared to outsourcing production businesses. Additionally, the focus on employee skill development and the preservation of brand savoir-faire aligns luxury with social and cultural sustainability. Brands like Hermes, Chanel, and Bulgari have long implemented projects that combine creativity with craftsmanship excellence (Chevalier & Mazzalovo, 2020).

Eventually, these arguments support the idea that luxury serves as an ideal foundation for designing and marketing products that are consistent deeply connected to social and environmental values, sustainable development, natural beauty, and excellence. Therefore, we can affirm that luxury and sustainability are consistent, with luxury naturally embracing sustainable principles and driving sustainable development (Chevalier & Mazzalovo, 2020).

Given the awareness of the alignment between luxury and sustainability, the current challenge for luxury brands is to develop the right communication strategy to convey their commitment to sustainability to their stakeholders (Athwal et al., 2019; Kunz et al., 2020).

Challenges in Building Trust with Sustainability Communication in the Luxury Market

Recent studies highlight that stakeholders increasingly demand luxury brands operate ethically and responsibly regarding social and environmental issues. Strong perceived sustainability can maintain solid corporate relationships with stakeholders and provide competitive advantages (Lee, 2020). For instance, CSR practices enhance staff job satisfaction (Sourvinou & Filimonau, 2018) and increase job retention (Sharma et al., 2022). Similarly, a strong commitment to CSR can enhance a luxury brand's image and reputation among consumers.

Given that companies with robust CSR initiatives are increasingly viewed favorably among stakeholders, effectively communicating social responsibility actions has become more crucial than ever. However, the literature reveals that luxury brand companies still weakly communicate their commitment to sustainability (Luo et al., 2021). Most luxury companies prioritize information for shareholders over information about sustainable practices (Jestratijevic et al., 2020). For example, while most luxury brands provide stakeholders with sustainability reports, only a few create advertising campaigns focused on CSR messages (Pankiw et al., 2021). Under-communicating CSR efforts can negatively impact the brand. Even if a company is performing well in sustainability, a lack of transparency can give the impression that the company is not as transparent or ethical as it could be.

The hesitance of communicating CSR among luxury companies is driven by the awareness that simply communicating about ethics and sustainability does not guarantee success. Jahdi and Acikdilli (2009) reveal that sustainability messages can backfire, leading to skepticism and mistrust if stakeholders perceive a disconnect between the brand's actions and its CSR claims, potentially damaging the brand's reputation (Sthapita et al., 2017; Torelli et al., 2012). This occurs when a company over-communicates its CSR efforts with inauthentic and manipulative messages, resulting in "greenwashing," where a company misleads about its environmental practices to attract a larger consumer base (Jahdi & Acikdilli, 2009).

Research suggests that the sustainability message content must reflect the brand's core values and maintain authenticity (Cervellon & Shammas, 2013). For example, consumers react positively to communications about genuine initiatives, such as sustainable practices in products or processes (Amatulli et al., 2021; Karatzas et al., 2019; Ozuem et al., 2023b). This agrees with findings from De Ven (2008) and Hur et al. (2014), who suggest that stakeholders trust messages showcasing sincere efforts toward sustainability.

Civera et al. (2018) provide valuable insights on effective CSR communication, emphasizing the importance of "integrated CSR communication." This approach ensures the company's social responsibility promises (mission, vision, goals) correspond with its actual CSR performance. The closer this match, the more likely the company is to create social value and build a strong reputation (Werther & Chandler, 2005). In practice, integrated CSR communication involves emphasizing tangible CSR outputs, such as sustainable products/services, processes (traceability, reduction of emissions, waste management), and policies (training, welfare, code of ethics). Conversely, overstressing vague promises without concrete results can harm the brand's image and reduce consumer trust (Pomering & Dolnicar, 2009). With luxury consumers increasingly active online, any discrepancies between a company's CSR statements and actions are easily detected, making authenticity in communication crucial (Fieseler et al., 2010; Kaplan & Haenlein, 2010).

Digital Channels for Communicating Sustainability in the Luxury Industry

In his paper "Making Sense of CSR Communication," Ziek (2009) identified seven key techniques businesses can use to share details about their CSR operations both internally and externally: annual report, annual shareholders letter, organizational codes, nonfinancial report, information on philanthropy, sustainable KPIs, and a web page about sustainability. Literature indicates that nonfinancial reporting is a standard tool for presenting sustainability performance to stakeholders. Previously, the implementation of such reporting was not mandatory, but the Corporate Sustainability Reporting Directive (CSRD) now requires all companies with more than 500 employees to provide it to stakeholders starting in 2024 (Mosca & Greco, 2024).

As Cerin (2002) noted, "The sustainability report offers a previously unavailable window into corporate environmental and social strategy and performance." Studies reveal that sustainability report has become the primary channel for communicating CSR activities even among luxury brands (Di Leo et al., 2023; Mosca & Chiaudano, 2022).

However, some authors argue that communicating sustainability through nonfinancial reports has significant limitations (Confetto & Covucci, 2021; Ozuem et al., 2023a; Wells et al., 2021). First, CSR communication in financial reports is focused exclusively on results at the conglomerate level rather than analyzing individual brands' CSR activities as demonstrated by Wells et al. (2021). They found inconsistencies due to the lack of brand-level reporting when analyzing the nonfinancial disclosures of Kering and LVMH. Second, another criticism of sustainable reports emerged from the study of Confetto and Covucci (2021) who suggest, that sustainability reports have low engagement power both as communication means and in the type of content delivered.

In an increasingly interactive world, the strategic challenge for luxury firms is to develop communication strategies that inform stakeholders about sustainable activities and goals by offering a higher level of involvement and making information more accessible and attractive (Chomvilailuk & Butcher, 2018; Lim & Greenwood, 2017; Rossi & Tarquinio, 2017). Today, the audience for how companies manage sustainability is not limited to shareholders. A large panel of stakeholders, including consumers, employees, suppliers, and academics, are increasingly interested in sustainability actions performed by luxury brand companies. Therefore, luxury brand companies must utilize new communication tools beyond the traditional nonfinancial report to provide all stakeholders with information in more engaging ways. Recently, scholars and marketing professionals widely recognized the online environment as an effective channel for creating more engaging messages about sustainability (Mosca & Civera, 2017). Particularly, scholars agree that luxury companies' presence on websites and social media can enhance information dissemination and distinctive communication about sustainability (Eberle et al., 2013; Kaplan & Haenlein, 2010; Lee et al., 2013; Mosca & Civera, 2017; Ozuem & Willis, 2022). Unlike traditional tools, online channels significantly enhance business-stakeholder interaction by allowing people to connect with brands in an "inexpensive, simple, and fast way" (Jose & Lee, 2007, p. 308). Web 2.0 has facilitated the merging of various types of content, making it interactive, extensive, and engaging. Websites are particularly effective for communicating about sustainability because they allow luxury companies to customize and update content tailored to their target audience, unlike traditional media which tend to create static and self-referential content (Da Giau et al., 2016; Herzig & Godemann, 2010; Luo et al., 2021). Thus, creating and managing websites represents an opportunity for luxury companies to share their actions and performance aimed at creating environmental well-being (D'Anolfo et al., 2017; Luo et al., 2021). Given the growing importance of digital platforms, luxury companies have also recognized social media as a powerful tool for delivering CSR messages by opening a research stream on sustainability communication of social media.

Social Media for Communicating CSR in the Luxury Industry: The State of the Art

Social media platforms are widely acknowledged as essential tools for brands to implement their content strategies, aimed at not only attracting new consumers but also meeting the needs of existing customers and enhancing overall brand engagement (Ajitha & Sivakumar, 2017). These platforms play a crucial role in engaging with consumers and shaping positive shopping experiences (Ozuem et al., 2021; Waqas et al., 2021). Consequently, there has been a growing interest in studying how luxury and fashion companies utilize digital technologies and social media to communicate their sustainability efforts and responsible management practices.

Current research predominantly focuses on popular platforms such as Instagram, Facebook, and X (Twitter). Studies analyzing tweets from fashion retailers suggest that sustainability-related tweets, particularly those addressing social sustainability, significantly boost customer engagement (Yuen et al., 2021). Another line of research explores brand purpose communication on X, revealing that values like solidarity and sustainability are frequently highlighted, although the luxury sector has yet to fully exploit this potential (Rudeloff & Michalski, 2023). Moreover, investigations into the social media activity of luxury brands like Gucci, Prada, and Ermenegildo Zegna, across platforms such as Instagram, Facebook, and TikTok, indicate that their CSR content often revolves around sustainable materials and environmental protection (Castillo-Abdul et al., 2024). Notably, videos and collaborative posts tend to garner the most interaction, underscoring the strategic significance of social media in reaching diverse audiences, including vital markets like Asia. Additionally, research examines the influence of sustainable communication on electronic word-of-mouth (eWOM) and purchase intentions across various cultural contexts (Kong et al., 2021).

Despite valuable insights from existing studies, several research gaps remain. Few studies explore the sustainability efforts of luxury brands outside the narrow scope of fashion marketing and communication, leaving other luxury sectors like leather goods, cosmetics, and hard luxury not investigated enough (Rudeloff & Michalski, 2023). Additionally, most research adopts a customer-centric approach, focusing mainly on the impact of sustainability-related content on consumers, rather than considering all stakeholders of luxury businesses, including less consumer-focused platforms like LinkedIn (Oguntegbe et al., 2023).

To address these gaps, our chapter aims to enrich the literature on sustainability in the luxury market by expanding the scope of sustainability-related content analysis to include LinkedIn, alongside the more commonly studied platforms like Facebook, Instagram, and TikTok. Additionally, we broaden our focus beyond fashion brands to include 50 luxury brands across various sectors such as cosmetics, perfume, automotive, hospitality, leather goods, and hard luxury. Our goal is to assess the extent to which luxury brand companies prioritize actual sustainability performance over mere promises, emphasizing the importance of integrated CSR communication. This approach, as Civera et al. (2018) suggest, is the most effective way to convey sustainability messages.

Findings

Based on prior research and insights, we examined Facebook, Instagram, TikTok, and LinkedIn as platforms for delivering sustainability-oriented posts. Then, we opted for LinkedIn as the sole platform for analysis for two main reasons.

First, our initial investigation revealed that LinkedIn stands out for the number of sustainability compared to other platforms. While Facebook and Instagram predominantly serve commercial purposes, showcasing new collections, brand updates, and fashion events, with occasional heritage-related content, a few luxury brands communicate about sustainability on TikTok. Secondly, LinkedIn, as a professional network, curates content that is not purely commercial, unlike other consumer-focused platforms (Instagram, Facebook, and TikTok). Consequently, LinkedIn offers a unique perspective for exploring online sustainability communication.

The analysis of luxury brand content on LinkedIn from 50 luxury brands across apparel, leather goods, perfume, cosmetics, hard luxury, hospitality, and automotive reveals that the main content delivered is related to three topics:

1. ***Protection of planet Earth***: content about actions dedicated to sustainable development and events to increase public awareness about sustainability;
2. ***Social inclusion***: content concerning how luxury brands address gender diversity, support for marginalized communities, and employee empowerment;
3. ***Sustainability in materials and processes***: content related to practices like circular economy, reducing emissions, plastic use, and resource management.

Figure 18.1 summarizes the main topics communicated online that are deeply investigated in the following paragraphs.

Protection of Planet Earth

Luxury brands use LinkedIn as a platform to showcase their commitment to sustainability, highlighting actions taken to safeguard the planet for future generations. This involves sharing information about partnerships with global organizations tackling significant environmental threats such as plastic pollution, climate change, overfishing, and poaching. For instance, on World Environment Day, Louis Vuitton celebrated its collaboration with "*People For Wildlife*" on LinkedIn, focusing on efforts to restore 400,000 hectares of habitat in the Apudthama reserve.

Additionally, luxury brands leverage their LinkedIn profiles to spotlight events aimed at raising sustainability awareness among consumers and stakeholders. These events, which can include conferences or

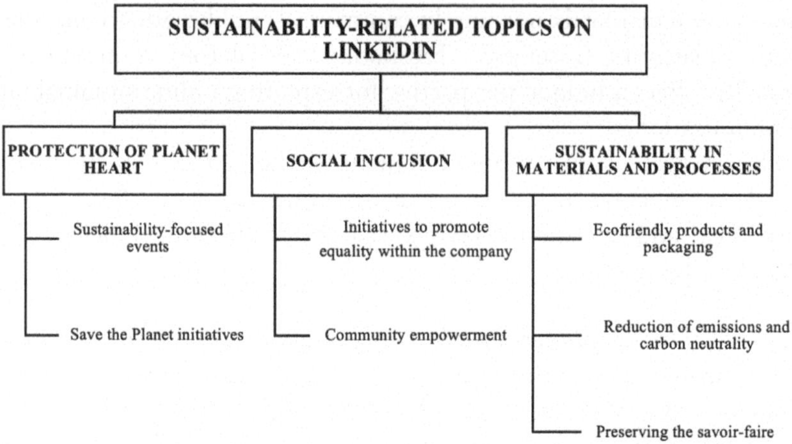

Fig. 18.1 Sustainability-related content on LinkedIn (*Source* Authors' elaboration)

parties, provide platforms for interaction with artisans, fostering an understanding of craftsmanship and heritage preservation. For example, Hermès organized the event "*Hermès in the Making*" where participants could engage with artisans across various crafts, exploring themes such as artisanal know-how, exceptional materials and the value of the Made In. This event serves as a celebration of Hermès' sustainable business model, which has been integral to the company's identity since its foundation in 1837.

Social Inclusion

On LinkedIn, luxury brands are actively engaged in promoting inclusion and supporting women, youth, communities, and employees through targeted initiatives and programs. Gender diversity, aligned with the fifth Sustainable Development Goal of achieving gender equality and empowering women and girls, is one of the most shared themes. Brands emphasize their commitment to gender equality by highlighting through LinkedIn the significant percentage of women in their workforce and organizing mentorship programs to promote women's empowerment.

On LinkedIn, Dior calls for active engagement in combating inequalities through the international mentoring and educational program WOMEN@DIOR, in collaboration with UNESCO. Its main objective is to ensure that all individuals, regardless of gender or sexual orientation, have access to quality education and improved opportunities in the market. Moreover, automotive brands such as Porsche, Lamborghini, and McLaren use LinkedIn to raise awareness and encourage women's participation in transportation and STEM fields.

Local community empowerment is another focus of LinkedIn posts, with luxury brands promoting training programs in underdeveloped countries in collaboration with nonprofit organizations and fundraising initiatives to support social causes. For example, Guerlain provides an interesting example of female empowerment and support for the local community. On the World Bee Day 2022, Guerlain, together with UNESCO, joined forces for the "*Women for Bees*" training program in Cambodia for female beekeepers. This partnership will help women to train as beekeepers and become part of a network of other entrepreneurs worldwide. Even Shangri-La attests its commitment to the local community by communicating on LinkedIn that it has been taking care of the environment in which it operates through the Sanctuary project, working with local partners to preserve local biodiversity and ecology. Additionally, many brands highlight on LinkedIn their support for the education of young people through donations to training institutions. This happened with Gucci, a brand strongly linked to craftsmanship skills and know-how that collaborates with the Istituto Secoli to promote Made in Italy and support young talents who represent the key to future innovation, especially in terms of sustainability. Similarly, the Coach Foundation has announced on LinkedIn its commitment to providing 5,000 scholarships by 2025, partnering with nonprofit organizations worldwide to address inequalities in higher education faced by underrepresented students. Additionally, in 2022, the Coach brand shared with the LinkedIn audience the Coach (Re) Loved Craftsperson Apprenticeship Program, a new one-year leather craftsmanship training program. This program was conceived as part of the Maison's commitment to contribute to creating a better future through better things.

Workplace inclusion, creating environments where all employees feel welcome and valued, is also a significant theme communicated on LinkedIn by luxury brands. Many luxury companies show to join international organizations advocating for equality and inclusion, furthering their commitment to fostering diverse and inclusive workplaces. For example, Moncler demonstrated its commitment to establishing procedures and policies supporting Diversity, Equity & Inclusion (DE&I) by publishing a DE&I Manifesto and forming a DE&I Committee in 2023.

Sustainability in Materials and Production Processes

Our analysis reveals that sustainability-related content on LinkedIn also highlights luxury brand companies' commitment to sustainability in materials and production processes, aligning with SDG 7 (sustainable energy) and SDG 12 (sustainable production and consumption). Key topics include circular economy, animal welfare, reducing emissions and plastic use, and resource management.

Considering the circular economy, luxury brands' communication on LinkedIn addresses circular economy practices across various aspects. Some posts focus on research and innovation for circular product design and processes like upcycling and recycling. Then we also found information about partnerships with organizations like the Ellen MacArthur Foundation (EMF) to facilitate the integration of circular economy principles. This is the case of Ralph Lauren and Estée Lauder who inform their LinkedIn audience about their collaboration with EMF to monitor and test circular alternatives, reducing waste and environmental impact.

Concerning animal welfare, some brands operating in the fashion luxury context like Moncler and Dior have announced on LinkedIn the permanent elimination of fur. Others like Gucci frequently showcase their eco-innovation activities and share on LinkedIn the news about the launch of Gucci Equilibrium, a whole portal dedicated to explaining and providing updates on its social and environmental best practices.

In the cosmetics sector, sustainability-related communication primarily focuses on reducing plastic usage and minimizing the environmental impact of packaging. Most luxury companies, including

Guerlain, Pola Orbis, and Shiseido, have committed to offering refills, reducing the weight of jars and bottles, adjusting cardboard packaging, exploring ways to separate components at end-of-use, and researching recycled or biosourced materials. Other common themes communicated on LinkedIn also include reducing CO2 emissions and achieving carbon neutrality by transitioning to renewable energy sources. For example, Salvatore Ferragamo announced on LinkedIn that it has been awarded an "A" score for climate change due to its reducing emissions, mitigating climate risks, and developing a low-carbon economy. In the automotive industry, some brands highlight their efforts toward a green transition, such as hybridization and the development of fully electric models. However, communication about emissions and waste reduction often results in social media content where promises outweigh actual performance details. For instance, instead of sharing data on CO2 emission performance, automotive companies announce on LinkedIn their plans to hybridize all car models and introduce their first fully electric vehicle in the coming years to meet Agenda 2030 goals.

Implications and Future Research Agenda

This chapter contributes to research on sustainable luxury communication in several ways. First, while luxury brand communication has received extensive attention in recent years by focusing on Facebook, Instagram, Twitter, and TikTok, our study offers a unique perspective by examining social media communication on LinkedIn. Our initial investigation highlights LinkedIn as the primary platform utilized by luxury brands to disseminate sustainability-related content. Unlike Instagram and Facebook, which predominantly target consumers, LinkedIn fosters professional connections within the business environment, enabling more specialized and technical communication. The analysis of LinkedIn provides us with the opportunity to understand how luxury brands engage a broader spectrum of stakeholders, including employees, potential talents, and business partners such as associations, suppliers, and consumers.

Second, our analysis of social media posts reveals a shift in luxury companies' sustainability-related communication toward integrated CSR, emphasizing concrete actions and achievements over mere intentions relate to world preservation, inclusion, and sustainable products and processes. By adopting an integrated CSR communication approach, luxury brands can enhance transparency and credibility in their sustainability efforts, moving away from under-communication and mitigating the risk of greenwashing.

Despite these valuable insights, this study is subject to certain limitations that open new avenues for future research. While we focus on communication strategies, we do not assess the actual impact and effectiveness of the communicated content. Future research should aim to delve deeper into the outcomes and consequences of sustainable luxury communication efforts by implementing empirical studies to measure the impact of each identified communication theme (protection of the planet Earth, social inclusion, and sustainable product and process) in terms of user engagement metrics such as likes and comments.

Furthermore, considering the ever-changing nature of the social media landscape, continuous research updates are crucial. For example, future research could explores the effectiveness of sustainability communication on platforms like TikTok to gain a deeper understanding of its potential impact on stakeholder perceptions and behavior within the luxury sector. As TikTok's popularity is growing, it has the potential to become a powerful platform for brands and organizations to engage a diverse range of stakeholders and raise their awareness about environmental and social issues.

Bibliography

Achabou, M. A., & Dekhili, S. (2013). Luxury and sustainable development: Is there a match? *Journal of Business Research, 66*(10), 1896–1903.

Ajitha, S., & Sivakumar, V. J. (2017). Understanding the effect of personal and social value on attitude and usage behavior of luxury cosmetic brands. *Journal of Retailing and Consumer Services, 39*, 103–113.

Amatulli, C., De Angelis, M., & Donato, C. (2021). The atypicality of sustainable luxury products. *Psychology & Marketing, 38*(11), 1990–2005.

Athwal, N., Wells, V. K., Carrigan, M., & Henninger, C. E. (2019). Sustainable luxury marketing: A synthesis and research agenda. *International Journal of Management Reviews, 21*(4), 405–426.

Castillo-Abdul, B., Ortega Fernandez, E., & Romero-Rodriguez, L. M. (2024). Corporate social responsibility communication of male luxury fashion brands: Analysis on Instagram, Facebook and TikTok. *Management Decision, 62*(2), 471–491.

Cerin, P. (2002). Communication in corporate environmental reports. *Corporate Social Responsibility and Environmental Management, 9*(1), 46–65.

Cervellon, M. C., & Shammas, L. (2013). The value of sustainable luxury in mature markets: A customer-based approach. *Journal of corporate citizenship*, (52), 90–101.

Chevalier, M., & Mazzalovo, G. (2020). *Luxury brand management in digital and sustainable times* (4th ed.). John Wiley & Sons.

Chomvilailuk, R., & Butcher, K. (2018). The impact of strategic CSR marketing communications on customer engagement. *Marketing Intelligence & Planning, 36*(7), 764–777.

Civera, C., Casalegno, C., Mosca, F., & Maple, P. (2018). Customers' judgments and misjudgments of corporate responsibility communication: A cross-country investigation of the effects on confidence and trust within the banking sector. *Psychology & Marketing, 35*(2), 138–149.

Confetto, M. G., & Covucci, C. (2021). A taxonomy of sustainability topics: A guide to setting corporate sustainability content on the web. *The TQM Journal, 33*(7), 106–130.

Da Giau, A., Macchion, L., Caniato, F., Caridi, M., Danese, P., Rinaldi, R., & Vinelli, A. (2016). Sustainability practices and web-based communication: An analysis of the Italian fashion industry. *Journal of Fashion Marketing and Management, 20*(1), 72–88.

D'Anolfo, M., Amatulli, C., De Angelis, M., & Pino, G. (2017). Luxury, sustainability, and corporate social responsibility: Insights from fashion luxury case studies and consumers' perceptions. In M. Gardetti (Eds.), *Sustainable management of luxury environmental footprints and eco-design of products and processes* (pp. 427–448). Springer Singapore.
De Ven, B. (2008). An ethical framework for the marketing of corporate social responsibility. *Journal of Business Ethics, 82*(2), 339–352.
Di Leo, A., Sfodera, F., Cucari, N., Mattia, G., & Dezi, L. (2023). Sustainability reporting practices: An explorative analysis of luxury fashion brands. *Management Decision, 61*(5), 1274–1297.
Eberle, D., Berens, G., & Li, T. (2013). The impact of interactive corporate social responsibility communication on corporate reputation. *Journal of Business Ethics, 118*(4), 731–746.
Fieseler, C., Fleck, M., & Meckel, M. (2010). Corporate social responsibility in the blogosphere. *Journal of Business Ethics, 91*(4).
Freeman, R. E., & Dmytriyev, S. (2017). Corporate social responsibility and stakeholder theory: Learning from each other. *Symphonya Emerging Issues in Management, 1*, 7–15.
Herzig, C., & Godemann, J. (2010). Internet-supported sustainability reporting: Developments in Germany. *Management Research Review, 33*(11), 1064–1082.
Hur, W. M., Kim, H., & Woo, J. (2014). How CSR leads to corporate brand equity: Mediating mechanisms of corporate brand credibility and reputation. *Journal of Business Ethics, 125*(1).
Jahdi, K. S., & Acikdilli, G. (2009). Marketing communications and corporate social responsibility (CSR): Marriage of convenience or shotgun wedding? *Journal of Business Ethics, 88*(1), 103–113.
Jestratijevic, I., Rudd, N. A., & Uanhoro, J. (2020). Transparency of sustainability disclosures among luxury and mass-market fashion brands. *Journal of Global Fashion Marketing, 11*(2), 99–116.
Jose, A., & Lee, S.-M. (2007). Environmental reporting of global corporations: A content analysis based on website disclosures. *Journal of Business Ethics, 72*(4), 307–321.
Joy, A., Sherry, J. F., Jr., Venkatesh, A., Wang, J., & Chan, R. (2012). Fast fashion, sustainability, and the ethical appeal of luxury brands. *Fashion Theory, 16*(3), 273–295.
Kapferer, J.-N. (2010). All that glitters is not green: The challenge of sustainable luxury. *European Business Review*, 40–45.

Kaplan, A. M., & Haenlein, M. (2010). Users of the world, unite! The challenges and opportunities of social media. *Business Horizons, 53*(1).
Karatzas, S., Kapoulas, A., & Priporas, C. V. (2019). Consumers' perceptions on complexity and prospects of ethical luxury: Qualitative insights from Taiwan. *Australasian Marketing Journal (AMJ), 27*(4), 224–232.
Kong, H. M., Witmaier, A., & Ko, E. (2021). Sustainability and social media communication: How consumers respond to marketing efforts of luxury and non-luxury fashion brands. *Journal of Business Research, 131*, 640–651.
Kunz, J., May, S., & Schmidt, H. J. (2020). Sustainable luxury: Current status and perspectives for future research. *BuR—Business Research, 13*(2), 541–601.
Latapí Agudelo, M. A., Jóhannsdóttir, L., & Davídsdóttir, B. (2019). A literature review of the history and evolution of corporate social responsibility. *International Journal of Corporate Social Responsibility, 4*(1).
Lee, E. M., Park, S., & Lee, H. J. (2013). Employee perception of CSR activities: Its antecedents and consequences. *Journal of Business Research, 66*.
Lim, J. S., & Greenwood, C. A. (2017). Communicating corporate social responsibility (CSR): Stakeholder responsiveness and engagement strategy to achieve CSR goals. *Public Relations Review, 43*(4), 768–776.
Luo, S., Henninger, C. E., Le Normand, A., & Blazquez, M. (2021). Sustainable what...? The role of corporate websites in communicating material innovations in the luxury fashion industry. *Journal of Design Business & Society, 7*(1), 83–103.
Mosca, F., & Greco, E. (2024). *Purpose governance and the new competitive scenarios*. EGEA.
Mosca, F., & Chiaudano, V. (2022). *How could well-being-centered business strategies increase competitiveness and innovation among luxury firms?* Routledge.
Mosca, F., & Civera, C. (2017). *Digital channels and social media management in luxury markets*. Routledge.
Oguntegbe, K. F., Di Paola, N., & Vona, R. (2023). Communicating responsible management and the role of blockchain technology: Social media analytics for the luxury fashion supply chain. *The TQM Journal, 35*(2), 446–469.
Ozuem, W., Willis, M., Ranfagni, S., Howell, K. E., & Rovai, S. (2023a). Examining the role of social media influencers in service failure and recovery strategies: An empirical investigation of millennials' views. *Information Technology & People*.

Ozuem, W., Willis, M., Howell, K., Ranfagni, S., & Rovai, S. (2023b). Examining user-generated content, service failure recovery and customer–brand relationships: An exploration through commitment-trust theory. *Internet Research.*

Ozuem, W., Ranfagni, S., Willis, M., Rovai, S., & Howell, K. (2021). Exploring customers' responses to online service failure and recovery strategies during Covid-19 pandemic: An actor–network theory perspective. *Psychology & Marketing, 38*(9), 1440–1459.

Ozuem, W., Ranfagni, S., Willis, M., Salvietti, G., & Howell, K. (2024). Exploring the relationship between chatbots, service failure recovery and customer loyalty: A frustration–aggression perspective. *Psychology and Marketing.*

Ozuem, W., & Willis, M. (2022). *Digital marketing strategies for value co-creation: Models and approaches for online brand communities.* Palgrave Macmillan.

Pankiw, S. A., Phillips, B. J., & Williams, D. E. (2021). Luxury brands' use of CSR and femvertising: The case of jewelry advertising. *Qualitative Market Research an International Journal, 24*(3), 302–325.

Pomering, A., & Dolnicar, S. (2009) Assessing the prerequisite of successful CSR implementation: are consumers aware of CSR initiatives? *Journal of Business Ethics, 85*(2S).

Rathi, R., Garg, R., Kataria, A., & Chhikara, R. (2022). Evolution of luxury marketing landscape: A bibliometric analysis and future directions. *Journal of Brand Management, 29*(3), 241–257.

Rossi, A., & Tarquinio, L. (2017). An analysis of sustainability report assurance statements: Evidence from Italian listed companies. *Managerial Auditing Journal, 32*(6), 578–602.

Rudeloff, C., & Michalski, P. (2023). How corporate brands communicate their higher purpose on social media: Evidence from top global brands on Twitter. *Corporate Reputation Review.*

Sharma, A., Soni, M., Borah, S. B., & Haque, T. (2022). From silos to synergies: A systematic review of luxury in marketing research. *Journal of Business Research, 139*, 893–907.

Sourvinou, A., & Filimonau, V. (2018). Planning for an environmental management program in a luxury hotel and its perceived impact on staff: An exploratory case study. *Journal of Sustainable Tourism, 26*(4), 649–667.

Sthapita, A., Yun-yong, H., & Jo, G.-Y. (2017). Communicating responsible luxury brand: The role of luxury-CSR fit and dispositional consensus on brand evaluation. *Journal of Distribution Science, 15*(2), 7–14.

Torelli, C. J., Monga, A. B., & Kaikati, A. M. (2012). Doing poorly by doing good: Corporate social responsibility and brand concepts. *The Journal of Consumer Research, 38*(5), 948–963.

Waqas, M., Hamzah, Z. L., & Mohd Salleh, N. A. (2021). Customer experience with the branded content: A social media perspective. *Online Information Review, 45*(5), 964–982.

Wells, V., Athwal, N., Nervino, E., & Carrigan, M. (2021). How legitimate are the environmental sustainability claims of luxury conglomerates? *Journal of Fashion Marketing and Management, 25*(4), 697–722.

Werther, W. B., Jr., & Chandler, D. (2005). Strategic corporate social responsibility as global brand insurance. *Business Horizons, 48*(4), 317–324.

Wong, J. Y., & Dhanesh, G. S. (2016). Luxury industry: Managing CSR-luxury par-adox online through acceptance strategies of coexistence and convergence. *Management Communication Quarterly, 25*.

Yuen, K. M., Zeng, F., & Lo, C. K. Y. (2021). Sustainable communication and customer engagement on social media. In *Advances in national brand and private label marketing* (pp. 105–113). Springer International Publishing.

Ziek, P. (2009). Making sense of CSR communication. *Corporate Social Responsibility and Environmental Management, 16*(3), 137–145.

19

Metaverse Fashion Ecosystem: A Sustainable Marketing Perspective

Mostafa Mohamad, Fandi Omeish, and Anna Tarabasz

Introduction

The metaverse idea was first researched in the 1980s and has grown to be potentially the hypertext cusp of future computing. It can be described as an application that is the culmination of virtual reality and the merging of physical reality and virtual spaces, including the sum of all virtual worlds, augmented reality, and the internet. This concept can be utilized in many practical fields, from medicine and education to business and

M. Mohamad (✉) · F. Omeish · A. Tarabasz
College of Interdisciplinary Studies, Zayed University, Abu Dhabi Campus, Zayed City, Abu Dhabi, UAE
e-mail: mostafa.mohamad@zu.ac.ae

F. Omeish
E-Marketing & Social Media Department, Princess Sumaya University for Technology, Aman, Jordan

A. Tarabasz
College of Interdsciplinary Studies, Zayed University, Dubai, United Arab Emirates

W. Ozuem et al. (eds.), *Sustainable Digital Marketing for Fashion and Luxury Brands*, https://doi.org/10.1007/978-3-031-82467-8_19

entertainment. A metaverse environment is considered much cheaper to conduct business than in the real world. It has many benefits, including global virtual meetings and faster visual data and concepts exchange. This can be done with less environmental impact, playing a massive part in behavior toward sustainability and constructing an ecosystem. In the case of this research, the focus is on understanding the effectiveness of sustainable marketing in the Metaverse Fashion Ecosystem (MFE) for a better lifestyle and the consumption of fashion products with minimum environmental impact.

The fashion industry has struggled to find positive literature in recent years. Much research has been conducted into how fashion can leave a more positive footprint on society, mainly investigations of the effects of fast fashion and how this can develop a more sustainable approach (e.g., Ozuem et al., 2024; Ray & Nayak, 2023; Yan, 2022). Sustainability has progressed within the luxury sector. However, future predictions could be more robust due to the general growth of the fashion sector and companies choosing to stay with traditional business forms and not research more environmentally friendly practices, marketing, and sales segmentation. With continuous uncertainty in promotion, pricing, place, and segmentation, fashion marketing needs help conforming to sustainable modes of practice. This uncertainty is a crucial area to be researched, as marketing impacts a company's development of sustainable products, place in the market, targeted consumer audience, and how consumers interpret and pursue sustainable fashion products. There is a need to discover more sustainable modes of marketing for fashion and how this can affect consumer behaviors and implement more sustainable consumption methods.

This research defines Metaverse Fashion as an Ecosystem (MFE) that includes human–computer interactions, social networks, and organizational policies to deliver sustainable marketing. The authors offer a systemic view of the MFE based on the multiple perspective theory (Mohamad et al., 2020; Phillips & Linstone, 2016), including a Kantian trio-perspective: technical, organizational, and personal.

The Concept of Metaverse Fashion Ecosystem

The concept of Metaverse Fashion involves the integration of virtual environments with the fashion industry, offering new opportunities for marketing, customer engagement, and virtual fitting experiences. Fashion brands like Balenciaga, Dolce & Gabbana, Nike, Gucci, and others are exploring the Metaverse to target younger generations (Dewalska-Opitek, 2023; Zbuchea & Pinzaru, 2023). Virtual fitting systems based on the Metaverse are being developed to bridge the gap between the digital and physical worlds, enhancing the authenticity and timeliness of virtual experiences (Jiang et al., 2023).

The Metaverse presents significant research interest due to its potential to revolutionize fashion through virtual digital humans and fashion-related tasks, especially in AI development and the COVID-19 pandemic (Mu et al., 2024). As the Metaverse evolves, personalized avatars and innovative marketing strategies are expected to shape the future of fashion and retail industries, particularly appealing to Generation Z (Periyasami & Periyasamy, 2022).

The realm of MFE incorporates sustainable materials, including fish skin, bacterial cellulose (BC) film produced from the fermentation of Kombucha tea, and porous electronics. Historically, Arctic communities have utilized fish skin, but it is now processed using eco-friendly methods for garment manufacturing (Yan, 2022). BC film, sourced from Kombucha tea fermentation, presents distinctive characteristics; however, meticulous drying is necessary to preserve its deformation properties (Periyasami & Periyasamy, 2022). Porous electronics, constructed on porous substrates such as silicon or gallium nitride, undergo significant property alterations at microscopic scales, which unlocks new functionalities and enhances performance in electronic devices pertinent to the metaverse era (Zabel et al., 2023). These materials are pivotal in advancing sustainable practices within metaverse fashion by providing environmentally conscious alternatives and innovative solutions for design and production.

Schöbel and Leimeister (2023) emphasize four essential components of Metaverse Platform Ecosystems as follows:

- ***Digital domains and environments***: Within the Metaverse, diverse digital domains and environments coexist, each forming a distinct universe with its assets, collaborators, and capabilities.
- ***Integrated meta-ecosystem***: The Metaverse is an expansive, interconnected meta-ecosystem comprising real-time rendered 3D virtual realms. It facilitates synchronized and enduring interactions for collaborators and users, enriching engagement through collaborative creativity supervised by orchestrators and facilitated by platform proprietors.
- ***Roles and obligations***: Establishing metaverse ecosystems and consolidated platforms assign specific roles and obligations to collaborators, users, platform proprietors, and orchestrators. This framework delineates the engagements and contributions within the metaverse platform ecosystem.
- ***Viewpoints***: The concept of metaverse platforms is delineated and refined through four distinct viewpoints: innovation, production, transactions, and social engagement. These viewpoints delineate the functionalities and operations of the metaverse platform ecosystem, propelling digital advancements and infrastructures across various sectors of the digital realm.

In their insight, Schöbel and Leimeister (2023) analyze the metaverse ecosystem as a digital forefront, but they might be oversimplifying the inherent complexities and challenges involved in creating and maintaining these ecosystems. Despite addressing the critical pillars of MFE, they seem to underestimate the practical challenges of the metaverse implementation, such as interoperability, security, and intellectual property rights. The reference to a "one-stop-shop meta-ecosystem" overlooks the substantial technological and regulatory obstacles that must be overcome to facilitate real-time, synchronized interactions. Additionally, while necessary, the designation of specific roles and responsibilities may encounter resistance due to conflicting stakeholder interests and potential power imbalances among platform owners, users, and orchestrators. The authors believe that the abovementioned quadratic perspective fails to address the legal and ethical issues associated with adopting metaverse technologies. Data privacy and user consent are privacy issues that require more attention to ensure the equitable and responsible development of metaverse platforms. The following section highlights how MFE facilitates sustainable marketing and addresses the complexity of this system.

Sustainable Marketing in the MFE

Integrating sustainability into metaverse fashion is rapidly evolving through various innovative approaches. Within the digital social landscape of the Metaverse, new methods are emerging across the fashion industry's stages of design, production, and communication, promoting circular economy models and reducing environmental impact (Ozuem et al., 2023a; Yan, 2022). Augmented and virtual reality technologies are being employed to enhance sustainability in fashion, aiming to decrease waste, educate consumers, and lessen dependence on physical resources. Despite these advancements, challenges such as high energy consumption and skill shortages remain (Mesjar et al., 2023). Additionally, the practice of upcycling existing garments and utilizing computational technology in garment creation allows designers to produce stylish, sustainable clothing, addressing consumer concerns about fashion's ecological and social impacts (Richa & Dushyant, 2021).

In the MFE, contemporary trends and strategies in sustainable marketing are transforming traditional practices. The Metaverse enables significant fashion design, production, and communication shifts to foster sustainability (Yan, 2022). Virtual fashion design in the Metaverse also serves as a medium for preserving cultural heritage, overcoming physical limitations, and reaching a broader audience (Ray & Nayak, 2023). Sustainable fashion marketing examines consumer behaviors and purchase patterns to address the gap between attitudes and actions, exploring opportunities in B2B marketing, circular economy initiatives, and sustainability-focused innovations (Mogaji et al., 2024).

Leading luxury brands like Gucci, Louis Vuitton, Burberry, and Dolce & Gabbana are adopting metaverse marketing strategies through virtual products, gaming experiences, and NFT collections, diversifying their marketing and communication efforts (Sung et al., 2024). Additionally, research highlights the relationship between time, sustainable practices, and fashion design, emphasizing the emotional aspect of time and its effect on fashion trends (Gazzola et al., 2020).

Benefits and Challenges of Sustainable Marketing in MFE

The MFE presents both benefits and challenges. Marketing sustainability within the MFE presents a myriad of advantages. By incorporating sustainable methodologies such as circular economy models and minimizing ecological impact (Yan, 2022), fashion brands can actively contribute to preserving cultural heritage through virtual design initiatives (Periyasami & Periyasamy, 2022). The Metaverse offers opportunities for personalized avatars and innovative advertising techniques, enriching the marketing strategies employed by fashion brands (Weiss, 2022). Virtual stores within the Metaverse offer immersive spatial experiences and entertainment options that outstrip conventional retail channels (Ray & Nayak, 2023). Moreover, the growing awareness of waste reduction and re-commerce trends in the fashion industry underscores the significance of sustainability, fostering a culture of mindful consumption (Ozuem et al., 2023b; Pérez & Bernabéu, 2017). Sustainable marketing in the MFE advances environmental and cultural sustainability, elevates customer engagement, and fosters brand loyalty.

Weiss (2022) referred to four main advantages of sustainable marketing in the MFE, including *enhanced brand perception, increased interaction with consumers, outreach to a competitive edge, and sustainable long-term growth.*

Sustainable marketing initiatives in the Metaverse enable fashion brands to position themselves as socially accountable and environmentally aware, thereby enhancing their "*brand perception*" and attracting consumers with ethical inclinations. By advocating sustainability within the Metaverse, fashion "*brands can engage with consumers*" more profoundly, fostering loyalty and confidence. This interaction can elevate customer retention rates and amplify brand advocacy. In addition, it helps "*distinguish fashion brands*" from competitors, mainly as consumers prioritize environmental consciousness and actively seek ethical brands. This differentiation can confer a competitive advantage within the market landscape. Above all, Weiss (2022) argues that sustainable marketing endeavors within the Metaverse contribute to the "*enduring growth of fashion brands*" by aligning their values with those of environmentally conscious consumers. This alignment ensures continued relevance and success amid the dynamic shifts in the retail industry.

Challenges include the need for interoperable and secure architectures for widespread adoption (Patruti et al., 2023) and ethical considerations regarding user behavior and design in virtual environments (Weiss, 2022). However, the integration of fashion into the Metaverse offers significant advantages. It revolutionizes fashion marketing communication, attracting younger generations and bridging the gap between gamers and non-gamers (Blowers et al., 2023). Furthermore, the Metaverse enables the development of sustainable practices in the fashion industry, such as circular economy models, and minimizing environmental damage while meeting consumer needs (Crespo-Pereira et al., 2023). The Metaverse's fusion of digital and physical elements creates a dynamic space for social connection and immersive brand experiences, driving innovation in the fashion and retail industries (Ullah et al., 2023).

Mu et al. (2024) referred to four significant challenges that warrant attention in the MFE as follows:

- ***Fashion retrieval difficulty***: One prominent obstacle designers encounter is the difficulty in efficiently seeking inspiration through perusing existing fashion items within multimedia databases. While fashion parsing in the Metaverse holds promise to alleviate this issue, it remains an evolving domain.
- ***Unexplored application scenarios***: Despite garnering increasing interest from academia and industry, numerous potential fashion application scenarios within the Metaverse still need to be explored. This lack of exploration hinders further development and practical implementation in this realm.

- ***Controllability and attribute disentanglement***: Current research highlights the importance of addressing issues such as identifying distorted fashion items, mapping attributes across different domains, and exploring methods for attribute disentanglement to facilitate the retrieval of unlabeled fashion items. Advancements in controllability within fashion intelligence systems are imperative to tackle these challenges effectively.
- ***Counterfeiting concerns***: The ease of digitization in replicating Metaverse fashion items has raised legitimate concerns regarding illegal copying and counterfeiting activities. Safeguarding the authenticity and originality of fashion items in the virtual space poses a significant challenge that necessitates proactive measures and innovative solutions.

The challenges discussed by Mu et al. (2024) appear credible. Nevertheless, recent progress in AI, blockchain, and AR technologies is actively tackling these issues. For instance, Liu et al. (2023) showcased how AI-driven systems have improved multimedia classification and retrieval. Additionally, the emergence of intuitive user interfaces and AR applications has streamlined the process of retrieving fashion inspiration. Smith et al. (2022) highlighted technological advancements, such as virtual fashion shows and digital try-ons, indicating considerable practical strides in implementation. These developments are poised to foster collaboration among designers, technologists, and VR experts, propelling innovations in this domain. Furthermore, Zhang and Chen (2023) delved into sophisticated AI models that leverage blockchain technology to enrich attribute mapping, addressing the challenges related to controllability and attribute disentanglement. Moreover, the issue of counterfeiting was also addressed by Marr (2021), who advocated for using NFTs and blockchain to establish immutable records and thwart unauthorized replication. Collectively, Mu et al. (2024) provide an encompassing view of the challenges in sustainable MFE, consolidating various previously examined aspects in isolation.

Multiple Perspective Theory as a Lens for MFE

Based on the above discussion of MFE and its applications of sustainable marketing, we are addressing a complex system that includes a virtual reality space where users can exponentially interact with a computer-generated environment and each other in real time (Table 19.1).

Our research proposes the multiple perspectives theory (Phillips & Linstone, 2016; Yoo, 2021) to address such complexity on three fronts: Technical, Organizational, and Personal (or TOP).

By addressing the technical components of metaverse platforms, organizational strategies for their effective deployment, and users' personal experiences, this analysis aims to understand how MFE works as a tool for sustainable marketing (Zhichang, 2010). This tripartite perspective provides a comprehensive understanding of its potential implications and the societal changes prompted by this innovative platform (Mitroff & Kilmann, 2021).

The TOP framework has been adopted across various disciplines and industries, facilitating the dissection and analysis of complex systems by breaking them down into smaller, interconnected components (Linstone & Turoff, 2011). A holistic comprehension of the system's

Table 19.1 TOP framework for complex system

System's elements	Technological	Organizational	Political
Ontology	Scientific, causality, & Problem Solving	Social construction, group belief, and institutional logic	Kantian, self-interest, and pragmatic
Epistemology	Explanatory	Exploratory	Predictive/ futuristic
Ethics of actions	Objectivity	Justice & Sustainability	Morality & prestige
Spam of effect	Strategic	Medium-term	Urgent, intuitive
Uncertainty/ Complexity of decision making	High Uncertainty	Moderate Uncertainty	Low Uncertainty
Rish Criteria	Predictive & Calculative	Mitigative & Political	Loss-gain compromise

The authors (based on Phillips and Linstone [2016] and Mohamad et al. [2020])

structure, behavior, and functionality can be developed by examining the interrelationships among these components (see Fig. 19.1). From a technical standpoint, MFE relies heavily on advanced virtual reality platforms and robust technological infrastructure. Key considerations include hardware and software requirements, network connectivity, user interfaces, and social media tools. Numerous studies have examined the technical dimensions of the Metaverse fashion, highlighting their capabilities for immersive user experiences (Aburbeian et al., 2022) and the challenges associated with providing low-latency interactions (Xi et al., 2011). Nevertheless, these studies did not address the sociotechnical interaction between fashion manufacturers, users, and the Metaverse and how they evolve as an ecosystem. The technical side of the Metaverse fashion is shaped by the sociomateriality of the developers, the manufacturers, and the user's behavior.

From an organizational perspective, MFE involves the strategic planning and implementation methodologies necessary for sustainable marketing. The organizational perspective is an epistemological tool to capture the social construction of groups, institutions, and networks and how their societal consciousness and culture evolve with technological

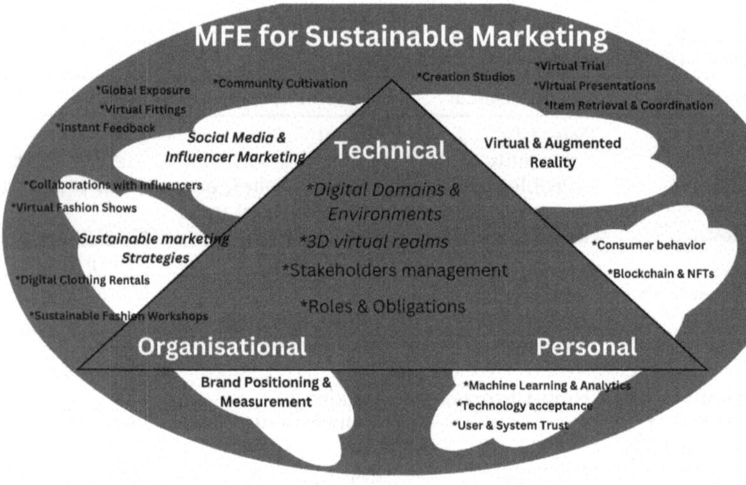

Fig. 19.1 MFE for sustainable marketing (*Source* The authors)

advances (Phillips & Linstone, 2016). There is limited research on how fashion manufacturers develop branding and positioning strategies in the Metaverse and how they measure the success of their sustainable marketing. Accordingly, this study uses the organizational perspective to point out the common practices followed by fashion manufacturers to set these crucial strategies and policies.

The personal perspective addresses user experiences, attitudes, and acceptance in MFE. Numerous studies have investigated shoppers' experiences in the Metaverse, highlighting cognitive, affective, and behavioral aspects (Haikel-Elsabeh, 2023; Lee et al., 2021). These studies underscore the significance of user engagement, motivation, and the potential for addressing customized preferences.

Adopting the TOP framework to analyze sustainable marketing in the MFE emphasizes the multifaceted nature of this emerging platform. The technical perspective highlights the requisite technological infrastructure and the resources required to develop the system. The organizational perspective underscores the necessity of strategic planning, stakeholder collaboration, and policy considerations. The personal perspective accentuates user experiences, engagement, and customized preferences. Collectively, these perspectives offer a comprehensive understanding of the transformative potential of MFE for sustainable marketing.

Technical Perspective of Sustainable Marketing in the MFE

In this section, we discuss the resource-based view of sustainable marketing in MFE and explain the accelerating use of social media, influencer marketing, and augmented reality in immersive reality fashion shops.

Social Media and Influencer Marketing in the MFE

Social media marketing within the metaverse fashion landscape is swiftly evolving. Brands harness the power of social media platforms and the Metaverse to enrich connections and perceptions between consumers and brands. The Metaverse introduces immersive encounters, enabling users to engage with brands within interactive 3D environments (Singhal & Ahuja, 2023). Also, influencer marketing within the Metaverse is gaining momentum as influencers guide their followers from social media platforms to virtual realms, fostering a more dynamic and collaborative atmosphere for brand partnerships (Sharma & Bansal, 2023). Fashion enterprises utilize the Metaverse to unveil virtual collections and interact with a global audience, presenting diverse styles through virtual showcases (Karabacak & Güngör, 2023). Consumers are keenly interested in the Metaverse, particularly drawn by its potential for remote communication and its influence on corporate and content consumption patterns (Madhura & Panakaje, 2022).

Singhal and Ahuja (2023) emphasize that social media marketing enriches MFE's customer experiences via the following mechanisms.

- ***Global exposure***: Social media platforms like Instagram and TikTok provide metaverse fashion brands instant access to a worldwide audience, amplifying brand visibility and engagement.
- ***Virtual fittings***: Leveraging social media, metaverse fashion labels can introduce virtual fitting experiences, enabling customers to try on clothing items before purchasing virtually. This immersive approach enhances the shopping journey and diminishes the necessity for physical retail spaces.
- ***Collaborations with influencers***: Social media influencers play a pivotal role in endorsing Metaverse fashion brands. Partnerships with influencers for sponsored content or virtual fashion presentations can significantly enhance brand recognition and credibility within the metaverse community.
- ***Instant feedback***: Social media platforms facilitate real-time feedback and interaction with metaverse fashion consumers. Brands can promptly respond to consumer preferences, gather valuable insights, and tailor their offerings to meet the evolving needs of the virtual fashion sphere.
- ***Community cultivation***: Social media platforms foster the establishment of online communities centered around metaverse fashion brands. By nurturing a sense of community and involvement, brands

can cultivate robust relationships with their virtual clientele, resulting in heightened brand loyalty and advocacy.

Singhal and Ahuja (2023) offered a water drop model of sustainable practices within the MFE. The authors referred to Instagram and TikTok as virtual forefronts that offered metaverse fashion brands a global outreach. However, this accelerated exposure can weaken brand identity in a saturated digital landscape where numerous brands vie for attention (Kaplan & Haenlein, 2010).

Virtual fittings create an immersive shopping experience and reduce the necessity for physical retail locations—however, a limited number of studies address the technology underpinning virtual fittings. Verhagen et al. (2014) highlight that technical constraints and user interface problems can negatively affect the overall user experience. Additionally, there are significant concerns about data privacy and security when personal measurements and images are used in virtual try-ons.

Influencer marketing plays a crucial role, as emphasized by Singhal and Ahuja, but the influencers' trust might be doubtful when followers recognize endorsements as commercial transactions rather than a relationship-building process. Indeed, this leads to short-term and seasonal attention to the products/services rather than long-term brand loyalty (Audrezet et al., 2020; Ozuem & Willis, 2022).

The ability to receive real-time feedback via social media allows brands to swiftly adapt to consumer preferences, which is a considerable advantage. However, the continuous flow of feedback can lead to hasty, short-term decisions instead of well-thought-out, long-term strategies (Paniagua & Sapena, 2014). Additionally, the process of managing and analyzing vast amounts of user-generated content can be both resource-intensive and challenging for brands.

Creating online communities around metaverse fashion brands helps foster a sense of loyalty and belonging among consumers. However, maintaining these communities requires ongoing engagement and valuable content, which can be resource-demanding. Moreover, community dynamics can be unpredictable, with negative sentiments potentially spreading quickly and harming the brand's reputation (Muniz & O'Guinn, 2001; Ozuem et al., 2021).

While Singhal and Ahuja (2023) provide a comprehensive overview of the benefits of social media marketing for MFE, it is crucial to acknowledge the inherent challenges. Issues such as overexposure, technical limitations, authenticity concerns, reactive decision-making, and the demanding nature of community management need careful consideration. Future research should delve deeper into these challenges to offer a more balanced perspective on the role of social media marketing in the sustainable fashion metaverse.

Virtual Reality and Augmented Reality in the MFE

Virtual Reality (VR) and Augmented Reality (AR) hold significant importance in the MFE (Gupta et al., 2023; Wang et al., 2023). VR technology facilitates the development of virtual fitting systems that bridge the gap between physical and digital realms, thereby enhancing the integration of the garment industry with the Metaverse (Soyoung & Seo-Young, 2022). Conversely, AR, alongside other emerging technologies such as XR and MR, supports collaborative platforms that enable immersive shopping experiences free from temporal and spatial constraints, thereby shaping the future of fashion commerce within the Metaverse (Dewalska-Opitek, 2023). These advancements not only transform how fashion brands interact with consumers but also present novel avenues for users to engage with virtual fashion items and experiences, ultimately reshaping the landscape of the fashion industry in the digital domain (Mu et al., 2024). In this paper, the authors refer to five applications of VR in MFE, as follows.

- ***Virtual fashion presentations***: Within the Metaverse, designers can organize virtual fashion presentations where digital avatars showcase their latest collections. This approach enables global participation unrestricted by physical constraints, thereby broadening accessibility and audience reach.
- ***Virtual trial experiences***: Leveraging VR technology, consumers can virtually test clothes, accessories, and makeup before committing to a purchase. This immersive experience enhances the online shopping journey by offering a more realistic preview of products.

- ***Digital fashion creation studios***: Designers have the capability to utilize VR tools for crafting and manipulating digital fashion pieces within a virtual setting. This facilitates swift prototyping, customization, and visualization of designs, streamlining the overall design process.
- ***Digitization of fashion items***: Transitioning real-world fashion items into the Metaverse allows for seamless replication and sharing. Nonetheless, this practice also triggers concerns regarding intellectual property rights and counterfeiting, given the ease of copying and disseminating items.
- ***Fashion item retrieval and coordination***: VR applications aid both designers and consumers in efficiently locating and coordinating fashion items based on specific attributes and characteristics. This encompasses tasks like identifying flawed items, categorizing attributes, and exploring attribute disentanglement to enhance retrieval processes.

Organizational Perspective of Sustainable Marketing in the MFE

This section of our chapter addresses the plurality of MFE stakeholders and the metaverse fashion supply side. In doing so, it addresses the strategies followed by Metaverse fashion brands to develop sustainable marketing. It also discusses the branding and positioning techniques, the ethical considerations, and the evaluation methods for sustainable marketing strategies in MFE.

Strategies for Sustainable Marketing in the MFE

Strategies for sustainable marketing in the MFE involve leveraging digital fashion to enhance industry sustainability, cultural heritage preservation, and consumer engagement (Yan, 2022). By integrating traditional garments into the virtual world, fashion brands like Gucci and Louis Vuitton are pioneering metaverse marketing through virtual products and NFT collections (Ray & Nayak, 2023). Sustainable fashion marketing emphasizes consumer behavior, circular economy, and sustainability-oriented innovations (Kim & Lee, 2022). Based on Buen Vivir's principles, cultural innovation can drive sustainable change in the fashion value chain (Freire, 2021). Through digital fashion design in the Metaverse, companies can overcome physical limitations and reach a wider audience while promoting cultural sustainability (Silva et al., 2022). These strategies benefit the environment and cater to evolving consumer needs, ultimately advancing the fashion industry's sustainability in the Metaverse.

Our analysis identified four key strategies and business models for sustainable marketing in the MFE, namely, virtual fashion shows, digital clothing rentals, collaborations with virtual influencers, and interactive sustainable fashion workshops.

Virtual fashion shows: Hosting virtual fashion shows in the Metaverse provides a sustainable alternative to physical events, reducing carbon emissions related to travel and venue logistics. This environmentally conscious approach aligns with sustainable marketing principles, emphasizing promoting eco-friendly practices and mitigating environmental impact (Rodriguez & Garcia-Badell, 2022, July).

Digital clothing rentals: Establishing a platform for renting digital apparel in the Metaverse contributes to a circular economy by extending the lifespan of virtual garments. This initiative fosters sustainable consumption patterns and reduces textile waste, demonstrating a commitment to sustainability within marketing strategies (Periyasamy & Periyasami, 2023).

Collaborations with virtual influencers: Partnering with virtual influencers who advocate for sustainable fashion practices can effectively encourage eco-conscious behaviors among metaverse users. By endorsing sustainable brands and products, these influencers play a crucial role in raising awareness about environmental issues and promoting sustainable consumption in the virtual sphere (Haikel-Elsabeh, 2023).

Interactive sustainable fashion workshops: Hosting virtual workshops focused on sustainable fashion practices in the Metaverse engages users in learning about eco-friendly materials, ethical production processes, and responsible consumption habits. These interactive sessions instill sustainable values and educate participants on making environmentally conscious fashion choices within the virtual environment (Idrees et al., 2023).

Branding and Positioning in the MFE

Brands integrate sustainability in metaverse fashion by leveraging digital design to promote cultural heritage, revolutionize supply chain stages, and minimize environmental damage (Brydges et al., 2020). The Metaverse allows the creation of virtual assets like blockchain digital outfits, offering unique, sustainable fashion experiences (AL-Hawamleh et al., 2024). Sustainability in the fashion industry is crucial due to its environmental impact, with a focus on detoxing from hazardous chemicals and enhancing transparency in the supply chain (Nayak et al., 2020). By adopting sustainable design strategies and circular economy models, brands can meet consumer expectations for eco-friendly practices in the Metaverse, ensuring a balance between innovation and environmental responsibility.

Positioning in the MFE involves various aspects such as intellectual property rights, sustainability of cultural heritage, phygital experiences, and virtual retailing. Fashion brands are exploring the Metaverse for innovative retail strategies, offering unique spatial experiences and entertainment activities not easily achievable in physical stores (Kim & Chakraborty, 2024). Additionally, the convergence of fashion and the Metaverse presents opportunities for eco-friendly practices, NFT issuance, and digital value chain transformations (Karabacak & Güngör, 2023). Moreover, the digital fashion design in the Metaverse can contribute to cultural sustainability efforts by overcoming physical limitations and reaching a wider audience (Trujillo & Bacciu, 2023). The Metaverse allows for immersive experiences that drive fashion brands to strategize deliveries and build communities through compelling applications, utilizing NFTs and ensuring privacy protection (Patruti et al., 2023).

Evaluation of Sustainable Marketing Efforts in the MFE

The success of Metaverse fashion can be measured through various factors such as customer engagement, virtual store credibility, unique spatial experiences, and the ability to convey fantasy and entertainment (Dewalska-Opitek, 2023; Shin et al., 2023). Consumer responses to meta-fashion trends, including replacing celebrities with virtual humans, ownership of digital assets, and metaverse marketing by luxury fashion brands, also play a crucial role in determining success (Breiter & Siegfried, 2022). Understanding consumers' expectations and attitudes toward the Metaverse and their willingness to spend on digital fashion products is essential for evaluating success (Yücelbaş & Yücelbaş, 2023). Additionally, the appeal of Metaverse fashion marketing to younger generations, the benefits offered to customers, and the narrowing gap between gamers and non-gamers in consuming digital fashion content are key indicators of success in the realm of fashion marketing communication (Aygün et al., 2022).

Measuring customer engagement in MFE is based on tools like frequency analysis, TF-IDF, and LDA Topic-modeling that can help to effectively measure and enhance customer engagement in MetaFashion, providing valuable insights for brands operating in the Metaverse.

Frequency analysis in MFE involves examining the occurrence of specific terms or topics within the context of the Metaverse and the fashion industry. Research has shown that consumers exhibit specific interests in various aspects of Meta Fashion, such as replacing celebrities with virtual humans, ownership of digital assets in Metaverse games, graphics using deepfake technology, and metaverse marketing by luxury fashion brands (Kim & Lee, 2022). Furthermore, the Metaverse serves as a new distribution channel for clothing products, with fashion brands providing unique spatial experiences and entertainment activities in virtual stores that differ from traditional retail channels (Lee et al., 2023). Companies transitioning to the Metaverse have seen a significant increase in positive sentiment on platforms like Twitter, indicating a positive perception shift among potential users (Park et al., 2023).

Personal Perspective of the MFE

This section presents the persona level of MFE, where consumers follow customized behavior in their purchase (demand-side) and use of immersive reality fashion products and services. Consumer behavior in the MFE is influenced by various factors such as using nonfungible tokens (NFTs), virtual product purchase intention, avatar identification, and the impact on real-world purchasing behavior. Luxury fashion brands leverage blockchain-based NFTs to authenticate digital assets, maintain reputations, and attract consumers (Hadi et al., 2024). The Metaverse offers new opportunities for retailers to enhance consumer experiences through meta-commerce, emphasizing interactivity and vividness (Kovacova et al., 2022). Studies suggest that appearance similarity and avatar identification are crucial in driving consumer behavior toward virtual product purchases, affecting real-world purchasing intentions (Shen et al., 2021). Additionally, consumer responses in the MFE are influenced by trends such as replacing celebrities with virtual humans, metaverse marketing by luxury brands, and the ownership of digital assets in virtual games (Du et al., 2023).

Hadi et al. (2024) offered a framework for consumer behavior in MFE that includes five distinctive facets—it inhabits a digital realm, encompasses spatial dimensions, provides immersive encounters, fosters communal engagements, and operates in real time. The paper then examines how these components might collectively shape consumer behavior within three fundamental domains: consumer identity, social influence dynamics, and ownership patterns. That study signifies the inception of endeavors to delineate a transformative evolution unfolding in the market landscape and seeks to analyze, from the lens of consumer behavior, the diverse transformations it may usher in.

Conclusion

This chapter uses the multiple perspective theory to offer a comprehensive map of the Metaverse Fashion Ecosystem (MFE) as a transformative platform for sustainable marketing. This research defines the MFE as a dynamic interplay of human–computer interactions, social networks, and organizational policies aimed at sustainable marketing. By exploring the main pillars of MFE and defining sustainable marketing in this virtual forefront, we provide insight into how fashion giants like Gucci, Burberry, and Balenciaga deliver sustainable fashion into the Metaverse. Accordingly, this chapter contributes to defining metaverse fashion as an ecosystem that includes sustainable and other advanced marketing practices in the fashion industry.

Utilizing the multiple perspective theory, we dissect the MFE from technical, organizational, and personal angles. Our research highlights that social media and influencer marketing are pivotal technical tools for enhancing immersive experiences, social engagement, and visual representation within the MFE. On the organizational front, strategies for sustainable branding, market positioning, and performance metrics are identified as essential tools for driving sustainable marketing. From a personal perspective, the customization of consumer behavior through nonfungible tokens (NFTs) and blockchain technology is emphasized, showcasing how consumers can interact uniquely within this digital space.

This research offers the first attempt to adopt the TOP framework to analyze the phenomenon of metaverse fashion and migrate the multiple perspective theory (Phillips & Linstone, 2016) from the information system to marketing and fashion management disciplines. The TOP framework offers a nuanced understanding of how sustainable marketing can be integrated into the Metaverse. It provides a viable pathway for the fashion industry to reduce its environmental footprint and promote sustainability.

The fashion industry has grappled with sustainability challenges, particularly due to the negative implications of fast fashion. Previous studies (e.g., Caniato et al., 2012; Thorisdottir & Johannsdottir, 2019) have focused on the industry's potential for positive societal impact through more sustainable practices. Despite advancements in the luxury sector, the broader fashion industry is reluctant to adopt environmentally friendly business models. This resistance hampers progress in sustainable marketing, encompassing promotion, pricing, distribution, and market segmentation. Effective marketing is critical for developing sustainable products, defining market presence, targeting consumer segments, and influencing consumer behavior toward sustainable fashion. There is an urgent need to explore innovative marketing strategies that can drive consumer behavior toward more sustainable fashion consumption.

References

Aburbeian, A. M., Owda, A. Y., & Owda, M. (2022). A technology acceptance model survey of the metaverse prospects. *Ai, 3*(2), 285–302.

Al-Hawamleh, A., Altarawneh, M., Hikal, H., & Elfedawy, A. (2024). Blockchain technology and virtual asset accounting in the Metaverse: A comprehensive review of future directions. *International Journal of Computing and Digital Systems, 15*(1), 1595–1614.

Audrezet, A., de Kerviler, G., & Moulard, J. G. (2020). Authenticity under threat: When social media influencers need to go beyond self-presentation. *Journal of Business Research, 117**, 557–569.

Aygün, İ., Kaya, B., & Kaya, M. (2022, October). Detection of customer opinions with deep learning method for Metaverse collaborating brands. In *2022 International Conference on Data Analytics for Business and Industry (ICDABI)* (pp. 603–607). IEEE.

Blowers, M., Jaimes, N., & Williams, J. (2023, June). Benefits and challenges of a military metaverse. In *Disruptive Technologies in Information Sciences VII* (Vol. 12542, pp. 171–180). SPIE.

Breiter, D., & Siegfried, P. (2022). The metaverse: Exploring consumer expectations, their attitudes, and its meaning to the fashion industry. *eISSN*, 2683-5665.

Brydges, T., Retamal, M., & Hanlon, M. (2020). Will COVID-19 support the transition to a more sustainable fashion industry? *Sustainability: Science, Practice and Policy, 16*(1), 298–308.

Caniato, F., Caridi, M., Crippa, L., & Moretto, A. (2012). Environmental sustainability in fashion supply chains: An exploratory case based research. *International Journal of Production Economics, 135*(2), 659–670.

Crespo-Pereira, V., Sánchez-Amboage, E., & Membiela-Pollán, M. (2023). Facing the challenges of Metaverse: A systematic literature review from Social Sciences and Marketing and Communication. *Profesional de la información/Information Professional, 32*(1).

Dewalska-Opitek, A. (2023). Digital revolution in fashion industry–to what extent can metaverse become a predominant business-to-customer model in the digital era. *Humanitas University's Research Papers Management, 24*(2), 31–47.

Du, H., Ma, B., Niyato, D., Kang, J., Xiong, Z., & Yang, Z. (2023). Rethinking quality of experience for metaverse services: A consumer-based economics perspective. *IEEE Network*.

Freire, K. (2021). Strategic design for social innovation in the fashion system: The sustainable fashion ecosystem case. *Sustainable Fashion and Textiles in Latin America*, 87–103.

Gazzola, P., Pavione, E., Pezzetti, R., & Grechi, D. (2020). Trends in the fashion industry. The perception of sustainability and circular economy: A gender/generation quantitative approach. *Sustainability, 12*(7), 2809.

Gupta, J., Rani, L., & Kaur, M. (2023). AR/VR technologies in the metaverse ecosystem. In *Handbook of research on AI-based technologies and applications in the era of the metaverse* (pp. 127–143). IGI Global.

Hadi, R., Melumad, S., & Park, E. S. (2024). The Metaverse: A new digital frontier for consumer behavior. *Journal of Consumer Psychology, 34*(1), 142–166.

Haikel-Elsabeh, M. (2023). Virtual influencers versus real influencers advertising in the Metaverse, understanding the perceptions, and interactions with users. *Journal of Current Issues & Research in Advertising, 44*(3), 252–273.

Idrees, S., Vignali, G., & Gill, S. (2023). Interactive marketing with virtual commerce tools: Purchasing right size and fitted garment in fashion metaverse. *The Palgrave Handbook of interactive marketing* (pp. 329–351). Springer International Publishing.

Kaplan, A. M., & Haenlein, M. (2010). Users of the world, unite! The challenges and opportunities of Social Media. **Business Horizons, 53*(1), 59–68.

Karabacak, Z. İ, & Güngör, İ. (2023). The metaverse as influencer marketing platform: Influencer-brand collaborations of Parıs Hilton with 'Superplastic', 'Bohoo', and 'Levi's.' *Etkileşim, 11*, 176–199.

Kim, D. H., & Lee, J. H. (2022). A case study on metaverse fashion marketing of global fashion luxury brand. *Journal of Art & Design Research, 25*(1), 11–24.

Kim, H. M., & Chakraborty, S. (2024). Exploring the diffusion of digital fashion and influencers' social roles in the Metaverse: An analysis of Twitter hashtag networks. *Internet Research, 34*(1), 107–128.

Kovacova, M., Machova, V., & Bennett, D. (2022). Immersive extended reality technologies, data visualization tools, and customer behavior analytics in the metaverse commerce. *Journal of Self-Governance and Management Economics, 10*(2), 7–21.

Lee, M. J., Lee, J. M., & Shin, E. (2023). An analysis of user experience of metaverse fashion shows based on grounded theory-focusing on Schmitt's experiential marketing. *Fashion & Textile Research Journal, 25*(5), 578–592.

Linstone, H. A., & Turoff, M. (2011). Delphi: A brief look backward and forward. *Technological Forecasting and Social Change, 78*(9), 1712–1719.

Liu, Y., Wang, X., & Li, J. (2023). AI-driven systems for fashion retrieval: Advances and applications. *Journal of Fashion Technology, 12*(3), 45–60.

Madhura, K., & Panakaje, N. (2022). Social media as a promotional tool in the fashion industry: A case study on meta platforms Inc. *International Journal of Case Studies in Business, IT and Education (IJCSBE), 6*(1), 351–365.

Marr, B. (2021). How NFTs and blockchain are changing the fashion industry. *Forbes*. Retrieved from https://www.forbes.com/sites/bernardmarr/2021/03/12/how-nfts-and-blockchain-are-changing-the-fashion-industry/

Mesjar, L., Cross, K., Jiang, Y., & Steed, J. (2023). The intersection of fashion, immersive technology, and sustainability: A literature review. *Sustainability, 15*(4), 3761.

Minghua, J., Chang Long, Z. (2023). Garment metaverse: Parametric digital human and dynamic scene try-on. https://doi.org/10.1145/3590003.3590014

Mitroff, I. I., & Kilmann, R. H. (2021). Inquiry systems as coping mechanisms. *The psychodynamics of enlightened leadership: Coping with chaos* (pp. 33–36). Springer International Publishing.

Mogaji, E., Dwivedi, Y. K., & Raman, R. (2024). Fashion marketing in the Metaverse. *Journal of Global Fashion Marketing, 15*(1), 115–130.

Mohamad, M., Wood-Harper, T., & Ramlogan, R. (2020). Mobile financial services at the base of the pyramid: A systemic view for cross-sector governance and embedded innovation Sustainable Business: Concepts, Methodologies, Tools, and Applications, 1255.

Mu, X., Zhang, H., Shi, J., Hou, J., Ma, J., & Yang, Y. (2024). Fashion intelligence in the Metaverse: Promise and future prospects. *Artificial Intelligence Review, 57*(3), 67.

Muniz, A. M., & O'Guinn, T. C. (2001). Brand community. *Journal of Consumer Research, 27*(4), 412–432.

Nayak, R., Nguyen, L. V. T., Panwar, T., & Jajpura, L. (2020). Sustainable technologies and processes adapted by fashion brands. In *Sustainable technologies for fashion and textiles* (pp. 233–248). Woodhead Publishing.

Ozuem, W., Ranfagni, S., Willis, M., Salvietti, G., & Howell, K. (2024). Exploring the relationship between chatbots, service failure recovery and customer loyalty: A frustration–aggression perspective. *Psychology and Marketing*. https://doi.org/10.1002/mar.22051

Ozuem, W., Willis, M., Ranfagni, S., Howell, K. E., & Rovai, S. (2023a). Examining the role of social media influencers in service failure and recovery strategies: an empirical investigation of millennials' views. *Information Technology & People*. https://doi.org/10.1108/itp-05-2022-0371

Ozuem, W., Ranfagni, S., Willis, M., Rovai, S., & Howell, K. (2021). Exploring customers' responses to online service failure and recovery strategies during Covid-19 pandemic: An actor–network theory perspective. *Psychology & Marketing, 38*(9), 1440–1459.

Ozuem, W., & Willis, M. (2022). *Digital marketing strategies for value co-creation: Models and approaches for online brand communities*. Palgrave Macmillan.

Ozuem, W., Willis, M., Howell, K., Ranfagni, S., & Rovai, S. (2023b). Examining user-generated content, service failure recovery and customer–brand relationships: An exploration through commitment-trust theory. *Internet Research*. https://doi.org/10.1108/intr-07-2022-0580

Pandey, R., Pandit, P., Pandey, S., & Mishra, S. (2020). Solutions for sustainable fashion and textile industry. In *Recycling from waste in fashion and textiles: A sustainable and circular economic approach* (pp. 33–72).

Paniagua, J., & Sapena, J. (2014). Business performance and social media: Love or hate? *Business Horizons, 57*(6), 719–728.

Panja, M. (2018). Sustainability integration in the fashion retail industry.

Park, Y., Ko, E., & Do, B. (2023). The perceived value of digital fashion product and purchase intention: The mediating role of the flow experience in metaverse platforms. *Asia Pacific Journal of Marketing and Logistics, 35*(11), 2645–2665.

Patruti, P., Zbuchea, A., & Pînzaru, F. (2023). Fashion joining online gaming and the Metaverse. In *Proceedings of the international conference on business excellence* (Vol. 17, No. 1, pp. 1065–1074). Sciendo.

Pérez Curiel, C., & Aparicio Bernabéu, E. (2017). Sustainability and fashion brands a pact for eco-luxury. *International Review of Management and Business Research (IRMBR), 6*(2), 717–734.

Periyasami, S., & Periyasamy, A. P. (2022). Metaverse as future promising platform business model: Case study on fashion value chain. *Businesses, 2*(4), 527–545.

Periyasamy, A. P., & Periyasami, S. (2023). Rise of digital fashion and Metaverse: Influence on sustainability. *Digital Economy and Sustainable Development, 1*(1), 16.

Phillips, F., & Linstone, H. (2016). Key ideas from a 25-year collaboration at technological forecasting & social change. *Technological Forecasting and Social Change, 105*, 158–166.

Ray, S., & Nayak, L. (2023). Marketing sustainable fashion: Trends and future directions. *Sustainability, 15*(7), 6202.

Richa, G., & Dushyant, D. (2021). Sustainable trendsetters: Up-cycling and rejuvenation of textile apparel using computational technology. https://doi.org/10.1109/ICCCNT51525.2021.9579649

Rodriguez Sanchez, M., & Garcia-Badell, G. (2022, July). Dressing the metaverse. The digital strategies of fashion brands in the virtual universe. In *International Fashion and Design Congress* (pp. 387–397). Springer International Publishing.

Schöbel, S. M., & Leimeister, J. M. (2023). Metaverse platform ecosystems. *Electronic Markets, 33*(1), 12.

Sharma, A., & Bansal, A. (2023). Digital marketing in the metaverse: Beginning of a new era in product promotion. In *Applications of Neuromarketing in the Metaverse* (pp. 163–175). IGI Global.

Shen, B., Tan, W., Guo, J., Zhao, L., & Qin, P. (2021). How to promote user purchase in Metaverse? A systematic literature review on consumer behavior research and virtual commerce application design. *Applied Sciences, 11*(23), 11087.

Shin, J. Y., Suk, J., & Chung, J. E. (2023, February). Consumer responses to fashion in the Metaverse: A text-mining analysis on online news comments. In *Future of Information and Communication Conference* (pp. 12–24). Springer Nature Switzerland.

Silva, J. S. G., Turčínková, J., & Magano, J. (2022). Sustainable marketing orientation in the clothing industry: Slow or fast fashion? *Percursos & Ideias, 12*, 86–99.

Singhal, V., & Ahuja, V. (2023). Social media marketing and the world of fashion: Identification of determinants for building consumer brand relationship and shaping consumer brand perception. *International Journal of Management Practice, 16*(2), 186–211.

Smith, A., Jones, T., & Roberts, L. (2022). Virtual fashion shows and digital try-ons: Bridging the gap between physical and digital fashion. *International Journal of Fashion Studies, 10*(2), 120–135.

Soyoung, K., Seo-Young, K. (2022). A study on the current status of metaverse technology expansion and fashion brand collaboration. *Journal of Korean Traditional Costume*. https://doi.org/10.16885/jktc.2022.12.25.4.167

Sung, E., Kwon, O., & Sohn, K. (2023). NFT luxury brand marketing in the metaverse: Leveraging blockchain-certified NFTs to drive consumer behavior. *Psychology & Marketing, 40*(11), 2306–2325.

Thorisdottir, T. S., & Johannsdottir, L. (2019). Sustainability within fashion business models: A systematic literature review. *Sustainability, 11*(8), 2233.

Trujillo, A., & Bacciu, C. (2023, June). Toward blockchain-based fashion wearables in the metaverse: The case of Decentraland. In *2023 IEEE International Conference on Metaverse Computing, Networking and Applications (MetaCom)* (pp. 653–657). IEEE.

Ullah, H., Manickam, S., Obaidat, M., Laghari, S. U. A., & Uddin, M. (2023). Exploring the potential of metaverse technology in healthcare: Applications, challenges, and future directions. *IEEE Access*.

Verhagen, T., von Mierlo, B., & van der Heijden, H. (2014). Virtual customer service agents: Using social presence and personalization to shape online service encounters. *Journal of Computer-Mediated Communication, 19*(3), 529–545.

Wang, H., Liu, X., Jiang, M., & Zhou, C. (2023, March). Garment metaverse: Parametric digital human and dynamic scene try-on. In *Proceedings of the 2023 2nd Asia Conference on Algorithms, Computing and Machine Learning* (pp. 60–65).

Weiss, C. (2022). Fashion retailing in the Metaverse. *Fashion, Style & Popular Culture, 9*(4), 523–538.

Xi, N., Chen, J., Gama, F., Korkeila, H., & Hamari, J. (2024). Acceptance of the Metaverse: A laboratory experiment on augmented and virtual reality shopping. *Internet Research, 34*(7), 82–117.

Yan, R. (2022). A sustainable fashion industry Business model revolution based on the Metaverse: Practices and reciprocal processes. *Highlights in Business, Economics and Management, 4*, 363–369.

Yoo, C. B. P. (2021). Re-envisioning organizational Complexity using a multiple perspectives model. *Journal of Management & Organization, 27*(4), 751–767.

Yücelbaş, C., & Yücelbaş, Ş. (2023). Examining the success of information gain, pearson correlation, and symmetric uncertainty ranking methods on

3D hand posture data for metaverse systems. *Sakarya University Journal of Science, 27*(2), 271–284.

Zabel, C., O'Brien, D., & Natzel, J. (2023). Sensing the Metaverse: The microfoundations of complementor firms' dynamic sensing capabilities in emerging-technology ecosystems. *Technological Forecasting and Social Change, 192*, 122562.

Zhang, H., & Chen, Y. (2023). Advancements in AI for fashion attribute mapping and controllability. *IEEE Transactions on Fashion Computing, 9*(1), 78–88.

Zhichang, Z. (2010). Theorizing systems methodologies across cultures. *Systems Research and Behavioral Science: The Official Journal of the International Federation for Systems Research, 27*(2), 208–223.

Part III

Strategies and Techniques

20

Chatbots and Customer Experience in Luxury Fashion

Isolde Ward-Lubbe and Steven Mbeya

Introduction

The luxury fashion industry is renowned for its emphasis on high quality, exclusivity, and superior craftsmanship (Gurzki & Gurzki, 2020). This sector, deeply rooted in history, has evolved to meet the modern demands of customers who seek not only exceptional products but also meaningful experiences (Amatulli et al., 2017). In recent years, there has been a significant shift towards integrating technology within the luxury fashion industry to enhance customer experiences and promote sustainability (Javornik et al., 2021; Mekonnen, 2024). This transformation is particularly evident among millennials, a demographic that plays a crucial role in shaping market trends due to their preference for digital interactions and ethical consumption (Eastman & Iyer, 2021; Jasrotia et al., 2023).

Millennials, often described as digital natives, are driving the luxury fashion market with their inclination towards seamless, personalised, and

I. Ward-Lubbe (✉) · S. Mbeya
University of Johannesburg, Olifantsfontein, Gauteng, South Africa
e-mail: isoldel@uj.ac.za

W. Ozuem et al. (eds.), *Sustainable Digital Marketing for Fashion and Luxury Brands*,
https://doi.org/10.1007/978-3-031-82467-8_20

engaging customer experiences (Chopra & Bhilare, 2020; Nawaz, 2020). Despite the potential of this market, luxury fashion brands face challenges in providing satisfactory customer experiences that meet the high expectations of this tech-savvy demographic (Khan et al., 2021). The need to offer a seamless, personalised, and engaging customer experience is more pressing than ever.

Chatbots, advanced AI-driven interfaces, present a promising solution to these challenges. They can enhance customer engagement by providing instant, personalised service, facilitating real-time interactions, and delivering tailored advice based on individual preferences and behaviours (Boon-itt, 2015; Davenport et al., 2020). For example, a customer looking for a specific luxury handbag should be able to ask the chatbot about stock availability, get prompt confirmation, and even provide details on the nearest physical store. This capability is crucial in addressing the unique expectations of millennials who value convenience, authenticity, and sustainability (Chi et al., 2021; Modi & Zhao, 2021; Sadiq et al., 2024). By integrating chatbots, luxury fashion brands can not only improve customer satisfaction and loyalty but also drive the adoption of sustainable practices. This approach aligns with the growing demand for transparency and ethical behaviour in the luxury market, making chatbots a vital tool in the ongoing evolution of customer experience in the luxury fashion industry.

What Is Luxury and How Is It Defined in the Fashion Industry?

The term 'luxury' originates from the Latin words 'luxuria' and 'luxus', signifying extravagant living and opulence (Nath & Batra, 2019; Nueno & Quelch, 1998). The purchase of luxury goods dates back to Ancient Egypt, where luxury items included precious jewellery, pottery, and metals with unique markings (Berry, 1994). Cabigiosu and Cabigiosu (2020) and Turunen and Leipämaa-Leskinen (2015) suggest that luxury's symbolism derives from the exclusivity, uniqueness, and superior quality of products. Antola (2017) adds that displaying and using luxury goods brings esteem to the owner. However, current literature indicates that luxury is not easily defined, with no universally accepted definition due to its multifaceted nature (Cabigiosu & Cabigiosu, 2020). Liang et al. (2017) argue that the luxury concept is vague and context-dependent, a view supported by Nwankwo et al. (2014), who note that perceptions of luxury vary by time, space, and context.

In the fashion industry, luxury is defined by high quality, exclusivity, and superior craftsmanship (Gurzki & Gurzki, 2020). These products are crafted from the finest materials with meticulous attention to detail and are often produced in limited quantities, enhancing their desirability (Amatulli et al., 2017). They signify wealth, status, and success, symbolising prestige (Han et al., 2010). Exceptional aesthetics and design, frequently by renowned designers, further distinguish luxury fashion items. Many luxury fashion brands boast a rich history and heritage, adding to their value. Beyond the products themselves, luxury in fashion encompasses exceptional customer service and an overall superior purchasing and ownership experience (Belfanti, 2023; Brun & Castelli, 2013). Understanding these foundational aspects of luxury fashion sets the stage for exploring the latest trends shaping the industry today.

Trends in the Luxury Fashion Industry

Currently, the luxury fashion industry is undergoing a dynamic transformation shaped by numerous key trends. For example, soon after the COVID-19 pandemic, there has been a disruption in formal dress codes, and gender fluidity which has resulted in positive attitudes towards purchasing clothes across different genders (McKinsey, 2023). One of the other prominent luxury fashion trends is the rapid increase of integration of technology, with brands leveraging AI tools, such as Augmented Reality (AR), and Virtual Reality (VR) to enhance customer experiences through online try-ons, and immersive fashion shows (Javornik et al., 2021; Mekonnen, 2024). In the same light, Mohr et al. (2022) echo that technology helps to accelerate luxury fashion trends via broad exposure on social media, such as fashion week shows, Hollywood red carpet, and celebrity stories. There is also increased customer demand for greater environmental responsibility, as 90% of customers indicate that sustainability attributes are crucial in their purchasing decisions (Forbes, 2023). Luxury brands progressively adopt eco-friendly practices, from sourcing sustainable raw materials to ensuring ethical labour initiatives (Sadiq et al., 2024). Furthermore, the luxury fashion industry is modifying itself to meet the preferences of millennials, who more than ever constitute a significant 70% of luxury customers (Eastman & Iyer, 2021; Jasrotia et al., 2023; Statista, 2023a). This demographic highly values social responsibility, authenticity, and unique experiences, driving brands to innovate and align or adapt their marketing strategies (Cairns et al., 2022; Mohr et al., 2022). As millennials opt for online purchasing and social media engagement, they also propel the trend towards digital interaction, making luxury fashion brands strengthen their e-commerce and digital presence capabilities (Rahman et al., 2023). Humanlike languages make customers feel less formal, more intimate, and very friendly, and this combination makes a great positive difference (Nguyen et al., 2023). For example, luxury fashion brands may use the human likeness of chatbots, such as emojis in conversation with millennial customers, thereby, enhancing engagement especially of the luxury brand has high perceived credibility.

Millennials Driving the Luxury Fashion Industry

Scholars have differing views on the exact birth years that define the millennial generation (Bevan-Dye et al., 2012; Karashchuk et al., 2020). Millennials, also known as 'Generation Y' are individuals born from the early 1980s to the mid-1990s; some authors even state until the year 2000 (Rawlins et al., 2008; Velasco, 2020). This generation is unique as the first to mature in the new millennium and as the original digital natives (Velasco, 2020). With many millennials in their thirties and the majority beginning their careers, this generation is becoming a significant driving force in the economy, shaping customer choices and driving the shift towards more sustainable consumption practices (Guga & Peta, 2023; Muhyidin et al., 2024; Statista, 2024a). The considerable size of this group has led brands to pay more attention to their behaviour patterns and needs (Moreno et al., 2017). Known for their technological proficiency, millennials seek innovation and digital interaction, prompting brands to adopt and implement advanced technological solutions to meet their demands (Chopra & Bhilare, 2020; Nawaz, 2020; Sulistyawati et al., 2024). An influential cohort, millennials constitute, for example, just over a fifth of the entire United States population in 2022 (Statista, 2024b). In 2021 millennials became the largest generation in the United Kingdom, with an estimated population of 14.4 million (Statista, 2023b). With millennials having the highest global spending power, it is essential to understand their preference for diverse, emotionally resonant experiential purchases and seamlessly integrated technological experiences within the expanding experience economy, while also valuing luxury products (Nawaz, 2020; Rosa, 2020; Sulistyawati et al., 2024). Driven by their personal values and considerable purchasing power, millennials are inclined to spend significantly on luxury fashion, favouring high-end products that reflect their values and status (Lim et al., 2023).

Analysis of Millennials' Attitudes Towards Luxury Brands and Products

Attitudes, as learned predispositions (Ajzen & Fishbein, 2000), are subjective evaluations, either positive or negative (Fishbein & Ajzen, 2005). They consist of cognition, affect, and conation, involving learning, feeling, and doing (Schiffman & Wisenblit, 2015). The cognitive component includes understanding and perceptions of an entity's features, gained through experience or information sources (Fishbein & Ajzen, 2005; Schiffman & Wisenblit, 2015).

Millennials exhibit unique attitudes towards luxury brands and products, valuing authenticity, exclusivity, and quality over mere brand names (Dobre et al., 2021; Pattuglia & Mingione, 2017; Rodrigues & Rodrigues, 2019). They seek brands that resonate with their personal identity and lifestyle, often favouring those with a strong narrative and ethical practices. Their preferences are for luxury brands that are honest, ethical, authentic, and true (Batat & Batat, 2019; Lim et al., 2023). For millennials, luxury is not just about conspicuous consumption but also meaningful experiences and self-expression. They perceive luxury not only to enhance social value but also as a solution to promote their identity (Batat & Batat, 2019).

In their need for experience and assertiveness, luxury brands offer part of the answer to millennials who seek preservation and distinction with their community (Batat & Batat, 2019). Millennials prefer spending money on their lifestyles, positive experiences, and social media currency instead of tangible and physical products. The immersive service experience makes a difference (Batat & Batat, 2019; Javornik et al., 2021). They place image and aesthetics at the heart of their luxury buying experience, an experience that only makes sense if it is endorsed by their peers and shared through stories or online platforms (Batat & Batat, 2019). The emphasis on experience and emotion and the need to express one's identity make youth generation customers' expectations particularly well-matched with luxury brand responses (Batat & Batat, 2019).

Rodrigues and Rodrigues (2019) highlight that millennials value status differently from traditional views, focusing on personal achievements and identity rather than wealth displayed through luxury brands. They frequently use technology for entertainment, socialisation, and emotion regulation. Millennials favour brands that resonate with their image-conscious peers and prefer customised products and prestigious brands, finding significant enjoyment in shopping (Dobre et al., 2024; Williams & Page, 2011). Influenced by online reviews, they actively seek and provide consumer-generated product information, often purchasing products recommended by friends on social media, viewing these comments as transparent and blogs as objective. They use multiple channels to find variety and enhance their shopping experience (Nawaz, 2020). Luxury evaluation for millennials is influenced more by family and material status, shaped by cultural and social factors, rather than being specific to their generation (Atkinson & Kang, 2022).

Factors Influencing Millennials' Purchasing Decisions in Luxury Fashion

When exploring the factors influencing millennials' purchasing decisions in the luxury fashion sector, key elements include the importance of experiences, sustainability concerns, and the role of chatbots (Forbes, 2023; Javornik et al., 2021; Mekonnen, 2024; Mohr et al., 2022; Murtarelli et al., 2023). Millennials, more receptive to new technologies than previous generations, find chatbots particularly suitable for online interactions (Murtarelli et al., 2023). They prioritise experiences over material possessions, seeking meaningful and immersive interactions with brands (Batat & Batat, 2019; Eastman et al., 2013; Stępień et al., 2018). Consequently, luxury fashion brands that offer exclusive events, personalised services, and engaging brand stories tend to attract this demographic (Batat & Batat, 2019; Nawaz, 2020; Rodrigues & Rodrigues, 2019). In addition, sustainability is a significant factor for millennials, who prefer brands committed to eco-friendly materials, ethical labour practices, and supply chain transparency (Chi et al., 2021; Modi & Zhao, 2021; Sadiq et al., 2024). Brands that effectively communicate their sustainability efforts often gain a competitive edge in the market (Abumalloh et al., 2023).

Furthermore, when purchasing luxury brands, millennials highly value the quality, craftsmanship, uniqueness, and sustainability of products, favouring items that demonstrate superior construction, exclusivity, and ethical production practices (Slaton & Hurst, 2023; Wong & Park, 2023). Brand authenticity and ethical values are crucial, with millennials gravitating towards brands with a strong identity, and clear values (Batat & Batat, 2019; Mohr et al., 2022; Rodrigues & Rodrigues, 2019). Immersive and personalised brand interactions, such as exclusive events, custom styling services, and engaging brand stories, enhance their shopping experience (Batat & Batat, 2019; Dhama et al., 2024; Zeng et al., 2023). In addition, seamless digital integration, AI-driven chatbots, virtual and augmented reality, and active social media engagement are vital technological elements that appeal to tech-savvy millennials (Arrington, 2021; Nawaz, 2020). By addressing these factors, luxury fashion brands can better cater to millennial preferences, ensuring a more successful and engaging shopping experience.

Millennial Experiences in Luxury Fashion: The Role of Technology

Experience can be defined as 'the outcomes of the interactions between organisations, related systems/processes, service employees and customers' (Bitner et al., 1997: 193). Everything an organisation does contributes to this customer experience, which is highly valued by customers (Kayton, 2018; Lubbe & Ngoma, 2021). With the rise of technology, the number of touchpoints between customers and organisations has increased significantly (Kushwaha et al., 2021). Customers now interact with brands through various intertwined interfaces, and any single touchpoint that fails to meet expectations can negatively impact their overall experience and attitudes (Van de Sand et al., 2020).

For millennials, experiences are paramount, especially when it comes to luxury fashion (Helal et al., 2018). Extreme luxury for these customers equates to simplicity, but it also requires uninterrupted, immersive interactions that fit seamlessly into their consumption habits (Johri et al., 2024). Omnichannel approaches that emphasise image and aesthetics are essential, as these elements are central to their luxury buying experience (Batat & Batat, 2019; Han et al., 2024). This experience must be validated by their peers and communities, often through stories or online games, to be truly meaningful (Batat & Batat, 2019; Ozuem et al., 2021). For instance, the Karl Lagerfeld boutique integrates user experience into its digital practices by offering the same conveniences as its website, along with constant community advice, illustrating how aesthetics, emotions, and brand experiences are significant when shared within their communities (Batat & Batat, 2019).

Incorporating advanced technology into these experiences is crucial for luxury fashion brands aiming to cultivate loyalty among millennials (Khan et al., 2021). Self-service technology, such as chatbots, enhances how customers interact with brands by providing personalised, efficient, and interactive services without human assistance (Boon-itt, 2015;

Davenport et al., 2020). AI-driven chatbots, for example, can offer tailored styling advice and instant customer service, aligning with the Fourth Industrial Revolution's technological advancements, including Internet of Things (IoT), AI, VR, and robotics (Schwab, 2015). Positive interactions with these technologies are vital, as they can significantly enhance customer satisfaction and loyalty (Zhu & Morosan, 2014).

However, for these technologies to be effective, they must provide a seamless and enjoyable user experience, which is integral to overall customer satisfaction and a competitive advantage (Mosavi et al., 2018). Apart from satisfaction, it is worth knowing that in an online environment, customer-service communication precedes trust (Chung et al., 2020). For example, luxury fashion brands can utilise previous online communication to derive inspiration for future personalised or customised products. When luxury brands effectively utilise technology to create engaging and effortless experiences, they meet the high expectations of millennial customers, ultimately driving customer satisfaction and brand loyalty (Bilgihan et al., 2016; Djelassi et al., 2018; Shahid Iqbal et al., 2018). Through interaction and positive experiences, chatbots have significant potential to motivate people towards more sustainable lifestyles through personalised advice, education, behavioural nudges, tracking and feedback, community engagement, incentives, and integration with smart devices (Åberg, 2017).

Sustainability in the Luxury Fashion Industry

In the luxury fashion context, sustainability can be viewed from different perspectives based on people's beliefs, experiences, and values (Mok et al., 2022). Scholars, such as Elkington (1994, 1998), Mok et al. (2022), and Slaper and Hall (2011) define sustainability as being grounded in the so-called triple bottom line framework (economic prosperity, social justice, and environmental quality). In luxury fashion, it is also known or interchangeably referred to as green eco, and ethical fashion (Mohr et al., 2022). Not only does considering the three components of the triple bottom line framework broaden the issue of sustainability, but it also encompasses several corporate behaviours and policies (Akrout &

Guercini, 2022). In other words, sustainability concepts suggest that for a business to be successful, it must not only focus on profits (traditional bottom line) but also consider its influence on the environmental and social aspects (Akrout & Guercini, 2022; Karaosman et al., 2020). For example, in the luxury fashion industry companies should be able to manufacture exclusive or unique, superior quality and durable products that are sold at a premium price without compromising their environment but also make a positive impact in the communities they trade in, such as being directly or indirectly involved in social causes. The modern consumer is becoming more and more sustainability inquisitive and seeks to purchase ethically produced products including luxury fashion brands, as well as receiving well-informed sustainability marketing messages from the brand (McKinsey, 2023). From a luxury fashion perspective, the strategic importance of sustainability is clear and needs to be greatly considered, implemented, and practised to build a positive reputation, return current customers, and attract new ones.

Trends in Sustainability in the Luxury Fashion Industry

The use and adoption of environmentally friendly materials started to evolve in 2017 (Mok et al., 2022) and show no signs of slowing down. Several current trends, such as changing consumer behaviour, investor expectations, and social norms, have prompted a greater emphasis on sustainability within the luxury fashion industry (Karaosman et al., 2020). As customers become more conscious of sustainability, they prefer luxury fashion products that can be recycled, reused, or is biodegradable (Mohr et al., 2022). To cater for the ever-evolving needs of sustainability-sensitive customers, luxury fashion brands have embarked on using more organic materials, such as polyester, cotton, and other innovative substitutes that reduce the environmental footprint and promote more sustainable purchases (Singh, 2023). In the same light, customers are seeking transparency from luxury fashion brands about the source of raw materials, and manufacturing processes assisting them to make more sound decisions (Garcia-Torres et al., 2022).

In terms of ethical labour practices, luxury brands are constantly seeking strategies to provide safe working conditions, and fair wages while respecting their employees' rights (Garcia-Torres et al., 2022). To enhance and simplify working conditions, luxury brands are embracing innovation and technology, such as using 3D printing, chatbots, and other artificial intelligence tools in their manufacturing and customer service activities to reduce waste and be more efficient and effective (Akinsola et al., 2022; Mok et al., 2022). On a different note, manufacturers of luxury brands collaborate with sustainability-focused brands to drive positive change and identify other innovative ways to address sustainability issues (Todeschini et al., 2020). Aside from producing luxury clothing in an eco-friendly manner, buying second-hand luxury clothing is another alternative to enhance sustainability practices (Mohr et al., 2022). For sustainability-sensitive customers, purchasing second-hand luxury clothing is regarded as being more sustainable by extending the lifespan of high-quality products (Turunen et al., 2020).

Millennials and Sustainability

Millennials have emerged as a very significant cohort in promoting sustainability. Research demonstrates that they are environmentally and socially conscious as they are willing to pay a premium price for products that enhance their health, are produced from organic raw materials or benefit the ecological environment (Eastman & Iyer, 2021; Jasrotia et al., 2023). They have greater eco-awareness, perceive products concerning their environmental impact and are willing to view sustainable luxury as fulfilling luxury needs (Eastman & Iyer, 2021). In terms of advocacy and activism, millennials are heavily involved in participating in signing petitions, protests, and supporting organisations or others that work towards sustainability goals (Jasrotia et al., 2023). In the same light, millennials think sustainability is a priority to purchasing products and leveraging technology to create and encourage sustainable consumption online via social media platforms (Sarkar et al., 2023). Other millennials have gone further and started innovative businesses that aim to drive sustainability, such as zero-waste stores, renewable energy, and sustainable fashion brands (Cairns et al., 2022; Mohr et al., 2022). Some of the driving factors towards sustainable behaviour among millennials are the negative environmental impacts of the luxury fashion industry, such as pollution, waste, degradation, and deforestation which results in preferences for eco-friendly products and ethical production practices (Akrout & Guercini, 2022; Cairns et al., 2022; Chen et al., 2023; Elkington, 1994; McKinsey, 2023).

The Importance of Technology in Sustainability

In online shopping environments, technology has played a pivotal role in advancing sustainability in the luxury fashion industry. To enhance the shopping experience while creating further sustainability awareness, luxury fashion brands, such as Louis Vuitton (over 3 million Facebook/Meta followers), have optimised AI-based chatbots to provide customised, more stylish, conversational, and visual online shopping experiences (Rahman et al., 2023). The implementation of machine learning and deep learning chatbots that use customer data to determine their purchasing behaviour, recommend sustainable luxury products and remind customers of the importance of using environmentally friendly products (Azemi & Ozuem, 2023; Dhama et al., 2024; Zeng et al., 2023). Using this approach, a company offers a tailored online experience, presenting various products to its intended target market based on their usage patterns. Apart from that, technology has assisted in reducing fossil fuel usage through renewable energy, such as hydroelectric power, solar, and wind energy, which might also act as an indirect catalyst in providing a good experience to customers who buy from brands that adopt eco-friendly energy in their manufacturing of luxury fashion brands (Irfan et al., 2021).

Promoting Sustainable Practices Through Chatbots

Chatbots are AI-powered digital assistants that are developed to simulate human-like interaction and assist existing and potential customers in answering various product questions through written or voice interfaces on online platforms (Klímová et al., 2023). Prevailing literature reveals that there are primarily three types of chatbots; dialogic chatbots as described by Peng et al. (2019), designed to comprehend oral inputs from users and discern their expectations; rational chatbots which use external knowledge bases and common sense to address human enquiries (Cuayáhuitl et al., 2019). Lastly, embodied chatbots, the earliest iteration, are favoured by non-technical users (Goli et al., 2023). Typically, they furnish users with tailored content information (Tran & Luong, 2020). In recent times, the adoption of chatbots has been ever-increasing across industries due to their ability to answer customer service queries at any time of the day, provide a convenient customer experience, provide a natural way of engaging with customers, and allow companies to understand the facets of online customer service experiences (Goli et al., 2023). In the foreseeable future, chatbots will become very smart in several sectors, such as health, customer service, the education environment, and the banking sector, and will play a dominant role in driving sustainability goals (Adamopoulou & Moussiades, 2020; Hwang & Chang, 2023). For luxury fashion brands, chatbots provide the opportunity to offer personalised purchasing experiences and provide a customer-tailored service based on individual preferences and product recommendations (Dhama et al., 2024; Zeng et al., 2023). In the context of sustainability, chatbots can educate and engage customers about eco-friendly initiatives and practices, suggest sustainable products, and improve transparent communication about a brand's environmental practices in online settings, such as e-commerce (Ozuem et al., 2024a, 2024b; Sadiq et al., 2024).

Since millennials are open to new or emerging technologies that previous generations did not experience, chatbots are the most suitable AI tools to interact with online (Murtarelli et al., 2023). This makes millennials unquestionably important players in shaping the landscape of chatbots and user experiences (De Cicco et al., 2020). Their attitudes towards such online interactive technologies are vital in understanding the direction of digital interactions (De Cicco et al., 2020). An extensive analysis of the existing literature on millennials' attitudes indicates a growing acceptance and a greater preference for chatbot tools, especially in sectors like luxury fashion (De Cicco et al., 2020; Murtarelli et al.,

2023; Richad et al., 2019). Attributes influencing millennials' behaviour and their adoption of chatbots include convenience, personalised cognitive engagement, and efficiency (Ling et al., 2021). Consequently, it has been predicted that in the future businesses will develop more chatbots than traditional mobile apps (Ling et al., 2021).

In the luxury fashion industry, millennials expect personalised shopping experiences and seamless service from brands on the use of AI tools especially chatbots (Ozuem et al., 2024a, 2024b). Chatbot technology is crafted to cultivate future connections between luxury brands and customers (Chung et al., 2020). For instance, Louis Vuitton offers a chatbot service tailored to provide information about its worldwide offline stores, facilitate access to personal service agents for product care enquiries, and engage users in conversational interfaces showcasing the craftsmanship behind their products (Chung et al., 2020). Drawing on theories of customer experience and customer engagement, it is apparent that millennials' shopping behaviour is increasingly influenced by their digital experiences, making chatbots a pivotal element in their purchasing journey (Adeola et al., 2020; Appiah & Watson, 2024).

Theoretical Framework

Understanding how millennials interact with chatbots to enhance sustainable behaviour in the luxury fashion industry requires a robust theoretical foundation. Customer experience theory and customer engagement theory are particularly relevant to this investigation.

Kim et al. (2023) suggest that the customer experience theory was coined by Brakus (2001). Kim et al. (2023) further add that the theory explains how customers' experiences are five kinds; social interaction, emotion, feeling, body and intelligence, and how customers react to several experiential stimuli, such as surroundings and packaging. In other words, it provides a comprehensive understanding of how customers perceive and interact with a brand throughout their entire journey and the overall holistic experience (Brakus, 2001). On a different note, this theory helps businesses to position themselves including their branding strategies (Becker & Jaakkola, 2020). From the luxury fashion industry perspective, it focuses on producing rare and exclusive luxury brands and the significance of delivering and maintaining seamless, omnichannel interactions across all touchpoints, from online stores to brick-and-mortar stores (Hyun et al., 2022). By prioritising factors, such as convenience, brand consistency, and visual aesthetics, luxury fashion brands can improve customer satisfaction and loyalty.

Another important theoretical grounding is the customer engagement theory. Rosado-Pinto and Loureiro (2020) claim that in the marketing domain, the customer engagement theory is still in its infancy. Rosado-Pinto and Loureiro (2020) further propose that if customers are highly satisfied, it leads to an emotional connection and drives engagement. This theory alludes to how customers connect and interact with products or brands with the sole purpose of building long-term relationships (De Oliveira Santini et al., 2020). In the context of a chatbot customer experience, this theory assists in explaining the role of chatbots in accelerating meaningful and personalised interactions between brands and their target, millennial customers (Murtarelli et al., 2023). By leveraging artificial intelligence and customer data, chatbots improve online engagement by addressing queries, delivering timely responses, and guiding customers through their purchasing journey (Cuayáhuitl et al., 2019; Klímová et al., 2023). Not only does it enhance a positive customer experience but is also essential in increasing conversion rates, market reach to potential customers and cost efficiency from both a business and customer's perspectives (Murtarelli et al., 2023).

The Future of Chatbots Enhancing Experiences for Sustainability

The future of chatbots in customer experience management looks promising, with advancements poised to revolutionise the fashion industry. Predictions suggest that chatbots will become increasingly sophisticated, using artificial intelligence and machine learning to offer highly personalised and intuitive customer interactions (Dhama et al., 2024; Zeng et al., 2023). In the fashion industry, this could manifest in several practical ways. For example, chatbots might analyse a customer's browsing history, previous purchases, and social media activity to provide tailored fashion recommendations that align with their personal style (Følstad & Skjuve, 2019; Kushwaha et al., 2021; Majeed et al., 2021). They could offer real-time styling advice, suggesting outfits based on current trends, the customer's wardrobe, and even upcoming events on their calendar (Campbell et al., 2020; Vaccaro et al., 2018).

In addition, chatbots could use machine learning algorithms to predict future fashion trends and stock availability, helping brands manage inventory more effectively and ensuring customers have access to the latest styles (Alduraywish et al., 2021). Virtual try-on features powered by AR, guided by chatbot interactions, would allow customers to see how clothes would look on them without physically trying them on, enhancing the online shopping experience (Aslam, 2023; Kumar et al., 2024).

Furthermore, these chatbots could provide proactive customer service by sending personalised notifications about sales, new arrivals, and restocked items of interest (Adam et al., 2021; Krishnan et al., 2022). By analysing customer feedback and engagement data, chatbots could also identify common pain points and preferences, enabling brands to refine their products and services continuously (Aslam, 2023; Kushwaha et al., 2021). This level of personalisation and responsiveness would help fashion brands build stronger relationships with customers, increase satisfaction, and drive loyalty in an increasingly competitive market.

Recommendations for Marketers

To make sustainability more accessible, engaging, and rewarding, marketers should leverage chatbots. Chatbots can play a crucial role in driving the adoption of eco-friendly practices by providing real-time, personalised interactions that educate and encourage users (Sadiq et al., 2024). As technology advances, the effectiveness of chatbots in promoting sustainability will likely increase, making them valuable tools in global environmental efforts. To effectively engage millennial customers in the luxury fashion sector, chatbots should be used to enhance the overall customer experience (Khan et al., 2021; Samala et al., 2020). For example, in retail, AI chatbots guide customers towards sustainable shopping by offering insights into the environmental impact of products, suggesting eco-friendly alternatives, and advising on responsible disposal methods (Kushwaha et al., 2021). This not only helps customers make informed choices but also encourages companies to adopt more sustainable practices. AI chatbots in corporate environments can play a key role in reducing energy consumption by automating and optimising usage (Matharaarachchi et al., 2024). They monitor patterns and make real-time adjustments, like lowering heating in empty areas or maximising natural light to reduce reliance on artificial lighting. Although these changes may seem small, they can result in substantial energy and cost savings, highlighting the importance of AI in environmental management (Alexiadis et al., 2022).

In the fashion sector, chatbots can play a pivotal role in promoting sustainability by conveying detailed information about a brand's eco-friendly practices, such as the use of sustainable materials and ethical labour practices, which resonate with millennials who prioritise ethical consumption (Chi et al., 2021; Modi & Zhao, 2021; Sadiq et al., 2024). Chatbots can offer tailored styling advice and outfit suggestions by analysing individual preferences, purchase history, and current trends. This not only meets millennials' desire for unique and customised experiences but also promotes more thoughtful and sustainable shopping habits by reducing overconsumption and waste (Del Prete, 2022). By integrating these capabilities, chatbots streamline the shopping process, enhance customer engagement, and reinforce compelling brand narratives, attracting and retaining millennial customers who value personalised, ethical, and immersive experiences (Abumalloh et al., 2023). To meet these expectations and foster long-term customer loyalty, marketers should prioritise the implementation of advanced chatbot technologies.

Lubbe and Ngoma's (2021) research highlights the importance of customer experience in the successful implementation of chatbots. While chatbots offer cost-reduction benefits, their true value lies in enhancing customer experiences (Kannan & Bernoff, 2019). Millennials, who are comfortable with new technologies, value highly the engaging and personalised experiences chatbots provide (Arnold, 2018; Bizcommunity, 2018). Chatbots can improve customer experience by offering real-time engagement, presenting next-best offers and recommendations based on AI analysis, and being accessible 24/7 (Kreutzer & Sirrenberg, 2020; Toader et al., 2020). For instance, a chatbot should be able to provide instant exclusive access to limited products to its loyal customers by giving them the new upcoming products, allowing them to pre-order before making them available to all customers. Furthermore, if a chatbot cannot answer a query immediately, it can schedule a follow-up at a convenient time for the customer.

Given millennials' dependence on technology, information must be readily available and personalised, allowing them to control their user experience (Adam et al., 2021; Arnold, 2018). Positive chatbot interactions lead to satisfied customers, who are more likely to recommend the product or service (De Haan et al., 2018; Djelassi et al., 2018). To achieve customer satisfaction, marketers should focus on personalisation and customisation of chatbot interactions. This can include adjusting the chatbot's persona, such as changing its gender, and ensuring it addresses specific customer queries effectively (Toader et al., 2020). For example, when a customer purchases a luxury fashion item, a chatbot could use sophisticated algorithms to suggest pairing the gown with limited-edition pearl earrings, adding a touch of elegance to the ensemble. Additionally, loyal customers like Emma might be offered early access to exclusive collections, enhancing their shopping experience and reinforcing brand loyalty.

Product recommendations generated by chatbots based on past searches and interactions can significantly enhance customer engagement and satisfaction. Providing multi-channel options ensures customers receive consistent service across various platforms, including websites, social media, and mobile applications (Nguyen, 2019). One effective strategy for luxury fashion chatbots to build customer loyalty is through brand storytelling. For instance, when a customer engages with the chatbot, it could share the rich history and craftsmanship behind the brand's iconic pieces. By weaving narratives about the brand's heritage, values, and the meticulous creation process of each item, the chatbot fosters a deeper emotional connection with the customer. This personalised storytelling not only enhances the shopping experience but also strengthens the customer's loyalty to the brand. By guaranteeing a seamless and consistent experience, regardless of the platform, organisations can strengthen customer loyalty and satisfaction. In conclusion, marketers should prioritise the integration of chatbots to deliver personalised, engaging, and sustainable experiences. This approach not only enhances customer satisfaction but also promotes eco-friendly practices, aligning with the values of millennial customers.

References

Åberg, J. (2017). Chatbots as a means to motivate behavior change: How to inspire pro-environmental attitude with chatbot interfaces.

Abumalloh, R. A., Nilashi, M., Ooi, K. B., Wei-Han, G., Cham, T. H., Dwivedi, Y. K., & Hughes, L. (2023). The adoption of metaverse in the retail industry and its impact on sustainable competitive advantage: Moderating impact of sustainability commitment. *Annals of Operations Research*, 1–42.

Adam, M., Wessel, M., & Benlian, A. (2021). AI-based chatbots in customer service and their effects on user compliance. *Electronic Markets, 31*(2), 427–445.

Adamopoulou, E., & Moussiades, L. (2020). Chatbots: History, technology, and applications. *Machine Learning with Applications, 2*, 100006. https://doi.org/10.1016/j.mlwa.2020.100006

Adeola, O., Ehira, D., & Ibelegbu, O. (2020). Application of digital technologies and social media to enhance customer service experience. In *Customer Service Management in Africa* (pp. 107–120). Productivity Press.

Ajzen, I., & Fishbein, M. (2000). Attitudes and the attitude-behavior relation: Reasoned and automatic processes. *European Review of Social Psychology, 11*(1), 1–33.

Akinsola, J. E. T., Adeagbo, M. A., Oladapo, K. A., Akinsehinde, S. A., & Onipede, F. O. (2022). *Artificial intelligence emergence in disruptive technology*. CRC Press.

Akrout, H., & Guercini, S. (2022). Sustainability in fashion and luxury marketing: Results, paradoxes and potentialities. *Journal of Global Fashion Marketing, 13*(2), 91–100. https://doi.org/10.1080/20932685.2021.2017320

Alduraywish, M., Unhelkar, B., Singh, S., & Prasad, M. (2021, October). Application of artificial intelligence in recommendation systems and chatbots for online stores in fast fashion industry. In *International Conference on Intelligent Vision and Computing* (pp. 558–567). Springer International Publishing.

Alexiadis, A., Veliskaki, A., Nizamis, A., Bintoudi, A. D., Zyglakis, L., Triantafyllidis, A., ... & Tzovaras, D. (2022). A smarthome conversational agent performing implicit demand-response application planning. *Integrated Computer-Aided Engineering, 29*(1), 43–61.

Amatulli, C., De Angelis, M., Costabile, M., & Guido, G. (2017). *Sustainable luxury brands: Evidence from research and implications for managers*. Springer.

Antola, L. M. O. (2017). *Motivational drivers behind second hand luxury consumption: A qualitative exploration of consumption motivations in Finland* (Bachelor's thesis). Aalto University. Available from https://core.ac.uk/reader/84756560

Appiah, D., & Watson, A. (2024). Smartphones and digital customer's journey. In *Digital transformation for fashion and luxury brands: Theory and practice*. Springer International Publishing.

Arnold, A. (2018). How chatbots feed into millennials' need for instant gratification. *Forbes*. Retrieved January 3, 2020 from https://www.forbes.com

Arrington, D. W. (2021). The luxury, social media, and e-commerce conundrum: How can luxury brands respond to the digital world and remain exclusive, aspirational, and alluring? In *In fashion: Culture, commerce, craft, and identity* (pp. 113–132). Brill.

Aslam, U. (2023). Understanding the usability of retail fashion brand chatbots: Evidence from customer expectations and experiences. *Journal of Retailing and Consumer Services, 74*, 103377.

Atkinson, S. D., & Kang, J. (2022). New luxury: Defining and evaluating emerging luxury trends through the lenses of consumption and personal values. *Journal of Product & Brand Management, 31*(3), 377–393.

Azemi, Y., & Ozuem, W. (2023). How does retargeting work for different Gen Z mobile users? *Journal of Advertising Research*, 2023-023. https://doi.org/10.2501/jar-2023-023

Batat, W., & Batat, W. (2019). How millennials and post-millennials are reshaping luxury. *The new luxury experience: Creating the ultimate customer experience*, 187–210.

Becker, L., & Jaakkola, E. (2020). Customer experience: Fundamental premises and implications for research. *Journal of the Academy of Marketing Science, 48*, 630–648. https://doi.org/10.1007/s11747-019-00718-x

Belfanti, C. M. (2023). 17 cultural heritage, intangible assets, and fashion branding. *The Routledge history of fashion and dress, 1800 to the present*, 323.

Berry, C. J. (1994). *The idea of luxury: A conceptual and historical investigation* (30th ed.). Cambridge University Press.

Bevan-Dye, A. L., Garnett, A., & De Klerk, N. (2012). Materialism, status consumption and consumer ethnocentrism amongst black generation Y students in South Africa. *African Journal of Business Management*. https://doi.org/10.5897/AJBM11.1803

Bilgihan, A., Kandampully, J., & Zhang, T. (2016). Towards a unified customer experience in online shopping environments: Antecedents and outcomes. *International Journal of Quality and Service Sciences, 8*(1), 102–119.

Bitner, M. J., Faranda, W. T., Hubbert, A. R., & Zeithaml, V. A. (1997). Customer contributions and roles in service delivery. *International Journal of Service Industry Management, 8*(3), 193–205.

Bizcommunity. (2018). *5 expectations of the African millennial consumer. CRM opinion Africa*. Bizcommunity. Retrieved January 3, 2020 from https://www.bizcommunity.africa/Article/410/458/179653.html

Boon-Itt, S. (2015). Managing self-service technology service quality to enhance e-satisfaction. *International Journal of Quality and Service Sciences, 7*(4), 373–391.

Brakus, J. (2001). *A theory of consumer experiences*. Unpublished doctoral dissertation, Columbia University, New York, NY.

Brun, A., & Castelli, C. (2013). The nature of luxury: A consumer perspective. *International Journal of Retail & Distribution Management, 41*(11/12), 823–847.

Cabigiosu, A., & Cabigiosu, A. (2020). *An overview of the luxury fashion industry*. Digitalization in the Luxury Fashion Industry: Strategic Branding for Millennial Customers, 9–31.

Cairns, H. M., Ritch, E. L., & Bereziat, C. (2022). Think eco, be eco? The tension between attitudes and behaviours of millennial fashion customers. *International Journal of Consumer Studies, 46*(4), 1262–1277. https://doi.org/10.1111/ijcs.12756

Campbell, C., Sands, S., Ferraro, C., Tsao, H. Y. J., & Mavrommatis, A. (2020). From data to action: How marketers can leverage AI. *Business Horizons, 63*(2), 227–243.

Chen, X., Xu, L., Ren, Z., Jia, F., & Yu, Y. (2023). Sustainable supply chain management in the leather industry: A systematic literature review. *International Journal of Logistics Research and Applications, 26*(12), 1663–1703.

Chi, T., Ganak, J., Summers, L., Adesanya, O., McCoy, L., Liu, H., & Tai, Y. (2021). Understanding perceived value and purchase intention toward eco-friendly athleisure apparel: Insights from US millennials. *Sustainability, 13*(14), 7946.

Chopra, A., & Bhilare, P. (2020). Future of work: An empirical study to understand expectations of the millennials from organizations. *Business Perspectives and Research, 8*(2), 272–288.

Chung, M., Ko, E., Joung, H., & Kim, S. J. (2020). Chatbot e-service and customer satisfaction regarding luxury brands. *Journal of Business Research, 117*, 587–595. https://doi.org/10.1016/j.jbusres.2018.10.004

Cuayáhuitl, H., Lee, D., Ryu, S., Cho, Y., Choi, S., Indurthi, S., & Kim, J. (2019). Ensemble-based deep reinforcement learning for chatbots. *Neurocomputing, 366*, 118–130. https://doi.org/10.1016/j.neucom.2019.08.007

Davenport, T., Guha, A., Grewal, D., & Bressgott, T. (2020). How artificial intelligence will change the future of marketing. *Journal of the Academy of Marketing Science, 48*, 24–42.

De Haan, H., Snijder, J., Van Nimwegen, C., & Beun, R. J. (2018). *Chatbot personality and customer satisfaction.* Bachelor thesis, Utrecht University, Netherlands. Available from http://research.infosupport.com/wp-content/uploads/2019/05/

De Cicco, R., Silva, S. C., & Alparone, F. R. (2020). Millennials' attitude toward chatbots: An experimental study in a social relationship perspective. *International Journal of Retail & Distribution Management, 48*(11), 1213–1233. https://doi.org/10.1108/IJRDM-12-2019-0406

De Oliveira Santini, F., Ladeira, W. J., Pinto, D. C., Herter, M. M., Sampaio, C. H., & Babin, B. J. (2020). Customer engagement in social media: A framework and meta-analysis. *Journal of the Academy of Marketing Science, 48*, 1211–1228.

Del Prete, M. (2022). Mindful sustainable consumption and sustainability chatbots in fast fashion retailing during and after the COVID-19 pandemic. *Journal of Management and Sustainability, 12*, 19.

Dhama, A., Kaur, A., Döngül, E. S., & Singh, N. (2024). *Artificial intelligence and sustainable green fashion industry.* CRC Press.

Djelassi, S., Diallo, M. F., & Zielke, S. (2018). How self-service technology experience evaluation affects waiting time and customer satisfaction? A moderated mediation model. *Decision Support Systems, 111*, 38–47.

Dobre, C., Milovan, A. M., Duțu, C., Preda, G., & Agapie, A. (2021). The common values of social media marketing and luxury brands. The millennials and Generation Z perspective. *Journal of Theoretical and Applied Electronic Commerce Research, 16*(7), 2532–2553.

Eastman, J. K., & Iyer, R. (2021). Understanding the ecologically conscious behaviors of status motivated millennials. *Journal of Consumer Marketing, 38*(5), 565–575. https://doi.org/10.1108/JCM-02-2020-3652

Eastman, J. K., Iyer, R., & Thomas, S. P. (2013). The impact of status consumption on shopping styles: An exploratory look at the millennial generation. *Marketing Management Journal, 23*(1), 57–73.

Elkington, J. (1994). Towards the sustainable corporation: Win-win-win business strategies for sustainable development. *California Management Review, 36*(2), 90–100. https://doi.org/10.2307/41165746

Elkington, J. (1998). *Cannibals with forks: The triple bottom line of 21st century business*. New Society.

Fishbein, M., & Ajzen, I. (2005). Theory-based behavior change interventions: Comments on Hobbis and Sutton. *Journal of Health Psychology, 10*(1), 27–31.

Følstad, A., & Skjuve, M. (2019, August). Chatbots for customer service: User experience and motivation. In *Proceedings of the 1st International Conference on conversational user interfaces* (pp. 1–9).

Forbes, (2023). *The luxury fashion trend taking Australia by storm*. Available from https://www.forbes.com.au/life/fashion/luxury-fashion-trends-net-a-porter/

Garcia-Torres, S., Rey-Garcia, M., Sáenz, J., & Seuring, S. (2022). Traceability and transparency for sustainable fashion-apparel supply chains. *Journal of Fashion Marketing and Management: An International Journal, 26*(2), 344–364. https://doi.org/10.1108/JFMM-07-2020-0125

Goli, M., Sahu, A. K., Bag, S., & Dhamija, P. (2023). Users' acceptance of artificial intelligence-based chatbots: An empirical study. *International Journal of Technology and Human Interaction (IJTHI), 19*(1), 1–18.

Guga, E., & Peta, E. (2023). Exploring the factors influencing entrepreneurial behavior among Albanian Millennials. *International Journal of Professional Business Review, 8*(8), e03636–e03636.

Gurzki, H., & Gurzki, H. (2020). Perspectives on luxury: An integrative model. *The Creation of the Extraordinary: Perspectives on Luxury*, 63–145.

Han, D. I. D., Melissen, F., & Haggis-Burridge, M. (2024). Immersive experience framework: A Delphi approach. *Behaviour & Information Technology, 43*(4), 623–639.

Han, Y. J., Nunes, J. C., & Drèze, X. (2010). Signaling status with luxury goods: The role of brand prominence. *Journal of Marketing, 74*(4), 15–30.

Helal, G., Ozuem, W., & Lancaster, G. (2018). Social media brand perceptions of millennials. *International Journal of Retail & Distribution Management, 46*(10), 977–998.

Hwang, G. J., & Chang, C. Y. (2023). A review of opportunities and challenges of chatbots in education. *Interactive Learning Environments, 31*(7), 4099–4112. https://doi.org/10.1080/10494820.2021.1952615

Hyun, H., Park, J., Hawkins, M. A., & Kim, D. (2022). How luxury brands build customer-based brand equity through phygital experience. *Journal of Strategic Marketing*, 1–25.

Irfan, M., Zhao, Z. Y., Rehman, A., Ozturk, I., & Li, H. (2021). Customers' intention-based influence factors of renewable energy adoption in Pakistan: A structural equation modeling approach. *Environmental Science and Pollution Research, 28*, 432–445. https://doi.org/10.1007/s11356-020-10504-w/

Jasrotia, S. S., Darda, P., & Pandey, S. (2023). Changing values of millennials and centennials towards responsible consumption and sustainable society. *Society and Business Review, 18*(2), 244–263. https://doi.org/10.1108/SBR-01-2022-0013

Javornik, A., Duffy, K., Rokka, J., Scholz, J., Nobbs, K., Motala, A., & Goldenberg, A. (2021). Strategic approaches to augmented reality deployment by luxury brands. *Journal of Business Research, 136*, 284–292. https://doi.org/10.1016/j.jbusres.2021.07.040

Johri, A., Sayal, A., Chaithra, N., Jha, J., Aggarwal, N., Pawar, D., & Gupta, A. (2024). Crafting the techno-functional blocks for metaverse—A review and research agenda. *International Journal of Information Management Data Insights, 4*(1), 100213.

Kannan, P. V., & Bernoff, J. (2019). Does your company really need a chatbot? *Harvard Business Review Digital Articles*, 2–6. Retrieved March 28, 2019, from https://hbr.org

Karaosman, H., Perry, P., Brun, A., & Morales-Alonso, G. (2020). Behind the runway: Extending sustainability in luxury fashion supply chains. *Journal of Business Research, 117*, 652–663. https://doi.org/10.1016/j.jbusres.2018.09.017

Karashchuk, O. S., Mayorova, E. A., Nikishin, A. F., & Kornilova, O. V. (2020). The method for determining time-generation range. *SAGE Open, 10*(4), 2158244020968082.

Kayton, D. (2018, September 17). Don't talk to me, talk to my chatbot. *BizCommunity*. Available from https://www.bizcommunity.com/Article/

Khan, S. A. R., Zia-ul-haq, H. M., Umar, M., & Yu, Z. (2021). Digital technology and circular economy practices: A strategy to improve organizational performance. *Business Strategy & Development, 4*(4), 482–490.

Kim, J. J., Lee, J. S., & Han, H. (2023). Tangible and intangible hotel in-room amenities in shaping customer experience and the consequences in the with-corona era. *International Journal of Contemporary Hospitality Management, 35*(2), 657–681. https://doi.org/10.1108/IJCHM-01-2022-0014

Klímová, B., & Ibna Seraj, P. M. (2023). The use of chatbots in university EFL settings: Research trends and pedagogical implications. *Frontiers in Psychology, 14*, 1131506.

Kreutzer, R. T., & Sirrenberg M. (2020). *Fields of application of artificial intelligence—Customer service, marketing and sales. In Understanding Artificial Intelligence. Management for Professionals.* Springer, Cham.

Krishnan, C., Gupta, A., Gupta, A., & Singh, G. (2022). Impact of artificial intelligence-based chatbots on customer engagement and business growth. *Deep learning for social media data analytics* (pp. 195–210). Springer International Publishing.

Kumar, A., Gupta, N., & Bapat, G. (2024). Who is making the decisions? How retail managers can use the power of ChatGPT. *Journal of Business Strategy, 45*(3), 161–169.

Kushwaha, A. K., Kumar, P., & Kar, A. K. (2021). What impacts customer experience for B2B enterprises on using AI-enabled chatbots? Insights from Big data analytics. *Industrial Marketing Management, 98*, 207–221.

Liang, Y., Ghosh, S., & Oe, H. (2017). Chinese customers' luxury value perceptions–a conceptual model. *Qualitative Market Research: An International Journal, 20*(2), 247–262.

Lim, X. J., Cheah, J. H., Ngo, L. V., Chan, K., & Ting, H. (2023). How do crazy rich Asians perceive sustainable luxury? Investigating the determinants of customers' willingness to pay a premium price. *Journal of Retailing and Consumer Services, 75*, 103502.

Ling, E. C., Tussyadiah, I., Tuomi, A., Stienmetz, J., & Ioannou, A. (2021). Factors influencing users' adoption and use of conversational agents: A systematic review. *Psychology & Marketing, 38*(7), 1031–1051. https://doi.org/10.1002/mar.21491

Lubbe, I., & Ngoma, N. (2021). Useful chatbot experience provides technological satisfaction: An emerging market perspective. *South African Journal of Information Management, 23*(1), 1–8.

Majeed, M., Owusu-Ansah, M., & Ashmond, A. A. (2021). The influence of social media on purchase intention: The mediating role of brand equity. *Cogent Business & Management, 8*(1), 1944008.

Matharaarachchi, A., Mendis, W., Randunu, K., De Silva, D., Gamage, G., Moraliyage, H., ... & Jennings, A. (2024). Optimizing generative AI chatbots for net-zero emissions energy Internet-of-things infrastructure. *Energies, 17*(8), 1935.

McKinsey. (2023). *The state of fashion 2023*. Available from https://www.mckinsey.com/~/media/mckinsey/industries/retail/our%20insights/state%20of%20fashion/2023/the-state-of-fashion-2023-holding-onto-growth-as-global-clouds-gathers-vf.pdf

Mekonnen, A. (2024). Augmented Reality (AR) in retailing: Customers' experience in luxury fashion. In *Digital transformation for fashion and luxury brands: Theory and practice*. Springer International Publishing.

Modi, D., & Zhao, L. (2021). Social media analysis of consumer opinion on apparel supply chain transparency. *Journal of Fashion Marketing and Management: An International Journal, 25*(3), 465–481.

Mohr, I., Fuxman, L., & Mahmoud, A. B. (2022). A triple-trickle theory for sustainable fashion adoption: The rise of a luxury trend. *Journal of Fashion Marketing and Management: An International Journal, 26*(4), 640–660. https://doi.org/10.1108/JFMM-03-2021-0060

Mok, A., Yu, H., & Zihayat, M. (2022). The trends of sustainability in the luxury fashion industry: A Triple Bottom Line analysis. *Journal of Global Fashion Marketing, 13*(4), 360–379. https://doi.org/10.1080/20932685.2022.2085601

Moreno, F. M., Lafuente, J. G., Carreón, F. Á., & Moreno, S. M. (2017). The characterization of the millennials and their buying behavior. *International Journal of Marketing Studies, 9*(5), 135–144.

Mosavi, S. M., Sangari, M. S., & Keramati, A. (2018). An integrative framework for customer switching behavior. *The Service Industries Journal, 38*(15–16), 1067–1094.

Muhyidin, A., Imal, I., Sutar, S., & Maswanto, M. (2024). Towards sustainable consumption: The role of knowledge, environment, and promotion for the millennial generation. *BISMA (Bisnis dan Manajemen)*, 144–166.

Murtarelli, G., Collina, C., & Romenti, S. (2023). "Hi! How can I help you today?": Investigating the quality of chatbots–millennials relationship within the fashion industry. *The TQM Journal, 35*(3), 719–733. https://doi.org/10.1108/TQM-01-2022-0010

Nath, V., & Batra, M. B. (2019). Decoding the millennial luxury consumer. *Think India Journal, 22*(4), 8558–8574.

Nawaz, I. Y. (2020). Characteristics of millennials and technology adoption in the digital age. In *Handbook of Research on Innovations in Technology and Marketing for the Connected Consumer* (pp. 241–262). IGI Global.

Nguyen, D. (2019). *Influences of multi-channel distribution related to consumer buying behavior and profits growth rate*. Vaasan Ammattikorkeakoulu University of Applied Sciences.

Nguyen, M., Casper Ferm, L. E., Quach, S., Pontes, N., & Thaichon, P. (2023). Chatbots in frontline services and customer experience: An anthropomorphism perspective. *Psychology & Marketing, 40*(11), 2201–2225. https://doi.org/10.1002/mar.21882

Nueno, J. L., & Quelch, J. A. (1998). The mass marketing of luxury. *Business Horizons, 41*(6), 61–68.

Nwankwo, S., Hamelin, N., & Khaled, M. (2014). Consumer values, motivation and purchase intention for luxury goods. *Journal of Retailing and Consumer Services, 21*, 735–744. https://doi.org/10.1016/j.jretconser.2014.05.003

Ozuem, W., Ranfagni, S., Willis, M., Salvietti, G., & Howell, K. (2024). Exploring the relationship between chatbots, service failure recovery and customer loyalty: A frustration–aggression perspective. *Psychology and Marketing*. https://doi.org/10.1002/mar.22051

Ozuem, W., Ranfagni, S., & Willis, M. (2024a). *Digital transformation for fashion and luxury brands*. Springer.

Ozuem, W., Willis, M., Howell, K., Lancaster, G., & Ng, R. (2021). Determinants of online brand communities' and millennials' characteristics: A social influence perspective. *Psychology & Marketing, 38*(5), 794–818.

Pattuglia, S., & Mingione, M. (2017). Towards a new understanding of brand authenticity: Seeing through the lens of Millennials. *Sinergie Italian Journal of Management, 35*(May–Aug), 35–55.

Peng, Z., Kim, T., & Ma, X. (2019). GremoBot: Exploring emotion regulation in group chat. *Conference Companion Publication of the 2019 on Computer Supported Cooperative Work and Social Computing*, 335–340.

Rahman, M. S., Bag, S., Hossain, M. A., Fattah, F. A. M. A., Gani, M. O., & Rana, N. P. (2023). The new wave of AI-powered luxury brands online shopping experience: The role of digital multisensory cues and customers' engagement. *Journal of Retailing and Consumer Services, 72*, 103273. https://doi.org/10.1016/j.jretconser.2023.103273

Rawlins, C., Indvik, J., & Johnson, P. R. (2008). Understanding the new generation: What the Millennial cohort absolutely, positively must have at work. *Journal of Organisational Culture, Communications and Conflict, 12*(2), 1.

Richad, R., Vivensius, V., Sfenrianto, S., & Kaburuan, E. R. (2019). Analysis of factors influencing millennial's technology acceptance of chatbot in the banking industry in Indonesia. *International Journal of Civil Engineering and Technology, 10*(4), 1270–1281.

Rodrigues, C., & Rodrigues, P. (2019). Brand love matters to Millennials: The relevance of mystery, sensuality and intimacy to neo-luxury brands. *Journal of Product & Brand Management, 28*(7), 830–848.

Rosa, Á. A. D. (2020). *Experiences over possessions: Millennials and the experience economy*. Master's thesis. Marketing, Operations and General Management, ISCTE Business School, Lisbon.

Rosado-Pinto, F., & Loureiro, S. M. C. (2020). The growing complexity of customer engagement: A systematic review. *EuroMed Journal of Business, 15*(2), 167–203. https://doi.org/10.1108/EMJB-10-2019-0126

Sadiq, M. W., Akhtar, M. W., Huo, C., & Zulfiqar, S. (2024). ChatGPT-powered chatbot as a green evangelist: An innovative path toward sustainable consumerism in E-commerce. *The Service Industries Journal, 44*(3–4), 173–217. https://doi.org/10.1080/02642069.2023.2278463

Samala, N., & Katkam, B. S. (2020). Fashion brands are engaging the millennials: A moderated-mediation model of customer-brand engagement, participation, and involvement. *Young Consumers, 21*(2), 233–253.

Sarkar, J. G., Sarkar, A., & Sreejesh, S. (2023). Developing responsible consumption behaviours through social media platforms: Sustainable brand practices as message cues. *Information Technology & People, 36*(2), 532–563. https://doi.org/10.1108/ITP-01-2021-0044

Schiffman, L. G., & Wisenblit, J. (2015). *Consumer Behavior.* 11th Edition Global Edition.

Schwab, C. (2015, December 12). The fourth industrial revolution. *Foreign Affairs*. [Online]. Retrieved January 3, 2020 from, https://www.foreignaffairs.com/articles/2015-12-12/fourth-industrial-revolution

Shahid Iqbal, M., Ul Hassan, M., & Habibah, U. (2018). Impact of self-service technology (SST) service quality on customer loyalty and behavioral intention: The mediating role of customer satisfaction. *Cogent Business & Management, 5*(1), 1.

Singh, S. (2023). *Fashion marketing*. LWRN Studio.
Slaper, T. F., & Hall, T. J. (2011). The triple bottom line: What is it and how does it work. *Indiana Business Review, 86*(1), 4–8. http://www.ibrc.indiana.edu/ibr/2011/spring/pdfs/article2.pdf
Slaton, K., & Hurst, J. L. (2023). What does luxury really mean to millennial customers? *International Journal of Consumer Studies, 47*(2), 736–750.
Statista. (2023a). *Share of customers who follow luxury brands on social media worldwide as of October 2021, by generation.* Available from https://www-statista-com.eu1.proxy.openathens.net/statistics/1359716/customers-following-luxury-brands-on-social-media-worldwide-by-generation/
Statista. (2023b, December 20). *Millennials in the UK—Statistics & facts.* Published by D. Clark. Available from https://www.statista.com/topics/11102/millennials-in-the-uk/#topicOverview
Statista. (2024a, March 6). *Millennials statistics and facts.* Statista. Statista Research Department. Available from https://www.statista.com/topics/2705/millennials-in-the-us/
Statista. (2024b, February 15). *U.S. Gen Z & millennials: consumer goods and shopping behaviour - statistics & facts.* D. Tighe. Available from https://www.statista.com/topics/1780/us-millennials-shopping-behavior/
Stępień, B., Lima, A. P., & Hinner, M. (2018). Are millennials a global cohort? Evidence from the luxury goods sector. *Journal of Intercultural Management, 10*(2), 139–158.
Sulistyawati, D., Santosa, I., Wahjudi, D., & Junaidy, D. W. (2024). Millennial experience through the utilization of feature technology in coffee shop interior design. *Environment and Social Psychology, 9*(5).
Toader, D. C., Boca, G., Toader, R., Măcelaru, M., Toader, C., Ighian, D., & Rădulescu, A. T. (2020). The effect of social presence and chatbot errors on trust. *Sustainability, 12*(1), 256.
Todeschini, B. V., Cortimiglia, M. N., & De Medeiros, J. F. (2020). Collaboration practices in the fashion industry: Environmentally sustainable innovations in the value chain. *Environmental Science & Policy, 106*, 1–11. https://doi.org/10.1016/j.envsci.2020.01.003
Tran, O. T., & Luong, T. C. (2020). Understanding what the users say in chatbots: A case study for the Vietnamese language. *Engineering Applications of Artificial Intelligence, 87*, 103322. https://doi.org/10.1016/j.engappai.2019.103322
Turunen, L. L. M., Cervellon, M. C., & Carey, L. D. (2020). Selling second-hand luxury: Empowerment and enactment of social roles. *Journal*

of Business Research, 116, 474–481. https://doi.org/10.1016/j.jbusres.2019.11.059

Turunen, L. L. M., & Leipämaa-Leskinen, H. (2015). Pre-loved luxury: Identifying the meanings of second hand luxury possessions. *Journal of Product & Brand Management, 24*(1), 57–65. https://doi.org/10.1108/JPBM-05-2014-0603

Vaccaro, K., Agarwalla, T., Shivakumar, S., & Kumar, R. (2018, April). Designing the future of personal fashion. In *Proceedings of the 2018 CHI Conference on Human Factors in Computing Systems* (pp. 1–11).

Van de Sand, F., Frison, A. K., Zotz, P., Riener, A., & Holl, K. (2020). The battle for attention. In Van de Sand et al., *User experience is brand experience: The psychology behind successful digital products and services* (pp. 1–16). Springer, Cham.

Velasco, J. C. (2020). Millennials as digital natives: Examining the social media activities of the Philippine Y-generation. *Pertanika Journal of Social Sciences and Humanities, 28*(3), 1939–1957.

Williams, K. C., & Page, R. A. (2011). Marketing to the generations. *Journal of Behavioral Studies in Business, 3*(1), 37–53.

Wong, K. Y. J., & Park, S. Y. (2023). That's so Gucci: A comparison of cultural values and the influence of perceived values on luxury goods attitudes and purchase intention among Korean and Dutch millennials. *Asian Business & Management, 22*(5), 1804–1829.

Zeng, N., Vignali, G., & Ryding, D. (2023). Understanding the application of AI-enabled chatbots in luxury fashion retailing. In *The garment economy: Understanding history, developing business models, and leveraging digital technologies.* Springer International Publishing.

Zhu, W., & Morosan, C. (2014). An empirical examination of guests' adoption of interactive mobile technologies in hotels: Revisiting cognitive absorption, playfulness, and security. *Journal of Hospitality and Tourism Technology, 5*(1), 78–94.

21

Sustainability than Digitalization: Prato and the Global Fashion Supply Chain

Daniela Toccafondi

Introduction

The fashion industry forms part of a larger social and cultural phenomenon known as the "fashion system", a concept that embraces not only the business of fashion but also the art and craft of fashion, and not only production but also consumption (Major & Steele, 2024). Sustainability is a dynamic and continuous process; it is not a steady state. In the fashion system, an item is considered sustainable not only because it is made with sustainable raw materials but also because it is the result of a sustainable process in compliance with good working conditions. The three spheres of the sustainability framework include not only the environmental sphere but also economic and social spheres (O'Connor, 2006). Sustainability begins at the outset of the supply chain and plays a significant role in the initial phases. It means respect for production processes, working conditions, workers'

D. Toccafondi (✉)
University of Florence, Firenze, Italy
e-mail: daniela.toccafondi@unifi.it

W. Ozuem et al. (eds.), *Sustainable Digital Marketing for Fashion and Luxury Brands*,
https://doi.org/10.1007/978-3-031-82467-8_21

rights, and attention to poverty and those in need. Moreover, sustainable growth is desirable (ILO, 2015, p. 4) because it supports more balanced growth, promotes greater levels of innovation, and tackles environmental pollution: "Managed well, transitions to environmentally and socially sustainable economies can become a strong driver of job creation, job upgrading, social justice, and poverty eradication". Combatting global warming involves far more than just adhering to environmental compliance.

The relationship between luxury and sustainability is an ongoing complex issue. Luxury and sustainability might seem incompatible. Luxury is based on the abundance and quality of raw materials regardless of cost, whereas sustainability is based on the limited use of materials and process efficiency. Luxury fashion is often associated with excess, high-end materials, and seasonal trends. These factors raise environmental concerns because of pollution from dyes and chemicals, water usage in production, and textile waste. "Luxury products are sophisticated, expensive, have a reasonably high quality, and claim a very strong and attractive brand name" (Chevalier & Gutsatz, 2012). A study suggests that young generations and their perception of luxury and sustainability is at a nascent stage (Ozuem et al., 2024; Pencarelli et al., 2019), but there is strong evidence that young people look for sustainable items.

People's increased interest in spirituality, especially the younger generation, is an extremely intriguing phenomenon. Many surveys on consumer orientations report that people seek satisfaction less and less in material things and more and more in life experiences. This search for meaning in life is playing a central role in reshaping corporate culture and global communication in many companies in the fashion system. Companies must provide indications of their performance not only from an economic point of view but also from a "humanistic" one. Some (Re, 2017) suggest that we are dealing with a *new Humanism* that considers companies responsible for social welfare and environmental sustainability in addition to economic growth. The sustainable wardrobe of 2030 will be greener and more responsible if everyone can take care of their garments and accessories: an increasingly sustainable choice is to pay careful attention to laundry, to minimize the environmental impact of clothes during washing, and to prevent the dispersal of microplastics into seas and oceans. Consumers seem ready and willing, but what about clothing manufacturers? The situation is very complex and differs greatly between the lower segments of the market (fast fashion) and the top-of-the-range ones, but, in many ways, the outcome appears to be the same.

If fashion brands were transparent about their policies and the impacts of their products, then consumers could make more informed purchasing decisions. Fashion Revolution published the "Fashion Transparency Index 2017", which reviewed and ranked a 100 of the biggest global fashion brands according to how much information they disclosed about their suppliers, supply chain policies and practices, and social and environmental impacts. The Index revealed that most fast fashion supply chains were not transparent, but even the supply chains of large luxury brands did not reveal the names of all their suppliers (Datheridge, 2017; Ozuem et al., 2023a). This makes little sense because many luxury brand supply chains are grouped under the same ownership (Kering, LVMH, Gucci). The time has come for greater transparency in the fashion system. In today's society, it is important to introduce a *digital product passport*, which informs the consumer about all steps of the supply chain, in order to be sure that everything has been created in full compliance with environmental regulations.

A European citizen consumes on average almost 26 kg of textile products per year and disposes of approximately 11 kg of them. The growth of fast fashion has played a fundamental role in increasing consumption, but, more importantly, it has disproportionately increased the amount of unsold clothing to be disposed of (Thomas, 2019). The majority (87%) of used clothing is incinerated or brought to landfills (Thomas, 2019). In 2019, over 12.6 million tonnes of textile waste were produced and sent to incinerators/landfills or were exported (European Parliament, 2020). New strategies to tackle this issue include campaigns to raise awareness among consumers; these campaigns encourage consumers to buy less and they promote new consumption patterns: clothing rental, clothes designed and made in such a way to allow reuse, easier recycling (circular fashion), and high-quality items (sustainable fashion). The aim is to guide consumer behaviours towards more sustainable options.

However, given the massive overproduction, this approach seems insufficient. Something could change with the introduction by producers, and with the acceptance of consumers, of the concept of "circular economy". According to the Ellen MacArthur Foundation (n.d., para. 1), one of the world's leading institutes in this field: "In a circular economy, products and materials are kept in circulation through processes like maintenance, reuse, refurbishment, remanufacture, recycling, and composting".

In the last century, the world population has quadrupled and resource consumption has increased 16-fold (Girardet, 2023). In consideration of the fact that only 22% of post-consumer textiles are reused, the European Commission is working on a waste framework directive that includes textile products. In March 2020 the European Commission proposed the first package of measures to accelerate the transition towards a circular economy, as announced in the EU Action Plan for a Circular Economy. This is in line with the objective of climate neutrality by 2050. Proposals include boosting sustainable products, empowering consumers towards a green transition, and reviewing sustainable textile materials' regulation and strategy. The textile district of Prato, Italy, is the place where a circular economy has been part of everyday life for over a hundred years. Before looking at Prato specifically, it is essential to provide an overview of the European fashion industry.

The European Textile and Fashion Industry

Textile clothing is considered one of the most polluting economic sectors due to the intense use of soil to grow natural fibres and for cattle farming, the enormous quantity of water used in production processes, and the use of dyes and chemical substances in some phases of the production chain. An estimated 20% of the world's drinking water pollution is attributed to the textile industry. To manufacture one cotton t-shirt 2700 L of water are needed. According to Euratex (2024), in 2020, an average of 400 square metres of land, 9 L of water, and 391 kg of raw materials were needed to supply every single EU citizen with shoes and clothes. Many fashion brands have now introduced a lot of sustainable raw materials in their collections, such as organic cotton and recycled silk, vegetable leather, and some fibres obtained from recycled substances. Furthermore, they are heavily investing in research to reduce waste and to optimize processes; they seek to use advanced technologies to improve precision and reduce errors, and to reduce water and energy consumption.

The fashion system is characterized by an enormous variety of items with a short life cycle, frequent releases of collections, and apparel made in fragmented supply chains (Ozuem et al 2021). From small businesses and independent designers to the most sophisticated luxury brands' chains, different suppliers or sub-suppliers are involved in a complex international supply chain, which makes it difficult to understand how the principles of ethical and environmental sustainability are respected throughout this supply chain. Luxury brands are responding by using organic materials, recycled fabrics, and low-impact dyes. In addition, some are focusing on timeless designs and high-quality garments that are meant to last. But what about their subcontractors?

In Europe, there are 197,000 companies engaged in the textile and fashion sector. These companies employ 1.3 million workers and are mostly unbranded; they mainly specialize in one or two phases of the supply chain. The bulk of this industry is small, family-owned enterprises, with decades of tradition and craftsmanship. But change is coming. The European strategy for sustainable and circular textiles intends to create a coherent framework for the green transition of the ecosystem. For this to happen, the sector must soon apply technological advances to transform its labour-intensive practices to increasingly capital-intensive practices; this would reflect a trend that emerged at the beginning of the twenty-first century (Ozuem & Willis, 2022; Sabel, 2004), but which has greatly accelerated in the post-COVID-19 years when "the return to normalcy was not snapping back to old ways of working" (Allen, 2021). Nowadays, the introduction of new information and communications technologies requires companies to adjust their internal systems and in-service activities. People are talking about a new manufacturing renaissance and changes are expected in all productive models. In a short time, 16 pieces of legislation are waiting to reshape the regulatory context for the European textile and fashion industry. Recent skills trends and occupational profile developments are moving towards medium and higher-skilled employees.

The European textile, clothing, leather, and footwear (TCLF) industries produce added value and create opportunities for investment and innovation. According to estimated data for 2023, the overall turnover amounted to €170 billion, and 75% of the total value of output came from manufacturing (clothing, furnishing, home textiles, and technical textiles), which is the final part of the supply chain (Euratex, 2024). Although the value of pre-manufacturing (i.e. production and trade of fibres, yarn production, finishing, and dyeing phase) seems small when considering the sector's overall turnover, it is far more significant when it comes to sustainability.

The main European producers are concentrated in Germany, Spain, France, Italy, and Portugal with over 40% of EU apparel produced in Italy (European Parliament on Eurostat data). Italy plays a dominant role in the European scene, both in clothing consumption and manufacturing production. By the end of the Second World War, industrialization in Italy was characterized by the presence of a high number of small and medium-sized enterprises mainly specialized in particular activities of a localized industry. According to Giacomo Becattini (2001), it was the age of the Italian industrial districts and the age of the Italian "economic miracle". The Italian industrial districts were not dominated by big firms or companies with state participation, but comprised interrelated small companies that specialized in each phase of the entire supply chain; these industrial districts were mainly localized in a territory with a high level of manufacturing specialization. The rise of the industrial districts with a myriad of autonomous manufacturing units reshaped industry all over Italy (Becattini, 2015) and was the beginning of the affirmation of made-in-Italy products all over the world.

The Textile District of Prato

The textile district of Prato is currently one of the most important textile districts in Europe in terms of the number of companies involved and the number of people employed. Before the Second World War, Prato primarily produced wool blankets, but after the "economic miracle" companies specialized in fabrics for apparel and fancy yarns for knitwear;

Prato increasingly focused on high-quality productions and the high-end market segment. Around 1950, Prato manufacturers abandoned the formula of vertical integration within the firm and moved towards a model of "open team" of specialized firms. After that period, despite an increasingly turbulent world market, textiles continued to be the most relevant sector of the area; companies improved the quality and the range of products, they looked for a niche market, and they expanded their product portfolio from wool to include cotton, linen, silk, and other fabrics dedicated to the spring/summer season.

Due to profound changes in the international markets during the 1980s, a lot of medium-sized corporations emerged in Prato and the rest of Italy. These were characterized by a high level of internationalization and an ability to dominate the typical made-in-Italy sectors in world markets. The origins of these medium-sized corporations can often be found in the traditional production organization of the districts based upon networks and subcontracting. Linked to the world of the districts, these pocket multinational enterprises showed a considerable degree of similarity and continuity with the diffused model of small entrepreneurship (Colli, 2002; Coltorti, 2006, 2009, 2011, 2018). It is interesting to note that small and medium-sized businesses in Prato formed both official and informal groups, but the revival of vertical phase integration ran into several obstacles. Today, all the major international fashion brands buy items from Prato: fancy yarns, fabrics, and items for the higher level of the market. It seems clear, therefore, that to guarantee the levels of sustainability promised to the consumer at increased prices, these companies must control all processing within the production chain very carefully, even those carried out under subcontract.

The TCLF industries are an important artery of the Italian manufacturing industry as far as national employment is concerned. They are marked by a long and ancient tradition that in recent years has come up against the need to acquire know-how on the use of the new technologies that have been introduced in these sectors. Central Italy accounts for more than one-third of TCLF employment; Tuscany represents 23.1% of all TCLF national employment (Skill4smart, 2022). In other words, almost a quarter of the entire Italian labour force in the TCLF sector is in

Tuscany. Prato is a historic textile hub known for its quality and craftsmanship and a centuries-old tradition of repurposing wool from rags, scraps of packaging, and leftover clothing. Interestingly, Prato can be a valuable partner in sustainable luxury fashion for:

Innovation—Prato is a centre for textile research and development. Many companies are pioneering sustainable practices like using recycled cashmere or innovative dyeing techniques that reduce water consumption.

Tradition and transparency—Prato's small and medium-sized businesses often have close relationships with their suppliers. This allows for greater transparency in the supply chain, which is a key factor for sustainable production. According to the new European requirements, it is time to adopt common "standard reporting and measurement" to make communication even more effective and information more transparent outside the district and among consumers.

Flexibility and customization—Prato's manufacturers are known for their adaptability. Luxury brands can collaborate with them to create unique, sustainable materials that meet their specific design needs. The most striking feature of many of Prato's companies is that they know how to process reclaimed raw materials by reviving a centuries-old tradition (Toccafondi, 2011). Prato companies were implementing a circular economy when the concept of circular economy was not yet well understood by the market. A circular economy is a crucial goal that needs to be accomplished soon because, despite recent improvements, the textile and fashion industry has never valued this ability and has not effectively communicated it to the consumer.

Public and Private Sector Collaboration in a Circular Economy

In recent years, Europe has shown an unprecedented commitment to the 2030 Agenda for Sustainable Development with a special focus on the Green Deal, social rights, and digital transition. Prato has a well-established tradition of respecting environmental and ethical issues with great expertise in a circular economy and the reuse of materials from the fashion world (Bettizza, 2020). More than a matter of process, it is a matter of culture and mental attitudes of the entire community. The same can be said for the great attention paid to the preservation of the ecosystem and the living and working environment. With the enactment of a law for the protection of water resources (Merli Law No. 319 of May 10, 1976), which regulated wastewater, Prato equipped itself with a sewage treatment plant. Gida Spa was established in 1981 to provide the citizens and companies of Prato with environmental services in the fields of wastewater and liquid waste (Gida Spa—https://www.gida-spa.it). Gida Spa is a public–private company that has three partners: Municipality of Prato (46.92% of total shares), the Association of Local Industries (45.08%), and the company that manages the garbage services (8%). Of course, some of the young people who extol the conscious processing of water in manufacturing were not even born. Today, Gida Spa is more prepared than ever to accept the new challenges through research and application of innovative technologies with low energy consumption: developing recycling processes of wastewater through an industrial aqueduct, enhancing the platform aimed at disposing of liquid waste, recovering the energy potential of the sludge resulting from water depuration, and finally active collaboration in the construction of a separate sewer for industrial wastewater (Gida Spa—https://www.gida-spa.it). Together with other organizations, mostly university institutes, most notably the University of Florence, the corporation has demonstrated an impressive commitment to research, study, and experimentation. This example of good practice represents concrete evidence of how important issues are addressed in the Prato district through concerted private–public actions (in this case trade associations with help from local institutions), as companies are generally too small in size to address issues independently. It is quite clear that in a situation like this, public institutions, private companies, and local citizens play their part to achieve common goals.

In dealing with issues related to the territory's competitiveness, the Prato district has traditionally relied on cooperation between public institutions and private companies. This collaborative approach has been particularly effective in addressing major topics. However, paradoxically, in the case of sustainability, local companies are all working independently rather than in concert. This situation highlights a significant departure from the district's usual method of cooperation. Instead of leveraging the collective strength and shared resources of a coordinated effort, businesses in Prato are pursuing sustainability initiatives on their own. This independent approach could lead to a variety of challenges, such as duplication of effort, inconsistent standards, and missed opportunities for innovation and cost savings that often arise from collaboration. The shift towards individual action on sustainability issues may be due to several factors. These could include differing priorities and capabilities among companies, the lack of a unified framework or incentives for collaboration in this area, or perhaps a competitive mindset where businesses see sustainability as a means to differentiate themselves in the market.

To interpret the district's disposition for sustainability in a more modern way, and to maintain the value of cooperation, stakeholders in Prato might consider the following steps:

1. **Maintain a permanent sustainability task force**—a dedicated group involving representatives from key public institutions and private companies to coordinate sustainability efforts.
2. **Develop a shared vision and goals**—formulate a common sustainability agenda that aligns with the district's economic and environmental objectives to ensure that all parties work towards the same targets.
3. **Facilitate knowledge sharing**—organize regular forums, workshops, and networking events where companies can share best practices, technological innovations, and lessons learned in their sustainability journeys.
4. **Incentivize collaboration**—introduce incentives for collaborative projects, such as grants, tax breaks, or recognition awards for joint sustainability initiatives.
5. **Implement standardized metrics**—develop and adopt common sustainability metrics and standards reporting to ensure consistency and enable benchmarking across the district.

To reintroduce cooperation in terms of sustainability, Prato must first initiate a common communication strategy that conveys the area's true vocation. Numerous efforts have already been made by the Municipality of Prato to foster aggregated communication through initiatives aimed at promoting environmental respect and a circular economy. Examples include the "Città di Prato" website, the Recò Circular Economy Festival in 2019 and 2020, and, more recently, the "Prato Circular City" project, an integrated strategy that involves, among other things, Prato's membership in the European network of circular cities. In addition to strengthening the image of Prato as a circular city, a permanent working group with local stakeholders has been set up to build circular governance. The topics covered concern four different lines of intervention:

- Textile district and clothing,
- Management of urban resources,
- Circular consumption, and
- Sustainable urban agricultural systems.

Since 2016, Prato has also represented Italy in the EU Urban Agenda on Circular Economy. Additionally, Prato, along with Florence in Tuscany, has been selected by the European Commission to be one of the 100 climate-neutral smart cities by 2030. There are only nine of these in Italy. According to ambitious goals inspired by the Green Deal, these cities are committed to reducing emissions by 55% by 2030 in order to achieve climate neutrality.

Recycling Second-Hand Garments

In Prato, there is a centuries-old tradition of using natural fibres in the production process and of reusing recycled carded mechanical wool as raw material for the textile industry. Every year, tens of thousands of clothes pass through the province of Prato. These garments are destined for the recycling stage. Once the first selection phase is over, there is a sorting of the fabrics, which is currently carried out by the touch of skilled workers. From 1850 to the present day, a regenerated wool supply chain has been possible thanks to the extraordinary skills of capable and irreplaceable professional figures, the *cenciaioli* (rag merchants). A rag man's job is hard to describe and is the result of great tactile experience. A rag man can identify the composition of a second-hand garment just by touching it. There are no schools that teach it, only long experience. However, in the next few years sophisticated machinery, with new infrared technology equipment, will sort second-hand garments according to the type of material, colour, and weight. This will be taken care of by Next Technology Tecnotessile, which is a specialized research centre that has been in the area since 1972. Next Technology Tecnotessile is a public–private organization. It works to improve the technological innovation and competitiveness of Prato's companies and it is registered as a research laboratory by Italy's Ministry of University and Research (Tecnotessile—https://www.tecnotex.it).

Those clothes that have passed the selection process will become so-called *new used clothes* or they will be used in the production cycle of carded fabrics and regenerated yarns for the textile industry, garments, and knitwear. Moreover, Italian literature has dealt with this "Prato matter". It can be found in the writings of the Italian writer Curzio Malaparte, who lived and studied in Prato. In 1956, when most people were not familiar with the concept of circular economy, he wrote, "All the history of Italy and Europe ends in Prato: all in rags!" (Malaparte, 1956). One wonders why, with this established tradition, there has not been a communication campaign to highlight the ways Prato's companies work. Before environmental awareness emerged in the European Community, companies in Prato felt uncomfortable about not using pure virgin wool in their production processes; consumers did not appreciate products made from recycled raw materials because they considered them to be of poorer quality. These are the factors that have prevented more people from learning about Prato's extraordinary professionalism and knowledge.

It is quite clear that sustainability is not a real problem for companies in the Prato district that boast long-standing traditions on mechanical production processes that reuse natural fibres. In the last ten years, it has not even become a communication problem. Prato today is proud of consolidated behaviour and good practices in line with the objectives of the European agenda.

In recent years, some research, including research carried out at Tecnotessile, is introducing innovative machinery designed to control volumes of used clothing and textile waste. This is the biggest project and, within a few years, it will help consolidate the role of the Prato district as a technological and operational hub for textile recycling at the European level (Prato Circular City—https://www.pratocircularcity.it). The project leader is Alia Spa Environmental Services, which currently collects and separates garbage for households and businesses in Tuscany. As usual in many districts, private entities (the industrial and artisan associations of the enterprises) and public institutions (Municipality) will be present in the consortium. Next Technology Tecnotessile is being entrusted with the scientific supervision and consulting of the project. An investment of about €20 million, including €3.5 million from National Recovery and Resilience Plan funds, is planned. The plant is to be built by December 2026. Through this project, people are trying to apply traditional talents to a working methodology that takes advantage of the newest technological advancements. The quantities that are expected to feed the processing (about 34,000 tonnes each year of used clothing and textile waste) go far beyond the needs of local industry, and should stimulate a very large inbound and outbound trade that needs consistent regulations in every country. In this case, technology is radically changing production processes and, in general, it will affect the entire global trade. Many vendors in Prato are sceptical about the machine's capacity to effectively separate items; while it may be necessary to combine certain processing with human intervention, the primary issue is instigating a cultural shift among numerous operators.

Sustainability for the Future: Digitalizing the Supply Chain and Certification

Working together, luxury fashion brands and the Prato textile district can redefine the luxury of the future. Sustainable practices do not mean sacrificing design; on the contrary, they call for more commitment to eco-design that can consider the garment's use after consumption. Sustainable practices can also improve a brand's image and attract the many consumers who claim to be environmentally conscious. The luxury industry has reached $1.5 trillion worldwide in 2023 (D'Arpizio et al., 2024). It is estimated that by 2025, Gen X and Gen Z will represent 78% of the luxury market. To gain their favour, many brands are restructuring their sales strategies and opening up to collaborations and cross-fertilization, such as Gucci + Balenciaga or Tiffany + Supreme for sportswear (DigIt Export. Il portale per l'export digitale—https://www.digitexport.promositalia.camcom.it).

Although Prato's manufacturers appear to have embraced the principles of sustainability and the circular economy (Bernardini, 2023), there is still more work to be done to inform customers and consumers about the expertise and technology required; this will also enable complete transparency (Gambi, 2024). Along the value chain, the bargaining power of international fashion brands greatly exceeds the power of the micro-enterprises in the industrial districts. Upstream companies are too weak, dispersed, and fragmented in their relations with their customers. In Europe, there is a clear trend to demand sustainability efforts by manufacturing companies, such as saving water, saving energy, and limiting the use of chemical substances in processes. These are supportable and desirable orientations, but measuring production values objectively requires a great deal of ability. It is not easy to switch from an emotional approach to a rational one. A notable attempt is the REMOkey project, which was set up a few years ago to calculate, communicate, and give visibility to the benefits of using recycled materials in clothing (REMO—https://www.remokey.com).

There is a great debate in Prato on the strategies single companies can use to focus on sustainability efforts. One interesting example is a network of companies that repurpose deadstock merchandize, particularly in the context of bioconstruction (Wetex Srl—https://www.wetex.it). To effectively manage and govern sustainable practices, there is a need to increase investments in digitalizing processes to handle information flow in real time; this may represent the only serious problem for the textile district of Prato. Digitalizing processes can be challenging for smaller companies that may lack resources for substantial investments in this area. Given the urgency of knowledge transfers, many entrepreneurs are asking institutions to provide incentives to avoid limiting or delaying the necessary process of change. Companies are not yet fully addressing the situation head-on, even though most entrepreneurs have realized the need to take action very soon. These decisions need to be made swiftly if the entire supply chain is to remain competitive. If the upstream phases remain sluggish, it will be difficult for fashion brands to boast transparency of information to consumers. Each phase in the supply chain has its dignity, and the upstream phases bear greater responsibility because they are more involved in the manufacturing process. While waiting to promote urgent and significant investments in digitalization, companies are protecting themselves from criticism by resorting to certifications that attest to their respect for environmental and ethical sustainability in production processes.

Fashion brands buy products and services from small companies, but, at the same time, they demand the signing of very detailed sales specifications. Activating a business relationship, or maintaining it, requires long and difficult bureaucratic procedures, which require enormous effort from small companies that notoriously rely on the work of a few employees. In addition, sustainability values could be distorted by the introduction of fibres derived from a second raw material made from clothes produced many years ago when certain restrictions (especially chemical ones) were not shared; this could cause fluctuations outside the established parameters and/or specifications. Europe could give Prato's mechanical wool producers a distinction from other generically understood supply chains because of their all-natural processes and unconditional approach to the canons of the circular economy. This desire for many local producers has never been seriously considered. In May 2024, an association that includes approximately a hundred local companies launched a new standardized information document about every product they produce. The Municipality of Prato has committed to presenting this project at the European level and has confirmed its participation in it (the "Cardato Riciclato Pratese"—www.cardatoriciclatopratese.it). Many could complain that Prato producers demand asymmetrical market conditions. In this case, it could be true. It depends on the peculiarity of the production process of reusing rags and seeking natural colours without the need for a dyeing stage, thus leveraging a circular economy. Prato's companies have been leaders in this production process for decades.

To clarify such confusion, sustainability certifications have become more and more important. They have the merit of enhancing the value of the many companies that want to move towards absolute transparency. Unfortunately, it has become difficult to find one's way around the many textile and fashion certifications for the consumer as well as the companies. The most important is Life Cycle Assessment: a systematic methodology that evaluates the environmental footprint of a product throughout its entire life cycle. Furthermore, we have OEKO-TEX®, ISO 14001, Eu Ecolabel, Cradle to Cradle, and so on. Each customer demands different specific certifications and the cost of obtaining them is very high. Perhaps within the fashion system, there is space for new professionals: young digital natives who can assist companies in finding their way through the jungle of certifications. Moreover, there are opportunities within the district for new professional consultancy roles to handle the bureaucratic practices of sustainability certification for many small companies. These companies often struggle to provide guarantees to customers due to their low number of employees and the challenges they face in providing detailed, timely, and calibrated information, particularly regarding the district's business model based on subcontracting. Regarding ethical sustainability, the Prato district finds itself in a paradoxical situation. Inside the industrial districts, and Prato in particular, there has always been a system of workers' compensation that is higher than in other places. Practical skills learnt on the job are highly valued. Working conditions under special agreements are often better than the national labour contract (Becattini, 2002).

In this particular *industrial atmosphere* with a real network of people and companies, with a real exchange of experiences and a *special production environment*, Giacomo Becattini launched the hypothesis that we can speak of a *production chorality* based not so much on the technical, spatial, and cultural proximity of enterprises, but on a cultural homogeneity of families (Becattini, 2015). The Chinese-owned companies make clothes for fast fashion, while the others produce yarns and fabrics for the high-level end of the market (*The Economist*, 2022; Toccafondi,

2011). For the sake of transparency, it is therefore necessary to have more certifications. In Prato there are not yet many companies that apply for ethical certifications (the most important are: Fairtrade, Fair Wear Foundation, Get it Fair); some companies are much more inclined to use a certification that attests to full compliance with animal welfare standards (such as Responsible Wool Standard, Responsible Mohair Standard). From the perspective of area communication, it draws the attention of newspapers and television to specific and episodic events that risk damaging the overall image of the area, ignoring the predominance of good practices and positive intentions. It is quite clear that there is a deep connection between digitalization and sustainability. It is evident that in Prato sustainability is a point of strength for most local enterprises. The same cannot be said about digitalization of processes: some companies are at early stages of digitalization, whereas others have adopted digitalization. The volume of information to be monitored in real time is such that the typical organizational model of the industrial districts is losing the flexibility that characterized it since the Second World War.

Larger and more structured companies seem aware of the urgency of this new digital transformation, which can also account for the sustainability efforts undertaken by the companies. Smaller subcontracting companies, on the other hand, are quite reluctant to introduce major changes. The reason for this may be that the digitalization of processes requires significant investments, which are not within everyone's reach. To make innovation easier for these small businesses, there is a need for shared platforms, which can be made possible by exceptional cooperation between public and private institutions. In 2019, the Ministry of Economic Development experimented in collaboration with IBM to explore the use of blockchain methodology in the fashion supply chain. The model has proved to have a positive impact in terms of supply chain governance and the use of incentives for each component. More recently, eight European Digital Innovation Hubs were created in Italy with the support of the European Commission to provide financial guidance, technical expertise, and support for small to medium-sized enterprises to upgrade their processes in a digital transformation. The presence is regional, but they are part of a pan-European network. The Italian government intends to finance and strengthen the role of these competence centres to help smaller companies overcome the stalemate in the use of new technologies, which, according to Istat, is below the European average: In general, the leading companies in digital transition represent between 5 and 10 per cent of the total and the digitalization models they adopt are not immediately transferable to other business profiles. The transition process appears, firstly, to be marked by necessary phases—such as infrastructure development and the awareness of the need for cybersecurity investments—before measurable productivity gains can be achieved (Istat, 2024).

Once again, Prato does not stand still, although the COVID-19 pandemic period has slowed down the ongoing transformation processes. The municipal administration has cabled the entire city with "Fibre to the Home", which represents a competitive advantage over other territories. With the Support Program for the 5G Emerging Technologies (Decree of the Ministry of Economic Development of March 26, 2019) financed with resources from the Development and Cohesion Fund, the PRISMA project was created. This project supports digital transition through the use of emerging technologies, such as blockchain, artificial intelligence, and the internet of things. A strategic project partner is PIN scarl, the University Campus of Prato (a public–private consortium involving the University of Florence, several private companies, and local stakeholders). To make the entire supply chain transparent and to encourage organizational changes based on information coming from databases and monitoring processes, it is necessary to implement digital twin processes. This means converting every link in the supply chain into a digital element, and simulating and experimenting with every possible change digitally. This is particularly complex in sectors with differentiated and variable demand, such as the fashion system. Each company in Prato proposes around 500 new articles in its collection every six months; they have to guarantee, in addition to the creativity effort, every bit of information on the savings of raw materials used and the degree of sustainability achieved. The proposed item must be accompanied by all the certifications required by customers. It is impossible to imagine all this without adequate digitization of processes. In the 2024 budget law, a new measure to support the textile districts was introduced for an amount of €10 million. Part of this financing covers the costs of an experimental lab, located at the PIN scarl, called The Digital District Platform; this is a project in which all the economic stakeholders of Prato are involved.

Conclusion

The fashion system is predicted to undergo significant changes, including the introduction of new technology, a greater focus on sustainability, and more standardized and focused procedures that lead to a stronger circular economy culture. Prato represents Italy in the Urban Agenda for the EU's circular economy and has been included among the pioneering nine Italian cities striving to achieve climate neutrality, or carbon neutrality, by 2030. The textile industry in Prato boasts a unique tradition of environmental and ethical sustainability that involves all the historic companies in the area. The approach to sustainable production in Prato is a cultural matter. Many entrepreneurs are becoming increasingly aware of the urgency to equip products with a digital passport and to invest more in process automation, as well as in the creation of blockchain systems for better resource control and greater transparency towards consumers. Collaboration between the public and private sectors remains a significant strength, and the municipal administration and local institutions are doing a great deal to equip the area with the necessary infrastructure. However, the urgency of digitalization is creating, perhaps for the first time, marked differences between companies; it distinguishes those that can make significant investments from those that are relying on more traditional production models.

Even in places that have for centuries been the world's point of reference for sustainability, like the industrial textile district of Prato, great changes are expected to adapt production processes to the fashion of the future. Two challenges will likely be crucial in the coming years. First, the investment into an aggregated area's communication; thus, making it easier for individual companies to show their great know-how accumulated over time in recovery and recycling. Second, the securement of substantial investments for all the companies along the supply chain, even the smallest, the subcontractors, and the artisan companies. Only in this way can luxury brands be sure to control the global fragmented supply chain. Organizational models may alter dramatically if businesses do not update and if institutions do not support their digital transformations. One possible outcome could be increased aggregation or acquisition between companies, possibly facilitated by investment funds, to drive dimensional growth and expedite the necessary digital transition. These changes are likely to make the next few years intense, and potentially lead consumers to new frontiers of experience and knowledge. This underscores the importance for companies to stay agile and responsive to technological advancements in order to remain competitive in today's rapidly evolving landscape.

References

Allen, J. (2021, December 22). *Roadmap for a Post-Pandemic World*. https://www.bain.com/insights/roadmap-for-a-post-pandemic-world-video/

Becattini, G. (2001). *The caterpillar and the butterfly*. Mondadori Education.

Becattini, G. (2002). *Miti e paradossi del mondo contemporaneo*. Donzelli Editore.

Becattini, G. (2015). *La coscienza dei luoghi*. Donzelli Editore.

Bernardini, G. (2023, April 3). Il viaggio degli abiti usati da Prato al resto del mondo: solo il 2% finisce in discarica. *Il Corriere Fiorentino*.

Bettizza, S. (2020). *Prato: The Italian town turning rags into new clothes*. BBC News. https://bbc.com/news/av/world-europe-55267992

Chevalier, M., & Gutsatz, M. (2012). *Luxury retail management: How the world's top brands provide quality product and service support*. John Wiley & Sons.

Colli, A. (2002). *Il quarto capitalismo, un profilo italiano*. Marsilio Editore.

Coltorti, F. (2009). Medium-size firms, groups and industrial districts: An Italian Prospective. In G. Becattini, M. Bellandi, & L. De Propis (Eds.), *A handbook of industrial districts* (pp. 441–456). Egdar Elgar.

Coltorti, F. (2011). Il ruolo dell'Industria: grandi e medie imprese. In L. Paolazzi (Ed.), *Libertà e benessere in Italia. 150 anni di storia unitaria e i traguardi del futuro* (pp. 131–167). Editori Laterza.

Coltorti, F. (2018). Distretti, grandi imprese e quarto capitalism. In N. Bellanca & M. Dardi (Eds.), *Giacomo Becattini* (pp. 113–123). Il Ponte Editore.

Coltorti, F. (2006). Areas of large enterprise and industrial district in the development of pot-war Italy: A preliminary study. *European Planning Studies, 14*(8), 1105–1138. https://doi.org/10.1080/09654310600852415

D'Arpizio, C. Levato, F., Steiner, A., & De Montgolfier, J. (2024, January 18). *Long live luxury: Converge to expand through turbulence.* https://www.bain.com

Datheridge, A. (2017). Fashion change: la consapevolezza come processo. In *Fashion change* by Out of Fashion. Connecting Cultures Editions.

Ellen MacArthur Foundation. (n.d.). *What is a circular economy?* https://www.ellenmacarthurfoundation.org/topics/circular-economy-introduction/overview

Euratex. (2024, March 19). Facts & Key Figures—EURATEX. http://euratex.eu/facts-and-key-figures-2024.pdf

European Parliament. (2020, December 29). *L'impatto della produzione e dei rifiuti tessili sull'ambiente.* 29/11/2020, 20201208ST093327.

European Parliament. https://single-market-economy.ec.europa.eu/sectors/textile-ecosystem

Gambi, S. (2024, May 11) *SoloModaSostenibile.* https://open.substack.com/pub/solomodasostenibile/p/185-il-riciclo-tessile-in-mezzo-alla?r=qzzox&utm_campaign=post&utm_medium=email

Girardet, H. (2023, August 1). The future-what future? *The Ecologist special series: Megamorphosis.* Brendan Montague.

ILO—International Labour Organization. (2015). Guidelines for a just transition towards environmentally sustainable economies and societies for all.

Istat—Istituto Nazionale di Statistica. (2024). *Rapporto sulla competitività dei settori produttivi.* Roma.

Major, J. S., & Steele, V. (2024, September 13). The fashion system. *Encyclopedia Britannica.* https://www.britannica.com/art/fashion-industry/Fashion-retailing-marketing-and-merchandising#ref1086321

Malaparte, C. (1956). *Maledetti Toscani.* Vallecchi.

O'Connor, M. (2006). The "Four Spheres" framework for sustainability. *Ecological Complexity, 3*(4), 285–292. https://doi.org/10.1016/j.ecocom.2007.02.002

Ozuem, W., Ranfagni, S., Willis, M., Rovai, S., & Howell, K. (2021). Exploring customers' responses to online service failure and recovery strategies during Covid-19 pandemic: An actor–network theory perspective. *Psychology & Marketing, 38*(9), 1440–1459.

Ozuem, W., Ranfagni, S., Willis, M., Salvietti, G., & Howell, K. (2024). Exploring the relationship between chatbots, service failure recovery and customer loyalty: A frustration–aggression perspective. *Psychology and Marketing*. https://doi.org/10.1002/mar.22051

Ozuem, W., & Willis, M. (2022). *Digital marketing strategies for value co-creation: Models and approaches for online brand communities*. Cham: Palgrave Macmillan.

Ozuem, W., Willis, M., Howell, K., Ranfagni, S., & Rovai, S. (2023a). Examining user-generated content, service failure recovery and customer–brand relationships: An exploration through commitment-trust theory. *Internet Research*. https://doi.org/10.1108/intr-07-2022-0580

Ozuem, W., Willis, M., Ranfagni, S., Howell, K. E., & Rovai, S. (2023b). Examining the role of social media influencers in service failure and recovery strategies: an empirical investigation of millennials' views. *Information Technology & People*. https://doi.org/10.1108/itp-05-2022-0371

Pencarelli, T., Ali Taha, V., Skerhakova, V., Valentiny, T., & Fedorko, R. (2019). Luxury products and sustainability issue from the perspective of young Italian consumers. *Sustainability, 12*(1), 245. https://doi.org/10.3390/su12010245

Re, M. (2017). Promuovere la cultura della moda sostenibile. In *Fashion Change*, by Out of Fashion, Connecting Cultures Editions.

Sabel, C. (2004). *District on the move.* Note on Tedis Survey of the Internationalisation of District Firms, June 18/19.

Skill4smart TCFL 2030. *Sectoral skills strategy for the EU TCLF industries. Final Report- The case for Italy* (2022). https://s4tclfblueprint.eu/wp-content/uploads/2022/07/NAFD421.pdf

The Economist. (2022, December 20). The three knife trilogy. *The Economist, 445*(9327), 40-43.

Thomas, D. (2019). *Fashionopolis: The price of fast fashion and the future of clothes.* Apollo.

Toccafondi, D. (2011). Prato's textile district and Chinese ethnic businesses. In G. Johanson, J. G. Smyth, & R. French. *Living outside the walls: The Chinese in Prato* (pp. 66–80). Cambridge Scholar Publishing.

Toccafondi, D. (2018). Giacomo Becattini, Prato e i pratesi. In N. Bellanca & M. Dardi (Eds.), *Giacomo Becattini, 2* (pp. 59–67). Il Ponte Editore.

22

Black Swan Events: Mitigating Disruption to a Supply Chain Using Blockchain and Artificial Intelligence

Gordon Bowen, Hamid Jahankhani, and Imad Nawaz

Introduction

Geopolitical events ranging from the pandemic to the war in Ukraine have impacted supply chain activities and economics (KPMG, 2023; Statista, 2023). Global political tensions in 2023 have made partnerships between nations less certain. The attitude to supply chains is cautiousness. Governments and firms are exploring domestic self-efficiency and building "friendshoring" relationships; friendshoring refers to governments encouraging businesses to restructure their supply chains and move production of critical imports from geopolitical rivals to allies and like-minded countries. There are moves afoot to replace global supply chains with nearshoring (i.e., supply chain relationships are with countries that are geographically close). The fashion industry is shifting from

G. Bowen (✉)
Anglia Ruskin University, Cambridge, UK
e-mail: gordon.bowen@aru.ac.uk

H. Jahankhani · I. Nawaz
Northumbria University, London, UK

W. Ozuem et al. (eds.), *Sustainable Digital Marketing for Fashion and Luxury Brands*,
https://doi.org/10.1007/978-3-031-82467-8_22

fast fashion to slow fashion but it requires an ecosystem. The change in ecosystem for the fashion industry will have consequences that are financial and also changing the expectations of customers. However, the challenge is to have similar advantages by changing the supply chain infrastructure to friendshoring and nearshoring. The geopolitical events identified above could be classified as black swan events because they are difficult to predict and how long the events will last is uncertain. KPMG (2023) suggested that the effects of current geopolitical tensions on supply chains could be minimised by taking the following actions:

Develop scenarios that include geopolitical situations that could impact supply chains negatively.
Supply chain infrastructure should build nearshoring and friendshoring attributes.
Clearly identify actions and work arounds that will be needed if access is denied to important components or material. Will product reformulation be required? How will it impact customer satisfaction and product specification? Will it have an impact on the regulatory environment of the product? Will additional costs be incurred if new suppliers or new markets are used? How can these additional costs be minimised? Where are the trade-off and risks likely to occur?
Recognise the impact friendshoring and nearshoring will have on lead times and time to market. Can you become more agile, responsive, and reduce working capital? Implementation of the nearshoring and friendshoring infrastructure becomes critical and a supply sustainable chain strategy will require developing from scratch.

The recommendations and actions suggested by KPMG (2023) are apt consideration for the fashion industry. The global size of the fashion industry is $171 billion in 2021, which was accompanied by global growth in the footwear and fashion apparel industry of 18.1% at current prices in 2020–2021. Global industry contributes 2% of the global GDP (FashionUnited, 2024). According to McKinsey post-Covid-19, the global fashion revenues declined by 20% (McKinsey, 2023).

Stakeholder intervention is required in black swan events and the challenge is getting all the stakeholders to work and co-ordinate their actions.

Government intervention is also likely, which will impact how firms respond to black swan events. However, governments need to be proactive when black swan events are identified and put the necessary resources in place. Intervention by governments can lead to unexpected outcomes (due to poor government performance or a lack of urgency and behaving proactively). The application of technologies such as blockchain and artificial intelligence (AI) has a role in minimising black swan events in the supply chain: AI would facilitate the identification of likely events of a geopolitical nature that could influence supply chain performance, and blockchain architecture would help to isolate impacted parts of the supply chain, because of its decentralised governance structure, and reconfigure elements of the supply chain. AI can develop scenarios that could aid in the prediction of likely black swan events. Thus, AI and blockchain working simultaneously could keep the supply chain ecosystem working and establish flexibility, reliability and resilience; this would give firms leadership and management of the supply chain in the event of its breakdown in a black swan event.

Disaster management (DM) is viewed from three perspectives: hazard, vulnerability, and holistic view (Berg & De Majo, 2017). The objective of this paper is to take a holistic and a vulnerability view of DM in the context of unpredictable situations (black swan events). Thus, the objective is not to decide on the constructs of resilience and sustainability but to view the problem holistically. The vulnerability paradigm focuses on the social consequences of political upheavals (Perry, 1998). The holistic paradigm takes a strategic perspective of DM. Supply chain disaster situations need to be discussed from an inter-paradigm approach and not viewed from one perspective.

The aim of this conceptual paper is to demonstrate how blockchain and AI can work in unison to reestablish a supply chain ecosystem after a black swan event, an event beyond the control of the firm and its stakeholders, with minimal disruption. The paper refers to the fashion industry because it is an industry that has been affected by geopolitical and global economic crisis. Resilience and sustainability might both be expected from stakeholders during a black swan event, although a trade-off will be required which could be achieved with blockchain and AI technologies.

The paper discusses supply chain governance and DM, blockchain in the supply chain, leadership and management in the supply chain, and the application of AI technology to oversee the discrete elements of the supply chain and manage overall control to supplement supply chain management. The paper closes with a discussion of the implications followed by a brief conclusion.

Supply Chain Governance and DM

Many organisations recognise that they can be held responsible for the environmental, social, and economic impacts of their internal activities and their suppliers' activities (Hartmann & Moeller, 2014). Thus, supply chain management is based on social, economic, and environmental sustainability and their integration in the supply chain (Tundys, 2020). However, the implementation of supply chain management utilising social, economic, and environmental parameters over geographical distances is challenging (Koberg & Longoni, 2019). Barriers to the implementation of sustainable supply chain management (SSCM) are related to sustainable parameters (economic, social, and environmental), which are influenced by different expectations that arise from cultural differences (Wu & Pullman, 2015). There is also the issue of transparency between suppliers and sub-suppliers and between developing countries that have environmental regulations and developing countries where regulations are not always enforced (Carter et al., 2015).

Sustainable supply chains incorporate the management of materials, information, and capital flows and co-operation between companies in the supply chain, while meeting the environmental, economic, and social obligations that are linked to customer and stakeholder requirements (Seuring & Müller, 2008). The implementation of sustainable parameters will enable a sustainable competitive advantage (Handfield & Nichols, 1999). However, a sustainable supply chain is about co-ordination of supply change management based on economic, environmental, and social parameters, which leads to voluntary integration of the parameters (Ahi & Searcy, 2013). It is necessary to achieve this efficient management of materials, information, and capital flows, which are linked to the procurement and distribution of products and services, to meet the requirements of stakeholders to improve profitability and competitiveness. "The role of SCM [supply chain management] is to ensure competitive advantage for the supply chain members through close collaboration, which includes trust, open communication and real-time data sharing, joint planning, and managing supplier relationships" (Milovanović et al., 2021, p. 74).

Simply creating a pro-environmental and pro-social environment in the supply chain does not necessarily lead to long-term profitability. There needs to be a balance between the pressures of social factors and the pressures of environmental factors. Creating the "right" environmental and social conditions requires long-term decision-making to give rise to long-term economic improvement (Tundys, 2020). The challenge is that sustainability in the supply chain is not just linked to the elements of the supply chain but also to overall supply chain management.

According to Carter and Easton (2011, p. 49), SSCM requires the following logic:

1. Strategy—holistically and purposefully identifying individual SSCM initiatives which align with and support the organization's overall sustainability strategy.
2. Risk management, including contingency planning for both the upstream and the downstream supply chain.
3. An organizational culture which is deeply ingrained and encompasses organizational citizenship, and which includes high ethical standards and expectations (a building block for SSCM) along with a respect for society (both within and outside of the organization) and the natural environment; and
4. Transparency in terms of proactively engaging and communicating with key stakeholders and having traceability and visibility into upstream and downstream supply chain operations.

Figure 22.1 illustrates SSCM logic.

According to Carter and Easton (2011), the theoretical lenses applied to supply chain management include stakeholder theory (Freeman, 1984), which is the most widely applied, the resource-based view (RBV),

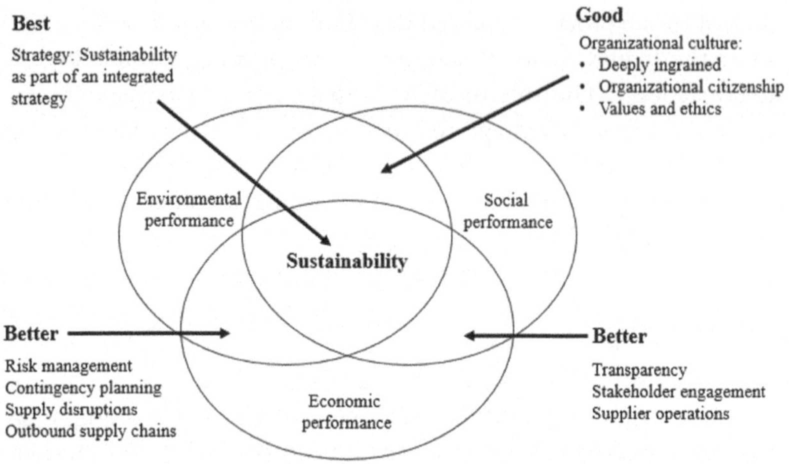

Fig. 22.1 Sustainable supply chain management (*Source* Carter and Easton [2011] adapted)

which is the next most widely applied, and natural RBV. RBV incorporates the strategic capability and natural RBV links to competitive advantage, such as pollution prevention leading to lower costs, product stewardship leading to pre-empting competitors, and sustainable development leading to future position (Hart, 1995). Other theoretical models applied include dynamic capabilities in achieving competitive advantage in sustainable global supply chain management (Reuter et al., 2010). Furthermore, the application of brand equity theory to achieve competitive advantage derived from sustainability (Brown et al., 2000; Flint & Golicic, 2009) employs efficacy theory to predict safe employee behaviour.

Table 22.1 reviews the literature in disaster performance management context with reference to emerging technologies, such as AI and blockchain. Performance management is preparing the context for performance (Lebas, 1995). Performance management is the whole process starting with defining the process, application targets and outcome of the results (Lebas, 1995).

Table 22.1 The role of AI and blockchain technologies in disaster performance management

Technology	Process description	Application	DM outcome
AI	Machines than can learn from past experiences. AI systems can assist with human decision making (Duan et al., 2019)	Process and task automation; machine learning algorithms to aid cognitive understanding patterns and trends; Cognitive engagement Language processing	Mitigation or prevention
Blockchain	Blockchain is a ledger system that uses peer-peer architecture (Felin & Lakhani, 2018)	BC is used in financial sector, supply chain, logistics, food safety, health care, food care art market and agriculture	Relief and disaster management

Source Vermiglio et al. (2021) adapted

Blockchain in the Supply Chain

In the past, focus on the supply chain was economic, but with environmental damage created by supply chain activities there is a shift towards SSCM based on environmental, social, and economic parameters (Gupta et al., 2020). This is particularly the case in the fashion industry; however, the pace of change to SSCM in the fashion industry is not always consistent. How can a balance be struck between these competing parameters? According to de Oliveira et al. (2018) and Manupati et al. (2019), pressure from governments and other stakeholders, such as regulatory organisations and customers, is forcing firms to redesign their supply chain architecture internally and externally due to environmental and social concerns.

Supply chain innovation faces many challenges; according to Chowdhury et al. (2019) these include: permission for access and control; legal and regulatory compliance; computing power data management;

efficiency and performance; knowledge, skills, and expertise; standard platform; operational costs; organisational resistance (inside an organisation); organisational resistance (between firms); privacy; scalability; security; strategy; suitability; and trust in automated software.

In a black swan event, which challenges are of the greatest significance? This will be addressed in Sect. 22.6 (Implications).

Chowdhury et al. (2019) reviewed five pilot cases in which blockchain technology was applied. These all have relevance to a black swan event. The main findings of each pilot case are discussed in sub-sections 'Food Supply Chain' to 'Banking'.

Food Supply Chain

An imperative for a food supply chain is freshness of food because of the health risks involved. Provenance (2015), a food supply firm, invested in blockchain architecture to improve transparency in the food supply chain. Provenance (2015) suggested that a centralised system is not supportive of transparency. Blockchain's data are driven by consensus and different elements of the blockchain will require certification to gain access to the different blocks (Chowdury et al., 2019). Blockchain in the food supply chain has the potential to improve traceability, which reduces duplication and paperwork. It enables marketplace innovation by connecting customers and suppliers, which encourages data sharing among operators in the supply chain and can lead to increased access to capital investments and improving customer payments.

Energy

Implementation of a fully decentralised system is another potential application of blockchain. Electrify (2023), an energy company, has employed blockchain technology in their electricity network since 2018 to accelerate growth and enhance AI applications. Blockchain technology is especially pertinent to the Electrify network because of the energy market deregulation in Singapore. PwC (2023) suggested that blockchain can be used for billing and the archiving of billing data, and that blockchain can be integrated with smart devices.

Relief and Disasters

Governments, non-governmental organisations, charities, and civil organisations need to collaborate and co-operate in relief or disaster situations. With so many stakeholders involved in these situations, co-ordination and control are required to prevent duplication of efforts. Blockchain has a role in improving traceability, transparency, immutability, and information sharing. The US government realised blockchain can be utilised to develop a decentralised system and enhance collaboration (Akilo, 2023). Blockchain can also facilitate donations and financial transactions in disaster situations (Phil, 2023).

Housing

An example of the application of blockchain technology to housing is the Kenyan National Housing Fund, which provides government funding for families in need. The Kenyan National Housing Fund had been open to corruption and fraudulent activities (Aki, 2021). James Macharia, Cabinet Secretary for Transport and Housing, at a meeting at the World Bank in Nairobi said that the nascent technology would be used to distribute housing to deserving applicants in a bid to address past issues concerning "graft fears arising from beneficiaries and even legislators ... Kenya will use blockchain technology to ensure the rightful owners live in government-funded housing projects" (Aki, 2021).

Sharma (2018), on behalf of the Blockchain Council, stated that blockchain technology enables transparency in the allocation of housing because blocks cannot be altered once added to the blockchain. The illegal adding or removing of information from a land registry housing database would be recorded using blockchain technology. The embezzlement of funds would be more challenging, and bribery would be considerably reduced.

Banking

Although blockchain is linked to cryptocurrency, it is an ideal way to improve financial transactions. Finextra (2018) is a collaboration between 10 banks; HSBC is the lead bank on the We.Trade platform. HSBC has spearheaded the use of blockchain in financial banking. In 2018, HSBC (2023) set up a transaction using R3's Corda scalable blockchain for a Cargill's shipment of soybeans from Argentina to Malaysia. The test was to reduce the transaction time (from days to less than 24 hours) and abandon the use of multiple systems and instead share one application. Ganesh et al. (2018) demonstrated that trade can be digitalised and lead to a reduction in fraud in letters of credit and the introduction of streamlined procedures.

Chowdhury et al. (2019) captured themes from a systematic review of the literature on the implementation of blockchain in supply chain scenarios; the themes they identified were: interoperability, platform dependency, trust in rule-based automation software, and consensus among supply chain actors. The technical requirements were interoperability and platform dependency, and the social requirements were trust in rule-based automation software and consensus among supply chain actors. The outcomes for the five pilot areas are summarised below.

Food supply chain: *Operability*—must operate in a wide range of industries from retail to fishing. *Platform dependency*—multiple platforms with differing stakeholder requirements. *Trust in rule-based automation software*—rule agreement and development can have significant influence on the supply chain. *Consensus among supply chain actors*—acceptance of technology innovation can be challenging.

Energy: *Operability*—decentralised technology requires similar requirements for users/producers for recording. *Platform dependency*—complex platform with many nodes, which is a single platform for users/producers. *Trust in rule-based automation software*—GDPR requirements and data sharing rules require designing. *Consensus among supply chain actors*—access rules are agreed upon and practice is consistent.

Relief and disasters: *Operability*—varying levels of technological competence among actors, especially donors. *Platform dependency*—multiple platforms with software not consistent or easily integrated. *Trust* *in rule-based automation software*—different stakeholders will need to agree the rules and who will be making them and how to integrate the stakeholders. *Consensus among supply chain actors*—combination of private and public funding and the impact on the different stakeholders; decision-making on how much information is shared and how it is shared.

Housing: *Operability*—technological competence in blockchain and data collection and recording specifications. *Platform dependency*—governmental organisations need access to the systems and integration with different parts of the system. *Trust in rule-based automation software*—GDPR requirements' complexity, the level of sharing of personal data and level of access. *Consensus among supply chain actors*—involvement of contractors/suppliers and government officials to identify type of data to be shared and the participants.

Banking: *Operability*—consistency in technology competence for all actors. *Platform dependency*—multiple platforms can become a single platform. *Trust in rule-based automation software*—agreement on how much data can be shared and who will define the rules and modification if required. *Consensus among supply chain actors*—banks and government officials need to agree on what data are useful for transactions and level of access for the various parties.

It is notable that examples of the application of blockchain technology in the fashion industry are limited. Tripathi et al. (2021) stated that very little is known about blockchain technology in the fashion industry although the technology is exponentially growing in popularity. The decentralisation, immutability, and consensus characteristics of blockchain technology have the potential to enhance the fashion industry by adding an additional level of security and trust. An important role for blockchain technology is the detection of fake products, which have an impact on brand image and identity. A function of blockchain in the supply chain is to protect and secure digital identity and establish authenticity.

Supply Chain Leadership and Management

Leadership in sustaining a blockchain-centric supply chain requires firms to reduce the negativity of environmental and social effects of their supply chain (Gupta et al., 2021; Rejeb & Rejeb, 2020). Sustainability in the supply chain is an opportunity for firms to redesign their supply chain. Incorporation of big data and AI can help firms achieve sustainability goals connected to traceability, security, environmental degradation, and social ethics (Munir et al., 2022). There is limited knowledge of the circular economy, but developing countries are taking a prominent role in its adoption and application (Kalmykova et al., 2018). This has implications for supply chains that traverse developing countries. However, the concept of a circular economy is changing, and the current focus is on transforming products into new products after their usefulness has ended (Munir et al., 2022; Ozuem et al., 2023).

Society is more focused on the environment and the social impact of supply chains (Munir et al., 2022). The core components of blockchain that are supportive of the sustainability of the environmental and social aspects of a supply chain include decentralisation, secure transactions, information transparency, and smart contracts (Kouhizadeh & Sarkis, 2018; Leng et al., 2019). Firms are focusing on technical improvement of their supply chain without affecting the triple bottom line (Casino et al., 2019). Customers should be made aware of the use of blockchain in a sustainable supply chain to enable green manufacturing. If manufacturing becomes green, then the environmentally aware customer will prefer purchasing the green product (Munir et al., 2022). The drive to green the supply chain will increase as awareness of sustainability increases and spreads to firms and customers. Thus, it is a matter of when and not if.

It is expected that managers of a global supply chain will protect the rights of workers and ensure they have a safe working environment. However, violations of these rights, regulations, and rules can occur in reputable organisations and this is not unusual. Blockchain is committed to providing social sustainability (Munir et al., 2022). Measures of the success of sustainable supply include "regional development, the welfare of workers, humanitarian supply chain, animals' health, transparency, fraud mitigation, trust development, and food security" (Munir et al., 2022, p. 16). Leadership in a social sustainable supply chain includes humanitarian supply chain areas of research with the following objectives (Munir et al., 2022):

Application and acceptance of blockchain in the traceability system in the meat supply chain (Sander et al., 2018). An application that is used in the fashion industry.
Evaluation and assessment of blockchain on fraud mitigation, welfare, animal health, food security, and transparency (Sander et al., 2021). An application that is used in the fashion industry.
Blockchain to facilitate social sharing dynamics (Pazaitis et al. 2017).
Social influence model on blockchain adoption and verified with Brazilian professionals (Queiroz et al., 2020).
Co-operation between stakeholders in disaster and relief situations (Dubey et al., 2020).
Barriers for blockchain adoption in the humanitarian supply chain (Sahebi et al., 2020).
The role of senior management participation, market pressure, market changes, and regulatory concerns on the use of blockchain (Wong et al., 2020).
Delphi method to gain knowledge from experts on economic, social, and technical influences of blockchain on supply chains (Kopyto et al., 2020).
Blockchain—social relationship between supplier and buyer (Benzidia et al., 2021).
Blockchain can improve clarity and trust in social media analytics (Choi et al., 2020).
Understanding the behaviour in blockchain adoption in India and United States (Queiroz & Fosso Wamba, 2019).
Development of a verifiable framework on how blockchain can increase social sustainability (Nikolakis et al., 2018).
Quality of data on the sustainability of supply chains (Choi & Luo, 2019).

Countries such as Japan and the United States are leading in the application of blockchain technology in sustainable supply chains. Blockchain supply architecture is gaining momentum in developed countries, but many African and Asian countries are also participating and implementing blockchain technology in their supply chain network. However, sustainable supply chain architecture is embryonic because green practices in procurement and regulatory requirements are not always adhered to (Munir et al., 2022).

Fast fashion is a global trend that changes the production process to increase consumption. Fashion retailers need to respond quickly to fast-moving fashion trends and consumers' changing tastes. Examples of fast fashion retailers are H&M, Top Shop, and Zara. The timescale from catwalk to fashion retailer is six months (Joy et al., 2012).

Slow fashion is a response to changing expectations of the fashion industry, such as sustainability, and to the overproduction of apparel leading to increased waste. Characteristics of slow fashion include small-scale production, sourcing local material and markets for production, season-less fashion, slower production times to focus on quality durable products, and pricing that is based on ecology and social aspects (Fletcher, 2010).

Slow fashion will require a blockchain supply chain where decisions are decentralised and independent to protect the integrity of the fashion chain supply chain. Slow fashion is dependent on a circular economy to maximise its effectiveness (Munir et al., 2022).

AI Technology in the Supply Chain (Integrator/Controller)

The uncertainty of decision-making in sustainable supply chain ecosystems is a significant problem (Gumus et al., 2010); this is compounded by black swan events. The characteristics of decision-making in sustainable supply chain ecosystems include variety and complexity, and decisions are made based on asymmetric information. For example, estimating demand for the different elements of a sustainable supply chain with changing order volumes is a challenge (Gherabi et al., 2023).

Provost and Fawcett (2013) suggested a data-driven decision-making approach that includes facts, metrics, and data to assist in the execution of business strategy so that a firm can achieve its objectives, which will influence policies, practices, and activities (Tan et al., 2015). SSCM decision-making will require sophisticated data and information with improved analytics; arguably, this will lead to a competitive advantage and drive data capture innovation.

Supply chain activities in which AI could play a role include demand forecasting, flow management, and optimising logistics performance, which would contribute to the overall customer experience (Gherabi et al., 2023). Real-time data from social media and forums can supplement demand forecasting (Chae, 2015). Improved forecasting will lead to better sales forecasts and stretch the product life cycle (Lau et al., 2018). AI technology could improve flow management, which includes sales management, and optimise inventories; thus, leading to improved finances (Gherabi et al., 2023; Ozuem et al., 2021). Amindoust et al. (2012) proposed the application of fuzzy logic to identify sustainable suppliers due to uncertainty in the decision-making process. They identified several criteria and sub-criteria that sustainable suppliers employ in their decision-making processes including: economic (sub-criteria are profitability, product quality, delivery performance, and service), environmental (sub-criteria are environmental management system and environmental competences), and social (sub-criteria are actors' rights, and health and safety at the workplace and for people).

The application of AI in SSCM is in its infancy. However, what is the role of AI in the sustainable supply chain process: decision-maker (controller) and/or technical (integrator)?

Implications

The implementation of sustainable supply chains is challenging because of the balance required between social and environmental dimensions, which will impact economic success and consequently long-term profitability. Thus, sustainability in "normal" business environments is challenging. However, the implementation and management of sustainable supply chains in business environments that experience black swan events is even more challenging. This does not mean that preparation for such an event should not occur, but the supply chain management must be proactive to such an event occurring. This is especially important for fashion retailers because the supply chain is fragmented, although it is less fragmented in a slow fashion ecosystem. Supply chain management and governance requires flexibility that gives rise to agility. The dimensions of the supply chain culture should include proactiveness, agility, and openness to changes in the business environment, which will have a major impact on the operational ability of the supply chain to function and deliver the outcomes required by the stakeholders. Thus, the cultural dimensions necessary for supply chains to function and deliver the economic, social, and environmental dimensions for SSCM and governance require integration with the elements of the supply chain and across the whole supply chain. The complexity of integrating the cultural fit is compounded by black swan events. How to legitimise the cultural dimensions across geographical boundaries with different cultures and sub-cultures of different countries is truly a challenge. The above discussion links to the vulnerability paradigm, which requires social, economic, and political environmental considerations (Buckle, 2005; Cutter, 1996). The traditional approach (hazard paradigm) is to consider disasters as hazards, which is reactive and focuses on short-term solutions. Black swan events require strategic thinking and the development of a strategic process to identify them (scenario planning).

The pressure to change the supply chain architecture due to environmental and social issues is an opportunity to apply emerging technologies to streamline and improve the design of supply chain activities to make them sustainable. However, there are many challenges in the implementation of blockchain technology in supply chains, such as access and control of data management, privacy, security, computing power, and trust in the automated software (Chowdhury et al., 2019; Ozuem et al., 2024). Developing countries have a substantial part of the fashion supply chain, but they do not have access to funds to use the latest technology, which hinders their ability to develop sustainable fashion supply chain processes (i.e., developing a slow fashion supply chain). Although Chowdhury et al. (2019) did not identify all the challenges, the ones they did identify will be of great importance in black swan events. In a black swan situation, control will require access being restricted to ensure peer-to-peer communications to make sabotage less likely to occur. Thus, the supply chain becomes a series of peer-to-peer connections with limited integration to minimise disruption. Although the supply chain will have improved security, because of the decentralised management system, it becomes more challenging to gain an overall picture of the supply chain's performance. Does blockchain architecture require an ability to integrate peer-to-peer activities so an overall analysis from a centralised command and data management can be achieved? This would only be a requirement in black swan events where threats to the supply chain will be heightened. The complexity of managing the application of blockchain would be less challenging where nearshoring and friendshoring can be accomplished. Slow fashion requires a blockchain architecture that is flexible so the supply chain can move from centralised to decentralised, especially to ensure quality. The era of slow fashion is about using material and resources that are closer to markets.

Reducing the complexity would be an overriding consideration in black swan events. However, should this not always be the goal to reduce the complexity of the supply chain? Supply chains require co-ordination, collaboration, and integration, but in black swan events these are not necessarily feasible or desirable. Thus, in black swan situations, the ability of the supply chain to operate in an optimal way is compromised. The application of the holistic paradigm is a necessary technique to resolve black swan events because they impact the economic, political, and social environment. The application of technological tools, such as blockchain and AI, could help to overcome the complexity of managing supply chains in black swan events. Taking a strategic perspective requires a trade-off between sustainability and resilience. Stakeholders will want both constructs to be operational in black swan events, so a choice needs to be made.

The role of AI needs to be defined in sustainable supply chain systems. Previously, it was noted that the role could be an integrator of the elements that provide the sustainable supply chain system, so it holistically controls the overall sustainable supply chain. In black swan events this will not be necessarily desirable and individual control via the use of blockchain technology would be preferable. Even in black swan events, blockchain as part of the decision-making process would be desirable. Nevertheless, allowing AI to be a decision-maker depends on actors' confidence in the software and platform (technical considerations). Black swan events compound the challenges experienced by SSCM and these will need prioritising to enable functionality. Arguably, black swan events will hit developing countries the hardest because they do not have the training, knowledge, and experience to navigate the application of blockchain technology integrated with AI. The severity of the impact of black swan events will be dependent on the geographical location (developed or developing countries), the sector, and the type of black swan event. The fashion industry is very dependent on developing countries and black swan events are likely to have a severe impact on the fashion supply chain in developing countries.

In a black swan event will customers still expect sustainable supply chain conditions even if the cost of maintaining the quality of a product would lead to increases in price? Customers will likely expect sustainability and resilience in the supply chain in black swan events. Under normal conditions a green customer would be less forgiving if the social and environmental dimensions of a sustainable supply chain were compromised. However, in black swan events would green customers be more forgiving and empathetic? Decision-makers in the sustainable supply chain system will also need to have an empathetic disposition because the accuracy of AI is questionable and could lead to false data/information, which would compromise the integrity of decision-making. In black swan events, culture, people, and legal factors could play a more decisive role in the use of technologies. Confidence in research relating to AI and blockchain in the sustainable supply chain system could be low due to limited research, especially of a longitudinal nature. One must also bear in mind that AI and blockchain technologies are in their infancy. More research into the technology from a standalone to an integrated approach would help to accelerate the implementation of these technologies in a sustainable supply chain environment. Also, firms need more exposure to the technologies, which requires more training and wider applications of the technologies in firms' sustainable supply chain systems and in other parts of the business.

The combination of blockchain and AI technologies has the potential to leverage the competitive advantage of a firm. However, the competitive advantage is based on statistical algorithms and probability (Bayesian statistics). Can one put trust and privacy of the data to one side and have confidence in the outcomes? Are blockchain and AI disruptive technologies for social innovation or just incremental technologies that have very low strategic significance in supply chain sustainability?

Conclusions

Ensuring social, environmental, and economic success in each element of the supply chain and transferring that success to the management of the overall supply chain is a pressing requirement for industries such as the fashion industry. Black swan events will disrupt sustainable supply chain systems but with careful use of blockchain technology and AI the risks can be contained or minimised. However, the accuracy of AI is a barrier to wide-scale adoption and to decision-making in sustainable supply chain. The combination of blockchain and AI is going to disrupt sustainable supply chain technology, but how wide-scale will the disruption be—niche or global? It is inappropriate to view black swan events through a single paradigm because these events have strategic as well as social, political, and economic consequences and require an inter-paradigm approach.

References

Ahi, P., & Searcy, C. (2013). A comparative literature analysis of definitions for green and sustainable supply chain management. *Journal of Cleaner Production, 52*, 329–341. https://doi.org/10.1016/j.jclepro.2013.02.018

Aki, J. (2021, March 4). *Kenyan Government to use blockchain to distribute affordable housing*. Available online https://www.ccn.com/kenyan-government-to-use-blockchain-to-distribute-affordable-housing (Accessed on 12 January 2024).

Akilo, D. (2023). *U.S. military explores blockchain for disaster relief*. Available online https://businessblockchainhq.com/business-blockchain-news/us-military-explores-blockchain-for-disaster-relief/ (Accessed on 29 December 2023).

Amindoust, A., Ahmed, S., Saghafinia, A., & Bahreininejad, A. (2012). Sustainable supplier selection: A ranking model based on fuzzy inference system. *Applied Soft Computing, 12*(6), 1668–1677. https://doi.org/10.1016/j.asoc.2012.01.023

Benzidia, S., Makaoui, N., & Subramanian, N. (2021). Impact of ambidexterity of blockchain technology and social factors on new product development: A supply chain and industry 4.0 perspective. *Technological Forecasting and Social Change, 169*, 120819, https://doi.org/10.1016/j.techfore.2021.120819

Berg, M., & De Majo, V. (2017). Understanding the global strategy for disaster risk reduction. *Risk, Hazards and Crisis in Public Policy, 8*(2), 147–167.

Brown, K. A., Willis, P. G., & Prussia, G. E. (2000). Predicting safe employee behavior in the steel industry: Development and test of a sociotechnical model. *Journal of Operations Management, 18*(4), 445–465.

Buckle, P. (2005). *Disaster: Mandated definitions, local knowledge and complexity*. In R. W. Perry and E. L. Quarantelli (Eds.), *What is a disaster? New answers to old questions* (pp. 173–200). Xlibris. Philadelphia, PA.

Carter, C. R., & Easton, P. (2011). Sustainable supply chain management: Evolution and future directions. *International Journal of Physical Distribution & Logistics Management, 41*(1), 46–62. https://doi.org/10.1108/09600031111101420

Carter, C. R., Rogers, D. S., & Choi, T. Y. (2015). Toward the theory of the supply chain. *Journal of Supply Chain Management, 51*(2), 89–97.

Casino, F., Dasaklis, T. K., & Patsakis, C. (2019). A Systematic literature review of blockchain-based applications: Current status, classification and open issues. *Telematics Informatics, 36*, 55–81. https://doi.org/10.1016/j.tele.2018.11.006

Chae, B. (2015). Insights from hashtag #supplychain and Twitter analytics: Considering Twitter and Twitter data for supply chain practice and research. *International Journal of Production Economics, 165*, 247–259. https://doi.org/10.1016/j.ijpe.2014.12.037

Choi, T.-M., Guo, S., & Luo, S. (2020). When blockchain meets social-media: Will the result benefit social media analytics for supply chain operations management? *Transportation Research Part E—Logistics Transportation Review, 135*, 101860. https://doi.org/10.1016/j.tre.2020.101860

Choi, T.-M., & Luo, S. (2019). Data quality challenges for sustainable fashion supply chain operations in emerging markets: Roles of blockchain, government sponsors and environment taxes. *Transportation Research Part e: Logistics and Transportation Review, 131*, 139–152. https://doi.org/10.1016/j.tre.2019.09.019

Chowdhury, S., Rodriguez-Espindola, O., Beltagui, A., & Mackenzie, L. (2019). If Blockchain is the answer what is the question? *Computer Science, Blockchain*, 1–10.

Cutter, S. L. (1996). Vulnerability to environmental hazards. *Progress in Human Geography, 20*(4), 529–539.

de Oliveira, U. R., Espindola, L. S., da Silva, I. R., da Silva, I. N., & Rocha, H. M. (2018). A systematic literature review on green supply chain management: Research implications and future perspectives. *Journal of Cleaner Production, 187*, 537–561. https://doi.org/10.1016/j.jclepro.2018.03.083

Duan, Y., Edwards, J. S., & Dwivedi, Y. K. (2019). Artificial intelligence for decision making in the era of Big Data—Evolution, challenges and research agenda. *International Journal of Information, 48*, 63–71.

Dubey, R., Gunasekaran, A., Bryde, D. J., Dwivedi, Y. K., & Papadopoulos, T. (2020). Blockchain technology for enhancing swift-trust, collaboration and resilience within a humanitarian supply chain setting. *International Journal of Production Research, 58*(11), 3381–3398. https://doi.org/10.1080/00207543.2020.1722860

Electrify. (2023). *Asia's electric marketplace*. Available online https://electrify.asia/ (Accessed on 28 December 2023).

Felin, T., & Lakhani, K. (2018, September 11). What problems will you solve with blockchain? *MIT Sloan Management Review*. Available online https://sloanreview.mit.edu/article/what-problems-will-you-solve-with-blockchain/

Finextra. (2018, July 3). *We.trade blockchain platform goes into live production*. Available online https://www.finextra.com/newsarticle/32342/wetrade-blockchain-platform-goes-into-live-production (Accessed on 1 January 2023).

Fletcher, K. (2010). Slow fashion: An Invitation for systems change. *Fashion Practice, 2*(2), 259–266.

Flint, D. J., & Golicic, S. L. (2009). Searching for competitive advantage through sustainability: A qualitative study in the New Zealand wine industry. *International Journal of Physical Distribution & Logistics Management, 39*(10), 841–860.

Freeman, R. E. (1984). *Strategic management: A stakeholder approach*. Prentice-Hall.

Ganesh, S., Olsen, T., Kroeker, J., & Venkatraman, P. (2018, October 21). *Blockchain points the way to a comprehensive digital approach in the paper-based documentary trade business*. Available online https://www.bain.com/insights/rebooting-a-digital-solution-to-trade-finance (Accessed on 1 January 2024).

Gherabi, Y., Benjouid, Z., El Montassir, El-K., & Nabil, N. (2023). Application of artificial intelligence in performance supply chain management. *International Journal of Strategic Management and Economic Studies, 2*(3), 755–757.

Global Fashion Industry Statistics (fashionunited.com). Accessed 16 March 2024.

Gumus, A. T., Guneri, A. F., & Ulengin, F. (2010). A new methodology for multi-echelon inventory management in stochastic and neuro-fuzzy environments. *International Journal of Production Economics, 128*(1). 248–260. https://doi.org/10.1016/j.ijpe.2010.06.019

Gupta, H., Kumar, A., & Wasan, P. (2021). Industry 4.0, cleaner production and circular economy: An integrative framework for evaluating ethical and sustainable business performance of manufacturing organizations. *Journal of Cleaner Production, 295*, 126253, https://doi.org/10.1016/j.jclepro.2021.126253

Gupta, H., Kusi-Sarpong, S., & Rezaei, J. (2020). Barriers and overcoming strategies to supply chain sustainability innovation. *Resources, Conservation and Recycling, 161*, 104819. https://doi.org/10.1016/j.resconrec.2020.104819

Handfield, R. B., & Nichols, E. L., Jr. (1999). *Introduction to supply chain management* (pp. 1–29). Prentice Hall.

Hart, S. L. (1995). A natural-resource-based view of the firm. *Academy of Management Review, 20*(4), 986–1014.

Hartmann, J., & Moeller, S. (2014). Chain liability in multi-tier supply chains? Responsibility attributions for unsustainable supplier behavior. *Journal of Operations Management, 32*(5), 281–294. https://doi.org/10.1016/j.jom.2014.01.005

HSBC. (2023). *HSBC and ING execute groundbreaking live trade finance transaction on R3's Corda Blockchain platform*. Available online https://www.hsbc.com/news-and-views/news/media-releases/2018/hsbc-trade-blockchain-transaction-press-released (Accessed on 1 January 2024).

Joy, A., Sherry, J. F., Jr., Venkatesh, A., Wang, J., & Chan, R. (2012). Fast fashion, sustainability, and the ethical appeal of luxury brands. *Fashion Theory, 16*(3), 273–295.

Kalmykova, Y., Sadagopan, M., & Rosado, L. (2018). Circular economy—From review of theories and practices to development of implementation tools. *Resources, Conservation and Recycling, 135*, 190–201. https://doi.org/10.1016/j.resconrec.2017.10.034

Koberg, E., & Longoni, A. (2019). A systematic review of sustainable supply chain management in global supply chains. *Journal of Cleaner Production, 207*, 1084–1098. https://doi.org/10.1016/j.jclepro.2018.10.033

Kopyto, M., Lechler, S., von der Gracht, H. A., & Hartmann, E. (2020). Potentials of blockchain technology in supply chain management: Long-term judgments of an international expert panel. *Technological Forecasting and Social Change, 161*, 120330. https://doi.org/10.1016/j.techfore.2020.120330

Kouhizadeh, M., & Sarkis, J. (2018). Blockchain practices, potentials, and perspectives in greening supply chains. *Sustainability, 10*(10), 3652. https://doi.org/10.3390/su10103652

KPMG. (2023). *The supply chain trends shaking up 2023*. Available online https://kpmg.com/xx/en/home/insights/2022/12/the-supply-chain-trends-shaking-up-2023.html (Accessed on 28 December 2023).

Lau, R. Y. K., Zhang, W., & Xu, W. (2018). Parallel Aspect-oriented sentiment analysis for sales forecasting with big data. *Production and Operations Management, 27*(10), 1775–1794. https://doi.org/10.1111/poms.12737

Lebas, M. J. (1995). Performance measurement and performance management. *International Journal of Production Economics, 41*(1/3), 23–35.

Leng, J., Jiang, P., Xu, K., Liu, Q., Zhao, J. L., Bian, Y., & Shi, R. (2019). Makerchain: A blockchain with chemical signature for self-organizing process in social manufacturing. *Journal of Cleaner Production, 234*, 767–778. https://doi.org/10.1016/j.jclepro.2019.06.265

Mangla, S. K., Kazancoglu, Y., Ekinci, E., Liu, M., Özbiltekin, M., & Sezer, M. D. (2021). Using system dynamics to analyze the societal impacts of blockchain technology in milk supply chainsrefer. *Environmental Science, Business, Agricultural and Food Science, Sociology, Transportation Research Part E-Logistics and Transportation Review, 149*, 102289. https://doi.org/10.1016/j.tre.2021.102289

Manupati, V. K., Schoenherr, T., Ramkumar, M., Wagner, S. M., Pabba, S. K., & Inder Raj Singh, R. (2019). A blockchain-based approach for a multi-echelon sustainable supply chain. *International Journal of Production Research, 58*(7), 2222–2241. https://doi.org/10.1080/00207543.2019.1683248

The State of Fashion 2024: Findings pockets of growth as uncertainty reigns. McKinsey (2023, November). The State of Fashion 2024 report|McKinsey. Accessed 17 March 2024.

Milovanović, V., Paunović, M., & Avramovski, S. (2021). The impact of COVID-19 on the hotel supply chain management. *Hotel and Tourism Management, 9*(2), 63–78.

Munir, A. M., Habib, M. S., Hussain, A., Shahbaz, M. A., Qamar, A., Masood, T., Sultan, M., Mujtaba, M. A., Imran, S., Hasan, M., Akhtar, M. S., Ayub, H. M. U., & Salman, C. A. (2022). Blockchain adoption for sustainable supply chain management: Economic, environmental, and social perspective. *Frontier in Energy Research, 10*, 1–24. https://doi.org/10.3389/fenrg.2022.899632

Nikolakis, W., John, L., & Krishnan, H. (2018). How blockchain can shape sustainable global value chains: An evidence, verifiability, and enforceability (EVE) framework. *Sustainability, 10*(11), 3926. https://doi.org/10.3390/su10113926

Ozuem, W., Ranfagni, S., Willis, M., Rovai, S., & Howell, K. (2021). Exploring customers' responses to online service failure and recovery strategies during Covid-19 pandemic: An actor–network theory perspective. *Psychology & Marketing, 38*(9), 1440–1459.

Ozuem, W., Ranfagni, S., Willis, M., Salvietti, G., & Howell, K. (2024). Exploring the relationship between chatbots, service failure recovery and customer loyalty: A frustration–aggression perspective. *Psychology and Marketing*. https://doi.org/10.1002/mar.22051

Ozuem, W., Willis, M., Ranfagni, S., Howell, K. E., & Rovai, S. (2023). Examining the role of social media influencers in service failure and recovery strategies: An empirical investigation of millennials' views. *Information Technology & People*. https://doi.org/10.1108/itp-05-2022-0371

Pazaitis, A., De Filippi, P., & Kostakis, V. (2017). Blockchain and value systems in the sharing economy: The illustrative case of backfeed. *Technological Forecasting and Social Change, 125*, 105–115. https://doi.org/10.1016/j.techfore.2017.05.025

Perry, R. W. (1998). Definitions and the development of a theoretical superstructure for disaster research. In E. L. Quarantelli (Ed.), *What is a disaster? Perspectives on the question*. Routledge.

Phil, L. (2023). *How blockchain could change the future of disaster response teams*. Available online https://medium.com/littlephilnews/how-blockchain-could-change-the-future-of-disaster-response-teams2a42e9e3176 (Accessed on 30 December 2023).

Provenance. (2015, September 21). *Blockchain: The solution for transparency in product supply chains.* Available online https://www.provenance.org/news-insights/blockchain-the-solution-for-transparency-in-product-supply-chains (Accessed on 28 December 2023).

Provost, F., & Fawcett, T. (2013). Data science and its relationship to big data and data-driven decision making. *Big Data, 1*(1), 51–59. https://doi.org/10.1089/big.2013.1508

PwC. (2023). *Blockchain—An opportunity for energy producers and consumers?* Available online https://www.pwc.com/gx/en/industries/assets/pwc-blockchain-opportunity-for-energy-producers-andconsumers.pdf (Accessed on 28 December 2023).

Queiroz, M. M., & Fosso Wamba, S. (2019). Blockchain adoption challenges in supply chain: An empirical investigation of the main drivers in India and the USA. *International Journal of Information Management, 46*, 70–82. https://doi.org/10.1016/j.ijinfomgt.2018.11.021

Queiroz, M. M., Fosso Wamba, S., De Bourmont, M., & Telles, R. (2020). Blockchain adoption in operations and supply chain management: Empirical evidence from an emerging economy. *International Journal of Production Research, 59*(20), 6087–6103. https://doi.org/10.1080/00207543.2020.1803511

Rejeb, A., & Rejeb, K. (2020). Blockchain and supply chain sustainability. *Logforum, 16*(3), 363–372. https://doi.org/10.17270/j.log.2020.467

Reuter, C., Foerstl, K., Hartmann, E., & Blome, C. (2010). Sustainable global supplier management: The role of dynamic capabilities in achieving competitive advantage. *Journal of Supply Chain Management, 46*(2), 45–63.

Sahebi, I. G., Masoomi, B., & Ghorbani, S. (2020). Expert oriented approach for analyzing the blockchain adoption barriers in humanitarian supply chain. *Technology in Society, 63*, 101427. https://doi.org/10.1016/j.techsoc.2020.101427

Sander, F., Semeijn, J., & Mahr, D. (2018). The acceptance of blockchain technology in meat traceability and transparency. *British Food Journal, 120*(9), 2066–2079. https://doi.org/10.1108/BFJ-07-2017-0365

Seuring, S., & Müller, M. (2008). From a literature review to a conceptual framework for sustainable supply chain management. *Journal of Cleaner Production, 16*(15), 1699–1710. https://doi.org/10.1016/j.jclepro.2008.04.020

Sharma, K. (2018, November 13). *Africa to use blockchain for affordable housing*. Available online https://www.blockchain-council.org/blockchain/africa-to-use-blockchain-for-distribution-of-affordable-housing/ (Accessed on 30 December 2023).

Statista. (2023). *Global supply chain management—Statistics & facts*. Available online https://www.statista.com/topics/7150/global-supply-chain-management/#topicOverview (Accessed on 28 December 2023).

Tan, K. H., Zhan, Y., Ji, G., Ye, F., & Chang, C. (2015). Harvesting big data to enhance supply chain innovation capabilities: An analytic infrastructure based on deduction graph. *International Journal of Production Economics, 65*, 223–233. https://doi.org/10.1016/j.ijpe.2014.12.034

Tripathi, G., Tripathi Nautiyal, V., Ahad, M. A., & Feroz, N. (2021). Blockchain technology and fashion industry-opportunities and challenges. In S. K. Panda, A. K. Jena, S. K. Swain, S. C. Satapathy (Eds.), *Blockchain technology: Applications and challenges* (Vol. 203). Intelligent Systems Reference Library. Springer, Cham. https://doi.org/10.1007/978-3-030-69395-4_12

Tundys, B. (2020). Sustainable supply chain management—Past, present and future. *Research Papers of Wroclaw University of Economics and Business, 64*(3), 187–207.

Vermiglio, C., Noto, G., Bolivar, M. P. R., & Zarone, V. (2021). Disaster management and emerging technologies: A performance-based perspective. *Medtari Accountancy Research, 30*(4), 1093–1117.

Wong, L.-W., Leong, L.-Y., Hew, J.-J., Tan, G.W.-H., & Ooi, K.-B. (2020). Time to seize the digital evolution: Adoption of blockchain in operations and supply chain management among Malaysian SMEs. *International Journal of Information Management, 52*, 101997. https://doi.org/10.1016/j.ijinfomgt.2019.08.005

Wu, Z., & Pullman, M. E. (2015). Cultural embeddedness in supply networks. *Journal of Operations Management, 37*, 45–58. https://doi.org/10.1016/j.jom.2015.06.004

23

Artificial Intelligence and Sustainability in Fashion: A Triple Bottom Line Approach

Emily Rosa Shahaj

Introduction

As luxury fashion looks towards recovery strategies following drastic market fluctuations, the incorporation of generative artificial intelligence (AI) is at the top of agendas for maximising profit, minimising costs, and building relationships with consumers. A Deloitte survey published in December 2023 found that 99% of surveyed corporate leadership believed that generative AI will transform their organisation (Deloitte, 2023). This technology is projected to add $150 billion to $175 billion in operating profits for the fashion and luxury sector over the next three to five years (Harreis et al., 2023). In fact, within the fashion industry, the luxury fashion sector may be uniquely positioned to benefit most from the proliferation of AI, due to the nature of its creative methods and its emphasis on a personalised experience. Compared to the potential

E. R. Shahaj (✉)
University for the Creative Arts, School of Fashion and Textile, Epsom KT18 5BE, UK
e-mail: emily.shahaj@uca.ac.uk

W. Ozuem et al. (eds.), *Sustainable Digital Marketing for Fashion and Luxury Brands*,
https://doi.org/10.1007/978-3-031-82467-8_23

financial upsides of adopting generative AI, its potential environmental sustainability benefits are less extensively documented (Khakurel et al., 2018). These include corporate exaggeration of sustainability claims (Dauvergne, 2020), sustainability being dependent on regional electricity sources (Kopka & Grashof, 2022), and efficiency not being a priority metric in AI development (Cowls et al., 2023). However, with AI's potential benefits also come a range of distinct sustainability risks. Given the immense energy draw and ecological footprint of AI, the implementation of AI tools by luxury fashion brands in the interest of sustainability must be approached deliberately and with the benefit of all available data.

Closely following the hype-and-bust cycles of cryptocurrency, non-fungible tokens (NFTs), and the Metaverse, generative AI has emerged as another major trending tech innovation impacting business decisions and headlines. Its boom began in late 2022 with the public releases of OpenAI's ChatGPT text generator, which reached a record-breaking 100 million users within two months of its launch (Hu, 2023), spurring tech giant Google to publicly release their own generative AI tool and Microsoft to invest billions into OpenAI. One year later, such tools could already be found in the fashion sector. Examples include Kering Group's AI-powered personal shopper, 'Madeline'; Stitch Fix's use of AI-processed consumer data to enhance styling recommendations; Zegna X's AI-powered tool to transform the tailored luxury shopping experience (van Gastel, 2023a); and AI-inspired runway looks such as Collina Strada's Spring 24 collection (Garcia-Furtado, 2023). These are early incarnations; in the hands of developers, these tools will soon lead to many more creative and transformative use cases.

However, throughout history, the development of new technologies has almost always ignored sustainability considerations, concentrating instead on proverbial arms races to maximise innovation and profit. In economics, the so-called Jevons Paradox describes the tendency for technologically influenced efficiency gains to rebound into greater consumption and, as a consequence, ecological damage (Polimeni & Polimeni, 2006). At present, generative AI is following the same course, on track to cause the same environmental consequences. The potential sustainability gains from incorporating AI into fashion business processes must be weighed against the environmental impact of its use. According to the triple bottom line (TBL) principle, whilst financial security is important for an organisation's long-term sustainability, so too are its actions towards the sustainability of people and planet (Elkington, 1994). As of December 2023, 91% of corporate leadership felt that generative AI would increase their company's productivity (Deloitte, 2024). What are the costs of this increased productivity—and possibly increased consumption of goods with substantial environmental impact—to the planet and its people?

Publicly available generative AI is emerging in an epoch of climate crisis, and the two must be considered together. Most information on these impacts is held privately by hardware manufacturers, developers and distributed data centres, making the true impacts difficult to monitor and predict (Cowls et al., 2023; Luccioni et al., 2022). AI emissions impacts are extensive due to energy usage throughout its lifespan, including data collection, model experimentation, model training, model optimisation, immediate impacts of deploying, data storage, and end-user inference (Kaack et al., cited in Luccioni et al., 2022; Wu et al., 2022). Each stage here requires individual inferences on emissions impact. Studies estimate that OpenAI's GPT-3, the engine behind ChatGPT as of 2020,[1] emitted between 223,920kg (Cowls et al., 2023) and 544,310kg (Luccioni et al., 2022) of CO_2-equivalent emissions in a single training. At the low end of this range, this single training run would equal the yearly emissions of 49 cars (Cowls et al., 2023). However, in the course of research and development, a single model may need to be trained thousands of times (Strubell et al., 2019). A significant—and revealing—part of the problem is that generative AI models are evaluated primarily on the basis of accuracy, not efficiency (Cowls et al., 2023); the consequences of this priority may be exacerbated exponentially in the case of more accurate machine learning models, which require more computation—sometimes vastly more—to achieve minute improvements (Cowls et al., 2023). This increased training, as well as the testing required to confirm it, requires more electricity; therefore, advancements in AI accuracy are directly responsible for increased carbon

[1] OpenAI did not publicly release the required data to perform these calculations for the more recently released GPT-4 (Heaven, 2023), but it can be reasonably assumed this more-accurate model was several times larger than its predecessor.

emissions (Cowls et al., 2023; Ozuem et al., 2024). As computational needs grow, so does the need for ever more powerful hardware. The manufacture of this new hardware requires mining of rare earth minerals, manufacturing and global shipping, and eventually contributes to the global issue of e-waste (Dauvergne, 2020; Luccioni et al., 2022). For most of the population, the inner workings of AI are mysterious, and its environmental implications (unseen by end users) are easily unknown and ignored. As the training of machine learning models expands, its environmental impacts must be addressed by experts and regulatory bodies with the knowledge and authority to mitigate them.

Legislation such as the landmark European Union Artificial Intelligence Act seeks to address the environmental impact of AI, but these measures are secondary to the mitigation of negative societal impacts. In November 2023, the managing director of Google France ranked AI's environmental burden fourth among its major risks, behind intellectual property infringement, misinformation, and societal impact on employment (Guinebault, 2024). Similarly, Deloitte's January 2024 report on the state of generative AI within enterprises found that 44% of surveyed leaders were at least highly confident about their organisation's expertise in generative AI. However, nearly two-thirds of those leaders also expressed they were unprepared to address concerns about talent, governance or risk related to generative AI adoption (Deloitte, 2024). This suggests that whilst the majority of organisations foresee integration of generative AI in their organisations, the majority are doing so without any plan to mitigate potential negative impacts.

This limited consideration of sustainability factors in AI is further reflected in legislation and governance. Although the European Union Artificial Intelligence Act (2024) mentions the environment multiple times in its example list of potential benefits, it does not mention environmental harm in its much shorter list of potential risks. Similarly, the EU Ethics Guidelines for Trustworthy AI (European Commission, 2024) list seven ethical principles for AI to 'help ensure that AI is trustworthy and ethically sound', the very last of which is 'social and environmental well-being and accountability'. It is also worth noting that these ethical principles are non-binding. Overall, although environmental and societal considerations of AI are 'making the list', it would appear that they are being treated as mere afterthoughts, as is the case in many other sectors and technologies.

This chapter defines sustainability according to the TBL principle, emphasising that organisational sustainability encompasses long-term thinking around the organisation's interactions with planet, people, and profit. TBL asserts that whilst organisations are well acquainted with financial sustainability, they cannot sustain operations in the long term without also making sustainable decisions around people and planet (Elkington, 1994). This chapter therefore critically evaluates AI's broad implications for the sustainability of the fashion industry in regard to the planet, people, and profit. Research around the subject can be categorised as either 'AI for sustainability' or 'the sustainability of AI' (van Wynsberghe, 2021). This chapter attempts to address facets of both as they relate to the fashion industry. Following established definitions and frameworks from prior literature, this chapter explores the impact of generative AI tools on profit, people, and planet within the fashion industry.

Understanding Artificial Intelligence

The European Union's Artificial Intelligence Act of 2024 defines artificial intelligence as 'a machine-based system that, for explicit or implicit objectives, infers, from the input it receives, how to generate outputs such as predictions, content, recommendations, or decisions that can influence physical or virtual environments' (EU Artificial Intelligence Act, 2024). In other words, AI is a computer programme that uses large amounts of existing data, called a 'data set', to predict something new. These predictions have a vast range of use cases across virtually every medium.

Most such machine predictions fall within a range of categories and subcategories. The following three types are particularly relevant to consumer-facing companies: machine learning, computer vision, and generative AI. The latter two can be considered subcategories of machine learning, which is a computer programme with the coded ability to 'study' a given data set to derive averages in order to form predictions. Use cases include personalisation or product recommendations. Computer vision is the ability of a machine learning computer programme to 'study' raw visual input including images, videos, and audio to derive averages in order to form predictions of what fits or does not fit the input. Use cases include fit recommendations from a photo, or detecting manufacturing errors in a production line. Generative AI is the ability of a computer vision programme to create an output in kind of its input, based on what is most likely to follow an adjacent word or pixel or byte. The input could be any form of 'unstructured' data—such as raw text, images, and video—and output new media in formats ranging from scripts to realistic virtual models (Harreis et al., 2023). Often, generative AIs are trained on massive general data sets but create a specific output based on a specific prompt from a user. These cases include text generators such as ChatGPT and image generators such as Midjourney. Fundamental differences between humans and computer programmes make generative AI useful as a collaborator on tasks where machines uniquely excel, leaving the uniquely human tasks, such as empathy and critical thinking, to humans. Overall, the potential use cases and associated impacts of all types of machine learning are vast and growing rapidly.

Framing Sustainability with a Triple Bottom Line

The TBL framework posits that an organisation's evaluation of its bottom line should not consist solely of financial profit, but should also consider people and planet. If an organisation seeks to survive and thrive in the long term, it must also take a long-term view of sustaining the environment and the people it relies on to operate (Elkington, 1994). We see many examples of fashion brands neglecting their bottom lines of planet and people, and of the consequences such neglect has on their financial bottom line. The garment industry is well recognised for its immense global carbon emissions (Thomas, 2020), thereby contributing to the effects of climate change, including the unpredictability of weather. This self-inflicted phenomenon is now inducing visible knock-on effects for an industry whose revenues rely on predictable seasonable garment purchase behaviours. In 2023, British high street fashion brands, including Marks & Spencer and Next, lost more than £500 million in market value due to 'unseasonable weather' in the UK (Lindell, 2023). Similarly, garment manufacturing hub Bangladesh is now named among the world's most climate-vulnerable nations, threatening its already-vulnerable workers as well as fashion's manufacturing operations (Bag et al., 2023). The increased unpredictability of climate, in part induced by the unsustainable behaviours of the garment industry, is now impacting that industry's financial sustainability and threatening its long-term existence.

With the rollout of the EU Strategy for Sustainable and Circular Textiles, fashion sustainability is being legislated for all clothing sold in the European Union, with initiatives rolling out up to 2030 (European Commission, 2024). Fashion brands aiming to sell to European consumers will no longer have the choice of whether or not to genuinely foster sustainability of people and planet within their operations. The European Union Artificial Intelligence Act of 2024 will similarly shape the incorporation of generative AI within European fashion houses and how this technology may be legally used. Luxury fashion firms must incorporate and interlink both sustainability and technology for the sake of their long-term business success.

AI and Financial Well-Being

The potential effects of AI on brands' financial well-being are by far the most touted and analysed of the three bottom lines of corporate sustainability. However, in accordance with the TBL framework, it is critical that a brand's drive for financial well-being not overwhelm their drive for planet or people sustainability. This section addresses the possible financial opportunities as well as the risks for luxury fashion brands' adoption of AI tools within their operations.

Generative AI tools open the possibility of next-generation product personalisation in accessories and apparel. Such personalisation features could enable customers to influence the design of garments in more advanced ways than they can using current modular tools. The customer could interact with such apps via a customised, AI-constructed consumer profile, or through conversation with a virtual personal assistant who would generate prototypes for the user's consideration. Advancements in manufacturing technologies such as 3D printing, 3D knitting, and 3D garment sampling would facilitate the manufacture of these custom products. The potential hyper-personalisation of products facilitated by generative AI may include generating eyewear to complement a user's facial topography (Harreis et al., 2023), printing textiles to complement skin tone, or modifying garment patterns to flatter body shape. The resulting engagement and purchase of such items would boost brand loyalty, raise willing purchase price, and extend the garment's more-sustainable longevity.

AI also opens possibilities for newly personalised brand interaction experiences. AI's ability to generate insights from raw customer data, such as shopping behaviour, consumer sentiment and omnichannel data, enables individual online shopping experiences. These insights could facilitate immense personalisation, from individual customer journeys in online fashion retail to finely honed product descriptions (Harreis et al., 2023). In terms of firms' financial bottom lines, estimates indicate that such one-on-one brand engagement drives 75% more spending (van Gastel, 2023a). Such AI-enabled marketing approaches could also power brand ambassadors on brand websites, social media, or gaming platforms. If executed correctly (insofar as it maintains the brand's character while appealing to an individual's character), and with the advantage of being among the first to successfully implement AI-powered brand ambassadors, this application could inspire powerful brand loyalty. For example, brands could provide customers with an AI-powered, personalised shop assistant to converse with the customer in the way a human shop assistant would, advising on fit and flattery, styling, and colour match to the customer's existing wardrobe. It is even possible that customers may be more willing to provide personal information, such as body scan data, to an AI assistant than to a human, because machines don't pass judgement. Such features could facilitate online luxury fashion sales in areas where current e-commerce falls short.

With the rise of online fashion retail, consumers' expectation of free returns has imposed a financial burden on the fashion industry, amounting to $743 billion in sales, or 14.3% of total retail sales (Zwieglinska, 2024). Broadly, the problem is split between two customer groups of 'heavy returners' driven by different motivations: One group returns because they want to ensure they have chosen the right fit and therefore over-order a range of sizes with the intention of returning the rest; accordingly, 46% of US consumers cite 'poor fit' as their prime reason for returning garments (Scurfield, 2023). The other group purchases with the intention of wearing garments once, keeping the tags intact, and then returning them for a full refund (Zwieglinska, 2024). A brand must adopt different approaches to mitigating these two groups' behaviours, but in both cases it is necessary to identify them swiftly. AI tools finally hold the potential to distinguish between these motivations, predicting them with minimal customer data, to correctively nudge the behaviour of problem customers while meeting the needs of customers with good intentions. For this purpose, a new generation of AI-powered virtual try-on tools and personalised sizing plugins is arriving on the market. For example, Zalando's AI-powered tool uses a customer-uploaded photo to predict measurements and sizes. A recent study from Coresight Research suggests that 85% of retailers intend to use such technology (Scurfield, 2023). If such widespread adoption results in a correspondingly large reduction in returns, it would have significant impacts on both sustainability and finances for affected fashion brands.

Within the design process, AI offers several advantages to luxury fashion brands, including more accurate trend prediction, spotting nuances and moderating effects undetectable by humans (Dauvergne, 2020; Ozuem & Willis, 2024). For luxury designers, mastery of prompting generative AI tools is, and will continue to be, a valuable skill for those seeking creative roles to inspire fresh ideas. When incorporating generative AI tools into their creative development process, fashion brands must consider the legal risks of 'plagiarism, copyright infringement... lack of transparency, explainability, and accountability; and systemic bias' (Deloitte, 2024). When it is unclear what data sources an AI tool is pulling from—and is therefore unclear how original the outputs are or whose copyrights they may be infringing—brands inadvertently risk committing plagiarism and inviting lawsuits. With data sources currently being considered proprietary information of the developers of generative AI tools, the lack of transparency behind the sources of the output makes it difficult to use these tools in commercial settings without risk of inadvertent copyright infringement. Generative AI only copies to predict averages; it does not add original alterations like human designers would. This legal risk may put discourage brands from using generative AI in design, or at least prompt them to add an element of resource-consuming human research into the AI's sourcing before proceeding with a generated design. This burden would likely affect fast fashion more than luxury due to the rate of output and premise of manipulating existing designs. Although there are great possibilities for automation of the fashion design process, legal problems and tracing sources may hinder this possibility.

In the longer term, fashion brands must also consider the risk of consumer pushback to a brand's overuse of AI tools, such as from poorly considered virtual shopping assistants and boycotts in solidarity with generative AI's negative impacts on people or planet. Historically, sweeping new digital technologies have provoked a nostalgic analogue reaction from consumers. For example, the rise of email broadly inspired a renewed sense of value in physical letters. Similarly, the rise of music streaming inspired a renewed interest in vinyl records. The proliferation of AI-generated content may well inspire backlash demand for genuine human-made media or products, as well as in-person or co-present experiences, given the convincing facsimile of recorded images. Similarly, we've seen each generation of digital natives becoming increasingly sceptical of, and resistant to, digital advertising tactics. It is foreseeable that consumers heavily exposed to AI tools will recognise and reject them, or at least be highly sceptical of them, in favour of human-created content. Fashion brands as well as physical retail spaces may take advantage of this pattern by taking a strong stance on generative AI use from the start and holding to it—positioning themselves as pro-human creation, much like we see brands taking strong stances on environmental sustainability and social matters today. Such transparent and publicly proactive measures, if taken now, may help shield brands from future generative AI backlash.

AI and Societal Well-Being

Commonplace use of generative AI and other machine learning tools holds significant implications for individuals and societies, from job security to data security. There are yet many unknowns in how the technology's uses will develop and how those uses might be regulated. Indeed, minimising the negative consequences for humanity is the focus of most ethical concerns towards AI and resulting legislation efforts towards AI (European Union Artificial Intelligence Act, 2024). Fashion has, historically and today, shown little regard for ethical treatment or well-being of its workers. As fashion employs one of every six working people on the planet (Thomas, 2020), a brand's decisions regarding its workers affect many lives, families, and communities across the world and across its span of operations. The fashion industry's incorporation of AI tools will have sweeping impacts on workers, but with concerted consideration from the start, these impacts could be positive.

Broadly, machines and humans are good at different things. Machines are good at processing and storing large amounts of information. As long as human data entry is good, and the human-made code that reads the data is good, machines do not make mistakes. They are therefore more efficient than humans at numerical tasks, reading, checking, and memory. Humans, on the other hand, have lived experiences through complex biological systems and a correspondingly wider range of input. They are uniquely capable of flexibility, judgement and common sense (Autor, 2015). AI, as with past waves of automation, will likely replace low-level monotonous tasks, leaving space for higher-level tasks where humans are inherently more adept than machines, such as critical thinking, teamwork and creativity (Budhwar et al., 2023; Smith, 2023). Whilst generative AI programmes can provide useful outputs, humans must still manually assess the outputs for accuracy and value.

At present, many humans work at jobs that do not make full use of their uniquely human capacities. This is because they are performing tasks that a machine could do, but for which no such machine yet exists (at least, no affordable machine). As generative AI applications evolve and become more broadly accessible and affordable, it will become easier to programme AI to perform tasks at which machines are already adept. This phenomenon has prompted widespread fears of unemployment induced by generative AI. Several studies have indicated that across both the US and UK, more than 50% of 18–24 year-olds are worried that AI will impact their future job prospects (Smith, 2023). However, Autor (2015) points out that labour has never before been wiped out by automation; rather, automation has historically complemented human tasks: For example, many of today's human jobs could not have been imagined prior to the development of electricity. A 1966 U.S. commission report on the potential for automation unemployment, prompted by similar fears in that era, succinctly concluded, 'The basic fact is that technology eliminates jobs, not work' (Bowen, 1966, cited in Autor, 2015). Automation will eliminate some jobs, but it will also create new ones, as it has always done.

Accordingly, many jobs within the fashion industry will likely be disrupted by the automation provided by generative AI. Employees whose jobs may be affected also stand to benefit by learning how to best use AI tools in their work, while also making adjacent use of their uniquely human qualities. In fashion (as in all industries), the role for such human qualities varies, being more central to some jobs than others. For example, fashion models, who provide themselves as images, perform a task that is more wholly substituted by generative AI than complemented by it. When generative AI can automate the creation of a fashion image, fashion models are vulnerable to replacement unless their primary outputs are reconsidered. This threat is different from that facing the job of a fashion designer, for example, who can use generative AI as an automated tool for inspiration but whose skilled human judgement is still needed to prompt the AI algorithms and to select from among generated images.

Furthermore, some demographics of workers within fashion are more susceptible to job loss than others. An increased need for digital skillsets, particularly within an industry that has long resisted digital transformation, puts certain groups at greater risk on the societal level. This will include the ageing workforce, those with limited access to technology, or those otherwise lacking digital skillsets (Budhwar et al., 2023). Optimistically, Deloitte's (2024) report on AI among corporate leadership claims that 36% of corporate executives surveyed were 'making a high or very high effort to... reskill workers impacted by generative AI' (Deloitte, 2024). When seeking directions for reskilling these existing workforces that perform tasks susceptible to replacement by generative AI, leadership need not look far:

> Workers are more likely to benefit directly from automation if they supply tasks that are complemented by automation, but not if they primarily (or exclusively) supply tasks that are substituted... A bank teller who can tally currency but cannot provide 'relationship banking' is unlikely to fare well at a modern bank. (Autor, 2015)

In fashion, the complementing of jobs versus full replacement of jobs by generative AI can already be illustrated by the differences in designers' and models' respective responses to the technology. Designers are lauding the technology as a new tool for creativity: With the emergence of generative AI tools such as Midjourney, designers can construct a prompt and receive a series of designs for their consideration. This use case has been publicly celebrated, making headlines with Collina Strada's Spring 24 AI-inspired collection (Garcia-Furtado, 2023). It is quite possible that further AI tools will soon emerge that can replicate other lower-level designer tasks, such as the production of tech packs. This impending automation demands a shift in the tasks required of lower-level creatives—who are unlikely to be fully replaced by generative AI—likely towards a mastery of generative AI prompts (Van Gastel, 2023b). Within the luxury fashion sector, originality of design is highly valued. If they become totally reliant on generative AI tools, luxury brands will fail to innovate, instead regurgitating averages derived from past collections. This would be disadvantageous to their core value propositions, and avoiding such a fate will require creative human input. The designers may be inspired by generative AI, but not wholly reliant on it. To illustrate, Richard Hobbs, CEO of Web3 fashion company Brand New Vision, emphasises, 'A lot of generative AI is bad... the level of creativity and quality of the output will be determined by the skill of the individual' (Van Gastel, 2023b).

These limitations inherent within the generation mechanisms of AI may always require human talent, and may always require top human talent for true originality. In contrast to fashion designers, for whom generative AI has more complementary applications, fashion models are pushing back against the possibility that they may be replaced altogether by AI-generated imagery, due to the nature of their skillset. These foreseeable risks have influenced a labour movement among fashion models demanding legislation to protect their rights and jobs, alongside strikes by screenwriters motivated by similar concerns (Lee, 2023). Models also demand transparency into the datasets on which AI models are trained. The AI could very well be generating its images of models based on human models' faces, meaning that a brand profits while the influencing models receive nothing. The labour movement's demand would require a generative AI to report what input it uses to develop its outputs (Lee, 2023). To date, such information has been considered proprietary—and technologically implausible to produce. Private-sector compliance with these workers' demands will likely require legislation to force change, including 'explainable' AI sourcing and the payment of royalties to those from whom input imagery was sourced (Lee, 2023). The drastic contrast between different fashion roles' responses to the same technology foreshadows the challenges and divisions to come.

Due to the formidable challenges of automating physical labour outside controlled environments, such as in factories (Autor, 2015), it is possible that fashion-industry garment workers will be largely unaffected by AI, at least in the medium term. To date, the technological advances possible in fashion manufacturing have largely failed to actually change the ways garments are being produced. Of the factories in developing nations and the fashion brands that contract them, few have invested in upgrading their factory floors (Thomas, 2020). The possibilities of AI efficiency will likely not affect garment workers' manual labour jobs until the enabling software and hardware (i.e. robots) becomes cheaper than the humans' manual labour. On a global scale, this modernisation of garment factories has yet to happen despite decades of ever-cheaper digital computing influencing industrial revolution in other sectors. Unless sweeping legislation from either brand-side or manufacturing-side governments forces investment in technological upgrades, change will continue slowly. Therefore, the short- and medium-term effects of

AI on people sustainability in the fashion industry will be largely seen in technology-saturated nations among consumers and skilled workers.

AI is also poised to transform fashion marketing campaigns. Although positive examples are already emerging, it is possible that the shift will be poorly received by audiences, particularly around diversity and representation. In benefit of sustainability, using AI to generate marketing imagery can help reduce the physical production of samples required (which a human model may wear only once) as well as the physical waste and travel emissions associated with a photo shoot. For example, Maison Valentino Essentials successfully utilised AI-generated marketing images for a 2023 campaign (Lee, 2023), embracing the visual quirks of the outputs as part of the aesthetic. However, the use of AI tools to generate marketing imagery poses risks to diversity and representation. Because AI is trained on existing digitised information and can produce output based only on that which is already aggregated and digitised, the already-digitised regions and cultures currently overrepresented on the internet will be proliferated and exacerbated by AI tools. This inherent bias is an important consideration when contemplating the impacts of AI on global inequality and representation. Similarly, generative AI may also exacerbate existing demographic biases. For example, in October 2023, a TikTok post from Taiwanese-American fashion model Shereen Wu lambasted designer Michael Costello for altering a runway photo of her by changing her head to that of a white model. The ensuing dispute went viral, viewed by over 3.5 million people (Lee, 2023). The altercation raises important questions around the ethics of AI image manipulation and the rights of those humans from whom the images are sourced.

The proliferation of AI-generated images in fashion marketing comes at a time when fashion brands are being called upon to represent more diverse models. It is critical that fashion brand marketing teams resist the temptation to model human diversity using AI-created models. Levi's learned this in a March 2023 campaign wherein the denim brand piloted advertisements using AI-create 'diverse fashion models', for which it received fierce backlash. Across social media, users asked why Levi's did not simply pay real, underrepresented human beings (Lee, 2023). It is foreseeable that as AI-generated marketing images become the standard and consumers push back, fashion brands—particularly luxury brands—will feature a 'premium' of real human models in their marketing campaigns. Models are also in a better position than AI-generated images to be leveraged for their individual, 'real' personalities as influencers within marketing campaigns. The potential for consumer backlash against AI-generated fashion marketing—as well as luxury's position as both a premium and slower-paced, higher-quality product—places the luxury fashion sector in a good position to *resist* use of generative AI in marketing imagery. Instead, luxury brands could utilise generative AI only where it improves creativity or furthers the concept of a collection, rather than merely to save on creative costs.

AI has the potential to reduce monotonous manual tasks for humans and allow humans to do what they are uniquely better at—namely, genuine empathy, relatability, creation, and critical thinking. Along these lines, some claim that the true value of AI is its 'role as a complement to human expertise, not a replacement' (Zaczkiewicz, 2024). However, this outcome requires concerted efforts for employers to reskill their workers into needed roles, many of which likely do not currently exist, but which would be created by new needs arising alongside generative AI tools. Education will also play a key role in reskilling across the working population (Khogali & Mekid, 2023). However, in order to reskill the working population across age and experience demographics, the initiative to reskill towards AI-adjacent roles must come from both educators and employers.

AI and the Planet's Well-Being

The incorporation of AI into the broad span of luxury fashion's operations presents both opportunities and risks for greater environmental sustainability. We begin here by first discussing the opportunities before delving into the risks.

AI has the potential to positively affect the entire fashion supply chain. Starting from the ground level, so to speak, AI is being used to optimise fertiliser use in crops such as rice, which in test cases roughly halved fertiliser and pesticide usage (Chen et al., 2023). This could have massive implications for cotton growing, which is presently the globe's most pesticide-reliant agricultural product (Thomas, 2020) and a key raw material for the fashion industry. AI's ability to calculate new synthetic materials has helped scientists develop new methods of treating toxic textile dyeing sludge that would otherwise be left to poison ecosystems (Ding et al., 2022). AI can help predict, and therefore help to mitigate, climate change-caused natural disasters and flooding in key garment manufacturing countries such as Bangladesh, which is ranked among the world's most climate-vulnerable nations (Bag et al., 2023). AI-based supplier relationship management, implemented by fashion brands, can enhance climate change adaptation and disaster risk reduction capabilities among complex garment industry supply chains (Bag et al., 2023). AI can also help brands determine the most suitable sustainable suppliers for their specific ideal needs and social impact objectives (Naz et al., 2022). Furthermore, AI can play a key role in enabling digital product passports to enhance traceability through fashion-industry supply chains (Alves et al., 2024), assisting in the industry's regulatory compliance to avoid labour violations arising from opaque subcontracting (Thomas, 2020). Further, AI can optimise shipping and logistics to reduce expenditures and lower per-product carbon emissions in transportation by avoiding delays and inefficient loadings (Dauvergne, 2020; Srhir et al., 2023). Generative AI has a broad range of use cases that stand to benefit the fashion industry, and more will emerge as the technology continues to develop.

Whilst much has been made of the use of generative AI within the garment design process (Lee, 2023), less attention has been paid to the potential for AI models to simultaneously consider the environmental impact of the manufacturing of the garments they generate. Going beyond image generation based on prompts, AI models with a more robust understanding of flat garment patterns and garment construction could understand the fabric usage, pattern piece arrangement, and material specifications of the generated garment. Such a tool could consider and generate the most material-efficient arrangement of pattern pieces on a given bolt of fabric, adjusting the pattern where needed, and thereby reducing pre-consumer waste. The resulting garment pattern layout, general environmental impact, and likely cost of materials for the generated design would be presented to the human designer in a series of iterated options for their consideration beyond aesthetics. Furthermore, transcending improved efficiency of production, generative AI tools also make it possible to consider the sustainability implications of a given design in the earliest phases, rather than as an afterthought. They could also reduce the need for repeated and iterative physical sampling of collections as well as the material waste—and, often, global shipping emissions—that have been typical of this standard manufacturing practice. However, a significant hurdle to this concept is a lack of garment pattern data with which to train an AI model. Due to the scarcity of fashion patterns that have been digitised in a standardised, computer-readable format, the creation of a training data set to recognise or create garment patterns would be highly burdensome and expensive. This limitation exemplifies how industries that have been slower to digitise their practices, such as fashion, are at a disadvantage when it comes to integrating AI.

Technologies associated with the fourth industrial revolution, including AI and big data analytics, can facilitate circularity in the garment industry. As part of a wider circular economy, circularity entails design and planning for the reuse and recycling of a product when it reaches the end of its lifecycle, rather than a linear system of products that end up in landfills (Ellen MacArthur Foundation, 2024). For fashion, this requires many changes, from product design to textile composition, and from brand behaviour to customer behaviour. AI can help facilitate these changes (Roberts et al., 2024; Wiegand & Wynn, 2023). For example, AI can be used at the end of a garment's lifecycle for improved recycling and, thus, circularity. At present, small amounts of elastane (Lycra, Spandex) in a textile render a garment unrecyclable. Computer vision tools such as PICVISA can use artificial vision and AI to detect the chemical composition of a garment's fabric and sort it for appropriate recycling. This process could save up to 2200 tons of textile waste annually (Recycling Inside, 2022). When undertaken by humans, however, this process takes impractical amounts of time and skill, and is not necessarily effective in detecting small percentages of materials within a given fabric. This inaccuracy and cost of sorting discarded garments using human labour has significantly hampered garment recycling efforts. AI tools can also be leveraged in garment recycling to accurately and broadly predict the amount of recycled material that will come out of the process, to help sell the recycled raw material more efficiently. Such use of AI could be the factor that makes widespread garment recycling feasible, and it is in alignment with the EU Strategy for Sustainable and Circular Textiles's emphasis on textile recyclability (Bag, 2022; European Commission, 2024).

Within fashion retail, AI tools will transform the customer journey for a more customised, tailored shopping experience. As this shopping experience becomes the norm and even the expectation, brands that are slow to adopt will be at a disadvantage among consumers. Whilst this improved digital customer experience could easily be used to simply encourage *more* purchasing (Dauvergne, 2020), ideally it could be used more responsibly to encourage *wiser* purchasing of fewer—but more durable—products (Sun et al., 2021) that persist longer within a brand's ecosystem. Like Apple's ecosystem of hardware products linked by clever software interconnectivity, smarter fashion brand ecosystems could be used to foster brand loyalty and repeat purchase through the convenience of remaining within the retailer's centralised ecosystem. For example, retailers could leverage AI tools to better understand an individual customer's lifestyle, taste, price sensitivity, and current wardrobe to present highly personalised recommendations and even product customisations. Over time and with repeated interactions, the model would learn and improve its accuracy, yielding increased understanding of the customer's existing wardrobe and more accurate product predictions. For the customer, this more refined model incentivises increased interaction and repeat purchases instead of starting over with new brands. Luxury brands and luxury multi-brand retailers are well poised for initial adoption because their retail model is already more centred on client relationships and customer service, compared to fast fashion brands.

Furthermore, such consumer-facing AI-powered retail tools can utilise wardrobe analysis and purchase history to encourage more prudent purchase behaviours by consumers. This could include restyling tips to match newer trends without making new purchases, as well as recommendations against buying products similar to those the customer likely still has, instead offering tips for new styling. Such tools could also help customers set and adhere to annual carbon budgets through their purchases, helping to balance more-sustainable decisions with splurges and keeping sustainability front-of-mind at the point of the sale. Dissuading customers from certain or excessive purchases would be an unusual approach for a retailer when evaluating the recent decades of consumer culture and the consumer–brand relationship. However, the culture and approach around unconsidered and unmitigated purchasing must change for the sake of the planet and for the sake of a brand's TBL. In fact, such a consistent 'don't buy' message has burnished the brand image of premium brands like Patagonia and REI (Thompson & Kumar, 2022). Brands investing in such strategies stand to increase customer trust and loyalty over the long term.

Further, the use of AI to generate retail imagery before launching physical production can facilitate new retail business models, such as by allowing brands to calculate consumer response before manufacturing a new product, thereby enabling them to adopt a made-to-order model. This practice is exemplified by the pricing model of Swedish clothing brand Atacac, which uses computer-generated imagery to sell designs before closing the window for orders, after which they manufacture only enough to supply what was pre-sold (Atacac, 2024). This practice eliminates the deadstock materials and products rampant in the typical fashion business model of overproduction.

Despite these promising use cases, AI tools that aim to reduce the fashion industry's environmental impact might also exacerbate that impact through the hardware and electricity needed to train these models and run them. Unless tempered by deliberate measures to significantly mitigate negative environmental impacts, the high electricity draw and manufacture of intensive computing hardware involved in generative AI tools could very well worsen the fashion industry's environmental cost. Furthermore, the persuasive power of personalised AI tools might easily be used irresponsibly by fashion brands to encourage consumer overconsumption and thereby magnify individual consumers' environmental impacts (Dauvergne, 2020). Indeed, the fashion industry has a poor history of self-regulation when it comes to sustainability matters (Thomas, 2020), although emerging governance from key fashion markets such as the EU Strategy for Sustainable and Circular Textiles (European Commission, 2024) may incentivise European luxury fashion brands to align with these approaches as they incorporate AI tools.

Conclusion

When considering how AI is implemented within an organisation, brands ought to strive towards their positive brand values. If integrity, authenticity, or quality are among their values, their AI tools must demonstrate the same, both those internally and consumer-facing.

With the rise of AI tools come many opportunities for the fashion industry to maximise profit and minimise costs, which have been explored by the fashion industry since their emergence. However, the implications for people and the planet in the use of this technology have been largely overlooked. On broader economic scales, 51% of surveyed corporate executives expected generative AI to worsen economic inequality (Deloitte, 2024). Avoiding these economic consequences requires careful handling and planning by both brands and policy-makers to find ways for the benefits of AI tools to touch the majority of humanity from the start, rather than consolidating the benefits for a powerful minority.

The overarching consideration of this complex subject is that AI has very real potential to do more harm than good (Chen et al., 2023; Dauvergne, 2020; Khogali & Mekid, 2023; Scola, 2021; Shumskaia, 2022; Wagner & Kalbalska, 2022), particularly in regard to the bottom lines of people and planet. Yet, with careful consideration, imagination and a purposeful, data-driven approach, these new tools could instead reduce the impact of implicit negative factors while making aspects of a fashion brand's operations significantly more socially and environmentally positive. To turn these aspirations into realities by achieving such positive impacts, it will be necessary to implement conscious decision-making at the earliest planning stages and user-centric design from end to end. Given its questionable record of self-regulation, the fashion industry requires careful planning and coordinated governance to ensure that the sustainability gains of AI are sufficient to offset the costs.

References

Alves, L., Sá, M., Cruz, E. F., Alves, T., Alves, M., Oliveira, J., Santos, M., & Rosado da Cruz, A. M. (2024). A Traceability platform for monitoring environmental and social sustainability in the textile and clothing value chain: Towards a digital passport for textiles and clothing. *Sustainability, 16*(1), 82. https://doi.org/10.3390/su16010082

Atacac. (2024). *Price model*. Available at https://shop.atacac.com/pages/price-model (Accessed 10 April 2024).

Autor, D. H. (2015). Why are there still so many jobs? The history and future of workplace automation. *Journal of Economic Perspectives, 29*(3), 3–30.

Bag, S., Sabbir Rahman, M., Rogers, H., Srivastava, G., & Harm Christiaan Pretorius, J. (2023). Climate change adaptation and disaster risk reduction in the garment industry supply chain network. *Transportation Research Part E: Logistics and Transportation Review, 171*, 103031. https://doi.org/10.1016/j.tre.2023.103031

Bag, S., Dhamija, P., Bryde, D. J., & Singh, R. K. (2022). Effect of eco-innovation on green supply chain management, circular economy capability, and performance of small and medium enterprises. *Journal of Business Research, 141*, 60–72. https://doi.org/10.1016/j.jbusres.2021.12.011

Budhwar, P., Chowdhury, S., Wood, G., Aguinis, H., Bamber, G. J., Beltran, J. R., Boselie, P., Cooke, F. L., Decker, S., DeNisi, A., Dey, P. K., Guest, D., Knoblich, A. J., Malik, A., Paauwe, J., Papagiannidis, S., Patel, C., Pereira, V., Ren, S., & Rogelberg, S. (2023). Human resource management in the age of generative artificial intelligence: Perspectives and research directions on ChatGPT. *Human Resource Management Journal, 33*(3), 606–659.

Chen, L., Chen, Z., Zhang, Y., Liu, Y., Osman, A. I., Farghali, M., Hua, J., Al-Fatesh, A., Ihara, I., Rooney, D. W., & Yap, P.-S. (2023). Artificial intelligence-based solutions for climate change: A review. *Environmental Chemistry Letters, 21*,. https://doi.org/10.1007/s10311-023-01617-y

Cowls, J., Tsamados, A., Taddeo, M., & Floridi, L. (2023). The AI gambit: Leveraging artificial intelligence to combat climate change—Opportunities, challenges, and recommendations. *AI & Society, 38*, 283–307. https://doi.org/10.1007/s00146-021-01294-x

Dauvergne, P. (2020). Is artificial intelligence greening global supply chains? Exposing the Political Economy of Environmental Costs. *Review of International Political Economy, 29*(3), 696–718. https://doi.org/10.1080/09692290.2020.1814381

Deloitte. (2024). *Deloitte's state of generative AI in the enterprise quarter one report.* Available at https://www2.deloitte.com/content/dam/Deloitte/us/Documents/consulting/us-state-of-gen-ai-report.pdf (Accessed 10 April, 2024).

Ding, Z., Chen, Z., Liu, J., Evrendilek, F., He, Y., & Xie, W. (2021). Co-combustion, life-cycle circularity, and artificial intelligence-based multi-objective optimization of two plastics and textile dyeing sludge. *Journal of Hazardous Materials, 426*, 128069–128069. https://doi.org/10.1016/j.jhazmat.2021.128069

Elkington, J. (1994). Towards the sustainable corporation: Win-win-win business strategies for sustainable development. *California Management Review, 36*(2), 90–100. https://doi.org/10.2307/41165746

Ellen MacArthur Foundation. (2024). *The fashion remodel*. Available at https://www.ellenmacarthurfoundation.org/the-fashion-remodel/overview (Accessed 25 July, 2024).

EU Artificial Intelligence Act. (2024). Available at https://artificialintelligenceact.eu/the-act/ (Accessed 10 April 2024).

European Commission. (2024). *EU strategy for sustainable and circular textiles.* Available at https://environment.ec.europa.eu/strategy/textiles-strategy_en (Accessed 10 April 2024).

Garcia-Furtado, L. (2023). *Collina Strada Sprint 2024 ready-to-wear.* Available at https://www.vogue.com/fashion-shows/spring-2024-ready-to-wear/collina-strada (Accessed 10 April 2024).

Guinebault, M. (2024). *From product sheets to design, AI is changing the fashion industry.* Available at https://ww.fashionnetwork.com/news/From-product-sheets-to-design-ai-is-changing-the-fashion-industry,1588471.html (Accessed 10 April 2024).

Harreis, H., Koullias, T., Roberts, R., Te, K. (2023). *Generative AI: Unlocking the future of fashion.* Available at https://www.mckinsey.com/industries/retail/our-insights/generative-ai-unlocking-the-future-of-fashion (Accessed 10 April 2024).

Heaven, W. D. (2023). *GPT-4 is bigger and better than ChatGPT—But OpenAI won't say why.* Available at https://www.technologyreview.com/2023/03/14/1069823/gpt-4-is-bigger-and-better-chatgpt-openai/ (Accessed 23 July 2024).

Hu, K. (2023). *ChatGPT sets record for fastest-growing user base.* Available at https://www.reuters.com/technology/chatgpt-sets-record-fastest-growing-user-base-analyst-note-2023-02-01/ (Accessed 10 April 2024).

Recycling Inside. (2022). *Hyperspectral vision and the classification of textiles for recycling.* Available at https://recyclinginside.com/recycling-technology/separation-and-sorting-technology/hyperspectral-vision-and-the-classification-of-textiles-for-recycling/ (Accessed 10 April 2024).

Khogali, H. O., & Mekid, S. (2023). The blended future of automation and AI: Examining some long-term societal and ethical impact features. *Technology in Society, 73*, 102232.

Kopka, A., & Grashof, N. (2022). Artificial intelligence: Catalyst or barrier on the path to sustainability? *Technological Forecasting and Social Change, 175*,. https://doi.org/10.1016/j.techfore.2021.121318

Lee, A. (2023). *Top 10 stories of 2023: Top 10 moves that accelerated AI in fashion.* Available at https://wwd.com/business-news/technology/top-10-ai-fashion-2023-artificial-intelligence-1236085150/ (Accessed 10 April 2024).

Lindell, K. (2023). *Warm weather knocks over £500 million off M&S and next.* Available at https://www.bloomberg.com/news/articles/2023-10-09/warm-weather-knocks-over-500-million-off-m-s-and-next?embedded-checkout=true (Accessed 10 April 2024).

Luccioni, A. S., Viguier, S., & Ligozat, A.-L. (2022). *Estimating the carbon footprint of BLOOM, a 176B parameter language model*. Preprint at arXiv. https://doi.org/10.48550/arXiv.2211.02001

Naz, F., Agrawal, R., Kumar, A., Gunasekaran, A., Majumdar, A., & Luthra, S. (2022). Reviewing the applications of artificial intelligence in sustainable supply chains: Exploring research propositions for future directions. *Business Strategy and the Environment, 31*(5). https://doi.org/10.1002/bse.3034

Ozuem, W., & Willis, M. (2024). Artificial intelligence and Predictive analytics: Towards a praxis of personalised shopping experiences. In W. Ozuem, S. Ranfagni, M. Willis (Eds.), *Digital transformation for fashion and luxury brands*. Palgrave Macmillan.

Ozuem, W., Ranfagni, S., Willis, M., Salvietti, G., & Howell, K. (2024). Exploring the relationship between chatbots, service failure recovery and

customer loyalty: A frustration–aggression perspective. *Psychology and Marketing*. https://doi.org/10.1002/mar.22051
Polimeni, J. M., & Polimeni, R. I. (2006). Jevons' Paradox and the myth of technological liberation. *Ecological Complexity, 3*(4), 344–353.
Roberts, H., Zhang, J., Bariach, B., et al. (2024). Artificial intelligence in support of the circular economy: Ethical considerations and a path forward. *AI & Society, 39*, 1451–1464. https://doi.org/10.1007/s00146-022-01596-8
Scola, L. (2021). *Artificial intelligence against climate change.* Lecture notes in networks and systems, 378–397. https://doi.org/10.1007/978-3-030-80126-7_29
Scurfield, H. (2023). *Tech tools for combating poor fit and returns: data analytics, AI and VR.* FashionUnited. Available at https://fashionunited.uk/news/business/tech-tools-for-combating-poor-fit-and-returns-data-analytics-ai-and-vr/2023101772138 (Accessed 25 July 2024).
Shumskaia, E. I. (2022) *Artificial intelligence—Reducing the carbon footprint?* (pp. 359–365). Springer eBooks. https://doi.org/10.1007/978-3-030-79496-5_33
Smith, S. (2023). *Students are worried about AI taking their jobs.* Available at https://www.dazeddigital.com/life-culture/article/61524/1/students-are-worried-about-ai-artificial-intelligence-taking-their-jobs (Accessed 10 April 2024).
Srhir, S., Jaegler, A., & Montoya-Torres, J. R. (2023). Uncovering Industry 4.0 technology attributes in sustainable supply chain 4.0: A systematic literature review. *Business Strategy and the Environment, 32*(7), 4143–4166. https://doi.org/10.1002/bse.3358
Strubell, E., Ganesh, A., & McCallum, A. (2019). *Energy and policy considerations for deep learning in NLP.* Proceedings of the 57th Annual Meeting of the Association for Computational Linguistics. https://doi.org/10.18653/v1/p19-1355
Sun, J. J., Bellezza, S., & Paharia, N. (2021). Buy less, buy luxury: Understanding and overcoming product durability neglect for sustainable consumption. *Journal of Marketing, 85*(3), 28–43. https://doi.org/10.1177/0022242921993172
Thomas, D. (2020) *Fashionopolis: Why what we wear matters.* Penguin Publishing Group.
Thompson, C. J., & Kumar, A. (2022). Analyzing the cultural contradictions of authenticity: Theoretical and managerial insights from the market logic of conscious capitalism. *Journal of Marketing, 86*(5), 21–41. https://doi.org/10.1177/00222429221087987

van Wynsberghe, A. (2021). Sustainable AI: AI for sustainability and the sustainability of AI. *AI and Ethics, 1*(1). https://doi.org/10.1007/s43681-021-00043-6

van Gastel, T. (2023b). *AI's role as fashion design assistant: Tommy Hilfiger, AI Fashion Week, and Text-to-Design.* Available at https://jingdaily.com/posts/artificial-intelligence-fashion-design-assistant-tommy-hilfiger-midjourney (Accessed 10 April 2024).

van Gastel, T. (2023a). *From Kering to Zegna: How brands can use AI to supercharge luxury shopping.* Available at https://jingdaily.com/posts/luxury-brand-shopping-ai-kering-zegna#cd8b6bae31ee (Accessed 10 April 2024).

Wagner, R., & Kabalska, A. (2022). Sustainable value in the fashion industry: A case study of value construction/destruction using digital twins. *Sustainable Development, 31*(3). https://doi.org/10.1002/sd.2474

Wiegand, T., & Wynn, M. G. (2023). Sustainability, the Circular Economy and Digitalisation in the German Textile and Clothing Industry. *Sustainability, 15*(11), 9111–9111. https://doi.org/10.3390/su15119111

Wu, C-J., Raghavendra, R., Gupta, U., Acun, B., Ardalani, N., Chang, G., Behram, F.A., Huang, J., Bai, C., Gschwind, M., Ott, M., Melnikov, A., Candido, S., Brooks, D., Chauhan, G., Maeng, K., Gupta, A., Lee, B., Lee, H-S., Akyildiz, B., Balandat, M., Spisak, J., Jain, R., Rabbat, M. & Hazelwood, K., (2022) *Sustainable AI: Environmental implications, challenges and opportunities.* Proceedings of the 5th MLSys Conference, Santa Clara, CA, USA.

Zaczkiewicz, A (2024) *Harnessing Generative AI: The New Frontier for Fashion Retailers.* Available at: https://wwd.com/business-news/technology/ai-tips-for-business-amazon-accenture-synchrony-1236163776/ (Accessed 10 April 2024).

Zwieglinska, Z (2024) *Luxury Briefing: How LVMH is tackling luxury returns with AI.* Available at: https://www.glossy.co/fashion/luxury/luxury-briefing-how-lvmh-is-tackling-luxury-returns-with-ai/ (Accessed 10 April 2024).

24

Artificial Intelligence: Building Sustainability in the Implementation of SDGs

Gordon Bowen, Janakan Sothinathan, Richard Bowen, Deidre Bowen, and Atul Sethi

Introduction

The fashion supply chain tends to use resources from developing countries where poverty and inequality have a significant impact on society and economic progress. Fast fashion has become synonymous with the fashion industry. Fast fashion production and delivery to market are

G. Bowen (✉)
Anglia Ruskin University, Cambridge, UK
e-mail: gordon.bowen@aru.ac.uk

J. Sothinathan
Business School, Northumbria University London Campus, London, UK

R. Bowen
Darwin Home, California, USA

D. Bowen
Mental Health UK, Operations, London, UK

A. Sethi
Business School, Ulster University London Campus, London, UK

W. Ozuem et al. (eds.), *Sustainable Digital Marketing for Fashion and Luxury Brands*,
https://doi.org/10.1007/978-3-031-82467-8_24

swift; designs are changed to keep the flow of fashion items moving. Consequently, a fast fashion product's lifecycle is shortened, which could increase the risk of overproduction (Fletcher, 2010). This chapter will argue that fashion has negatively impacted the implementation of sustainable development goals (SDGs), especially SDG 5, gender equality, and SDG 1, no poverty, which has made economic growth in developing countries much slower than anticipated. However, the introduction of "slow fashion" could contribute to the achievement of no poverty and gender equality and concurrently improve economic growth (SDG 8). Slow fashion involves longer production lead times, the use of local materials, and a focus on sustainability and quality (Fletcher, 2007). One could view fast fashion through the prism of greed because more products are produced that lead to more sales that deliver ever-increasing profits. However, this is at the expense of workers' rights (leading to inequality) and exploitation (leading to poverty). Living better, designing better, and consuming better are the hallmarks of slow fashion; this approach requires designers, buyers, retailers, and consumers to do things differently. All the stakeholders understand the impact of fashion products on workers, communities, and ecosystems (Azemi & Ozuem, 2023; Fletcher, 2007). The main hypothesis of this chapter is that adopting a slow fashion approach could improve employment and economic conditions in emerging developing countries that have the fashion industry as their main industry. A supplementary hypothesis is that artificial intelligence (AI) could help to drive the fashion ecosystem to the slow fashion paradigm. Slow fashion is an attempt to counterbalance the negative impacts of fast fashion, and AI could help in achieving a new equilibrium in the fashion industry.

The topics in this chapter are the fashion industry, SDGs (economic growth, gender equality, and no poverty), supply chain and AI implementation, consumer behaviour in the slow fashion ecosystem, and models of societal behaviour, the last two sections are implications and conclusion.

Fashion Industry

A McKinsey & Company report (Balchandani et al., 2023) on the fashion industry suggested that storm clouds are gathering over the fashion industry, but it continues to do well. The luxury segment of the fashion industry continued to show strong growth in 2022 with a 36% rise in profit over 2021. Even the non-luxury fashion segments showed strong growth in 2022 leading to the fashion industry achieving at least double the growth it experienced in the period 2011–2020, except for one year.

According to the website FashionUnited, the largest retail markets globally are USA, China, United Kingdom, Germany, and Japan (FashionUnited, n.d.). The fashion industry faced many challenges in 2023, which included persistent slow growth in Europe and the USA throughout 2023. China maintained strong growth part of the year, but it faded towards year-end. The luxury fashion segment started well in 2023 but faded towards the end of 2023 due to weakening demand. The business environment in the fashion industry faced uncertainty, which led to slowing economic growth and a high level of inflation (compared to recent historical levels), which was persistent and led to weak consumer confidence. An improvement is predicted for 2024 with a top-line growth of 2 to 4%. The expectation is that the luxury fashion segment will have the strongest growth (3 to 5% globally). Fashion industry executives have cited geopolitical instability as the greatest impediment to growth with economic uncertainty and inflation the next biggest impediments to growth (Balchandani et al., 2023).

According to Balchandani et al. (2023), the themes for the 2024 fashion market include an unsettling global economic outlook with the major fashion markets facing economic headwinds, climate change issues, and changes in consumer attitudes, such as an increase in travel now the pandemic is in the rearview mirror, following new fashion brand influencers, and embracing a healthier lifestyle that will drive sales of outdoor clothing (gorpcore). The other themes identified were: the capturing of value in the fashion industry with the application of generative AI; competition from challengers such as Shein and Temu that are lowering prices and giving customers a new experience with increased speed; an emphasis on brand marketing that fosters emotional connections with consumers to build long-term branding; sustainability as a driver that will end self-regulation for the fashion industry, and sustainability requirements that cross many jurisdictions and require changes to business models; and the bullwhip effect could resonate due to customers cutting back, which could lead to order volatility and unpredictability in supply chains. Strategic partnerships will add pressure to suppliers as retailers focus on brands and transparency.

According to Bhardwaj and Fairhurst (2010), fashion is under-researched, and researchers focus on quick or fast fashion in the research context of buyer–supplier relationships (Forza & Vinelli, 1996; Ozuem et al., 2023), role of the supplier in fast-moving fashion (Doyle et al., 2006), buyer behaviour (Bruce & Daly, 2006), and financial performance (Hayes & Jones, 2006). The lifecycle of fashion pre-1980s had four stages: introduction of a fashion product and adoption by leaders of fashion (fashion conscious); maturity, which was characterised by public acceptance leading to growth; the final stage was decline and obsolescence of the fashion (Bhardwaj & Fairhurst, 2010). There have been several major changes in the fashion industry since the pre-1980s. One of these changes was a reduction in the low-cost mass production and standardisation of product styles and the infrequent change of designs that characterised the 1980s (Brooks, 1979). The demise of the mass production of fashion led to consumers becoming more fashion conscious and more sensitive to style (Bailey, 2001). In response to fashion conscious consumers the fashion industry introduced colour and texture, which led to more co-ordination between outfits for women and some men (Donnellan, 1996). Fashion trends evolve with the change in seasons; this is considered a temporary phenomenon that is a cyclical process (Ozuem et al., 2024; Sproles, 1979). Increasing the variety of fashion apparel products in the market led to an increase in phases in the fashion season (Bhardwaj & Fairhurst, 2010); three to five mid-seasons put additional pressure on suppliers to deliver fashion items in smaller bundles with reduced lead times (Tyler et al., 2006).

Another major change in the fashion industry was the demise of several large retailers in the late 1980s, which increased competition in the fashion industry (Barnes & Lea-Greenwood, 2006). Structural changes since the late 1980s include outsourcing of material and offshoring manufacturing to places with low-cost economies that have low labour costs (Bhardwaj & Fairhurst, 2010). The benefits of outsourcing were not necessarily complementary to streamlining because lead times were increased, diverse geographical supply chains impacted management of the supply chain on both the supply and retail side, and the import/export procedures were more complex (Bruce & Daly, 2006). The savings expected from outsourcing were a mirage that increased inventory costs and led to mark downs to shift the excess stock (Christopher et al., 2004). The shortcomings caused by the issues mentioned above forced more changes in the fashion industry, such as just-in-time techniques; from 1994 to 1995, the percentage of retailers implementing the just-in-time technique grew from 60 to 72% (Jones, 1995). Given the documented issues that arose from the introduction of fast fashion techniques, consumer behaviour is likely to change and the desire to purchase throwaway fashion apparel is likely to diminish, especially among younger generations.

Is the slow fashion paradigm an enabler to overcome some of the challenges and themes identified? How can slow fashion minimise the economic headwinds and geopolitical instability? Sustainability and unpredictability of fashion supply chain activities could be improved with a slow fashion approach that incorporates the SDGs that link to inequality and poverty. These topics will be returned to in the Implications section of the chapter.

SDG 8 Economic Growth, SDG 5 Gender Equality, and SDG 1 No Poverty

The politics of sustainability and innovation in the fast fashion industry will determine the success of SDGs in the fashion industry. The concepts of sustainability and innovation emerged simultaneously along parallel paths (Pérez-Bou & Cantista, 2023). The fashion industry's commitment to building a sustainable framework of social and economic success needs to be underpinned by innovation in the fashion industry (Pérez-Bou & Cantista, 2023). Sustainability in the fashion industry requires national models of sustainability, such as the national innovation system proposed by Nelson and Rosenberg (1993). They identified important factors of innovation capacity: economic power by companies, the power of education and training, the power of politics, and the power of finance (Nelson & Rosenberg, 1993: 4).

Economic Growth (SDG 8)

The fashion industry is one of the most polluting industries in the world: textiles require high levels of water and raw materials, and they are a major contributor to greenhouse gases (EU, 2020).

Actions undertaken by two leading fashion companies towards achieving SDGs are discussed below.

Inditex

Inditex, in its 2022 annual report (Inditex, n.d.), specifically mentions sustainability in its organisational strategy. It bases sustainability on four pillars: unique fashion proposal, increasingly engaging shopping experience, extraordinary team, and sustainability and responsibility (Inditex, n.d.). The company claims it can adapt to changes in the marketplace or changes in fashion processes that may require a change in processes. Inditex states that a significant weight of geographical manufacturing is close to its headquarters in Spain and analysis of the locations they operate globally this is an accurate account. The customer experience is based on innovative technological stores with cutting-edge energy systems in prime locations around the world. Inditex makes the point that they employ 160,000 "passionate and curious people" that form an extraordinary team. How the firm interacts with the surrounding environment is described as sustainable and responsible. The outcome is quality fashion apparel at an attractive price. Inditex has also adhered to the United Nations Global Compact since 2001. Inditex SDG milestones include good health and well-being (SDG 3), gender equality

(SDG 5), decent work and economic growth (SDG 8), responsible consumption and production (SDG 12), climate action (SDG 13), and partnerships for the goals (SDG 17) (Inditex, n.d.).

H&M

The key economic and social goals for H&M include a reduction in carbon dioxide emissions by 2030 against a 2019 baseline, and net-zero emissions by 2030. Both goals are science-based targets. Products are designed with the circular economy in mind; H&M works in partnership with the Ellen MacArthur Foundation, which has a vision for a circular economy for fashion. H&M's aim is that by 2025 at least 30% of its source material is recyclable and, by 2030, 100% of commercial goods will be recyclable or sustainable. Another goal is to reduce packaging by 25% by 2025 using a 2018 baseline (it appears to be making very good progress on this metric) and to use 100% recyclable or sustainable packaging by 2030. In 2030, suppliers must be compliant with the ZDHC Manufacturing Restricted Substances List (there appears to be very good progress on this metric). Water goals include a reduction in absolute total freshwater use by 10% by 2025 using a 2022 baseline and a reduction in absolute total freshwater use by 30% by 2030 against a 2022 baseline. Fair and equal goals include an annual increase in percentage terms of female supervisors for Tier 1 suppliers (27%) and an annual increase in percentage terms for worker representation for Tier 1 suppliers (2022—63%) using a baseline 2022 (H&M Group, n.d.). Interestingly, SDG metrics are not explicitly assigned but one can deduce them from the website report.

Gender Equality (SDG 5)

SDG 5 is about gender and not sex, which is a biological process. The differences between men and women and gender are influenced by social status, religion, ethnicity, environment, and age (Pathania, 2017). Gender equality is a concept in which all genders have equal rights and freedoms in all social settings, the work environment (salary ratio, gender ratio), education, and voting (Shastri, 2014).

The aim of SDG 5 is to end all forms of discrimination against women and girls; this includes ending violence, giving them access to sex health and reproductive health, ending child marriages, and sexual exploitation. Women must be more visible in society and enter all the spheres in society (Stuart & Woodroffe, 2016). Although gender inequality is decreasing, women still face challenges (Küfeoğlu, 2020). Gender equality is a universal issue; women and girls make up approximately 50% of the global population and consequently a significant part of the global population could face discrimination (UN Women, 2021).

No Poverty (SDG 1)

According to the World Bank, poverty is a significant lack in well-being (Malmberg Calvo et al., 2000). According to Haughton and Khandker (2009), well-being is concerned with monetary advantage, such as command over income or consumption. People experiencing poverty do not have an adequate level of income or consumption. People experiencing poverty do not have control over specific consumption, such as housing, food, and health quality. In a broad sense poverty is about individuals being able to function in society. Measuring poverty keeps its importance upfront. Interventionalist strategies can be applied to aid people experiencing poverty and the effectiveness of organisations' projects and policies to help them can be monitored and evaluated.

The fashion industry uses labour in developing countries and thus has direct responsibility for the level of poverty of its employees and their families. The effectiveness of the fashion industry's activities and policies to alleviate poverty is not necessarily directly included in its SDG metrics.

The drivers of poverty include globalisation, increasing population, inflation, economic crisis, and growth rates; all these drivers need to be continually confronted and SDG 1 is an aspirational goal (Küfeoğlu, 2020). Unfortunately, the drivers identified are not normally predictable. Individual countries can face economic issues; thus, global economic issues are not always the cause of a country's poverty (Jolliffe et al., 2015). The eradication of poverty is a long-term objective which will be challenging to achieve even with the application of technology.

The SDG goal for no poverty includes income poverty and human deprivation in many dimensions, such as eradicating extreme poverty, universal primary education, getting rid of gender inequality in primary and secondary schooling, reducing infant mortality by two-thirds, reducing maternal mortality by three-quarters, universal access to reproductive health services, and the implementation of national sustainable strategies in every country (Haughton & Khandker, 2009).

Strategies to overcome poverty, according to the World Bank, include promoting opportunities for people experiencing poverty, such as giving them access to financial services, jobs, schools, sanitation, and skills. Another strategy is giving people living in poverty access to public services and market opportunities; however, access in this context requires political influence and requires people experiencing poverty to collaborate, which could lead to changes in governance and the removal of institutional barriers. The final strategy suggested by the World Bank is that people living in poverty need to be insulated from economic shocks, natural disasters, ill health, disability, and personal violence. Overall, a strengthening of democratic institutions and processes will help people experiencing poverty to progress and this will give them social mobility (Haughton & Khandker, 2009). A driver of reducing poverty is the adoption of the circular economy and sustainability strategies in general, particularly in the fashion industry.

Supply Chain and AI to Implement SDGs and Build Sustainability

Some consider generative AI to be beneficial but dangerous and that the benefits outweigh the dangers. Bengel (2020), Elon Musk, Stephen Hawkins, and Bill Gates have warned that AI could increase global poverty and that it is a threat to humankind. The acceptance of AI is based on multiple and interrelated variables that are classified into five significant dimensions: organisational, individual, financial, technological, and societal.

Artificial general intelligence (AGI) has the potential to displace jobs on a mass scale and it could have a more significant impact on job losses than generative AI (also known as narrow AI). AGI could have a significant effect on the following SDGs: SDG 1 (no poverty), SDG 9 (industry, innovation, and infrastructure), SDG 8 (decent work and economic growth), and SDG 10 (reduced inequalities). AGI could have the greatest impact on developing countries that have few social rights: labour rights and employment protection (Goralski & O'Connor, 2020).

Not all researchers agree that AGI will be a panacea; some think that AGI could cause an increase in income inequality (SDG 10). The use of AGI will be concentrated in developed countries and not equally distributed globally. It is unlikely the developers of AGI will distribute it equally. Thus, the wealth will be concentrated in countries that have access to AGI, which is generally not developing countries (Goralski & O'Connor, 2020).

AI has been used to benefit SDG projects, such as the application of AI to manage water management systems (smart water management). AI achieves this by mimicking human decision-making on investments in water management infrastructure (Hill, 2018). Another application of AI is in agriculture, for example, the PlantVillage project focuses on bringing AI benefits to small farmers who farm 2 hectares or less, which is the "standard size" for farms in developing countries (Lohr, 2018); "in low-income countries that lack human capital in fields like agricultural science, there is an opportunity to use AI to help break the cycle of poverty" (Hughes, 2018, as cited in Lohr, 2018: 5). The final example is AI and sanitation and health (Datafloq, 2018); a critical problem for the world, including developing countries, is testing and confirming that water is clean, which requires expensive test equipment and analysis of the data that is carried out manually. PeterMa a software innovator at Intel has developed an algorithm that uses pattern recognition and machine learning to detect bacteria.

The examples discussed demonstrate that AI can be harnessed by the developed world and shared with the developing world to decrease inequality and improve productivity, which would lead to a reduction in poverty.

Consumer Behaviour—Perception of Sustainability of Fast Fashion

Times have changed from the past decade to the present; sustainability and ethical conduct are now more important and have more prominence in the fashion industry than they did before (Emberley, 1998; Moisander & Personen, 2002). Sustainability is often linked to social corporate responsibility (Aguilera et al., 2007). Seidman (2007: 58) stated that "sustainability is about much more than our relationship with the environment; it's about our relationship with ourselves, our communities, and our institutions". Joy et al. (2012: 274) opined that "sustainability involves complex and changing environmental dynamics that affect human livelihoods and well-being, with intersecting ecological, economic, and sociopolitical dimensions, both globally and locally". The fashion supply chain has global reach, which leads to fragmentation that results in complexity, which in turn leads to a lack of transparency in the industry (Mihm, 2010; Partridge, 2011).

Fast fashion is at a crossroads; thus, sustainability and fast fashion are in conflict. Is modifying fashion to slow fashion enough? H&M's and Zara's fashion product cycle from catwalk to consumer is a mere few weeks, previously it was six months, which heightens profitability (Tokatli, 2008). To keep customers coming back, retailers source new trends and purchase them on a weekly basis to introduce new fashion items and to replenish existing stock (Tokatli & Kizilgun, 2009). The exclusiveness of fashion is lost, and mass exclusiveness replaces it (Schrank, 2004). Is this not a contradiction of exclusiveness in fashion style? Mass production of fashion leads to higher volumes and lower unit costs and increasing profitability. In addition, fashion retailers such as Zara use Turkey to make fashion items instead of China due to the faster manufacturing turnaround from Turkey: shipping from China takes three weeks and from Turkey five days (Tokatli, 2008). To sustain fast fashion requires high disposable incomes or ready availability of credit; this can lead to immediate self-gratification and temporary self-identification (Bauman, 2005). However, fast fashion retailers are facing a backlash from consumers. Joy et al. (2012: 277) stated, "consumers are also aware that individual consumption fosters organizational production, creating an ongoing cycle of appetite, simultaneously voracious and insatiable". According to Binkley (2008), anti-consumerism encompasses a multitude of ethical and political positions and is a mediator in consumer choice at an everyday level through a critical discourse of the market. Binkley's (2008) comments suggest anti-consumer sentiment is an influencer on consumer behaviour and product decision-making.

Joy et al. (2012) employed a methodology to examine subconscious metaphors and combined interviews with Zaltman Metaphor Elicitation Technique to access subliminal thoughts (Zaltman, 1997). Their research took place in Hong Kong and Canada. Joy et al.'s (2012) findings suggest that consumers in Hong Kong and Canada showed concern for the environment and the social impact of non-fashion items, but this concern did not extend to fashion items. Thus, social and environmental considerations influence decision-making for non-fashion items but not for fashion items. Thomas (2008: 525) defined ethical fashion as "the positive impact of a designer, a consumer choice, a method of production as experienced by workers, consumers, animals, society, and the environment". The contradiction with the findings of Joy et al. (2012) is unsurprising and is like the findings on consumer values (Moisander & Personen, 2002). The themes that dominate the research of Joy et al. (2012: 281) are "speed and style at low cost" and "disposability and limited durability". These themes enable consumers to constantly change their identity.

The "speed and style at low cost" theme is linked to consumers wanting to look different in a fashion context and consumers do not want to wait. One respondent likened it to fast food restaurants that are visited once a week and where customers do not want to wait. Another respondent related the theme to Flash Gordon—gone in a flash. Fast fashion is seen as cheap chic. The "disposability and limited durability" theme set expectations that fashion apparel will only last a few washes and this concept was implanted by the fashion retail industry that suggests garments will last for at least 10 washes (Joy et al., 2012).

Joy et al.'s (2012) analysis of luxury fashion identified three fashion themes: desire/dream, history/heritage, and elegance/art. Fast fashion allows dreams of luxury to come true according to one participant. Style is achievable even if the quality is not the best. Even if the beauty and elegance of the fashion item is not as good as the "real" thing, at least consumers can afford the item. Luxury fashion product ownership is an aspiration according to the participants. The history/heritage of luxury fashion products is aspirational and, thus, participants showed a sense of pragmatism. The participants understood that fast fashion products are substitutes for luxury fashion products. The theme of elegance and art was discussed by one participant in the context of pearls that give a feeling of luxury, because pearls are elegant, bright, luminous, expensive, and gloriously beautiful.

The findings from research will have profound implications for sustainability in the fashion industry. Consumers around the world understand the implications of environmental issues but, in the words of Bonini and Oppenheim (2008: 56), "when it comes to actually buying green goods, words and deeds often part ways". Clark (2008: 428) was of the opinion that slow fashion could be a way to get consumers to apply ethical fashion (eco-fashion) ideas to fast fashion decision-making and not just other consumables by emphasising the fashion "buzz" (what is seen and heard). Joy et al. (2012: 291) opined, "However, the promise is evident, provided the focus is shifted from fashion as image, to the materiality of fashion".

Models of Societal Behaviour

Unprecedented changes in the global environment due to climate change leading to global warming require a rethink of the fashion industry's business models. According to Islam and Iyer-Raniga (2023), the circular economy offers some radical and innovative approaches to energy and material reduction and taking care of people and business. Incorporating the ideas of a circular economy into a business model is an appropriate direction of travel to get the best of all worlds (environment, social, and business); it would convert a linear economy into a circular business model (CBM).

Many definitions of the circular economy exist, such as "the core of circular economy is the circular (closed) flow of materials and the use of raw materials and energy through multiple phases" (Yuan et al., 2006: 5). Furthermore, Bocken et al., (2016: 309) categorised the characteristics of a circular economy as "design and business model strategies [that are] slowing, closing, and narrowing resource loops". The final definition given here is by the Ellen MacArthur Foundation (2013: 23):

> 'circular economy' denotes an industrial economy that is restorative by intention and design. In addition to meeting current demand/consumption needs, a circular economy also actively invests in improving resource systems and increasing their resilience to ensure their continuing availability in the future. In short, it replaces a throughput- and efficiency-driven view that ultimately degrades capital with one where capital rebuilding and maintenance offers an upward spiral or virtuous cycle, and a continuous flow of materials and products. In a circular economy, agricultural practices aim at optimising yields while also improving the quality of soil, water, and air. It views the long-term health of our agricultural systems as our best chance for long-term performance.

The CBM tool originally only applied circular economy strategies (Geissdoerfer et al., 2020) and was not underpinned with theory (Islam & Iyer-Raniga, 2023). According to Islam and Iyer-Raniga (2023), revamping of the CBM by Geissdoerfer et al. (2020) included several theories; these theories are discussed below.

The CBM reflects theories on customers' needs and wants and how business can meet them and do it profitably (Teece, 2007). Another underpinning theory is that the business model emphasis is on the value proposition, which identifies the appropriate technology and features, and the target market segments that help to define value chain activities; thus, it identifies potential costs and profit (Chesbrough & Rosenbloom, 2002). CBM is discussed by many researchers in the context of sustainability-related business models that support the development of frameworks on circular and sustainability models; this approach leads to innovation in business model theory (Cardeal et al., 2020; Giourka et al., 2019). Lewandowski (2016) considered the circular economy an important concept in the development of business model theory. However, sceptics such as Nußholz (2017) disagreed that resources efficiency theory can be implemented in CBM. There are gaps in our understanding of what makes a business circular (Islam & Iyer-Raniga, 2023).

The building blocks of sustainable CBM frameworks are varied and many CBM and sustainable CBM frameworks exist. The Triple Bottom Line Business Model Canvas is a sustainable CBM; its purpose is to provide a unified business model that focuses on social, economic, and environment dimensions (Joyce & Paquin, 2016). The Circular by Design model is a circular economy-related model that focuses on circular design and product/process with an emphasis on the lifecycle (Ballie & Woods, 2018). Mentink (2014) developed the Circular Business Model Innovation framework that is based on the business model canvas to aid development of circular supply chains. The sustainability attributes of the circular economy business model canvas (Pollard et al., 2023) are in the dimensions of social responsibility and eco-design within logistics and distribution with consideration of skills and training. The business models described in this section focus on sustainability (Joyce & Paquin, 2016) or a circular economy (Mentink, 2014), but some focus on both (Pollard et al., 2023).

Implications

The fashion industry has been affected by recent events in the global business environment, such as geopolitical tensions in the Middle East and Ukraine, the cost of living, and slowing or stationary economic growth. The fashion industry is not immune to these environmental changes that have proved not to be transitionary. Changes in the fashion industry, as discussed in this chapter, have not mitigated the current global economic performance but the headwinds are starting to abate. Over-reliance on a fast fashion paradigm that appears to thrive in economies that are not experiencing economic and political headwinds requires a different approach from all industries, especially the fashion industry. How to future proof the global fashion industry when substantial economic and geopolitical storms occur is a pressing problem.

The ready to wear fashion ecosystems give fast fashion retailers the ability to gain profitably because of the competitive advantages that the retailers can accrue. How long can the low-cost and disposable fast fashion industry exist without eventually harming fashion retailers' profitability and exacerbating environmental concerns that will manifest in global climate warming and potentially scar the world permanently. Will environmental concerns lead consumers to apply the constructs of ethical fashion (eco-fashion) not only to other products but also to the fashion industry? Sustainability does not always get the airing it should and not all fast fashion retailers put the same amount of focus and emphasis on sustainability one would expect (e.g. H&M versus Inditex).

Fast fashion's approach of feeding consumers products weekly will likely lead to consumer fatigue. Fatigue could exhibit itself due to global economics and geopolitical situations, which impact fashion supply chains or cause economic havoc for consumers. The global cost of living crisis that started in 2021/22 has cut living standards, which has led to less global disposable income. There is also the anti-consumerism brigade, which started with Gen Z but is spreading across other generations; it is also likely to add to the woes of the fast fashion industry. Furthermore, not all fashion retailers are comprehensively embracing sustainability, which could lead to pressure from consumers to change (Pérez-Bou & Cantista, 2023). Fashion firms need to put the SDGs front, centre and back of their strategy and ensure they influence the decision-making process. The context of the fashion industry must change from economic profitability to sustainability that is tangible and visible, if fashion is not to be accused of greenwashing. Sustainability and innovation are inextricably linked to improving economic growth, which leads to improving profitability; these are the reasons for the fashion industry to harness the opportunities provided by sustainability and innovation. Applying innovation and sustainability ingenuity will increase profits and, at the same time, not damage consumer trust and confidence in the industry, with accelerating price increases to compensate for the "alleged" additional costs of implementing sustainability techniques and policies.

How to the change the industry context is a real challenge for the industry. Two recommendations are suggested in this chapter: a social contract between developed countries and developing countries based on the new business models (models of societal behaviour) in the deployment and implementation of AI. The second recommendation is that the fashion industry changes radically to move to a slow fashion approach. These recommendations are discussed below.

The characteristic of fast fashion is to persuade consumers that fashion style is everything and it is a substitute for aspirational fashion brands (Joy et al., 2012). Is this akin to brainwashing leading to manipulation of fashion consumers? To afford the increasing rapid changes in style requires increasing disposable income or to be eligible for credit using options such as buy now pay later. Is this a sustainable proposition for fashion consumers? The reverse of fast fashion is slow fashion. The idea of slow fashion originated in Italy in response to the imagery of fast fashion (Fletcher, 2007). The concept of slow fashion is not to literally slow fashion down the fashion supply chain; the purpose of slow fashion is to develop holistically a sustainable supply chain process to include design, transparent production sourcing, and consumer education (Clark, 2008; Fletcher, 2010), which would lead to less consumption and less waste (Hall, 2018). Slow fashion characteristics include understanding the impact of fashion on communities and ecosystems, and increased awareness of how fashion items are produced with the possibility to have experiential contact with the production process (Hall, 2018). Slow fashion is an evolving object and its business model has various names, "...terms, such as sustainable new, eco fashion, ethical fashion, locally made, vintage and second-hand, under one unified movement" (Cataldi et al., 2013: 24). The slow fashion approaches challenge existing approaches based on the fast fashion concept. These challenges are identified below (Clark, 2008: 429):

> These slow approaches: • challenge existing hierarchies of "designer," "producer," and "consumer;" • question the notion of fashion being concerned exclusively with the "new;" • challenge fashion's reliance on image; • present fashion as a choice rather than as a mandate; • highlight collaborative/cooperative work—providing agency especially to women.

The change to a slow fashion approach requires a cultural change in the fashion industry, the fashion retailers, and the fashion consumers. To successfully implement a slow fashion approach requires the fast industry to lead, if not then Gen Z and other generations will become an enabler of change. Change identifies new opportunities and new competitors that see the future as slow fast, which could displace the fast fashion retailers, especially with the harnessing of AI making it more probable than less.

The implementation of slow fashion requires a social contract between the developed and developing countries to engage in, and encourage, sustainability holistically and particularly in the fashion industry. What is the social contract going to look like? It must treat the developing countries as equals despite most of the funding coming from the West and developed countries. The social contract needs to be underpinned by models similar to those identified in the section "Models on societal behaviour". Stakeholders in the social contract should include governments, society, businesses (wider businesses), consumers, non-governmental organisations, charities, fashion suppliers, fashion retailers, the press, and online influencers. The greater the stakeholders' representation, the more likely the contract will be implementable. The social contract would issue in a wind of change in the fashion industry that focuses on sustainability and not exclusively on profitability (obviously, profit is a necessary requirement but how it is made is also a consideration in the social contract). Implementation of the social contract will help to overcome the scepticism of the circular economy from some stakeholders. The use of emerging technologies, such as blockchain and AI, has many benefits for the fashion industry, such as dealing with fake brands, mitigating fraud, and traceability in the supply chain. However, some of the other applications of blockchain and AI are not applied in the fashion industry, such as building a social relationship between supplier and buyer. The developing countries will have to resist the concentration of technology in the West and developed countries. The need to share technology competences will be necessary, but this could be challenging. Leveraging technology give businesses a competitive advantage, which they are reluctant to share. Otherwise, the benefits of slow fashion will not be fully realised, and sustainability will become further away. However, the fashion industry needs to embrace sustainability models and develop strategies that incorporate them at all levels of the organisation. Integrating sustainability models into the strategic planning and business decision-making processes is a challenge for the fashion industry, but one it needs to accept, so that it can work towards a solution for the good of society and all stakeholders.

To reduce poverty and inequality in developing and developed countries requires a social contract implemented by government and organisations with people experiencing poverty. This will require the strategies identified by the World Bank being championed and implemented by organisations that rely on developing countries to underpin and drive their economy, which is virtually all the developed countries. The fashion industry relies heavily on supply chains that extend to developing countries. Moving to a slow fashion approach will require a social contract with the developing countries that is implemented fairly and ethically. Implementation of the social contract will require the fashion industry to shift to new business models where sustainability and the circular economy are central to the way business is done. Poverty and inequality could be diminished to an extent that developing countries level up to a better quality of life for a vast majority of the population. Technology will aid improvement in tackling inequality and poverty, and support economic growth, but technology will require the participation of society to eradicate inequality and poverty, which requires a binding social contract.

Conclusion

The fashion industry is at a crossroads due to geopolitical and economic circumstances, which have impacted global economic growth and led to fashion consumers to retract their spending habits and at least temporarily change their behaviour. The challenge for the fashion industry is to make the changes in consumer behaviour permanent, but in the context of a fashion industry that identifies with innovation and sustainability. How can slow fashion minimise the economic headwinds and geopolitical instability that afflict the fashion industry? Is the slow fashion paradigm an enabler to overcome some of the challenges and themes identified? These are questions that require further research. However, the view of the researchers is that AI, sustainability, and innovation in a culture that embraces slow fashion and truly implements SDGs can minimise the unpredictability of fashion supply chain activities. To ensure that SDGs on no poverty and inequality in the developing world are achieved requires a social contract between the "haves" and the "have nots"; this approach requires the distribution of AI technology from the developed countries to the developing countries. Will developed countries continue to concentrate technology in the West and developed countries or share it for all of humankind?

References

Aguilera, R. V., Rupp, D. E., Williams, C. A., & Ganapathi, J. (2007). Putting the S back in corporate social responsibility: A Multi-level theory of social change in organizations. *Academy of Management Review, 32*(3), 836–863.

Azemi, Y., & Ozuem, W. (2023). How does retargeting work for different Gen Z mobile users? *Journal of Advertising Research*, 2023-023. https://doi.org/10.2501/jar-2023-023

Bailey, T. (2001). Organizational innovation in the apparel industry. *Industrial Relations, 32*(1), 30–48.

Balchandani, A., Starzynska, E., Barrelet, D., Berg, A., D'Auria, G., Rölkens, F., & Amed, I. (2023, November 29). *The state of fashion 2024: Findings pockets of growth as uncertainty reigns*. McKinsey & Company. https://www.mckinsey.com/industries/retail/our-insights/state-of-fashion. Accessed 17 March 2024.

Ballie, J., & Woods, M. (2018). Circular by design: A model for engaging fashion/textile SMEs with strategies for designed reuse. In R. Crocker, C. Saint, G. Chen, & Y. Tong (Eds.), *Unmaking waste in production and consumption: Towards the circular economy* (pp. 103–121). Emerald Publishing Limited, Leeds. https://doi.org/10.1108/978-1-78714-619-820181010

Barnes, L., & Lea-Greenwood, G. (2006). Fast fashioning the supply chain: Shaping the research agenda. *Journal of Fashion Marketing and Management, 10*(3), 259–271.

Bauman, Z. (2005). *Liquid life*. Polity Press.

Bengel, D. (2020). *Organizational acceptance of artificial intelligence*. Springer.

Bhardwaj, V., & Fairhurst, A. (2010). Fast fashion: Response to changes in the fashion industry. *The International Review of Retail Distribution and Consumer Research, 20*(1), 165–173.

Binkley, S. (2008). Liquid consumption. *Cultural Studies, 22*(5), 599–623.

Bocken, N. M. P., de Pauw, I., Bakker, C., & van de Grinten, B. (2016). Product design and business model strategies for a circular economy. *Journal of Industrial and Production Engineering, 33*(5), 308–320. https://doi.org/10.1080/21681015.2016.1172124

Bonini, S., & Oppenheim, J. (2008). Cultivating the green consumer. *Stanford Social Innovation Review,* Fall, 56–61.

Brooks, J. (1979, November 12). A friendly product. *The New Yorker*, 58–94. Accessed 24 March 2024.

Bruce, G., & Daly, L. (2006). Buyer behavior for fast fashion. *Journal of Fashion Marketing and Management, 10*(3), 329–344.

Cardeal, G., Höse, K., Ribeiro, I., & Götze, U. (2020). Sustainable business models–canvas for sustainability, evaluation method, and their application to additive manufacturing in aircraft maintenance. *Sustainability, 12*, 9130.

Cataldi, C., Dickson, M., & Grover, C. (2013). Slow fashion: Tailoring a strategic approach for sustainability. In M. Gardetti & A. Torres (Eds.), *Sustainability in fashion and textiles: Values, design, production and consumption* (pp. 22–46). Greenleaf.

Chesbrough, H., & Rosenbloom, R. S. (2002). The role of the business model in capturing value from innovation: Evidence from Xerox Corporation's technology spin-off companies. *Industrial and Corporate Change, 11*, 529–555.

Christopher, M., Lowson, R., & Peck, H. (2004). Creating agile supply chains in the fashion industry. *International Journal of Retail and Distribution Management, 32*(8), 367–376.

Clark, H. (2008). Slow + fashion—An oxymoron—Or a promise for the future? *Fashion Theory, 12*(4), 427–446.

Datafloq. (2018, May 7). *AI-driven test system detects bacteria in water*. Intel. https://datafloq.com/read/ai-driven-test-system-detects-bacteria-in-water/. Accessed 2 April 2024.

Donnellan, J. (1996). *Merchandise buying and management*. Fairchild Publications.

Doyle, S. A., Moore, C. M., & Morgan, L. (2006). Supplier management in fast moving fashion retailing. *Journal of Fashion Marketing and Management, 10*(3), 272–281.

Ellen MacArthur Foundation. (2013). Towards the circular economy: Opportunities for the consumer goods sector TCE_Report-2013.pdf (ellenmacarthurfoundation.org). Accessed 29 March 2024.

Emberley, V. (1998). *Venus and Furs: The cultural politics of Fur*. I. B. Tauris & Co.

FashionUnited. (n.d.). *Global fashion industry statistics*. FashionUnited. https://fashionunited.com/global-fashion-industry-statistics. Accessed 16 March 2024.

Fletcher, K. (2007). Slow fashion. *The Ecologist, 37* (5). Slow fashion (theecologist.org). Accessed 17 March 2024.

Fletcher, K. (2010). Slow fashion: An invitation for systems change. *Fashion Practice, 2*(2), 259–266.

Forza, C., & Vinelli, A. (1996). An analytical scheme for the change of the apparel design process towards quick response. *International Journal of Clothing, 8*(4), 28–43.

Geissdoerfer, M., Pieroni, M. P., Pigosso, D. C., & Soufani, K. (2020). Circular business models: A review. *Journal of Cleaner Production, 277*, 123741.

Giourka, P., Sanders, M. W., Angelakoglou, K., Pramangioulis, D., Nikolopoulos, N., Rakopoulos, D., Tryferidis, A., & Tzovaras, D. (2019). The smart city business model canvas—A smart city business modeling framework and practical tool. *Energies, 12*(24), 4798.

Goralski, M., & O'Connor, M. (2020). Artificial intelligence and sustainable development. *The International Journal of Management Education, 18*(1), 1003. https://doi.org/10.1016/j.ijme.2019.100330

Hall, J. (2018). Digital Kimono: Fast fashion, slow fashion? *Fashion Theory, 22*(3), 283–307. https://doi.org/10.1080/1362704X.2017.1319175

Haughton, J., & Khandker, S. R. (2009). *Handbook on poverty + inequality*. World Bank.

Hayes, S. G., & Jones, N. (2006). Fast fashion: A financial snapshot. *Journal of Fashion Marketing and Management, 10*(3), 282–300.

Hill, T. (2018, March 5). *How artificial intelligence is reshaping the water sector*. Water Finance & Management. Retrieved from How Artificial Intelligence is Reshaping the Water Sector - Water Finance & Management (waterfm.com). Accessed 2 April 2024.

H&M Group. (n.d.). *Annual and sustainability report 2022*. H&M Group. https://hmgroup.com/about-us/. Accessed 25 March 2024.

Inditex. (n.d.). *Inditex annual report 2002*. Inditex. Accessed 25 March 2024.

Islam, M. T., & Iyer-Raniga, U. (2023). Circular business model value dimension canvas: Tool redesign for innovation and validation through an

Australian case study. *Sustainability, 15*, 11553. https://doi.org/10.3390/su15151155

Jolliffe, D., Lanjouw, P., Chen, S., Kraay, A., Meyer, C., Negre, M., Prydz, E. B., Vakis, R., & Wethli, K. (2015). *A measured approach to ending poverty and boosting shared prosperity: Concepts, data, and the twin goals, policy research report*. World Bank Group.

Jones, J. (1995). Forces behind restructuring in US apparel retailing and its effect on the US apparel industry. *Industry, Trade, and Technology Review*, March 23–30.

Joy, A., Sherry, J. F., Jr., Venkatesh, A., Wang, J., & Chan, R. (2012). Fast fashion, sustainability, and the ethical appeal of luxury brands. *Fashion Theory, 16*(3), 273–295. https://doi.org/10.2752/175174112X13340749707123

Joyce, A., & Paquin, R. L. (2016). The triple layered business model canvas: A tool to design more sustainable business models. *Journal of Cleaner Productivity, 13*(5), 1474–1486.

Küfeoğlu, S. (2020). Emerging technologies: Value creation for sustainable development. *Springer*. https://doi.org/10.1007/978-3-031-07127-0

Lewandowski, M. (2016). Designing the business models for circular economy—Towards the conceptual framework. *Sustainability, 8*, 43.

Lohr, S. (2018). From agriculture to art—The AI wave sweeps in. *New York Times,* Business Day. Retrieved from https://www.google.com/search?client=firefox-b-d&q=Agriculture+to+Art+—+the+A.I.+Wave+Sweeps+In+-+The+New+York+Times+(nytimes.com). Accessed 2 April 2024.

Malmberg Calvo, C., Das Gupta, M., Grootaert, C. N., Kanbur, R., Kwakwa, V., & Lustig, C. (2000). *World development report 2000–2001: Attacking poverty—Overview.* World Development Report, World development indicators. World Bank Group. http://documents.worldbank.org/curated/en/673161468161371338/World-development-report-2000-2001-attacking-poverty-overview

Mentink, B. (2014). *Circular business model innovation: A process framework and a tool for business model innovation in a circular economy*. Master's Thesis, Lahti University of Technology, Lappeenranta, Finland.

Mihm, B. (2010, June). Fast fashion in a flat world: Global Sourcing strategies. *International Business and Economics Research Journal, 9*(6), 55–63.

Moisander, J., & Personen, S. (2002). "Narratives of sustainable ways of living: Constructing the self and others as a green consumers. *Management Decisions., 40*(4), 329–342.

Nelson, R. R., & Rosenberg, N. (1993). Technical innovation and national systems. In R. R. Nelson (Ed.), *National innovation systems—A comparative analysis*. Oxford University Press.

Nußholz, J. L. (2017). Circular business models: Defining a concept and framing an emerging research field. *Sustainability, 9*(18).

Ozuem, W., Ranfagni, S., Willis, M., Salvietti, G., & Howell, K. (2024). Exploring the relationship between chatbots, service failure recovery and customer loyalty: A frustration–aggression perspective. *Psychology and Marketing*. https://doi.org/10.1002/mar.22051

Ozuem, W., Willis, M., Ranfagni, S., Howell, K. E., & Rovai, S. (2023). Examining the role of social media influencers in service failure and recovery strategies: An empirical investigation of millennials' views. *Information Technology & People*. https://doi.org/10.1108/itp-05-2022-0371

Partridge, D. J. (2011). Activist capitalism and supply chain citizenship: Producing ethical regimes and ready-to-wear clothes. *Current Anthropology, 52*(S3), S97–S111.

Pathania, K. (2017). Sustainable development goal: Gender equality for women's empowerment and human rights. *International Journal Research, 5*(4), 72–82. https://doi.org/10.29121/granthaalayah.v5.i4.2017.1797

Pérez-Bou, S., & Cantista, I. (2023). Politics, sustainability and innovation in fast fashion and luxury fashion groups. *International Journal of Fashion Design, Technology and Education, 16*(1), 46–56.

Pollard, J., Osmani, M., Grubnic, S., Díaz, A. I., Grobe, K., Kaba, A., Ünlüer, Ö., & Panchal, R. (2023). Implementing a circular economy business model canvas in the electrical and electronic manufacturing sector: A case study approach. *Sustainable Production and Consumption, 36*, 17–31.

Schrank, A. (2004). Ready to wear development? Foreign investment, technology transfer, and learning by watching in the apparel trade. *Social Forces, 83*(1), 123–156.

Seidman, D. (2007). *How we do anything means everything*. John Wiley & Sons.

Shastri, A. (2014). Gender inequality and women discrimination. *IOSR Journal of Humanities and Social Science, 19*, 27–30. https://doi.org/10.9790/0837-191172730

Sproles, G. (1979). *Fashion: Consumer behaviour toward dress*. Burgess Publishing Company.

Stuart, J., & Woodroffe, J. (2016). Leaving no-one behind: Can the sustainable development goals succeed where the millennium development goals lacked? *Gender Development, 24*, 69–81. https://doi.org/10.1080/13552074.2016.1142206

Teece, D. J. (2007). Explicating dynamic capabilities: The nature and microfoundations of (sustainable) enterprise performance. *Strategic Management Journal, 28*, 1319–1350.
Thomas, S. (2008). From "Green Blur" to eco fashion: Fashioning an eco-Lexicon. *Fashion Theory, 12*(4), 525–540.
Tokatli, N. (2008). Global sourcing insights from the clothing industry: The case of Zara, a fast fashion retailer. *Journal of Economic Geography, 8*, 21–38.
Tokatli, N., & Kizilgun, O. (2009). From Manufacturing garments for ready to wear to designing collections: Evidence from Turkey. *Environment and Planning, 41*, 146–162.
Tyler, D., Heeley, J., & Bhamra, T. (2006). Supply chain influences on new product development in fashion clothing. *Journal of Fashion Marketing and Management, 10*(3), 316–328.
UN Women. (2021). *United Nations women, sustainable development goal 5: Gender equality*. UN Women. https://www.unwomen.org/en/news/in-focus/women-and-the-sdgs/sdg-5-gender-equality. Accessed 20 April 2024.
Yuan, Z., Bi, J., & Moriguichi, Y. (2006). The circular economy: A new development strategy in China. *Journal of Industrial Ecology, 10*(1–2), 4–8.
Zaltman, G. (1997). Rethinking market research: Putting people back in. *Journal of Marketing Research, 34*(4), 424–432.

25

Kering's Strategy for Digital and Sustainable Transformation: Twin Transition Through NFTs in the Luxury Industry

Stefania Masè and Elena Cedrola

Introduction

The inception of the twenty-first century has been marked by a transformative shift toward digitalization and sustainability, propelling industries into a new era where technology and social stewardship become intertwined (Ozuem & Willis, 2024; Uggla & Lashgari, 2012). This dual transition highlights the interconnectedness of digital innovation and sustainability as complementary drivers of economic, social, and environmental progress (Colapinto & Masè, 2025; Jones & Wynn, 2021). In this evolving context, the luxury sector, traditionally steeped in exclusivity and heritage, is at a pivotal stage, compelled to redefine its identity

S. Masè (✉)
IPAG Business School, Nice, France
e-mail: s.mase@ipag.fr

E. Cedrola
University of Macerata, Macerata, Italy
e-mail: elena.cedrola@unimc.it

W. Ozuem et al. (eds.), *Sustainable Digital Marketing for Fashion and Luxury Brands*, https://doi.org/10.1007/978-3-031-82467-8_25

and operational strategies to meet changing consumer demands and global sustainability objectives (Osburg et al., 2021).

The concept of a twin transition, which underscores the synergy between digitalization and sustainability (Bernardi et al, 2022), becomes a critical strategy for industries navigating the complexities of today's challenges while promoting innovation, efficiency, and inclusivity (Vial, 2019). Particularly for the luxury industry, this transition sets unique expectations; brands must preserve their allure and exclusivity while integrating digital transformation and embracing robust sustainable practices (Kapferer & Bastien, 2012). This balancing act raises pertinent questions about the feasibility of integrating cutting-edge technologies with environmental and social governance principles without diluting the intrinsic value of luxury goods, a twin transition increasingly important also in the near future (Bain & Company, 2022).

With a celebrated history of strategic transformations and bold decisions, Kering embodies the essence of luxury redefined for the digital and sustainable era. The company's interest in a digital-first approach, coupled with a deep-rooted commitment to sustainability, exemplifies a forward-thinking strategy that aligns with the Triple-Bottom-Line (TBL) framework (Elkington, 1997). According to TBL, a sustainable company minimizes its ecological impact by optimizing production, reducing waste, and using responsible materials while also respecting the health and rights of workers, consumers, and communities of interest (Elkington, 1997). However, since there seems to be a correlation between corporate sustainability and financial performance through energy and water savings and reduced costs related to regulatory requirements, many companies invest in innovative solutions for the green to save money and reduce costs, and not because sustainability is a core value (Cedrola & Trabaldo Togna, 2020). In any case, this framework, which advocates a holistic consideration of profit, people, and planet, sets a new standard for how luxury brands can navigate the complexities of modern business practices.

Kering's journey from a regional distributor to a global luxury leader showcases a narrative of strategic foresight, innovative prowess, and a steadfast commitment to sustainability principles (Colapinto & Masè, 2025; Correia, 2019). The company's strategic operations toward sustainability in a broader sense are not merely reactions to market trends but are part of a broader vision to lead the luxury sector toward a future that is innovative, responsible, and inclusive. Kering's sustainability endeavors reflect a profound understanding of the luxury industry's impact on the planet and its communities. The company's ambitious 2025 sustainability strategy demonstrates a recognition of the luxury sector's potential to influence broader societal shifts toward environmental stewardship and social responsibility (D'Adamo & Lupi, 2021; Fiorani et al., 2022; Kering, 2023b). On the other side, Kering's foray into digitalization, from its embrace of e-commerce and digital platforms to most recent NFTs adoptions, illustrates a keen understanding of digital's role in reshaping consumer interactions and expectations (Ferrini et al., 2023; Park & Lim, 2023). These initiatives are not just about adapting to a digital future but about leading the charge in defining what luxury can mean in a digitally connected world.

The integration of sustainability and digital innovation speaks to a deeper strategic vision in Kering, presenting these two areas as interconnected opportunities for growth and transformation. Kering's initiatives, from blockchain for supply chain transparency to AI for enhanced customer experiences, showcase a holistic approach to integrating technology and sustainability (Kering, 2023b; Ozuem et al., 2023, 2024a, 2024b).

We examine Kering's position in the wider framework of the luxury industry's dual approach toward digitalization and sustainability, emphasizing the important perspectives the company provides on the future of luxury as resilient, pertinent, and ethical.

In the following section, we present the history and a global overview of the company, setting the stage to explore its strategies for digitalization and sustainability. We then focus on a specific digital tool, the Non-Fungible-Tokens, to show how the company adopted it to integrate digital innovation, the arts, and sustainable practices, as evidenced by a detailed press analysis we performed. Adopting the Triple-Bottom-Line approach we propose a taxonomy about how to use NFTs to merge digital and sustainable strategies. We conclude the chapter by summarizing an exemplary case of twin transition proposed by Kering, merging NFTs with the arts, social, and environmental goals, and we conclude the chapter highlighting managerial implications for luxury companies embarking on a sustainable and digital twin transition.

Digitalization and Sustainability in Luxury

Luxury conglomerates and brands are progressively embedding digital innovations and sustainable practices within their strategic frameworks, adapting to the shifts in the global market (Fiorani et al., 2022). The luxury sector has recognized the need for transformation, adopting digital platforms and sustainability as critical elements for their future development and brand values.

Digital transformation in the luxury sector has been profound, spanning from enhanced e-commerce capabilities to the adoption of artificial intelligence (AI), blockchain technology, and the Internet of Things (IoT) to refine customer experiences and streamline operations (Sestino & Amatulli, 2023; Sestino et al., 2022a, 2022b). For instance, the acceleration of online sales has become a significant focus for brands such as Gucci, Saint Laurent, and others within the Kering portfolio, highlighting the shift toward omnichannel retailing as a response to changing consumer behaviors (Rangel & Lopez, 2022). This digital push is not just about expanding into e-commerce but also about creating immersive, seamless experiences that bridge the physical and digital worlds, ensuring luxury consumers receive unparalleled service and engagement online as they would in-store (Ozuem et al., 2024a, 2024b).

Simultaneously, sustainability has become a central pillar in the luxury industry's evolution, with brands increasingly recognizing their role in promoting environmental stewardship and social responsibility. Luxury brands are implementing initiatives aimed at reducing their carbon footprint, enhancing supply chain transparency, and promoting sustainable consumption practices among their clientele (Lopez et al., 2023). The adoption of sustainable materials, investment in green technologies, and efforts to achieve carbon neutrality underscore the industry's commitment to a sustainable future (Jin & Cedrola, 2018). Notably, Kering's ambitious 2025 sustainability strategy sets a blueprint for integrating environmental considerations deeply into business operations, targeting significant reductions in greenhouse gas emissions and championing sustainable sourcing (Kering Press Release, 2023a).

The integration of digital technologies such as AI and blockchain into sustainability efforts illustrates the luxury sector's innovative approach to addressing environmental challenges. For example, blockchain technology is utilized to verify the authenticity and sustainability credentials of luxury items, thereby combating counterfeiting and ensuring ethical sourcing practices (Lin & Yu, 2023; Rangel & Lopez, 2022).

The journey toward digitalization and sustainability in the luxury industry reflects a broader transformation within the sector, driven by the need to adapt to a rapidly changing global landscape and align with the values of a new generation of consumers who prioritize environmental sustainability and digital engagement. This shift is visible in both developed and emerging markets where consumers are also increasingly conscious of the sustainability credentials of the brands they patronize (Young et al., 2023). Luxury consumers worldwide show sustainability-driven purchasing behaviors, which necessitate tailored approaches from global luxury brands to align with these values effectively. As luxury brands navigate this evolving terrain, their efforts to blend digital innovation with sustainable practices not only enhance their competitiveness but also contribute to the development of a more responsible and resilient luxury industry, as shown by the exemplary case of Kering luxury conglomerate.

Kering: An Exemplary Case Study for Sustainability and Innovation

Founded in 1963 as a modest building materials company, Kering has transformed into a leader within the global luxury sector, noted for its strategic vision and innovative approach (Kering, 2021). The transformation began in earnest with the acquisition of Gucci in 1999, a move that not only solidified Kering's commitment to the luxury industry but also set the stage for the inclusion of other prestigious brands such as Yves

Saint Laurent, Bottega Veneta, and Balenciaga (Kering, 2021; Kering, 2024d).

In the early 2000s, Kering began divesting non-core businesses to focus more on luxury and sports & lifestyle, under the leadership of François-Henri Pinault. By the late 2000s, Kering had honed its focus on the high-margin luxury market, culminating in 2018 with a full shift to exclusively luxury offerings. The strategic sale of Puma in 2018 reaffirmed Kering's dedicated focus on the luxury segment, allowing for more targeted investments in sustainability and brand development.

Despite a downturn in annual revenue in 2023 reflecting the volatile global market (Kering, 2023b), Kering continues to expand its brand portfolio and presence. Recent initiatives such as the launch of Kering Beauté and the acquisition of Creed highlight its efforts to dominate the beauty market (Kering, 2024b).

Today, Kering is celebrated for its distinctive luxury brands such as Gucci, Saint Laurent, and Bottega Veneta, which skillfully blend rich heritage with modern appeal to target a global clientele. This blend underscores Kering's enduring commitment to innovation, sustainability, and luxury, setting it apart in the dynamic world of high fashion.

Kering's narrative from regional distributor to luxury icon underscores its strategic evolution and excellence commitment. As the luxury market continues to evolve, Kering's emphasis on creativity, sustainability, and strategic brand development equips it to navigate future challenges and opportunities.

Lately, Kering has sharpened its emphasis on sustainability and digital innovation, reflecting current industry trends and the demand for environmentally conscious, technology-driven luxury. The downturn in 2023 revenues is largely due to strategic initiatives such as the overhaul of Gucci, indicative of the company's commitment to long-term growth and enhanced brand appeal (Kering, 2022, 2023b). Kering's endeavors to rejuvenate Gucci, focusing on increasing its market presence and exclusivity, highlight the company's dedication to merging traditional appeal with contemporary innovation. Kering's investments in artisanal quality and cutting-edge technology demonstrate its drive to position itself at the forefront of a sustainable and innovative luxury industry (Kering, 2024b).

Sustainability at Kering

In the luxury and fashion sector, the Kering Group stands out for its pioneering commitment to sustainability, laying the groundwork for a more responsible future in the luxury fashion industry. Kering's leadership in the luxury fashion industry's shift toward sustainability reflects a profound understanding of the need for a holistic approach that balances economic success with environmental protection and social responsibility. Under the leadership of François-Henri Pinault, Kering has embraced sustainability as a core aspect of its business model, embedding it across all levels of its operations. This strategic focus is evident in Kering's (2025) sustainability plan, which targets significant reductions in carbon emissions, sustainable sourcing of materials, and improvements in social welfare across its supply chain, and markets (Azemi & Ozuem, 2023; Kering, 2024c; Lahbib et al., 2023).

The group's efforts in incorporating renewable resources and pursuing energy-efficient practices align with the broader industry trend toward a circular economy. This commitment to sustainability reflects Kering's vision for the future of luxury fashion: responsible, innovative, and inclusive. Kering's initiatives, including its pioneering work in sustainable materials and its partnerships for biodiversity conservation, are setting new benchmarks for the industry (D'Adamo & Lupi, 2021; Fiorani et al., 2022).

Moreover, Kering's approach to corporate social responsibility underscores a commitment to social welfare that goes beyond traditional business objectives. By ensuring the well-being and fair treatment of its workforce and fostering positive community impacts, Kering is leading by example in the luxury sector. These efforts highlight the interconnectedness of social and environmental sustainability, demonstrating how responsible supply chain management can respect both people and the planet (Fiorani et al., 2022).

Kering's economic strategy, recognizing the complementarity of sustainability and profitability, aligns with changing consumer preferences. This strategic alignment ensures Kering's long-term viability and market position by catering to a growing demand for sustainable luxury products. The Group's investments in sustainable materials and processes not only mitigate its environmental impact but also cater to a consumer base that values ethical and sustainable practices (D'Adamo & Lupi, 2021; Fiorani et al., 2022).

Kering's leadership in the luxury fashion industry's shift toward sustainability reflects a profound understanding of the need for a holistic approach that balances economic success with environmental stewardship and social responsibility. Under the leadership of François-Henri Pinault, Kering has embraced sustainability as a core aspect of its business model, embedding it across all levels of its operations. This strategic focus is evident in Kering's (2025) sustainability plan, which targets significant reductions in carbon emissions, sustainable sourcing of materials, and improvements in social welfare across its supply chain.

The group's efforts in incorporating renewable resources and pursuing energy-efficient practices align with the broader industry trend toward a circular economy. This commitment to sustainability is not merely about compliance but is a reflection of Kering's vision for the future of luxury fashion—one that is responsible, innovative, and inclusive. Kering's initiatives, including its pioneering work in sustainable materials and its partnerships for biodiversity conservation, are setting new benchmarks for the industry (D'Adamo & Lupi, 2021; Fiorani et al., 2022).

Moreover, Kering's approach to corporate social responsibility underscores a commitment to social welfare that goes beyond traditional business objectives. By ensuring the well-being and fair treatment of its workforce and fostering positive community impacts, Kering is leading by example in the luxury sector. These efforts highlight the interconnectedness of social and environmental sustainability, demonstrating how responsible supply chain management should respect both people and the planet (Fiorani et al., 2022).

Recognizing the complementarity of sustainability and profitability, Kering aligns with changing consumer preferences. This strategic alignment ensures Kering's long-term viability and market position by catering to a growing demand for sustainable luxury products. The Group's investments in sustainable materials and processes not only mitigate its environmental impact but also cater to a consumer base that values ethical and sustainable practices (D'Adamo & Lupi, 2021; Fiorani et al., 2022).

The analysis of the integration of sustainability and social responsibility into Kering's competitive strategies illuminates the depth of the company's commitment showing how the company has not only embraced sustainable practices but has woven these principles into the very fabric of its brand identity and strategy, reflecting a broader shift in the luxury industry toward sustainable development (Pavione et al., 2016). It is not by chance that the analysis of how conglomerates have navigated challenges of sustainability, digital innovation, and market expansion, positioning Kering as a pioneer in embracing organizational change and sustainability as key drivers of competitive advantage (Donzé & Fujioka, 2018).

Despite the efforts, challenges remain in the global luxury industry, including the need for greater transparency in sustainability reporting and communication. Research indicates a gap in communicating sustainability initiatives, particularly on e-commerce platforms, which underscores the necessity for enhanced consumer engagement in sustainability efforts (San Miguel et al., 2021). Additionally, critical examinations of environmental sustainability claims by luxury conglomerates raise questions about the legitimacy of these claims, emphasizing the need for consistent, transparent, and comprehensive sustainability reporting (Wells et al., 2021).

With its recent strategical choices toward sustainability in its broad definition, Kering is paving the way for a sustainable future in the luxury sector; its holistic approach sets a benchmark for the industry, demonstrating the viability of sustainable luxury and the potential for luxury brands to lead global sustainability efforts (D'Adamo & Lupi, 2021; Fiorani et al., 2022).

Digital Strategy at Kering

Tracing the trajectory of Kering's digital strategy reveals a visionary journey, charting the evolution from foundational e-commerce developments to the cutting-edge exploration of Non-Fungible Tokens (NFTs) and virtual worlds. This progression underscores Kering's proactive stance in harnessing digital innovation to redefine luxury fashion in the modern era, from the initial steps toward online retailing to the forefront of digital artistry and sustainability (Noris et al., 2021).

E-commerce remains a critical element for Kering, particularly for its leading brands (La revue du digital, 2021). Digital platforms not only aim to attract a growing group of consumers who appreciate the convenience of online shopping but also strive to provide a flawless omnichannel experience that integrates both online and offline interactions (Ozuem et al., 2024a, 2024b). The appointment of Grégory Boutté as Chief Client and Digital Officer in December 2017 marked a pivotal moment, setting the stage for an accelerated digital transformation across Kering's luxury houses (McDowell, 2019). Under Boutté's leadership, e-commerce emerged as the fastest-growing channel, demonstrating the Group's commitment to integrating digital solutions seamlessly across customer touchpoints (Press Release Kering, 2018).

Initiatives such as developing a suite of applications in partnership with Apple, aimed at enhancing the in-store experience, showcased Kering's dedication to offering personalized services through real-time access to stock levels and customized recommendations; this seamless integration of digital tools within the physical retail space illustrated Kering's innovative approach to enriching customer engagement and service (Press Release Kering, 2018).

Moving beyond the foundational elements of e-commerce and omnichannel experiences, Kering embarked on a broader digital transformation, aiming to incorporate digital innovation throughout the value chain. This included the internalization of e-commerce site management for its houses, leveraging data science for personalized customer communication, and exploring advanced technologies like 3D design for product development (Jin et al., 2019). Such endeavors not only streamlined operations but also fostered a culture of creativity and innovation within the Group, paving the way for more sustainable and responsive business models (Kering's Chief Client & Digital Officer on Digital Innovation Strategy, 2022; New Business Models for the Fashion of Future | Kering, 2024a, 2024b, 2024c).

Kering's commitment to sustainability became intricately linked with its digital strategy, evident in initiatives aimed at upgrading the supply chain for e-commerce growth and implementing blockchain technology for the traceability of materials. These efforts underscored a holistic approach to sustainability, where digital tools and platforms played a crucial role in ensuring responsible sourcing and reducing environmental impacts (New Business Models for the Fashion of Future | Kering, 2024a, 2024b, 2024c).

At the forefront of Kering's digital evolution lies its exploration of NFTs and virtual worlds, marking a bold foray into the intersection of digital, fashion, and sustainability. Collaborations with gaming platforms like Roblox and investments in digital art and NFT platforms reflect Kering's ambition to engage with younger, tech-savvy consumers through innovative mediums (Kering, 2021). NFTs, in particular, offer a unique blend of exclusivity, creativity, and digital ownership, resonating with the luxury sector's values while opening new avenues for sustainable and interactive consumer experiences. These initiatives not only enhance brand visibility and appeal to specific market segments but also pioneer new forms of digital engagement and community building within the luxury fashion realm (Ferrini et al., 2023; Sestino et al., 2022a, 2022b). It is always via its most iconic brand that Kering introduced its first foray into NFTs through one of its most iconic brands, Gucci. The brand released its first NFT in June 2021, a film inspired by its Aria collection, which was auctioned at Christie's for $25,000 (Baticka, 2022; Christie's, 2021). This marked a significant step for Kering into the digital and blockchain space, leveraging NFT technology to bridge luxury fashion with the burgeoning world of digital art and collectibles. The proceeds from this auction were designated for UNICEF USA to support the COVAX initiative, aligning with Gucci's commitment to social impact (Journal du Luxe, 2021). This first journey into digital arts Kering faced with its flagship brand immediately testify the twin transitional approach of the brand, navigating the digital world via NFTs, with attention to creativity, sustainability, and strategic brand development positioning Kering to face future challenges and opportunities clearly stated in their official communication to their stakeholders and not only (Kering, 2024a, 2024b; Sung et al., 2023).

A Special Focus on NFTs at Kering: Bridging Sustainability and Digital Strategy

Kering's digital strategy, from its early days to its current engagements with NFTs and virtual realms, showcases a proactive evolution toward embedding digital innovation and sustainability at the core of luxury fashion. This discussion illustrates how Kering has skillfully navigated the digital domain, consistently adapting and pioneering to meet changing market demands, thereby establishing new benchmarks for the broader luxury sector.

The following analysis explores how Kering utilizes NFTs to meet its environmental, social, and profit objectives, demonstrating how Kering is actively merging sustainability initiatives with its digital strategies.

Utilizing document analysis (Bowen, 2009), we have examined data to derive empirical insights (Corbin & Strauss, 2008) regarding Kering's integration of digitalization with sustainability from a Triple-Bottom-Line approach. This examination involved reviewing official press materials issued by Kering since 2018—the year following Grégory Boutté's appointment as Chief Client and Digital Officer in December 2017. This was complemented by a thorough press review utilizing major databases such as Factiva and Google, with «Kering» and «NFT» as the primary keywords, exploring a broad spectrum of sources (Morgan, 2022). The review period matched the years analyzed in Kering's internal documents. Initial research produced 19 items, while a deeper dive into online databases revealed 140 items, which were refined by focusing on pertinent content. Additional filters specific to «Kering» reduced the selection to 34 articles, and the term «Gucci» brought up 22 more. Results from Google searches were narrowed down to 20 articles. After eliminating duplicates, the final press review database included 43 articles, which underwent a detailed content analysis to extract, categorize, and summarize key themes and findings (Miles et al., 2014).

Consequently, we present a taxonomy that outlines the various sustainable uses of NFTs by Kering, adopting a Triple-Bottom-Line (TBL) approach and showcasing some of the most pertinent excerpts in Table 25.1. The entire dataset is available upon request. Following a brief overview of the table, we delve into a specific case: the launch of an NFT that symbolizes a collaborative effort between Kering, a digital artist, and a non-profit initiative, encapsulating Kering's strategy of merging the pillars of the TBL approach through a twin transition strategy that could be decisive for the entire luxury sector.

This table captures Kering's innovative use of Non-Fungible Tokens (NFTs) from a Triple Bottom Line (TBL) approach, intricately woven with their digital and sustainability strategies. The 'People' aspect highlights how Kering's digital endeavors enhance community engagement through initiatives such as the KNXT project, fostering cultural engagement and inclusivity in the fashion metaverse (Marion Abou, 2022). Environmentally, the table notes the reduction of physical waste through digital means, as Kering's commitment to eco-friendly practices extends to minimizing the environmental footprint of their operations (Ryder, 2023).

Economically, the table showcases innovative revenue streams through the integration of NFTs in luxury fashion. An illustrative example is Kering's sale of virtual bags on Roblox, which effectively merged digital presence with luxury branding, commanding prices that surpass their physical counterparts (The Wall Street Journal Online, April 1, 2022). This approach not only opens new markets but also aligns with the evolving digital landscape where digital assets hold tangible value.

Drawing on the theoretical insights from Joy et al. (2022), Kering's strategy reflects a broader industry shift toward digital transformation. The research highlights the role of NFTs and AI in transforming consumer experiences and expanding the luxury market into digital realms, suggesting a paradigm shift where digital and physical luxury coexist and complement each other. This integration exemplifies how luxury brands can navigate the complexities of modern consumer demands, leveraging technology to enhance brand value and sustainability, thus redefining the luxury experience in the digital age. The value creation potential of NFTs through the establishment of unique digital ownerships, enhance both the exclusivity and authentication of luxury items (Kaczynski & Kominers, 2021). Additionally, the increasing time the younger demographics spend online, underlines the necessity for luxury brands to integrate new technologies to attract these digitally native consumers (Williams, 2021).

Table 25.1 Kering NFT from a TBL perspective

TBL	Details and sources
PEOPLE	Articles highlighting community impacts, employee engagement, social responsibilities, ethical considerations, and inclusivity efforts in luxury fashion. Most representative sources: Zwieglinska (2022), Harley-McKeown (2023), LS:N Global (n.d.), Marion Abou (2022), Journal du Luxe (2021), Arab News FR (2022) • Gucci's efforts in inclusivity, shaping a narrative that supports societal benefits and employee engagement (Zwieglinska, 2022) • Gucci uses NFTs to outfit existing digital collections, creating unique digital apparel that enhances brand engagement and authenticity (Harley-McKeown, 2023; LS:N Global, n.d.) • Supports sustainable and ethical art and fashion projects, contributing to social responsibility and cultural preservation Harley-McKeown, L. (2023); LS:N Global (n.d.) • Kering's KNXT project aims to integrate the fashion community into the metaverse, offering interactive experiences that promote cultural engagement and social connection (Marion Abou, 2022)
PLANET	Discussions on environmental sustainability, reducing carbon footprints, implementing eco-friendly practices, and exploring digital solutions to minimize physical waste. Most representative sources: Hirschmiller (2023), The Peninsula Newspaper (2022), Fusionchat AI (2023), Ryder (2023), Marion Abou (2022), LS:N Global (n.d.) • Gucci's commitment to sustainability and managing environmental impact. (Hirschmiller, 2023) • Companies' broader strategies on the Metaverse that often touch on reducing physical waste through digital initiatives (The Peninsula Newspaper, 2022; Fusionchat AI, 2023; Ryder, 2023; Marion Abou, 2022) • NFTs offer potential for future applications in supply chain transparency, allowing for enhanced traceability and verification of luxury products' authenticity and sustainability credentials (*LS:N Global,* n.d.); • Minimizes environmental footprint by reducing the need for physical samples and products. Fusionchat AI (2023), Ryder (2023), Marion Abou (2022)

(continued)

Table 25.1 (continued)

TBL	Details and sources
PROFIT	Articles on profit maximization through innovative strategies like NFTs, digital fashion collections, and virtual experiences that open new revenue streams. Most representative sources: Moss (2022), Hirschmiller (2022), Maddyness (7 March 2022), Journal du luxe (n.d.), Harley-McKeown, L. (2023); LS:N Global (n.d.); etc • Kering SA, via its Balenciaga and Gucci brands, adopts a proactive «test and learn» digital strategy, exemplified by Gucci's sale of 400 digital Dionysus bags on Roblox, where frenzied trading led to a player paying over $4000 for a virtual bag, surpassing its real-life price (The Wall Street Journal Online, 1st April, 2022); • Métavers, NFT... L'industrie du luxe mise sur le virtuel pour créer de nouveaux revenus (Hirschmiller, 2022) • Pre-order access for NFT holders to «hyper-limited» collections (Maddyness, 7 March 2022); Journal du luxe (n.d.) • Kering explores innovative revenue streams through NFTs and digital fashion, enhancing brand value and creating new market opportunities. Harley-McKeown (2023); LS:N Global (n.d.)

Conclusion

Kering's strategic navigation through the twin transitions of digitalization and sustainability marks a significant pivot in the luxury industry, illustrating a future where tradition and innovation coalesce to foster a new era of responsible luxury (Lopez et al., 2023). This journey is not merely a response to contemporary challenges but a proactive redefinition of luxury's role in a rapidly evolving global landscape. Through its commitment to the Triple-Bottom-Line (TBL) framework, Kering transcends conventional business metrics, integrating economic success with environmental stewardship and social responsibility, thereby redefining the essence of true luxury in the twenty-first century (Elkington, 1997; Colapinto & Masè, 2025; Correia, 2019).

Kering's approach to sustainability, characterized by ambitious goals such as significant reductions in its carbon footprint and the championing of sustainable sourcing, exemplifies a forward-thinking mindset that not only addresses environmental concerns but also anticipates the evolving expectations of luxury consumers (D'Adamo & Lupi, 2021;

Fiorani et al., 2022; Kering, 2023). The integration of digital innovations, from blockchain technology to enhance supply chain transparency to AI-driven customer experiences, underscores Kering's recognition of digital transformation as a pivotal component of sustainable luxury (Ferrini et al., 2023; Park & Lim, 2023).

This integration reflects a broader industry imperative to adapt to the values of a new generation of consumers who demand transparency, sustainability, and ethical practices, alongside a seamless digital experience (Bain & Company, 2020; Kapferer & Bastien, 2012). Kering's initiatives serve as a blueprint for operational excellence and strategic alignment with these changing consumer preferences, ensuring the group's continued relevance and leadership in the luxury market.

Furthermore, Kering's pioneering efforts in the realm of digital art and NFTs exemplify the luxury sector's potential to lead in the adoption of new technologies, offering unique, sustainable, and engaging consumer experiences. These ventures not only enhance brand visibility and appeal but also signify a commitment to innovation and creativity, aligning luxury with contemporary cultural trends (Ferrini et al., 2023). Such initiatives are indicative of Kering's broader vision to redefine luxury, making it not just about exclusivity and heritage, but also about leading the way in digital engagement and sustainable practices.

However, the journey toward this integrated vision of digital and sustainable luxury is not without its challenges. The need for greater transparency in sustainability reporting and enhanced consumer engagement in sustainability efforts highlights areas where the luxury industry, including Kering, must continue to evolve (San Miguel et al., 2021; Wells et al., 2021). The complexity of aligning the traditional tenets of luxury with the imperatives of sustainability and digital innovation calls for continuous innovation and strategic foresight.

Despite these challenges, Kering's strategic integration of digitalization and sustainability within its operations and brand narratives positions it as a luminary in the luxury sector, setting benchmarks for how luxury brands can achieve economic success while fostering environmental and social responsibility. The company's journey underscores the potential for luxury brands to lead global sustainability efforts, demonstrating the viability of sustainable luxury and the pivotal role of digital innovation in shaping the future of the luxury industry.

In conclusion, Kering's dual focus on digitalization and sustainability heralds a new paradigm in the luxury industry, where responsibility, innovation, and tradition converge to redefine the contours of luxury. By embedding sustainability and digital innovation at the core of its strategy, Kering not only navigates the complexities of the modern business environment but also seizes the opportunities presented by these global shifts. As the luxury sector continues to evolve, Kering's journey offers valuable lessons on the transformative power of integrating sustainability and digital innovation into the fabric of luxury business models.

As we look to the future, the luxury industry stands at a critical juncture, with Kering leading the charge toward a more sustainable, digitally integrated, and ethically responsible luxury landscape. The success of this transition will not only shape the future of luxury but also contribute to the broader narrative of global sustainability and technological advancement. In this context, Kering emerges not just as a leader in luxury but as a beacon of innovation and responsibility, guiding the industry toward a future where luxury and sustainability are inextricably linked.

References

Arab News. (2022, March 6). Métavers, NFT: l'industrie du luxe se met à la mode du virtuel. Available at https://www.arabnews.fr/node/212776/%C3%A9conomie

Azemi, Y., & Ozuem, W. (2023). How does retargeting work for different Gen Z mobile users? Customer expectations and evaluations of retargeting via the expectancy-theory lens. *Journal of Advertising Research, 63*(4), 384–401. https://doi.org/10.2501/JAR-2023-023

Bain & Company. (2022). *Renaissance in uncertainty: Luxury builds on its rebound*. Bain & Company, Inc. Available at https://altagamma.it/media/source/Summary%20Altagamma-Bain%20WW%20Monitor%202022.pdf

Bernardi, A., Cantù, C. L., & Cedrola, E. (2022). Key success factors to be sustainable and innovative in the textile and fashion industry: Evidence from two Italian luxury brands. *Journal of Global Fashion Marketing, 13*(2), 116–133. https://doi.org/10.1080/20932685.2021.2011766

Bowen, G. A. (2009). Document analysis as a qualitative research method. *Qualitative Research Journal, 9*(2), 27–40.

Cedrola, E., & Trabaldo Togna, L. A. (2020). *Eccellenze italiane. Internazionalizzazione ed ecosostenibilità del distretto tessile biellese*, Pearson Italia.

Colapinto, C., & Masè, S. (2025). Introducing twin transitions in family businesses: A triple-bottom-line perspective. *Buiness Ethics, The Environment & Responsibility,* Early view. https://doi.org/10.1111/beer.12786

Corbin, J., & Strauss, A. (2008). *Basics of qualitative research: Techniques and procedures for developing grounded theory* (3rd ed.). Sage.

Correia, M. S. (2019). Sustainability: An overview of the Triple Bottom Line and sustainability implementation. *International Journal of Strategic Engineering, 2*(1), 1–15. https://doi.org/10.4018/IJoSE.2019010103

D'Adamo, I., & Lupi, G. (2021). Sustainability and resilience after COVID-19: A circular premium in the fashion industry. *Sustainability, 13*(1861). https://doi.org/10.3390/su13041861

Donzé, P.-Y., & Fujioka, R. (eds.). (2018). *Global luxury: Organizational change and emerging markets since the 1970s.* Springer Nature.

Elkington, J. (1997). *Cannibals with forks: The Triple Bottom Line of 21st century business.* Capstone.

Ferrini, G., Huber, S., Batt, V. (2023). How do luxury brands utilize NFTs to enhance their brand image?. In N. Sabatini, T. Sádaba, A. Tosi, V. Neri & L. Cantoni (Eds.), *Fashion Communication in the Digital Age. FACTUM*. Springer Proceedings in Business and Economics. Springer. https://doi.org/10.1007/978-3-031-38541-4_8

Fiorani, G., Bosco, F., & Di Gerio, C. (2022). Measuring sustainability in the luxury fashion sector: A comparison between LVMH and Kering. *Modern Economy, 13,* 356–369. https://doi.org/10.4236/me.2022.133020

Fusionchat AI. (2023, May 12). Kering launches KNXT: An innovative fashion marketplace for NFTs and AI Personal Shopper. *Fusion Chat AI News.* Available at https://fusionchat.ai/news/kering-launches-knxt-an-innovative-fashion-marketplace-for-nfts-and-ai-personal-shopper

Harley-McKeown, L. (2023, February 15). Amazon, Google and Kering back NFT animation studio making "synthetic celebrities". *The Block,* 1:12 PM EST. Available at https://www.theblock.co/post/212048/amazon-google-and-kering-back-nft-animation-studio-making-synthetic-celebrities

Hirschmiller, S. (2023, September 22). Gucci's Milan fashion week show debuts on roblox and zepeto. *Decrypt*. Available at https://decrypt.co/198384/guccis-milan-fashion-week-show-debuts-on-roblox-and-zepeto

Jin, B., & Cedrola, E. (2018). Product Innovation: Core to Continued Success. In B. Jin & E. Cedrola (Eds.), *Product innovation in the global fashion industry. Palgrave studies in practice: global fashion brand management* . Palgrave Pivot. https://doi.org/10.1057/978-1-137-52349-5_1

Jin, B. E., Cedrola, E., & Kim, N. (2019). Process innovation: Hidden secret to success and efficiency. In B. Jin & E. Cedrola (Eds.), *Process innovation in the global fashion industry. palgrave studies in practice: Global fashion brand management*. Palgrave Pivot. https://doi.org/10.1057/978-1-137-52352-5_1

Jones, P., & Wynn, M. (2021). The leading digital technology companies and their approach to sustainable development. *Sustainability, 13*(12), 6612. https://doi.org/10.3390/su13126612

Journal du Luxe. (2021). *NFT: Gucci se lance sur le marché de l'art numérique*. Available at https://www.journalduluxe.fr/fr/mode/nft-gucci-se-lance-sur-le-marche-de-l-art-numerique

Journal du Luxe. (2022, October 4). Gucci relance ses pré-commandes pour ses détenteurs de NFTs. *Journal du Luxe*. Available at https://www.journalduluxe.fr/fr/mode/gucci-pre-commandes-nft. (Accessed: 23 April 2024).

Joy, A., Zhu, Y., Peña, C., & Brouard, M. (2022). Digital future of luxury brands: Metaverse, digital fashion, and non-fungible tokens. *Strategic Change, 31*(3), 337–343. https://doi.org/10.1002/jsc.2502

Kaczynski, S., & Kominers, S. (2021). How NFTs create value. *Harvard Business Review*. Available at https://hbr.org/2021/11/how-nfts-create-value

Kapferer, J.-N., & Bastien, V. (2012). *The luxury strategy: Break the rules of marketing to build luxury brands*. Kogan Page.

Kering. (2018). *Kering announces new developments in its digital strategy*. [Press release]. Available at https://www.kering.com/en/news/announces-new-developments-in-its-digital-strategy/

Kering. (2023a). *2023 activity report*. [Press release]. Available at https://www.kering.com/en/group/discover-kering/activity-report/

Kering. (2023b). *2023 annual results*. [PDF document]. Available at https://www.kering.com/api/download-file/?path=Kering_Press_release_2023_Full_year_results_3388f09c4c.pdf

Kering. (2024a). *New business models for the fashion of future*. Available at https://www.kering.com/en/sustainability/innovating-for-tomorrow/new-business-models/

Kering. (2024b). *2023 Full year results.* [PDF document]. Available at https://www.kering.com/api/download-file/?path=Kering_Press_release_2023_Full_year_results_3388f09c4c.pdf

Kering. (2024c). *Crafting tomorrow's luxury.* Available at https://www.kering.com/en/sustainability/crafting-tomorrow-s-luxury/

Kering. (2024d). *Group history.* Available at https://www.kering.com/en/group/culture-and-heritage/group-history/

Lahbib, O., Kessous, A., & Valette-Florence, P. (2023). Toward a better understanding of the phenomenon of ambivalence in the endorsement of sustainable luxury. *Décisions Marketing, 110*, 217–246.

Lin, Y., & Yu, J. (2023). Study on the modernization of supply chain management of the luxury industry in the context of the digital economy. *Academic Journal of Management and Social Sciences, 4*(1). https://doi.org/10.54097/ajmss.v4i1.11454

Lopéz, B., Rangel Perez, C., & Fernandéz, M. (2023). Innovative strategies for sustainability in luxury brands. *Journal of Business Research, 157*. https://doi.org/10.1016/j.jbusres.2022.113607

LS:N Global. (n.d.). *Kering embraces NFTs and ChatGPT with AI personal shopper*. Available at https://www.lsnglobal.com/AI/article/29446/kering-embraces-nfts-and-chatgpt-with-ai-personal-shopper

Maddyness. (2022, March 7). *Métavers, NFT... L'industrie du luxe mise sur le virtuel pour créer de nouveaux revenus.* Available at https://www.maddyness.com/2022/03/07/metavers-nft-lindustrie-du-luxe-mise-sur-le-virtuel-pour-creer-de-nouveaux-revenus/

Marion, A. (2022, July 31). *KNXT by Kering.* Available at https://marionabou.com/2022/07/31/knxt-by-kering/

Miles, M. B., Huberman, A. M., & Saldaña, J. (2014). *Qualitative data analysis: A methods sourcebook* (3rd ed.). SAGE Publications Inc.

Morgan, H. (2022). Conducting a Qualitative Document Analysis. *Qualitative Report, 27*(1).

Moss, T. (2022, April 1). A $300,000 Dolce & Gabbana Tiara you can only wear in the metaverse; Dolce & Gabbana, Gucci, Burberry and other luxury-goods companies see promise in digital markets where—just as in real life—rarity and exclusivity can translate into high prices. *The Wall Street Journal Online*. Available at https://www.wsj.com/articles/a-300-000-dolce-gabbana-tiara-you-can-only-wear-in-the-metaverse-11648817988

Noris, A., Nobile, T. H., Kalbaska, N., & Cantoni, L. (2021). Digital fashion: A systematic literature review. A perspective on marketing and communication. *Journal of Global Fashion Marketing, 12*(1), 32–46. https://doi.org/10.1080/20932685.2020.1835522

Osburg, V. S., Davies, I., Yoganathan, V. et al. (2021). Perspectives, opportunities and tensions in ethical and sustainable luxury: Introduction to the thematic symposium. *Journal of Business Ethics, 169*, 201–210. https://doi.org/10.1007/s10551-020-04487-4

Ozuem, W., Ranfagni, S., & Willis, M. (eds.). (2024a). *Digital transformation for fashion and luxury brands: Theory and practice* (Illustrated ed.). Springer International Publishing.

Ozuem, W., Ranfagni, S., Willis, M., Salvietti, G., & Howell, K. (2024b). Exploring the relationship between chatbots, service failure recovery and customer loyalty: A frustration–aggression perspective. *Psychology and Marketing, 41*(10), 2253–2273. https://doi.org/10.1002/mar.22051

Ozuem, W., Willis, M., Ranfagni, S., Howell, K., & Rovai, S. (2023). Examining the role of social media influencers in service failure and recovery strategies: An empirical investigation of millennials' views. *Information Technology & People, 37*(5), 2035–2068. https://doi.org/10.1108/ITP-05-2022-0371

Park, H., & Lim, R. E. (2023). Fashion and the metaverse: Clarifying the domain and establishing a research agenda. *Journal of Retailing and Consumer Services, 74*(C). https://doi.org/10.1016/j.jretconser.2023.103413

Pavione, E., Pezzetti, R., & Dall'Ava, M. (2016). Emerging competitive strategies in the global luxury industry in the perspective of sustainable development: The case of kering group. *Management Dynamics in the Knowledge Economy, 4*(2), 241–261. https://www.managementdynamics.ro/index.php/journal/article/view/162

Rangel, C., & Lopez, B. (2022). Digital transformation in luxury brands. In *Challenges in an uncertain world*. Routledge.

Ryder, B. (2023, April 11). Kering taps the power of AI, NFTs with new tech-first fashion marketplace. *Jing Daily*. Available at https://jingdaily.com/posts/kering-ai-nft-fashion-marketplace

San Miguel, P., Pérez-Bou, S., Sádaba, T., & Mir-Bernal, P. (2021). How to communicate sustainability: From the corporate web to E-commerce. The case of the fashion industry. *Sustainability, 13*(20), 11363. https://doi.org/10.3390/su132011363

Sestino, A., & Amatulli, C. (2023). *New technologies in luxury consumption.* Springer International Publishing. https://doi.org/10.1007/978-3-031-26082-7

Sestino, A., Giraldi, L., Cedrola, E., Zamani, S. Z., & Gianluigi, G. (2022b). The business opportunity of blockchain value creation among the Internet of value. *Global Business Review.* online. https://doi.org/10.1177/09721509221115012

Sestino, A., Guido, G., & Peluso, A. M. (2022a). *Non-fungible tokens (NFTs)—Examining the impact on consumers and marketing strategies.* Palgrave Macmillan. https://doi.org/10.1007/978-3-031-07203-1

Sung, E. C., Kwon, O., & Sohn, K. (2023). NFT luxury brand marketing in the metaverse: Leveraging blockchain-certified NFTs to drive consumer behavior. *Psychology & Marketing, 40*(11), 2306–2325. https://doi.org/10.1002/mar.21854

The Peninsula Newspaper. (2022, August 4). *Luxury brands Gucci, Tiffany dive into NFTs despite slump.* The Peninsula Qatar. Available at https://thepeninsulaqatar.com/article/04/08/2022/luxury-brands-gucci-tiffany-dive-into-nfts-despite-slump

Uggla, H., & Lashgari, M. (2012). Brand portfolio prerogative: Five challenges and research themes within brand portfolio management. *The IUP Journal of Brand Management, 9*(3), 7–20. https://ssrn.com/abstract=2180741

Vial, G. (2019). Understanding digital transformation: A review and a research agenda. *The Journal of Strategic Information Systems, 28*(2), 118–144. https://doi.org/10.1016/j.jsis.2019.01.003

Wells, V., Athwal, N., Nervino, E., & Carrigan, M. (2021). How legitimate are the environmental sustainability claims of luxury conglomerates? *Journal of Fashion Marketing and Management, 25*(4), 697–722. https://doi.org/10.1108/JFMM-09-2020-0214

Williams, R. (2021). Gucci's Robert Triefus on testing luxury's allure in the metaverse. *Business of Fashion.* Available at https://www.businessoffashion.com/articles/luxury/the-state-of-fashion-2022-bof-mckinsey-gucci-robert-triefus-metaverse-virtual-nft-gaming.

Young, H., Su, X., Shion, K. (2023). Sustainable luxury purchase behavior in the Post-Pandemic Era: A grounded theory study in China. *Frontiers in Psychology, 14*, 1061369. https://doi.org/10.3389/fpsyg.2023.1260537

Zwieglinska, Z. (2022, November 27). Weekend briefing: Luxury brands' big week of exits and controversy. *Glossy.* Available at https://www.glossy.co/fashion/weekend-briefing-luxury-brands-are-crumbling-amid-controversies-and-exits/

26

Elevating the Luxury Brand Digital Engagement Using Chatbots

Nicole Cunningham

Introduction

The Covid-19 pandemic shifted how consumers purchase goods and made them more comfortable using online shopping. Prior to 2020, the luxury industry reported relatively low online sales with the value reaching €33 billion in 2019. This increased substantially post the Covid-19 pandemic with the amount more than doubling to €75 billion in 2022 (Sabanoglu, 2023). This demonstrates that given the Covid-19 pandemic, many luxury consumers were willing to purchase luxury brands online and continue to do so, with Sabanoglu (2024) predicting that 25% of luxury sales will be made through online channels by 2025. Historically, luxury brands have predominantly relied on the in-store luxury experience as a driver of sales due to the exclusivity and management of the customer experience within the store (Fatima, 2024).

N. Cunningham (✉)
Department of Marketing Management, College of Business & Economics, University of Johannesburg, Johannesburg, South Africa
e-mail: ncunningham@uj.ac.za

W. Ozuem et al. (eds.), *Sustainable Digital Marketing for Fashion and Luxury Brands*,
https://doi.org/10.1007/978-3-031-82467-8_26

However, as with all industries, luxury brands are shifting towards integrating more digital technologies to adapt to the changing consumer preferences (Klaus, 2020).

The challenge faced by luxury brands specifically is that simply offering their products online would not cater to the experience that luxury brands offer consumers within the stores. Often, when entering a physical luxury brand's store, a customer is usually greeted by a sales representative who provides a personalised shopping experience. When shopping online for generic products like groceries and books, the expectation of a personalised shopping experience is not heightened, however, due to the nature of luxury brands, this is still an expectation. As consumers are becoming more familiar and comfortable with digital technologies and shopping online, many industries have incorporated various types of digital technologies given the benefits they offer. However, it appears as though the luxury brand industry has been slow to adopt the use of chatbots, integrated into their digital platforms.

Based on the above, several gaps are evident—(1) the use of chatbots within the luxury brand industry is underexplored. Although some studies, i.e., Lin and Shin (2022), Hoang, Kousi and Martinez (2023) have focused on emoticons of chatbots and online customer engagement within the luxury industry, their practical analysis of how luxury brands are using chatbots is lacking. (2) With an increased amount of customers using digital platforms like mobile apps and social media as a source of information and to purchase products, the way in which luxury brands could use chatbots to ensure an omni-channel experience is underexplored. (3) Lastly, the reasons for integrating chatbots into the luxury brand's digital presence (in the context of luxury specifically) are lacking.

Therefore, this chapter will provide a discussion of luxury brands and how they are building their digital presence by focusing on the platforms they operate on and the execution of the platform. In addition, the way in which chatbots have been integrated into the luxury brand industry and how specific brands are executing the use of chatbots is also explored. The chapter concludes with a discussion of how luxury brands can make use of chatbots as a tool to secure customer engagement through their online channels.

Luxury Brands and the Digital Environments

Consumers are increasingly using the internet to search, compare, and purchase goods and this has led to many industries developing and introducing digital marketing strategies to reach today's consumers. The growing reliance of the internet is showcased in the fact that Google, the largest search engine, processes 99 000 search queries every second with an average person conducting, on average, three to four searches per day (Flensted, 2024). In addition, a new trend has shown that consumers also rely on social media as a source of information (Iskiev, 2023). This demonstrates the significant presence that the internet plays and the potential opportunities for various industries to secure their presence using digital platforms. Most commonly, brands have attempted to secure their presence by either introducing a website, making use of social media or introducing online sales channels. The latter has been found to be successful amongst fashion and the consumer electronics industry where the largest amount of retail sales is observed (van Gelder, 2024).

Luxury brands have been somewhat reluctant to make use of digital marketing strategies, particularly the introduction of online sales channels. This was primarily due to luxury brands being seen as exclusive, aspirational brands that offered a personalised shopping experience that online sales channels could not replicate (Kapferer, 2009; Ozuem et al., 2024). In 2017, the four most common reasons for opting to purchase luxury brands in-store were: (1) I need to see and touch the product before buying, (2) I prefer the in-store experience with a sales assistant, (3) I am concerned that some products sold online may not be genuine, and (4) I have enough opportunities to visit stores near where I live, work or when I travel (Statista, 2017). Many luxury brands relied on these four reasons to avoiding a digital presence. However, during the Covid-19 pandemic, luxury brands experienced significant decreases in their sales due to their brands not being easily available via online channels which can be seen in the significant decline in sales in both Europe and the USA over the 2020 and 2021 year with both regions declining by over 20 per cent (McKinsey & Company, 2021). This prompted luxury brands to revise their digital marketing strategies by enhancing their digital presence and introducing various online sales channels to increase their exposure to consumers and increase their sales. This has shown to be successful for several luxury brands, for instance, Louis Vuitton reported the highest online sales in 2022 across the top 10 luxury brands with US$2.61 billion generated through online sales channels (Koutsou-Wehling, 2024). The need for enhancing a digital presence and online sales channels within the luxury industry is further supported by the fact that 78% of luxury consumers conduct research using digital platforms beforehand (Emilie, 2023). This suggests that luxury brands need to have a presence on digital platforms where at the very least, consumers are exposed to the luxury items and at the most, able to purchase the luxury items. Table 26.1 below summarises the top 10 luxury brands, according to their brand value (Brand Finance, 2023) and their digital presence on their websites and Instagram. Instagram was selected as the social media site to review due to Instagram's visual nature and benefits of connecting, engagement and s-commerce which are important for luxury brands.

Based on the above different luxury brands appear to be integrating their digital presence ranging from fully integrated (i.e., opportunity to use augmented reality to try a product on) to limited integration (i.e., not having a mobile app). Although some may argue that limiting the digital presence speaks to the luxury brand's need to remain unique and exclusive. For example, the Birkin Bag is one of the most sought-after handbags in the world that cannot be easily bought, let alone online. The Hermès website does provide some information about the handbag; however, there is no opportunity to purchase the bag nor the price. Although this may be in line with Hermès need to remain exclusive, in this digital environment, limiting your digital presence can harm a brand's performance. Therefore, understanding how technology can be used to enhance the exclusivity while offering the personalised engagement is where luxury brands can make use of chatbots.

Research has been conducted on luxury brands and their use of digital environments however, research has been limited due to luxury brands lagging in the adoption of digital environments (Willersdorf et al., 2020). The Table 26.2 provides an overview of various studies conducted on luxury brands and their use or adoption of tools within the digital environment, ranging from gamification to online shopping to social media.

Table 26.1 Top 10 luxury brands digital presence

Brand	Official website	Official Instagram & mobile app
Porsche	Online information available (i.e., vehicle comparisons, model information, service information, dealer information, etc.) and allows the purchase of accessories, clothing, equipment and home and lifestyle items. Vehicles can be configured online (i.e., model, colour, interior) but cannot be purchased online, instead consumers are directed to a dealer	Customers can view a range of posts that are primarily focused on their vehicles and their capabilities. If customers choose to shop for accessories, they are prompted to the website to make the purchase Various mobile apps are available for different functions—i.e., track precision, dashcam and in-vehicle connection
Louis Vuitton	Various products are available for purchase via the website (i.e., handbags, accessories, shoes, etc.). Each product has the product information available including a description, dimensions, the sustainability information (where applicable) and product care. Customers can also personalise some items according to their preferences (i.e., colours and initials)	Customers can view different posts focusing on various fashion items and accessories. Messaging and shop facilities are available—shop facilities are linked to the official website The mobile app offers customers information, shopping facilities and services (similar to the website)
Chanel	Provides information about products and allows customers to try on items like sunglasses and watches using virtual reality. Products cannot be purchased online and customers are prompted to find a store near them	A range of posts focusing on fashion, make-up, fragrances, jewellery, etc. No shop link built into Instagram however, customers are provided the link to the official website Mobile app provides product information and directs customers to the website

(continued)

Table 26.1 (continued)

Brand	Official website	Official Instagram & mobile app
Gucci	Various products are available to purchase via the website. Each product includes the product details, dimensions. In addition, various products can be seen using 3D technology	Posts focusing on fashion items on Instagram with customers given the opportunity to email Gucci Mobile app provides similar functionality to the website however, online services are managed through the website
Hermès	Products are available to purchase via the website. Information relating to the product, care details and gifting options are also available. Some products also have videos available on how to use the product (i.e., putting on a bracelet)	Various posts focusing on the brand and fashion items. Message and shop functionality available (linked to website) on the Instagram page No mobile app available
Dior	Various products (fashion, accessories, beauty and fragrances) are available via the website with customers being able to purchase the items directly from the website. Information relating to the description of the product and dimensions is available	Various posts focusing on the brand and fashion items. Message and shop functionality available (linked to website) on the Instagram page A mobile app available for customers who wish to register
Cartier	Certain products are available for purchase on the website (i.e., handbags, fragrances and accessories) however certain jewellery items cannot be purchased through the website—presumably due to their cost. The website also includes a live augmented reality experience where for example, customers can try on watches	Different posts focusing on jewellery and watches. No shop functionality available however, customers are directed to the website No mobile app available

(continued)

Table 26.1 (continued)

Brand	Official website	Official Instagram & mobile app
Rolex	Product information is available as well as 360-degree views of the various products. No products can be purchased through the website and customers are encouraged to visit a Rolex retailer however, customers can configure their watches through the website	Various watches are showcased on the Instagram page. No shop functionality available A mobile app is available focusing on providing product information
Tiffany & Co	Product description, design explanation and the purchase of various products are available through the website. In addition, certain items provide usage guidelines like how to open and close a bracelet	Jewellery is mostly displayed on the Instagram page. A message and the shop functionality are available with customers being directed to the website to make a purchase An exhibition mobile app is available showing some of the products and how they are crafted
Ferrari	Customers cannot purchase vehicles online, however, product information is available with customers also being able to configure their chosen vehicle using 3D and 2D technology (i.e., interior, exterior design, equipment) and then enquire about the design. Other products like accessories (i.e., handbags, gifts) can be purchased via the online store	Various vehicles are displayed on the Instagram page focusing on the brand (limited product information available) A mobile app is available for owners

Source The official website and social media sites of Porsche, Louis Vuitton, Chanel, Gucci, Hermès, Dior, Cartier, Rolex, Tiffany & Co and Ferrari (note searches completed in May 2024 using the United Kingdom as the location)

Based on the above, researchers have focused on a range of different digital environment applications within the luxury industry making it challenging to compare different results as there is not a clear roadmap on how luxury brands use the digital environment. However, based on the studies above, the digital environment can offer luxury brands opportunities to encourage favourable responses ranging from a basic

Table 26.2 Summary of studies conducted on luxury brands and digital environments

Authors	Summary
Milanesi et al. (2023)	The study focused on MZQ's introduction of VER5, a gaming app that combines gaming, socialising and shopping. It was reported that users spent ten times more time on the app than the e-commerce website, offering the luxury retailer an opportunity to expose users to additional luxury products. The study revealed that there are three levels within the app: creating virtual avatars, competing in luxury fashion challenges and aspiring to be luxury virtual influencers
Javornik et al. (2021)	The study focused on the deployment of Augmented Reality (AR) in order to convey luxury brand's attributes. The study focused on four strategic approaches: ephemeral elevation, auratic amplification, bespoke personalisation and effortless continuation within a luxury context. The study found that the deployment of AR within the luxury industry should be done in alignment with the luxury brand's characteristics—i.e., reiterating the craftmanship, using luxurious visualisations, using holograms, metaverses—rather than applying mainstream automated processes that other brands use when using AR
Kim (2020)	The study focused on how males and females differ in their perceptions of the e-service quality of a luxury website. The findings revealed that order and delivery management impacted e-satisfaction amongst males (i.e., goal-orientated) while order and delivery management, customer service, personalisation, trust and entertainment value all influenced female's e-satisfaction of the luxury brand's website
Fazeli et al. (2020)	The study focused on four different studies focusing on how promotion-focus, prevention-focus and regulatory focus influence the intention to purchase luxury online as well as the moderating role of self-construal. The study found that promotion-focused consumers have an increased online shopping frequency for luxury items and spend more than prevention-focused consumers (online and offline). The study also showed the importance of regulatory fit in influencing prevention-focused consumers to purchase more
Kumar et al. (2022)	The study focused on how luxury brands engage consumers through social media. The study found that luxury brand's social media activities have the opportunity to encourage engagement amongst luxury brand consumers. In addition, the study found that content (MGC) developed by the luxury brand moderated the relationship between social media marketing and customer-brand engagement

introduction (i.e., using social media) to more complex activities like introducing an online shopping platform or gamification.

Chatbots

Chatbots have been in existence since the 1960s with the first chatbot offering automated responses based on a decision-tree format which offered simplistic interactions (Hasal et al., 2021). Chatbots progressed in the 1990s where limited artificial intelligence was integrated to identify an accurate response using the information records it had available (Kuhail et al., 2023). However, in the 2000s, with the introduction of natural language processing and machine learning, chatbots were able to interpret and respond to organic prompts and questions as opposed to the set list of questions previously permitted (Shah et al., 2023). The use of natural language processing and machine learning only progressed further and allowed for enhanced engagements where various industries like retail, banking, education and tourism use chatbots in order to enhance customer engagement and service on digital platforms (Hari et al., 2022; Singh et al., 2023). More specifically, chatbots can be used to offer customer service, offer product suggestions and provide feedback based on enquiries (Nithuna & Laseena, 2020). Table 26.3 below highlights how different industries are making use of chatbots.

Table 26.3 How different industries are using chatbots

Industry	Use of chatbots to
Hospitality and tourism	Assist with travel planning, making travel bookings, offering customer support, providing recommendations and assisting customers with any travelling challenges (Pillai & Sivathanu, 2020)
Fashion industry	Provide personalised shopping experiences, provide recommendations and enhance customer engagement (Aslam, 2023)
Banking	Respond to customer queries quickly, provide information and offer the opportunity of a direct communication channel with a bank representative (Hari et al., 2022)
Education	Enhance student engagement and answer queries (Hwang & Chang, 2023)

Whilst chatbots are essentially a once-off investment, it is still vital that businesses consider both the benefits and challenges of using chatbots.

Benefits

Chatbots offer a range of benefits for businesses. Firstly, chatbots are simplistic in nature and offer businesses the opportunity to engage without the need of a human to facilitate the engagement (Adamopoulou & Moussiades, 2020). Secondly, according to a study conducted by Li and Shin (2023), a chatbot is able to encourage four times more sales compared to an inexperienced human. Cheng and Jiang (2020) add that chatbots offer increased engagement due to their ability to mimic speech to improve the customer's experience. Meaning that chatbots have the ability to adapt the way in which they engage with different customers which may be why they are able to encourage more sales. Thirdly, further to the enhanced engagement, chatbots also provide businesses with access to data such as customer queries, purchase behaviour, contact information, customer interests and motivations for making or not making a purchase (Joy et al., 2022). Lastly, chatbots offer customers the opportunity of receiving personalised recommendations according to their queries and requests (Myin & Watchravesringkam, 2024).

Challenges

As with the use of any technology, there are some challenges that businesses need to be aware of before implementing a chatbot. Firstly, there is a perception that a chatbot cannot provide the assistance that a human being can and often customers end the conversation when they realise that they are not speaking to a human being (Hasal et al., 2021). Secondly, customers feel a risk in sharing too much information, particularly personal information with a chatbot due to chatbots being able to summarise large amounts of information and form patterns according to the information shared (Murtarelli et al., 2021). Thirdly, chatbots and their execution differ from industry to industry meaning that customers may have similar expectations of what the chatbot can do based on their experience with other chatbots which may limit the use of a certain chatbot or on the extreme affect the perceived performance of the chatbot based on customer expectations (Chong et al., 2021).

Chatbots & Luxury

As mentioned, most luxury brands are investing in an online presence due to changes in consumer preferences. However, as the digital environment has the potential to diminish the exclusivity and the experience that the customer experiences within a luxury store, luxury brands have invested in the use of chatbots to offer assistance and engagement via their digital platforms (Zeng et al., 2023). In addition to the chatbot being used to positively enhance the customer's experience with the luxury brand (in the absence of a salesperson), chatbots have become an expectation of certain industries like luxury where a superior service is expected (Chung et al., 2020; Ozuem et al., 2021). This makes it imperative that luxury brands provide chatbots that match or exceed customer expectations as the experience that luxury brands offer via their online platforms has a significant impact on customer experience, brand awareness and retention (Majeed et al., 2024). In addition, Generation Z and Alpha consumers are expected to account for 45% of the global population by 2030 and will be the largest potential customer segment for luxury brands (Roberts, 2023). As these consumers prefer digital channels and assistance, their minimum expectation would be that a chatbot is available to offer convenient assistance via a shopping platform that they prefer (Li & Shin, 2023). Therefore, the implementation of chatbots for luxury brands is considered an investment for luxury brands.

Reasons Motivating the Use of Chatbots for Luxury Brands

Chatbots are designed to offer the business operational efficiencies while enhancing the customer's engagement and convenience while engaging on digital platforms like websites and social media (Chung et al., 2020; Li & Shin, 2023). Generally, luxury brand chatbots are used to offer product information, recommendations, shopping assistance and enhance the shopping experience (Hindolia & Arya, 2022; Zeng et al., 2023). The uses relate to four reasons motivating the use of chatbots for luxury brands: (1) personalisation; (2) the 24/7 availability; (3) the seamless omni-channel experience; and (4) enhanced customer service.

Personalisation

When customers go to the luxury brand's physical store customers are very rarely left to roam around the store without assistance or being approached by a sales representative. This type of service is what sets luxury brands and other brands apart because this offers the customer's unique needs and preferences (Eken, 2024). Simply offering their products online for customers to view and possibly purchase would diminish the personalised service that luxury brand customers receive in store. Therefore, by incorporating chatbots into their digital platforms, luxury brands are still able to offer personalisation and a unique shopping experience (Hoyer et al., 2020; Li & Shin, 2023; Ozuem & Willis, 2022) as it appears as though the customer is having a one-on-one conversation in real-time (Sidlauskiene et al., 2023). This ensures that luxury brand customers feel valued, as they would in the store. In addition, chatbots offer luxury brands the benefit of accessing an abundance of customer data. Data is important for luxury brands as it allows for a more customer-centric approach by understanding customer preferences, requests, purchases and consumption (Bertrand & Glebova, 2024). As chatbots collect and analyse the data that customers provide (Shahzad et al., 2024), luxury brands have the benefit of forming patterns of various customer inputs and improve the functionality of their chatbots in order to produce more specific responses to current and future chatbot users (Misischia et al., 2022; Ozuem et al., 2023), making the customer feel unique. Further to this, chatbots have the ability to recall customer preferences and therefore offer enhanced personalisation depending on the customer's previous engagements and preferences (Aslam, 2023). This in turn offers luxury brands the opportunity to learn from customer inputs—for example, Gucci is known to design products based on customer preferences (Cheng & Jiang, 2022).

24/7 Availability

Although luxury brand's physical stores are operational during certain hours and days, the nature of digital platforms implies 24/7 availability. This suggests that luxury brands must be prepared to assist customers who visit their digital platforms at any time, particularly since luxury customers demand enhanced retail experiences (Carufel, 2023). Using a chatbot that is available 24/7 ensures that customers are given the assistance they require at any time and potentially reduce uncertainty (Hoyer et al., 2020; Misischia et al., 2022). This provides luxury brands with the opportunity to satisfy customer needs outside of in-store operational hours, thus enhancing the potential for increased sales while still maintaining the relationship with the customer (Youn & Jin, 2021). Therefore, by integrating a chatbot into their digital platforms, luxury brands can engage with their customers at any time, satisfying the expectation of immediate assistance (Pappasa et al., 2023).

Seamless Omni-channel Experience

A seamless omni-channel experience is defined successful when customers regard a retailer's various sales as one and their experience using the one channel is the same as another channel (Bertrand & Glebova, 2024). From a luxury brand perspective, this would simply mean that the customer would have the same shopping experience regardless of whether they select the in-store or online shopping experience. For a luxury brand, this would be the desired outcome (Amatulli et al., 2021). This is a very important reason motivating the use of chatbots for luxury brands who want to ensure that they offer support, product information and assist throughout the shopping process, as an in-store sales assistant would (Araújo & Casais, 2020). For instance, if a customer was reviewing a particular item of clothing on the luxury brand's website and they wanted a suggestion in terms of shoes, the chatbot could offer guidance and recommendations almost as an in-store sales assistant would.

Enhanced Customer Service

Within an in-store environment, there are a certain amount of sales assistants which creates a restriction in amount of customers who can be serviced at one-time. However, the use of chatbots is able to attend to numerous customers at once and manage engagements effectively which decreases the potential for frustration as customers receive an instantaneous response (Araújo & Casais, 2020). In addition to this benefit, chatbots offer consistent levels of customer service that are not impacted by human fatigue, inconsistent information provided or unavailability (Pappasa et al., 2023). As shown in Table 26.1, although luxury brands have a digital presence, very few use chatbots effectively. Instead, when visiting the digital platforms, customers are generally only able to engage via chat when an agent is available, meaning that luxury brands are not taking advantage of the opportunity that chatbots offer in providing enhanced engagements via digital platforms when the live agent is not available.

Based on the discussion presented above about the various benefits, challenges, and reasons for using chatbots, Table 26.4 below provides an overview of how the top 10 luxury brands are making use of chatbots across their websites and mobile apps.

The above shows that a significant of luxury brands are not integrating chatbots into their service offering. It appears most are relying on the live-chat facility to ensure the personalised engagement that a

Table 26.4 Top 10 luxury brands use of chatbots

Brand	Platform	Functionality
Porsche	Website, Instagram, mobile app	No chatbot available on the website or mobile app however, business chat available on Instagram however, this is a live-chat facility (no timeline specified)
Louis Vuitton	Website, Instagram, mobile app	No chatbot available on the website, Instagram or mobile app, only live-chat facility that allows engagement with an agent (within 8 hours)
Chanel	Website, Instagram, mobile app	No chatbot available on the website or mobile app however, business chat available on Instagram however, this is a live-chat facility (no timeline specified)
Gucci	Website, Instagram, mobile app	No chatbot available, only a chat facility with a client advisor. Instagram allows for business chat however, this is a live-chat facility (no timeline specified)
Hermès	Website, Instagram, mobile app	No chatbot available on the website or mobile app however, business chat available on Instagram however, this is a live-chat facility (no timeline specified)
Dior	Website, Instagram, mobile app	No chatbot available on the website or mobile app however, business chat available on Instagram however, this is a live-chat facility (no timeline specified)
Cartier	Website, Instagram, mobile app	No chatbot available, only a chat facility that allows engagement with a live Cartier ambassador via the website
Rolex	Website, Instagram, mobile app	No chatbot available, customers are prompted to engage with the brand through official channels (i.e., social media sites)
Tiffany & Co	Website, Instagram, mobile app	Chatbot available via the website however, most requests lead to the chatbot linking the chat to a client advisor. A chatbot is available through Instagram where customers are prompted using questions and recommendations are made
Ferrari	Website, Instagram, mobile app	No chatbot available, only a live-chat facility

Source The official website and social media sites of Porsche, Louis Vuitton, Chanel, Gucci, Hermès, Dior, Cartier, Rolex, Tiffany & Co and Ferrari (note searches completed in May 2024 using the United Kingdom as the location) customer may expect in a store—i.e., Louis Vuitton, Chanel, Hermès and so on. However, Tiffany & Co's chatbot (available through Instagram Messaging) provides personalised engagement whereas the website's chatbot does not understand most of the queries and tends to request that an agent joins the chat. Although the use of chatbots may be used reluctantly due to the perception of them being impersonable, chatbots offer luxury brands the benefit of meeting the need for personalisation while ensuring a seamless omni-channel experience. Table 26.5 below provides a summary of studies focusing on chatbots within the luxury industry.

Table 26.5 Studies focusing on the deployment of chatbots within the luxury industry

Authors	Summary
Chung et al. (2020)	The study focused on whether luxury fashion brands could offer personalisation through chatbots. The five-dimension model measuring the chatbot's marketing efforts (interaction, entertainment, trendiness, customisation and problem-solving) leading to communication quality (accuracy, credibility and communication competence) resulting in satisfaction. The study found that the chatbot's marketing efforts impacted the accuracy and credibility with regards to communication quality but did not impact communication competence. Further, the study found that accuracy and credibility impacted satisfaction yet communication competence did not
Li and Shin (2022)	The study focused on whether luxury chatbots should use emoticons and the impact on perceived brand status. The results of the two studies conducted reveal that luxury brands should consider not using emoticons due to the potential dilution of brand status perception. However, this only applied for traditional luxury brands and not for masstige brands
Jin and Youn (2023)	This study focused on anthropomorphism (human-likeness, animacy, intelligence), social presence, imagery processing, psychological ownership and continuous intention as factors driving consumer's use of chatbots. The study found that the perceived human-likeness positively influences social influence and imagery processing whilst animacy and intelligence did not have a positive influence. Social presence in turn influenced the chatbot continuous intention whilst imagery processing influenced psychological ownership and the chatbot continued intention. Therefore, revealing the importance of perceived human-likeness of a chatbot within the luxury industry

Based on the above, there is limited research being conducted on how luxury brands are using chatbots in an effort to engage consumers, highlighting a potential research gap in the understanding of how chatbots can be used to enhance customer engagement. The next section provides practical recommendations on how luxury brand could embrace the use of chatbots.

Recommendations for Luxury Brands and Use of Chatbots

As mentioned, chatbots offer a range of advantages, particularly to luxury brands who want to offer a digital experience yet do not want to diminish the personalised engagement. Therefore, the below recommendations provide practical recommendations of luxury brands who would like to introduce chatbots—from the most basic form of a chatbot to a comprehensive version:

1. Personalised recommendations—when customers make use of digital platforms that are very visually appealing, there is an expectation that they will resemble the individual or the aesthetic that they see online. Within a store, given luxury brands and their ability to provide a positive perception, receiving personalised recommendations may be one of the basic introductions of a chatbot. For example, a customer may be reviewing a new pair of jeans on the Dior website and as they are clicking on different parts of the page, the chatbot may pop up and ask if the customer requires any further assistance or would like to see a recommendation. In a way, this mimics what a sales representative may start with within an in-store environment.
2. Providing product information and support—by incorporating a chatbot, customers are able to engage with the luxury brand at any point in time. A customer may have a very straightforward question that they don't necessarily need a live agent to provide. For example, a customer may want to know if they can engrave a certain product and may not want to read through the website information. Thus,

incorporating a chatbot allows for customers to obtain information in a manner that is convenient to them.

3. Assisting with the live-chat performance—many of the luxury brands listed in Table 26.3 made use of a live-chat facility that was available at certain times through different platforms. Although this is a satisfactory start with merging technology and in-person engagement, the frustration of the live-chat facility may leave customers frustrated. Thus, by including a chatbot to pre-empt queries (i.e., booking an appointment) and guide customers as much as possible, a chatbot may result in more satisfied customers and less strain on the live-chat agents who may be inundated with queries that a chatbot may have been able to manage.
4. Humanisation—although chatbots are digital, a level of humanisation is encouraged in order to secure the personalised engagement. However, luxury brands should be careful of offering too much humanisation. For example, in a study conducted by Lin and Shin (2022), it was found that emoticons decrease the brand status perception of luxury brands simply because the use of emoticons and luxury brands are not synonymous. Therefore, luxury brands can implement some humanisation elements (i.e., giving the chatbot a human-like name and engaging with the customer as though they were in the store) however, ensuring that the humanisation is aligned with the luxury brand's identity is paramount.

Based on the above, luxury brands can use chatbots to alleviate the demand on synchronous online engagement (online customer and live agent) whilst ensuring that customers receive the personalised assistance that they would receive in the luxury brand store. Therefore, using chatbots as a technology to aid in providing personalised engagements would result in customers who use digital platforms whilst still remaining true to what the luxury brand aims to provide.

Conclusion

This chapter provided an overview of how chatbots are being and can be used by luxury brands. Although the review of various luxury brands shows that many don't adopt the use of chatbots in their true sense and rather make use of digital platforms to link customers to live agents, it is clear that luxury brands are missing the opportunity to utilise technology like chatbots effectively. The reasons for being reluctant to adopt chatbots are mostly related to the luxury industry itself and the way in which it prides itself on providing customers with personalised engagements in the in-store environment. However, if luxury brands invest in developing comprehensive chatbots that are able to personalise their offerings, answer customer questions and queries and provide human-like interactions, luxury brands would still be able to offer their products using digital platforms while ensuring a seamless omni-channel experience. Customers are not opting to use luxury brand digital platforms, therefore, the onus is on luxury brands to adapt their digital marketing presence—using chatbots—as a way to ensure a consistent customer experience.

References

Adamopoulou, E., & Moussiades, L. (2020). Chatbots: History, technology, and applications. *Machine Learning with Applications, 2*, 100006.

Amatulli, C., De Angelis, M., Sestino, A., & Guido, G. (2021). Omnichannel shopping experiences for fast fashion and luxury brands: An exploratory study. In *Developing successful global strategies for marketing luxury brands* (pp. 22–43). IGI Global.

Araújo, T., & Casais, B. (2020). Customer acceptance of shopping-assistant chatbots. In *Marketing and smart technologies: Proceedings of ICMarkTech 2019* (pp. 278–287). Springer Singapore.

Aslam, U. (2023). Understanding the usability of retail fashion brand chatbots: Evidence from customer expectations and experiences. *Journal of Retailing and Consumer Services, 74*, 103377.

Bertrand, M., & Glebova, E. How digital transformation impacts customer experience in the hard luxury industry: Consensus on Omnichannel Strategy.

Carufel, R. (2023). *Luxury consumers prefer in-store shopping—But demand superior retail experiences*. Available from https://www.agilitypr.com/pr-news/public-relations/luxury-consumers-prefer-in-store-shopping-but-demand-superior-retail-experiences/ [Accessed 1 May 2024].

Cheng, Y., & Jiang, H. (2022). Customer–brand relationship in the era of artificial intelligence: Understanding the role of chatbot marketing efforts. *Journal of Product & Brand Management, 31*(2), 252–264.

Chong, T., Yu, T., Keeling, D. I., & de Ruyter, K. (2021). AI-chatbots on the services frontline addressing the challenges and opportunities of agency. *Journal of Retailing and Consumer Services, 63*, 102735.

Chung, M., Ko, E., Joung, H., & Kim, S. J. (2020). Chatbot e-service and customer satisfaction regarding luxury brands. *Journal of Business Research, 117*, 587–595.

McKinsey & Company. (2021). *The state of fashion 2021*. Available from https://www.mckinsey.com/~/media/mckinsey/industries/retail/our%20insights/state%20of%20fashion/2021/the-state-of-fashion-2021-vf.pdf [Accessed 30 April 2024].

Brand Directory. (2023). *Luxury and premium: The annual report of the most valuable and strongest luxury and premium brands*. Available from https://brandirectory.com/rankings/luxury-and-premium [Accessed 10 May 2024].

Eken, Y. (2024). *Custom couture: High-end lessons in marketing personalisation from luxury brands*. Available from https://segmentify.com/blog/marketing-personalisation-lessons-from-luxury-brands/ [Accessed 16 April 2024].

Emilie. (2023). *Understanding and attracting luxury consumers thanks to digital technology*. Available from https://www.buybox.net/en/blog/understanding-attracting-luxury-consumers-digital-technology [Accessed 20 May 2024].

Fatima, N. (2024). *Luxury goods market: Net sales development, online & offline sales*. Available from https://ecommercedb.com/insights/the-global-luxury-market-ecommerce-growth-rate-surpasses-that-of-non-luxury/4672 [Accessed 15 April 2024].

Fazeli, Z., Shukla, P., & Perks, K. (2020). Digital buying behavior: The role of regulatory fit and self-construal in online luxury goods purchase intentions. *Psychology & Marketing, 37*(1), 15–26.

Flensted, T. (2024). How many people use google? *Statistics & Facts*. Available from https://seo.ai/blog/how-many-people-use-google [Accessed 10 May 2024].

Hari, H., Iyer, R., & Sampat, B. (2022). Customer brand engagement through chatbots on bank websites–examining the antecedents and consequences. *International Journal of Human-Computer Interaction, 38*(13), 1212–1227.

Hasal, M., Nowaková, J., Ahmed Saghair, K., Abdulla, H., Snášel, V., & Ogiela, L. (2021). Chatbots: Security, privacy, data protection, and social aspects. *Concurrency and Computation: Practice and Experience, 33*(19), e6426.

Hoyer, W. D., Kroschke, M., Schmitt, B., Kraume, K., & Shankar, V. (2020). Transforming the customer experience through new technologies. *Journal of Interactive Marketing, 51*(1), 57–71.

Iskiev, M. (2023). *The way people search the web is changing: 4 stats marketers & SEOs should know [HubSpot Data].* Available from https://blog.hubspot.com/marketing/how-search-behaviors-are-changing [Accessed 15 May 2024].

Javornik, A., Duffy, K., Rokka, J., Scholz, J., Nobbs, K., Motala, A., & Goldenberg, A. (2021). Strategic approaches to augmented reality deployment by luxury brands. *Journal of Business Research, 136*, 284–292.

Jin, S. V., & Youn, S. (2023). Social presence and imagery processing as predictors of chatbot continuance intention in human-AI-interaction. *International Journal of Human-Computer Interaction, 39*(9), 1874–1886.

Joy, A., Zhu, Y., Peña, C., & Brouard, M. (2022). Digital future of luxury brands: Metaverse, digital fashion, and non-fungible tokens. *Strategic Change, 31*(3), 337–343.

Kapferer, J. N., & Bastien, V. (2012). *The luxury strategy: Break the rules of marketing to build luxury brands.* Kogan Page Publishers.

Kim, J. H. (2020). Luxury brands in the digital age: Perceived quality and gender difference. *The International Review of Retail, Distribution and Consumer Research, 30*(1), 68–85.

Klaus, P. P. (2020). The end of the world as we know it? The influence of online channels on the luxury customer experience. *Journal of Retailing and Consumer Services, 57.*

Koutsou-Wehling, N. (2024). *Louis Vuitton analysis: Sales, online to offline, B2B vs. D2C.* Available from https://ecommercedb.com/insights/louis-vuitton-generated-us-2-8-billion-in-net-sales-online-by-2022/4701 [Accessed 28 April 2024].

Kuhail, M. A., Alturki, N., Alramlawi, S., & Alhejori, K. (2023). Interacting with educational chatbots: A systematic review. *Education and Information Technologies, 28*(1), 973–1018.

Kumar, V., Khan, I., Fatma, M., & Singh, A. (2022). Engaging luxury brand consumers on social media. *Journal of Consumer Marketing, 39*(1), 121–132.

Li, Y., & Shin, H. (2023). Should a luxury Brand's Chatbot use emoticons? Impact on brand status. *Journal of Consumer Behaviour, 22*(3), 569–581.

Majeed, M. U., Aftab, H., Arslan, A., & Shakeel, Z. (2024). Determining online consumer's luxury purchase intention: The influence of antecedent factors and the moderating role of brand awareness, perceived risk, and web atmospherics. *PLoS One, 19*(2), e0295514.

Milanesi, M., Guercini, S., & Runfola, A. (2023). Let's play! Gamification as a marketing tool to deliver a digital luxury experience. *Electronic Commerce Research, 23*(4), 2135–2152.

Misischia, C. V., Poecze, F., & Strauss, C. (2022). Chatbots in customer service: Their relevance and impact on service quality. *Procedia Computer Science, 201*, 421–428.

Murtarelli, G., Gregory, A., & Romenti, S. (2021). A conversation-based perspective for shaping ethical human–machine interactions: The particular challenge of chatbots. *Journal of Business Research, 129*, 927–935.

Myin, M. T., & Watchravesringkan, K. (2024). Investigating consumers' adoption of AI chatbots for apparel shopping. *Journal of Consumer Marketing, 41*(3), 314–327.

Nithuna, S., & Laseena, C. A. (2020, July). Review on implementation techniques of chatbot. In *2020 International Conference on Communication and Signal Processing (ICCSP)* (pp. 0157–0161). IEEE.

Ozuem, W., Ranfagni, S., Willis, M., Rovai, S., & Howell, K. (2021). Exploring customers' responses to online service failure and recovery strategies during Covid-19 pandemic: An actor–network theory perspective. *Psychology & Marketing, 38*(9), 1440–1459.

Ozuem, W., Ranfagni, S., Willis, M., Salvietti, G., & Howell, K. (2024). Exploring the relationship between chatbots, service failure recovery and customer loyalty: A frustration–aggression perspective. *Psychology and Marketing*. https://doi.org/10.1002/mar.22051

Ozuem, W., & Willis, M. (2022). *Digital marketing strategies for value co-creation : Models and approaches for online brand communities*. Palgrave Macmillan.

Ozuem, W., Willis, M., Ranfagni, S., Howell, K. E., & Rovai, S. (2023). Examining the role of social media influencers in service failure and recovery strategies: An empirical investigation of millennials' views. *Information Technology & People*. https://doi.org/10.1108/itp-05-2022-0371

Pappasa, A., Fumagallib, E., Rouziouc, M., & Bolanderc, W. (2023). More than machines: The role of the future retail salesperson in enhancing the customer experience.

Pillai, R., & Sivathanu, B. (2020). Adoption of AI-based chatbots for hospitality and tourism. *International Journal of Contemporary Hospitality Management, 32*(10), 3199–3226.

Roberts, F. (2023). *Five ways Gen Z is transforming luxury and fashion.* Available from https://www.euromonitor.com/article/five-ways-gen-z-is-transforming-luxury-and-fashion#:~:text=Consumption%20patterns%20evolving%20as%20Gen,for%20luxury%20and%20fashion%20brands. [Accessed 10 April 2024].

Sabanoglu, T. (2023). *Value of the online personal luxury goods market worldwide from 2004 to 2022.* Available from https://www.statista.com/statistics/246133/value-of-the-online-personal-luxury-goods-market-worldwide/. [Accessed 10 April 2024].

Sabanoglu, T. (2024). *E-commerce share of personal luxury good sales worldwide from 2017 to 2025.* Available from https://www.statista.com/statistics/1092062/e-commerce-share-of-personal-luxury-good-sales-worldwide/. [Accessed 15 April 2024].

Shah, I., Jhawar, S., Khater, A., Jacob, A., & Potdar, G. (2023). Chatbot development through the ages: A survey.

Sidlauskiene, J., Joye, Y., & Auruskeviciene, V. (2023). AI-based chatbots in conversational commerce and their effects on product and price perceptions. *Electronic Markets, 33*(1), 24.

Singh, A., Sharma, K. K., Kumar, P., & Vats, S. K. (2022, September). Chatbots: Understanding their world, classification, and their current state. In *International Conference on Emergent Converging Technologies and Biomedical Systems* (pp. 421–429). Springer Nature Singapore.

Statista. (2017). *Why have you not made your luxury product purchases online?* Available from https://www.statista.com/statistics/804281/consumers-reasons-for-not-purchasing-luxury-goods-online-worldwide/. [Accessed 10 May 2024].

van Gelder. (2024). *E-commerce worldwide—Statistics & facts.* Available from https://www.statista.com/topics/871/online-shopping/#topicOverview. [Accessed 12 May 2024].

Willersdorf, S., Hazan, J., Ricci, G., Prénaud, A., Bianchi, F., Seara, J., & Yang, V. (2020). A new era and a new look for luxury. *BCG Global.*

Youn, S., & Jin, S. V. (2021). In AI we trust?" The effects of parasocial interaction and technopian versus luddite ideological views on chatbot-based customer relationship management in the emerging "feeling economy. *Computers in Human Behavior, 119*, 106721.

Zeng, N., Vignali, G., & Ryding, D. (2023). Understanding the application of AI-enabled chatbots in luxury fashion retailing. *The garment economy: Understanding history, developing business models, and leveraging digital technologies* (pp. 369–388). Springer International Publishing.

27

The Role of Blockchain in Sustainable Luxury Fashion

Silvia Ranfagni, Massimo Rosati, and Michele Di Giura

Introduction

In the increasingly industrialised and globalised landscape of high fashion, attention to sustainability has become a very important issue in recent years. Consumers are increasingly distinguished by their sensitivity and attention to their consumption choices and what consequences these may have for the Planet. The pressures that not only consumers but also institutions have begun to exert are pushing companies to review and renew their supply chain management strategies. In this context, technological innovation emerges as a huge opportunity to help organisations improve the transparency, efficiency and sustainability of production and supply chains.

In this context, technological innovation is a huge opportunity to help organisations manage and shape their production supply chains. The aim

S. Ranfagni (✉) · M. Rosati · M. Di Giura
Department of Economics and Business, University of Florence, 50127 Florence, Italy
e-mail: silvia.ranfagni@unifi.it

W. Ozuem et al. (eds.), *Sustainable Digital Marketing for Fashion and Luxury Brands*,
https://doi.org/10.1007/978-3-031-82467-8_27

of this chapter is, therefore, to describe the potential of blockchain, one of the most disruptive technologies introduced by Industry 4.0, within high-fashion supply chains, paying particular attention to how this tool can contribute to the sustainability of supply chains (Ranfagni, 2022; Ranfagni & Salvietti, 2015; Ranfagni et al., 2018, 2021). Through an in-depth analysis of the key concepts of supply chain and blockchain, this study aims to offer a clear and comprehensive view of the opportunities, benefits, risks and critical issues arising from the implementation of blockchain in the most exclusive fashion industry.

The first part of the chapter will introduce the topic of supply chains, focusing on the world of luxury and the production chains of this exclusive sector, as well as on so-called sustainable supply chains, in which environmental and social impacts play a key role in shaping processes. Finally, the most important technological innovations that can become part of production chains nowadays will be introduced. Among this, one of the most promising tools is the so-called blockchain, the analysis of which will focus on its principal characteristics, its birth and evolution, the rules of operation, the current areas of application, the potential and difficulties that have determined its development and diffusion. It will also be analysed how and for what purposes it can be considered a useful tool in supply chain management, looking at the advantages and limitations that its implementation can bring about. The last section will introduce the results of research based on a content analysis, carried out by collecting texts from heterogeneous sources (secondary data and academic sources), which were processed through the T-Lab software. This application was used to carry out a co-occurrence analysis, which was useful in exploring the relationships between blockchain, the luxury fashion supply chain and sustainability. Employing various sources allows for a comprehensive exploration of this subject from multiple perspectives. This approach aims to ascertain the present utilisation of this technology within the luxury sector while accentuating its prospects, constraints and prospective advancements. A particular emphasis is placed on examining the frequency with which the theme of sustainability appears in the chosen sources. This serves to underscore how blockchain can be connected to more sustainable practices by organisations that opt to integrate this intricate technology into their supply chain. In conclusion, this study seeks to enrich the discourse surrounding the integration of blockchain technology in the supply chains of luxury fashion. It aims to illuminate the role, applications, opportunities and challenges that define this domain at present.

The Supply Chain

The supply chain consists of all parties involved, directly or indirectly, in the entire production process of a product. It is a complex and integrated system involving organisations, activities, people, information and resources involved in the movement and transformation of goods and services from suppliers to end customers, encompassing all the stages necessary to meet market demand, and which, simplified, consists of three basic moments: procurement, production and distribution. In this system, multiple actors coexist simultaneously, constituting complex networks, the management of which is essential to ensure the proper functioning of the chain, and which therefore constitutes the subject of supply chain management. Among these players, there are producers, suppliers, distributors and customers. Supply chain management can therefore be conceived as a complex, relational system formed and driven by the behaviours of the various actors involved. These behaviours shape a set of decisions and processes designed to integrate the activities of procurement, production and delivery of products and services to customers.

Lambert et al. (1998) define eight processes, which, taken together, constitute a supply chain management framework: (1) customer relationship management, (2) customer service management, (3) demand management, (4) order fulfilment, (5) production flow management, (6) supplier relationship management, (7) product development and marketing, and finally (8) returns management. This framework makes it clear that the efficient and effective management of production chains is a far from simple challenge for organisations, especially those in which a very large multitude of actors, each driven by different interests, coexist simultaneously.

However, one of the interests that has been increasingly permeating production and supply chains recently is related to sustainability. Sustainability has been defined in 1987 by the World Commission on Environment and Development within the Brundtland Report as meeting the needs of the present generation without compromising those of the future generation. It has become such an important issue that it has led to the emergence of concepts such as Green Supply Chain Management (GSCM), described by Srivastava (2007) as the fusion of green thinking in supply chain management. In particular, GSCM includes the ecological design of products, the procurement of environmentally sustainable materials and components, the reorganisation of production processes to make them more environmentally friendly and the management of the return of products after their use through reverse logistics. Such an approach not only aims to reduce waste and pollution, but also aims to generate and increase value creation throughout the supply chain processes. One of the factors that has certainly led to increased awareness of sustainability issues stems from regulations. A clear example of this is the recent European Union's Corporate Sustainability Reporting Directive (CSRD) in force since 2023, which has extended the obligation to report on environmental, social and economic impact according to standardised criteria at the European level. It forces not only public interest entities and large companies, but also small and medium-sized listed companies to undergo these constraints and prepare so-called sustainability reports.

Relationships Between Luxury and Sustainability

Based on etymology and their traditional definition, combining the concepts of luxury and sustainability can be a real oxymoron. The term luxury comes from the Latin word "luxus", which, starting from the root (lux), means light, magnificence and splendour. However, from "luxus" we also derive the word "luxuria", which reflects the idea of excess and unrestraint. It is clear how the term itself evokes two opposing meanings: on the one hand, we have sumptuousness, light, while on the other we have debauchery, viciousness. This is why it is a concept often associated with excess and superfluous. On the opposite, the concept of sustainability values saving, reducing environmental impacts, promoting equity and utility. This is why, as pointed out by Guercini and Ranfagni (2013), luxury is believed to be the exact opposite of sustainability precisely because it is superfluous, showy and excessive, lacking any utilitarian use. In fact, if we consider the definition of the concept of luxury, we can see that sustainability constitutes a fundamental element of its DNA (Ranfagni & Ozuem, 2022). From this perspective, sustainable products share "essential" characteristics similar to those of luxury goods: they require a high level of creativity and design, are made of high-quality materials, are considered rare and have a high cost. Therefore, the two concepts do not appear so far from each other (Hashmi, 2017; Ozuem et al., 2023). This awareness has generated the concept of "Sustainable Luxury", which reflects a return to the roots of the concept of luxury in its earliest form. This concept embraces the idea of thoughtful consumption, artisanal production and appreciation of the beauty of materials in the broadest sense, along with respect for social and environmental issues.

However, just as it cannot be said that sustainability concerns exclusively environmental issues, but rather involves a large number of indicators and issues, succinctly contained within the acronym ESG (Environment, Social, Governance), one cannot observe the luxury fashion sector as a single sector. In fact, it is crucial to emphasise that the concept of luxury represents a sector within which there are brands that belong to different segments. The three main ones are accessible luxury, intermediate luxury and exclusive luxury. The first level consists of luxury produced and distributed on a large scale, in which exclusivity is not due to the intrinsic characteristics of the product, but rather to the brand that produces them (Hugo Boss and Michael Kors are examples). The second segment, also known as aspirational luxury, is represented by brands such as Louis Vuitton, Gucci or Prada, i.e., products of high quality and prestige whose distribution takes place through extremely curated channels, at decidedly high prices. Finally, products that are mostly provided by traditional brands with a long-standing legacy and recognised elitism represent exclusive luxury. Brands in this category usually offer one-of-a-kind offers or highly customised products whose price positioning combines a rational and an irrational component, where rarity, also found in the use of an extremely small number of sales channels, justifies the final price (Hermès and Van Cleef & Arpels are some examples).

This segmentation is crucial to understanding the factors that determine the configuration of the supply chain of a brand as belonging to one sector rather than another. Therefore, the configuration of supply chains depends primarily on the level of luxury (Castelli & Sianesi, 2015; Ozuem et al., 2024).

Segmentation is also critical to understanding which critical success factors are most applicable to a particular segment rather than another. Quality and uniqueness, however, represent the transversal objectives along the entire supply chain, that is, fundamental in all three segments, although they grow in importance as one moves up towards the top of the luxury pyramid, represented in Fig. 27.1. Other critical success factors relate to traceability, which is fundamental both to prevent image damage due to counterfeiting and to guarantee the focal company optimal control over the processes that occur within the chain. Nevertheless, it poses a highly intricate challenge, particularly for the accessible luxury segment, distinguished by swift and abundant flows, along with decentralised channels. Sustainability is another important critical factor: in accessible luxury, the focus is on the huge volume of exchanges and processes involved, while in exclusive luxury, the focus is on the use of scarce and valuable resources, such as diamonds and precious stones embedded within watches, bags and jewellery. Despite the discrepancy between the terms luxury and sustainability, sustainable innovation, understood as the improvement of existing products and processes and the development of new products from an environmental sustainability perspective, is increasingly permeating the luxury world. Bernardi et al. (2021) identify two main drivers that foster sustainable innovation in high fashion: territory and communication. First, in a luxury industry, especially if it is the highest segment of the pyramid, the value of "Made In" is fundamental. In addition, a strong connection to territory can allow luxury fashion companies to be perceived as sustainable and responsible through job creation and the use of local resources

(Fletcher, 2008). However, especially when it comes to brands that are part of accessible luxury, production chains have an international, sometimes even global, character, and therefore, the value of "Made In" is replaced by that of "Made by". In this case, to be perceived as sustainable, brands must be able to provide a lot of timely and correct information regarding all production processes. Thus, the key role of traceability of production and raw materials emerges. The role of communication becomes crucial here, as it should meticulously elucidate the production processes, emphasising the intricacies involved and the provenance of raw materials. Communication should not only encompass the company's declarations regarding its implemented sustainable practices and material traceability but also strive to inspire consumers to embrace more sustainable purchasing habits (Fletcher, 2008). This involves promoting concepts such as the circular economy, reuse, recycling and prioritising quality over quantity in purchases.

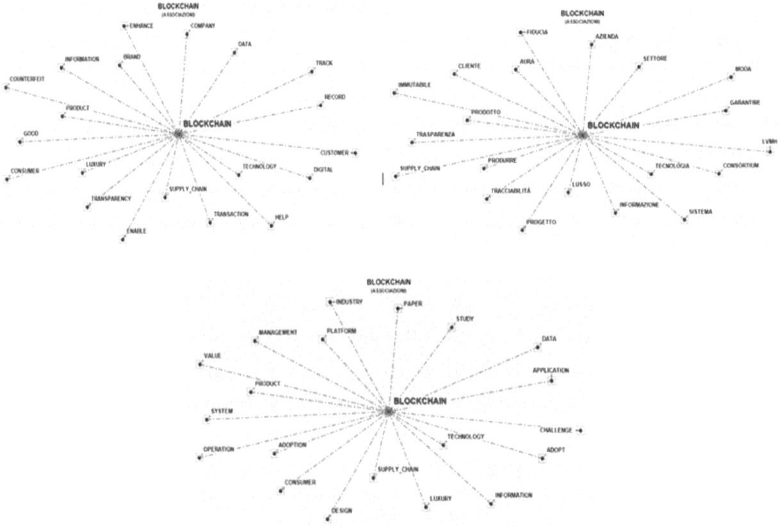

Fig. 27.1 Radial plot of co-occurrence analysis, made on the dataset of popular sources in English, in Italian and academic sources. Focus on "blockchain" (*Source* Our elaboration on T-lab)

In this context, technology emerges as a vital tool for the supply chains of luxury fashion striving to enhance traceability within their supply networks. Certainly, Industry 4.0 has facilitated the integration of innovative practices into production processes, progressively digitising them and yielding significant outcomes. Nishal et al. (2024), citing an analysis by the Boston Consulting Group, contend that digitalising the supply chain has the potential to increase EBITDA and revenue by up to 6 per cent, achieve cost savings of up to 20 per cent and enhance customer service satisfaction by up to 30 per cent. There are several technologies that can be implemented within supply chains; these include the use of big data, the Internet of Things (Iot), which in an industrial context is called Industrial Internet of Things (IIoT), cloud computing and artificial intelligence. In this study, however, the focus was placed on one technology in particular: the blockchain.

The Blockchain Technology and Its Applications

First introduced in 2008 by an anonymous collective known as Satoshi Nakatomo, blockchain was considered in the early years of the last decade, one of the most important revolutions since the advent of the Internet, capable of disrupting today's economic and social landscape. In reality, the expectations associated with it have dwindled over the years, although it has been confirmed as a technology with incredible potential. Nevertheless, the global market for blockchain technologies has been valued at $11.02 billion in 2022, with forecasts claiming that it will reach the extraordinary amount of $265.01 billion by 2028, reflecting a growing demand for solutions and services based on this tool (Research & Markets, 2023).

But what is blockchain actually? Trying to simplify the discussion, one can describe this technology as a decentralised virtual ledger, capable of storing the digital data of a transaction simultaneously on multiple computers or devices, i.e., a secure and decentralised digital ledger created by a network of computers, which continuously and simultaneously store blocks containing information about transactions, in a highly secure and verifiable way. The key principles on which it is based are three: decentralisation, transparency and immutability (Kshetri, 2022). The first refers to the fundamental principle whereby control and management of the blockchain are distributed among multiple participants, rather than being concentrated in a single central authority acting as an arbitrator. Data are not owned by a single unit, but are shared among all participants in the network. This technology, in which nodes communicate directly with each other and there is no central operator, is called peer-to-peer (P2P) (Ghiani, 2022). Transparency means that all activities that are carried out within the chain are stored and well identified. This implies that it is consistently feasible to track down the originator of an action and acquire comprehensive information regarding said action. Finally, immutability means that data, once recorded, become permanent and immutable: after information is added to a block and the block is incorporated into the blockchain, retroactively changing that data becomes extremely difficult and virtually impossible without the consent of the majority of the network. There is therefore a zero chance of tampering. This feature of the chain is attributed to a function called *cryptographic hasher*. This is a very complex system, the operation of which, in summary, is as follows: when data is entered, a kind of unique alphanumeric computer code is generated that identifies that information, this is the block. The various blocks of information are then concatenated together using mathematical functions, called "hash", so that each block contains the hash of the previous block and the linkage between the blocks creates the chain structure. Thus, there is chaining between blocks, which results in the impossibility of changing the information contained within a node (Kshetri, 2022).

Over the years, different types of blockchain have developed, although the main ones are: public, private and consortium based. The three types vary depending on the areas in which they are to be implemented. This is because, although it originated in parallel with bitcoins and the world of cryptocurrencies (i.e., the digital currencies born with the aim of eliminating the role of central financial authorities), there are different areas of application of this technology. Indeed, it has found its place in various sectors including the medical field, public administration, art, music and entertainment, as well as agrifood. Consequently, there is a multitude of applications, ranging from managing health data or digital identity to creating unique intangibles, often conceptualised as art forms (known as Non-Fungible Tokens or NFTs), or even novel forms of entertainment.

It appears evident that due to its secure and reliable nature for storing, tracking and sharing information, one of the areas where it could significantly expand its implementation is within production chains. Indeed, it can play a crucial role in supply chain management, affecting various aspects such as traceability, sustainability and chain transparency. Therefore, the supply chain represents one of the best areas for application of this technology, among several possible alternatives. In fact, the intricacies of contemporary supply chains render sole reliance on vast databases insufficient for its effective management as modern supply chains encompass numerous interdependent variables, including supplier relationships, logistics networks, demand fluctuations and regulatory compliance, among others. Attempting to encapsulate such complexity within massive databases inevitably leads to oversimplification and overlooks nuanced operational dynamics. Moreover, due to their often-global reach, a central authority risks losing control over them (Kshetri, 2022). Blockchain can therefore connect the different participants in a supply chain, making the flow of production and information more transparent.

An article published by McKinsey & Company (2019) points out that value creation due to blockchain mainly concerns three areas. The first pertains to minimising inefficiency, opacity and fraud. The second, applicable to some sectors, is related to the modernisation and digitisation of processes, which should make them more efficient and collaborative. Finally, companies looking to enhance their reputation and showcase their commitment and capability to innovate can implement blockchain technology.

In this respect, its applications throughout the supply chain are abundant. For instance, within procurement, blockchain technology can play a crucial role through the utilisation of "smart contracts"—digital codes that provide a set of assurances under predefined conditions mutually agreed upon by the involved parties. This facilitates the regulation and optimisation of contracts, thereby enhancing transaction transparency. In fact, the smart contract contains all the data of the two parties involved, the conditions of sale, the characteristics of the products involved in the exchange, the timing, leading to a reduction in costs and time associated with the negotiation, and constituting a very effective tool in case of litigation. Another application lies within production processes, where blockchain presents the opportunity to uniquely identify the origins of raw and semi-finished materials. This capability is crucial for ensuring the quality and safety certification of products, particularly in instances where such certifications are mandated, as exemplified by the designation of origin requirements within the agrifood supply chain. This tool could also offer numerous benefits to logistics by enabling the identification of accompanying documents for goods, such as bills of lading or customs forms. This enhanced security would minimise the risk of forgery or loss. Regarding reverse logistics, returns management could also benefit from the implementation of blockchain, as it would provide a range of information related to the product and material returned by the customer.

It is evident, therefore, that blockchain's role extends well beyond mere product tracking, a responsibility assumed by other technologies. Instead, its primary function lies in guaranteeing the accuracy and consequently, the credibility of data furnished by other systems, thereby fostering a crucial element of trust. Undoubtedly, trust has emerged as a paramount concern for companies, as they recognise that today's customers are considerably more discerning and vigilant. Traceability stands out as the foremost factor in bolstering trust within consumer purchasing behaviours. The results of a survey conducted by IBM in 2020 stated that 73 per cent of surveyed consumers identified traceability as one of the key issues in their purchasing behaviours and that 71 per cent of them were willing to pay more for products that were the result of traceable production.

The Harvard Business Review in 2020 stated that blockchain, besides being at the core of Bitcoin and the cryptocurrency network, where it has emerged as a potential game-changer in the financial context, holds enormous potential also in supply chain management where it plays a distinctly different role compared to the crypto world. In the world of digital currencies, blockchain technology enables private and secure transactions among countless anonymous parties without the need for a central intermediary. Conversely, integrating blockchain into supply chains entails empowering a restricted pool of identifiable participants to safeguard their transactions from nefarious entities, all the while enhancing operational efficiency (Gaur, 2020). Blockchain is being touted as a possible solution to several limitations related to the use of traditional ERP (Enterprise Resource Planning) systems, i.e., those software systems used to manage business operations that increase performance in terms of error reduction, faster decision-making and better management of conflicts within the supply chain. The transactions that occur within a supply chain consist of three types of flows: information, inventory and financial. Current ERP systems are unable to simultaneously and effectively oversee all three flows, while blockchain has the ability to do so. Today, a common approach to improving operations within the supply chain is to verify transactions through auditing, a process necessary to ensure compliance with contracts, but of little help in improving decision-making in the event of operational shortcomings (Gaur, 2020; Ozuem et al., 2021). Larger companies then find themselves using multiple ERP systems simultaneously, which makes managing the highlighted flows even more complicated. Thus, if activities such as inventory or order management are supported by blockchain technology, all assets are assigned unique identifiers, which act as digital tokens (similar to bitcoins), while blockchain participants are assigned unique identifiers, or digital signatures, which they use to sign the blocks they add to the blockchain. Each step in the transaction is noted on the blockchain as the movement of the appropriate token from one participant to another. The blockchain is thus valuable because it represents a chronological sequence of blocks that integrates all three types of flows within the transaction. Each block is encrypted and distributed to all participants, who therefore maintain their own copies of the blockchain, making the system secure and immutable. The blockchain provides a comprehensive, reliable and tamper-immune audit trail of the three types of flows typical of the chain. It, therefore, has the potential to greatly reduce, if not eliminate, problems of execution, traceability and coordination. Given that participants possess their own unique copies of the blockchain, each party is empowered to verify transaction status, identify errors and ensure accountability among counterparts. No participant in the blockchain can change data that has already been recorded, as this would require changing all subsequent blocks on all shared copies of the blockchain. However, it should be emphasised that the blockchain is not intended to replace the ERP systems currently in use, but to offer a supplementary solution, aimed at improving their security and efficiency.

Interconnectedness Between Blockchain, Luxury and Sustainability

In order to investigate how blockchain is nowadays implemented within high fashion production chains, a content analysis was conducted on secondary data from both popular and academic sources. Specifically, three datasets were employed: one comprised popular sources in the Italian language, another consisted of popular sources in English, and the last encompassed academic sources in English. Subsequently, articles from those sources underwent meticulous examination and processing with T-lab Software to conduct a co-occurrence analysis, focusing on the interconnectedness of the topics of blockchain, supply chain, luxury and sustainability. Co-occurrence analysis consists of a widely used research methodology in the field of text analysis, aimed at identifying semantic relationships between terms based on the extent to which they appear simultaneously within texts. This methodology aims to identify the terms most commonly associated with the concept of "blockchain" and to visualise the differences between the scientific literature, which focuses more on theoretical aspects, and the popular literature, which can offer a more practical perspective.

In conducting the co-occurrence analysis, the initial crucial step involved constructing radial diagrams corresponding to each type of utilised source, as illustrated in Fig. 28.1. The diagrams allow the relationships between terms with the highest correlations to be visualised graphically. The following section describes the main findings that emerged from the research.

This study holds significant value as it provides a first attempt to carry out a comprehensive exploration of blockchain implementation in the luxury industry from various perspectives. Secondary data of a popular nature provided a practical point of view related to current trends and major events, while papers of a scientific nature contributed to a better understanding of the theoretical foundations underlying this phenomenon.

One notable discovery is the frequent association of the term "technology" with "blockchain". This outcome is hardly unexpected, primarily due to the inherent nature of blockchain, which is categorised as a technology in popular discourses. Further arguments emphasising this tight correlation include its positioning within the context of innovations introduced by Industry 4.0. This framing is crucial for better elucidating both the nature of this innovation, which the general public often superficially grasps without fully understanding the mechanisms governing its operation and its scope of application, and to underline that it is usually accompanied by other innovations. Moreover, the association with the term "technology" indicates that implementing blockchain requires the synergistic use of other technologies, foremost among them being IoT.

Luxury fashion has proven to be one of the most interested in this technology, seizing its possible opportunities and investing heavily in this direction. This aspect emerged particularly from the analysis of the dataset based on Italian sources. Very important in this regard is the establishment by LVMH, in collaboration with Prada Group, Cartier, and OTP Group, of the Aura Blockchain Consortium. This is a project that promotes the use of a single global blockchain solution, open to all luxury brands worldwide, to provide consumers with greater transparency and traceability. The Aura consortium was created with the goal of establishing a technology standard in the luxury sector. It currently has more than 23 million products registered on its blockchain and 40 member brands, with the potential to accommodate additional brands and groups, thus following the ever-growing nature of blockchain technology. Among the various benefits offered by Aura is the ability to create unique digital identities for products to ensure their authenticity (Ranfagni, 2018; Ranfagni et al., 2015), enable traceability of the entire supply chain up to the end consumer (who can also resell the product by transferring ownership), and create NFTs. One of the main services offered by the consortium is Aura SaaS, accessible through APIs (Application Programming Interfaces, i.e., solutions that allow two softwares to communicate with each other using a set of specific definitions and protocols), which enables smart contract generation, product ownership management, product registration on the blockchain and product-related content management. In addition, the blockchain can host so-called Digital Product Passports (DPPs), which record the lifecycle of a product and verify its authenticity. The distinctive features of blockchain technology make it an excellent platform for storing these DPPs, which are essential for countering the counterfeit market and monitoring environmental and sustainability performance (Buttol, 2024).

Blockchain finds a seamless integration within luxury supply chains, where this technology is recognised as a key tool for luxury companies to demonstrate unprecedented transparency and innovation, meeting ever-increasing consumer expectations (The Fashion Law, 2023). One of the most important findings that emerged from English-language popular sources is related to the effects that blockchain produces within the luxury world. This evidence aligns with the findings of Arianee.com (2024), which outline four primary impacts that blockchain is poised to generate within the luxury supply chain in the forthcoming years:

1- Counterfeiting will be an outdated problem. The author promises that in the last few years, blockchain-supported productions will be able to eliminate counterfeit products.
2- A fully transparent supply chain will soon become a reality. With consumers showing growing interest in the origins of their clothing purchases, fashion brands are compelled to maximise the accessibility of information. Customers are increasingly willing to pay a premium for products sourced from transparent supply chains. This new level of transparency will also indirectly impose ethical and environmentally sustainable practices within the luxury industry.
3- There will be a greater connection between brands and consumers: blockchain offers luxury brands a new channel of direct communication with the owners of their products, enabling them to transparently convey the stories and value of their items. Brands then have the ability to identify customers and the products they own, improving relationship management and demonstrating a concrete commitment to transparency.

4- In the long run, products will gain even more value. In fact, by decreasing the presence of counterfeit products on the market, at the same time the value of authentic products increases, which become rarer and are certified for their quality. Finally, blockchain will enable companies to reduce the costs associated with anti-counterfeiting systems, allowing them to direct more resources to product development and innovation.

By embracing this and other 4.0 technologies, luxury brands can enhance their reputation for quality, authenticity and excellence while meeting the growing expectations of modern consumers. As technology advances, the role of blockchain and artificial intelligence in the luxury industry will become increasingly prominent, leading to continued business impact and growth (Ambolis, 2024).

However, while this technology offers significant opportunities for enhanced transparency, traceability and process efficiency through reliable, secure and accurate data, as well as fostering a more innovative brand image, its widespread adoption within production contexts has been hindered by substantial limitations over the years. This aspect emerged in all three datasets. In particular, in the one based on academic sources the terms "obstacles" and "challenges" were among the 20 most correlated.

The first stumbling block concerns the lack of specific technical knowledge on the topic. For example, in 2018, of the 20 million software developers in business, only 0.1 per cent were competent on blockchain-related codes and languages. Only 6000 developers were considered to possess the necessary skills to develop quality blockchain-based solutions (Mishchenko, 2019). These numbers are certainly not able to meet a demand that, as pointed out by the Global Blockchain Employment of 2021, tends to increase by 300–500 per cent each year (The Blockchain Academy, 2021).

Another obstacle is in relation to costs. In organisations that opt to integrate technology into their production processes, there is a need for employee training. This incurs additional costs for companies, which are subsequently compounded by expenses in essential infrastructure like software, IoT-equipped machinery, sensors, etc. These necessary investments create a barrier to the widespread adoption of such solutions especially for companies operating in rural or disadvantaged regions. This poses an additional level of complexity for supply chains, such as those in jewellery or electronics, which heavily depend on precious metals sourced primarily from poor countries. These nations often lack industrialisation and endure decades of economic stagnation, as well as insufficient regulatory oversight. Furthermore, for small companies contemplating investments in technologies whose full utility and potential may not be comprehensively grasped, embracing blockchain represents a formidable decision owing to the inherent complexity of these tools. Additionally, integrating advanced technology within companies characterised by an older workforce lacking specialised technological skills could potentially impede efficiency rather than bolstering it. Such scenarios may result in process slowdowns, confusion and ultimately, an exacerbation of overall complexity.

Another impediment hindering the advancement of blockchain within organisations pertains to interoperability—a concept denoting the capacity of two or more blockchains to communicate and interact seamlessly, facilitating the exchange of data and transactions without necessitating external intervention or intricate conversions. This is a fundamental concept, the lack of which has led to a fragmented blockchain landscape, with many networks operating in isolation. Therefore, connecting them can help reduce fragmentation and form a more unified ecosystem that provides greater scalability, efficiency and pursuit of innovation. One possible solution that has recently emerged is due to the use of cross-chain networks, which allow communication and exchange of data and value between different blockchains in a transparent and secure way, without the need for an intermediary (Crypto.com).

Additional hurdles this innovation continues to confront include fragmented and ambiguous regulatory frameworks, substantial energy costs required for operation, privacy concerns and a lack of awareness, particularly among individuals less immersed in today's rapidly evolving technological landscape. Finally, one of the most serious limitations of blockchain is its scalability: for example, Ethereum can process up to 20 transactions per second (Mearian, 2020), a number extremely lower than Visa's average of about 1700 TPS (transactions per second). Within very large and congested networks, this can also be a very serious problem. Consider the application in the medical field: responses in very long-time frames would not be contemplated.

Lastly, an inherent challenge persists with this technology. While it significantly enhances transparency in transactions and related operations, blockchain fails to resolve the "first mile problem". This highlights that blockchain alone cannot guarantee the accuracy and complete alignment with the reality of the information it receives. To gain a deeper comprehension of this issue, let us consider a case in point: a supply chain associated with the extraction of precious minerals. This encompasses intricate processes, like excavation, filtration and gem cleaning, which pose challenges for seamless integration with other technologies. Thus, relying solely on blockchain may not mitigate the risk of errors or fraudulent activities during these pre-chain stages. The initial data could potentially be tampered with even before its entry onto the blockchain, a critical step presumed to ensure complete security and reliability (Kshetri, 2022). Fortunately, leveraging blockchain in conjunction with the aforementioned technologies mitigates these risks, emphasising the crucial integration between blockchain and the other innovations emerging from the fourth industrial revolution.

Finally, we would like to delve into the relationship between blockchain and sustainability. Sustainability seems to be among the objectives facilitated by blockchain, albeit not a primary focus. In fact, in the research conducted, sustainability did not prominently feature in the radial diagrams, indicating a relatively low correlation with the term "blockchain". However, within a sustainable supply chain framework, blockchain can fulfil various roles. Primarily, it enables the tracking of sustainability metrics, such as carbon emissions, in a quantifiable and immutable manner. Its potential contribution lies in enhancing transparency and traceability in supply chain operations. Nonetheless, further advancements by companies in this area, coupled with insights from literature, are imperative to fully leverage blockchain's capabilities in fostering sustainability.

The research findings underscore that blockchain technology within the luxury industry possesses the potential to instigate significant transformations, impacting both production methodologies and communication strategies adopted by luxury *maisons*. While traditionally associated with enhancing transparency and traceability, the applications of blockchain extend beyond these realms to encompass digital creations and the emerging metaverse landscape. These concepts, albeit nascent, remain uncertain in their trajectory, leaving their eventual widespread adoption or relegation to mere reminiscence uncertain. Sustainability emerges, albeit not directly. It seems that traceability and transparency bring about greater accountability within supply chains concerning green and sustainable issues. However, the primary objectives for maintaining a secure and verifiable trace are primarily linked to authenticity, combating counterfeiting—identified as a much more central issue, and production quality, rather than sustainability.

Conclusions

In conclusion of this chapter, we aim to highlight the prospects of blockchain in supply chain and sustainable fashion supply chains. Much like the cryptocurrency industry, which is currently going through a period of uncertainty and has not yet fully expressed its potential, the use of blockchain in the luxury fashion industry is also at only an early stage, the future developments of which will be determined by several factors, including, the resolution of the hurdles that have not yet been overcome to date. Only by overcoming these hurdles can the application of blockchain in the fashion supply chain become a key element in effectively combating the black market of counterfeiting, and for companies intent on achieving the goals set by the European Union's 2030 agenda. The prospects of blockchain in the sustainable fashion supply chain remain promising and suggestive. Its ability to provide complete traceability and authenticity to products, coupled with the possibility of optimising logistical processes and improving overall supply chain efficiency, as well as the opportunity to provide new shopping experiences for consumers, has the potential to bring profound changes to the entire industry. This transformation will have to be made by overcoming current stumbling blocks, which may one day diminish or disappear, given the ever-changing pace of technological progress. In order to overcome these hurdles, it is necessary not only for blockchain to be implemented while also integrating the other technologies, which are projected to become more and more powerful in the future, but it is also crucial that there be a collaborative attitude among the various brands in order to shape a more transparent, authentic and sustainable future for the fashion industry. In conclusion, blockchain is emerging as a very important technology for the luxury fashion industry, although it is still in an embryonic stage, with quite a few problems to be addressed. Contrary to what was initially believed; however, sustainability is not, at least for the moment, the central reason for this implementation.

References

Ambolis, D. (2024, February 16). Top 10 ways luxury brands are leveraging blockchain and AI for business impact. *Blockchain Magazine*. Retrieved from https://blockchainmagazine.net/luxury-brands-are-leveraging-blockchain/

Bernardi, A., Cantù, C. L., & Cedrola, E. (2021). *Fattori chiave di successo per l'innovazione sostenibile nel settore tessile e moda. Best practices di due luxury brand del Made in Italy* (Issue 2, pp. 1349–1376). L'industria, Società editrice il Mulino.

Buttol, D. V. (2024, March 6). *Lusso e Innovazione: il ruolo chiave della Blockchain*. Affidaty Blog. Retrieved from https://affidaty.io/blog/it/2024/03/lusso-mercato-nft-tecnologia-blockchain/

Castelli, C., & Sianesi, A. (2015). Supply chain strategy for companies in the luxury-fashion market: Aligning the supply chain towards the critical success factors. *International Journal of Retail and Distribution Management, 43*(10/11), 940–966.

Fletcher, K. (2008). *Sustainable fashion & textiles: Design journeys*. Earthscan.

Gaur, V. (2020, April 14). Building a transparent supply chain. *Harvard Business Review*. Retrieved from https://hbr.org/2020/05/building-a-transparent-supply-chain

Ghiani, A. (2022). *Blockchain: linee guida. Dai casi pratici alla regolamentazione*. Giappichelli.

Guercini, S., & Ranfagni, S. (2013). Sustainability and luxury: The Italian case of a supply chain based on native wools. *The Journal of Corporate Citizenship, 52*, 76–89.

Hashmi, G. (2017). Redefining the essence of sustainable luxury management: The slow value creation model. In M. A. Gardetti (Ed.), *Sustainable management of luxury* (pp. 3–27). Springer.

Higginson, M., Nadeau, M., & Rajgopal, K. (2019, January 4). *Blockchain's Occam problem*. McKinsey & Company. Retrieved from https://www.mckinsey.com/industries/financial-services/our-insights/blockchains-occam-problem?cid=other-eml-alt-mip-mck&hlkid=flff/216a70%E2%82%AC4041951d60293978a0ea&hctky=2762145&hdpid=95e9bdfa-0709-4b4d-8252-f401bcaac86d

Impacts Blockchain will have on Luxury. (2024, March 15). Arianee.com. Retrieved from https://www.arianee.com/post/4-impacts-blockchain-will-have-on-luxury

Kshetri, N. (2022). *The rise of blockchains, disruptive economies and transforming societies*. Elgar.

Lambert, D. M., Cooper, M. C., & Pagh, J. D. (1998). Supply chain management: Implementation issues and research opportunities. *The International Journal of Logistics Management, 9*(2), 1–20.

Mearian, L. (2020, February 3). MIT's blockchain-based "Spider" offers 4X faster cryptocurrency processing. *Computerworld*. Retrieved from https://www.computerworld.com/article/1677757/mits-blockchain-based-spider-offers-4x-faster-cryptocurrency-processing.html

Mishchenko, A. (2019, April 26). How much does it cost to hire a blockchain developer in 2018? Salary overview and hiring trends. *Medium*. Retrieved from https://medium.com/hackernoon/how-much-does-it-cost-to-hire-a-blockchain-developer-in-2018-salary-overview-and-hiring-trends-908488615142

Nishal, M., Prasad, K. R., & Kumanan, R. (2023). Digital supply chain paradigm. *Environmental footprints and eco-design of products and processes*, 1–23.

Ozuem, W., Ranfagni, S., Willis, M., Rovai, S., & Howell, K. (2021). Exploring customers' responses to online service failure and recovery strategies during Covid-19 pandemic: An actor–network theory perspective. *Psychology & Marketing, 38*(9), 1440–1459.

Ozuem, W., Ranfagni, S., Willis, M., Salvietti, G., & Howell, K. (2024). Exploring the relationship between chatbots, service failure recovery and customer loyalty: A frustration–aggression perspective. *Psychology and Marketing*. https://doi.org/10.1002/mar.22051

Ozuem, W., Willis, M., Ranfagni, S., Howell, K. E., & Rovai, S. (2023). Examining the role of social media influencers in service failure and recovery strategies: An empirical investigation of millennials' views. *Information Technology & People*. https://doi.org/10.1108/itp-05-2022-0371

Ranfagni, S. (2018). Autenticità e Imprenditorialità. Il tempo come risorsa. Franco Angeli.

Ranfagni, S. (2022). Cultural-based authenticity and luxury as a bridge to cultural sustainability, social well-being, and innovation: The case of Giuditta Brozzetti's textile workshop. In *The rise of positive luxury* (pp. 61–78). Routledge.

Ranfagni, S., & Salvietti, G. (2023). How to combine sustainability and authenticity in luxury brands: An insight into the case of La Milanesa. In *Made in Italy and the Luxury Market* (pp. 225–239). Routledge.

Ranfagni, S., Burresi, A., & Rosati, M. (2015). Generating brand authenticity: Cases of Tuscan wine companies. *Global Fashion Management Conference., 6*(2015), 222–227.

Ranfagni, S., & Ozuem, W. (2022). Luxury and sustainability: Technological pathways and potential opportunities. *Sustainability, 14*(9), 5209.

Ranfagni, S., Runfola, A., & Sarti, D. (2018). International expansion based on a locally authentic brand: Issues and findings from Italian case studies. *Journal of Marketing Development and Competitiveness, 12*(1), 124–136.

Research and Markets. (2023). *Global Blockchain Market: Analysis by component, by type, by enterprise size, by application, by industry vertical, by region size and trends With impact of COVID-19 and forecast up to 2028*. Retrieved from https://www.researchandmarkets.com/r/aicvv4.

Srivastava, S. (2007). Green supply-chain management: A state-of-the-art literature review. *International Journal of Management Reviews, 9*(1), 53–80.

28

Certification Standards and Ecolabelling for Sustainability and Traceability in the Textile Supply Chain

Leonardo Borsacchi

Introduction

In recent years, there has been an increasing interest in understanding how certified management systems (MS) can contribute to sustainable supply chain management in the manufacturing industry. Global demand for sustainability compels organisations to be accountable for their environmental and social impacts. Textile enterprises should consider implementing certified MSs to improve the efficiency and effectiveness of their value chains, as this fosters a comprehensive process management strategy. Currently, sustainability-driven innovations in textiles focus on durability, recyclability, and waste utilisation (Dominidiato et al., 2023). Therefore, process innovations must incorporate circular economy principles, enhance traceability, and reduce water and chemical usage, applying technical improvements and supplier-customer

L. Borsacchi (✉)
ARCO, PIN Foundation—Prato Campus of University of Florence, Piazza Dell'Università, Prato, Italy
e-mail: leonardo.borsacchi@pin.unifi.it

W. Ozuem et al. (eds.), *Sustainable Digital Marketing for Fashion and Luxury Brands*,
https://doi.org/10.1007/978-3-031-82467-8_28

relationships (Borsacchi & Pinelli, 2020). Environmental issues are now prioritised on enterprises' agenda. The challenge for these organisations lies in producing authentic products that harness market potential by blending modern styles with local influences, particularly in relation to their territories, as local textile makers aim to captivate consumers with collections that evoke the natural world (Ranfagni & Guercini, 2014). Traditional production processes require innovation capable of optimising various phases in terms of necessary inputs and outputs. Moreover, in a globalised market, organisations' policies must comply with international regulations and standardised procedures. Hence, organisations engaged in eco-friendly practices are urged to create a narrative around their products or services to explain how they relate to sustainability and circularity (Borsacchi et al., 2020). Effective business communication should operate on multiple levels to reach a wide audience, particularly stakeholders. Product quality is traditionally associated with intangible values, such as beauty, excellence, durability, and performance. Today, it also encompasses attributes that increasingly attract consumers' attention, who demand that organisations commit to safety, energy consumption reduction, and minimising environmental impacts (Testi et al., 2023). Furthermore, supply chains have become increasingly complex, stretching globally across countries and involving numerous actors. This complexity makes it more challenging to monitor supply chains effectively and exacerbates issues related to product quality or counterfeiting (Marucheck et al., 2011; Pettit et al., 2013; Zhang et al., 2020). Consequently, traceability has recently become an increasingly relevant issue, calling for greater scrutiny and transparency (Garcia-Torres et al., 2022). For several years, major international political and economic institutions, responding to growing social pressure to improve environmental quality, have initiated campaigns to promote positive environmental behaviours, fostering sustainable development, economic growth, and well-being compatible with environmental respect and a more careful resource policy. Here, the textile sector plays a significant role in environmental degradation and climate change, creating substantial impacts on the socio-economic and environmental aspects of sustainability (Raut et al., 2019), particularly given the technical waste generated at various stages along the supply chain (Yasin & Sun,

2019). The pressure has been growing, especially from regulations and customers, due to the need for ecological production that reduces environmental impacts (Gomes et al., 2024). Thus, companies are pushed to make informed decisions aimed at minimising these impacts. It is crucial to possess data encompassing inputs such as water, energy, chemicals, and raw materials, as well as outputs such as emissions to air, land, and water occurring throughout the production process and along the supply chain (Edirisinghe et al., 2024). The intensity and type of environmental impact of a single textile product vary based on the type of fibre used and the properties desired, as this determines the production steps the raw material undergoes. Therefore, some yarns have a greater impact on certain aspects, while others affect different aspects more significantly. According to an Ellen MacArthur Foundation's (2017) report, textile production uses nearly 100 billion cubic metres of water annually, representing 4% of global freshwater withdrawal. Institutions and governments endorse environmental labels and sustainability standards to encourage the "eco-friendliness" of textiles. To be considered environmentally responsible, a product must maintain eco-friendliness throughout its entire life cycle, including manufacturing, usage, maintenance, and disposal (Plakantonaki, 2023). Thus, product design must integrate ecological, social, and economic considerations, and independent organisations certify products that are safe for human health and the environment. Despite these efforts, there is a significant lack of consumer awareness about eco-friendly products and their life cycles (Lin & Ma, 2023). Among the methods organisations can consider for external communication to main stakeholders and consumers are globally recognised tools such as certifications, labels, and traceability. External verification is vital due to consumers' low trust in large firms. Given that consumer activities also contribute to CO_2 emissions, educating and motivating the public to adopt sustainable behaviours is crucial for the success of ecolabels (Plakantonaki et al., 2023).

Standardised Management Systems

Fashion companies require independent third-party verification for their claims to gain consumer trust, making brands struggle due to differing global regulations, evolving production methods, and the introduction of new materials. Hence, international standards and third-party certifications assist in regularly updating requirements and tracking legal and industry developments (Zaczkiewicz, 2020). An illustrative example is the International Organization for Standardization's (ISO) standard that is an internationally recognised guideline established through global consensus to facilitate trade and cooperation. Some of its key standards include ISO 9001 for quality MS and ISO 14001 for environmental MS, both last revised in 2015 to create simplified requirements applicable to organisations of all sizes and types. Such a standard allows for flexible implementation of MSs tailored to demonstrate effective process control and continuous improvement. ISO 9001 primarily enhances internal processes and supply chain cooperation, with some influence on environmental practices. Conversely, ISO 14001 significantly advances environmental processes within organisations (Zimon et al., 2020). Integrating the above-mentioned standards yields both advantages and challenges in terms of fulfilling their objectives. For instance, in the textile sector, organisations often adopt certifications at clients' requests rather than strategically. Looking at the number of certified organisations in Italy specifically, the adoption of ISO certifications by textile enterprises remains limited compared to other industries. In Italy, there were 40,030 registered textile enterprises in 2023, including 11,495 in ATECO code 13 (textile products) and 28,535 in code 14 (clothing items). According to Accredia data, in 2023, there were 1,305 textile enterprises certified with ISO 9001 (representing 0.95% of all ISO 9001-certified companies in Italy), 572 certified with ISO 14001 (1.4%), and only 66 certified with ISO 45001 (1.02%). The deployment of an integrated system (based on multiple standards) can enhance positive outcomes (Hernandez-Vivanco et al., 2019). This integration primarily aims to streamline and optimise processes within the organisation and ensure the collaboration of individual MS while considering external processes implemented by suppliers and subcontractors (Foster,

2008). To effectively establish a quality MS within the supply chain, it is essential to identify the activities and processes executed through its components (e.g. suppliers, subcontractors, or distributors) (Zimon et al., 2020). To optimise product flow and customer service in the supply chain, management processes should be identified, assessed, and corrected as needed. Integrating these processes into the MS ensures proper execution and helps balance conflicting goals. Combining the ISO 9001 standard, which focuses on internal processes, with ISO 14001, which emphasises environmental solutions, can support sustainable supply chain management (Zimon et al., 2020). The more features these standards share, the better they facilitate the integration of environmental concerns into the organisation's daily activities (Borsacchi et al., 2020). Regardless of the sector, it is advisable to first implement an ISO 9001-based system, which can then be expanded with additional certifications (Borsacchi, 2012). Process mapping, required as an initial step by ISO 9001, can be conducted jointly and integrated with the initial environmental analysis required by ISO 14001. Both systematic analyses examine site location, production processes, regulatory frameworks, production-environment relationships, and managerial aspects, identifying compliance and improvement priorities. The initial environmental analysis assesses how production activities interact with the environment, ensuring regulatory compliance and organising data for environmental policies and work programmes. Environmental aspects are classified as direct (e.g. emissions and waste) and indirect (e.g. product impact on consumers), with evaluations considering normal, abnormal, and emergency conditions to determine impact significance. Organisations can also demonstrate commitment to social responsibility and sustainability by adhering to standards like SA 8000 or following ISO 26000 guidelines (Borsacchi et al., 2020). Figure 28.1 explains the approach that a textile sector organisation must follow to implement an MS according to a certifiable standard.

The organisation's activities are governed by a framework defined by pertinent legislation and market demands. Within this framework, the organisation must develop its MS in accordance with the standard's requirements. This involves defining roles and responsibilities through effective and appropriate leadership, as outlined in section 5

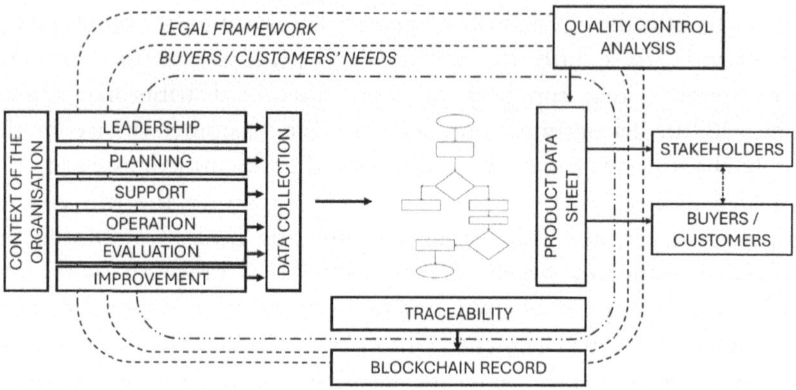

Fig. 28.1 MS and certification framework

of ISO 9001. This leadership is responsible for planning organisational activities (section 6 of ISO 9001) and identifying the required resources, including human resources, equipment, and infrastructure (section 7). Resource definition at the organisational level should encompass more than just production quality and efficiency. In the context of integrated systems and multiple certification schemes, attention to workers' employment and contractual conditions, including corporate welfare elements, constitutes significant strategies and policies for companies, especially from a communication standpoint. Notably, parts of the textile supply chain continuously struggle with labour exploitation and inadequate safety conditions (Biggeri et al., 2022). Additionally, in resource allocation, prioritising environmental protection and reducing impacts can drive organisations to adopt specific production processes or technologies with lower environmental footprints. The organisation's operational activities, as defined in reference to section 8 of ISO 9001, are aligned with planning and available resources and can be illustrated through one or more flowcharts. Collecting process data is crucial for evaluating and improving system performance, following a continuous improvement approach or the PDCA cycle, and for providing qualitative and quantitative production data. Certified organisations recognise the value of ongoing improvements by employing methodologies such as PDCA or Lean Six Sigma (LSS). The effectiveness of LSS implementation significantly depends on the product type, with items related to safety necessitating a focus on defect minimisation (Nedra, 2022). A key element of MS is a structured documentation system that enables process control and provides production information. This information, combined with product quality control analyses, can be utilised to create technical production sheets that satisfy customer requirements and, more broadly, stakeholder expectations. Furthermore, all system information can contribute to a traceability system throughout the production stages. A certifiable MS must include documented information as required by the relevant standard, along with any additional documentation the organisation deems necessary to ensure the system's effectiveness. The scope and format of MS documentation can vary between organisations based on factors such as size, nature of activities, process complexity and interactions, and personnel competence. This documentation can be maintained in any format or medium. ISO standards mandate organisations to maintain documented information to support process operation and retain documented information to ensure processes are conducted as planned. Indeed, document requirements are structured into a three-tier pyramid: the top tier includes high-level documents establishing an MS, the second tier consists of specific documents conveying necessary operational information, and the third tier comprises records that provide evidence of achieved results (Pinelli &Borsacchi, 2016). Organisations that adopt ISO standards demonstrate a proactive approach to improving operational efficiency and product quality. This adherence not only ensures compliance with legal standards but also fosters a culture of continuous improvement. By addressing additional criteria, companies can achieve significant advancements in environmental stewardship, such as reducing emissions, minimising waste, and optimising resource use. Furthermore, voluntary certification schemes encourage companies to enhance their social responsibility. This includes creating safer and healthier working conditions, promoting fair labour practices, and engaging in community development initiatives. By prioritising the welfare of their employees and the surrounding community, organisations can establish stronger, more resilient relationships with their stakeholders. Moreover, companies that participate in these schemes often play a pivotal role in local and regional development. Their commitment to sustainability can drive economic growth, create job opportunities, and promote sustainable practices within the community. This holistic approach not only benefits the company but also contributes to the overall well-being and prosperity of the region in which it operates. In this regard, the concept of corporate citizenship combines socially responsible practices, thus contributing to a higher quality of life for the communities that surround them while still maintaining high profitability for stakeholders (Borsacchi et al., 2018). Indeed, there are several key areas where textile organisations can demonstrate responsible and ethical practices, contributing positively to both their workforce and the wider community. In terms of employees' welfare, organisations could be encouraged to proactively develop the well-being of their workers and their families. This can be achieved by offering services and benefits that go beyond what is legally required, through the development of specific policies and negotiated welfare practices. Such actions not only enhance the quality of life for employees but also foster a more motivated and loyal workforce. Actions of "corporate citizenship" involve organisations engaging in activities that promote social cohesion (Borsacchi et al., 2016). This can include organising social, cultural, or sports events that bring the community together. By doing so, organisations help to build stronger, more cohesive communities, demonstrating their commitment to social responsibility. The adoption of these practices could significantly promote ethical production (Borsacchi et al., 2018). In the realm of certifiable standards, SA 8000 and ISO 45001 stand out as essential frameworks designed to ensure ethical and safe working conditions. These standards, grounded in principles of human rights and occupational safety, offer a comprehensive approach to managing workplace dynamics and promoting worker welfare. Both apply to organisations in all sectors, but in textiles, they can enhance engagement towards ethics and worker protection (Borsacchi et al., 2013). Indeed, SA 8000 is an internationally recognised standard for social accountability, deeply rooted in the principles of international human rights and labour standards, including the Universal Declaration of Human Rights and International Labour Organisation (ILO) conventions. The core aim of SA 8000 is to ensure ethical working conditions and respect for workers' rights across all industries. Key aspects of SA 8000 include (i) prevention of child and forced labour; (ii) non-discrimination; (iii) health and safety; and (iv) freedom of association and fair remuneration. SA 8000 certification, like ISO standards, requires rigorous third-party verification, giving organisations global recognition for social accountability and ethical labour practices. ISO 45001, replacing OHSAS 18001, sets a worldwide standard for occupational health and safety management to reduce workplace risks and create safer working conditions, thus protecting employees from work-related injuries and illnesses. By achieving ISO 45001 certification, organisations demonstrate their commitment to a safe working environment and compliance with OHS laws, which can improve their reputation and efficiency. In the textile sector, adopting these standards ensures worker protection and promotes a sustainable, socially responsible business model. Moreover, adherence to ISO voluntary certification schemes fosters continuous improvement in processes, environmental performance, and social responsibility. By integrating various MSs, textile organisations can effectively demonstrate their commitment to sustainability and ethical practices, ultimately benefiting their stakeholders and contributing to broader societal goals (Biggeri et al., 2022).

Ecolabels and Life Cycle Assessment

Environmental labels, or "ecolabels," are certifications awarded to products or services that meet specific environmental performance criteria. These labels are intended to help consumers identify and choose products that have a reduced environmental impact throughout their life cycle (Ranasinghe & Jayasooriya, 2021). Ecolabels, also adopted in textile production, can cover a wide range of criteria, including resource use, energy efficiency, emissions, waste management, and the use of hazardous substances. Ecolabels are categorised into three types: Type I, Type II, and Type III (Global Ecolabelling Network, 2004). Type I ecolabels are established according to ISO 14024 and include examples such as the Nordic Swan and Blue Angel, as well as the EU Ecolabel (which covers several product groups, including textiles, and aims to establish a unified standard of environmental excellence across Europe). According to UNOPS (2009), Type I ecolabels are independent and reliable, focusing on stringent environmental quality criteria and assessing all environmental impacts throughout a product's life cycle, including energy and water consumption, waste disposal, and emissions. In contrast, Type II ecolabels, adhering to ISO 14021, are self-declared and not verified by an independent authority (Global Ecolabelling Network, 2004). Type III ecolabels comply with ISO 14025 and involve third-party audits, thus requiring environmental parameters to be evaluated by an independent third party. Ecolabels can also be classified as voluntary or mandatory. Government-issued ecolabels include Blue Angel (Germany) and White Swan (Nordic European Countries). In contrast, private organisations issue labels such as Oeko-Tex from Germany and Green Seal from the United States (Sinha & Shah, 2010). Some ecolabels are country-specific, like Eco Mark in Japan and Green Label in Thailand, while others are globally recognised, such as Bluesign and Oeko-Tex Standard 100 (Plakantonaki et al., 2023). Among the prominent ecolabels, Blue Angel (i.e. "Blauer Engel") covers various products and focuses on ensuring high standards of environmental protection and consumer health, reflecting its 40-year reputation as a mark of environmentally friendly products and services. The Bluesign, developed by textile industry stakeholders, sets environmental standards and consumer safety criteria throughout the textile manufacturing process across the supply chain. Label Global Organic Textile Standard (GOTS) is the leading global standard for organic fibres, covering ecological and social criteria. GOTS aims to unify existing standards and set internationally recognised criteria for organic textile production, ensuring that textiles are produced sustainably along the chain. The Nordic Swan, established in 1989, is the official ecolabel of Nordic countries. It aims to reduce environmental impacts from production and consumption by setting strict sustainability criteria for harmful substances. These ecolabels help consumers make informed choices about the sustainability of textile products and encourage manufacturers to adopt more responsible practices. Adherence to voluntary certification schemes in accordance with ISO standards obligates organisations to ensure continuous improvement in their management processes and the products they manufacture. This commitment is undertaken while complying with relevant regulatory requirements and meeting stakeholders' expectations (i.e. customer satisfaction). By adhering to these schemes, enterprises voluntarily commit to additional requirements beyond those mandated by law, which can lead to enhanced environmental performance, increased social responsibility towards their employees, and contributions to regional growth and development. Umbrella labels might also be used. Their concept is to create a single label that signifies compliance with various ecolabels, each featuring different focus areas. By integrating multiple ecolabels, the umbrella label provides a holistic certification that covers the essential criteria of each label. Thus, strengthening well-performing ecolabels like the Blue Angel through information campaigns could increase consumer awareness and pressure companies to adopt labelling practices (Diekel et al., 2021). Fashion brands have progressively incorporated more stringent environmental criteria into their purchasing specifications, often exceeding the mandatory legal requirements. These specifications also involve additional social responsibility criteria.

Traceability and Digital Solutions

According to new European legislation on sustainable textiles (i.e. "EU strategy for sustainable and circular textiles"), one of the new requirements for textile organisations is adopting a European digital product passport (DPP) aimed at improving traceability, circularity, and transparency within the textile industry. Indeed, to enhance the EU textile industry's traceability, sustainability, and business strategies, it is essential to identify where added value can be generated. Companies can utilise traceability to ensure the quality of their products, adhere to regulations, authenticate product origins and identity to combat fraud and counterfeiting (Dabbene et al., 2014), efficiently manage recalls of defective items with minimal economic and logistical impact (Dai et al., 2015), and build trust with supply chain partners by sharing traceability information (Ramon-Jeronimo et al., 2017). Considering the recognition of blockchain as a promising technology in the context of increasingly global and complex supply chains, integrating DPP with blockchain for traceability should be considered. Blockchains, with their transparency, immutability, decentralisation, and disintermediation, increase trust among supply chain stakeholders by protecting against corruption and opportunistic behaviours. Immutable traceability data can be easily retrieved, aiding in fraud detection, especially when combined with machine learning. Additionally, the decentralised nature of blockchains secures data against cyber threats, enabling reliable peer-to-peer data sharing without third-party intervention (Testi et al., 2023). Currently, legislative and technological barriers may impede the transition from a linear to a circular economy in the textile industry. Waste management legislation requires precise identification of waste origins and detailed characterisation of materials. An effective traceability system can significantly aid in complying with these regulations. Some countries already have waste flow accounting systems to track waste from production to final disposal, implying that a structured and documented traceability system could effectively identify waste suitable for recovery, recycling, or reuse. Implementing waste traceability through blockchain technology can identify special waste, trace its flows, and determine possible destinations for recovery and reuse as secondary raw materials. This approach can be especially effective in homogeneous production districts or urban industrial areas (Dei Ottati, 2018; Ozuem et al., 2024). Tracing material flows, such as waste and secondary raw materials, can optimise their destinations and encourage reuse within a circular framework. These destinations can be within the same supply chain, forming a closed cycle, or in another supply chain, creating industrial symbiosis.

Recently, in the textile industry, blockchain technology has been employed to ensure supply chain traceability. Organisations should implement systems that document relevant evidence, ensuring that every step of the production process is traceable. This not only enhances transparency but also fosters trust with consumers and other stakeholders (Saccani et al., 2023). To effectively trace flows and determine destinations, blockchain-encrypted codes can identify waste based on origin and quality. Large companies already practise traceability procedures to monitor inputs and ensure quality and quantity, but these practices are less common among smaller businesses. While blockchain has been used primarily in the food sector for supply chain traceability and marketing, its new application involves tracking waste flows at the urban level, addressing information gaps by coding waste according to the productive sector rather than composition or production paths. Blockchain platforms allow organisations to store and share information along supply chains (Borsacchi et al., 2020; Testi, 2023).

Circular Economy in Textiles: New Certification Opportunities

The circular economy envisions a system where waste is eliminated through innovative design strategies applied to materials, products, systems, and business models (Ellen MacArthur Foundation, 2015). This paradigm primarily intersects with environmental economics and industrial ecology. Industrial hubs, characterised by diverse production activities, inevitably generate a multitude of by-products. An industrial ecosystem emerges when businesses collaborate, exchanging materials and by-products to minimise waste (Glavič & Lukman, 2007), a phenomenon known as industrial symbiosis (Chertow, 2000). Such ecosystems optimise the consumption of energy, raw materials, and water, as by-products from one process become inputs for another. Industrial symbiosis is defined as a collaborative approach where distinct industries exchange physical resources like materials, energy, water, and by-products to gain a competitive edge (Pinelli & Borsacchi, 2018). At the micro level, strategic planning can foster a closed-loop system by connecting producers, distributors, consumers, and recyclers. Ecodesign plays a critical role in this context, underscoring the use of recycled, renewable resources and the creation of durable, maintainable, upgradeable, and recyclable products (Mestre & Cooper, 2017). By minimising resource consumption and maximising recycling rates, ecodesign contributes to substantial waste reduction (Nieminem et al., 2006). The Ecodesign Directive, which mandates environmental and energy efficiency standards for energy-related products, offers a regulatory framework to support these objectives (EU, 2009). The textile industry, particularly the fast fashion segment, is a significant contributor to environmental pollution and waste generation. The linear production model prevalent in this industry, characterised by rapid design, production, and consumption cycles, leads to excessive resource depletion, water contamination, and textile waste accumulation. To address these concerns, the circular economy suggests a transformative approach that emphasises resource optimisation, waste reduction, and extended product lifespans. Industrial symbiosis principles can be effectively applied within the textile industry to foster circularity. Textile manufacturers can collaborate to exchange by-products such as fabric scraps, yarn waste, and wastewater treatment residuals, transforming them into valuable inputs for other processes. This collaborative approach reduces waste, creates new business opportunities, and strengthens supply chain resilience. Yarn producers in the textile industry continue to play a crucial role in process innovation. However, companies that interact more directly with the end consumer better understand market demands for new sustainable products (Dominidiato et al., 2023; Ozuem et al., 2023). Ecodesign principles are fundamental to creating circular textiles. Textile manufacturers can significantly reduce their environmental footprint by prioritising the use of recycled and renewable materials, designing for durability, and incorporating disassembly and recyclability considerations (European Commission, 2022). Additionally, adopting transparent and traceable production practices can enhance consumer trust and promote sustainable purchasing decisions. Extended Producer Responsibility (EPR) schemes can serve a focal part in driving circularity in the textile industry. By placing financial and logistical responsibility for end-of-life management on producers, EPR incentivises the design of durable, recyclable products and promotes the establishment of efficient collection and recycling systems. Engaging consumers through education and awareness campaigns can encourage sustainable consumption habits, such as extending garment lifespans through proper care, repair, and resale. Transitioning from fast fashion to a circular textile system necessitates a comprehensive approach encompassing industry-wide collaboration, policy interventions, and consumer engagement. By embracing circular economy principles, the textile industry can prepare for a more sustainable future, minimising its environmental impact and creating long-term value for all stakeholders.

Enterprises have been immensely challenged in obtaining environmental certifications, driven by national governments and international brands (i.e. companies like Adidas, H&M, and Burberry have targeted incorporating recycled or degradable materials by 2025). These brands use green certifications as a criterion for supplier evaluation and have set goals for using recycled materials (Lin & Ma, 2023). Textile companies are frequently required to conduct life cycle studies of their products. Although these studies follow a standardised methodology, they face reliability challenges when applied to typical textile production processes. Relatedly, a Life Cycle Assessment (LCA) is a systematic method for evaluating the environmental impacts associated with all stages of a product's life cycle, from raw material through production, use, and disposal or recycling. LCA aims to identify and quantify the energy and materials used, as well as the waste and emissions released, and to assess the potential environmental impacts of these inputs and outputs (Nieminem et al., 2006). This comprehensive analysis is carried out according to international standards (ISO 14040:2006 and ISO 14044:2006) that ensure that LCAs are conducted similarly, enabling reliable comparisons of the results. It should be noted that individual LCA studies offer limited significance for assembling a comprehensive life cycle of textiles due to numerous varying parameters, especially in terms of quality. The same fabric can have different environmental impacts depending on the production technology, equipment, or formulas used (Nieminem et al., 2006). Collecting high-quality data on the environmental impact of fibre and textile production is key to conducting an effective LCA study. For a quantitative assessment, secondary data provide averaged insights into environmental impacts, enabling LCAs without primary data (Sacchi et al., 2022). Thus, databases are crucial for facilitating LCAs, offering comprehensive information on the average environmental impact of various materials and processes used in everyday life and national economies (Edirisinghe et al., 2024). Therefore, an LCA analysis conducted for the same fabric but produced with different technologies and inputs will yield different results (Bacci, 2009). The evolution of materials technologies, together with progressively changing market demands, has led to a profound transformation in both industrial processes and the use of materials, and the textile sector is now involved in new paradigms of digitalisation and sustainability (Borsacchi et al., 2023). Transitioning to a circular economy is challenging, especially for organisations with linear processes, requiring investments in new technologies and worker training. Circularity uses by-products as raw materials, but technological, economic, or legislative constraints may hinder progress. The textile industry consumes significant resources like water, energy, and fibres, impacting the environment. Europe discards 6 million tons of garments annually, with only 25% recycled (WRAP, 2017). EU policies underline sustainability and circularity, especially in textiles (Ghisellini et al., 2016; RESET, 2018). Recycling in the textile-fashion sector can be done through different methodologies: mechanical, chemical, and thermal recycling. Each method applies specific technologies, uses different sources, and results in various impacts on the environment (i.e. according to a recent study published by the European Commission, mechanical recycling is among those with the lowest environmental impact).

The Global Recycled Standard (GRS) is an international, voluntary standard that sets requirements for the third-party certification of recycled content, chain of custody, social and environmental practices, and chemical restrictions in the textile industry. It is administered by Textile Exchange, a non-profit organisation dedicated to sustainable practices in the textile and apparel industries. The GRS was developed in response to the growing demand for recycled textiles and the need for a robust certification standard to ensure the authenticity and credibility of recycled content claims. The comprehensive standard addresses all aspects of the recycled textile supply chain, from the collection of pre-consumer and post-consumer waste materials to the final production and sale of finished products. To achieve GRS certification, companies must be independently audited by an accredited certification body. To obtain certification, products must contain at least 20% certified recycled content by weight and recycled materials must be tracked from the point of origin to the final product (i.e. a chain of custody). GRS also outlines requirements for the organisation's MS, including social practices, environmental protection, and restrictions on using hazardous chemicals in their production processes. The guidelines specify requirements for environmental, chemical, and social standards for GRS certification, highlighting its global importance. Companies must appoint a responsible individual, track environmental indicators, set annual goals, and train staff on environmental management. Energy and water use must be monitored monthly, with efficiency targets reviewed annually. Wastewater and emissions must comply with legal standards with proper monitoring and management. Waste management must also align with national laws, emphasising staff training, hazardous waste handling, and sustainability goals. Chemical usage must be documented, with safety data sheets maintained for each substance. Prohibited substances are defined under REACH, with monitoring by trained personnel. GRS guidelines prohibit forced or child labour and ensure contracts do not involve worker fees or document retention. Workers have the right to unionise and bargain collectively without discrimination. Equal opportunities are mandatory, ensuring a respectful workplace. Organisations must provide a safe and hygienic working environment, with emergency procedures and medical facilities. Regular employment contracts and fair wages must meet legal standards, covering basic needs and discretionary income. Working hours must not exceed 48 per week, excluding overtime, and must include rest breaks and days off.

From this brief overview of the main requirements that GRS-certified organisations must meet, it is evident that an organisation adopting an integrated MS based on ISO 9001, ISO 14001, and SA 8000 can equally fulfil the provisions set by GRS (Borsacchi et al., 2023). Standardisation bodies have begun developing technical standards for implementing circular economy principles at the organisational level. The first such technical standard, developed by the British Standard (BS), is BS 8001:2017—"Framework for implementing the principles of the circular economy in organizations." It serves as a guide on how to adapt business processes to a circular model, including design and traceability. Similarly, the French standard AFNOR XP X30-901:2018 applies to organisations intending to modify their production processes to align with circular principles. It requires compliance with social, economic, and environmental obligations. This standard can be integrated with other ISO management standards. In 2024, the work of various ISO technical committees at the international level led to the publication of ISO 59004:2024 "Circular Economy—Vocabulary, Principles and Guidance for Implementation." ISO 59004 is part of the ISO 59000 family designed to promote a circular economy. It provides comprehensive guidance for organisations, including defining key terms and concepts, outlining a vision for a circular economy, explaining core principles, and suggesting practical steps towards sustainability. This document defines key terms, establishes a vision and principles for a circular economy, and gives guidance, including possible actions, for an organisation to implement. It applies to organisations seeking to understand and commit to or contribute to a circular economy while supporting sustainable development. These organisations can be private or public, acting individually or collectively, regardless of type or size, and located in any jurisdiction or position within a specific value chain or value network. Adhering to ISO 59004 allows organisations to create and share societal value while ensuring ecosystem quality and resilience, supporting a sustainable future. This standard, combined with other ISOs, may become a valuable reference for implementing circular MS (with respect to quality, environmental protection, social responsibility, and traceability) even for textile organisations that wish to stand out for their commitment to the sustainability of their production.

References

Bacci, L. (2009). Tessile: sostenibilità e innovazione. Ricerca trasferimento innovazione.

Biggeri, M., Borsacchi, L., Braito, L., & Ferranini, A. (2022). Measuring the compliance of management system in manufacturing SMEs: An integrated model. *Journal of Cleaner Production, 382*.

Borsacchi, L. (2012). Integrated management systems for sustainable development and business innovation. In C. M. Bartolini, E. Bertacchini, A. Romani, L. Borsacchi, & M. Ciani Scarnicci (Eds.), The innovation strategy to overcome the crisis: The innovative entrepreneur from *Schumpeter to the present day* (pp. 121–131).

Borsacchi, L., Ciani Scarnicci, M., & Laino, A. (2013). Politiche integrate di responsabilità sociale di impresa: il caso Rohan. In M. Ciani Scarnicci, A. Laino, P. Pinelli, A. Romani, & P. Vignolini (Eds.), *Estratti naturali da piante medicinali e tessili–tintorie Caratterizzazione ed usi innovativi di ortica, daphne, lavanda e tannini da castagno Resoconto del Progetto PRIN 2008* (pp. 333–346).

Borsacchi, L., Biggeri, M., & Ferranini, A. (2016). Application and review of an integrated checklist to promote legal compliance and socially responsible behaviors among ethnic enterprises. In *20th IGWT Symposium, Commodity Science in a Changing World* (pp. 733–740).

Borsacchi, L., Biggeri, M., & Ferrannini, A. (2018). Corporate citizenship in Prato textile organisations: Design and experimentation of the "responsible business textile" label. In Laboratorio Phytolab (Pharmaceutical, Cosmetic, Food Supplement Technology and Analysis)—DiSIA Università degli Studi di Firenze. *XXVIII Congresso Nazionale Di Scienze Merceologiche*, Firenze, 326–332.

Borsacchi, L., & Pinelli, P. (2020). Sustainable and innovative practices of small and medium-sized enterprises in the water and waste management sector. In *Innovation strategies in environmental science* (pp. 255–290). Elsevier.

Borsacchi, L., Feligioni, G., Ferrini, A., & Lockwood, C. (2023). The on-going project FLOWTEX (dynamic FLOW diagrams for circular TEXtile) in the textile district of Prato (Italy): Implementation and future perspectives. In Rasyikah Md. Khalid et al. (Eds.), *29th International Sustainable Development Research Society (ISDRS) Conference 2023—Proceedings* (pp. 558–568).

Chertow, M. R. (2000). Industrial symbiosis: Literature and taxonomy. *Annual Review of Energy and the Environment, 25*(1), 313–337.

European Commission. (2022). *Strategy for textiles.* https://single-market-economy.ec.europa.eu/industry/sustainability/strategy-textiles_en

Dabbene, F., Gay, P., & Tortia, C. (2014). Traceability issues in food supply chain management: A review. *Biosystems Engineering, 120*, 65–80. https://doi.org/10.1016/j.biosystemseng.2013.09.006

Dai, H., Tseng, M. M., & Zipkin, P. H. (2015). Design of traceability systems for product recall. *International Journal of Production Research, 53*(2), 511–531. https://doi.org/10.1080/00207543.2014.955922

Dei Ottati, G. (2018). Marshallian industrial districts in Italy: The end of a model or adaptation to the global economy? *Cambridge Journal of Economics, 42*(2), 259–284.

Diekel, F., Mikosch, N., Bach, V., & Finkbeiner, M. (2021). Life cycle based comparison of textile ecolabels. *Sustainability, 13*(4), 1751.

Dominidiato, M., Guercini, S., Milanesi, M., & Tunisini, A. (2023). Supplier-customer relationships for sustainability-led innovation in the textile industry. *Journal of Business & Industrial Marketing, 39*(13), 15–26.

Edirisinghe, L. G. L. M., de Alwis, A. A. P., & Wijayasundara, M. (2024). Sustainable circular practices in the textile product life cycle: A comprehensive approach to environmental impact mitigation. *Environmental Challenges*, 100985.

Ellen MacArthur Foundation. (2015). *Growth within: A circular economy vision for a competitive Europe.*

Ellen MacArthur Foundation. (2017). *A new textile economy: Redesigning fashion's future.*

Foster, S. T. (2008). Towards an understanding of supply chain quality management. *Journal of Operations Management, 26*, 461–467.

Garcia-Torres, S., Rey-Garcia, M., Sáenz, J., & Seuring, S. (2022). Traceability and transparency for sustainable fashion-apparel supply chains. *Journal of Fashion Marketing and Management: An International Journal, 26*(2), 344–364.

Ghisellini, P., Cialani, C., & Ulgiati, S. (2016). A review on circular economy: The expected transition to a balanced interplay of environmental and economic systems. *Journal of Cleaner Production, 114*, 11–32.

Glavič, P., & Lukman, R. (2007). Review of sustainability terms and their definitions. *Journal of Cleaner Production, 15*(18), 1875–1885.

Global Ecolabelling Network. (2004). *Information paper: Introduction to ecolabelling.*

Gomes, C., Pires, I., Monteiro, L., Lima, T. M., & Gaspar, P. D. (2024). Empowering eco-friendly choices: An environmental impact assessment decision support system for textiles and clothing. *Applied Sciences, 14*(2), 659.

Hernandez-Vivanco, A., Domingues, P., Sampaio, P., Bernardo, M., & Cruz-Cázares, C. (2019). Do multiple certifications leverage firm performance? A dynamic approach. *International Journal of Production Economics, 218*, 386–399.

Lin, H. J., & Ma, H. W. (2023). Analysis of green certification standards related to recycled materials involving textiles based on life cycle thinking. *Sustainable Production and Consumption, 41*, 107–120.

Marucheck, A., Greis, N., Mena, C., & Cai, L. (2011). Product safety and security in the global supply chain: Issues, challenges and research opportunities. *Journal of Operations Management, 29*(7–8), 707–720. https://doi.org/10.1016/j.jom.2011.06.007

Mestre, A., & Cooper, T. (2017). Circular product design: A multiple loops life cycle design approach for the circular economy. *The Design Journal, 20*(sup1), S1620–S1635.

Nedra, A. (2022). Effect of ISO (9001) certification and article type produced on Lean Six Sigma application successes: A case study within textile companies. *Fibres & Textiles in Eastern Europe, 151*(2), 17–22. https://doi.org/10.2478/ftee-2022-0003

Nieminem, E., Linke, M., Tobler, M., & Vander Beke, B. (2006). EU COST Action 628: Life cycle assessment (LCA) of textile products, eco-efficiency and definition of best available technology (BAT) of textile processing. *Journal of Cleaner Production, 15*(13–14), 1259–1270.

Ozuem, W., Ranfagni, S., Willis, M., Salvietti, G., & Howell, K. (2024). Exploring the relationship between chatbots, service failure recovery and customer loyalty: A frustration–aggression perspective. *Psychology and Marketing*. https://doi.org/10.1002/mar.22051

Ozuem, W., Willis, M., Howell, K., Ranfagni, S., & Rovai, S. (2023). Examining user-generated content, service failure recovery and customer–brand relationships: An exploration through commitment-trust theory. *Internet Research*. https://doi.org/10.1108/intr-07-2022-0580

Pettit, T. J., Croxton, K. L., & Fiksel, J. (2013). Ensuring supply chain resilience: Development and implementation of an assessment tool. *Journal of Business Logistics, 34*(1), 46–76. https://doi.org/10.1111/jbl.12009

Pinelli, P., & Borsacchi, L. (2016, September 12–16). From documented procedure to documented information: The new approach of ISO 9001:2015. In *20th IGWT Symposium—Commodity Science in a Changing World* (pp. 89–95). University of Economics—Varna.

Pinelli, P., & Borsacchi, L. (2018, June 18). Circular economy and industrial symbiosis: The role of the municipality of Prato within the EU Urban Agenda partnership. In *Proceedings of the 24th International Sustainable Development Research Society Conference: Actions for a sustainable world: From theory to practice* (pp. 716–722). The Organizing Committee of the ISDRS Conference.

Plakantonaki, S., Kiskira, K., Zacharopoulos, N., Chronis, I., Coelho, F., Togiani, A., & Priniotakis, G. (2023). A review of sustainability standards and ecolabeling in the textile industry. *Sustainability, 15*(15), 11589.

Ramon-Jeronimo, J., Florez-Lopez, R., & Ramon-Jeronimo, M. (2017). Understanding the generation of value along supply chains: Balancing control information and relational governance mechanisms in downstream and upstream relationships. *Sustainability, 9*(8), 1487. https://doi.org/10.3390/su9081487

Ranasinghe, L., & Jayasooriya, V. M. (2021). Ecolabelling in textile industry: A review. *Resources, Environment and Sustainability, 6*, 100037.

Ranfagni, S., & Guercini, S. (2014). On the trail of supply side authenticity: Paradoxes and compromises emerging from an action research. *Journal of Consumer Behaviour, 13*(3), 176–187.

Raut, R., Gardas, B. B., & Narkhede, B. (2019). Ranking the barriers of sustainable textile and apparel supply chains: An interpretive structural modelling methodology. *Benchmarking: An International Journal, 26*, 371–394.

RESET. (2018). *RESET*. https://www.cittadiprato.it/EN/Sezioni/337/RESET-European-project/

Saccani, N., Bressanelli, G., & Visintin, F. (2023). Circular supply chain orchestration to overcome circular economy challenges: An empirical investigation in the textile and fashion industries. *Sustainable Production and Consumption, 35*, 469–482.

Sacchi, R., Terlouw, T., Siala, K., Dirnaichner, A., Bauer, C., Cox, B., Mutel, C., Daioglou, V., & Luderer, G. (2022). Prospective environmental impact assessment (premise): A streamlined approach to producing databases for prospective life cycle assessment using integrated assessment models. *Renewable and Sustainable Energy Reviews, 160*, 112311. https://doi.org/10.1016/j.rser.2022.112311

Testi, N. (2023). Blockchain technology for supply chain traceability: The case of SMEs of the Made in Italy. *Piccola Impresa/Small Business* (2).

Testi, N., Borsacchi, L., & Spigarelli, F. (2023). Blockchain technology for supply chain traceability: A literature review. *L'industria, 44*(1), 77–100.

Yasin, S., & Sun, D. (2019). Propelling textile waste to ascend the ladder of sustainability: EOL study on probing environmental parity in technical textiles. *Journal of Cleaner Production, 233*, 1451–1464.

Zaczkiewicz, A. (2020). *Combating "greenwashing" with third-party textile certifications*. WWD: Women's Wear Daily. https://wwd.com/feature/oeko-tex-ben-mead-1203535837/

Zhang, A., Zhong, R. Y., Farooque, M., Kang, K., & Venkatesh, V. G. (2020). Blockchain-based life cycle assessment: An implementation framework and system architecture. *Resources, Conservation and Recycling, 152*, 104512. https://doi.org/10.1016/j.resconrec.2019.104512

Zimon, D., Madzik, P., & Sroufe, R. (2020). The influence of ISO 9001 and ISO 14001 on sustainable supply chain management in the textile industry. *Sustainability, 12*(10), 4282. https://doi.org/10.3390/su12104282

Standards

ISO 9001:2015 "Quality Management Systems—Requirements".
ISO 14001:2015 "Environmental Management Systems—Requirements with Guidance for Use".
ISO 26000:2010 "Guidance on Social Responsibility".
ISO 45001:2018 "Occupational Health and Safety Management Systems—Requirements with Guidance for Use".
ISO 59004:2024 "Circular Economy—Vocabulary, Principles and Guidance for Implementation".
SA8000:2014.
Textile Exchange, GRS-101 Global Recycled Standard (GRS).

Correction to: Luxury Hotels' Corporate Social Responsibility Communications and Online Brand Communities

Mei Kun (Vicky) Loi

Correction to:
Chapter 7 in: W. Ozuem et al. (eds.), *Sustainable Digital Marketing for Fashion and Luxury Brands*,
https://doi.org/10.1007/978-3-031-82467-8_7

The original version of Chapter 7 was previously published with an incorrect author name, which has now been corrected. The chapter has been updated with the changes.

The updated version of this chapter can be found at
https://doi.org/10.1007/978-3-031-82467-8_7

W. Ozuem et al. (eds.), *Sustainable Digital Marketing for Fashion and Luxury Brands*,
https://doi.org/10.1007/978-3-031-82467-8_29

Index

W. Ozuem et al. (eds.), *Sustainable Digital Marketing for Fashion and Luxury Brands*,
https://doi.org/10.1007/978-3-031-82467-8

T

U

V

The manufacturer's authorised representative in the EU is Springer Nature Customer Service Centre GmbH, Europaplatz 3, 69115 Heidelberg, Germany. If you have any concerns regarding our products, please contact ProductSafety@springernature.com

Printed and bound by CPI Group (UK) Ltd, Croydon, CR0 4YY
01/10/2026
02225953-0016